AF605933

LEGENDS OF THE BUILDING OF OLD PEKING

"Nezha naohai" (Nezha Stirring up the Sea)
Mural, Foreign Visitors Lounge, Beijing International Airport, c. 1985
(Photo by Hok-lam Chan)

Legends of the Building of Old Peking

Hok-lam Chan

The Chinese University Press

University of Washington Press
Seattle

The Chinese University Press ISBN 978–962–996–313–2
University of Washington Press ISBN 978–0–295–98782–8

Published for North America by:
University of Washington Press
PO Box 50096
Seattle, WA 98145-5096
www.washington.edu/uwpress

Published for the rest of the world by:
The Chinese University Press
The Chinese University of Hong Kong
Sha Tin, N.T., Hong Kong
Fax: +852 2603 6692
+852 2603 7355
E-mail: cup@cuhk.edu.hk
Web-site: www.chineseupress.com

Library of Congress Cataloging-in-Publication Data
Chan, Hok-lam.
Legends of the building of old Peking / Hok-lam Chan. — 1st ed.
p. cm.
Includes bibliographical references and index.
ISBN 978-0-295-98782-8 (hardback: alk. paper)
1. Beijing (China)—History. 2. Beijing (China)—Legends. I. Title.
DS795.3C43 2008
951'.156—dc22 2007051641

The paper used in this publication meets the minimum requirements of American National Standard for Information Sciences—Permanence of Paper for Printed Library Materials, ANSI Z39.48–1984.

TO THE MEMORY OF FREDERICK W. MOTE

Teacher, Scholar, Friend

Contents

Note on Spelling ix

List of Illustrations xi

Acknowledgements xiii

Preface xv

Introduction 1

The Historical Background 1

The Cosmological Concepts of Imperial Cities 8

The Planning of Imperial Cities 15

Legends of Dadu and Peking 24

PART I The "Nezha City" of Old Peking: Origins and Transformations 33

Chapter 1 Liu Bingzhong, Nazha, and the Building of Yuan "Great Capital" 35

The Historical Background 35

Liu Bingzhong's City Plan 44

The Nazha Cheng Legend 63

The Nazha Saga 66

Myth and Reality 79

Chapter 2 Liu Bowen, Nezha, and the Building of Ming Peking 87

The Historical Background 87

The Genesis of the "Northern Capital" 91

The Imperial City Plan 100

New Nazha Cheng Legend 121

Liu Bowen's Legends 138

Nezha Cheng Legend Analyzed 155

PART II "Siting by Bowshot": Locating the City of Ming Peking 171

Chapter 3 The Mongolian Story of How Emperor Yongle Built the City of Peking 173

The Historical Background 173
Anatomy of the Folkloric Legend 177
Impact on the Nezha Cheng Legend 199
Another Mongolian Legend 202

Chapter 4 The Stories of Liu Bowen, Yao Guangxiao, and Shen Wansan Building the City of Peking 207

The Folkloric Background 207
"Liu Bowen Built the City of Peking" 215
Liu Bowen, Xu Da, and Shen Wansan 215
Liu Bowen, the Dragon King, and Warrior Gao Liang 221
Gao Liang, Shen Wansan, and the Dragon King 226
"How was the City of Peking Built?" 231
Yao Guangxiao and the Prince of Yan 231
The Prince of Yan and Shen Wansan 236
The Folkloric Legacy 241

Epilogue 249

PART III Appendices 261

1. The Eight-armed Nezha City (1) 263
2. The Eight-armed Nezha City (2) 266
3. Book of the Story of How Emperor Yung-lo of the Great Ming Built the City of Peking—The Yüan Prince—The True Prince 270
4. Liu Bowen Built the City of Peking 277
5. How was the City of Peking Built? 283

Glossary 289
Notes 291
Bibliography 345
Index 375

Note on Spelling

1. Peking/Beiping/Pei-p'ing/Beijing

The postal spelling Peking 北京 (Northern Capital) is retained for the name of the Ming and Qing capitals in modern Beijing. Beiping 北平 (Northern Peace) was the new name for Yuan Dadu in early Ming before it was renamed Peking. Pei-p'ing, the Wade-Giles spelling equivalent to Beiping , refers to the changed name of Peking from 1928 to 1949 when the national capital of the Republic of China was moved to Nanking 南京, the Ming southern capital which is present-day Nanjing. Whenever Beijing is used, it refers to the national capital of the People's Republic of China.

2. Nanking/Nanjing

The spelling Nanking is retained for the Ming southern capital.

3. Nazha/Nezha

Both spellings refer to the same Buddhist child deity. Nazha 那吒 is generally used in pre-Yuan and Yuan literature, but in post-Yuan orthography, it is usually written as Nezha 哪吒, with the "mouth" radical added to the left side of the character Na. Both spellings are adopted in order to distinguish different usages in Yuan and Ming and post-Ming literature.

4. Although the Hanyu pinyin system is used throughout the text, the Wade-Giles spelling is retained for the citation of certain older English-language source materials, such as the works of E. T. C. Werner, L. C. Arlington and Wm. Lewisohn, and H. Serruys's and O. Lattimore's translations of the Mongolian texts.

5. Units of linear measure of the Yuan and Ming periods

(a) Yuan (b) Ming

1 *chi* 尺 (10 *cun* 寸) = 0.3078 m (a); 0.3178 m (b)

1 *bu* 步 (5 *chi*) = 1.54 m (a); 1.59 m (b)

1 *zhang* 丈 (10 *chi*) = 3.078 m (a); 3.178 m (b)

1 *li* 里 (360 *bu*) = 1,800 *chi* = 0.554 km (a); 0.572 km (b)
Source: Li Xieping, *Mingdai Beijing ducheng yingjian congkao* (2006), pp. 92–103.

List of Illustrations

Figure 1. Site of Ji and Peking (p. 3)

Figure 2. Plan of Liao Nanjing and Jin Zhongdu superimposed on Yuan Dadu and Ming-Qing Peking (p. 6)

Figure 3. Four animal images as shown on eave tiles from the Former Han (p. 11)

Figure 4. (a) The circular *xiantian* arrangement of the Eight Trigrams; (b) The circular *houtian* arrangement of the Eight Trigrams (p. 12)

Figure 5. Diagram of circumpolar *fenye* (p. 14)

Figure 6. The Purple Palace Enclosure; The Privy Council Enclosure; The Celestial Markets Enclosure (p. 16)

Figure 7. Wangcheng *tu* (p. 18)

Figure 8. The Diviner (*taibao*) inspects a site for a dwelling (p. 21)

Figure 9. Portrait of Qubilai Qaghan (p. 38)

Figure 10. Portrait of Liu Bingzhong (p. 38)

Figure 11. Plan of Yuan Dadu superimposed on Jin Zhongdu (p. 49)

Figure 12. Zhongdu, Dadu, the lakes, rivers, and canals (p. 51)

Figure 13. Plan of Dadu superimposed on the "Diagram of the Posterior Heavens" (p. 54)

Figure 14. Portrait of Heavenly King Vaiśravana in Tang Buddhist text (p. 68)

Figure 15. Portrait of Prince Nazha in Tang Buddhist text (p. 71)

Figure 16. Portrait of Nazha in *Soushen daquan* (p. 78)

Figure 17. Portrait of Nezha (dubbed "Crimson Kid") (p. 80)

Figure 18. Portrait of Ming Taizu (Zhu Yuanzhang) (p. 90)

Figure 19. Plan of Nanking (p. 92)

Figure 20. Portrait of the Yongle Emperor (Ming Chengzu) (p. 93)

Figure 21. Bust of the Statue of the Dark God in the Qin'andian (p. 97)
Figure 22. Plan of Ming Peking (early stage) superimposed on Yuan Dadu (p. 101)
Figure 23. Ming Peking—Forbidden City within the Imperial-city (p. 104)
Figure 24. Plan of the Ming Forbidden City (p. 108)
Figure 25. Plan of the Ming Imperial-city (p. 112)
Figure 26. Ming Peking—Capital-city in the later stages (p. 116)
Figure 27. Plan of Mid-Qing Peking from *Qianlong jingcheng quantu* (p. 119)
Figure 28. Image of Nezha superimposed on plan of Peking (p. 131)
Figure 29. Portrait of Nezha (p. 134)
Figure 30. Images of the Dragon King (p. 137)
Figure 31. Portrait of Liu Ji (Bowen) (p. 141)
Figure 32. Liu Bowen dressed in a Daoist garment performing ritual before an altar in *Yinglie zhuan* (p. 145)
Figure 33. Liu Bowen prognosticating before Ming Taizu in *Shaobing ge* (p. 152)
Figure 34. Portrait of the Iron-cap Daoist Zhang Zhong (p. 153)
Figure 35. Portrait/Statue of Monk Daoyuan (Yao Guangxiao) (p. 164)
Figure 36. Bronze statues of the Dark God from Mt. Wudang's Zhenwu Temple (p. 188)
Figure 37. Statuettes of Vaiśravana as Kubara, God of Wealth (p. 190)
Figure 38. Shen Wansan as the fisherman receiving help from the Dragon King in a Qing woodblock print (p. 211)
Figure 39. Shen Wansan as the God of Wealth in a Qing clay figurine (p. 214)
Figure 40. Portrait of Xu Da (p. 220)

Acknowledgements

To Harrassowiltz Verlag, Wiesbaden, Germany, for permission to reprint materials from Owen Lattimore, "A Mongol Legend of the Founding of Peking", published in *Central Asiatic Journal*, Vol. XXIII (1979), pp. 237–239.

To Program in East Asian Studies, Princeton University, New Jersey, for permission to reprint materials from Hok-lam Chan, "A Mongolian Legend of the Building of Peking", published in *Asia Major*, third series, Vol. 3, Part II (1990), pp. 65–93.

To The Mongolian Society Publications, Indiana University, Bloomington, Indiana, for permission to reprint materials from Henry Serruys, "A Manuscript Version of the Legend of the Mongol Ancestry of the Yung-lo Emperor", published in *Analecta Mongolica: Dedicated to the Seventieth Birthday of Professor Owen Lattimore*, edited by John G. Hangin and U. Onon (1972), pp. 19–61.

To National Palace Museum, Taipei, for permission to reprint the Portrait of Qubilai Qaghan, the Portrait of Ming Taizu (Zhu Yuanzhang), and the Portrait of the Yongle Emperor (Ming Chengzu).

To Beijing chubanshe, Beijing, for permission to reprint four pictures from Jin Shoushen, *Beijing de chuanshuo* (2003), pp. 9, 29, 115.

To Zijincheng chubanshe, Beijing, for permission to reprint three pictures from Wang Zilin, *Zijin cheng fengshui* (2005), pp. 271, 275, 276.

Acknowledgments

Preface

Peking (now spelled Beijing), the historical capital of the Chinese empire and the national capital of the People's Republic of China, evokes not only a paragon of a multifunctional modern capital but also the majesty of a grand humanistic civilization. Both anglicized names mean "Northern Capital", but Peking is used in this study to denote the historical past, in order to distinguish it from the contemporary applications. The name was coined when the powerful Yongle emperor of the Ming dynasty built his new capital in present-day Beijing in 1406–1420, inaugurating the first Chinese imperial capital in the region. It traced its antecedents to the capital cities of Dadu of the Yuan, Zhongdu of the Jin, and Nanjing of the Liao—all founded by non-Han dynastic regimes. Peking remained the imperial seat of the Ming to the end of its rule and was refurbished by the Manchu rulers as the capital of the Qing dynasty. After the founding of the Chinese Republic in 1911, Peking became the primary capital under several short-lived northern governments until the ascendancy of the Guomindang (Nationalist Party) of Chiang Kai-shek (Jiang Jieshi) in 1928, when Nanking (Nanjing) was designated the national capital of a united country. At that point the city's name was changed to Pei-p'ing (Northern Peace), as it had been known after the Ming founding and well before the Yongle emperor made it his new capital. Peking, under the changed spelling Beijing, was restored as the national capital upon the inauguration of the People's Republic in 1949, ushering in a new phase of extensive urban development against a richly variegated historical and cultural backdrop.

The building of the imperial capital has won acclaim as a unique accomplishment in Chinese architectural history. It combines a fortuitous siting based on classical cosmological ideology with the collective ingenuity and skill of traditional architects and artisans. Peking, the capital of the last major dynasties that spanned over five centuries, with antecedents in the three preceding powerful non-Han ruling dynasties, is a gem unrivaled by other imperial cities.

There is no lack of historical literature lauding the city's ingenious architectural design and painstaking construction, and effusively describing its splendid buildings, imposing monuments, and grand urban landscape. This literature gives a vivid testimony to Peking's past grandeur and majesty, and bears silent witness to the corrosion and destruction of its walls and gates brought about by the tumultuous political and physical changes which have taken place in the modern era. At the same time, equally impressive and spectacular to the city's inhabitants and observers alike, is the profusion of dramatic popular legends surrounding the building of the capital which have found lively expression in literary miscellanies, folktales, and other forms of oral communication. These legends have enthralled the popular imagination and have blossomed into fanciful stories about the building of Peking in recent centuries.

The earliest version of the Peking legend, that of the Nazha cheng legend of the Yuan dynasty capital Dadu and its transformation in modern times in reference to the Ming dynasty capital Peking, is the central focus of the present study. It alleges that Liu Bingzhong, the Buddhist-Daoist adviser of Qubilai Qaghan, designed a city plan in the likeness of Nazha (later written as Nezha), the spiritual child deity of Tantric Buddhism. According to the legend Dadu was laid out with eleven walled gates in the outer-city symbolizing the three heads, six arms and two feet of Nazha's transformed body. It was thought that the Great Capital of the Sino-Mongolian empire, which often suffered water shortages due to drought, needed spiritual protection. Nazha, who could subdue demons and had fought the Dragon King who dominated the Eastern Sea, was the ideal guardian-protector. In the late Qing and early Republican era the old myth resurfaced in a new form as the legend of Liu Bowen building the Eight-armed Nezha City of Peking, wherein the chief architect was said to be the early Ming imperial adviser Liu Ji, who had been intensely mythologized as a clairvoyant prognosticator and champion of Han ethnic restoration. The city plan again bore the likeness of Nezha's body in order to invoke his presence to protect the capital city and to subdue the Dragon King in order to release his control of the water resources.

Publicized in folk tales and folk songs, and animated in various forms of oral entertainment, this engrossing legend of the building of Peking has left the metropolitan residents spellbound and remains a public fixation down to the present day. Vivid testimony to such popularity was a huge multicolored mural called "Nezha naohai" (Nezha Stirring up the Sea) which was mounted inside the "foreign visitors" lounge of Beijing International Airport shortly after its opening in the early 1980s. Painted by Zhang Ding, a veteran artist, it features the child deity battling the sea dragons superimposed on the layout of old Peking, all of which is surrounded by tiny dragons fluttering amid layers of colored clouds and flags (see Frontispiece). In the painting Nezha, embraced by an elliptical ring of fire, emerges like a baby bursting out of the womb, alive with energy, golden light beaming from his eyes. He has a full head of curls, a pinkish face, and red lips. On his upper body he wears a red damask halter and his legs and feet are bare. In his left hand he holds a golden ring, his right hand grips a red ribbon, and each of his ankles are fitted with a golden bracelet. Such vivid animation undoubtedly enhanced public awareness of the legend as an indigenous icon for the national capital, even though the painting was removed after a few years to accommodate remodeling and expansion of the airport.

Besides the Nezha City saga, two other equally riveting traditions inspired by a Mongolian folk tradition about the origin of Peking, with or without affinity to the Nezha tradition, have thrived. The dominant theme in these legends is "Siting by bowshot, locating the city of Peking", and is featured in both Mongolian and Chinese versions. The Mongolian version relates that the site of Peking was chosen by the nomadic custom of shooting arrows in four directions with the fallen arrows becoming the boundaries of the future city. The Chinese version has a single arrow shot toward the north by a powerful archer, a prominent early Ming general, and the spot where the arrow fell would become the center of the city where construction was to begin. In both instances Liu Bowen is present in plotting strategies and executing the construction. These animating stories begot still more sensational stories extracted from the Nezha legend about the treachery of the Dragon King. They narrate how the ingenious Liu Bowen bettered the dragon family over the control of water in the Peking region and enlisted his nemesis Yao Guangxiao to coerce the eccentric and wealthy Shen Wansan to deliver hoarded gold and silver ingots to finance the building of the city. They are inspiring and enchanting folktales, exalting and glamorizing the building of Peking from the respective ethnic perception and imagination which are prominently accentuated in these legends. A judicious investigation can highlight a neglected area of Peking's history and illuminate a significant aspect of popular culture in an urban setting in Chinese civilization.

As a lone researcher in the field of Peking legends I approach the subject from the vantage of decades of research into Yuan and Ming political and religious history, with occasional excursions into Mongolian and Altaic studies. I have benefited from my intensive work on the biography and legend of Qubilai's eminent adviser Liu Bingzhong, and particularly the mythologization of his junior namesake, the early Ming imperial adviser Liu Ji (Liu Bowen), who was the principal figure in most of the Peking legends. A happy confluence of fortuitous circumstances and opportunities criss-crossing the Pacific over the last three decades, especially the last ten-year niche teaching alternately at the University of Washington, Seattle, and the Chinese University of Hong Kong, has kindled my intellectual curiosity, sustained my bilingual scholarship, and provided the scarce resources to bring this investigation to fruition. This work saw its first publication—a paper on the genesis of the legend of the Nazha City of Yuan Dadu—in a Chinese journal in Taiwan in 1985, and progressed by fits and starts, with an essay on the Mongolian legend of the siting by bowshot of the building of Peking published in *Asia Major* in 1990 and another piece on a contemporary Chinese adaptation of the same Mongolian story with additional fantasies published in a festschrift volume in Liaoning in 1993. They culminated in a monograph in Chinese on the legend of Liu Bowen building the Nezha City of Peking published in Taipei in 1996. At the invitation of Professor Kristopher Schipper of the CNRS-EPHE, an English synopsis of this legend was presented to the International Conference on "Beijing as a Holy City: Liturgical Structures and a Civil Society" held in Paris in October 1999. It forms the backbone of the first part of the present work.

Drawing substantially on primary materials and on my earlier research, my book is concerned with the evolution of the old Peking legends from earlier sources and with the interactions of various historical and cultural traditions, those of the Han Chinese and the Mongols, from the dynastic periods to recent times. As such it involves a careful investigation and analysis of multifarious historical, literary, and folkloric materials at various levels and from different points of views. Though a complex scholarly undertaking, it is the only means to get to the bottom of the story and I sincerely hope that such an approach will not deflect the interest of non-specialists and laymen. In the course of research and writing I have benefited from the prolific scholarly publications on Peking in the Chinese press and from the theoretical stimulation provided by several recent studies on the old capital from the viewpoint of comparative religion and urban cultural history. Presented in two separate parts in four chapters, each has its own focus. But each is symbiotic to the others and some replications are unavoidable. It is hoped that they will reinforce each other, providing a basis for comparative introspection, and will not disrupt the flow of comprehension or the pleasure of reading.

I would like to acknowledge my indebtedness to many friends and colleagues who have shown keen interest in my work and have offered valuable advice and assistance over the years. Many of them have already received mention in my Chinese monograph, *Liu Bowen yu Nezha cheng* published in 1996, but I wish to reiterate my foremost gratitude to the late Professor F. W. Mote, my academic mentor at Princeton University. Through his erudition, unfailing advice, and warm-hearted friendship he helped broaden my views on Sinology and history and sharpen my research and methodological skills. The present work is dedicated to his memory. I also wish to thank again Professor Liu Tsun-yan of the Australian National University; Professor Hou Renzhi of Peking University; Su Tianjun of the Beijing Academy of Social Sciences; Chen Gaohua, Du Wanyan, and Wang Chunyu of the Chinese Academy of Social Sciences, Beijing; and Professor Hsieh Min-ts'ung, formerly of Tamkang University, Taipei.

In addition, I have been much inspired by the thoughtful comments of several reviewers of my Chinese monograph from China, Taiwan, Japan, and the U.S. since its publication, in particular Professor Kin Bunkyō of the Institute for Research in Humanities, Kyoto University, and Mr. Wang Wenbao, a senior member of the Chinese Folk Literature Research Association in Beijing. I am grateful to Professor Nancy S. Steinhardt of the University of Pennsylvania for reading my draft chapters and writing the endorsement, and also to Felicia Hecker of the Jackson School of International Studies, the University of Washington, Seattle, for judicious editorial assistance during the preparation of the manuscript.

I want to thank Professor Jenny So of the Institute of Chinese Studies, The Chinese University of Hong Kong, for providing a publication subsidy. Grateful acknowledgements are also due to Dr. Steven K. Luk, former Director of The Chinese University Press, for his enthusiastic support; the two anonymous reviewers for helpful suggestions; and Lisa Tang, Senior Editor, for her meticulous care in seeing the manuscript through to publication. I also owe thanks to Pat Soden and Lorri Hagman, Director and Senior Editor of the University of Washington Press, for sponsoring the publication of the North American edition of the book.

Finally, my special gratitude goes to my family: to my sons Enoch and Erwin, for help in improvising the computer program for indexing; to my daughter Eugenia for her interest in her father's work; and to my spouse Kin May for her warm affection and unreserved support over the years. Their love and understanding have sustained my professional career and enabled me to give undivided attention to the completion of this and many other scholarly projects.

Seattle, August 2007
Hok-lam Chan

Introduction

The Historical Background

No more magnificent and imposing monuments attest to the splendor and durability of Chinese history and civilization than the cluster of imperial capitals that have dotted the North China plain since antiquity and flourished through the centuries. Representative of these were Chang'an 長安 and Luoyang 洛陽 of the Han 漢 and Tang 唐 dynasties, Bianliang 汴梁 (Kaifeng 開封) or Dongjing 東京 of the Song 宋, Dadu 大都 of the Yuan 元, and Peking of the Ming 明 and Qing 清 dynasties.[1] As multifunctional metropolises, each endowed with a unique historical legacy, these imperial cities served not only as the political and administrative capital of the empire but also as a residence of the ruling sovereign and his family, and of senior government officials, as well as a commercial and cultural center. Each capital played an important role in history, bequeathing a legacy that continues to radiate today. However, in historical import and contemporary significance none equals Peking, the present-day Chinese national capital Beijing.[2]

The area where Beijing stands and where a succession of cities and capitals of states and dynasties had been founded over the centuries is located between 115°25′–117°30′ east longitude and 39°26′–41°03′ north latitude in the semi-humid, warm temperate zone. It nestles at the foot of the Yan Mountains 燕山 on the northern tip of the North China Plain, some 140 km from the Gulf of Bohai 渤海 to its southeast, and is semi-enclosed by the Taihang Mountains 太行山 to the west. It is in the corridor connecting the North China Plain in the northeast and the Mongolian Plateau in the north with the Yellow River in the south. South of the Yan Mountains and east of the Taihang Mountains is an alluvial plain which geographers have dubbed the "Gulf of Beijing". This sub-plain is protected by two mountain ranges, with several important passes created by rivers cascading through their valleys. It is sandwiched between two tributaries of North China's ancient rivers—the Yongding River 永定河 to the west and the Chaobai 潮白 to the east, which have been a source of flood disasters because of constant silting. The first historical city was founded more than three thousand years ago north of the Yongding River, at the confluence of crossings from several directions. It was the home of *Homo erectus Sinanthropus pekinensis* or "Peking man", who lived there about 700,000 to 200,000 years ago, when it was less menaced by floods and where a network of rivers and lakes facilitated communication. The area had a continental climate of the monsoon type, with long, cold, dry winters and warm, humid summers punctuated by protracted drought and incessant rain, but it provided a strategically secured and economically fertile environment for the growth of communities, cities, and states that nourished high culture.[3]

The first walled city founded in the Beijing sub-plain was Ji 薊, a fief granted to the descendants of the ancient Lord Yao 堯帝 by King Wu 武王 in the year after the conquest of the Shang 商 and the establishment of the Zhou 周 kingdom. The date has been established as 1045 B.C. and so this would be Ji's birth date. At the same time the King also enfeoffed the descendants of the Duke of Zhao 召公 at the state of Yan in the Fangshan 房山 county. About four centuries later Yan annexed its neighbor and made Ji its capital, located in the Western District section of present-day Beijing near the White Cloud Shrine (Baiyunguan 白雲觀). This area was in the cradle of ancient Chinese civilization distinguished by bronze culture, sociopolitical organizations, and humanistic civilization (Figure 1).

Under the Qin 秦 and Han dynasties Ji became a frontier county south of the Great Wall guarding the borders against the intrusion of the nomadic tribes. It grew into an administrative city and commercial center under several regional political states after the fall of the Han, and was incorporated into the Youzhou 幽州 prefecture under the Sui 隋 in A.D. 583 and remained the same under the Tang. As the prefectural capital, Ji henceforth became known as the city of Youzhou. It was a typical medieval walled city, nine *li* 里 long from north to south, seven *li* wide from east to west, and with a perimeter of thirty-two *li*. There were ten walled gates and twenty-six *fang* 坊 or wards of residential quarters. It flourished as a political, commercial, and industrial center with over a hundred thousand inhabitants in its

Figure 1 Site of Ji and Peking

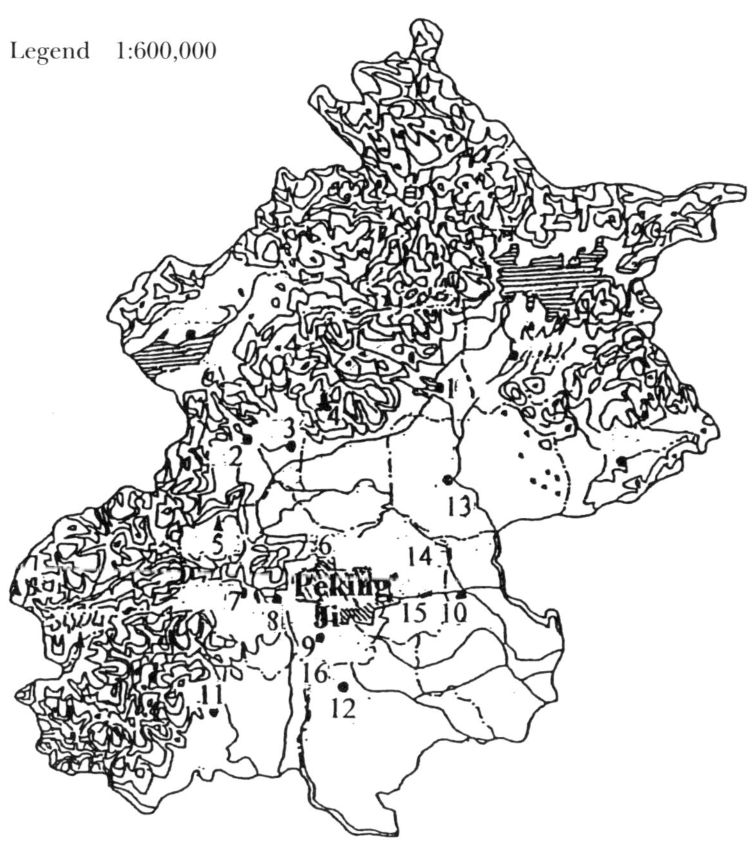

1. Huairou
2. Nankou
3. Changping
4. Tianshoushan
5. Miaofengshan
6. Haidian
7. Mentougou
8. Shijingshan
9. Fengtai
10. Tongxian
11. Fangshan
12. Daxing
13. Chaobai River
14. Wenyu River
15. Tonghui Canal
16. Yongding River

Source: Hou Renzhi, *Beijing lishiditu ji*, I, frontispiece.

heyday; it also served as a forward base for the Chinese ruler's military campaigns against Koryŏ 高麗 and was eclipsed only with the disintegration of the Tang empire.[4]

In A.D. 938 Youzhou fell into the hands of the Khitans (Qidans 契丹), founders of the Liao 遼 dynasty, after they were ceded the sixteen northeastern prefectures from the Later Jin 後晉 state ruled by a former Tang warlord. The emperor Yelu Deguang 耶律德光 (Taizong 太宗, r. 927–947) upgraded Youzhou to be the Southern Capital, Nanjing 南京, also known as Yanjing 燕京. Liao Nanjing was essentially a Chinese-style imperial city. It was a multiwalled city with eight gates, consisting of an enclosed imperial area of 5 *li* with three interior and exterior gates; inside the imperial space was a palace sector in the southwest corner. The perimeter of the outer-city wall was probably 27 *li*, not 37 *li* as recorded in the *Liaoshi dilizhi* 遼史地理志. Within the city there were twenty-six wards of residential quarters criss-crossing the avenues in various shapes; a trade center with shops and markets was located in the north corner; and Buddhist monasteries took a prominent place. There was vivid evidence of Liao's devotion to Buddhism and its patronage by the imperial Khitan families.

In 1012, under Emperor Yelu Longxu 耶律隆緒 (Shengzong 聖宗, r. 983–1031), the prefectural administration was renamed Xijinfu 析津府.[5] The name Xijin originated from the ancient astral-geographical *fenye* 分野 or "field division" system devised during the Zhanguo 戰國 (Warring States) period (480 B.C.–221 B.C.), under which the stars in the Chinese sky were grouped under four seven-unit, twenty-eight "lunar lodges" (*xiu* 宿) along the equator, with each unit assigned to oversee certain geographical divisions or feudal states of the Zhou kingdom. Under the Han these lunar lodges were also regrouped into twelve "dwellings" or "habitations" (*shier ci* 十二次), corresponding to the "twelve stations" of the Jupiter cycle; they are analogous to the twelve signs of the Western zodiac (Capricorn, Aquarius, Pisces, Aries, etc.). A star named Yan was located in the Celestial Markets Enclosure (Tianshiyuan 天市垣), which covered the Ji 箕 (winnower) and Wei 尾 (tail) lodges; the latter were allotted to the *ximu* 析木 dwelling (i.e. Sagittarius) and corresponded to the terrestrial domain of Yan and Youzhou. It was called *ximu* because the habitation was also associated with the *yin* 寅 branch in the twelve "terrestrial branches" (*dizhi* 地支) of the celestial-terrestrial division system and was identified with Wood in the Five Agents or Phrases correlative scheme. Thence came the phrase *ximu weijin* 析木為津 (split wood to make a ferry) from which came the name Xijin for the Yan prefecture (see Figure 5).[6] As one of Khitan Liao's five capitals, and as the administrative center of the Chinese population, Yanjing was gradually renovated, boasting a multiethnic population of 250, 000. In 1036 the new emperor Yelu Zongzhen 宗真 (Xingzong 興宗, r. 1031–1055) gave an order to build additional palaces and official quarters to strengthen the subsidiary capital. This laid a strong foundation for a succession of imperial capitals built in the Beijing area down to the Qing dynasty.[7]

After the fall of Liao in 1125, Yanjing suffered a brief period of neglect under the succeeding Jin 金 rulers of the Wanyan 完顏 clan of the "savage" Jurchen (Nüzhen 女真), but it was soon to be revived. In 1151 the fourth emperor, Liang 亮 (Digunai 迪古迺, r. 1150–1161), a Sinophile, planning for the conquest of south China, decreed a move of the Jin capital from Shangjing 上京 (present-day Acheng 阿城 county, Heilongjiang) to Yanjing and gave orders for its extensive reconstruction. Upon its completion in 1153 the new capital, considered to be situated in the center of Zhongguo 中國, the Middle Kingdom under heaven, was called Zhongdu 中都 (Central Capital), and the name of the administrative prefecture was changed to Daxing 大興 (Great Prosperity). It was a rectangular concentric triple-walled capital city like Liao Nanjing and Song Dongjing; it retained Nanjing's northern wall but expanded outward into the western part of present-day Xuanwu 宣武 District of Beijing. With a perimeter of over 37 *li*, or 18,690 meters, it had three walled gates on each side; the palace- and imperial-cities were located in the south of the center of the outer-city. The new capital was notable for its plans to improve water supply and beautify the landscape. Water was diverted from the ancient West Lake (Xihu 西湖, present-day Lianhua Pond 蓮花池) into the Xima Ditch 洗馬溝 at the northwest of the city and drained in one direction into the Hucheng 護城 (Protective) Canal that surrounded the entire city, and in another into the lakes of the western part of the imperial-city to create a scenic park of lakes and gardens. The outer-city was divided into sixty-two wards, with an extended, active trade center located in the north replete with shops and markets, and under the Jurchen rulers' patronage Buddhist monasteries and Daoist shrines flourished. At the height of its development the Zhongdu administration registered a population in excess of 400,000, including many who were forced to migrate into the capital under imperial orders (Figure 2).[8]

Emperor Liang's ambitious plans ended with his death during the fatal campaign against the Southern Song in late 1161. He was posthumously demoted first to be the Prince of Hailing and then further to be a commoner by his successor Emperor Wulu 烏祿 (魯) (Shizong 世宗, r. 1161–1189). Hence he is known as Hailing wang 海陵王 in the *Jinshi* 金史 imperial annals. Wulu retained Yanjing as the imperial capital, and in the 1180s he added a cluster of summer palaces with the Daning 大寧 (or Wanning 萬寧) Palace in the center

Figure 2 Plan of Liao Nanjing and Jin Zhongdu superimposed on Yuan Dadu and Ming-Qing Peking

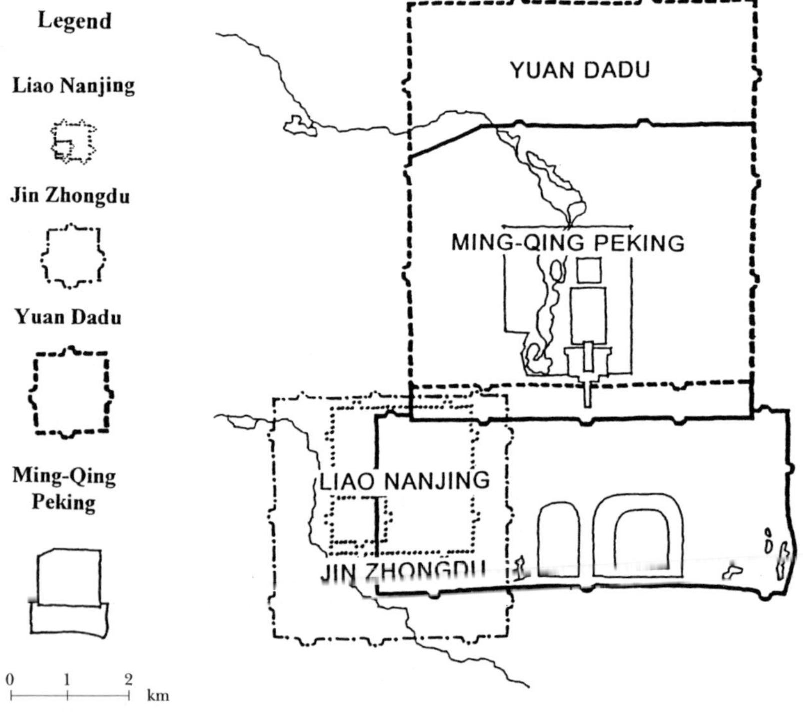

Source: *Beijing tongshi*, III, frontispiece.

at the northeast of the city where lakes and water resources were abundant. In addition, he and his successor Madage 麻達葛 (Zhangzong 章宗, r. 1190–1208) devoted considerable efforts to dredging what came to be known as the Jinkou 金口 Canal. It started from Jinkou on the northern slope of Shijing Hill 石景山 west of Zhongdu, and through the ancient Chexiang Canal 車廂渠 channeled the water of the Lugou 盧溝 (Yongding) River to present-day Yuyuan Pool 玉淵潭 north of the city, from where it flowed southward to the northern Hucheng Canal to drain the Zha 閘 (Watergate) Canal which connected the city with the Grand Canal 運河. The new canal, however, was not serviceable because of constant silting and flooding due to its steep slopes and shallow river beds. Another project was launched in 1205 to divert the water from the Yuquan 玉泉 (Jade Spring) Hill northwest of Zhongdu through the Wengshanbo 甕山泊 (a small lake below the Weng or Urn Hill) to the Gaoliang 高粱 River to serve two canals which ran across the city and joined the Grand Canal from different directions. One of them, starting from the Bailian 白蓮 Pool (later renamed Jishui 積水 [Gathered Waters] Pool) toward the east, joined the Ba 壩 (Dam or Embankment) Canal and exited the city toward Tongzhou 通州 via the Wenyu 溫榆 Canal (northern extension of the Grand Canal). The other, descending from the Bailian Pool to the south, joined the southwestern extension of the Gaoliang River to reach the northern Hucheng Canal and then the Zha Canal for its exit to the Grand Canal. These efforts made some improvement to Zhongdu's waterway communications and they laid an important foundation for the Yuan hydraulic projects. In the spring of 1214, under the pressure of the Mongol invasion directed by Chinggis Qan (r. 1206–1227), the newly enthroned emperor Wudupu 吾補睹 (Xuanzong 宣宗, r. 1213–1223) moved the capital to Bianliang, former capital of the Song, then to Jin's southern capital Nanjing. A year later Zhongdu surrendered to the Mongol forces and Nanjing remained the imperial capital of the Jin state until its annihilation by the Mongols in early 1234.[9]

Zhongdu, which was renamed Yanjing by the Mongol administration, returned to the historical spotlight half a century later when the Mongol-Yuan emperor Qubilai Qaghan (Shizu 世祖, r. 1260–1294) ordered his confidant, the Buddhist monk Zicong 子聰 (Liu Bingzhong 劉秉忠 [1216–1274]), to found a new capital there in 1267. In September 1264 Qubilai changed the name back to Zhongdu but renamed it Dadu (Great Capital) in March 1272. Construction work on the capital was completed in the 1280s. It lost its supreme status after the end of the Mongol domination when the founder of the Ming dynasty, Zhu Yuanzhang 朱元璋 or Ming Taizu 明太祖 (r. 1368–1398), who inaugurated the reign of Hongwu 洪武, chose Nanking to be the capital of the restored Chinese rule and entrusted his principal adviser Liu Ji 劉基 (1311–1375) with designing the city plan. Dadu was renamed Beipingfu 北平府 and became the fief of Taizu's fourth son Zhu Di 朱棣 (1360–1424), the Prince of Yan. It was rebuilt and transformed into Ming Peking (Northern Capital) after the Prince unseated his nephew Zhu Yunwen 朱允炆 (1377–1402?) the Jianwen 建文 emperor (r. 1399–1402), to become the Yongle 永樂 emperor (Taizong/Chengzu 成祖, r. 1403–1424) and designated the former Yuan imperial city as the new capital in 1403. After years of preparation, major construction was undertaken between 1416 and 1420. Peking became the principal Ming capital in the following year.[10]

The Manchu rulers of the Qing dynasty inherited Ming Peking and proceeded to make elaborate modifications and to expand the city and its western suburbs. It became the national capital of several northern governments after the founding of the Chinese Republic in 1911. The name was changed to Pei-p'ing 北平 in 1928, a year after the Nationalist Government of Chiang Kai-shek 蔣介石 (Jiang Jieshi [1887–1975]) chose Nanking to be China's national capital, which it remained for two decades. Peking was again made the nation's capital, renamed Beijing, with the inauguration of the People's Republic of China in October 1949.[11] The old imperial capital soon fell prey to urban expansion and modernization, and many of its inner and outer city walls and historic headquarters were demolished, but the palace-city, dubbed *Zijin cheng* 紫禁城 (Purple or Polar "Forbidden City"), remained intact. Renamed and renovated as the Palace Museum, it houses many treasures and artifacts of the imperial dynasties.

The Cosmological Concepts of Imperial Cities

A complex undertaking, the building of Dadu and Peking brought into play traditional philosophy, religious thought, ancient mythology, political ideology, power politics, historical traditions, and the architectural ingenuity of Chinese civilization. The ancient Chinese believed that Heaven was ruled by the mighty god Shangdi 上帝 (High Lord) or Taiyi 太一 (Grand Monad), and the Earth by his deputy, the Son of Heaven (Tianzi 天子), the temporal ruler, and that there was a close correlation between their courts and residence. The design of imperial cities therefore evoked a microcosm of the heavenly and earthly order and the speculative celestial-terrestrial correspondence system as formulated in ancient cosmogony and astrology. These cities represented an elaborate embodiment of the Chinese world view and value system drawn from strands of various pre-Qin schools of thought: the Confucian, Daoist, and the cosmologist, as expounded, *inter alia,* in the *Shijing* 詩經 (Book of Songs), *Shujing* 書經 (Book of Documents), *Yijing* 易經 (Book of Changes), and *Zhouli* 周禮 (Institutions of Zhou). During the Han dynasty they were reconstituted by the Confucian classicists through the incorporation of the dualist *yinyang* 陰陽 (feminine/masculine cosmic forces) and correlative metaphysical *wuxing* 五行 (Five Agents or Five Phases) theories derived from the *Book of Changes*, with corresponding ritual symbols.

This mythical concept of sky-earth correspondence emerged from early belief in the intimate relationship between the cosmic and political realms, the natural and human worlds, or between the macrocosm and microcosm, with the Son of Heaven as a critical nexus between them dedicated to maintaining the correspondences by proper ritual observances. Paul Wheatley, following the French architectural historian René Berthelot, defined this kind of cosmic arrangements as “astrobiology”, representing the “parallelism” between the astral and biological worlds.[12] This phenomenon was developed in two stages: first, the identification of the celestial constellations, which resulted in the complete “lunar lodges” equatorial divisions system in the pre-Qin era; and second, an idealistic reconstruction of imperial rulership and human society in the sky completed during the Han period. The sources were pre-Qin classics and other works such as the *Lüshi chunqiu* 呂氏春秋 (The *Spring and Autumn Annals* of Master Lü) ascribed to Lü Buwei 呂不韋 (?–235 B.C.). They were supplemented by the “Tianguan shu” 天官書 (Monograph on Celestial Officers) in Sima Qian’s 司馬遷 (145 B.C.–

86 B.C.?) *Shiji* 史記 (Records of the Historian), and by Former and Later Han works such as the *Huainan honglie* 淮南鴻烈 (Great Works of King of Huainan) by Liu An 劉安 (179 B.C.?–122 B.C.) and the *Chunqiu fanlu* 春秋繁露 (Luxuriant Dew of the Spring and Autumn Annals) by Dong Zhongshu 董仲舒 (179 B.C.–104 B.C.). The latter two works further expounded the philosophy of cosmological resonance known as *tianren ganying* 天人感應 (stimulus and responses between heaven and man) to dramatize the inter-relationship between the way of Heaven and human affairs, and laid the basis for Confucians to interpret unusual natural phenomena in terms of celestial vistas or prodigies.[13]

In ancient Chinese cosmology as conceptualized by pre-Qin and early Han astrologers, the sky or heaven was populated by a number of stars and constellations. The most important of these were grouped into four seven-unit, twenty-eight lunar lodges or mansions (*ershiba xiu* 二十八宿) marked along the ecliptic belt of the celestial sphere to serve as reference points for the motion of the sun, moon, and planets. Each seven-unit represented a precinct known as "palace" (*gong* 宮) in four cardinal directions: Eastern, Southern, Western, and Northern, reflecting the belief in a quadruple division of the world. Each palace was in turn represented by a distinct animal image (*xiang* 象): (E) Azure Dragon (Canglong 蒼龍), (S) Vermillion Bird (Zhuque 朱雀), (W) White Tiger (Baihu 白虎), and (N) Dark Warrior (Xuanwu 玄武) (Figure 3). With Sima Qian's attempt to reorganize the celestial sphere by adding the Central Palace (*zhonggong* 中宮), also known as Purple Palace (*zigong* 紫宮) occupying the North Pole, the palaces were increased to five. This celestial reconstruction also incorporated the *yinyang* and Five Agents/Phases theories of the *Book of Changes*. The four images, for example, adopted the symbolic correlations of the Five Agents with cardinal directions and colors: Wood (east, green); Fire (south, red); Earth (central, yellow); Metal (west, white); and Water (north, black).[14] They were also accommodated in the circular sequence of the Eight Trigrams (*bagua* 八卦) of the *Book of Changes*. There were two versions: the earlier *xiantian tu* 先天圖 ("Diagram of the Prior Heavens"), ascribed to the legendary Fuxi 伏羲; and the later *houtian tu* 後天圖 ("Diagram of the Posterior Heavens"), credited to King Wen 文王 of Zhou, which was more popular. The two diagrams had different circular sequence of the Trigrams. In the latter, starting

Figure 3 Four animal images as shown on eave tiles from the Former Han

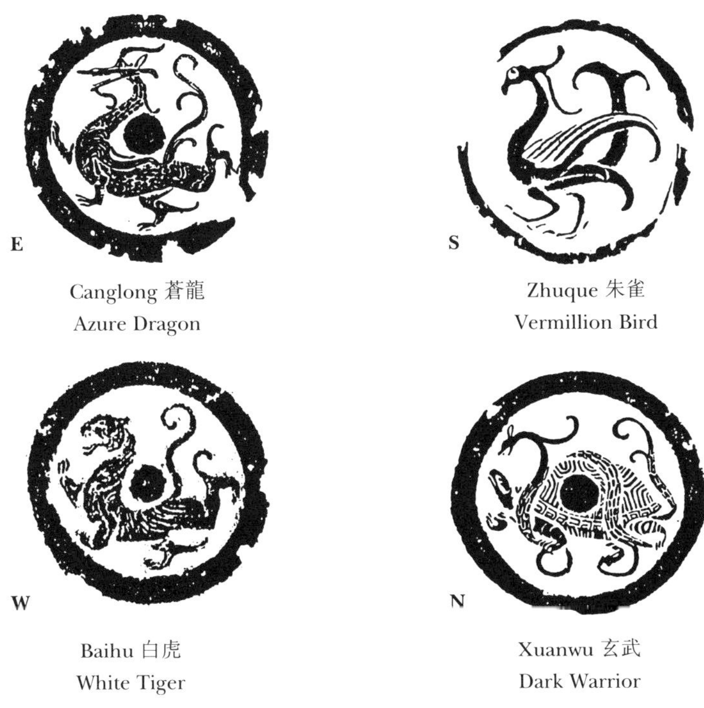

Source: Reproduction from Sun, *The Chinese Sky*, p. 118.

from the east in the clockwise direction, the cardinal points are *zhen* 震, *xun* 巽, *li* 離, *kun* 坤, *dui* 兑, *qian* 乾, *kan* 坎, and *gen* 艮, representing various symbolic correlations with topography and climate (mountain, wind, and water) in geomantic (fengshui 風水) applications (Figure 4). There were many symbolic correlations between the Five Agents/Phases and elements in the natural and divine worlds, such as seasons and calendar, musical notes, human growth, political succession, and even human virtues, and some of these ideas and symbols had significant impact on architectural and spatial conceptualizations in city planning in later periods.[15]

With the appearance of the *fenye* or "field division" system during

Figure 4 (a) The circular *xiantian* arrangement of the Eight Trigrams; (b) The circular *houtian* arrangement of the Eight Trigrams

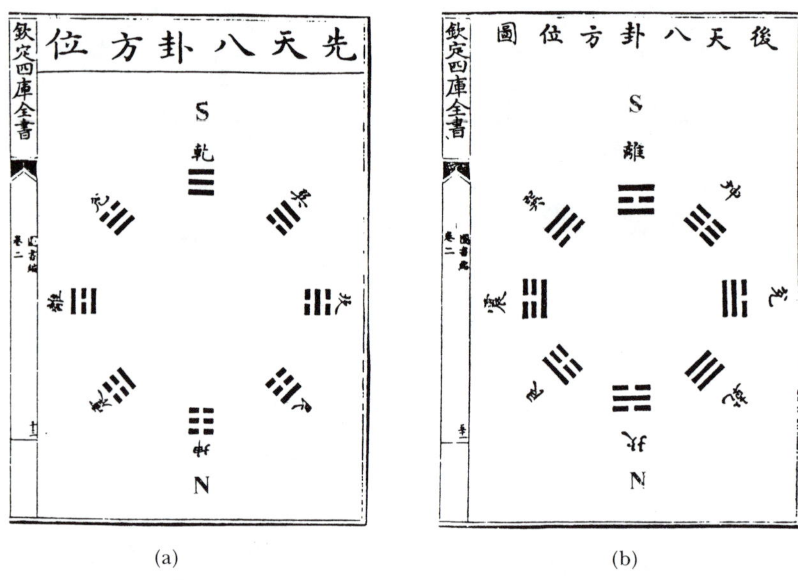

(a) (b)

Source: Zhang Huang, *Tushu bian* (1613), *SKQS* ed.

the Zhanguo period, some of the lunar lodges were assigned to "govern" a certain correlating regional feudal state as well as the royal Zhou house. According to the *Institutions of Zhou* and the *Records of the Historian*, the intent of the system was probably to cement the celestial coordinates and the earthly sociopolitical structure in order to bolster the waning royal authority. For instance, the lunar lodges of Jiao 角 (horn), Kang 亢 (neck), and Di 氐 (root) (Eastern Palace) were thought to correlate with the state of Han; those of Dou 斗 (dipper) and Niu 牛 (cow, or ox) (Northern Palace) with Wu 吳 and Yue 越; Kui 奎 (stride), Lou 婁 (lasso), and Wei 胃 (stomach) (Western Palace) with Lu 魯; and those of Liu 柳 (willow), Xing 星 (star), and Zhang 張 (extended net) (Southern Palace) correlate with Zhou and others. As noted earlier, this "field division" system was complemented by two other celestial-terrestrial division systems during the Han dynasty—the "twelve terrestrial branches" division on the one hand, and the "twelve dwellings/habitations" or "Jupiter station" system on the other. The former divided the sky into twelve terrestrial branch segments in the order of *zi* 子 to *hai* 亥, and the latter divided the sky into twelve "Jupiter stations" in the order of Xuanhao 玄枵 (murky hollow) to Zhouzi 諏訾 (loggerhead turtle). Both systems correlated with the four seven-unit twenty-eight lunar lodges and their corresponding geographical divisions on earth.[16] This practice of "field division" was continued in the compilation of local gazetteers to ascertain the correlation between the celestial stars and the terrestrial regions throughout the imperial dynasties and obviously played an important role in geomantic siting in the planning of cities and monuments (Figure 5).

The astrologers identified three distinctive sidereal regions in the celestial sphere collectively known as *san yuan* 三垣; the region was called *yuan* because it was enclosed by stars lined up like city "enclosures" or "walls". The Ziweiyuan 紫微垣, literally meaning Wall of the Purple Bright Constellation with Polaris, the pole star, in the Center, or simply Purple Palace Enclosure (purple being a regal color), occupied the Central Palace surrounding the North Pole. The Privy Council Enclosure (Taiweiyuan 太微垣) resided in the Southern Palace centered on the autumnal equinox; and the Celestial Markets Enclosure (Tianshiyuan), reconstructed and enlarged after Sima Qian's time, dwelled in the Eastern Palace. The constellating and naming of the stars, stemming from the astrologers' imagination, show clearly the ideological connections between the celestial and terrestrial or, more precisely, that the celestial configurations were regarded as a reflection of the human society impacting on the earthly imperial world order and human society.[17]

In earlier times, before the astrologers worked out the complex celestial system, according to the "Tianguan shu" the Central Palace or central celestial court was dominated by the stars of the constellation Beiji 北極 (North Pole), the pivot of heaven. The brightest star is the residence of Taiyi, the mighty god and ruler of heaven, the three stars next to it represent the three excellencies, and behind the Beiji are two separate groups of four and three stars representing the empress and concubines in the inner palace. The Taiyi was probably created as a superior deity equivalent to Shangdi and above other gods by an imperial cult in the Qin and Han in order

Figure 5 Diagram of circumpolar *fenye.* The inner circle contains the polar constellations, the next circle the 28 lunar lodges (*xiu*), and the outer ring the 12 dwellings. Peking's segment (Yan/Youzhou) is under the Celestial Markets Enclosure (3), as indicated in the chart.

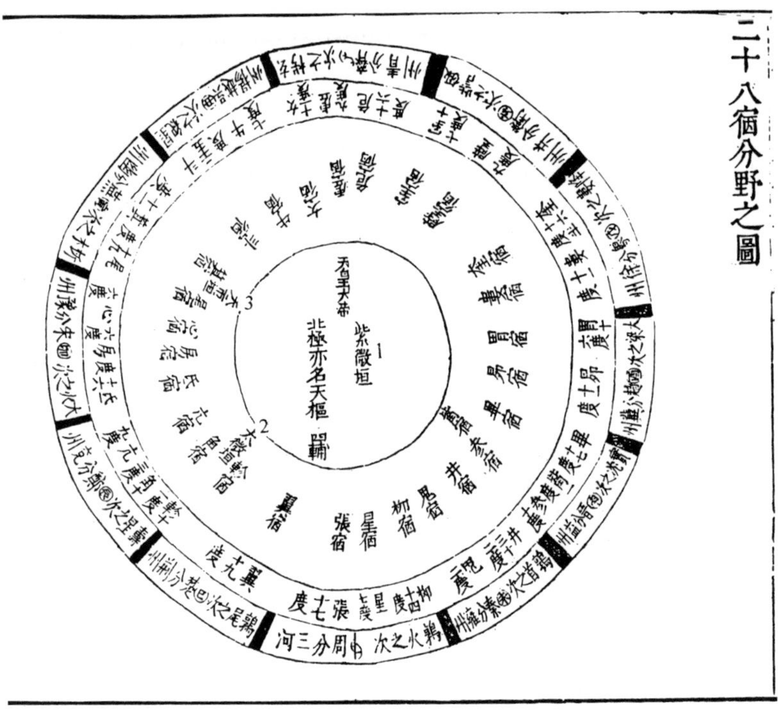

Source: Wang Qi, *Sancai tuhui* (1609), 3 *Tianwen:* 47a.

to enhance the power of the temporal sovereign. In the revised and expanded system of the Ziweiyuan, the brightest star in the North Pole was the Tianhuang dadi 天皇大帝, the High God or Great Emperor of Heaven. This name, created under the growing influence of Han Daoism as the ultimate deity of the Daoist hierarchy, combined four characters respectively meaning Heaven, Emperor, and Mighty Great Lord. Tianhuang dadi hence becomes the ultimate deity ruling in the office at the Pole and replaces Taiyi and Shangdi as the heavenly ruler in the mature celestial-terrestrial corresponding system.[18]

The Purple Palace Enclosure, which was enclosed and surrounded by fifteen stars, was the most prominent sidereal region in the Chinese sky because it represented the celestial imperial palace. Besides the legendary Great Emperor of Heaven, the stars were named after his Four Advisors (*sifu* 四傅) and other assistants, and they corresponded with their counterparts in the terrestrial imperial court headed by the August Emperor (*huangdi* 皇帝) and his bureaucracy. The Privy Council Enclosure, said to be the Spring (Southern) Palace of the Yellow Emperor (Huangdi 黃帝), consisted of ten stars. Their names, such as Dongxi Shangxiang 東西上相 (East and West Upper Ministers), Zuoyou Zhifa 左右執法 (Left and Right Law Administrators), Dongxi Shangjiang 東西上將 (East and West Upper Generals), and others, indicated that they corresponded with the administrative, judicial, and military personnel in the earthly government. The Celestial Markets Enclosure, reconstructed in the Later Han, consisted of twenty-two stars within an enclosure. Their names, such as Huanzhe 宦者 (Eunuch), Zongzheng 宗正 (Nobility's Head Servant), Zongren 宗人 (Nobility's Servant), Lieshi 列市 (Row of Shops), Chesi 車肆 (Wagon Shop), Tusi 屠肆 (Butcher Shop), and others, suggested that they represented the imperial court on the commercial market (Figure 6). These stars were also individually correlated to a number of the Han dynasty provinces (or states) in the empire in accordance with the astral-geographical "field divisions" system.[19]

The Planning of Imperial Cities

In time this concept of astral-geography came to be replicated in the construction of imperial capitals. Already in 514 B.C., when King Helu 闔閭 of the state of Wu entrusted his chief minister Wu Zixu 伍子胥 with the design of a state capital in present-day Suzhou 蘇州, Wu adopted the principle of *xiangtu changshui* 相土嘗水 ("divining the land and testing the water") and *fatian xiangdi* 法天象地 ("following the model of the sky and creating its counterpart on the earth").[20] Later planners of capitals, emulating the technique of *fenye*, designed the metropolitan layout to correspond to the celestial courts and the positions of the constellation stars. For example, the imperial residence corresponded to the region of the Purple Palace Enclosure; the administrative offices or official headquarters with the

Figure 6 The Purple Palace Enclosure (upper left); The Privy Council Enclosure (upper right); The Celestial Markets Enclosure (lower left)

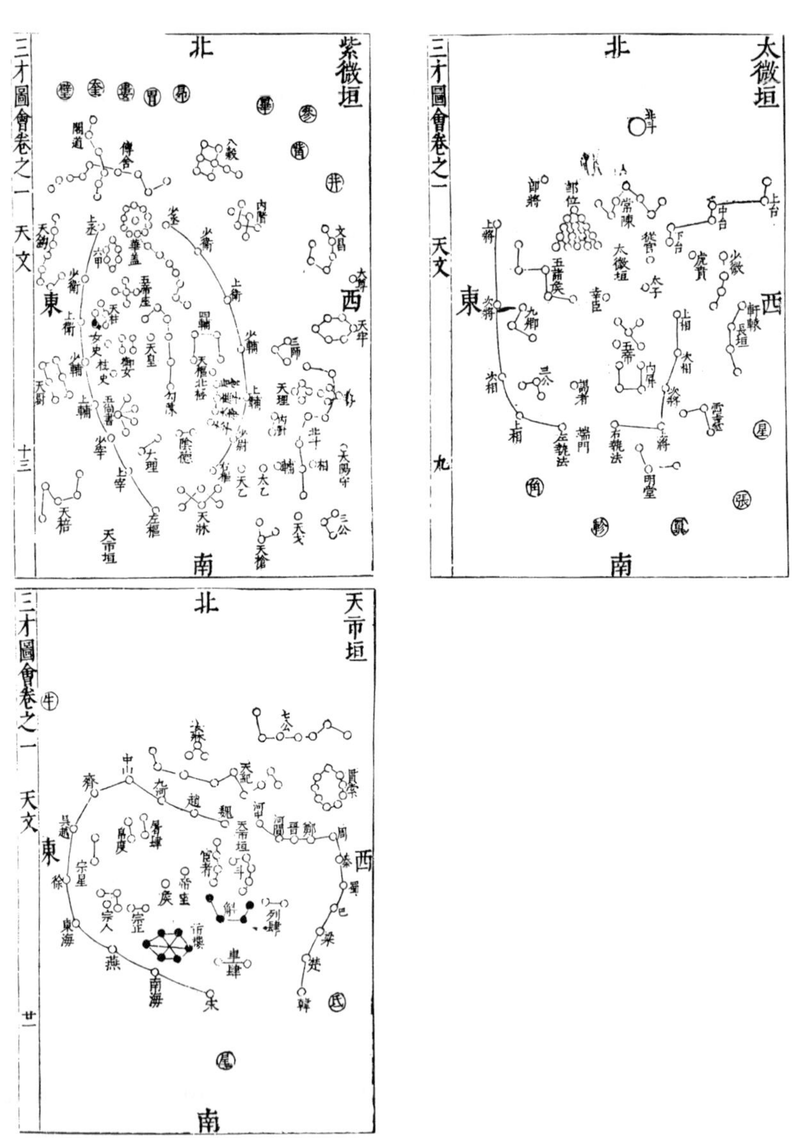

Source: *Sancai tuhui,* 1 *Tianwen.*

Privy Council Enclosure; the markets and trade centers with the Celestial Markets Enclosure; and sundry others. The names of many of the palaces and courts and the walled gates and avenues also matched those found in the celestial constellations.

The *locus classicus* of the layout of Chinese ancient capitals was the *Kaogong ji* 考工記 (Record of Construction), a document traceable to antiquity, which was substituted for a missing section of the *Institutions of Zhou* by Han classicists during the second half of the first century B.C. The section on the Wangcheng 王城 (ruler's city) of the Zhou king contains an idealized design of King Cheng's 成王 city Luoyi 洛邑, built under the supervision of the Duke of Zhou 周公. Under the heading "Jiangren yingguo" 匠人營國 the relevant passage reads: "The *jiangren* [i.e. architect] constructs the state [i.e. Royal Zhou] capitals. He plots a square with sides of nine *li*, each side having three gates. Within the capital are nine meridian and nine latitudinal avenues, each of the former being nine carriage-tracks in width. On the left [as one faces south, or, to the east] is the Ancestral Temple (Taimiao 太廟), and to the right [west] are the Altars of Soil and Grain (Shejitan 社稷壇). In the front is the Hall of Audience and behind the markets." (匠人營國，方九里，旁三門。國中九經九緯，經涂九軌。左祖右社，面朝後市。) (Figure 7). With the square-shaped city layout, the plan provided a multifunctional seat of sovereign power that structurally stressed the centrality of the royal kingdom in the universe and the supreme authority of the august ruler. It symbolically emphasized the interconnections between the gods and men and the harmony between the dualist cosmic forces and human socioeconomic activities. Three, nine, and twelve are significant emblematic numbers in the ancient cosmic mode of thinking which became prominent toward the end of the Former Han. "Three" represents the three sectors of the intelligible universe (heaven, earth, and man); "nine" is three times three and is also the number that represents the ancient Chinese world (the nine provinces established by the ancient emperor Yao); and "twelve" is the sum of three and nine and the number of months in a year.[21]

This classical Wangcheng scheme along with its celestial-terrestrial correlation mythology was subsequently canonized and was employed variably in the layout of great ancient capitals such as Chang'an and Luoyang of the Han and Tang. It was also adapted in the innovative triple-walled Song Dongjing and the Jin capital

Figure 7 Wangcheng *tu*

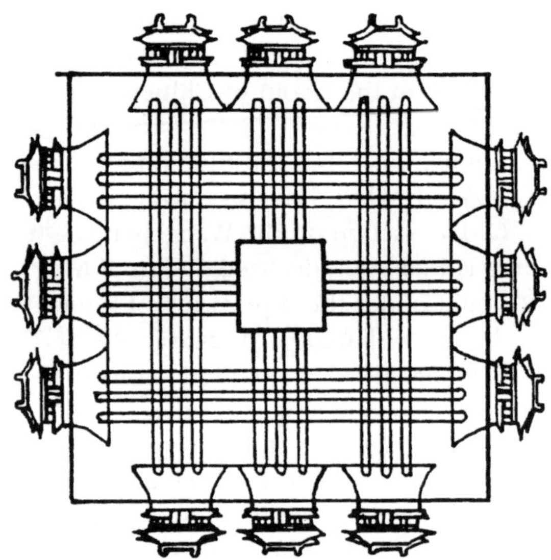

Source: (Song) Nie Chongyi, *Sanlitu jizhu* 4: 6a.

Zhongdu as well as in Dadu and Peking. As showcases of the concentric rectangular or square triple-walled grand imperial capital, Dadu and Peking each included the "palace-city" (*gongcheng* 宫城), "imperial-city" (*huangcheng* 皇城) (functionally an administrative city), and "outer-city" (*waicheng* 外城), providing a grandiose multi-purpose metropolis as well as a sacrosanct architectural monument for legitimating the imperial power. The palace-city, known as the Forbidden City in Ming and Qing times because it was the domicile of the Son of Heaven, was the enclosed residence of the august ruler and his clansmen. Besides the palaces, residential quarters, parks and lakes, the palace- and imperial-cities were studded with many ancestral temples, sacrificial altars and religious monuments whose layout and locations were designed and arranged according to cosmological or geomantic principles. For the outer-city, major north-south and east-west avenues criss-crossed each other with interconnected streets and lanes. Thoroughfares served as boundaries for a number of residential or commercial *fang* or wards that housed a heterogeneous population engaged in various professions. Dadu had fifty such wards corresponding to the "number of the total" (*dayan zhishu* 大衍之數) of the *Book of Changes*, whereas Peking had thirty-two wards, all bearing ritual-symbolic names derived from classical texts. These formal models of imperial capitals were richly documented in dynastic records, local gazetteers, and different literary genres, and formed an integral part of the official and élite traditions of the splendid Chinese civilization.[22]

In this context we should note that in various ways the planning and building of imperial cities had come under the influence of the popular proto-science known as fengshui, or geomancy in the West. The Chinese term, literally "winds and waters", did not mean merely the winds of everyday life, but rather the cosmic *qi* 氣 or *yuanqi* 元氣 (primal breath, ether, or energy)—dubbed the earth's blood—circulating through the veins and vessels of terrains and the windings of watercourses. According to the Chinese belief, the *qi* pervaded heaven, man, and earth; there was both auspicious and malefic *qi* and it could be nourished or manipulated to bring about wealth, happiness, and longevity and to avoid misfortune, disaster, and death. Every place had its special features which modified the local influences of the various *qi* of nature. Apart from the layout of landforms and directions of watercourses, the heights and forms of buildings, or the directions of roads and bridges, were also potent factors. In layman's terms, fengshui has been defined as "the art of adapting the residences of the living and the dead so as to cooperate and harmonize with the local currents of the cosmic breadth" (Joseph Needham). Experts were called in to produce the correct siting, seeking a balance of the *yang* and *yin* forces and a harmony of astrology, space, and directions for building the domicile of the living and preparing for the burial of the dead in order to achieve benefits for the occupant and his/her descendants. In much of Chinese history, fengshui had played an essential role in architecture as a system of rules for siting man-made structures in the landscape, i.e. cities, buildings, temples, tombs, and houses.[23]

To perform siting, before the magnetic compass was developed around the sixth or seventh century, the geomancers used a diviner's board (*shi* 式), one of several special instruments known in Han times under the term *kanyu* 勘輿, literally "canopy and carriage", representing heaven and earth. The term started as a description of the two parts of the instrument—the upper discoidal, corresponding to Heaven, and the lower square, corresponding to Earth, which enabled an operator to consult the stars regarding the choice of a time for activity and to prognosticate the good or bad results. Such experts came to be known as *kanyu jia*. As time passed, and the emphasis of fengshui came to lie more on the choice of place, it made use of the instrument directly descended from the *kanyu* of the Han. The term persisted, and *kanyu jia* became synonymous with *fengshui jia* 風水家. The geomancers' magnetic compass was known as the "dial-plate" (*luopan* 羅盤), a schematic representation of heaven and earth with a number of circles indicating the twenty-four directions. The compass is oriented at a site to the magnetic meridian and bearings are taken on local features across a number of concentric circles carrying the wind-rose, the Eight Trigrams, the Twelve Terrestrial Branches and Ten Celestial Stems, the Twenty-eight Lunar Lodges, and other symbols representing the interactions of heaven, earth, and man. It was the basic instrument used for geomantic and topographical siting down the centuries (Figure 8).[24]

The basic principles of fengshui were derived from the ancient Daoist and cosmological schools of thought on cosmology and cosmogony, astrology and geography, and the concept of change in the *Yijing* and the Five Agents/Phases pulsation theories. They were already apparent in the *Guanzi* 管子 of the Zhanguo period, which noted that the *qi* of the earth flowed in vessels comparable with those in the body of man and animals. A more refined system emerged at the beginning of the Han with the presence of diviners called *kanyu jia* who explored the relationship between heaven and earth. Guan Luo 管輅 (A.D. 209–256) of the Three Kingdoms (Sanguo 三國) period (221–265) is credited with the consolidation of the fengshui system; his manual, *Guanshi dili zhimeng* 管氏地理指蒙 (Guan's Geomantic Indicator), was the first comprehensive treatise on the subject of fengshui. In the fourth century Guo Pu 郭璞 wrote the famous *Zang shu* 葬書 (Burial Book) but it is not clear whether the present edition is his own work. Two famous treatises appeared in the Liu Song 劉宋 (420–479) and Tang periods. They were Wang Wei's 王微 *Huangdi zhaijing* 黃帝宅經 (The Yellow Emperor's House-Siting Manual), and the *Qingnang aozhi* 青囊奧旨 (Mysterious Principles of the Blue Bag [= the Universe]) ascribed to the famous geomancer Yang Yunsong 楊筠松 (c. 840–c. 888), which are still extant.

Figure 8 The Diviner (*taibao*) inspects a site for a dwelling

Source: Sun Jianai, *Shujing tushuo* (1905), 32: 2b.

From the late Tang dynasty onward, with the increasing use of the compass, geomancers were divided between two schools. The School of Forms (*xingshi* 形勢) from Jiangxi, following Yang Yunsong, held mainly to the older principles, stressing the observance of the shapes of the mountain and courses of the river in making prognostications. The School of Orientations (*fangwei* 方位) from Fujian, following a certain Wang Ji 王伋 of Song, regarded the compass as all-important for determining the indications of the topography. This same school also made more use of the Eight Trigrams of the *Yijing* and of astrological elements in their calculations. The division into the two schools was still evident in the Ming and Qing. During the Song, Neo-Confucian metaphysical philosophers such as the Cheng brothers, Cheng Yi 程頤 (1032–1085) and Cheng Hao 程顥 (1033–1107), and Zhu Xi 朱熹 (1130–1200) in particular, made favorable comments on the fengshui theories. New manuals and treatises, including new commentaries on earlier works, appeared in the Yuan and Ming. Some of these were ascribed to eminent personalities of the period such as Liu Bingzhong and Liu Ji, the renowned planner of Dadu and Nanking. The former, as noted later, was credited with a geomantic treatise known as the *Yuchi jing* 玉尺經 (Jade Ruler Canon), whereas the latter, besides being the alleged commentator, was credited with several popular treatises including the *Dili (kanyu) manxing* 地理(勘輿)漫興 (Agreeable Geomantic Aphorisms), which seems to have been an ascribed work. A sample of the essential literature on this subject is found in the *kanyu* section of the imperial commissioned encyclopedia *Gujintushu jicheng* 古今圖書集成 compiled during the early eighteenth century.[25]

In essence, the fengshui scheme is articulated in the precepts and terminology of the cosmological theories of the *Yijing*, the correlative Five Agents/Phases theories of the pre-Qin period, and the celestial-terrestrial correspondence system of the Han period. The dualist *yang* and *yin* ether are identified with the two animal symbols assigned to the eastern and western quarters of the sky—the Azure Dragon of spring and the White Tiger of autumn. Each of these is symbolized further by configurations of topography and direction. The four cardinal directions in the heaven-earth order have similar representations. The South, symbolized by the Vermillion Bird, is regarded as the source of warmth, light, and fire; the East and West are represented by the Dragon and Tiger; the North, represented by the Dark Warrior, is regarded as the cold dark plains. The entrance of a house or the site of the ruler's residence therefore favors facing the south with open spaces in front of it. The cyclical flux of the cosmic *qi* is described by a series of characters called the Twelve Palaces (*shier gong* 十二宮) which postulate the rise and wane of *qi* energy in a human life-cycle. As prominent animal symbols, the dragon and tiger represent different landscapes which betray the presence of *qi* in positive or negative form. The dragon, a cloud-emanating, rain-making protean spiritual being in Chinese mythology, is believed to have hidden and moved around in China's mountain ranges, causing various permutations with hills and ridges through the traversing rivers. The mythical Kunlun 崑崙 mountain range in the far northwest was considered to be the progenitor of all the mountains of the world since historical times. It then branched off into the northern range in the Yan and Taihang Mountains, and the middle range through the Huainan Mountains terminating with the southern range of mountains on the coast of the Yellow Sea. In geomantic parlance, the dragon's veins symbolize auspicious *qi*, the dragon's "cave" (*longxue* 龍穴) is where the *qi* of the heaven/earth and male/female converge and is the source of birth, happiness, and fortune. The confluences of watercourses are considered to be good geomancy as they contain yet do not obstruct the flow of *qi* of the terrain. This explains why followers of the Yang Yunsong school considered of foremost importance the forms and outlines of the terrain as indicators in making prognostications. In addition, as shown by the indicators on the magnetic compass, fengshui embraces and puts into operation the entire Chinese cosmology, such that siting involves observance of the Nine Moving Stars (*liuxing* 流星), consultation of the Twelve Branches of the calendar denoting compass directions as well as years, months, days, and hours, the astrological cycle of the Twelve Animals, the Twenty-four Mountains and Sixty-four Hexagrams, and coordination with the Five Agents/Phases scheme with their symbolic correlations. The latter, moving from Water to Wood to Fire to Earth to Metal in the four cardinal directions with earth in the center, are presented in a number of combinations with the seasons of the year, the 360 degrees, and the twenty-eight lunar lodges of the astrological constellation. It is believed that such a process will achieve a siting in harmony with nature and conducive to good fortune for building a house or preparing a burial ground, and it even applies to the building of a large-scale capital city.[26]

A survey of the literary records on Chinese imperial cities as well as research by contemporary scholars have underscored the varying influences of the fengshui principles in site selection, in the building of the city, and in architectural designs. Though not easy to construct a specific, verifiable case, there is already evidence of these practices in the design and construction of the older imperial capitals such as Chang'an, Luoyang, or Bianliang (Dongjing) of the Han, Tang, and Song. Somewhat clearer cases, however, are the building of Yuan Dadu and especially of Ming Peking. They show that belief in auspicious geomancy was an important consideration, if not a *post facto* rationalization, in the selection of Yanjing as the capital city, and that geomantic siting was applied to the building of Dadu's triple-walled cities and its various administrative buildings and that certain geomantic principles were observed in the construction of the waterways. There are even more specific references in the literature and contemporary opinions on the observance of geomantic principles in the planning of Ming Peking, especially in the design of the sovereign's domicile, the Forbidden City, and the architectural layout of its halls, palaces, and courtyards, which sought to achieve a balance between competing cosmic forces and harmonious interactions between heaven, earth, and man. A fengshui interpretation of Peking is feasible, but it will at best remain a patch-work because of the intuitive, tentative, and elusive nature of the data.[27]

Legends of Dadu and Peking

Against this rich historical background we shall examine the genesis and evolution of the dramatic and resilient popular traditions surrounding the building of Yuan Dadu and Ming Peking. The most popular and enduring of these was the legend of *Nazha cheng* 那吒城 (Nazha City), which emerged sometime after the completion of Dadu, the "Great Capital", and which was transmitted and elaborated upon in literary miscellanies of the period. After having built a capital city near Qubilai Qaghan's headquarters at Jinlianchuan 金蓮川 in Inner Mongolia—called Kaiping 開平, later known as Shangdu 上都 (Upper Capital)—the Buddhist-Daoist Liu Bingzhong received an order to found an imperial capital in the later Peking area shortly after the Prince's accession. Legend has it that he designed eleven gates among the outer-city walls, thatched them with hay and paved them with earth to build the Nazha City. The eleven gates symbolized the body of Nazha, a supernatural child deity in Tantric Buddhism who could transform himself at will into three heads, six arms, and two feet and perform miraculous tasks against demons and evil spirits. Eventually *Nazha cheng* became Dadu's popular name. It imparted a special historical and cultural legacy to a broad cross-section of the populace distinct from the official and élite traditions about the building of the multiethnic capital of the Sino-Mongolian empire.[28]

After the demise of Dadu the Nazha/Liu Bingzhong legend subsided, but in modern times it inspired a more elaborate and engrossing legend about the origin of Ming Peking called "Liu Bowen Building the Eight-armed Nezha City" (*Liu Bowen zhizao babi Nezha cheng* 劉伯溫製造八臂哪吒城). Liu Bowen was the courtesy-name of Liu Ji, a principal adviser of Ming Taizu, the dynastic founder. (In post-Yuan orthography, Nazha is usually written as Nezha, with the "mouth" radical added to the left side of the character Na.) Though a distinguished scholar-adviser who had designed the capital city of Nanking, Liu Ji was actually not involved in the building of Peking. Peking was planned and built in 1403–1420 under the third Ming emperor Yongle or Chengzu, several decades after Liu's death. The emperor Zhu Di, Taizu's fourth son, usurped the throne of his nephew the Jianwen emperor in July 1402 after a three-year civil war. In the legend Liu Bowen entered a contest with another imperial adviser, Yao Guangxiao 姚廣孝 (1335–1418), the former Buddhist monk Daoyuan 道淵, to design a plan for the imperial city. Unbeknownst to each other, both drew a plan to symbolize Nezha—who had remained a prominent supernatural deity in popular culture—in order to summon the guardian deity to exorcize the wicked Dragon King who controlled the water resources, but Liu won the trophy on a technical edge. Apparently, the legend transposed the Nazha/Liu Bingzhong saga onto Liu Ji who, like his namesake, has been intensely mythologized as an ingenious astrologer, geomancer, and prognosticator in the modern Chinese consciousness.[29]

There was yet another sequence of equally interesting legends surrounding the building of Peking, which originated with the Mongol communities but also engrossed the Chinese literati and local residents during the last century. These related the story that the site of the imperial city was chosen by the flight of arrows in the nomadic tradition, hence it is dubbed as "siting by bowshot—locating the city of Ming Peking" in our inquiry. In its indigenous form it featured an eerie legend about the Mongol maternity of the Ming emperor Yongle, which began to circulate in the seventeenth century. The story, entitled "How Emperor Yongle of the Great Ming Built the City of Peking", presents the future emperor, then known as the Prince of Yan, as the posthumous son of the last Mongol Yuan ruler Toghōn Temür (Shundi 順帝, r. 1333–1370) born to his

Mongol consort from the Qonggirad tribe after she became the "empress" of the Ming dynastic founder. Suspicious of his paternity, Ming Taizu sent the young prince away to the land of Yan in the northern border to establish a fief to secure the territory. The prince requested and obtained his father's permission to take Liu Bowen along as adviser. When they reached their destination, while out in the wilderness one day, a mysterious swarthy-faced black rider intercepted them. He took the prince's bow and shot arrows in four directions, asking him to instruct Liu Bowen to build the city at the place where the arrows fell. The prince then put his sagacious adviser to work and a majestic city was thus built, becoming the capital Peking when the prince was enthroned as the Ming emperor. Evidently the legend fused the Mongolian tradition about siting by bowshot in the building of monuments with the mythology of the Mongol maternity of the Yongle emperor, and incorporated the Chinese popular stories about Liu Bowen designing the first Ming capital Nanking transmitted to Peking in a new form.[30]

Two new versions of the legend of the building of Peking emerged in more recent times through incorporating dramatic episodes from the Mongolian tradition of siting by bowshot with the story of Liu Bowen designing the Nezha City of Peking, and fusing them with the miraculous feats of the mythologized early Ming wealthy landlord Shen Wansan 沈萬三 (Shen Fu 沈富) and the ingenious scheming of the Buddhist monk Yao Guangxiao. The first story, entitled "Liu Bowen built the City of Peking", introduces the early Ming general Xu Da 徐達 (1329–1383) as the archer of the bowshot, while Liu Bowen followed the flight of the arrow to locate the site, physically coercing Shen Wansan to reveal his hoarded gold and silver to finance the construction and fending off the wrath of the Dragon King who resented the intrusion of the city building on his turf. The second story, called "How was the City of Peking Built?", reverses the role of Liu Bowen and Yao Guangxiao; Yao becomes the principal actor, whom Liu Bowan recommended to the Yongle emperor to execute the building project based on his city plan. Desperate over the dearth of funds, Yao also sought out Shen Wansan and chained and whipped him repeatedly until he confided the whereabouts of the hidden treasure for financing the construction, in a series of actions resembling those taken by Liu Bowen. The Ming emperor was seen as deeply involved in supervising

Yao Guangxiao and threatening Shen Wansan and brought the city building to a satisfactory conclusion. In these two stories, the chicanery of the Dragon King and the miraculous feats of Shen Wansan were carefully exploited from fictional materials and skillfully crafted onto Liu Bowan and Yao Guangxiao to create another cycle of inspiring folklore. They provide another melodramatic component to the fanciful legends of the building of old Peking from the Yuan through the Ming that have lingered on into the twentieth century and hold contemporary scholars and the general public spellbound.[31]

As this book deals with a subject untreated in English language literature on Peking, it is pertinent to review briefly a few of the major studies on the old capital in recent scholarship to shed light on the comparative aspects of this and other studies on Chinese cities and urban culture. I have chosen three major books published within the last decade: Jeffrey F. Meyer, *The Dragons of Tiananmen: Beijing as a Sacred City* (1991); Susan Naquin, *Peking: Temples and City Life, 1400–1900* (2000); and Madeleine Y. Dong, *Republican Beijing: The City and Its Histories* (2003). Works that deal more with political and socioeconomic issues or general themes of modernity and Chinese city developments are excluded.[32]

Meyer's book, which carries the subtitle *Beijing as a Sacred City*, is the first work in the field of comparative religion to study religious symbolism in a Chinese imperial city. This field generally takes urban spaces to be sacred when they are laid out according to prevailing cosmological belief systems and when, as in the case of Peking, they unite the realm and the ruler in a pattern of sacred kingship. The same pattern can be seen in the ancient Near East, Rome, and in classical Mesoamerica, as well as in China where the proper cosmic orientation in space, combined with the appropriate foundation lore, transformed a new capital into a symbolic sacred city. In treating old Peking as a "sacred city" Meyer stresses the importance of both *symbol* and *place*, using the terms "warp" and "weft" of a tapestry to describe the structural unity. Although symbol and place represent two separate systems, they are woven together to form a seamless urban fabric. The "warp" of Peking is "the cosmic/astral system of symbols that identify it as the seat of government, the center of the earthly world, and the place where the emperor ruled as the Son of Heaven." It constitutes a general pattern that could be adopted and imitated in any imperial city in the pre-modern world; it was simply space organized in a certain special way. The "weft" of Peking, on the other hand, is place. "It is reflected in the complex of popular belief that made it a sacred place, a unique spot on the face of the land where gods, spirits, and heroes visited, where unrepeatable events took place, and where transcendent powers could be reached."[33]

Meyer's book therefore gives a detailed analysis of the cosmological structure of Peking under the rubric "Geometry of the Universe" and examines the significance of the suburban altars under the caption "Heaven is Round, Earth is Square". A succinct exposition of Peking in myth and legend follows—all of which seeks to support the argument of Peking as a "sacred city" in light of the paradigm of comparative religion and comparative history, which is well summarized in the conclusion. Similar approaches have also been taken by the French research group on "Pekin, Ville Sainte" at the CNRS-EPHE in Paris in recent years. While such approaches to the study of Chinese historical cities are not without merits in their own sphere, my study makes no attempt to tailor itself to the framework of comparative religion, although such explorations are fashionable in Western scholarship, particularly outside the realm of China.[34] My work is primarily focused on an investigation of the myths and legends of the building of old Peking in light of the rich intellectual and cultural traditions and historical precedents that enveloped the building of the imperial city. A unique feature in the backdrop of the analysis is the development and interactions between Han Chinese and non-Han popular culture relevant to Peking's urban development over the past centuries, which is outside the concern of most of the current studies. The transformation and renewal of these influences are strongly felt in the modern era as Peking shed its imperial past and entered the world of nations as the capital city of a republican government. As the urban residents struggle to define their identity and to preserve the glorious culture of the past under the pressure of modernization, the endurance of the popular heritage of this great Chinese capital and its eventual efflorescence merit special attention.

By contrast, Naquin's more recent book, *Peking: Temples and City Life,* is a lengthy compendium-like study of the religious organizations in the Chinese imperial capital and their impact on urban social and cultural life from 1400 to 1900. This ambitious and comprehensive book, a rare scholarly endeavor in recent years, covers five hundred years of history, and the author has processed information from over 2,500 Peking temples of the Ming and Qing periods and collected references and data from 2,400 stelae for documentation and analysis. Although temples figure prominently in the title and throughout the text, they are not the sole focus of this mammoth study of over seven hundred pages. In fact, near the end of the volume the author characterizes her work as a "study of religious organizations, public space, and urban identity in Peking". The purpose is to expand understanding of the variety of organizations in Chinese society, particularly in urban cities, before the twentieth century, and to illuminate the importance of religion and space in creating and sustaining networks and associations outside the state, community, or family. This particular interweaving of space, group identity, religion, and state and local affairs in reference to Peking or to any other cities in imperial or modern China has not been attempted before in any scholarship, and though the author is at home in the theoretical paradigm of such topics she lets the documents speak directly for themselves. The wealth of detail, as well as its relevance to such issues as urban organization and culture, social integration and power, and state-society relationships, all of which are important hallmarks in recent scholarship on Chinese cities and urban cultural development, make this study an important and valuable work.

With such an array of rich information and broad coverage of topics, ranging from the focused issues of the integrative potential of popular religion, the functioning of temples as space, the expansion of social associations based on networks and communities, to the general conceptions of state, private and public, the construction of civil identity, and sundry others, Naquin has provided a rich feast from which readers can pick and choose and her book will have a great impact on the study of Peking and other Chinese cities for years to come. My own work has a different and more specific agenda, but Naquin's rich discussions are stimulating and helpful to my conception and analysis of the genesis of legends and their dissemination in relation to the development of urban culture in the historical capital city. Although Naquin does not provide much detail about individual cases of either major temples or religious organizations, it is heartening that the legend of Nazha coming to

Peking to tame its waters by capturing the resident family of dragons and its fancied involvement in the planning of the capital city receives a short description in the introductory chapter. It is unfortunate, however, that the mythical Liu Bowen is not also mentioned, nor is the Nezha Temple built near the Black Dragon Pool (Heilongtan 黑龍潭) in Taoranting 陶然亭 (Pavillion of Merriment) inside the Yongding Gate given attention. The Temple, which was founded by the Sash and Girdle Manufacturing Guild (Tiaodaihang 縧帶行) in the early Qianlong 乾隆 reign (1736–1795) and survived into the 1950s, would give a fascinating illustration of the impact of god and temple on socioeconomic life in historical Peking.[35]

In her *Republican Beijing, the City and Its Histories*, Madeleine Y. Dong attempts to show how the old imperial capital, through the processes of modernization and the material and cultural practices of recycling to meet the residents' present needs, acquired a new identity as a consummately "traditional" cultural city in the early Republican period. The book, covering the years 1911–1937, is divided into three parts. Firstly it explores the city's spatial and administrative transformations, showing the pattern of power relations and of struggle among different forces to control urban spaces, and the state-sponsored projects to construct new public, symbolic, and ceremonial spaces. Next it discusses the urban residents' mode of material life, examining the city's economic conditions and pattern of consumption, with a case study of the bustling "recycling center" in the Tianqiao 天橋 (Heavenly Bridge) District bordering the Ancestral Altar of Agriculture (Xian'nongtan 先農壇) and Altar of Heaven (Tiantan 天壇) in the southeastern part of the city. Then it focuses on the cultural representations of the city produced by the older scholars and new intellectuals. The work concludes with reflections on the theoretical and methodological issues in the study of the capital city and how her study sheds new light on the conception and definition of modernity in comparative perspectives. The author draws heavily on the writings on Peking's history, customs, and styles of daily living produced by older scholars and new intellectuals, not out of pure nostalgia of the bygone era but in order to transform the material and cultural productions of the past for the residents' consumption and to define their needs in the struggle of urban renewal under modernization.

As the author surmises, the history of Republican Peking raises the question of what role the past plays in defining Chinese modernity and demands that we think about modernity not in terms of the framework of East versus West, or modern versus traditional, but instead in terms of a narrative that accommodates both imported and native resources. Dong adopts the idea of "recycling" from the social anthropologists and develops it into the theoretical framework of her book. It describes a primary mode of labor-intensive activities of cultural and material production and circulation engaged in by Peking residents in their search for the meaning of the past and the path to modernity. As she explains it, "Recycling, with its concomitant social and cultural elements, such as nostalgia, is a key of Chinese modernity" and the importance of such a definition is that "modernity was not brought to China by and from the West but created in and through China in its interactions with the rest of the world". In this regard, "China was not a site of passive reception of modernity as defined by Western experiences but an active participant in its creation." This idea of recycling fits well with my attempt to describe the process of the adaptation of old legends and stories surrounding the building of Peking by the ingenious folklorists and entertainers of various persuasions, the Han Chinese as well as the Mongols and Manchus, recreating and disseminating the existing materials to general and specific audiences in different venues in the old capital city. Dong does mention the recycling activities of the leading folklorist, the Manchu royal descendant Jin Shoushen 金受申 (1906–1968), but stops short of describing his work on the Peking legends, let alone the stories of Liu Bowen building the Nezha City of Peking and their significance, which would have provided an important supplement to her thesis—a shortcoming now hopefully made up in the present book.[36]

PART I

The "Nezha City" of Old Peking: Origins and Transformations

Chapter 1

Liu Bingzhong, Nazha, and the Building of Yuan "Great Capital"

The Historical Background

As in all legends of significant import in Chinese civilization, the "Nazha City" legend of the Mongolian Yuan "Great Capital" Dadu unfolded through a multifarious process of mythologization and metamorphosis of a number of distinctive entities: supernatural deities and historical personalities, as well as unique topography and environment. The principal actors were the chief architect Liu Bingzhong, the Buddhist-Daoist adviser of Qubilai Qaghan adept in astral-geography and the cosmological theories of the *Book of Changes* for city-planning; and the supernatural guardian Nazha or Nezha, the Tantric Buddhist child-deity endowed with miraculous powers in exorcizing demons and protecting cities against external threats. Equally important were the unusual topography and environment of the ancient northern city upon which the Yuan imperial capital was to be built, which provided an important source of historical and mythological inspiration. It all began shortly after Qubilai's enthronement in May 1260 at Kaiping (later Shangdu) in succession to his half brother Möngke (r. 1251–1259) as the Mongol qaghan and emperor of China. In 1267, Qubilai entrusted to his confidant, formerly the Chan monk Zicong, the task of founding a capital city in the present-day Beijing region to facilitate his administration and control of north China. This city later became known as Dadu.[1]

Born in 1216 under Jurchen Jin rule, Liu Bingzhong was a native of Xingtai 邢臺, Xingzhou 邢州, modern Hebei, the descendant of a military bureaucratic family from Ruizhou 瑞州, Liaoning. Liu's original name was Kan 侃 and his courtesy-name Zhonghui 仲晦. He took the name Zicong and the appellation Cangchun 藏春 when he converted to Buddhism c. 1238, at the age of twenty-two. He was later known as Liu Bingzhong by imperial decree. A precocious child under the tutelage of his father, Liu Run 潤 (?–1246), a talented musician and able administrator, he was outstanding for his broad learning and talents, but the family suffered after the Mongol invasion. His father submitted to the Mongols in 1220 and was later appointed an administrator of the Xing prefecture, and at the age of twelve Liu Bingzhong was sent to the military commander's headquarters as a hostage son to ensure the family's loyalty. In 1232 his father retired and Liu, then sixteen, was transferred to the Xingtai administration as a first-grade scribe. However, he soon grew tired of the routine and, after his mother née Ma's 馬 death in 1236, he left his post to live in seclusion in Mount Wu'an 武安, Henan. He associated himself with the Daoists of the Quanzhen 全真 sect but did not become a Daoist. Instead he was recruited by Monk Xuzhao 虛照 (1196–1252), a Chan master of the Caodong 曹洞 school from the Tianning Monastery 天寧寺, and converted to Buddhism two years later, becoming the monk Zicong.

Zicong's fortune took a sharp turn when in early 1242 Monk Haiyun 海雲 (1203–1257), master of the famed Linji 臨濟 sect of Chan Buddhism, was summoned by Qubilai, then a powerful and ambitious Mongol prince, to visit his court at Qaraqorum to advise on state and religious affairs. While passing through Xingtai on his way and meeting with Zicong, Haiyun was deeply impressed by his knowledge and personality and took him along as his secretary.[2] During the visit Zicong displayed erudition and wisdom. He was not only adept in Buddhism, but also conversant with Confucianism, Daoism, state affairs, and pseudo sciences including astrology, mathematics, the calendar, geomancy, divination, and different schools of rituals. Qubilai was delighted by his resourcefulness and asked Zicong to stay to render service; Zicong consented but left in late 1246 because of his father's death. However, sometime in 1249, Zicong returned to Qaraqorum at the prince's command. He submitted his famous "ten-thousand word memorial" in which he outlined a detailed plan for consolidating Mongol rule in China through the adoption of the "Han" methods of governance and employment of Chinese scholar-officials in state service. It became the most important document on this subject and was subsequently emulated and implemented by the new administration.[3]

During the next several years, before Qubilai's rise to power, Zicong performed various tasks for the prince that established the framework for Chinese-style government under Mongol rule. In 1251 he organized a corps of advisers, mostly ethnic Han subjects, drawn from capable scholars and grandees of North China with experience in government to serve the prince at his new headquarters in Jinlianchuan, near the future capital Shangdu. These men made important contributions to Qubilai's administration. In the following year, he and his colleagues administered a series of sweeping reforms in his native place Xingtai then plagued by maladministration and poverty. The spectacular results demonstrated the efficacy of the Han method of government and thus strengthened the new policy. In late 1253 Zicong and several of his associates accompanied Qubilai on his campaign against the Dali 大理 kingdom in Yunnan as military advisers. They all entreated the prince to refrain from indiscriminate slaughter and to avoid oppressive measures against the people; the kingdom surrendered without much bloodshed several months later. Then in April 1256, Qubilai assigned his confidant to design and build a capital city which lay between the pastoral and agrarian territories of his fiefdom. It was completed three years later, named Kaiping, and came to be known as Shangdu or Upper Capital. It became a subsidiary capital city of Dadu after the latter's completion and they functioned as twin centers of government and power in the new administration. All these accomplishments greatly pleased Qubilai. The work on Shangdu laid the ground for Zicong's design and the construction of the Great Capital in the following decade (Figures 9, 10).[4]

In the fall of 1259 Qubilai set out to invade the Southern Song in the Huai 淮 valley on Möngke's orders to complete the conquest of China. With Bātur (Bağatur) (?–1261), a grandson of the great Mongol general Muqali (1170–1223), and several Chinese miliarchy commanders leading the forces, he took Liu Bingzhong and some of his colleagues along as military advisers. During the campaign they again strongly remonstrated with Qubilai in order to restrain the commanders from wanton slaughter and plunder of the Chinese population. The Mongol armies successfully crossed the Huai River in September and had reached Ezhou 鄂州 (Wuchang 武昌, Hubei) when word came that Möngke had died (in August) fighting the Song in Hezhou 合州, Sichuan. In December, after adverse reports

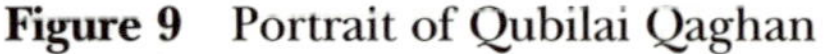

Figure 9 Portrait of Qubilai Qaghan

Source: Courtesy of National Palace Museum, Taipei, Taiwan.

Figure 10 Portrait of Liu Bingzhong

Source: Wang Qi, *Sancai tuhu*, 8 *Renwu*: 5a.

arrived that his brother Ariq Böke (?–1266) had been intriguing to seize the throne, Qubilai hurried north with his confidants leaving Bātur and others to prosecute the siege of Song cities. He won the election in succession to Möngke as Mongol qaghan and ruler of China.[5]

Shortly after Qubilai's enthronement Zicong submitted a memorial on the organization of a Chinese-style bureaucratic administration for the new government, restoration of the traditional Sinitic rites, music and similar ceremonial features, and the construction of a new imperial capital city. With the qaghan's strong endorsement Zicong, together with his close colleagues, devoted the next several years to these tasks. Throughout all this time Zicong remained as Qubilai's adviser in a monk's attire without official appellation. Then in September 1264, in recognition of his many outstanding contributions, Qubilai granted him the layman's name Liu Bingzhong, awarded him the honorific title Taibao 太保 (Grand Protector), and appointed him a councilor of the Secretariat (Canling Zhongshu 參領中書). In early 1267 he was entrusted by the qaghan to design a new capital city in Zhongdu. Nevertheless, Liu kept a low profile in political matters and shunned administrative duties in order to avoid confrontation with the powerful Mongol nobles and Central Asian Muslim officials. A year later he received permission to be relieved of his formal duties at the Secretariat and, apart from the construction of the capital, he occupied himself with other tasks. He collaborated with his colleagues in preparing a new set of rituals for the court ceremonies, in revising the calendar (known as *Shoushi li* 授時曆 upon completion in 1281 after his death), and labored in recruiting talented persons for governmental service in the absence of a competitive civil service examination.

In late 1271 Liu submitted another distinguished recommendation, the adoption of the Chinese state title Da Yuan 大元, meaning "great great" in the classical context, which corresponded to *yeke* in the Mongolian state name "Yeke Mongghol ulus" for the Sino-Mongolian dynasty. This was subsequently accepted. On January 18 1272 Qubilai decreed that Da Yuan replace the older Chinese title Da Chao 大朝, meaning "Great Dynasty", which had been in use as early as 1217 by the Mongol régime when Muqali, the commander-in-chief, was entrusted by Chinggis Qan with the consolidation of North China. During his later years, Liu Bingzhong retired to his private home in Nanping 南屏 Hill south of Shangdu, content with a simple, obscure life, and was deeply absorbed in the *Book of Changes* and Daoist philosophy while studying and practicing Daoist magic rituals. He had built in his house an altar dedicated to the Taiyi and Liuding 六丁 Daoist deities and the site was converted into the Taiyi Guangfu Wanshougong 太一廣福萬壽宮 (Grand One, Vast Prosperity, Myriad Longevity Palace) upon his death. Liu Bingzhong passed away in September 1274 at the age of fifty-nine, bequeathing a rich political legacy colored with myths and legends. The following year Qubilai bestowed upon him the posthumous rank Taifu 太傅 (Grand Tutor), with the accompanying investiture as Duke of the state of Zhao 趙國 and the canonized name Wenzhen 文貞 (Cultured and Faithful). His collected works, entitled *Cangchun ji* 藏春集, in six *juan*, with five *juan* of poems and one *juan* of essays and biographical accounts, is included in the *Siku quanshu* 四庫全書 collection.[6]

Being distinguished as Qubilai Qaghan's principal counselor with extraordinary accomplishments, Liu Bingzhong was given the lofty accolades and stereotyped attributes accorded to a corps of exemplary imperial advisers in Chinese history. The biographers of Liu Bingzhong followed the time-honored historiographical tradition by invoking exemplary historical models in their adulation of their hero. In his career as imperial adviser under Qubilai, his relationship with the qaghan and contribution to his regime was compared to distinguished personalities such as the Duke of Zhou of the Zhou kingdom; Zhang Liang 張良 (?–190 B.C.), counselor of Han Gaozu 高祖 (r. 206–195 B.C.); and Fang Xuanling 房玄齡 (578–648) and Du Ruhui 杜如晦 (585–630), prime ministers under Tang Taizong 太宗 (r. 627–649). However, no single model sufficed to portray his broad intellectual capabilities such as his knowledge of astrology, mathematics, physiognomy, Daoist magical rites, and his literary and artistic talent. The biographers, therefore, viewed him through a broad spectrum of historical examples.[7] This was vividly illustrated by Xu Shilong 徐世隆 (1206–1285) in his "Ji Taibao Liugong wen" 祭太保劉公文. In this funeral ode Liu Bingzhong is compared as an imperial advisor to Zhuge Liang 諸葛亮 (181–234) of the Three Kingdoms Shu 蜀 State. As a celebrated Buddhist, he is compared to Dao'an 道安 (312–385) of the Eastern Jin 東晉. As a monk turned political adviser, he is compared to Huilin 惠琳 of the Liu Song kingdom of the Southern Dynasties. His knowledge of mathematics and of the philosophy of the *Book of Changes* is compared to that of Shao Yong 邵雍 (1011–1077) of the Song. For his skill in poetry he is compared to Tang Xiu 湯休, also of the Liu Song kingdom, once a Buddhist convert. His talent in calligraphy and painting is compared to that of Zhao Feng 趙渢 of the Jurchen Jin. His ingenuity in leadership and in military strategy is compared to that of Wei Gao 韋皋 (746–806) of the Tang. His combined career as court adviser and military leader is compared to that of Du Yu 杜預 (222–284) of the Jin dynasty. His contentment to serve the state without caring for a noble title is compared to that of Li Mi 李密 (722–789) of the Tang. His capacity as builder of the capital is compared to that of the Duke of Zhao of the Zhou kingdom. In this setting, Liu Bingzhong becomes a kaleidoscopic figure.[8]

Like many outstanding historical personalities, Liu Bingzhong also became the subject of legend-making in popular fiction. His mysterious outlook as a Buddhist-Daoist, coupled with his role as a Confucian statesman, provided the germination point of this process. His exceptional qualities as a perspicacious politician and versatile scholar have been attributed to his possession of occult powers, while the myths thus created have blurred his biographical profile and transformed him into a legendary figure. Legends were already flourishing within less than a century of his death, for example, in the works of Tao Zongyi 陶宗儀 (c. 1320–1402), *Chuogeng lu* 輟耕錄, and Ye Ziqi 葉子奇 (fl. 1340–1385), *Caomu zi* 草木子. These mythical accounts, in one form or another, were transmitted through and subsequently multiplied in the flourishing popular literature of the Ming dynasty. Some of them, despite their fictitious trappings, contain certain historical truths which might add to our knowledge of his life; others, however, bequeathed to us an over-exaggerated, transmuted picture of the hero, reflecting the fantasy and obsession of a generation with special meaning.

Several of these stories were a mythologization of Liu Bingzhong's accomplishments. The motives behind his recommendation for the printing of paper notes is attributed to his foresight that coined money could be used only in bright regions and paper currency in dark regions. Since China is the bright region and the desert waste of the north is the dark region, the Mongols descended to rule China from the desert should adopt the paper currency. Otherwise, he predicted, chaos would occur.[9] The construction of the new capital city in Zhongdu (later Dadu) also provided an occasion for mystifying his political wisdom. It is said that in the construction process, tens of thousands of red-headed worms were unearthed at the foundation site. When Qubilai asked if he understood the implication, Liu replied that he perceived these creatures would bring ruin to the empire. There are also stories about his prophesizing the fortunes of the Mongols. For instance, Liu is said to have foreseen the successors to the Mongol throne after Qubilai to be the men from the "Western Regions".[10] Similarly, he is said to have composed a *ci* 詞 poem entitled "Xijiang yue" 西江月 (The Moon over the West River), predicting the demise of the last Yuan emperor and the rise of the Ming dynasty founder.[11] According to the same source, Liu's premonition about the men from the "Western Regions" cast a pall on Qubilai who had begun lavishing gracious offers on 'Phags-pa (1235–1280), an influential Tibetan Buddhist priest. The qaghan thought he was the ringleader of the men from the "Western Regions" and hoped that in this way he could perhaps buy off his potential enemy and ensure the security of his throne.[12] Liu's knowledge of mathematics likewise became another source of legend. According to late Ming accounts, his mathematical know-how enabled him to foresee that some hundred years after his death a thief named Li Huai 李淮 and his accomplices would come to plunder his grave and steal the mortuary objects. He had the robbers' names inscribed on an epitaph buried inside the grave, so that when the crime was actually committed in a certain year during the Jiajing 嘉靖 reign of Emperor Shizong 世宗 (r. 1522–1566), the authorities had no difficulties in catching the culprits.[13]

Not surprisingly Liu Bingzhong became a popular figure in Ming times. On the one hand, he was much praised as a minister of virtue whose advice and foresight deserved the attention of future generations. When Emperor Xuanzong 宣宗 (r. 1426–1435) ordered the compilation of the *Lidai chenjian* 歷代臣鑑 (Mirror of Exemplary Officials in Successive Dynasties) in 1426, Liu Bingzhong's memorial to Qubilai Qaghan on the adoption of the Chinese model for institutional reforms was included.[14] On the other hand, his dramatic role as a Chan Buddhist *cum* political adviser made him a paragon among some Ming officials such as the monk Daoyuan, later known as Yao Guangxiao. A native of Changzhou 長洲, Suzhou prefecture, Yao entered a Buddhist temple in his early teens and was tonsured in

1352 at the age of seventeen, but he was no ordinary monk. Besides studying Chan Buddhism he also read the Confucian classics and the works of early thinkers, practiced the writing of poetry and prose, dabbled in Daoism and cosmological studies, and became adept in military science. He is said to have forsaken his secluded life after a physiognomist, impressed by his extraordinary features, reportedly foretold his rise to power by calling him another Liu Bingzhong. In 1382 he responded to Ming Taizu's summons to the Yan prefecture to serve Zhu Di, the Prince of Yan, later the Yongle emperor, as a monk-in-attendance and became his most trusted counselor in civil and military affairs. It is said that through his skills in physiognomy he presaged the prince's imperial destiny and counseled Zhu Di with plans and stratagems in his usurpation of the throne of the Jianwen emperor. Daoyuan was a great admirer of Liu Bingzhong. According to an anecdote, when Daoyuan was residing at the "double-pagoda" Qingshou Monastery 慶壽寺 near the prince's headquarters in the then Beiping prefecture, he often dreamed of chatting with Liu Bingzhong.[15] Upon his accession the Yongle emperor bestowed on Daoyuan a lay name from which he became known as Yao Guangxiao. Some Ming writers suspected that when the emperor chose the name he may have had Liu Bingzhong in mind, for "Guangxiao" means "to broaden filial piety", which parallels "Bingzhong" meaning "to sustain loyalty". Daoyuan's obsession with his hero was so great that in the minds of his contemporaries and later historians, the two images became merged. For example the Qing scholar Qian Qianyi 錢謙益 (1582–1664) wondered, somewhat metaphorically, if the monk might be considered a reincarnation of Liu Bingzhong! In commenting on Yao Guangxiao's poem on a visit to Liu Bingzhong's grave, Zhu Yizun 朱彝尊 (1629–1709) also suggested that Yao's emulation of his hero might have prompted him to play an active role in the Prince of Yan's usurpation.[16]

The legends of Liu Bingzhong were frequently exploited by Ming writers in their effort to dramatize the founding of their own dynasty. The red-headed worms discovered during the construction of the capital, regarded as a bad omen, became a reference to the anti-Yuan Red Turban (*hongjin* 紅巾) insurgents who successfully overthrew the Mongols. It was held that Liu understood the implication, but was reluctant to divulge it. Liu's alleged prophecy that the men from the "Western Regions" would succeed to the Mongol throne also became a reference to the founder of the Ming. The legend-makers alluded to the fact that Ming Taizu's native place, Fengyang 鳳陽 (i.e. Zhongdu), modern Anhui, lay to the west of Peking (actually it was situated to the southwest), and they blamed Liu Bingzhong for not being more specific in his prediction.[17] Liu's capacities as the architect of two capitals, Shangdu and Dadu, apart from giving rise to dramatic legends that are the focus of the present study, were likewise exaggerated by geomancers of the Ming as being due to his special knowledge of astral-geography. In this connection he was purported to have written the geomantic treatise *Yuchi jing* whereas Liu Ji or Liu Bowen, chief adviser to Ming Taizu, was the attributed author of the commentary.[18] By the same token, Liu Bingzhong's astuteness in politics was also improperly exploited. For instance, in January 1475 an imperial decree was promulgated banning the circulation of some eighty "heterodox books" (*yaoshu* 妖書), among which there was one entitled *Liu Taibao xielou tianji* 劉太保洩漏天機 (Liu Taibao divulging the hidden plans of Providence). Appearing to be a prognostic text, it was most probably forged by seditious agents exploiting the legends around Liu Bingzhong for propaganda purposes.[19]

Liu Bingzhong's most significant impact in Ming times was that his magnetic qualities as imperial adviser, religious master, and versatile scholar became a source of mythologization of Liu Ji and, to a lesser extent, the monk Daoyuan or Yao Guangxi, two distinguished imperial advisers of the early Ming. In the course of time Liu Bingzhong's image and character traits became convoluted with those of Liu Bowen and Yao Guangxi, particularly with the former, and provided the germination of miraculous stories and bizarre legends which laid the basis of much of the mythology surrounding the building of Peking in recent centuries.

Liu Bingzhong's City Plan

Liu Bingzhong's biographies, including the main entry in the official *Yuanshi* 元史 compiled in the early Ming, give few details of his role in the building of Dadu, but contemporary references on his contribution are very specific. He is positively identified in the late Yuan gazetteer of the capital, the *Xijin zhi* 析津志 compiled by Xiong Mengxiang 熊夢祥, a one-time superintendent of Confucian studies of the Dadu circuit, as the ingenious architect who designed the city based on his broad knowledge of urban planning and the historical traditions of imperial cities. Although the biography of Zhao Bingwen 趙秉溫 (1159–1232), an academician knowledgeable in city building, also mentions that he had accompanied Liu Bingzhong "to inspect (the site) for a dwelling" (*xiangzhai* 相宅), and submitted a city plan to Qubilai qaghan, Liu was definitely the main contributor to the design and building of Dadu.[20] There were plenty of good reasons for Liu Bingzhong to choose this site: not only was it the seat of the imperial cities of Liao and Jin, where many important and magnificent architectures were still standing, but it was also believed that the capital was situated at the center of heaven and earth, and its terrain and waterways were blessed with auspicious geomancy.

Prior to this time, for example, Zhu Xi, the Southern Song doyen of Neo-Confucianism and an ardent exponent of fengshui, had used Yan's ancient name Jidu 冀都 to conjure up a favorable impression of the region, hailing it as the center of the terrain under heaven. Using the dragon and tiger images to pinpoint the striking features and the suggestive flow of auspicious cosmic breadth, he started with a poignant remark: "Jidu is situated in the center of heaven and earth; what a site of auspicious geomancy!" Then he continued: "There the mountain range originates from Yunzhong, the peak of the mountain's spine is right there. The water west of the spine flows west into Longmen and the West River, the water east of the spine drains into the Sea. In the front is the Yellow River encircling. On the right side is Mt. Hua, towering aloof; it is the Tiger. Passing Mt. Hua to the center is Mt. Song; this is the front row. Further away is Mt. Tai, towering on the left, it is the Dragon" (冀都是正天地中間，好箇風水。山脈從雲中發來，雲中正高脊處。自脊以西之水，則西流入於龍門，西河自脊以東之水，則東流入海。前面一條黃河環繞，右畔是華山，聳立為虎。自華來至中為嵩山，是為前案。逐過去為泰山，聳於左，是為龍。) That Zhu Xi invoked the archaic name in preference to Yan is interesting because the latter was then the capital of the Jurchen Jin, Song's arch rival. He could not openly relish the auspicious geomancy of the enemy's seat of authority, and he might have wished that a restored Song empire in the near future would plan its capital there.[21]

In Qubilai's time, a favorable opinion about You and Yan as the site of the new capital was expressed by Bātur, grandson of the eminent general Muqali, in response to an imperial enquiry before the start of the project. He said: "The topography of You and Yan looks like a 'coiling dragon' (*longpan*) and a 'crouching tiger' (*huju*); its landforms and terrains are mighty and impressive. It controls the Jiang-Huai region to the south, and joins the adverse deserts to the north. The Son of Heaven should sit in the center to receive audience from the four directions. If the great qaghan wished to rule the land under Heaven, the seat of residence should be none other than Yan." (幽燕之地，龍蟠虎踞，形勢雄偉，南控江淮，北連朔漠。且天子必居中以受四方朝覲。大王果欲經營天下，駐蹕之所，非燕不可。) This "dragon and tiger" metaphor was allegedly coined by Zhuge Liang, the sagacious minister of the state of Shu, in reference to the superior topography of the ancient city Jinling 金陵 (renamed Nanking by Ming Taizu, see later), then capital of the state of Wu, which he had commented on during a visit in an attempt to persuade its ruler Sun Quan 孫權 (181–252) to join forces against the state of Wei 魏 during the Three Kingdoms period.[22] Bātur accompanied Qubilai on his invasion of the Southern Song in 1259, with Liu Bingzhong serving as military adviser. It is quite possible that his comments on the geomancy of the region reflected the views of his mentor.

Shortly after Qubilai's reign Li Weisun 李洧孫 (1243–1329), a former Song scholar who was recruited to serve the Yuan government, wrote a glowing rhapsody on the newly completed Great Capital. In his "Dadu fu" 大都賦, citing the "Covering Sky" (*gaitian* 蓋天) cosmological theory from the classic *Zhoubi suanjing* 周髀算經 (Arithmetic of the Gnomon and the Circular Paths), he made the following comments on the region's geomancy:

> Heaven looks like a cover or a tilted bamboo-hat, the Lord's carriage is driving around from the center. The Northern Asterism (Beichen [i.e. Beiji]) remains stationary, taking command of the four directions and looking down at Youdu. Viewing the celestial phenomenon, North is the center of Heaven. The Kunlun mountain range coalesces its roots (in Yan Mountains), and its waterways flow eastward. Looking over Shanggu the Dragon is coiled, and heading toward the (southern) direction of the *li* and *ming* hexagrams the seat of orthodoxy has been laid. The soil is fertile; the water is sweet. Examining the "principles of the topography" (or "principle of the earth") (*dili*), Yan is the land of the superlative.[23]

天如倚蓋而笠欹，帝車運乎中央。北辰居而不移，臨制四方，下直幽都。仰觀天文，則北乃天之中也。維崑崙之結根，并河流而東馳。歷上谷而龍蟠，嚮離明而正基。厥土既重，厥水為甘。俯察地理，則燕乃地之勝也。

These lines evoked the popular belief in celestial-terrestrial correlation and relished the image of the Dragon, symbol of the auspicious *qi*, and the conjugation of good and sweet water as testimony to superior geomancy. Short of *de facto* glorification of the building of the capital, the rhapsody reflected the literati's consensus on the supremacy of the region. Liu Bingzhong, with his good knowledge of astrology and geomancy, was certainly well aware of its significance.

However, having decided to build the Yuan capital on the site of the former Jin Zhongdu, Liu Bingzhong and his colleagues ruled against renovating the existing Jin capital and advocated building a new city in its vicinity. There were apparently two practical reasons for this: first, many of the imperial palaces and official quarters in the old Jin capital had been severely damaged by the Mongol invasion in 1215 and were beyond repair; and second, the supply of water provided by the Lianhua Pond to the west of the old city was deemed inadequate for what would become a grand metropolis in the Mongolian state. In selecting the new imperial city—allegedly after having performed the divination of geomantic siting by examining the locale's fengshui, seeking a harmonious blend of the wind, mountains, and water—Liu favored the northeast of Zhongdu, with the old Jin summer palaces built by Emperor Wulu as the center. This was to take advantage of the water from an artificial lake called Taiye Pond 太液池—in the center of which was the famed Qionghua Island 瓊華島—which was supplied by the copious Gaoliang River to the west. The concentric triple-walled architectural model adopted was none other than the classical Wangcheng described in the *Institutions of Zhou,* with appropriate modifications to incorporate the existing Jin architecture and to meet the requirements of the multiple functions of the new capital. In this undertaking, Liu applied his knowledge of astral-geography and the cosmological theories of the *Book of Changes* to urban planning and designed a grand metropolis which, though it incorporated certain Mongolian tribal and pastoral features in architecture and decorations, was basically a traditional

Chinese imperial capital. The role of the new capital was to legitimate the Mongol sovereign as the Son of Heaven ruling from the center of the Universe.[24]

Under the supervision of a number of senior officials and experienced artisans, including a few of Central Asian origin, the construction was carried out in several stages. In February 1267 ground was broken for erecting the outer walls of the imperial-city. Construction of the imperial palaces and residential halls within the palace- and imperial-cities was started a year earlier and the building of the walled enclosures followed, while additional palaces, altars, temples, official quarters, and inner-city walls were built within the decade. In March 1272 the capital was renamed Dadu, followed by the completion of the palace-city. All the imperial palaces and sacrificial halls were completed in late 1274, and the initial phase of the building program was concluded by the end of 1276. The outer-city walls, made of tamped earth instead of bricks, along with other structures, reached their first stage of completion in 1283 together with the administrative offices, but they were not finished until August 1292. (Some parts of the northern sections of the earthen walls survived and are now incorporated into a Dadu Remains Public Park.) According to the Yuan record, the rectangular perimeter of Dadu was 60 *li* or 33.2 km, but it measured only 28,600 meters by an archaeological team, and had eleven gates along the outer-city walls protected all around by an artificial waterway with moats (Figure 11).[25]

In the meantime, several important waterworks projects were implemented under the supervision of the eminent astronomer, mathematician, and hydraulic engineer Guo Shoujing 郭守敬 (1231–1316). Already in 1263, shortly after Qubilai's accession, Guo had proposed to reopen the former Jin Jinkou Canal which had been used to channel the water of the Lugou River to the capital city through the old canals although the outflow was blocked during the war between the Mongols and the Jurchens. Guo argued that its reopening after careful management would be useful for both navigation and irrigation while safely draining away the excess water. His suggestion was adopted, and the renovated Jinkou Canal facilitated the transport of boulders and stones from the Western Hills (Xishan 西山) for the construction of Dadu, but with the passage of time it was again silted and inundated by flooding and had

Figure 11 Plan of Yuan Dadu superimposed on Jin Zhongdu

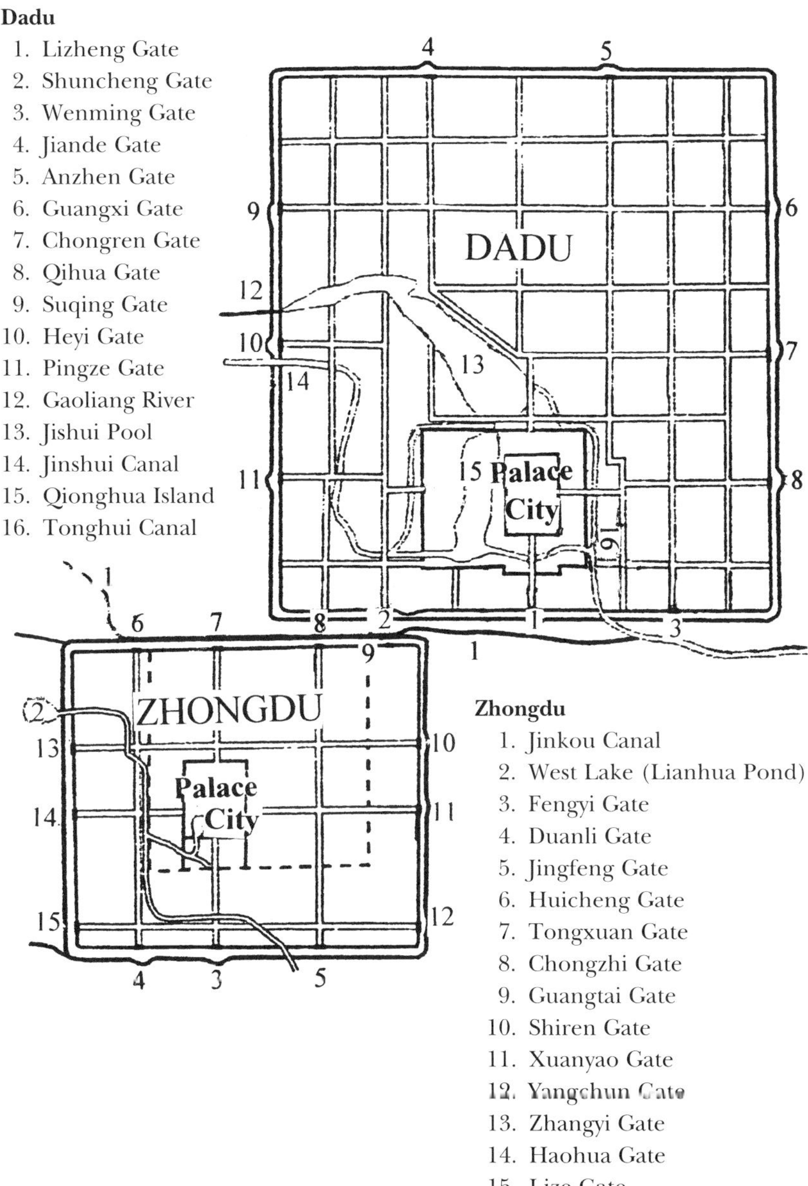

Source: Hou Renzhi, *Beijingcheng de qiyuan*, p. 82.

to be shut down in the early 1330s. In addition, Guo proposed to divert the water from the Jade Spring Hill of Dadu via the Jinshui Canal 金水 (Golden Water) into the Jishui Pool, then channeling it into the disused canal constructed by the Jin which ran across the capital city through the northeast corner and exited to join the Grand Canal. This led to the restoration of the old Dam or Embankment Canal in 1279, which provided the northern canal that connected Dadu with the Grand Canal.

Then in autumn 1293, shortly before Qubilai's death, Guo Shoujing launched an ambitious hydraulic work to improve the water supply and inland navigation of the capital. First he channeled the water from the affluent Baifu Spring 白浮泉 east of the Shen 神 (Spiritual) Hill in Changping 昌平 county through various canals running south into the Urn Hill Lake (i.e. Wengshanbo, known as Kunming Lake 昆明湖 since the Qing), and emptied it through the Gaoliang River into the Jishui Pool to be connected with the old canal. From there the renovated old canal descended downward around the eastern walls of the imperial-city and exited through the Wenming Gate 文明門 of the outer-city in the south, joining with the Grand Canal. The canal, installed with a series of lock-gates to regulate the water levels for the entire section between Dadu and Tongzhou and covering a distance of some 160 *li*, was completed a year later and Qubilai bestowed on it the name Tonghui 通惠 (Thorough and Beneficial). The project not only brought to Dadu a new source of water supply from the Baifu Spring through Urn Hill Lake into the Jishui Pool, but also greatly facilitated the navigation of grain boats from the southeastern provinces into the capital (Figure 12).[26]

The city plan of Dadu is well documented in extant fragments of the *Xijin zhi*, miscellaneous literary pieces, and recent archaeological finds. In the outer-city, a stone engraved with the phrase *zhongxin zhi tai* 中心之臺 (Central Platform) found near the Central Pavilion (Zhongxinge 中心閣), on the right of the Drum Tower (Gulou 鼓樓) north of the imperial-city points to a "center marker" of the entire triple concentric walled city. It must have been intended to be equidistant from the midpoints of each of the four outer-city walls. It also formed the main north-south axis through the imperial- and palace-city along which all major imperial buildings and gates were situated. The location of the imperial-city, however, deviated from

Figure 12 Zhongdu, Dadu, the lakes, rivers, and canals

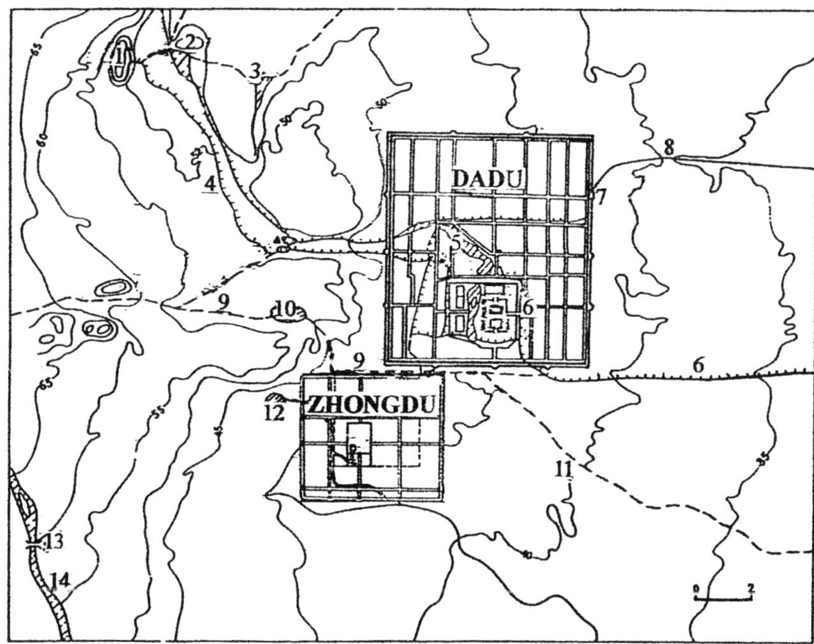

1. Yuquan Hill
2. Wengshan Lake
3. Gaoliang River
4. Jinshui Canal
5. Jishui Pool
6. Tonghui Canal
7. Guangxi Gate
8. Ba Canal
9. Jinkou Canal
10. Yuyuan Pool
11. Jinkou New Canal (1342)
12. Lianhua Pond
13. Lugou Bridge
14. Lugou River

Source: Hou Renji: *Beijing cheng de qiyuan*, pp. 71, 83.

the classical Wangcheng model because of the need to incorporate the existing Jin palaces and to adapt to the topographical features of the former summer capital. It was built slightly southeast of the "center marker" and the palace-city, known as Da Nei 大内 (Great Interior), though placed in the center of the city, shifted to the far right of the imperial-city. The lake area of Wanning Palace (present-day Beihai 北海 Park) northeast of Zhongdu became the center of the square-shaped imperial-city. Two imperial parks and a group of symmetrical residential palaces were built on the east and west shore of the picturesque artificial Taiye Pond. The palace-city, located at the east shore, included two palaces and three multihall compounds (Da Mingdian 大明殿, the hall of audience, in the front), arranged in a north-south direction along the main axis, and a Mongolian *ordos* for the empress was erected next to the northern palace-hall. Inside the palaces and halls were a number of residential pavilions decorated with Mongolian tribal furnishings and an area was provided within these walls for yurt tents. Enclosed by earthern walls 10.7 meters in height on four sides with one gate on each face, this vertical rectangular palace-city also had another distinctive feature. Modeled on the Song's Bianliang city plan via Jin's Zhongdu, a T-shaped Imperial Way (*huangdao* 皇道) was built extending from the southern gate through a huge court yard and a bridge into the corresponding gate of the imperial-city, leading to the exit of the outer-city and providing an outlet through the triple-walled cities.[27]

Liu Bingzhong's application of geomantic siting, and the astral-geography system that he allegedly adapted in designing the triple-walled capital, were alluded to in Xiong Mengxiang's *Xijin zhi* under the section captioned "Chaotang gongyu" 朝堂公宇. This section is focused on the principal administrative offices and buildings of the Yuan court in the imperial- and palace-cities. The preamble briefly states:

> On the *jichou* day of the second month of the fourth year of Zhiyuan (March 27 1267), starting at the northeast corner of Yanjing, [the planners] took compass bearings. They set up the state and established the capital, in so doing laying a foundation to all under heaven. On the *jiazi* day of the fourth month (April 30), construction was begun on the inner imperial-city. On that site the Honorable (i.e. Liu Bingzhong) marked the cardinal directions. Starting at the northern sector of the new capital's Fengchi Ward, he set up the Office of the Central Secretariat. . . . Relishing the site of the new capital as the cornerstone of security, he placed the administrative headquarters in [the location corresponding to the sidereal] Purple Palace Enclosure.
>
> 至元四年二月己丑，始於燕京東北隅，辨方位。設邦建都，以為天下本。四月甲子， 築內皇城，位置公定方隅，始於新都鳳池坊北立中書省。……奠安以新都之位置，居都堂於紫微垣。[28]

After a sketch of the geomantic siting to mark the Office of the

Central Secretariat in a location corresponding to the sidereal Purple Palace Enclosure, a more detailed description of the architectural layout follows:

> Office buildings of the Northern (Central) Secretariat were the first to be built. They were located north of the Fengchi Ward, and west of the Bell Tower.
>
> Office of the Central Secretariat. In the fourth year of Zhiyuan (1267), the Shizu Emperor (i.e. Qubilai Qaghan) gave an order to build the new walled capital. He commanded the Grand Protector Liu Bingzhong to take the compass bearings, and Liu sited the Secretariat north of the present-day Fengchi Ward. Planning the city against the terrain [in correlation with the celestial constellations], he marked several coordinates (i.e. corresponding realms) from the dwellings of the Purple Palace Enclosure.
>
> The Bureau of Military Affairs was placed at the dwelling of the Military Windings star (Wuquexing) (i.e. the Kaiyang star in the Big Dipper [Beidou] constellation); and the Censorate, atop the Left and Right Law Administrator Celestial Gates stars (Zuoyou Zhifa Tianmen) [in the Privy Council Enclosure]. The Ancestral Temple was sited in the *zhen* (eastern) cardinal direction; there it was the Blue (i.e. Eastern) Palace [of the universe].
>
> The Celestial Master Shrine (Tianshigong) was placed in the *gen* (northeastern) cardinal direction above the Ghost Household (Guihu) [lunar lodge?]. The designs of the inner and outer cities, the palaces and chambers, and the public buildings were all based on the sage ruler's recommendation. They were also verified by Liu Bingzhong according to the "warp" and "weft" of the topography (i.e. the longitude and latitude of the terrain), focusing on the region of the "ruler's emanation" (*wangqi*). As a result, he was able to assist the imperial enterprise and expand the grand plan and the great foundation; they were the standard rules of governance and would generate boundless dynastic fortune and longevity (Figure 13).[29]
>
> 北省始剏創公宇，宇在鳳池北坊，鐘樓之西。中書省。至元四年，世祖皇帝築新城，命太保劉秉忠辨方位，得省基，在今鳳池坊之北。以城制地，分紀於紫微垣之次。樞密院，在武曲星之次。御史臺，在左右執法天門上。太廟， 在震位，即青宮。天師宮，在艮位鬼戶上。其內外城制與宮室、公府，並係聖裁，與劉秉忠率按地理經緯，以王氣為主。故能匡輔帝業，恢圖丕基，迺不易之成規，衍無疆之運祚。

Figure 13 Plan of Dadu superimposed on the "Diagram of the Posterior Heavens"

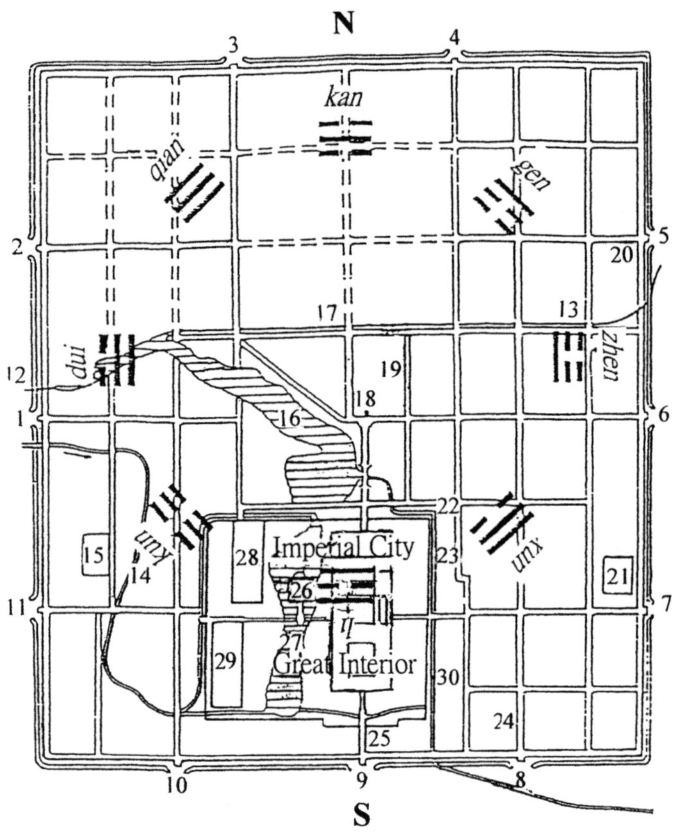

1. Heyi Gate
2. Suqing Gate
3. Jiande Gate
4. Anzhen Gate
5. Guangxi Gate
6. Chongren Gate
7. Qihua Gate
8. Wenming Gate
9. Lizheng Gate
10. Shuncheng Gate
11. Pingze Gate
12. Gaoliang River
13. Ba Canal
14. Jinshui Canal
15. Shejitan (Altars of Soil and Grain
16. Jishui Pool
17. Beisheng (Northern Central Secretariat)
18. Zhongxinge
19. Da Tianshou Wanningsi
20. Longwangtang
21. Taimiao (Ancestral Temple)
22. Tianshigong
23. Shumiyuan (Bureau of Military Affairs)
24. Yushitai (Censorate)
25. Zhongshusheng (Central Secretariat)
26. Qionghua Island
27. Taiye Pond
28. Xingsheng Palace
29. Longfu Palace
30. Tonghui Canal

Source: Yu, "*Zhouyi* xiangshu", p. 179.

Xiong Mengxiang may have idealized the building scheme. However, present evidence also shows that Liu Bingzhong, besides adopting the classical Wangcheng model, had adhered to the ancient astral-geographical precept of *fatian xiangdi* which harked back to city building in the pre-Qin era and the Han philosophical discourses. He emulated the celestial-terrestrial correlation system elucidated in Pre-Qin and Han astrological works to site the imperial- and palace-cities, as well as the principal official buildings and religious monuments. According to records, the Office of the Central Secretariat, Bureau of Military Affairs, and the Censorate were completed in 1268. The Central Secretariat came to be called the Northern Secretariat (Beisheng 北省) in 1290 when its offices were incorporated into the Shangshusheng 尚書省 (Presidential Council), a superior department principally in charge of finance established in 1270 in the Wuyun Ward 五雲坊 outside the south gate of the imperial-city. The latter was then called the Southern Secretariat (Nansheng 南省). (After 1308, the Southern Secretariat became the only Secretariat when the offices of the Northern Secretariat were taken over by the Hanlin Academy [Hanlinyuan 翰林院], which survived until the end of the dynasty.) The Bureau of Military Affairs was located in the Baotian 保天 Ward outside the east gate of the imperial-city, and the Censorate in the Chengqing 澄清 Ward to the southeast of the former. All were in the outer-city. The Celestial Master Palace (Tianshigong 天師宮) was built shortly after 1276 in honor of the Daoist Heavenly Master Zhang Zongyan 張宗演, and the Ancestral Temple was completed in 1280. The Shrine, renamed the Revered True Myriad Longevity Palace (Chongzhen Wanshougong 崇真萬壽宮) upon completion in 1296, was situated at the Penglai 蓬萊 Ward outside the northeastern wall of the imperial-city.[30]

The planners of Dadu also introduced certain significant modifications to the pattern of the celestial-terrestrial correlation system. The most important was the siting of the offices of the Central Secretariat (the Northern Secretariat) in the northern section of the outer-city. This location is said to have corresponded with the pre-eminent sidereal Purple Palace Enclosure surrounded by fifteen stars, which was traditionally identified with the celestial imperial palace and hence with the sovereign's residence. The Yuan imperial residence inside the palace-city, known as Da Nei, was located to the south of the Northern Secretariat. In celestial correspondence, it occupied the Privy Council Enclosure, said to be the Spring Palace of the Yellow Emperor guarded by ten stars including the Left and Right Law Administrator Celestial Gates. That the Bureau of Military Affairs and the Censorate were placed in the east and southeast of the walled imperial-city underscored this conceptual arrangement.[31] How the Da Nei was actually sited is not clear, but the *Xijin zhi* under the section "suiji" 歲紀 records a rather odd anecdote. It says that when Qubilai Qaghan asked Liu Bingzhong how he chose the site of the imperial residence, Liu pointed to a tall tree standing south of the third bridge outside the space of what later became the Lizheng Gate 麗正門 (present-day Tian'anmen 天安門), saying that it provided the guide of direction. The emperor applauded his choice and invested the tree as the "Single Tree General" (*dushu jiangjun* 獨樹將軍); henceforth lighted floral lamps were hung on its branches at night during special annual festivals.[32] Other architectural planning, however, reflected the traditional pattern. For instance, Liu adopted the "Diagram of the Posterior Heavens" of the *Book of Changes* ascribed to King Wen of Zhou and favored by the Song philosopher Shao Yong in assigning some of the prominent religious buildings. Therefore the Ancestral Temple was placed at the *zhen* (eastern) cardinal direction, which also adhered to the Wangcheng model, and the Celestial Master Palace at the *gen* (northeastern) cardinal direction, and each also corresponded respectively to specific stars or lunar lodges.

It is perplexing that the city planners (Liu Bingzhong in consultation with Qubilai Qaghan) embarked on this conceptual deviation from the traditional celestial-terrestrial correlation pattern. A recent researcher opines that shifting the Yuan imperial palace away from the correlative Purple Palace Enclosure suggests that the Mongol-Yuan ruler, under the influence of Mongolian shamanistic religion and Tibetan Buddhism, did not aspire to the celestial residence in the Chinese sky but rather revered the mystical forces of brightness, the sun and the moon. This reverence is reflected, for example, in the name of the main imperial hall and the walled gates of the palace-city. The main hall of the imperial palace was called Da Ming 大明 (Great Brightness), and so was the name of the main gate of the entrance, Da Mingmen. The left and right side gates were respectively named Rijing 日精-men and Yuejing 月精-men, alluding to the brightness of the sun and the moon. The central walled-gate on the outer-city which guarded the entrance to the imperial-city was called Lizhengmen. *Lizheng*, rendered as "clinging to brightness", was derived from the second line of the Commentary on the Decision of the *li* (The Clinging, Fire) hexagram of the *Book of Changes*: *Zhongming yi li hu zheng*" (重明以麗乎正). It has been translated as "Double Clarity (Brightness), clinging to what is bright". Literally, *zhongming* can mean sun and moon, and also "brightness and brightness" so the name therefore underpinned significant philosophical and religious aspirations.[33] However, another scholar makes the criticism that Liu Bingzhong's building of the Central Secretariat at the Fengchi Ward near the "center marker" of the entire tripled-walled city based on his divination of geomantic siting compromised the principle of functional effectiveness in urban planning. It placed the Secretariat at a considerable distance from the emperor's residence in the palace-city and undermined efficient communication. The later relocation of the original offices of the Central Secretariat in the north to those of the former Presidential Council in the south was an obvious correction.[34] The identification of the imperial palace with the Purple Palace Enclosure was also restored to the Forbidden City of Ming Peking with the resumption of Chinese rule.

In short, under this "Chaotang gongyu" section, Xiong Mengxiang had given a succinct exposé of Liu Bingzhong's geomantic siting to determine the location of the imperial- and palace-cities and the sites of the various government administrative offices. He also affirmed Liu's invocation of the celestial-terrestrial correlation system as a guiding principle in the architectural layout of the city with auspicious prognostication for the state's fortune. As he remarked, "They were verified by Liu Bingzhong according to the 'warp' and 'weft' of the terrain, focusing on the region of the 'ruler's emanation'; as a result, he was able to assist the imperial enterprise and expand the grand plan and the great foundation." Following this, Xiong made some observations on the role of fengshui in the founding of state capitals; he thought auspicious fengshui was fully realized in the construction of Dadu, but deplored that its principles were violated in the late Yuan resulting in a degradation of the capital's environment. He commented:

> Since then (i.e. the completion of Dadu), having gained experience, some (officials) had proposed to improvise changes in the system, and perverse consequences ensued. The fact is that in the "principle of the earth", for mountains, there are topographical features; for waters, there are fountainheads. Mountain is the base; water is the blood vein. Ever since ancient times when principalities and states were founded, people inspected the topographical features of the terrain, and sited the ruler's veins and arteries, such that they accomplished the grand enterprise. These were all closely intertwined, and it was an unaltered judgment. But recently the court often rashly adopted recommendations without seriously investigating the merits and demerits. Projects such as dredging the Jinkou Canal at Wuhua Hill (i.e. northeast of Shijing Hill), breaching the walled-city moats and dispersing the sea water were major construction works, but they disturbed the terrain's veins, sapped its "primal breath or energy", and the intended enterprise failed. Only then major criticisms were heard, but they offered no help to the grand undertaking.[35]
>
> 自後閱歷既久，而有更張改制，則乖戻矣。蓋地理，山有形勢，水有源泉。山則為根本，水則為血脈。自古建邦立國，先取地理之形勢，生王脈絡，以成大業。關係非淺，此不易之論。自後朝廷妄用建言，不究利害，往往如是。若五華山開金口，決城濠，泄海水，大修造，動地脈，傷元氣而事功不立。比及大議始出，則無補於事功矣。

Under a veiled criticism of deviation from the traditional principles by later planners, Xiong apparently alluded to Liu Bingzhong's embracing the fengshui precepts in designing Dadu in the statement that "Ever since ancient times when principalities and states were founded, people inspected the topographical features of the terrain, and sited the ruler's veins and arteries, such that they accomplished the grand enterprise." Xiong did not give specific illustrations, but Wang Zilin 王子林, a Chinese researcher from the Palace Museum who has recently written on the fengshui of the Forbidden City, has expanded on this. He opines that Dadu was favored because the planners believed that the Dragon's vein, i.e. a geomantically auspicious site, lay in the Jade Spring Hill west of the Urn Hill Lake in the Western Hills in the northwest, hence giving the imperial-city the source of its nourishment. In addition, according to the "indicator" of the great geomancer Guan Luo of the Three Kingdoms period, the three-way confluence of felicitous waterways inside the city would provide another venue of auspicious geomancy. He points out that clear natural water cascading from the Jade Spring

Hill was channeled through the man-made Jinshui Canal into the imperial-city and then turned south, splitting into two tributaries. One headed north and then east along the walls to drain into the Taiye Pond of the palace-city, while the other continued westward through the pond and crossed the imperial-city to join the Tonghui Canal where it exited the city. Dadu, and later Peking, never ceased to kindle geomantic imaginations.[36]

Xiong's criticism of later Yuan planners' violations of the fengshui principles in city planning referred specifically to the failed hydraulic work during the reign of the last Yuan emperor Toghōn Temür to reopen the old Jinshui Canal and extend the canal from south of the Lizheng Gate toward the southeast to reach the Grand Canal. After much heated debate at court, presided over by the aggressive right chancellor Tuotuo 脱脱 (1314–1355), over the transportation of the much needed coal from the Western Hills and grain from the southeastern provinces through waterways, the project was launched in early 1342, mobilizing one hundred thousand laborers and incurring enormous expense. The new canal, starting from the Western Hills and ending at the northern section of the Grand Canal, about 130 *li* in length, was completed in less than nine months. However, it soon proved to be ineffective as the steep slopes and shallow river beds caused constant silting and flooding; it was not navigable and brought extensive damage to the farmlands.[37] The failure caused a political uproar and two of the senior officials who proposed the project were executed. Charging that the project "disturbed the terrain's veins and sapped its 'primal breath'", Xiong clearly invoked the violation of the fengshui principles as the cause of the debacle. It was a skillful camouflage to lay blame on the reckless Yuan officialdom for one of the worst hydraulic disasters.

The imperial-city of Dadu, which incorporated the palace-city to the far right, was divided almost in the middle by the artificial Taiye Pond where there were two man-made islands joined by a marble bridge. In the north was the landscaped Qionghua Island adorned by its magnificent Wanshou 萬壽 or Wansui 萬歲-shan (Hill of Longevity or Myriad Years), which overlooked the entire city and provided an outstanding cosmological landmark. The stones and flowers that decorated the peak came from the magnificent Genyue 艮嶽 (*Gen* or Northeast Marchmount), a man-made hilltop pleasure park with purported auspicious geomancy to inspire imperial fertility which was built for the Northern Song emperor Huizong 徽宗 (r. 1101–1125) at Bianliang. This garden was pillaged by the Jurchen army when they took the capital in January 1127. Prized pieces of the garden were transported to Zhongdu to build the towering mount. It was taken over by the Yuan with additional decorations as the only remnant of the Jin capital that escaped destruction. The left side of the Taiye Pond included, in the north-south direction, a group of residential halls and pavilions for the empress and the crown prince, each with a private park located at both ends of the buildings. The square-shaped imperial-city was again enclosed by walls which, according to the estimates of modern research, had a perimeter of 8, 800 meters, longer on the north-south than the east-west, more than double that of the palace-city which had a perimeter of 3,480 meters, with two gates on the northern and southern walls and one each on the eastern and western walls. The former stood on the axis originating from the "center marker" and provided exits to the north and south; the latter stood on a subsidiary horizontal axis and provided exits to the east and west of the outer-city.[38]

The outer-city was a huge rectangular city enclosed by walls on four sides with eleven gates and the protective Hucheng Canal which served as a moat with bridges from all the gates. Inside the city the main lake, Jishui Pool, laid lopsided to the south of the Central Pavilion. In the rear was the enclosed imperial- palace-cities, and there was a large space in the north, east, and west, with a total area in excess of 50 sq. km. Within the city, major north-south and east-west avenues emerged from the northern and southern gates criss-crossing each other and inter-connecting with streets and alleyways (the latter were called *xiangtong* 衖通, from the Mongolian *qutung*, the predecessor of *hutong* in the Ming) in a checkerboard pattern. The thoroughfares served as boundaries for a number of enclosed areas of various sizes and shapes known as *fang* or wards.[39] The city's water supply came from two different man-made waterways originating from the mountains to the northwest. The one from the Baifu Spring passed through the Urn Hill Lake, then the Gaoliang River, down the Jishui Pool into the Huitong Canal, and passing by the eastern wall of the imperial-city served all the residents. The other, from the Jinshui Canal originating from the Jade Spring Hill and entering the imperial-city with split tributaries, one draining into the Taiye Pond which lay vertically inside the palace-city and the other flowing southwestward across the imperial-city to exit at the Tonghui Canal, supplied water for the imperial residents. However, these sources were inadequate and Dadu often suffered from an unstable supply of water, which became acute in times of flood or drought.

At the beginning there were fifty *fang* in the outer-city (the number later steadily multiplied), corresponding to the "number of the total" in the *Book of Changes*, and they provided the sites of various imperial temples, sacrificial altars, Buddhist monasteries, Daoist shrines, administrative offices, official residences, markets, and bazaars. Following the Wangcheng design, the Ancestral Temple was located to the far right north of Qihua 齊化 Gate on the eastern wall, and the Altars of Soil and Grain were on the far left north of Pingze 平則 Gate. The markets were situated in three locales: one called Xiejieshi 斜街市, located on the north shore of Jishui Pool near the Drum Tower, was the most prosperous trade center; another called Yangjiaoshi 羊角市, southwest of the imperial-city within Shuncheng 順承 Gate, catered to the animal trade; yet another called Jiu Shumiyuan jiaoshi 舊樞密院角市, situated in the southeast of the imperial-city near Wenming Gate, was a bustling market for daily amenities. In terms of the celestial-terrestrial correlative perception, the latter would fall within the dwellings of the Celestial Markets Enclosure. It was estimated that at the end of Qubilai's reign Dadu had a population close to or in excess of 900,000. Most of the populace resided in the wards to the south, but there were also people living in the old city, i.e. the former Jin Zhongdu in the southeast sector of the outer-city.[40]

The eleven gates of the outer-city walls require an explanation. In principle, the number and position of the gates in all the triple city walls were decided by the length of the wall and their correspondence to the philosophical precepts of the city plan. For the latter, as one scholar recently suggests, while the designer generally observed the Wangcheng model the layout of the gates and their names were based on the "Diagram of the Posterior Heavens" of the *Book of Changes*.[41] Since the triple-concentric enclosures were either square or rectangular, the gates of the walls should all be in even numbers, but those on the outer-city were an exception. The northern wall had two gates: Jiande 建德, Anzhen 安貞, and all the three other walls each had three gates: Guangxi 光熙, Chongren

崇仁, Qihua (eastern); Suqing 肅清, Heyi 和義, Pingze (western); Wenming, Lizheng, and Shuncheng (southern). It is puzzling that the northern wall had only two gates. A late Yuan scholar, Huang Wenzhong 黃文仲, offered an explanation in his "Rhyme prose on Dadu" (*Dadu fu*). He said: "Designing eleven gates, [the traffic] flows in all directions. This is because by emulating the *cosmos* (*yuan*) to create the image (*xiang*), it matches the numbers five and six, which give the sum of the numerals of the center of Heaven and Earth." (闢十一門，四達幢幢，蓋體元而立象，允合乎五六，天地之中。) This opinion evidently followed the cosmological numerology of the prominent Song philosopher Shao Yong, who declares in his *Huangji Jingshi shu* 皇極經世書 (Supreme Principles Governing the World) that all the odd numbers from one to nine are the numerals of Heaven, and all the even numbers from two to ten are the numerals of Earth.[42] In this sense, Liu Bingzhong may have been inspired by Shao's numerology to design eleven gates on the outer-city walls to symbolize the imperial capital as the center of heaven and earth. However, a clue to why he planned two gates on the right and left sides of the northern wall, leaving the center completely sealed, may also be found in King Wen's "Diagram of the Posterior Heavens" of the *Book of Changes*. In the due north was the *kan* 坎, which presents the image of a "double defile", with the character meaning a "pit", "perilous cavity", or "defile", and the commentary suggests that the prince or lord, facing such a dangerous situation, should fortify the city and uphold strenuous laws to secure his state. The absence of a gate in the center of the northern wall therefore, while concurring with the sagely admonition, was also sound for strategic considerations in order to bolster the security of the imperial capital.[43] Whatever may be the explanation, this odd-number of gates in the outer-city walls evoked the Nazha cult in Tantric Buddhism that inspired the dramatic legend about the building of Dadu in the popular imagination. If there had been an even number of walled gates, there may not have been the same legend!

Known in Mongolian transliteration as Daidu, in Turkic as Khanbalik, and as Cambulac (city of the Khans) to medieval European travelers through Marco Polo's *Description of the World*, Dadu was a grand metropolis with a population of multiple nationalities numbering about a million. Besides the majority Han Chinese it included Mongols, Jurchens, Tanguts, and many inhabitants of diverse Central Asian extractions. The city served not only as the imperial capital of the Mongol-Yuan empire, whose authority extended well beyond the Middle Kingdom, but also as an important world-class political as well as commercial city. It was also rich in culture founded on strong and diverse socioeconomic bases. With its deep-rooted foundation in Han élite and popular culture, it attracted various cultural traditions from not only Mongolia but also Central Asia and beyond.[44] Dadu had many strands of religious and cultural traditions, but in terms of popular tradition none was as dramatic and entertaining as the legends about the building of the city, which sharply contrast with the official or élite versions.

The Nazha Cheng Legend

The building of Dadu was renowned in the *Nazha cheng* legend traced to the design of the imperial city by Liu Bingzhong, which was transmitted in late Yuan literary miscellanies as an integral part of a growing mythology. As a prelude, there are several eerie episodes recorded in the *Caomu zi* by Ye Ziqi relating Liu's advice to Qubilai Qaghan on city planning. One of these states that when Liu Bingzhong chose the northern city of the old Jin capital to be the Yuan capital, he diverted the water from the western mountains through the Juyong Pass in order to irrigate the terrain. But still the state succumbed to disaster in less than a hundred years and people wondered whether this disaster was caused by tempting fate with geomancy. Another episode claims that when Qubilai asked Liu whether Shangdu or Dadu should be chosen as the imperial city after his enthronement, Liu commented that whereas Shangdu had a population noted for modest lifestyle, its lifespan was short; conversely, Dadu had a population noted for voluptuous lifestyle, but its lifespan was long, and so the latter was chosen. Yet another alleges that when Qubilai commanded Liu Bingzhong to build the capital city at the proposed site, and ground was broken, uncounted thousands of red-headed worms were revealed. When asked about his prognostication for this Liu replied that the creatures would bring ruin to the empire, alluding to the Red Turban rebels who later toppled Mongol rule.[45]

It appears that these anecdotes represented a few of the popular stories that were circulated, and whereas they focused their attention on the environment of the city, noting in particular its water resources and lifestyle of the residents, they tried to invoke them as prophecies of the misfortune of the Yuan state at a time when it was already rocked by sporadic popular uprisings. However, none of these episodes were as bizarre and resilient as the Nazha City legend. The story was first reported in one of a series of 102 poems on the imperial city entitled "Nianxia qu" 輦下曲 (Ballads from the Capital) by the late Yuan belle lettrist Zhang Yu 張昱 (1308?–1376+), which says:

> There are eleven gates around the [outer-city] walls of Dadu,
> 大都周遭十一門
>
> thatched with hay and paved with earth the Nazha City was built.
> 草苫土築那吒城
>
> The prophecy says if [the walls] were encased in brick and stone,
> 讖言若以磚石裹
>
> they will be as long as [the column of] the armored soldiers of the Heavenly King.[46]
> 長似天王衣甲兵

The first line reveals the number of gates on the outer-city walls of the capital, and the second line mentions that the city was also known as Nazha City, which was thatched with hay and paved with earth. The next two lines invoke a prophecy claiming that if the walls were encased in brick and stone, they would be very long like the column of armored soldiers of the Heavenly King, which means there would be drawn-out military confrontation. The Heavenly King, as noted later, refers to Vaiśravana, one of the four "Heavenly Kings" who was the guardian of the north in Tantric Buddhism. In China, King Vaiśravana later came to be identified with the mythologized early Tang general Li Jing 李靖 (571–649) who, in the legend to follow, personified the father of the hero Nazha. As a war god he allegedly had a metal body made of steel and, as stated later the armored soldiers included his sons, of which Nazha was the third and the youngest.

None of these make much sense but for the explanation offered by a junior contemporary Changgu Zhenyi 長谷真逸 (a pseudonym) in a follow-up account in his miscellany *Nongtian yuhua* 農田餘話 (Conversations from plowing the field):

> The city of Yan was designed by Liu Taibao. There were eleven walled-gates in order to symbolize Nazha's three heads, six arms, and two feet. Shizu (Qubilai Qaghan) was enthroned in the *gengshen* year (1260), and the state perished between the *wushen* (1368) and *siyu* (1369) years. Altogether one hundred and ten years had elapsed.[47]
>
> 燕城，係劉太保定制，凡十一門，作那吒神三頭六臂兩足。世祖庚申即位，至國亡于戊申己酉之間，經一百一十年也。

This passage positively identifies Liu Bingzhong as the designer of the city of Dadu and suggests that it was called *Nazha cheng* because it had eleven gates among its walls which symbolized the transformed body of the supernatural deity Nazha with three heads, six arms, and two feet. This would mean that the three southern gates represented his three heads (with the primary head represented by the Lizheng Gate), the six eastern and western gates represented his six arms, and the two northern gates represented his two feet. The statement points out that there were altogether one hundred and ten years from the time of Qubilai's enthronement to the termination of the Yuan state, and that this corresponds exactly with the tenfold "eleven" number of the main parts of Nazha's body. The suggestion then is that the legend, evoking mystical numerology, also prophesized the demise of Mongol rule and further dramatized the legend's implications for contemporary political affairs. This statement was probably inserted in the early Ming period.

In addition there was a related version of this legend which, though not focused on Dadu but on Shangdu, merits attention as it again refers to Liu Bingzhong's design of the twin capital cities against the backdrop of the Dragon mythology. It provides a useful frame of reference for explaining the origin of the Dadu legend. This story is recounted in the miscellany *Zhizheng zhiji* 至正直記 (Faithful Record of the Zhizheng Era) of the late Yuan scholar Kong Qi 孔齊 (?1318–1360+), a distant descendant of Confucius, under the caption "Shangdu bishu" 上都避暑 (Escaping Summer in Shangdu):

> Shangdu was originally grassland; the ground was high and was extremely cold. It was about one thousand *li* from Dadu. Legend has it that when Liu Taibao moved the capital [to Shangdu], because there was the Dragon's pool which could not be drained [for construction], he memorialized Shizu that they should borrow the land from the Dragon. This was agreed. That night at three strokes of the hour thunder roared,

> the Dragon had already spurted away. The next day, an order was given to build the foundation of the city wall with earth. It is still intact to this day. After the upheaval [of the anti-Yuan uprisings] the "imperial carriage" (alluding to the last Yuan emperor Toghōn Temür) was spared but we heard that the palaces and halls had been burnt down by the bandits. Everywhere within one thousand *li* of Shangdu there were Red [Turban] bandits. They illegitimately declared Longfeng (Dragon and Phoenix) as the reign-name, is this not fate?[48]

> 上都本草野之地，地極高甚寒，去大都一千里。相傳劉太保遷都時，因地有龍池，不能乾涸，乃奏世祖當借地于龍，帝從之。是夕三更雷震，龍已飛上矣。明日，以土築城基，至今存焉。亂後車駕免幸，聞宮殿已為寇所焚燬。上都千里皆紅寇，稱偽龍鳳年號，亦豈非數耶。

The story about Liu Bingzhong moving the capital is not quite accurate because Shangdu was built in 1256 before Dadu and after the latter was founded, Shangdu remained a subsidiary capital. Mongol administration retained a "dual capital" system for a long period. The significance here is that it reveals that Shangdu had marshy fields, lakes, and rich underground water from the flooding of the surrounding rivers, and they needed to be drained before construction could start. The legend of Liu Bingzhong proposing to borrow the land from the Dragon who allegedly lived in a lake should be read in this light, and it also has important bearing on the development of the Dadu legend. The last few lines alluded to the devastations of the anti-Yuan Red Turbans of the White Lotus-Maitreya Buddhist sects spearheaded by the prominent leader Han Shantong 韓山童 (?–1351), and Longfeng was the reign-name of the Da Song 大宋 (Great Song) state (1355–1367) founded by his son Xiao Mingwang 小明王 Han Liner 韓林兒 (?–1367), which was replaced by the Ming dynasty of Zhu Yuanzhang in 1368.[49]

So much for the stories. What was the origin of this riveting legend? Who was Nazha and what sort of supernatural power did he command that allegedly inspired Liu Bingzhong to design Dadu's outer-city walled gates in his likeness? And what was the impact of this legend on the popular traditions surrounding the building of Peking centuries later?

The Nazha Saga

An investigation of Nazha, the principal Buddhist character in this legend, should begin with a survey of his father, King Vaiśravana, a prominent deity known in Chinese as Pishamen *tianwang* 毘沙門天王 or deva-king in the Buddhist pantheon. He is one of the four "Heavenly Kings" in the lowest of the six heavens of desire in the universe, and is guardian of the North. In Brahmanic mythology, Vaiśravana, son of Viśravas, is originally a chief of evil spirits; later he is Kubara or Kuvera, the god of wealth, and ruler of the northern quarter. After he was borrowed by Buddhism from Brahmanism he became one of the four Maharajas-devas frequently mentioned in Sanskrit texts known through Chinese translations. According to the *Foshuo Chang Ahan jing* 佛説長阿含經 (*Dirghāgama*) translated by Buddhayaśas and Zhu Fonian 竺佛念 during the rule of the Later Qin 後秦 kingdom (384–417), the four are Dhritarāshtra (Chiguo [keeping the kingdom] tianwang 持國天王) in the East, who leads the musicians in heaven; Virūdhaka (Zengzhang 增長 [increase and growth] tianwang) in the South, who is the sovereign of the deformed demons; Virūpāksha (Guangmu 廣目 [broad-eyed] tianwang) in the West, who is king of the *Nagas* (scorpion or snake-like sea creatures translated into Chinese as *long* 龍 or *longwang* 龍王, i.e. dragon or dragon king) who dwell in their palaces at the bottom of lakes; and Vaiśravana (Duowen 多聞 [well-informed] tianwang) in the North, who is head of the *Yakṣa*, who are strong and brave genii. Vaiśravana acquired the title *duowen* or *puwen* 普聞, meaning one who hears much and is very knowledgeable, because he is said to have heard the Buddha's preaching.[50]

King Vaiśravana and his five children emerged from the esoteric literature of the Tantric School of Buddhism introduced to China during the early Tang dynasty as powerful heavenly deities in enforcing the dharma, defending the kings and kingdoms, and suppressing demons and evil spirits. Vaiśravana's fearsome image and martial prowess are vividly portrayed in the Tantric sutra *Beifang Pishamen tianwang suijun hufa zhenyan* 北方毘沙門天王隨軍護法真言 (The True Words of the Heavenly King Vaiśravana of the North, the Protector of the Army) translated by Monk Amoghavajra (Bukong 不空, 705–774): "All the practitioners who wish to chant this mantra (i.e. mantra prescribed by Vaiśravana) should first draw his portrait. Using color but not mixing with glue, draw a portrait of Vaiśravana deva on a white blanket. His suit of solemn-looking armor is adorned with the "seven treasures", his left hand clinches a forked halberd, and his right hand rests on his waist, and under his feet are two female Yakṣa genii, their body in dark color. Vaiśravana's face shows a very frightening gesture and his eyes give a stern look at all the evil spirits. The pagoda he is carrying is for worship of Buddha Śākyamuni . . ." (Figure 14).[51] (若行者受持此呪者，先須畫像，於彩色中並不得和膠，於白毡上畫一毘沙門神。七寶莊嚴衣甲，左手執戟矟，右手托腰上，其神腳作二夜叉鬼，身並作黑色。其毘沙門面作甚可畏形，惡眼視一切鬼神勢。其塔奉釋迦牟尼佛。……) This portrait is strikingly similar to that of Nazha described in a related sutra.

Figure 14 Portrait of Heavenly King Vaiśravana in Tang Buddhist text

Source: *TSD, tuxiang* (portraits), pp. 538–539.

Nazha, whose name was written as Nezha in post-Yuan literature, was Nata in Sanskrit and has been associated with several Chinese names deemed as alternate renderings of the Sanskrit variants of Nata. The *Mochizuki Būkkyō daijiten* 望月佛教大辭典 gives Naluojiupo 那羅鳩婆, Naluojuwaluo 那羅矩韈囉, Nazhajiuboluo 那吒鳩鉢羅, Nazhajufaluo 那吒倶伐羅, and others as the transliterations of Nalakūvara or Nalakūbala. Naluojiupo appears as early as in Monk Dharmaraksa's (Tanwuchen 曇無讖, 385–433) translation of the Sanskrit sutra *Buddhacarita-kāvya* (*Fosuoxingzan jing* 佛說行讚經) attributed to Aśvaghosa (Maming 馬鳴) during the Northern Liang 北涼 Kingdom (397–439) of the Northern Dynasties. He is mentioned as a son born to King Vaiśravana, whereupon all the hosts of heaven were thrilled with joy, but recently the Taiwanese scholar Xiao Dengfu 蕭登福 has contested that the name suggests he was only one of Vaiśravana's sons and does not specifically refer to Nazha. In most of the Tantric Buddhist texts Nazha appears as Vaiśravana's third son, and remains so through later times. The only exception is found in the sutra attributed to Monk Amoghavajra's other translated sutra cited below. There it states that Nazha was Vaiśravana's grandson, but this assertion has generally been ignored.[52]

Amogha's sutra, as the Chinese title *Beifang Pishamen tianwang suijun hufa yigui* 北方毘沙門天王隨軍護法儀軌 (Ceremonies in the Worship of the Heavenly King Vaiśravana of the North, the Protector of the Army) indicates, is concerned with the modes or regulations prescribed by King Vaiśravana for disciples taking part in military action and enforcing the dharma of the Buddha. It gives the first full description of Nazha in the Buddhist *Tripitaka*:

> At that time Prince Nazha, his [right] hand holding a halberd and his eyes giving a stern look to all around, said to the Buddha: "I am the grandson, the second son of the third prince of Vaiśravana, the Heavenly King of the North. . . . I enforce the Buddha's dharma, wishing to subdue the hateful people and snuff out the evil mind. I would daily and nightly stay on guard protecting the king, the grand ministers, and the hundred officials. I would kill the devils and the like; I, Nazha, would use the 'vajra (diamond) cane' to stab their eyes and heart." . . . At that time Vaiśravana's grandson Nazha also told the Lokajyestha (epithet for Buddha): "I would in the future subdue and destroy to ashes all the evil humans, and would protect the kingdom's borders. Here I am revealing the 'true words' to expose the wicked; lend me your ears."[53]

爾時那吒太子，手捧戟，以惡眼見四方白佛言：我是北方天王吠室羅摩那羅闍 (即毘沙門) 第三王子其第二之孫。……我護持佛法，欲攝縛惡人或起不善之心。我晝夜守護國王大臣及百官僚，相與殺害打陵，如是之輩者，我等那吒以金剛杖刺其眼及其心。……爾時毘沙門孫那吒，白佛言世尊：我為未來諸不善眾生，降伏攝縛皆悉滅散故，亦維持國界故，說自心暴惡真言，唯願世尊聽許。……

It shows that Nazha not only enforced the dharma, subdued evil, but also protected the king and his functionaries and secured the kingdom's borders. As well as the vajra stick, utterance of Nazha's "true words", a sort of spell, was a powerful weapon to disarm and destroy devils and wicked spirits. As a result Vaiśravana and Nazha became the objects of worship by the faithful and laymen since the Tang; monks from India even came to China "to invite" a portrait of King Vaiśravana to return home. Additional portraits of Vaiśravana were made in many of the monasteries and they were inherited by later dynasties.

Elsewhere the sutra shows that even in Nazha's absence, disciples could achieve the same objective by drawing the Prince's portrait and chanting his "true words":

All the practitioners who wish to chant this mantra should first draw the portrait. Using color but not mixing with glue, draw a portrait of King Vaiśravana's grandson the Nazha heavenly deity on a white blanket. The "seven treasures" [on his armor] look very solemn; his left hand holding tightly his mouth and teeth (?), his right hand resting on his waist and clinching a forked halberd, and under his feet is a female Yakṣa genie sitting cross-legged. . . . When chanting this mantra, the place must be cleaned of filth, and flora be displayed and incense be burnt. All the practitioners should wear clean upper and lower garments, and drain off their bodily wastes to protect themselves; they should initiate on the night of the fifteenth of the black month, and chant the mantra three hundred thousand times before the portrait. . . . (Figure 15).[54]

若行者受持此呪者，先須書像，于彩色中並不得和膠，于白氈上畫一毘沙門神其孫那吒天神七寶莊嚴，左手令執口齒，右手詫腰上令執三戟矟，其神足下作一藥叉女住趺坐。……若誦此呪時，就好地勿使有穢惡，種種花燒香供養，行者上下衣服並須一清，一廁行時當護身，黑月十五夜起首，對象前誦呪滿三十萬遍訖，然後取香泥供養尊像。……

This portrait of Nazha resembles closely his father as depicted in the Tantric sutra *Suijun hufa zhenyan*, and a Tang image of him preserved

Figure 15 Portrait of Prince Nazha in Tang Buddhist text

Source: *TSD*, *tuxiang*, pp. 566–567.

in the *Taishō daizōkyō* 大正新修大藏經 reflects the description. It is vastly different from Nazha's later images after he was given a popular Buddhist-Daoist transformation.

In a related sutra translated by Amogha, the *Pishamen yigui* 毘沙門儀軌 (Ceremonies in the Worship of Vaiśravana), it is mentioned that in A.D. 742, the first year of the Tianbao 天寶 era (742–755) of the Tang emperor Xuanzong 玄宗 (r. 712–755), when the city of Anxi 安西 (in modern Xinjiang) was besieged by the troops of five states—Tashkand (modern Taskent), Samarkand, and others, King Vaiśravana, responding to imperial summons, emerged above the tower of the city-gate with his celestial soldiers and defeated the invading troops. It says that "Previously, (Vaiśravana) defended the kingdom's borders to discharge the rescript of the Buddha. His third son Nata was ordered to accompany the Heavenly King holding up a pagoda with both hands . . ." (昔防援國界，奉佛教敕，令第三子那吒捧塔隨侍天王左右……), showing positively that Nata himself had seen military action alongside his father and two elder brothers. However, scholars have surmised that this reference to King Vaiśravana responding to the Tang emperor's summons and leading his children to defend the five states against foreign attacks, which did not appear in the earlier Tantric sutras, was apparently interpolated by Amogha himself to perpetuate the legend.[55]

In this context, we note that a later Tantric sutra, the *Foshuo zuishang mimi nanatian jing* 佛說最上秘密那拏天經 translated by Monk Fatian 法天 (i.e. Faxian 法賢, ?–1001) of the early Song, depicts a scene of the heavenly deity Nana deva presenting himself at a gathering before the Buddha and Vaiśravana as an exorcist of the Dragon. "At that time there is a heavenly deity named Nana, his looks and gesture are very strange and he has a smiling face. His hands are holding the 'sun and moon' (symbolic statues?) and other implements; his [armor's] solemn-looking decorative treasures shine brighter than the sun and moon. He used the Nantuo and Wubonantuo Dragon as his axilla, and made the Zhajia Dragon his waist belt. He is as powerful as Naluoyan (= Narayana, a hero of divine power) and presents himself before the Buddha."[56] (是時有天名曰那拏，色相殊妙，面現微笑。手持日月及諸器仗，朏寶嚴飾，光踰日月。以難陀、烏波難陀二龍為絡腋，得叉迦龍以為腰條。有大威力如那羅延，亦來集會坐於佛前。) In the same text, he declared to the Buddha that he possessed the "*xinming*" 心明, i.e. a magical spell that could be invoked to subdue the devils, demons, and also pacify the dragons. A number of formulas for subduing dragons so as to produce rain, including the beating of the dragon effigy with a magical wand and chanting of the mantra attributed to Nana, has been included in the second *juan* of this sutra.

Is Nana the same as Nazha? The *Mochizuki Būkkyō daijiten* thought so and included it as a possible alternate name for Nazha, but Xiao Dengfu disputes the claim. He points out that despite similarity in pronunciation Nazha is not to be confused with Nana, who in fact is a heavenly deity superior in rank to all the four "Heavenly Kings".[57] Nevertheless, the story of Nana deva's suppression of the dragons is an important Buddhist source for the later development of the Daoist legend of Nazha's feuds with the Dragon King and his family in the undersea world.

By the early Song, both King Vaiśravana and Nazha enjoyed prominence in Tantric Buddhist sutras as well as Chan Buddhist *gongan* 公案 (cases) and other genres of popular literature as powerful heavenly deities noted for their extraordinary abilities and magnificent feats. In the *Song Gaozeng zhuan* 宋高僧傳 by Zanning 贊寧 (919–1001), for instance, Vaiśravana and Nazha are cited in the biography of Amogha as enforcers of the dharma and are hailed for their military actions at Anxi in Tang times.[58] In a related collection of biographies of monks by Zanning entitled (*Da Song*) S*engshi lue* (大宋) 僧史略 it is reported that Emperor Tang Xuanzong, impressed by Vaiśravana's martial prowess, had given orders to the military commissioners (*jiedushi* 節度使) to house his image for worship in the northwestern corner of the walled gates of every prefectural and sub-prefectural cities, and also in special quarters in the Buddhist monasteries of the country.[59] Vaiśravana remained a revered deity of worship as a guardian-protector into the later Song. It was reported in Song sources that his statue was housed inside some of the government offices in the capital Dongjing for the offering of regular sacrifices, and that in Southern Song many military barracks erected a hall of worship called Tianwangtang 天王堂 (Heavenly King's Hall) inside their building to pay homage for his divine protection.[60]

But at the same time, both Vaiśravana and Nazha were credited with additional roles and their images also underwent gradual transformation in popular Buddhist works and miscellaneous literature under increasing Daoist influence. For example, in an inscription on a commemorative epitaph in the Temple of the Heavenly King Vaiśravana (Pishamen tianwangmiao 毘沙門天王廟) in Ninghua county, Fujian, composed c. 920, Vaiśravana is already said to have dwelled on the north of Mt. Sumeru, and in the *crystal palace*, as chief of the Yakṣa. This is the first reference to his domicile in the Crystal Palace, with access to the sea creatures, which apparently confused him with Virupaksha, who exercised control over the Nagas. The story is repeated in the late Song popular

Buddhist work *Da Tang San Zang qujing shihua* 大唐三藏取經詩話 (Poetic Talks on Great Tang's "Three Tripitaka" Master Journeying to obtain the Scriptures), where it reports that "The Vaiśravana of the Indra Heaven, the Guardian of the North, prepares vegetable dishes (to fete the Buddhist priests) in the Crystal Palace" (北方毘沙門天王水晶宮設齋).[61]

Nazha's image likewise underwent dramatic transformation in Chan Buddhist works, literary miscellanies, and Daoist literature. In the *Jingde chuandeng lu* 景德傳燈錄 compiled in the Jingde reign (1004–1007), Monk Daoyuan 道原 relates a story of a monk making an inquiry of his master: "Prince Nazha, after having a dispute with his father, cut his bones to return to his father, the flesh to his mother, and then seated in a lotus leaf to preach the dharma for his parents—what is left of Nazha's original body?" (問那吒太子析骨還父，析肉還母，然後於蓮華上為父母掊法，如何是那吒本來身？) The *Biyan lu* 碧嚴錄 by Monk Yuanwu Keqin 圓悟克勤 (1063–1135) notes that "Nazha suddenly burst into temper, displaying his three heads and six arms."[62] In the *Wudeng huiyuan* 五燈會元 by Monk Puji 普濟 (1179–1253), one entry also describes Nazha as a supernatural deity with "three heads and six arms, able to raise up heaven and earth". (In both accounts Nezha showed off "six arms" but in some Song/Yuan dramas he began to reveal "eight arms" and the latter became a standard feature in Ming works.) Another entry repeats the earlier eerie story about Nazha cutting off his bones and flesh. It reports that after Nazha accidentally killed an innocent Daoist, as an act of repentance "he cut his flesh to return to his mother and split his bones to return to his father, then manifested his original body and used his divine power to preach the dharma for the benefit of his parents."[63] (那吒太子析肉還母，析骨還父，然後現本身，運大神通，為父母說法。) Meantime, popular Daoism made Nazha a Daoist immortal endowed with magical spells. In the *Yijian zhi* 夷堅志 by Hong Mai 洪邁 (1123–1202) there is a story of a Maoshan 茅山 Daoist magician invoking Nazha's "fiery blanket spell" (*huotanzhou* 火毯咒) to fight off the intrusion of two frightening demons. Then in the late Song and early Yuan Daoist compendia of rituals, the *Daofa huiyuan* 道法會元, Nazha is placed on the list of the thirty-three (later thirty-six) *yuanshuai* 元帥 (marshals) in the Daoist pantheon under the epithet "Ganying tongxie dutaizi Nazha" 感應統懾都太子那吒 (The Responsive, Awe-inspiring Chief Prince Nazha).[64] All these attest to a significant transformation of Nazha from an austere heavenly deity in the Tantric tradition to a supernatural hero credited with many miraculous deeds and majestic achievements in popular Buddhism and religious Daoism.

In the late Song, however, much more dramatic changes took place in the dissemination of King Vaiśravana and Nazha's legends in folk belief and popular literature when they were inserted into the myths surrounding the early Tang general Li Jing and became Sinified supernatural heroes. An eminent general distinguished for his military exploits and political sagacity, Li Jing was steadily mythologized after his death, becoming a Daoist guardian with supernatural powers. His legends grew in intensity in the late Tang and early Song. In due course Chinese popular imagination incorporated Vaiśravana and Nazha into Li's mythological genealogy, and some of the most fanciful legends associated with King Vaiśravana were grafted onto this eminent historical figure. What emerged was a mythologized hero known as Pagoda-bearing Heavenly King Li Jing (*Tuota tianwang* Li Jing 托塔天王李靖). This new hero was already featured in the novels and dramas of Southern Song and his legends grew thereafter. As a result, Nazha acquired a new status as Li Jing's third son.[65]

In this setting, Nazha became the popular hero of a mythological cult and was well received in dramatic entertainment in Yuan times but increasingly susceptible to Daoistic apotheosization. A number of Yuan plays carried the theme of Nazha in many manifestations, such as the "Nazha ling" 那吒令 (A Short Syllabic Lyric about Nazha); "Dingding dangdang panergui" 叮叮噹噹盆兒鬼 ([The Jingling Ghost in the Tub], with two plots entitled "Heilian Nazha" 黑臉那吒 [Dark-face Nazha] and "Nazha fa" 那吒法 [Nazha's Law]); "Nazhataizi yanjingji" 那吒太子眼睛記 (A Tale of Prince Nazha's Eyes); "Erlangshen zuishe suomojing" 二郎神醉射鎖魔鏡 (The Second Elder Deity in Drunkenness Shot at the Locking Devil's Mirror); and the famous "Menglie Nazha sanbianhua" 猛烈那吒三變化 (The Three Transformations of the Ferocious Nazha). (It is striking that one of these plays presents Nazha as dark-faced, perhaps under the influence of the portrait of the Daoist Dark God Zhenwu 真武, a war god and guardian of the north, very popular in China.) In addition, Nazha's name became the title of the musical notes of the chantables and he was a frequent character in many genres of dramatic entertainments—in plays, songs, storytelling, and the like. The characterization of Nazha is the most dramatic in the "Menglie Nazha sanbianhua" play.[66] In a number of lively and uncanny plots the imaginative writer portrayed the hero as a supernational deity with three heads and six arms, capable of transforming himself at will and performing ever changing miraculous acts. As enforcer of the dharma and exorcist of evil, he was sent by the Buddha to conquer the hundreds of male and female devils and demons infesting the Yanmoshan 燄魔山 (Mount of Devils of Blazing Flames). After a string of life and death struggles in numerous skirmishes he successfully subdues and eliminates all the wicked devils to bring eternal peace to the area. The play not only bolstered Nazha's image but also provided an important source for continual fictionalization in later popular novels drawing on the legends of Li Jing and Nazha.

Lastly, as mythologization intensified, Nazha was treated to a Daoist hagiography whereby he was cast as a *daluoxian* 大羅仙 (the highest-ranked immortal) under the Jade Emperor (Yuhuang 玉皇, a later name for Tianhuang dadi), the highest deity in the Daoist hierarchy, and was involved in a chain of battles with evil beings, including the dragon family and several hundred devils and demons. He won all the fights and was enfeoffed as commander-in-chief of the thirty-six marshals of the Daoist pantheon and became leader of all the celestial commanders. This story appears in a Daoistic biography, "Naji (*sic.* for Nazha) taizi zhuan" 那叱(吒)太子傳 from a late Yuan collection titled *Huaxiang Soushen guangji* 畫像搜神廣記 (An Expanded Record of the Eminent Deities with Portrait). The original edition was lost but was copied into a Ming edition called *Huitu Sanjiao yuanliu Soushen daquan* 繪圖三教源流搜神大全 (A Compendium of the Sources and Eminent Deities of the Three Teachings) compiled by an anonymous editor.[67] The work provides an important link in the metamorphosis of the Nazha legend from the Yuan to Ming. The opening lines of the biography read:

> Nachi (Nazha) was initially a *daluoxian* under the Jade Emperor. He is six *zhang* (sixty feet) tall, his head wears a golden wheel, and he has three heads, nine eyes and eight arms. His mouth emits blue mist, his feet stand on the solid rock, and [one of] his hands holds an instrument representing the law. Whenever he howls, the cloud descends and the rain follows, both heaven and earth tremble. Because there are too many "devil princes" in the people's world, the Jade Emperor ordered him to

> descend to the world, and so he was reincarnated into the family of the Pagoda-bearing Heavenly King Li Jing. His mother Lady Suzhi gave birth to eldest son Junchi (*sic.* for Junzha), the second son was Muchi (*sic.* for Muzha), and the third, Nachi. Five days after birth Nachi went bathing in the Eastern Sea, he trampled on the Crystal Hall with his feet, and took a gallop ascending the Precious Pagoda Palace. Outraged by his trampling on the hall, the Dragon King challenged him to a duel, and in seven days Nachi killed the nine dragons, and the old dragon could do nothing but wail before the Emperor. Having been thus informed, Nazha intercepted the Dragon under the Heavenly Gate and fought, the Dragon met his death.[68] (Figure 16)

> 那叱 (吒) 本是玉皇駕下大羅仙，身長六丈，首帶金輪，三頭九眼八臂。口吐青雲，足踏盤石，手持法律。大喊一聲，雲降雨從，乾坤爍動。因世間多魔王，玉帝命降凡，以故托胎於托塔天王李靖。母素知夫人生下長子軍叱 (吒)，次木叱 (吒)，師三胎那叱 (吒)。生五日化身浴於東海，腳踏水晶殿，翻身直上寶塔宮。龍王以踏殿故，怒而索戰，師時七日即能戰殺九龍，老龍無奈何而哀帝。帥知之，截戰於天門之下，而龍死焉。

In this full biography Nazha is presented as one of the highest-ranked Daoist immortals under the Jade Emperor: sixty feet tall, wearing a golden wheel on his head and displaying three heads, nine eyes, and eight arms. The most dramatic element introduced into the saga, however, was the story of Nazha's feud with the dragon family: how his bathing in the Eastern Sea accidentally enraged the Dragon King who challenged him to a duel, and how in seven days Nazha killed his nine dragon sons, and finally the Dragon King himself, unleashing much pandemonium in the watery world. The source is not clear but it attests to the inroad of popular Daoism into the metamorphosis of Buddhist traditions about Naga or the Dragon King through infusion of Chinese mythology about the heavenly dragon as a rain-maker.

Known in Chinese as *long* or *longwang* and in English translation as dragon or dragon king, this mythical being appeared in ancient Chinese mythology as a protean heavenly spirit and sea creature that could bring rain, cause havoc in the watery realm, and deliver good fortune and misfortune. By Tang times, through the Chinese translation of the Sanskrit sutra, the scorpion or snake-like rain god Naga of Tantric Buddhism introduced from India became grafted onto this Chinese mythological figure in a cultural transfusion. In

Figure 16 Portrait of Nazha in *Soushen daquan*

Source: *Huitu Sanjiao yuanliu Soushen daquan*, 7: 13a.

due course the dragon/dragon king emerged in Chinese Buddhist sutra and mythology as a Sino-Indian composite rain or water deity and left a conspicuous imprint in religious canons and popular literature.[69] However, we should note that in the development of the Nazha saga, the conflict between the heavenly deity and the dragon in the Buddhist tradition plays a key role. It was already stated that Virupaksha, Heavenly King of the West, was assigned to govern the *Nagas* living in their palaces under the sea, and a superior heavenly deity, the Nana deva, was known to be a vigorous exorcist of the evil dragons and possessed magical formula for subduing the dragon to produce rain. There are several Buddhist sutras devoted to the stories of the guardian deities exorcizing the evil dragons who caused disturbance.[70] In so far as the story's bearing on Nazha's battle with the Dragon King is concerned, the depiction in late Song popular works of his father Vaiśravana living in the undersea Crystal Palace feting the Buddhist priests provides a very important source of the development of the legend. It paves an easy entry for Nazha into the undersea where his father had a domicile, and inspires the story of the Dragon King occupying the Crystal Palace and the feud between Nazha and his nemesis for control of the watery world against the backdrop of the animosity between the Buddhist heavenly deities and the mythical evil dragons.

This miraculous story in turn inspired a full-blown Nazha saga in the popular religious novels *Fengshen yanyi* 封神演義 (Tales of the Investiture of Gods) attributed to Lu Xixing 陸西星 (1520–c. 1601?), the *Xiyou ji* 西遊記 (Journey to the West) attributed to Wu Cheng'en 吳承恩 (c. 1506–c. 1582) in the sixteenth/seventeenth century, and others. These two novels synthesized much of the characterization of Nazha as Li Jing's son and his extraordinary exploits presented in the late Yuan sources and introduced imaginative features and episodes. (In both works the name was written as Nezha, and in the *Xiyou ji* Nezha is dubbed the Honghaier 紅孩兒 or "Crimson Kid" [Figure 17].) Particularly relevant to our inquiry are the reworked episodes of Nazha's adventures in the Eastern Sea and his feud with the dragon genii. Instead of dueling with the Dragon King, it features Nazha engaging his third son in a fierce combat and killing him; the Dragon King then complained to Li Jing and sought revenge by wrecking havoc in the deep seas. It was the stories about Nazha in these two novels along with their dramatization in drama, popular songs, and storytelling that captured the public's imagination and furthered their obsession with Nazha's divinity and his miraculous adventures, which continues to modern times.[71]

Myth and Reality

Against this rich historical and religious background, it is clear why Liu Bingzhong invoked the presence of Nazha by designing the walled gates of the outer-city of Dadu in the numerals representing the main parts of his body in the legend. Nazha, as the youngest son

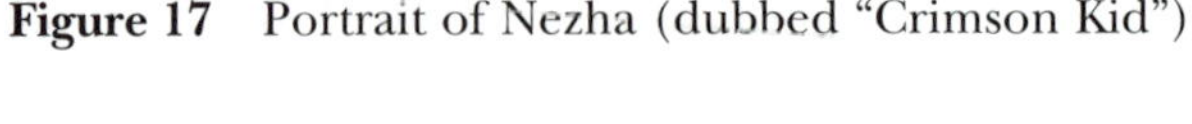

Figure 17 Portrait of Nezha (dubbed "Crimson Kid")

Source: Frontispiece of *Xiyou ji* (Guangxu ed.).

of King Vaiśravana, guardian of the North, was endowed with an extraordinary physique and divine power, capable of transforming himself at will and performing miraculous feats. He had allegedly assisted his father in defending the city of Anxi in modern Xinjiang against foreign invasion. Moreover, he possessed prodigious power and magical spells that could destroy evils and wicked spirits and was known to have battled and subdued the treacherous Dragon King and his sons in the Eastern Sea. Since Dadu was the imperial city and warranted the protection of a guardian deity, under the pervasive influence of Tantric Buddhism Nazha was a logical candidate, the more so given the perennial concern of Dadu's residents at that time, i.e. the water problem.

As records show, because of various climatic and ecological factors the Dadu district suffered from a high percentage of incessant rain alternating with protracted drought and other natural disasters throughout the entire Mongol-Yuan reign (1271–1268). A recent study shows that flood occurred in 52 years or 53% of the 97 years of Yuan rule, whereas drought occurred in 23 years or about 24% of the same duration. Heavy rain fuelled the water cascading from the mountains in the western region through various tributaries and inundated the plains, whereas drought dried the rivers and lakes and depleted the water supply for the population. In periods of drought, the Mongol-Yuan rulers from Qubilai Qaghan to Toghōn Temür used both Chinese classical rituals and Mongolian, Central Asian shamanistic practices to pray for rain to relieve the human suffering and, in a gesture of subservience to the traditional popular beliefs that a mystical dragon had controlling power over water, the last Yuan ruler also ordered sacrificial offering to the dragon for relief.[72] Folk beliefs attributed the havoc to the misdeeds of the Dragon King who resided in the lake region and manipulated the water resources. He had to be either worshipped or exorcized by a superior deity. According to the gazetteer *Xijin zhi*, under the section "suiji", during the second day of the second month of the year in Dadu a popular ritual, called *long taitao* 龍檯頭 (Dragon raising its head), was widely observed by the communities. It was believed that the Dragon, who had been in hibernation during winter, would emerge at the beginning of spring, bringing rain and facilitating crop growing. People scattered lime around their well dotting a white path into their house hoping they could lead the dragon inside to exterminate the worms and insects, and they were told not to sweep the floor on that day lest they disturb the dragon's eyes.[73]

In addition, the Dragon King was revered as a deity for calming the waters and offering blessing to waterway travels, and memorials had been built along the inland transport routes in Dadu. A prominent Dragon King Hall (Longwangtang 龍王堂) was built on the side of the aforementioned Dam or Embankment Canal at its outlet at the water gate of the Guangxi Gate on the upper northeastern walls of the outer-city. An old Jin canal renovated and expanded under Guo Shoujing's proposal, it started at the tip of the north bend of the Jishui Pool in the northwestern corner, ran across the imperial capital through its northeastern walls and then dipped southeast, with seven lock-gates to connect it with the Wenyu Canal, the northern extension of the Grand Canal. It was one of the two inland waterways (the other was the Tonghui Canal) through which the grain boats shipped provisions from the southeastern provinces. This shipping route was enforced from 1275 to 1283 before the inland waterway transport was superseded by maritime transportation which prevailed until the end of the Yuan dynasty. According to the *Xijin zhi*, each year when grain was put into storage, the officials in charge of shipping unloaded the cargo from the grain boats and delivered it inside the embankment, probably to the Qiansicang 千斯倉 (A Thousand Granary) in the adjacent area. At this juncture, they chanted and prayed before the Dragon King Hall in a ceremony to express gratitude for the supernatural spirit's blessing (Figures 12, 13).[74]

There was a similar Dragon King Hall on the edge of an island adjoining the northern bank of the Jishui Pool near the outlet of what was later the Tonghui Canal. It slithered southeastward along the outer walls of the imperial-city and exited through the Wenming Gate in the south of the outer-city to join the Grand Canal. A small worshiping memorial known as Huitong 匯通 or Huiquanci 匯泉祠 was established south of the island and at its rear was a six-foot five-inch fossil rock resting on a pedestal. On top of the rock were two artistically engraved statues of a four-inch cock and a seven-inch lion facing each other, with the cock on the left appearing to flee toward the prostrate lion on the right. South of the rock were also two similar but fossil statues shaped like a cock facing a lion, except that the lion appeared to be in a crouching position. These rocks were dubbed *Jishishi* 雞獅石 ("cock-lion" rock), hence the watery area was called Jishi—"cock-lion" or "cock-rock" pond (*jishi* 雞獅 or *Jishichi* 雞石池). After the completion of the Tonghui Canal, during which the pond—originally simply known as Haizi 海子—was expanded, it was named Jishui (Gathered Waters) Pool—a name which is similar in pronunciation to its original name. It is believed that when the grain boats were anchored at the banks of the Jishui Pool to unload cargo, similar ceremonies to pay homage to the Dragon King were held before they continued their journey through the locks of the Heyi Gate and exited to the northwest.[75]

The obeisance to the Dragon was most obvious in the case of drought. For instance in 1350, when Dadu was struck by this calamity, a certain Mongol administrative executive, hearing of the efficacy of a spiritual dragon at the Black Dragon Pool in the Fangshan county southwest of the capital, went there to offer Daoistic prayers and a downpour instantly followed. The official then gave orders to erect a temple and a shrine to pay homage, and regular sacrificial offerings were made thereafter. It was also reported that the last Yuan emperor Toghōn Temür habitually initiated sacrificial offerings to the dragon in the event of drought at the capital and seals bearing the impression of the "dragon deity" (*longshen* 龍神) used in the sacrifice were then buried under the walled gates of the imperial-city after successful results. A few of these seals were discovered under Peking's imperial-city walls in Qing times, thus furnishing direct material evidence of the performance of these rain-praying rituals in the Yuan capital.[76]

The above references did not mention Nazha along with the sacrificial offerings to the Dragon to relieve drought. But there was a piece of information about Nazha in the *Xinshi* 心史 (History written from the Heart), attributed to Zheng Suonan 鄭所南, popularly known by his style-name Sixiao 思肖 (1238–1315), a late Song scholar who became a hermit under Mongol rule. According to this, grand celebrations were held in Dadu on Nazha's birthday in the second month of the year, attesting to the popularity of the Nazha cult. Although *Xinshi* was allegedly discovered under a well in Suzhou in 1638 and its authenticity has been repeatedly challenged since, modern scholars have concluded that some of the information about the Yuan state is veracious. If so, this reference to Nazha is very valuable and we may even be tempted to relate the celebration to the concurrent ritual enactment observing the "Dragon Raising its Head" mentioned earlier.[77] Why was Nazha so well received in folk worship? He was adulated as a guardian-protector because people believed he could resolve water problems by subduing the Dragon King with his supernatural power and magical spells. In the earlier legend concerning the building of Shangdu, Liu Bingzhong is alleged to have used his instinct to communicate with the Dragon, borrow a lake site, and drain it to build the subsidiary capital city. Here in the Dadu legend, Liu Bingzhong used his power to invoke the presence of Nazha to serve a similar but more lasting objective, further strengthening the Nazha legend. But in the last analysis it must have been the metamorphosis of Nazha into a supernatural hero battling with the dragon family and subduing the vicious genii who controlled the watery world in the late Yuan Daoist hagiography that enchanted the Dadu residents and immortalized Nazha. This new development provided the catalyst for a more colorful Nazha, which subsequently captivated popular Ming fiction and helped carry the Dadu legend well beyond the Mongol period.

Who then may have been the makers or perpetuators of this engrossing Liu Bingzhong/Nazha City legend? Though lacking direct evidence, from the mythologization of Liu and Nazha, the candidates may well have been the Buddhist or Daoist cultists who sought to apotheosize their Han Chinese hero Liu Bingzhong through a connection with the popular deity Nazha. The stories could also have been conjured up by men of letters familiar with these popular traditions and propagated to enthrall the populace because they appealed to their craving for drama and fantasy and reflected their aspiration to living in peace and their seeking of solutions to practical problems in their daily life. As the stories were told and retold, they were embroidered with further imaginative exaggeration, thereby perpetuating an inspiring and durable legend. At the same time, this mythologization of a Han Chinese hero in the Mongolian setting must have also had a special meaning to the large indigenous population struggling for a precarious existence under alien rule. The very fact that the Nazha story, and related popular anecdotes about the planning of Dadu, were invoked and interpreted in the early Ming as a prophecy of the duration of Mongol-Yuan rule underlined the sociopolitical implication of this marvelous legend.

We should note, moreover, that the name *Nazha cheng* appeared to have been commonly accepted by late Yuan/early Ming literati as an alias for Yuan Dadu, when its glamour and vibrancy were in eclipse. A good example can be found in Yang Weizhen 楊維楨 (1296–1370), *Tieya gu yuefu* 鐵崖古樂府 (The Old *yuefu* of Tieya), a collection of poems patterned after the *yuefu* style of the Han dynasty. In this a series of lyrics eulogized the demise of the Mongol Yuan and glorified the triumph of Ming Taizu in reestablishing Han Chinese rule. No. 12 of the series was captioned: "The Imperial armies marched into Yan from the sea, the master of Yuan left the country en masse. The city was returned [to Chinese rule] without tainting one single sword with blood, unifying the prefectures of You and Ji." (王師由海入燕，元主大去其國，全城來歸，不血一刃，為統幽薊。) The first five lines of the poem read: "The [Yuan] state's fortune collapsed; the Six Armies [of the new ruler] have encamped. Here is the Nazha City. The master of Kucha took flight to the Luan Capital." (國運傾，六師駐。那吒城。龜玆主，走灤京。)[78] It is absolutely clear that the poem was referring to the Ming armies' taking of Dadu and the last Yuan emperor Toghōn Temür's hurried flight with his retinue to Luan prefecture, the summer capital Shangdu. It is interesting that while Nazha City was used to allude to the Great Capital, Kucha, the ancient kingdom in Chinese Turkestan situated to the northwest of modern Xinjiang was cited to disguise the Yuan emperor's origin. Perhaps they were just used as historical allusion which is so typical in Chinese literature, but the fact that *Nazha cheng* appeared in the works of a prominent late Yuan belle lettrist vividly attest to the legend's popularity and its acceptance by the literati.

Chapter 2

Liu Bowen, Nezha, and the Building of Ming Peking

The Historical Background

Ming Taizu's armies marched into Dadu on September 14 1368, four days after the hurried departure of Toghōn Temür for Kaiping (Shangdu) and then to Yingchang 應昌 in Inner Mongolia, where he reigned over the remnants of the Yuan regime, which the Chinese called Bei (Northern) Yuan, for two more years. The former Yuan capital was renamed Beipingfu (the "Northern Peace" Prefecture), whereas the dynastic capital Yingtian, the historical city Jinling in the southeast of the Yangzi River was named Nanking (Southern Capital). The supreme commander of the expeditionary force, General Xu Da, was instructed to avoid any deliberate destruction of the former capital and so contrary to rumor, Dadu remained unscathed. To protect the city from resurgent Mongol incursions the Ming command rebuilt the northern face of the outer walls with two gates 5 *li* or 2.9 km to the south behind the old canal which surrounded the entire rectangular city and exited at the southeastern end to join the Grand Canal. The length from the east to the west was 1,890 *zhang* or 6 km. As the canal was connected to the Gaoliang River which ran northeastward from the corner of the western city wall until it reached the Jishui Pool, the wall in this section therefore slanted in the same direction and the wall in the western city was shorter than its eastern counterpart.[1]

Having secured the northern walls of Beiping, Ming Taizu initiated plans to establish the fief of his fourth son Zhu Di, due to be invested as the Prince of Yan in May 1370, on the site of the former Yuan capital. It was the first step toward the eventual enfeoffment of all his twenty-four sons. In late 1369 the emperor appointed Zhao Yao 趙耀 as administrative vice commissioner of the prefecture, putting him in charge of safeguarding the deserted Yuan palaces. Zhao then submitted a copy of the *Beiping gongshi tu* 北平宮室圖 (Drawings of the palaces and chambers of Beiping) prepared by Minister of Works Zhang Yun 張允. Thereupon Taizu gave instructions to build a princely residence for his son within the old foundation of the Yuan imperial-city. Work started in 1371, and the residence of the Prince of Yan was completed in late 1379; it was a reconstruction of the old Yuan Da Nei, i.e. the palace-city. No major public work projects were undertaken in Beiping until after the Prince's accession as the Yongle emperor, when it was elevated to be the main capital.[2]

In the meantime, Taizu turned his attention to the imperial capital construction at his own power base in Yingtianfu 應天府 (Responsive to Heaven), the site of a historical city which he renamed Nanking after the founding of the dynasty. Known as Jinling county in Zhou times, under the names Jianye 建業 and Jiankang 建康 it was the capital of the Three Kingdoms state of Wu (222–280), and thereafter, despite name changes, the capital of the Eastern Jin, Song, Qi, Liang, and the Chen—known as the Southern Dynasties (317–589). The ancient name Jinling was restored in A.D. 625 under the Tang. Under the Yuan it was the seat of the Jiqing 集慶 district. There were important reasons favoring Jinling ("gold tumulus") as the capital city. It lay in rich alluvial land in the lower Yangzi valley at a meeting point with the north China plain across the River, shielded by mountains and ridges on the northeast and southwest, and watered by the Yangzi from the west and up north to the sea. As such, since historical times the site had been highly regarded for its strategic, geomantic as well as economic value—an ideal location for an imperial capital city. Zhuge Liang, the sagacious minister of the Three Kingdoms Shu state, allegedly left this perceptive comment: "Jinling, with Mount Zhong 鍾山 looking like a 'coiling lion' and Mount Shitou 石頭 (Boulder) a 'crouching tiger', is the site of a ruler's residence." This was subsequently reiterated by Ming Taizu's advisers commenting on the strategic supremacy of his future capital.[3]

In early 1355 Zhu Yuanzhang, having given his allegiance to the emerging Da Song state of Han Liner but still commanding an independent army in Anhui fighting against the Mongol Yuan and rival warlord forces, was appraised by his two comrades Tao An 陶安 (1312?–1368) and Feng Guoyong 馮國用 (1324–1359) of the importance of Jinling. Thus in July that same year he took his colleagues' advice, crossing the Huai River with his troops and seizing the old city in April of the following year as his forward base. Impressed by the walled city's topography and strategic value, he hailed it as a gift of Heaven and moved into it as his headquarters, renaming the district Yingtian.[4] Then in September 1366 Zhu Yuanzhang, now the Prince of Wu 吳王, commanded his confidant-adviser Liu Ji (Bowen) to administer the siting of a new capital city. According to a contemporary Yao Tongshou 姚桐壽, reminiscing in his memoir *Lejiao siyu* 樂郊私語 (Gossip from the Le Suburbs), Liu excelled in the discourse of "forms" of the Jianxi school of geomancy. In a conversation with Yao shortly before he entered Zhu Yuanzhang's service, Liu Ji confided that the south-bound dragon's veins originating from the Kunlun mountain range lay in the Haiyan 海鹽 county (northeast of Hangzhou 杭州). When asked who would merit the geomantic blessing, Liu predicted that only a sage like the Duke of Zhou or Confucius deserved it, hinting at the rise of a future prince.[5] Whether or not the story is apocryphal, Zhu Yuanzhang must have been impressed by Liu Ji's know-how to place such trust in him.

According to official records, Liu sited and designed a rectangular walled imperial-city with an interior palace-city north of Mt. Zhong, 2 *li* to the east of the old city, which is said to have spread over an area in excess of 50 *li* centered at the reclaimed Yanque Lake 燕雀湖 where the central palace was to be constructed. This was completed in late 1367, in time for Zhu Yuanzhang's inauguration of the Ming dynasty in January 1368 (Figure 18). Because of the need to adapt to the topography the imperial-city was situated at the extreme east of the outer-city, enclosed by irregular walls, leaving considerable space to the northwest for additional office quarters, domestic residences, and army barracks. Additional construction was stalled by discussions on choosing an alternate dynastic capital, as well as a preoccupation with building the massively expensive city of Zhongdu in Fengyang, Anhui, site of the emperor's birth and a potential candidate as the new imperial capital. It was only after Zhongdu's construction was suspended in May 1375 because of the

Figure 18 Portrait of Ming Taizu (Zhu Yuanzhang)

Source: Courtesy of National Palace Museum, Taipei, Taiwan.

excruciating fiscal burden and labor shortage that the building of Nanking restarted and took on new significance as the final choice of the imperial capital.[6]

When construction resumed in the autumn of 1375 the existing palaces and halls in the square walled palace-city, which was about 2 sq. *li* or l.3 sq. km in size, were modified or rebuilt according to the Zhongdu city plan which followed the design of the classical square-shaped Wangcheng model and the precedent of Yuan Dadu. The square walled palace-city, with the Wumen 午門 (Meridian or Noon Gate) at its south center, was entered by four gates, one on each side. It was approached by its own imperial way along an axis that included a row of palaces (*gong*) and halls (*dian*) divided into two symmetrical groups, three at the front, or south, and three behind, or north. The three front halls: Fengtian 奉天 (Commanded by Heaven), Huakai

華蓋 (Stately Umbrella), and Jinshen 謹身 (Cautious to Self), were "public", used for imperial audiences or proclamations. The three back halls, much smaller, consisted of two palaces: Qianqing 乾清 (Heavenly Purity) and Kunning 坤寧 (Earthly Tranquility), and one hall, Jiaotai 交泰 (Peaceful Unity); they were more private in function. Both groups had additional buildings on the sides. Encircling the city wall was the Hucheng Canal, the traditional protective canal serving as a moat with bridges from all the gates.

The palace-city was dubbed the Forbidden City because as the residence of the Son of Heaven it corresponded to the "Purple Bright Constellation with Polaris in the Center" (Purple Palace Enclosure), believed to be the celestial ruler's residence in the universe. It had great significance to Peking as its famed Forbidden City was a replica of the plan initially designed for Zhongdu and then adopted by Nanking. Thus began the close relationship, structurally as well as politically, between the three Ming imperial cities. According to the official record, the horizontal rectangular imperial-city had six gates on its enclosed wall with a perimeter of 59 *li* or about 33.7 km surrounded by a moat. It was the outer compound of the palace-city and the site of the altars, temples, official quarters, and markets—all of which were completed in 1378. The wall of the irregular outer-city was built in 1390, with sixteen gates and a perimeter of 120 *li* or 68.6 km, while additional construction of civil and military quarters and residences on the southern fringe of the imperial-city walls was ordered in 1392 and finalized in 1395, three years before Taizu's death (Figure 19).[7]

The Genesis of the "Northern Capital"

The building of a new capital city in Beipingfu over the former Yuan Dadu took place under the third Ming emperor Yongle, i.e. Zhu Di, temple-name first Taizong and later Chengzu (r. 1403–1424), after a tumultuous three years of civil war to unseat his nephew, the Jianwen emperor (Zhu Yunwen, r. 1398–1402), the dynastic founder's grandson and designated successor. Shortly after his enthronement following the successful *jingnan* 靖難 ("to clear away disasters") campaign, the new emperor was preoccupied with urgent tasks to consolidate his rule, legitimate his usurpation, and initiate institutional and policy changes for the new reign (Figure 20).[8] In

Figure 19 Plan of Nanking

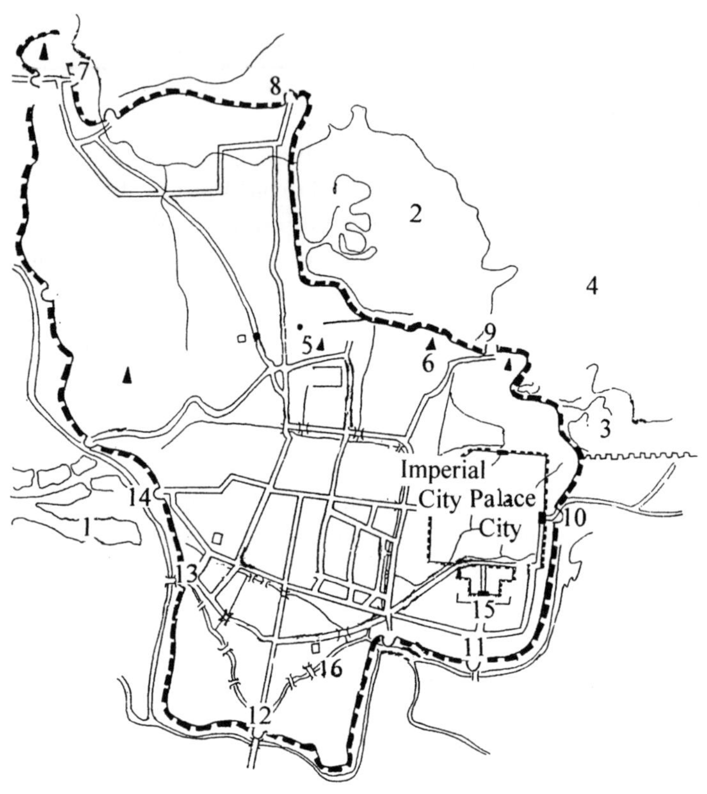

1. Mochou Lake
2. Xuanwu Lake
3. Yanque Lake
4. Mt. Zhong
5. Mt. Jilong
6. Mt. Fuzhou
7. Jinchuan Gate
8. Shence Gate
9. Taiping Gate
10. Chaoyang Gate
11. Zhengyang Gate
12. Jubao Gate
13. Sanshan (Shuixi) Gate
14. Shicheng Gate
15. Hongwu Gate
16. Qinhuai River

Source: *Gaoshusen: Jinling shichao diwangzhou*, p. 122.

Figure 20 Portrait of the Yongle Emperor (Ming Chengzu)

Source: Courtesy of National Palace Museum, Taipei, Taiwan.

selecting the capital the emperor, whose fiefdom was headquartered at Beipingfu, made a decision to designate it as the new seat of government, known as Peking, in present-day Beijing, with plans for major construction. His motives were linked to historical concerns and to the current political and military situation. Ming Taizu had early on shown dissatisfaction with Nanking as the capital of the empire and had considered relocating it to the north. But the new emperor's preference for Beipingfu, apart from attempting to solve his father's dilemma, reflected his perception that the north was the seat of his own power and that the new capital was the citadel of defense for the northern and western frontiers of the empire. Also, from the classical geomantic interpretation harking back to Yuan Dadu, lying in the center of the earth corresponding to the northern asterism, and well protected by lofty mountains and ridges to its west, north, and northeast in a horseshoe shape, with nine felicitous winding streams in a vast curved coastal plain, it was an auspicious site where vital energy gathered and was concentrated. Peking therefore surpassed all other sites in the then contemporary political and military considerations. Moreover it had been the imperial capital for several past dynastics and its architectural monuments and physical facilities remained largely intact, laying a solid foundation for its new resurgence.[9]

Those in favor of the relocation of the capital heaped praise on Peking's rich historical tradition and supreme topography and environs befitting the imperial city of a great empire. Several laudatory rhapsodies and essays containing extravagant descriptions of the new capital with rich classical allusions and literary accolades were presented to the Yongle emperor during the construction from 1403–1420. The most prominent of these were two essays both entitled "Huangdu dayitong fu" 皇都大一統賦 (Rhapsody of the Imperial Capital of Grand Unity), composed respectively by Yang Rong 楊榮 (1371–1440) and Jin Shan (Youzi) 金善 (幼孜) (1368–1431), and another, entitled "Beijing fu" 北京賦 (Rhapsody of Peking), was written by Li Shimian 李時勉 (1374–1450). All were members of the Hanlin Academy and the former two were also appointed to the Grand Secretariat; they made their submissions in January 1421 in commemoration of the completion of the imperial city.[10]

However, none of the above made specific references to geomancy and its relationship to city planning, and not until the later Ming era did such literature emerge, but it is apparent that geomancy did command Yongle's attention. For instance, in June 1409 he had directed Liao Junqing 廖均卿, a follower of the Jiangxi school of "forms" of geomancy, and other specialists to search for an auspicious site for the joint mausoleum of Empress Xu and himself. They identified the site in a yellow earth mount northeast of Changping county north of Peking, and it was subsequently renamed Tianshoushan 天壽山 (Mount of Heavenly Longevity) (see Figure 1), where the mausoleum Changling 長陵 ("Longevity Tumulus") was constructed.[11] Then in a rescript announcing his attendance at the newly completed imperial court to receive audience on the first day of the following calendar year (i.e. January 1421 in the nineteenth year of Yongle), in a gush of exhilaration and jubilation, the emperor emphatically declared: "Having inherited the mandate to rule, I set my mind to restore and expand the grand enterprise and make plans for the future. Always cherishing Peking, I made it the real metropolis. This is the instruction of Heaven, and is also affirmed by the verdict of the tortoise-shell and straws divination. (眷兹北京，實為都會。惟天意之所屬，實卜筮之攸同。) Hence I followed the ancient tradition, abided by the public opinion, instituted the two-capital system, and ordered the construction of the altars of sacrifice to Heaven and Earth, ancestral temples, and the palaces and chambers."[12] The last couplets underscored the prominence of the cosmological and geomantic precepts in the design and construction of the capital city and its facilities, which were distinctively revealed upon their completion.

In his recent book *Zijin cheng fengshui* 紫禁城風水 (Geomancy of the Forbidden City), Wang Zilin attempts to identify the cosmological and geomantic underpinnings of the imperial city through an investigation of the extant literature and verification with the structure and layout of the Forbidden City, now the Palace Museum. A seminal reference work was the *Renzi xuzhi zikao dili xinxue tongzong* 人子須知資考地理心學統宗 (Essential Knowledge of the Principles of Geomancy and Philosophy of the Mind to Posterity), in 39 *juan*. It was written by Xu Shanji 徐善繼 and Xu Shanshu 徐善述, two twin-brother geomancers of the Jianxi school, and was first printed in 1564. Echoing the findings of Zhu Xi and the Yuan commentators of Dadu, they opined that the dragon's vein of the Yan capital originated from the mythical Kunlun Mountain and coalesced at Mt. Tianshou, where the dragon transmitted the auspicious ether of the cosmos to the entire terrain and laid the geomantic foundation of the capital city.[13]

Wang seeks to reconstruct the complex cosmological and geomantic picture of the Forbidden City from several perspectives. First, he postulates that the dragon's vein from Mt. Tianshou ran south through the palace-city along the north to south axis and the dragon's cave lay in the Jiaotai Hall; it was midway between the emperor's and empress's private chambers where the intercourse of the male/female *yang/yin* essence germinated energy and nourishment. The dragon's vitality and blessings thus filled the halls and palaces where the Son of Heaven resided and discharged his mandate from the high lord and heavenly ruler within the cosmological celestial-terrestrial correspondence system. Second, he points out that the Forbidden City was patterned after the celestial Purple Palace Enclosure, where three main palaces of the inner court were flanked by six smaller palaces and halls on each side of the north-south axis, corresponding to the number of stars in the celestial constellation. The most sacrosanct edifice was the Huangjidian 皇極殿 (Hall of Imperial Supremacy) in the Ming, known as Taihe 太和 (Supreme Harmony) in the Qing, which lay at the center of the axis in the outer court where the emperor received audience. It was hailed in a Qing dynasty couplet "Long de zheng zhong tian, si hai yong xi fu guang yun" 龍德正中天，四海雍熙符廣運。The first line of the couplet was adapted from the explanation of the second *nine* line of the *qian* hexagram of the *Book of Changes*. The classical meaning was that the great man has the dragon's powers and occupies the central place, and as the sovereign had been mythologized as the dragon in imperial ideology he assumed similar powers in geomantic parlance. The second line of the couplet means "the four seas exude harmony and peace and they portend vast fortune".[14]

Third, the Wansuishan, an artificial mount erected north of the palace-city and facing the auspicious Mt. Tianshou, was regarded as the back of the dragon's cave lodged underneath. These led the dragon's vein into the inner courts of the Forbidden City, while to the south of the outer court, three different waterways headed by the Jinshui Canal formed an auspicious geomantic confluence generating energy to bolster the circulation of the dragon's ether. Fourth, the Dark God Zhenwu, who was deified as the Xuantian Shangdi 玄天上帝 (High Lord of the Dark Heaven) in 1304 by the decree of the Mongol ruler Chengzong 成宗 (Temür, r. 1295–1307), and who the Yongle emperor hailed for divine assistance in his *jingnan* campaign to ascend the throne, was revered as the spiritual guardian-protector. A bronze statue of Zhenwu was housed in the Qin'andian 欽安殿 (Hall of Blessed Peace) built in 1420 in the upper inner court facing the northern gate of the palace-city (see Figure 21). As an exponent of the fengshui system, however, the most significant phenomenon was the prominence of the cosmological principles of the Eight Trigrams of the *Book of Changes* and the correlative *yinyang* and Five Agents/Phases theories. They were ubiquitously manifested in the architectural designs, cardinal

Figure 21 Bust of the Statue of the Dark God in the Qin'andian

Source: Wang, *Zijin cheng fengshui*, p. 271.

directions of the buildings, multicolored symbols of the ornaments, and spatial layout of the monuments and courtyards, as well as the parks and sacrificial altars in and outside the concentric triple-walled capital cities. To sum up, the Forbidden City was a skillfully crafted mosaic that articulated the centuries-old Chinese beliefs in the omnipotence and universality of the magnificent imperial city that has no comparison in human civilization.[15]

Wang's account is provocative and stimulating but suffers from a weak and incomplete analytical scheme and incorrect and excessive use of some of the geomantic literature without careful verification with the existing architectural layout. Lacking documentary evidence of the city plan, it is impossible to authenticate or dispute the arguments of the fengshui system as it has been preconceived or conjectured, and even more so to ascertain whether or not such a presentation is a *post facto* intellectual elucidation. A factual description with less theoretical speculation and philosophical endorsement is a better approach in light of current scholarship on the imperial city.

The transformation of Peking into an imperial capital was a formidable task for the emperor and his advisers and it imposed heavy burdens on the people. Although some of Yuan Dadu's city walls and palaces were still preserved, the general plan of the city had to be altered and major construction was needed to meet the emperor's specifications. In addition, transportation facilities had to be improved to expedite massive shipments of grain and provisions from the southeastern provinces. Moreover, the military organization in the vicinity had to be restructured to handle the new situation. The basic institutional arrangements also had to be revamped, and the changes affected imperial agencies in Nanking and in other parts of the empire which had to be adjusted. The transfer of the capital to Peking was therefore the most complex and far-reaching imperial project undertaken during the Ming dynasty.

Construction of the capital took place in several stages and took over two decades to complete. In January 1403, on announcing his intention, the Yongle emperor formally gave the city the status of Northern Capital (Peking) and sent his eldest son Zhu Gaozhi 朱高熾, later Emperor Renzong 仁宗 (r. 1424–1425), to administer the new capital with a ministry to oversee the auxiliary branch offices of the central administration. From this time on until 1421 the seals of Peking bore the characters *xingzai* 行在, meaning "residence pro tempore", to reflect the institutional transition. The metropolitan prefecture was also renamed Shuntian 順天 (Obedient to Heaven) in order to match Nanking, i.e. Yingtian (Responsive to Heaven) and to link the emperor symbolically with his father to enhance his legitimate succession. In August 1406, after ordering that palace buildings be constructed in the following year, the emperor sent the Earl of Taining 泰寧, Chen Gui 陳珪 (1335–1419), an assistant commissioner-in-chief, Minister of Works Song Li 宋禮 (?–1422), and other civil and military officials to the provinces for the acquisition of building materials and recruitment of skillful artisans and laborers.

However, major construction was disrupted by the death of Empress Xu 徐 (born 1362) in August 1407 in Nanking. Much preparation was diverted to the construction of the joint imperial mausoleum in Mt. Tianshou in Changping county north of Peking. Between 1408 and 1409 only some minor offices were built, and the emperor still resided in Nanking and issued his orders in Peking through the heir-apparent. In ensuing years, piecemeal construction work was done on the palaces, halls, temples, residential quarters, walls, and bridges. But it was not until early 1417, after the completion of the mausoleum, Changling, the reconstruction of the Grand Canal and the completion of the emperor's Western Palace (Xigong 西宫), that massive capital construction was undertaken. Under the charge of Chen Gui and the Ministry of Works, hundreds of thousands of skillful artisans and laborers were mobilized. Some of these were drawn from military units, others were criminals, and some were prisoners of war, such as the outstanding Annamese architect Ruan An 阮安 (?–1453) who, having been made a eunuch, played an important role in the construction of the capital. By late 1417 most of the palace buildings in the palace- and imperial-cities had been built. In 1418 improvements were made to the moats, walls, and bridges, and the imperial grandson's palace and the princes' residences were under construction. In 1420 sections of the Yuan southern city wall were restored at 2 *li* to the south, about 2,100 *zhang* or 6.7 km in length; the Bell Tower (Zhonglou 鐘樓) and Altar of Heaven were also finished; and by early 1421 the basic works of the capital were complete. In January of that year Peking formally became the principal capital of the empire, and the central government was thoroughly reorganized. Nanking was reduced to subordinate status and so were the government offices and agencies there.[16]

Peking's new status and the consequent reorganization of the central government greatly affected the civil and military establishments in both Peking and Nanking. Most importantly the prefix *xingzai* for Peking was dropped and all the seals with this inscription were withdrawn. On the other hand, all the offices and agencies in Nanking were given new seals inscribed with the prefix "Nan-jing" (Southern Capital) to indicate their now subordinate status. These changes in terminology served to reflect political reality. However, all the new designations were reversed when the Yongle emperor's successor Renzong decided in 1425 to return the capital to Nanking, when he reinstituted the previous titles. But on his death late in 1425 the return to Nanking was halted. When Zhu Zhanji 朱瞻基 (1399–1435) ascended the throne as Emperor Xuanzong (r. 1426–1435) he again designated Peking as the principal capital, but continued to use the term *xingzai* for its offices, perhaps in anticipation of an eventual return to Nanking. It was not until 1441 under Emperor Yingzong 英宗 (Zhu Qizhen 朱祁鎮, r. 1436–1449; 1457–1464) that this prefix was finally removed from the titles of all government agencies in Peking.[17]

The Imperial City Plan

The building of Peking was not based on a novel imperial city plan in which a key architect, like Liu Bingzhong for Dadu, could be identified. Instead it drew on the blueprint of Dadu and adopted certain specifications from those of Ming Zhongdu and Nanking of the earlier reign, as attested by its physical layout. This was a stark contrast to the popular legend which credited Liu Bowen as the planner of Peking and other contemporary colorful historical figures as his close associates in the construction. There is not a shred of documentary record in the Ming sources concerning the design of the new capital or the specific personnel in charge of the building project at various stages. The imperial capital was a concentric triple-walled city like the Yuan capital, but was shorter in length from north to south because of the early Ming decision to pull back the northern wall 5 *li* southward in order to build a new defense against the Mongol invaders. Unlike the designers of Dadu, the planners of Ming Peking again conceptually correlated the palace-city with the Purple Palace Enclosure in the traditional celestial-terrestrial correspondence system, hence it was dubbed the Forbidden City. But the formal name *Zijin cheng* did not come into use until the reign of Emperor Shizong in the mid-sixteenth century. It was situated at the meeting point of the north-south, east-west axes inside the imperial-city over the former Yuan palace-city and flanked by an artificial protective canal. It was encircled by the rectangular imperial- or administrative-city which occupied the southern part of the center of the outer-city, later expanded by inclusion of the suburbs. In designing the imperial-city, like Dadu, a north to south axis was drawn starting from the Bell Tower in the north through the center of the palace-city to the south with exits at Zhengyang 正陽 (Facing Brightness) Gate and then Yongding (Eternal Security) Gate as the walled city later expanded its southern boundary. The axis was about 8 km long and divided the administrative-city into two halves; all the important monuments and buildings were built along the axis, and other collateral buildings and parks were also built in juxtaposition to or in harmony with this architectural planning (Figure 22).[18]

The Forbidden City—lying due south of the Tianshoushan which geomancers claimed to be the main mountain of the dragon's vein extending through the imperial-city, was a square enclosure

Figure 22 Plan of Ming Peking (early stage) superimposed on Yuan Dadu

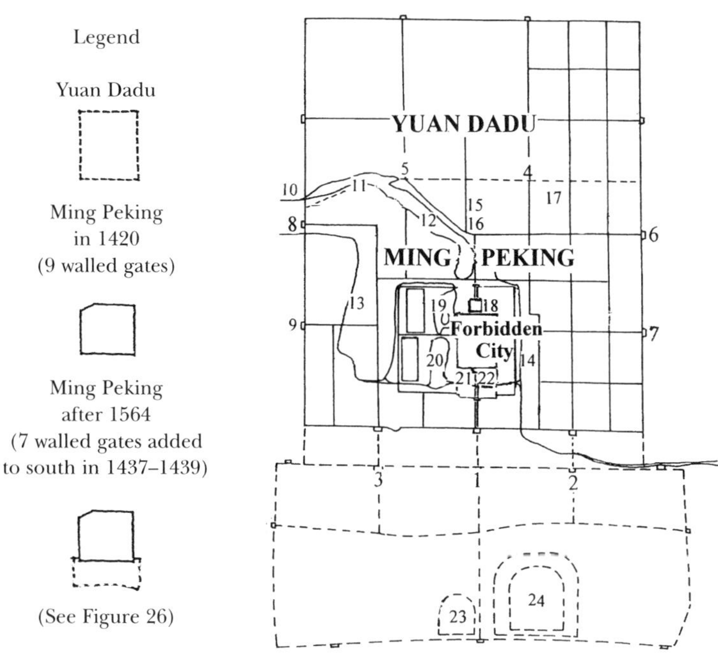

1. Zhengyang (*Lizheng) Gate
2. Chongwen (*Wenming) Gate
3. Xuanwu (*Shuncheng) Gate
4. Anding Gate
5. Desheng Gate
6. Dongzhi (*Chongren) Gate
7. Chaoyang (*Qihua) Gate
8. Xizhi (*Heyi) Gate
9. Fucheng (*Pingze) Gate
10. Gaoliang River
11. Jishui Pool
12. Shicha Sea
13. Jinshui Canal
14. Yu (Jade/Imperial) Canal
15. Zhonglou (Bell Tower)
16. Gulou (Drum Tower)
17. Wenmiao (Confucius Temple)
18. Wansuishan (Mei/Jingshan)
19. Qionghua Island
20. Taiye Pond (West Park)
21. Shejitan
22. Taimiao
23. Shanchuantan (Altars of Mountains and Rivers)
24. Tiantan (Altar of Heaven)

* Yuan names

Source: Based on *Kaogu* 1967, no. 6, p. 26.

occupying the former Yuan palace-city. It was moved slightly south, and an artificial waterway, the Hucheng Canal, was dug as a moat around the city. Bridges were extended over the moat at each gate on the four sides of the city. As the Son of Heaven's abode, its architectural model and spatial layout vividly reflected cosmological principles and the omnipotence of the sovereign in heaven and on earth. The city had a perimeter of 6 plus *li* or 3.4 km; its length from north to south was 960 meters and the width from east to west was 760 meters, with an area of 0.72 sq. km. It was enclosed by brick walls 7.9 meters in height, with four main gates. The city was laid along a north-south axis on which two groups of symmetrical palaces and halls were built in the middle. The main buildings were the Three Great Halls (*san dadian* 三大殿) of the outer court (south), and the smaller-scale replicas were the Rear Three Palaces (*hou sangong* 後三宮) (actually two *gong* and one *dian*; like Nanking, the *dian* was added later) of the inner court (north). The latter were flanked by six eastern and western smaller palaces and halls, both groups arranged in two clusters of three. The Three Great Halls were used for the emperor's administrative affairs and court audience, and the Rear Three Palaces were the residences of the emperor, empresses, and consorts. They were separated by the Qianqingmen 乾清門 (Heavenly Purity Gate). In geomantic parlance, the Jiaotai Hall, lying between the bed-chamber of the emperor and the empress, i.e. the Qianqing and Kunning (Earthly Tranquility) palaces in the inner court, was the "dragon's cave" where the *yang* and *yin* ether interacted and produced life and nourishment. This architectural arrangement and the dimensions of the palaces and halls in the Forbidden City all replicated the main capital of Nanking as a symbol of continuity and legitimacy. According to an extant tomb inscription, before construction was started, the Yongle emperor sent a eunuch Ni Zhong 倪忠 (1382–1441), who previously supervised the building of the mausoleum in Mt. Tianshou, to the Forbidden City in Nanking to note down all the measurements. This same eunuch might also have supervised the construction in Peking to assure conformity. On both sides of the front Three Great Halls and the rear Three Great Palaces there were various pavilions and chambers for the ladies-in-waiting and other imperial personnel. The southern walled gate, popularly known as Meridian (Noon) Gate, provided an entrance through a T-shaped Imperial Way from the imperial-city and beyond.[19]

The Forbidden City in Peking displayed ingeniously conceived, magnificent, variegated architectural designs and elegant, lavishly crafted multicolored physical adornments displaying the celestial-terrestrial correspondence myth of ancient Chinese cosmology adapted to the building of imperial-cities. The planners were inspired by the Han reconstruction of the celestial sphere and the correlated *yinyang* and Five Agents/Phases theories of the geomantic principles that had stoked the Chinese architectural imagination. The Forbidden City, situated in the center of the concentric rectangular triple-walled imperial capital, corresponded to the Purple Palace Enclosure occupying the Central Palace of the universe, which was modeled by the palace-city of Nanking. In correlating symbolism Ziwei, meaning "Purple Bright Constellation with Polaris in the Center" of the universe, equated with *jinzhong* 禁中 or *jinnei* 禁內, meaning "forbidden interior", the term used in pre-Tang texts for the restricted residence of the imperial ruler. A statement in the Monograph on Astronomy of the *Jinshu* 晉書 reads: "Ziwei forms the throne of the Great Emperor or High God [of Heaven] and the dwelling place of the Son of Heaven and governs the making of decrees and regulations." (紫微大帝之坐也，天子之常居也。) The term was formally used in the Tang dynasty, and set the precedent for the Ming and was followed by the Qing. Under Manchu rule the Forbidden City remained the imperial residence and was extensively refurbished; after the establishment of the Republic, the Manchu royal families were gradually relocated and in 1925 it was renamed Palace Museum, opening to the public a panoramic view of the magnificent grandeur of the historic capital (Figure 23).[20]

The similarity between the architectural arrangement of the palace-city in Peking and the conceptual correlation of the "Three Enclosures" with their coordinate stars in the celestial space is striking. Accordingly, the Rear Three Palaces are flanked by six palaces and halls on both the east and west side of the north-south axis of the walled inner court. The north-south axiality had great symbolic significance in the plan of Peking and other great Chinese capitals because it was the "line of dominion". The emperor's palace corresponds to the pole star, from which the high lord and heavenly emperor ruled and viewed the world of humankind to the south. In imitation the Son of Heaven on earth hence took the corresponding

Figure 23 Ming Peking—Forbidden City within the Imperial city

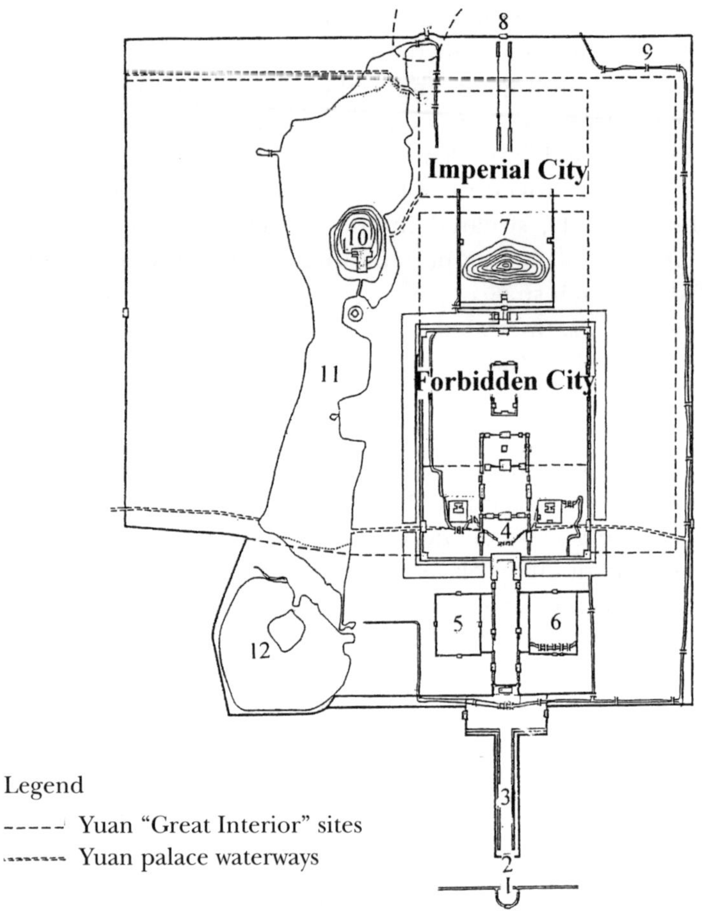

1. Zhengyang (Front) Gate
2. Da Ming (Great Brightness) Gate
3. Qianbulang (Thousand-pace Corridor)
4. Nei Jinshui (Interior Golden Water) Canal
5. Shejitan
6. Taimiao
7. Wansuishan (Jingshan)
8. Di'an Gate
9. Yu Canal
10. Qionghua Island
11. Taiye Pond
12. Xiyuan (West Park)

Source: Hou, *Beijing lishi ditu*, p. 34.

position. There are a total of fifteen buildings in the inner court in the Forbidden City, resembling the fifteen stars in the Purple Palace Enclosure and mirroring the celestial imperial palace. Outside the Tian'an (Heavenly Peace) Gate (i.e. Tian'anmen Square) directly in front of the imperial-city were four dragon "ornamented pillars" (*huabiao* 華表). They matched the five Heavenly Pillar (Tianzhu 天柱) stars outside the eastern enclosure of the Purple Palace, symbolizing the support for imperial authority. As corresponding symbols of the palaces in the four cardinal directions, guardians of the Polaris in the Central Palace, the planners named the north and south walled gates of the Forbidden City after the images of the celestial palaces. The south Meridian Gate, also known as Wufenglou 五鳳樓 (Five Phoenix Tower), alluded to the Vermillion Bird of the Southern Palace, the north Xuanwu Gate (renamed Shenwu 神武 [Divine Warrior] Gate under the Qing) equated with the Dark Warrior of the Northern Palace, the west Xihua 西華 Gate symbolized the White Tiger of the Western Palace, and the east Donghua 東華 Gate corresponded to the Azure Dragon of the Eastern Palace. A shrine named Sishenci 四神祠 (Shrine of Four Deities) was erected in the Imperial Garden (Yuhuayuan 御花園) outside the north gate of the Three Great Halls in the inner court in honor of these spiritual deities of the four directions, underscoring the heavenly protection of the imperial residence.[21]

The stars of the Privy Council Enclosure, situated in the Southern Palace of the universe as administrative offices, were represented in the architecture of the south end of the Forbidden City. It appears that the Three Great Halls of the Forbidden City corresponded to the three Mingtang 明堂 (Hall of Light) stars in the enclosure of the Privy Council, known as *santai* 三臺 (Three Terraces), where administrative offices were located. Just as the Left and Right Zhifa (Law Administrator) Celestial Gates stars flanked the Privy Council, there were left and right side gates with such names outside the Meridian Gate guarding the entrance to the Forbidden City. Furthermore, whereas the stars in the Celestial Markets Enclosure in the Eastern Palace symbolized the heavenly imperial court on the commercial market, there was a cluster of regularly scheduled markets known as Houshi 後市 (Rear Markets) outside the northern Bei'an 北安 Gate (renamed Di'an 地安 Gate under the Qing) of the imperial-city. There were also similar but more vigorous markets known as Chaoqianshi 朝前市 (Court's Front Markets) in what was known as Qipan (Chessboard) Street 棋盤街 on the left and right of Zhengyang Gate, dubbed the Front Gate (Qianmen 前門), the southern entrance into the imperial capital from the outer-city.[22] These star constellations flanked the celestial imperial palace and symbolically protected and extended the authority of the earthly sovereign and government.

The planners, said to be conscious of the distinctive fengshui features of Peking's topography and water resources, made meticulous references to the cardinal directions of the Eight Trigrams of the *Book of Changes* and the correlative *yinyang* and Five Agents/Phases theories. These made a conspicuous imprint on the architectural designs, spatial orientations, and decorative ornaments of the Forbidden City. Observing that the capital was bordered by mountains in the north and faced the sea in the east, that the land was raised in the north and dipped in the south, and thus conserved sunlight and accentuated drainage, the planners believed that the Forbidden City should replicate this auspicious topography. Thus they created an artificial elevation called Wansuishan (Hill of Myriad Years) at the back (north) of the Forbidden City, which the geomancers dubbed as the back of the dragon's cave in order to conserve the auspicious ether. It was popularly known as Meishan 煤山 (Coal Hill) but was renamed Jingshan 景山 (Scenic Hill) in 1655 under the Qing. They also dug a waterway called Nei Jinshui 內金水 (Interior Golden Water) Canal that flowed across the walls of the outer court (south) outside the Huangji (Imperial Supremacy) Gate, as geomancers believed that this would help nourish the ether emitted from the dragon's vein. The waterway, derived from the northwestern Hucheng Canal, then dipped into the southeastern section of the protective canal and joined the Wai Jinshui 外金水 (Exterior Golden Water) Canal, which originated at the South Sea west of the Forbidden City and flowed alongside the interior southern and northern walls of the imperial-city as its protective canal. This design was in accord with the fengshui principles defined by the configuration of the Eighth Trigram of the *Book of Changes*, which stipulate that water rises from the *qian* and retreats at the *xun* cardinal direction; thus the interior river entered the Forbidden City from the west (*qian*) and eventually exited in the southeast (*xun*). Also, according to the Five Agents correlation scheme, *jin* or Metal was associated with West, and since the river flowed through the Forbidden City it thus received the name Interior Golden Water Canal.[23]

The interactions of *yin* and *yang*, two opposite but complementary cosmic forces, were vividly reflected in the design and arrangement of the various units of the palaces and halls. Those in the outer court (south), symbolizing *yang* (brightness), were larger, taller, more lavish and spacious; whereas those in the inner court, symbolizing *yin* or darkness, were smaller, narrower, gloomier, and more cloistered, producing a contrasting but balanced physical and spatial harmony. Moreover, since *yang* represented odd numbers and *yin* represented even numbers, all the architectural dimensions in the outer court imperial halls were in odd numbers and all those in the rear court were in even numbers. A comparison between the Huangji Hall (renamed Taihe [Supreme Harmony] in the Qing) in the outer court and the Qianqing (Heavenly Purity) Palace in the inner court dramatically demonstrates the contrasting use of *yin* and *yang* principles. The Hall of Supreme Harmony, which symbolized the "superior *yang*", was a magnificent imperial audience hall in which the throne was the central focal point as it sat upon a nine-stepped platform, decorated with carved marble dragon, which corresponded to the nine layers of Heaven. The Palace of Heavenly Purity, symbolizing the "*yang* among the *yin*", was the more subdued and cloistered bed-chamber of the emperor and empress characterized by its remarkable serenity (Figure 24). Another example of the application of *yin* and *yang* harmony principles was the balance in location between the Altar of Heaven in the south and Altar of Earth (Ditan 地壇) in the north, and between the Altars of Soil and Grain on the left and the Ancestral Temple on the right, located respectively in the imperial- and outer-cities.[24]

Evidence of the Five Agents symbolic correlations is ubiquitous in the architectural planning and physical appearance of the Forbidden City. For instance, the buildings in the outer court facing south were used as administrative offices because according to the Five Agents principles "south" symbolized Fire and assumed charge of great affairs. However, those in the inner court facing north were used as imperial bed chambers because "north" symbolized Water and was an element that preferred concealment and withdrawal. Similarly, all the buildings on the east side of the axis of the palace-city performed

Figure 24 Plan of the Ming Forbidden City

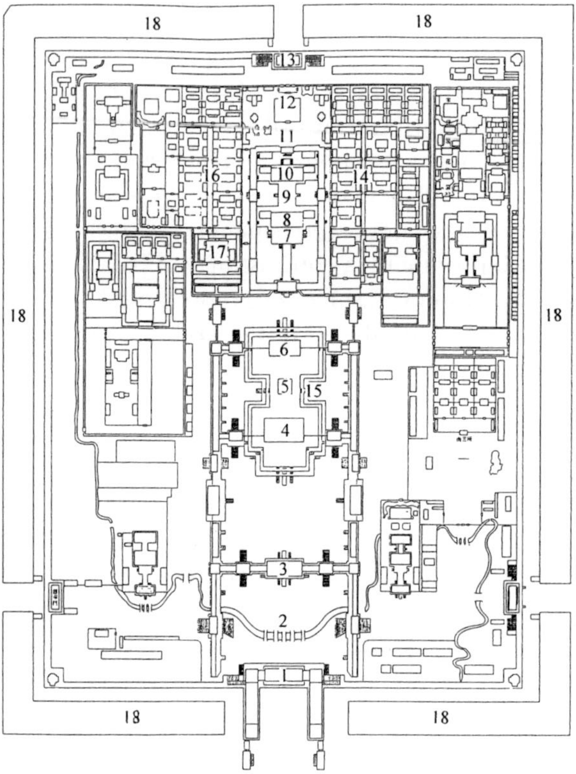

1. Wumen (Meridian Gate)
2. Nei Jinshui (Interior Golden Water) Canal
3. Huangjimen (Gate of Imperial Supremacy)
4. Huangjidian (Hall of Imperial Supremacy)
5. Zhongjidian (Hall of Middle Supremacy)
6. Jianjidian (Hall of Establishing Supremacy)
7. Qianqingmen (Heavenly Purity Gate)
8. Qianqinggong (Palace of Heavenly Purity)
9. Jiaotaidian (Hall of Peaceful Unity)
10. Kunninggong (Palace of Earthly Tranquility)
11. Yuhuayuan (Imperial Garden)
12. Qin'andian (Hall of Blessed Peace)
13. Xuanwumen (Dark Martial Gate)
14. *dong liugong* (Six Eastern Palaces)
15. *san dadian* (Three Great Halls)
16. *xi liugong* (Six Western Palaces)
17. Yangxindian (Nourishing Heart Palace)
18. Tongzi (Hucheng)-he (Protective Canal)

Source: Yu, *Zijin cheng gongdian* (1982), p. 11.

civil and cultural functions, but those on the west side performed military and punishment functions. The rationale was that "east" represented Wood and spring, which symbolized growth and prosperity, whereas "west" represented Metal and autumn, which symbolized force and the time of killing. As one faces south, the left to right location of the Ancestral Temple and the Altars of Soil and Grain can also be explained according to the Five Agents correlation of cardinal directions and human growth. The Ancestral Temple was located left or to the "east" because east corresponded with Wood and favored growth, hence symbolizing the perpetual expansion of the royal lineage. The Altars of Soil and Grain were located right or to the "west" because west corresponded with Metal and favored consolidation, thus symbolizing continuous labor for the welfare of the rulers and the people. In addition, the Five Agents scheme provided the most striking correlations between color configuration and cardinal directions: green/east, red/south, yellow/central, white/west, black/north. The palaces, halls, and walls were painted in red, symbolizing fire/greatness, and also in yellow, symbolizing earth/center; other imperial buildings and monuments, as well as decorative motifs, were painted in different colors in accord with the Five Agents correlation schemes. Altogether they formed a visually contrasting and auspiciously balanced multicolored microcosm of the universe, which was so carefully reproduced in the sacred imperial residence that it is unmatched in Chinese architectural history.[25]

The Forbidden City thus conceptually replicated the celestial imperial palace on earth, where, in harmonious cosmology, auspicious geomancy, and in lavish palaces and halls, the Son of Heaven ruled his myriad subjects from the center of the empire to the four corners of the world with ultimate authority. This configuration of human authority emulated precisely the Polaris in the center of the universe around which many stars and constellations revolved. The sky-earth correspondence mythology sanctioned the intimate relationship between the heavenly emperor and the earthly sovereign, and imputed powerful mystical symbols of supreme authority and legitimacy to the Ming and their successors, the Qing rulers. A laudatory passage describing the Forbidden City states: "Sky and earth meet, where the four seasons merge, where wind and rain are gathered in, and where *yin* and *yang* interacted are in harmony." (天地會合，四季融合，風調雨順，陰陽交泰之處。) It was the perfect setting for the august emperor who "stands in the center of the earth and stabilizes the people within the four seas", and allowed him to discharge his sacred heavenly mandate according to the benevolent and virtuous Confucian political ideology.[26]

The walled imperial- or administrative-city, which incorporated the Forbidden City, was built over the site of Dadu and was situated in the center of the outer-city. It had a perimeter of 18 plus *li* or 3,225 *zhang*, equivalent to 10.2 km, with four gates in the walls. The Forbidden City almost split the imperial-city into two halves. On the left was the artificial Taiye Pond, also called West Park (Xiyuan 西苑) in the Ming; it was divided into three parts, known as "Three Seas" (*sanhai* 三海): Beihai (North Sea), Zhonghai 中海 (Middle Sea), and Nanhai 南海 (South Sea). In the North was the celebrated man-made Qionghua Island; in the Middle was the former Yingzhou 瀛洲 Island on which the famous Qingshu 清暑 (Lucid Summer) Palace was built in the Ming; and in the South were several man-made islands and parks. Many exquisite palaces, halls, and gardens lined the shores. To the north of the Forbidden City situated in the center of the axis was the artificial Wansuishan rebuilt over the Yuan ruins, and further north outside the wall of the imperial-city was the Drum Tower and the Bell Tower. Wansuishan, popularly known as Coal Hill, was 46.67 meters in height with five peaks and commanded a panoramic view of the entire city. An elevation on its top was dubbed *zhenshan* 鎮山, i.e. "mount for suppression", to symbolize the Ming victory over the previous regime. It was renamed as Scenic Hill under the Qing. Under this architectural design the Forbidden City came to be flanked by an artificial mount in the north and man-made lakes to the west, conjuring up a landscape of auspicious geomancy for the sovereign. On both sides of the Imperial Way in front of the Meridian Gate of the Forbidden City stood the Ancestral Temple and the Altars of Soil and Grain. The most distinctive feature of the administrative-city was the extension of the T-shaped Imperial Way through the southern exit Chengtian 承天 (Received from Heaven) Gate into the walled outer-city exit called Da Ming Gate in the Ming and Da Qing 大清 (Great Purity) Gate in the Qing. It was renamed Zhonghua 中華 (Central Flower, i.e. China) Gate after 1911 and has been so known throughout the Republican period. In front of the Chengtian Gate was a gigantic square for public gatherings, and along the two sides of the Imperial Way flanked by the *qianbulang* 千

步廊 (thousand-pace corridor) were rows of buildings and chambers which housed the most senior civil and military administrative offices of the central government. This public square was further expanded in the Qing and as recently as the 1960s into the present-day Tian'anmen Square, making it the most spectacular landscape of the imperial city and the largest public square in a modern world capital (Figure 25).[27]

The outer-city was initially called capital-city but was popularly known as "great city" (*dacheng* 大城) until it was walled from the outside and became known as inner-city (*neicheng* 內城). It had a perimeter of 40 plus *li* or 23 km and all the walls measured 10 meters in height and were built with bricks. When general Xu Da rebuilt the outer wall, he moved the northern face 5 *li* to the south behind the old canal; as a result, it curved northeastward along the Protective Canal from the western corner until it reached the Jishui Pool, then ran horizontally to the eastern corner. In 1419 the southern face was moved back by more than 2 *li* and there were three gates in the wall. In 1436, during the reign of Yingzong, under the supervision of Ruan An, the nine walled gates were renovated to strengthen the defense capability against the northern tribesmen. A double tower was built on the gate; outside each gate a curved protective wall called *wengcheng* 甕城 was added and on the gate an arrow tower (*jianlou* 箭樓) was built. The work was completed in 1439. The Yuan names for the walled gates were changed but those given by the Ming founder were retained and the Ming names of the nine gates of the inner city: Desheng 德勝, Anding 安定 (northern); Dongzhi 東直, Chaoyang 朝陽 (eastern); Xizhi 西直, Fucheng 阜城 (western); Xuanwu, Zhengyang, and Chongwen 崇文 (southern), were all inherited by the Qing. In addition, following similar Five Agents cardinal directions, five major altars were built in four directions within the walled city: the Altar of Heaven and the Altars of the Mountains and Rivers (Shanchuantan 山川壇, later renamed Ancestral Altar of Agriculture) in the south, the Altar of Earth in the north, the Altar of the Sun (Ritan 日壇) to the east, and the Altar of the Moon (Yuetan 月壇) to the west, to be visited by the emperor and the imperial retinue regularly for solemn prayers and sacrificial offerings.

The shape of Peking remained unchanged until 1553 during the Jiajing reign of Emperor Shizong, when in order to defend the

Figure 25 Plan of the Ming Imperial-city

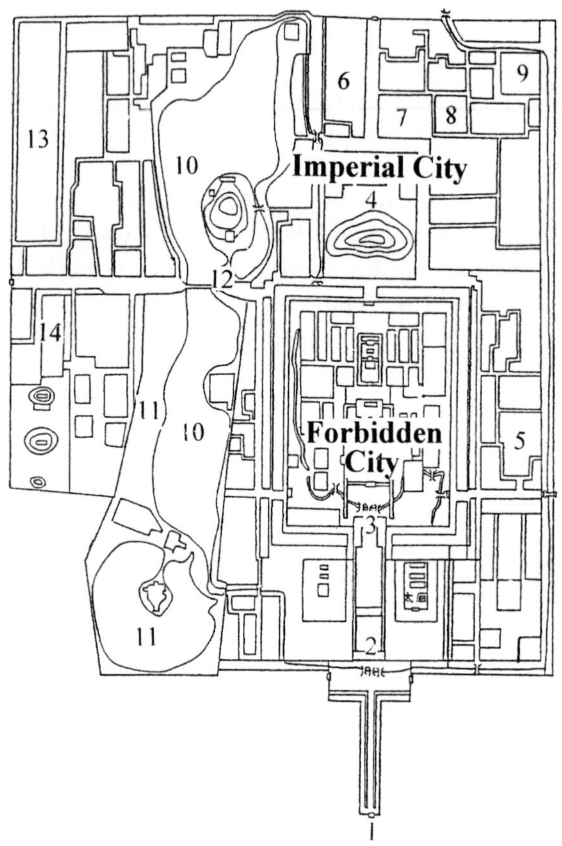

1. Da Ming Gate
2. Chengtian (Tian'an) Gate
3. Wu Gate
4. Wansuishan
5. Guanglusi (Court of Imperial Entertainments)
6. Neigongjian (Directorate of Eunuchs)
7. Shangyijian (Directorate of Clothing Service)
8. Silijian (Directorate of Ceremonial)
9. Nezhiranju (Palace of Weaving and Dyeing Service)
10. Taiye Pond
11. Xiyuan
12. Chengguangdian (Hall of Receiving Brightness)
13. Chengyunku etc. (various palace storehouses)
14. Da Guangmingdian (Hall of Great Brightness)

Source: Hou, *Beijing lishiditu ji*, p. 34.

capital against the threat of invasion of the Mongol tribes a new wall was built to encircle the southern extension to the city. This wall, called *wailuocheng* 外樓城, which included the 6 *li* or 6.7 km of the southern edge of the old city's outer wall, was 28 *li* or 16 km in perimeter. As a result an outer walled city appeared, called *waicheng*, and the original walled city came to be known as *neicheng*. The original plan was to extend the new outer wall all around the city but lack of funds meant only the southern section was completed, enclosing both the Altar of Heaven and the Altars of the Mountains and Rivers. Upon completion, new gates were added to the southern wall, so that Peking had nine inner walled gates and seven outer walled gates, altogether sixteen in number. These seven outer walled gates were named: Dongbian 東便, Guangqu 廣渠 (eastern); Xibian 西便, Guang'an 廣安 (western); You'an 右安, Yongding, Zuo'an 左安 (southern), and were all inherited by the Qing. The total area of the original walled city and the nearby walled southern extension was about 62 sq. km, making Peking not only China's but also the world's largest capital city.[28]

The capital-city was divided into thirty-six *fang*, twenty-eight in the inner-city and eight in the outer-city under the jurisdiction of five different supervisorates. Like Dadu, more than thirty vertical streets emanating from the northern wall ran to the south and equally numerous *hutong* or alleyways ran parallel from the eastern or western wall, criss-crossing each other like a checkerboard. According to an estimate of the mid-sixteenth century—there were 710 lanes and 459 *hutong*, an increase of almost three times over those of Dadu.[29] There were several commercial centers. One of them was situated in the Drum Tower and its vicinity. Small shops were scattered around the four gates of the imperial-city, around the Bell Tower and in the areas near the Chaoyang, Anding, Xizhi, Fucheng, and Xuanwu Gates because of the concentration of residential buildings and the consequent local trade. In addition, as grain transport was redirected from the Grand Canal to the land route at the southern wall, districts around the Zhengyang and Chongwen gates gradually grew into burgeoning commercial centers. The capital's busiest street, Chaoqian Market, was located outside the Zhengyang Gate. The Qipan Street outside the Da Ming Gate was the main east-west avenue; many important government offices were located on both ends of the street. To the east was the southern hall of the Huitongguan 會同館, a hostelry for foreigners, where exchanges of foreign products with local goods took place, making it one of the most commercially active locales in the city. Outside the Zhengyang Gate was an array of stalls, shops, and hotels. The residents of the Toutiao *hutong* 頭條胡同 were among the wealthiest. In addition, there were a number of markets all over the city specializing in trading rice, pigs, mules and horses, sheep, and fruits. Providing further commercial outlet were the "temple fairs" (*miaohui* 廟會), which were held regularly in famous monasteries and temples such as the Longfusi 隆福寺, Huguosi 護國寺, Dongyuemiao 東嶽廟 (Eastern Park Temple), Chenghuangmiao 城隍廟, Baiyunguan (White Cloud Shrine), and others. The cultural and educational district was located in the Anding Gate area. There the Guozijian 國子監 was the site of the National College for the Yuan through Qing dynasties and inside the college compound were Confucius's temple, lecture halls, and the state library and printing office. In addition, during the Wanli 萬曆 period (1573–1620) of Emperor Shenzong 神宗, a Gongyuan 貢院 or Examination Hall was built. The triennial civil service examinations in the Ming and Qing were all held there, making it an important cultural and educational locale of the imperial city.[30]

After the founding of the imperial capital under the Yongle emperor, a large number of religious buildings, such as Buddhist monasteries, Daoist shrines, Lamaist temples, and Islamic mosques were built outside the walled city. They numbered more than a thousand during the entire span of the Ming period. There were also numerous villas and gardens amid the parks and lakes outside Peking with the most glamorous architectural designs and artistic decorations, creating an exquisite kaleidoscopic landscape for the suburbs of the imperial capital. Mention must be made of the imperial mausoleums, popularly known as the Ming Tombs, at the foot of Mt. Tianshou in the Changping county outside Peking. Of the sixteen Ming emperors only thirteen had mausoleums at this site. Ming Taizu's mausoleum was in Nanking, the Jianwen emperor vanished without a trace, and the disgraced Jingtai 景泰 emperor (i.e. Zhu Chiyu 朱祁鈺, Daizong 代宗, r. 1450–1457) was denied an imperial mausoleum. Each of these mausoleums occupied a large compound with imposing monuments and buildings, significantly bolstering the architectural grandeur and enhancing the majestic solemnity of the imperial capital.[31]

As the imperial capital, Peking had undertaken extensive public work projects to increase its water resources but was still confronted with numerous problems. In the Yongle reign, because of the silting of the old Tonghui Canal due to drought and negligence, grain boats could no longer navigate through the Grand Canal and grain had to be transported overland. Moreover, at the time of the construction of the Forbidden City, because of a decision to expand the former Yuan imperial walled city, part of the land in the northeast and in the east including a section of the Canal were incorporated into the imperial-city. Grain boats could not sail directly into the imperial-city, and shipment had to depend on land transport, adding to the cost of operation. In later reigns various attempts were made to dredge the old Grand Canal but because of inadequate water flowing from Jade Spring Hill, the Canal remained unnavigable. In addition, water resources from the suburbs were not as plentiful as in Yuan times, largely because the construction of the imperial mausoleum had impeded the flow of the tributaries originating at the Baifu Spring on Spiritual Hill, later known as Longshan 龍山 (Dragon Hill). As a result the upper tributary of the Jinshui Canal had dried up, whereas the water from Jade Spring Hill, after draining into the West Lake (known as Urn Hill Lake in the Yuan, and Kunming Lake in the Qing), flowed through the old channels of Baifu Spring into the watergates of Desheng Gate. It then emptied into the Shicha Sea, where one tributary drained into the West Park (Xiyuan, i.e. the Three Seas) and another into the Yu (Jade or Imperial) Canal 玉(御)河, the upper section of the Tonghui Canal. In this way, the water supply of the palaces and halls in the Forbidden City came from the same source as that of the Grand Canal, thus reducing the resources of the city residents. The water shortage was further aggravated by cycles of protracted drought. This situation remained little changed despite repeated undertaking of similar hydraulic projects in the Qing and through the Republican period (Figure 26).[32]

Under the Yongle emperor and his immediate successors, Peking grew into an architecturally majestic imperial city and an all-powerful political and economic national capital. It was also the leading intellectual and cultural center, as well as the cosmopolitan metropolis of the Ming empire for diplomatic and commercial intercourse with foreign countries. These unique characteristics were made possible because as a planned imperial city, Peking was able to

Figure 26 Ming Peking—Capital-city in the later stages

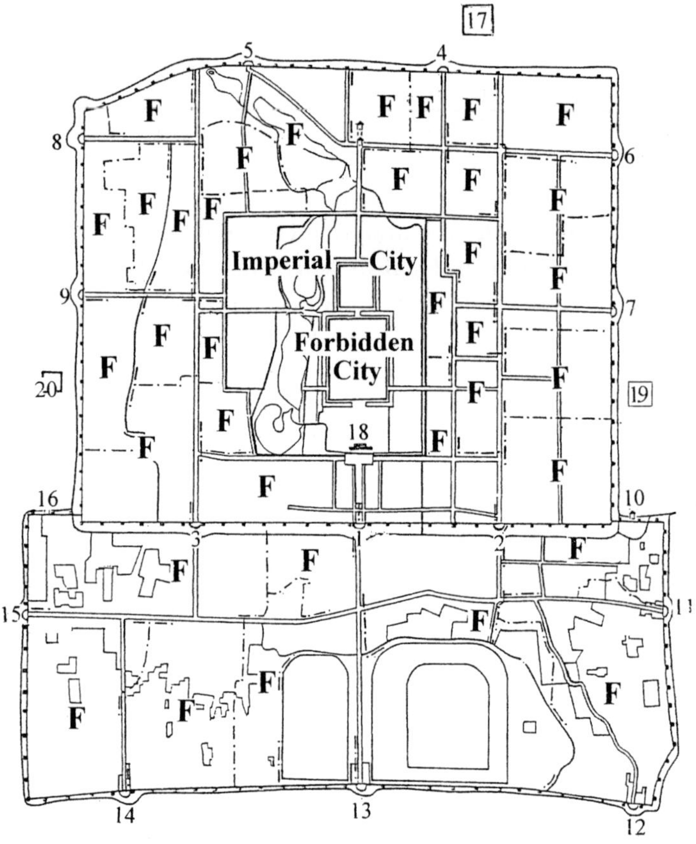

F = Fang/Ward (36 wards)

1. Zhengyang Gate
2. Chongwen Gate
3. Xuanwu Gate
4. Anding Gate
5. Desheng Gate
6. Dongzhi Gate
7. Chaoyang Gate
8. Xizhi Gate
9. Fucheng Gate
10. Dongbian Gate
11. Guangqu Gate
12. Zuo'an Gate
13. Yongding Gate
14. You'an Gate
15. Guangning Gate
16. Xibian Gate
17. Ditan (Altar of Earth)
18. Chengtian Gate
19. Ritan (Altar of Sun)
20. Yuetan (Altar of Moon)

Source: Hou, *Beijing lishiditu ji,* p. 32.

draw on the best models and tap the best resources from all over the empire. For instance, the builders of the Forbidden City drew on the architectural model of Nanking, and drafted artisans and labor forces from all over the empire together with personnel from foreign countries. To bolster the city's population, various means were used to attract inhabitants from all over the country, including mandatory migration. From the Yongle through the Wanli reign, several decrees were issued to induce qualified and wealthy people from Zhili 直隸 (i.e. Nanking), Suzhou, and Zhejiang to take up residence in Peking.[33] It was estimated that at the beginning of the seventeenth century, of the 700,000 plus population in the capital-city, a significant proportion originated from south of the Yangzi River. As the apex of state power and the terminus for the highest civil service examinations, aspirants for high government office and talented intellectuals and erudite scholars regularly flocked to the imperial capital, thereby facilitating intellectual and cultural intercourse and exchange. The city was also noted for cosmopolitanism by virtue of the presence of a large Mongol and northern tribal population in and around the capital and the frequent visits of envoys from foreign countries who came to China to offer tribute products under the tributary system. Last but not least, Peking was also the major consumer capital of the empire, which procured its daily necessities by land and sea routes from the production and manufacturing sites in the south and even from foreign countries. It was the consumer center for the goods and products of the empire, and effective maintenance of its supply system held the key to its wealth and power.[34]

The Manchu founders of the Qing dynasty, which ruled China until the Revolution in 1911, retained Peking as the imperial capital. The last Qing emperor and his family lived in the Forbidden City until 1924. Qing emperors from Shunzhi 順治 (r. 1644–1661) through Kangxi 康熙 (r. 1662–1722), Yongzheng 雍正 (r. 1723–1735) and Qianlong (r. 1736–1795), who had brought the country to its zenith of military and economic power, all devoted themselves to the renovation and addition of palaces, halls, parks, and gardens in the imperial-city. Beginning with Kangxi, while laboring to increase the water resources and improve the service system, they ordered the construction of the renowned "three mounts" and "five gardens" at the foot of Urn Hill overlooking present-day Kunming Lake in order to beautify the western suburbs, all of which were completed in the Qianlong era. They now lie scattered over the Haidian 海淀 District of present-day Beijing, in what is collectively called the Yiheyuan 頤和園 parks. Socially, however, radical changes occurred in the structure of the population in the inner-city brought about by the influx of the privileged Manchu bannermen with their military units as permanent residents. They were given fiefs and pastures and caused considerable sociopolitical and economic tensions with the predominantly Han ethnic population. Yet Peking remained a national center of intellectual and cultural life by virtue of the Qing emperors' patronage of imperial Confucianism, the arts and letters, and expansion of the civil service examination system. Chinese literary culture thus flourished alongside Manchu and Mongolian culture and Tibetan Lamaism among the multiethnic literati, while varieties of Han and Manchu popular culture with unique characteristics also left a permanent imprint on metropolitan culture (Figure 27).[35] As capital of the last Chinese empire with a predominantly Han population of a little over one million at the end of the Qing dynasty, Peking underwent radical changes in its political, socioeconomic, intellectual, and cultural scene as the empire was rocked by internal and external challenges in the late nineteenth century. The repeated failings to resolve the domestic and foreign crises inflamed the anti-Manchu revolutionary movement that brought down the empire, ushering in a new epoch for China and Peking with more radical changes and transformations.[36]

To conclude, however, we should note a phenomenon that had greatly impacted on Peking, namely the effects of climatic and ecological factors on the dynastic rulers and the capital population. As in Yuan Dadu, Peking under the Ming and Qing suffered a litany of natural disasters and calamities, especially the havoc wrought by excessive rains, floods, and protracted drought in varying seasons, as shown in statistics tabulated by recent researchers. Drought was more frequent and devastating than rains and floods in both Ming and Qing Peking. During the 277 years of Ming rule, 157 droughts were recorded, averaging almost one occurrence in every two years. On the other hand there were only 95 annual recordings of excessive rains and/or floods, averaging one occurrence in almost three years. The most severe and frequent droughts occurred in the Chenghua

Figure 27 Plan of Mid-Qing Peking from *Qianlong jingcheng quantu*

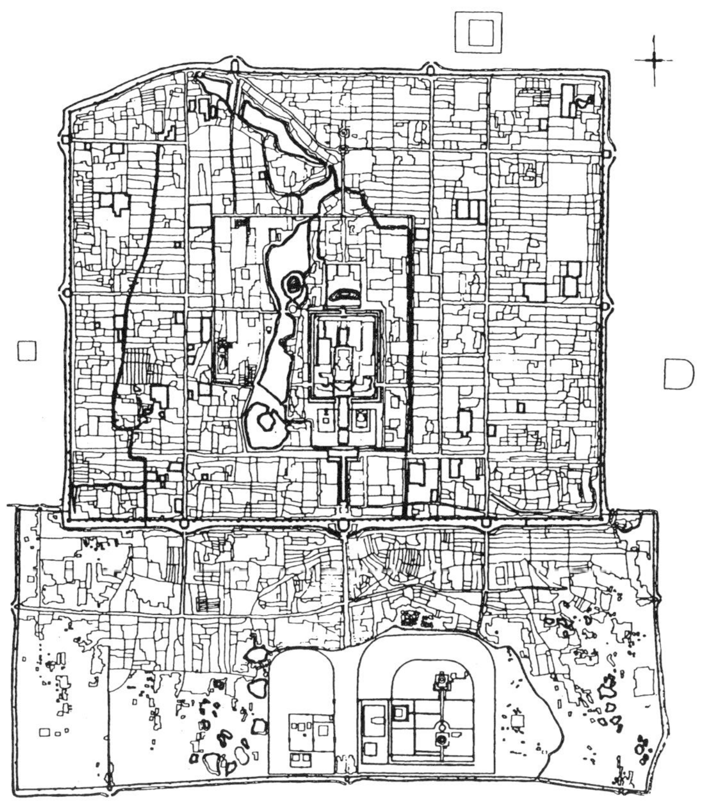

Source: *Zhongguo Jianzhu jiangshi* (1957), Figure 6-12.

成化 reign (1465–1487), in 16 successive years, and the Jiajing reign (1522–1567), in 8 and later 9 successive years, and Zhengde 正德 (1506–1521), Wanli (1573–1620), and Chongzhen 崇禎 (1628–1644) all recorded high yearly frequencies of drought. During the Qing, under 268 years of its rule, there were 161 droughts of various degrees compared to 129 yearly occurrences of excessive rains and floods. The most serious as well as the highest frequency of drought befell the reigns of Kangxi, Qianlong, and Guangxu 光緒 (1875–1908)—each recorded 33, 35, and 25 yearly occurrences respectively—the most devastating occurring in the Kangxi and the Qianlong reigns. On this the Kangxi emperor signed in an edict in 1717 toward the end of his reign: "In early summer rain was always scarce in the capital. I have reigned for fifty-seven years, and have conducted rain-prayers for almost fifty years!" The Qianlong emperor uttered a similar lament in a rain-prayer in 1759: "It has been twenty-four years since I was enthroned, but in no year was I not worried about the drought, and this year is the worst!"[37] The droughts had serious ramifications for people's livelihood and with this the political behavior and religious culture of the rulers and the population.

As a prominent political tradition influenced by the cosmological school of thought, Chinese rulers since the Han had regarded rain-praying as a sacrosanct duty of the sovereign in his role as mediator between Heaven and Earth, between the spirits and the people, to plead for relief of the people's suffering. Rain-praying was regularly performed by the Ming and Qing rulers, either in person or by their representatives, depending on the nature of the drought, at either outdoor altars or interior altars set up in the palaces within the imperial-city. The same duties applied to the prefects of the Shuntian Administration and other local officials. The Ming emperors conducted the traditional rain-praying rituals known as *yu li* 雩禮 (drought sacrifice) at the Altar of Heaven, Altars of Soil and Grain, Altars of the Mountains and Rivers, and at other altars in honor of the hundred deities. But some emperors, indulging in the popular belief of the occult power of the rain-making Dragon, also conducted sacrificial offerings to the Dragon King at the famed Black Dragon Pool in the Fangshan county and at various dragon shrines and dragon temples inside the imperial-city and its vicinity in times of drought. Following the Ming tradition, the Qing rulers abandoned shamanistic sacrifices and regularly performed the Chinese traditional rain-praying rituals not only at outdoor altars such as the Altar of Heaven and others, but also at special altars set up inside various halls and palaces in the Forbidden City. After the completion of the auxiliary imperial residence in the lakes and parks of the western suburbs, they also performed such rituals at special altars set up inside some of the newly built palaces and halls. In addition they too conducted rain-praying rituals and ceremonies to the mythical Dragon King at the same dragon pools, dragon shrines, and temples inside and outside the imperial-city. Under imperial initiatives, both in the Ming and Qing, local officials as well as district residents made sacrificial offerings at various alleged Dragon domiciles, and many shrines and temples honoring the Dragon King flourished in Peking and its vicinity. The mystical rain-making Dragon thus became a fixture in Peking's monuments and buildings and perpetuated the Dragon-worship that significantly influenced the florescence of a unique popular culture.[38]

New Nazha Cheng Legend

Against the rich historical tradition seen in the building of Peking and its development into one of the most glamorous imperial cities in recent history, the equally spectacular popular legend about the city's origin credited to Liu Bowen in association with Nezha made its debut and became a folkloric obsession. However, although the legend evidently represented a continuation of the Yuan saga and featured a Ming story, its manifestation in concrete form in popular literature is a relatively late modern phenomenon. Nazha, the protean Buddhist child deity now commonly known as Nezha, continued to enthrall the public imagination as a supernatural hero of miraculous power and extraordinary feats, especially after the appearance in the late sixteenth century of the popular novels *Tales of the Investiture of Gods* and *Journey to the West* and related dramas and storytelling. But the Yuan legend was hardly mentioned in literary miscellanies. Evidently, after the Han Chinese dynastic restoration and the construction of a new capital under the Yongle emperor, the old Yuan Dadu legend associated with Liu Bingzhong and the Mongol régime lost its contemporary relevancy.

Indeed, after the surge of anti-Mongol sentiment germinating from the Chinese debacle at the battle of Tumu 土木 fortress (Huailai 懷來 county, Hebei) against the Oirat-Mongol invasion in September 1449, when Emperor Yingzong was held in captivity in Inner Mongolia for a year as a prisoner of war, many of the eminent Chinese scholars and grandees who had served the Mongol court headed by Liu Bingzhong came to be discredited in Ming writings and their historical contributions were tarnished. Liu Bingzhong lost his glamour as a revered mythologized hero in the Chinese consciousness.[39] More importantly, with the construction of Ming

Peking under a different structure with only nine walled gates in the outer-city, the old legend of Liu Bingzhong designing eleven gates in order to symbolize Nazha's three heads, six arms, and two feet was no longer relevant. Without a historical super-hero at its helm and the architectural setting which sustained the mythology, even though the core of the old legend—Nazha serving as a spiritual-protector of cities and combating the Dragon King and his family to release their control of the watery world—remained popular folklore, the legend could no longer be associated with the building of Peking. Its propagandists had lost their cause and their audience. This situation prevailed well into the Qing when the Manchu rulers, though rehabilitating the Chinese grandees serving under the Yuan, retained the structure of Ming Peking and its conservative culture and the ground was not yet fertile for the legend to reinvent itself until the rise of a Chinese historical hero mythologized for his association with Peking in a new political and cultural environment.

Not surprisingly, this once captivating Nazha City legend lay dormant in the Ming and Qing and received only a passing reference in literary works. It was mentioned, for instance, in a poem by a mid-Ming scholar-official Yang Ziqi 楊子器 (1458–1513) as a nostalgic reminder of the faded glory of Yuan Dadu, and in a memoir by the late Qing eunuch Xin Xiuming 信修明. Yang's verse, captioned "Yong Shizu" 詠世祖 (A Song on Qubilai Qaghan), a seven-character quartet, reads:

> Towers and Terraces were raised above the Nazha City,
> 那吒城裏起樓臺，
>
> Tens of thousands of palace flowers blossomed.
> 萬朵宮花次第開。
>
> It is said that the good men and women of the Southern Dynasty,
> 見説南朝好兒女，
>
> Followed the Imperial Seal crossing the River from afar.[40]
> 遠隨帝璽渡江來。

In explicit praise of Qubilai Qaghan's achievement, Yang Ziqi alluded to the splendor and beauty of the grand metropolis and the migration of the literati from the south to the Yuan capital following the Mongol capture of the Song emperor Duanzong 端宗 (Zhao Shi 趙昰, r. 1276–1277) that marks the end of the Chinese dynasty.

However, on the other hand, writing three centuries later, Xin Xiuming relates that he overheard in the corridors of the Forbidden City gossip about an early Qing reference to a similar Peking Nezha City legend:

> Treading west after departing the Shenwu Gate, there is a well blocking the way on the northern bank of the Hucheng Canal. It was covered by a stone lid. Stories had it that if the well was exposed, the head eunuch would amass power. In the early Qing some people proposed that the well be clogged. But a geomancer commented: "This well should not be destroyed. Peking is a three-headed, six-armed Nezha City. This is Nezha's naval. If a person is deprived of the naval, he is physiologically deficient." Thus it was ordered to seal it with a huge rock.[41]
>
> 出神武門西行，護城河北岸有井擋路，上有石蓋。據傳此井如開，主太監有權。清初有人主張將井塞。風鑒家云：「此井毀不得。北京為三頭六臂哪咤城，此哪咤之肚臍也。人無肚臍，生理失缺。」因用大石封之。

Uncanny as it may be, this story attests to the continued belief in the legend of the Nazha City expressed in geomancy terms. It also suggests that with Nazha maintaining his appeal as a supernatural deity and popular hero, and since the ecological and urban environments that inspired the Buddhist miraculous exploits were very much the same in Peking, the grounds remained strong for the resurgence of the Nazha cheng mythology in a different form in later times.

The myth was rekindled in the early twentieth century after the founding of the Chinese Republic when Peking, spurred by the May Fourth Movement of 1919, returned to the spotlight as the center of the nation's sociopolitical activism. Liu Bowen was well received in the popular purview not only as a Ming hero championing the restoration of Han Chinese rule from alien domination, but also for his close connection with the building of old Peking. It was first reported by a foreign priest Alphonse Favier, the French vicar of the Catholic church, in his memoir, but he erred in stating that the city was built by Liu Bowen between 1524 to 1564. These were the dates for the building of the new wall encircling the southern extension of the imperial-city, but far after Liu Bowen's time.[42] Meanwhile, amid elderly residents' nostalgia for the lost old culture and the intellectual and cultural ferment to rebuild China after the end of Manchu rule, a popular story called "Liu Bowen building the Eight-armed Nezha City" captivated Peking residents, old and young, and gained instant publicity because of its colorful personalities and miraculous fantasies. It said that Peking was designed by Liu Bowen, Ming Taizu's principal adviser, modeled on the likeness of the body of the supernatural deity Nezha in order to protect the city and exorcize the evil demons. The provenance is a mystery but bits and pieces of the story had already appeared in Chinese as well as Western popular writings about Peking since the 1920s. In popular songs that flourished in Peking or Pei-p'ing during this time some featured the line "Liu Bowen" or "Liu Bowen xiansheng zhizao Beijing cheng" 劉伯溫先生製造北京城 (Mister Liu Bowen Building the City of Peking), and some of these songs originated as far south as Shandong, attesting to the story's widespread popularity.[43]

One of the earliest sources of Liu Bowen's alleged role in building Peking was the story reported by E. T. C. Werner in his much-cited *Myths and Legends of China* published in 1924. The story, with the lead title "Legend of the Building of Peking", features the vicissitudes of Zhu Di, the future Yongle emperor, the fourth son of Ming Taizu by a consort named Lady Weng 翁〔甕〕妃 (known in Chinese as Gongfei, see later), who was appointed by his father as the governor of the Yan country and hence was styled the Prince of Yan. He was given this post due to the persuasion of Lady Weng who was worried that her son might become involved in court politics over the succession and tried to keep him from harm's way. It is said that before the prince departed from Nanking, a Daoist priest named Liu Bowen, who had a great affection for him, put a "sealed packet" into his hand and told him to open it for instruction when he found himself in difficulty, distress, or danger. When the prince arrived in what was later Peking, he was distressed that the place was a mere barren wilderness, with few inhabitants and no city walls to afford protection to the people. Thus he unsealed the packet to read the instructions and found: "When you reach Pei-p'ing Fu you must build a city there and name it Nocha Ch'eng, the City of No-cha. . . . On the back of this paper is a plan of the city; you must be careful to act according to the instructions accompanying it. . . ." As a result the prince followed the instruction and a spacious, magnificent capital city, resembling that of the layout of Nanking, was built in due course.[44]

After this the prince resided in the city as emperor. Everything was tranquil and orderly until one day his ministers reported that "the wells are thirsty and the rivers dried up"—there was no water, and the people were in great distress. The scarcity was caused by a dragon couple who had resided for myriads of years in a cave at Peking's east gate. They were so disturbed by the workmen digging out the earth of their abode to build the city walls that they decided to move elsewhere, taking all of the city's water in baskets with them. They first transformed themselves into an old man and an old woman and appeared to the prince in a dream to explain their intent. When the prince woke up and heard the report of the scarcity of water, he became suspicious. Thus he consulted the packet which Liu Bowen had given him and learned that his dream-visitors had been dragons who had taken the waters of Peking away in their magic baskets. Following Liu Bowen's directions, the prince donned his armor, mounted his black steed and, spear in hand, dashed out of the west gate of the city in pursuit of the dragons. He pierced their baskets with a spear, and the water that gushed forth became a well that has provided Peking its water down to the present day. The dragons were subdued and confined and could no longer cause trouble.[45]

This story, though sketchy, was the first in Western works to mention Liu Bowen and his plan to build the Nezha City, and the problem of water shortage caused by the vicious scheming of the old dragon couple who thrived there based on local folkloric sources. It was an indigenous folk myth but, as examined in Chapter 3, it was also infused with a more elaborate Mongolian legend about the Mongol maternity of the Yongle emperor and the building of Peking, and other local stories about Liu Bowen's feud with the dragons over the control of the water resources in the popular media.

In fact, according to the reminiscences of former Peking residents, more elaborate stories about Liu Bowen and the Nezha City were in vogue in the old capital in the early Republican period. In one anecdotic account, an author recalled that he heard of a strange story about the Nezha city from his junior school geography teacher in the early 1920s, alleging that Liu Bowen imitated Nezha's body in building the city of Peking and pinpointing various supposedly architectural representations. For instance, Nezha's two curl hair was represented by the Altar of Heaven and the Ancestral

Altar of Agriculture; the "wind and fire" wheels under his feet by the Altar of Earth; his intestines by the underground waterway; and his two eyes by the openings of the Qianmen etc. It is indeed bizarre.[46] A collection of various similar stories about Liu Bowen's adventures in building Peking written in the vernacular was also available in the early 1930s. Appended to a primer on the Peking dialect, the *Beipinghua yuhui* 北平話語匯 by the author Yan Gongshang 嚴工上, a reputed male movie actor, it was presumably intended to use these local popular stories as instructional material. They included those about Liu Bowen building a pagoda to seal off the well to suppress the old dragon, fighting with the Dragon King and other dragon-like sea-creatures to protect Peking's "sweet" water, and employing the assistance of the warrior Gao Liang 高亮 to smash the treacherous scheme of the dragon and his spouse. They vividly attest to the popularity of the old legend.[47]

In effect, the appearance of such nuanced popular stories about Liu Bowen building the city of Peking and related episodes ushered in an era of intellectual and cultural transition between the old and new Peking. There was much nostalgia for the passing of the old culture and a craving for recovery of the old heritage in order to impute new meaning to the present as the historical city labored in search of a new image and cultural identity amid tumultuous modern transformation. As noted, Madeleine Dong develops the concept of "recycling" in her *Republican Beijing* to describe a primary mode of material and cultural production and circulation which characterizes much of the labor-incentive activities of the city's residents in the early Republican period.[48] In the literary and cultural realm these involved the editing and publication of gazetteers and handbooks on Peking's local history, the writing of books and essays on the city's old houses, buildings, temples and shrines, and on the city's past and present social customs and lifestyles, the production of popular entertainments of various kinds, and other activities that dwelt on the past but gave new meaning to their existence in the present. The emergence of folktales about Liu Bowen and the Nezha City legend presents a vivid case of "recycling" by repossessing the old Yuan Nazha City legend of Liu Bingzhong and recasting it in the name of Liu Bowen, with additional embroidery to make the old relevant to the new age.

Amid such a flurry of literary and cultural activity, however, it is in the most popular foreign account about the old capital, *In Search of Old Peking* by two English journalists, L. C. Arlington and William Lewisohn (1937), that we find several rudimentary excerpts of the legend of the building of the city that give very specific and elaborate identifications of the representations of Nezha's (No Cha's) body in the city's architectural plan based on local folklore. (Note: the Wade-Giles spelling system is used in the text.)

The first few paragraphs about Nezha in this book appear in a narrative of the imperial city of Peking, which Westerners dubbed the Tartar City, in the late Qing and early Republican period. After describing the glamour of the Qipan Street leading to the entrance of the gigantic Tian'anmen Square, the authors commented: "This square is interesting for another reason. It is the nose of the 'Man of Peking' and the two wells at the south corners are his eyes. We do not mean the Peking man (i.e. *Sinanthropus pekinensis*) recently dug up by anthropologists in these parts, but the symbolic figure for Peking, No Cha by name. Tradition tells us that when Prince Yen, afterwards the Emperor Yung Lo, first arrived in Peking, an eminent astrologer Liu Po-wen, gave him a sealed package which contained the lay-out of the new capital, to be called No Cha. These plans were based on the most approved principles of geomancy and allotted a certain building or open space to teach part of the human body. (Those interested in this subject will find further details in Appendix B; see below)." The latter part of the story, it appears, was derived from the Mongolian folktale about the building of Peking narrated by E. T. C. Werner in the aforementioned text.[49]

Further down the same account, the authors described how the two northern gates of the Imperial City resembled No Cha's feet: "Turning north up the main street we come to the An-ting Men (Gate of Fixed Peace). This gate, the easterly of the two north gates, . . . was occupied in 1860 by the British who dragged their guns up the ramp and posted them on the wall commanding the city. The only other point of interest about the gate is that, before it was reconstructed for the round-the-city railway, the outer gate, in the barbican, faced east, outwards, instead of west, inwards. The two northern gates were, therefore, not facing each other, as was the case with the pairs of gates on the other three sides. The reason for this is that Peking was built to resemble No Cha, a mythical personage, with three heads and six arms. The two northern gates, representing his feet, were

S
┌ ▽ ┐
O O O
Ch'ien Men 前門

—O O O—
—O O—
—O O O—

O O
L L

An-ting Men 安定門 Te-sheng Men 德勝門

N

therefore built with their outer gateways turned the same way like human feet. The following sketch will make this clear."[50]

The authors then elaborated how "(the imperial city plans) were based on the most approved principles of geomancy and allotted a certain building or open space to each part of the human body" in Appendix B of the book:[51]

No Cha's Body as Represented by the City of Peking

According to Liu Chi's plan the various parts of No Cha's body were represented by the following sites in Peking:

1. No Cha's head is represented by the Ch'ien Men (Front Gate; i.e. Cheng-yang Men 正陽門).
2. His ears by the two side-gates of same.
3. His nose by the Ch'i-p'an Chieh 棋盤街 (Street).
4. His mouth by the Chung-hua Men 中華門 (i.e. Da Ming Gate in the Ming, and Da Qing Gate under the Qing).
5. His eyes by the two wells on the south side of the Ch'i-p'an Chieh.
6. His right shoulder by the Hata Men 哈達門 (i.e. Ch'ung-wen Men 崇文門).
7. His left shoulder by the Shun-chih Men 順治門 (i.e. Hsuan-wu Men 宣武門).

8. His right hand by the Chao-yang Men 朝陽門, holding the Tung-yueh Miao 東嶽廟 (Temple), which represents No Cha's "Heaven and Earth" diamond bracelet (i.e. *Qianqun zuanzhuo* 乾坤鑽鐲).
9. His left hand by the P'ing-tse Men 平則門 (i.e. Fou-ch'eng Men 阜城門), holding the White Pagoda (on top of the Baita Monastery 北塔寺), which is symbolical of his "Precious Spear" (i.e. *huojianqiang* 火尖槍).
10. His hips are represented by the Tung-hua Men 東華門 and Hsi-hua Men 西華門. (Note: according to the city plan, No Cha's hips should be represented by Tung-an Men 東安門 and Hsi-an Men 西安門 [no. 16]).
11. His knee-pans by the Tung-chih Men 東直門 and Hsi-chih Men 西直門.
12. His feet by the An-ting Men and Te-sheng Men, treading on the "Yellow" and "Black" Temples which are symbolical of No Cha's "Wind and Fire" wheels (i.e. *fenghuolun* 風火輪). (Note: the "Yellow" Temples refer to the Dong [East] Huang Si 東黄寺 and Xi [West] Huang Si 西黄寺, the so-called Shuang Huang [Double Yellow] 雙黄寺 Monastery built outside the Anding Gate in the early Qing. The "Black" Temple refers to the Cidu Monastery 慈度寺 built outside the Desheng Gate, also in the early Qing.)[52]
13. The red-painted walls of the Imperial City are symbolical of No Cha's red silk stomach-protector with which he subdued the third son of the Dragon King.
14. His wind-pipe is represented by the "Imperial Way" (i.e. *huangdao*) leading north from the Chung-hua Men (i.e. Da Ming/Da Qing Gate).
15. The ante-chambers on either side of the way represent his shoulder blades.
16. His breasts are represented by the Tung-an Men and Hsi-an Men. (Note: according to the city plan, No Cha's breasts should be represented by the Tung-hua Men and Hsi-hua Men [no. 10].)
17. His lungs by the space in front of the T'ien-an Men 天安門.
18. His pericardium by the T'ien-an Men and Tuan Men 端門.
19. His heart by the Wu Men 午門.
20. The fold of the peritoneum by the T'ai-ho Men 泰和門.

21. The T'ai-ho Tien 泰和殿 (Hall) represents a duct which according to Chinese physicians connects the heart and the liver.
22. His liver is represented by the Chung-ho Tien 中和殿.
23. His gall by the Pao-ho Tien 保和殿.
24. His stomach by the Three Seas (*sanhai* 三海).
25. His spleen by the She-chi T'an 社稷壇 (Altars). (Note: this representation is wrongly placed because according to the city plan, She-chi T'an is situated south of Wu Men [no. 19], i.e. No Cha's heart.)
26. The open gutter in the West City (now covered-in) is his large intestine.
27. That in the East City his small intestine.
28. The Ch'ien-ch'ing Men 乾清門 is an anatomical point between the kidneys, supposed to be a fatal spot.
29. The Ch'ien-ch'ing Kung 乾清宮 (Palace) and Yang-hsin Tien 養心殿 are his kidneys.
30. A well with a small aperture located in the western section of the Forbidden City represents the navel.
31. The Shih-ch'a Hai 十剎海 (Sea) his bladder.
32. The bridge at the Hou Men 後門 (Rear Gate, i.e. Bei'anmen in the Ming and Di'anmen under the Qing) his membrum virile.[53]
33. The Hou Men at the end of his spine (Figure 28).

This most fanciful account about the various parts of Nezha's body being represented by different sites in Peking probably drew on the urban mythology flourishing among the Chinese residents rather than stemming from sheer concoction by the authors. Although it specifies the correspondence of Nezha's "internal organs" and other parts of his body with the layout of Peking's city plan, it presents Nezha as a normal "person" with one head and four limbs. This varied from the mythical three heads, six arms, two feet Nezha portrayed in the previous account. With a few exceptions, such as the representation of Nezha's hips by the Forbidden City's Tung-hua and Hsi-hua Gates, his breasts by the Imperial-city's Tung-an and Hsi-an Gates (nos. 10, 16), and his spleen by the She-chi Altars (no. 25), which are wide of the mark, the imagined drawing approximately reflects the correspondence of Nezha's body with the design of

Figure 28 Image of Nezha superimposed on plan of Peking

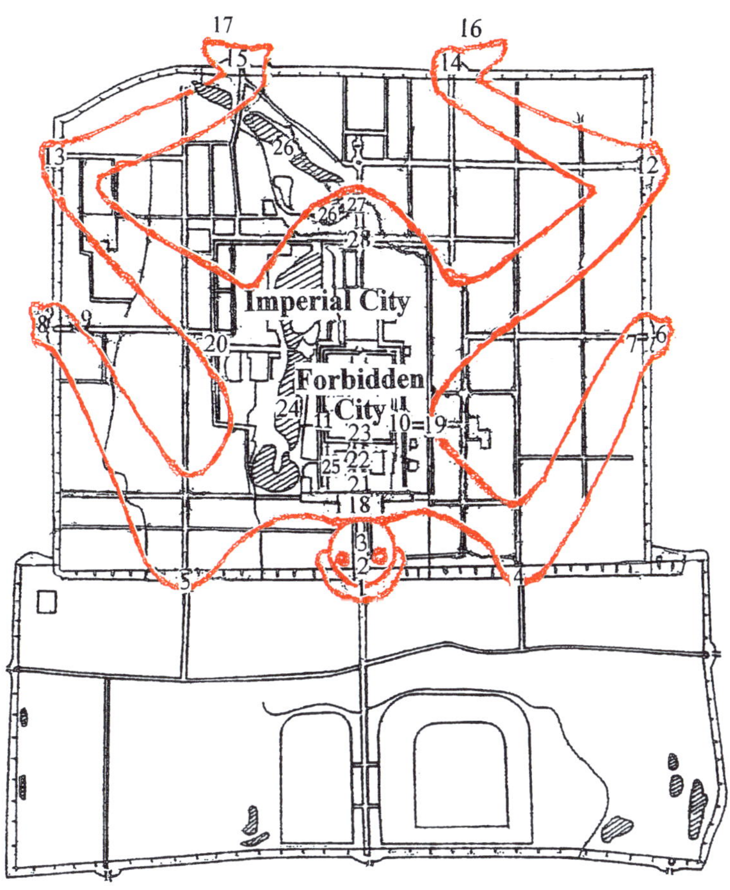

1. Zhengyang (Front) Gate
2. Qipan Street
3. Zhonghua (Da Ming/Da Qing) Gate
4. Hata (Chongwen) Gate
5. Shunzhi (Xuanwu) Gate
6. Chaoyang Gate
7. Dongyue Temple
8. Pingze (Fucheng) Gate
9. Baita Monastery
10. Donghua Gate
11. Xihua Gate
12. Dongzhi Gate
13. Xizhi Gate
14. Anding Gate
15. Desheng Gate
16. Shuang Huang (Double Yellow) Monastery
17. Cidu (Black) Monastery
18. *huangdao*
19. Dong'an Gate
20. Xi'an Gate
21. Tian'anmen
22. Duan Gate
23. Wu Gate
24. *sanhai*
25. Shejitan
26. Shicha Sea
27. Houmen Bridge
28. Di'an (Bei'an) Gate

Source: Based on Arlington, *In Search of Old Peking*, pp. 338–339.

Peking. Whatever the source of inspiration, the legend-makers' ingenious fantasies have significantly broadened the old Nazha City legend into specific conceptual identification of the different parts of Nazha's body with the actual architectural layout of the imperial city. It thus provided concrete details that enhanced the popularity of the legend and was subsequently bolstered by two similar, more refined versions of an equally sensational story about the episode. The story, entitled "The Eight-armed Nezha City", which featured Nezha with one head but "eight arms" since this was the more popular caricature of the supernatural deity since the Ming dynasty, was narrated and penned in the Peking vernacular by the leading Manchu folklorist Jin Shoushen and was published respectively in the 1950s and 1980s, but could have been written much earlier. English translations are presented in Appendices (1), (2).

The first version of the story, published in Jin's collection of Peking folktales, *Beijing de chuanshuo* 北京的傳説 (Beijing Legends) in 1957, is summarized as follows:

> When the Emperor (i.e. the third Ming emperor Yongle) decided to build a capital in Peking his Minister of Works panicked and tried to avoid the task, saying the site was the Bitter Sea Youzhou (*kuhai* 苦海幽州) where the dragons were exceptionally vicious. The Emperor then invited his two chief advisers, Liu Bowen and Yao Guangxiao, who knew all about heaven and earth, and spirits and devils, to take up the task, but they unfortunately despised each other. So they proposed a contest whereby the winner would claim all the credits for the plan. Liu was to stay in the east city and Yao in the west. They would meet after ten days, sit back to back, draw their plans for the city, and compare the results.
>
> During the first two days, they stayed apart and neither went out to survey the terrain, but both heard yet did not see a child who said: "Just copy me and you will do fine." On the third day both went out separately to survey the terrain and everywhere they went they each saw a child in a red jacket and short pants walking ahead of them. Then on the fourth day, they again separately saw the same child, still wearing a red jacket and short pants, the silk fringes dangling from the shoulders and rustling in the wind like arms. As they chased the child, they again heard the voice: "Just copy me and you will do fine." Then they each realized that this must be Nezha, that it had been his voice instructing them to draw a plan of the city in his image—the Eight-armed Nezha.
>
> As agreed upon, on the tenth day they came to the center of the city, and, sitting back to back, drew their plans. When both finished their

> work and each picked up the other's to examine it, both of them burst out laughing because their plans were identical—each being an Eight-armed Nezha city! Liu Bowen explained that the walled gate in the center due south, Zhengyangmen, was Nezha's head, the gates to its east and west were his ears, and the two wells inside the Zhengyangmen his eyes. On the east side of the Zhengyangmen, the Chongwenmen, Dongbianmen, and the Chaoyangmen, Dongzhimen on the east side of the city's walled gates were four of Nezha's arms. On the west side of the Zhengyangmen, the Xuanwumen, Xibianmen, and the Fuchengmen, Xizhimen on the west side of the city's walled gates were Nezha's other four arms. The Andingmen and Deshengmen were his feet.
>
> Yao Guangxiao agreed with this plan, but asked Liu if Nezha had only eight arms, and had no heart, liver, spleen, lungs or kidneys. "Nezha is very much alive, otherwise he could not subdue vicious dragons," Liu exclaimed. He pointed at his plan showing that the rectangular imperial-city is Nezha's viscera, and Tian'anmen at its entrance is the way into his viscera and it leads in the other direction to Zhengyangmen—his brain. The long level road between them is Nezha's gullet! Their plans were exactly alike, and so neither would outbid the other to claim all the credit. Liu Bowen did not mind, but Yao Guangxiao became so downcast that he went off to live as a monk, waiting to see how his rival would build Peking.[54]

Jin Shoushen provides a fictive account of the building of Peking in the context of a competition between Liu Bowen and Yao Guangxiao, purported to be the two principal advisers to the Ming emperor. Their encounter with Nezha is amplified so as to show that the inspirations for the planning of the city came directly from this supernatural deity. The details of the drawing of the city plan that allegedly matched the various parts of the body of Nezha manifested in one head but eight arms and two feet, reflect the architectural layout of Ming and Qing Peking—which remained relatively intact in modern Beijing until the demolition of the city walls in the 1950s. By fully portraying Nezha's body, Jin's "Eight-armed Nezha City" complemented the earlier sketches, transformed the legend into a more credible story and, with additional embroidery in the later version, made it the most engrossing folktale about the building of the Imperial-capital. Although Jin did not provide a graphic sketch of the Nezha City in his work, this was compensated for by the illustration in the English translation of his *Beijing Legends* by Gladys Yang. The latter features on the book cover a depiction of Nezha with three heads, eight arms and two feet superimposed on the layout of the imperial city, distinctively complementing the earlier descriptive and graphic illustrations (Figure 29).[55]

The second version, also written by Jin based on the folkloric materials he had gathered, was included in a sequel to his collection under the same title *Beijing de chuanshou* edited by Zhang Zichen 張紫晨 and Li Yuenan 李岳南 and was published in 1982. There are a few significant alterations and additions to the basic core of the old story, which make it more entertaining.[56]

First, after sketching the historical background, the second version presents Liu Bowen and Yao Guangxiao taking positions in the center of the city, drawing a line from north to south, then standing back to back at the mid-point. One walked toward the east, and the other toward the west, each covering 5 *li*, marking the edge of the city. Next they drew a east-to-west line along the places they had covered intersecting the north-to-south line, forming the shape of the character *shi* 十, i.e. "ten" (like a cross). Then they stood back to back on the same spot, one walked toward the south, and the other toward the north, each covering 7 *li*, marking the northern and southern edge of the city. After that they drew a frame around the miles of terrain they had covered and set the boundaries of the city.

Figure 29 Portrait of Nezha

Source: *Beijing Legends* (1982, book cover).

Second, the first version introduces Liu Bowen and Yao Guangxiao's encounter with Nezha. They heard a child's voice instructing them how to draw the plan of the city and realized the red-dressed child they saw in the street was Nezha, and on the ninth day they met again and executed the plan. The second version presents both Liu and Yao hearing the voice of the child as they slept. They met the mysterious red-dressed child the next day. It was the same day that they were to meet in the center of the city, sitting back to back to draw their plan. When they sat down and concentrated on their thoughts to start their brush strokes they each saw, without the other knowing it, the image of the child and became aware that he was Nezha, so they sketched his body and drew a plan known as the Eight-armed Nezha City.

Third, unlike the first version which is silent on what had happened when Liu Bowen and Yao Guangxiao were each drawing their city plan according to the image of Nezha's body, the second version reveals that when Yao started making his last brush stroke, a breeze suddenly arose, blowing away the lapel of Nezha's jacket, and he sketched it in as well. It turned out that both plans were exactly identical, and the explanations given by Liu Bowen to Yao Guangxiao's query as to why it was called the Eight-armed Nezha City are similar in both versions. The only flaw in Yao's drawing was that the northwestern corner of the outer wall did not form a true corner, but slanted off to the west in an oblique angle. Liu declared this was not appropriate for the city wall. Responding to Liu's criticism, which is reported only in the second version, Yao defended himself by saying that it was the shape of Nezha he saw with his own eyes, alluding to the fact that the breeze had distorted his vision of the supernatural deity.

Fourth, unlike the first version, which skips the aforementioned controversy, this second version reveals a row between Liu Bowen and Yao Guangxiao over who should claim credit for the Nezha City plan because of the flaw in Yao's drawing. The two then went before the Prince of Yan and the prince, though commending both for their good work, pointed out that because Liu's drawing was a proper square he should stay as Chief Adviser, whereas Yao's had a diagonal line thus he might stay as Deputy Adviser. The prince also gave orders that in building the city, the east city should follow Liu's plan and the west city follow Yao Guangxiao's. The story ends with the remark that after the city was completed it was revealed that Yao Guangxiao's slanted line was exactly the slope from the Deshengmen west to the Xizhimen, and that even to the present day the northwestern corner of Peking's city wall is still askew, lacking a ninety-degree angle at that point (Figures 26, 27)!

Summing up, the alterations and additions to the second version of the story significantly enhance the imaginative fiction and dramatic appeal of the popular legend. They seek to explain not only why, even though both Liu Bowen and Yao Guangxiao had drawn identical plans following their vision of Nezha's body, Yao's plan was judged inferior, but also why, when the building of the west city followed Yao's drawing, the northwestern corner of the city wall turned out to be askew rather than square. It was most ingenious to craft such an explanation of the peculiar shape of the northwestern corner of the city wall. In actual fact this feature was caused by the necessity of following the route of the protective canal. The story also offers an apt explanation of why Yao Guangxiao was considered inferior in stature when compared with Liu Bowen, which subtly reflected the popular denigration of the crafty adviser who threw in his lot with the "illegitimate" Yongle emperor.

Nezha's mystical prowess is not described in either version of this story, but in one of the spin-off stories called "Gao Liang's Race for Water"(*Gao Liang ganshui* 高亮赶水), Jin Shoushen reveals Nezha's extraordinary powers in a description of how people in old Peking were forced to live outside the city in the mountains to the northwest and led a wretchedly poor existence, while the city's water was made brackish by the inhabitation of a dragon king and his family. Then one day a young man named Nezha came along and, after fighting fiercely with the Dragon King and his son for nine consecutive days, captured the Dragon King and his wife and put the rest of the family to flight. After the battle was over the waters subsided and dry land appeared. Nezha imprisoned the two dragons in a large pool over which he built a large pagoda, and the people began to build houses in the city and dwell there. Thereafter the story proceeds with Liu Bowen's feuds with the dragon king and family and a warrior named Gao Liang emerges who desperately tried to save the waters carried off in two baskets by the dragons and lost his life, leaving Liu Bowen in difficulties (Figure 30).[57]

Jin probably wrote and published these stories much earlier in newspaper columns before they were brought into book form together with other stories about old Peking. A prolific writer of Manchu noble pedigree who had lived in Peking all his life, Jin was deeply immersed in the history, people, social customs, lifestyle, and legends of the city and he devoted most of his adult years to writing about and documenting the old capital and its present conditions. Many of his works are still extant. In many ways he was a great scholar of local *zhanggu* 掌故 (historical anecdotes and legends), and his writing, which tries to relate the past to the present, is an outstanding example of the "recycling" effort of the Peking men of letters in this era of transition. It is no surprise that he was able to replenish the material of the old Nazha City legend and resurrect it in new form for the modern audience as a piece of nostalgic popular history yet entertaining to all generations. It is also striking that since he published the refined versions of the Nezha City Legend in the heyday of the Communist state, the stories are distinctly laced with Maoist-Marxist leanings in their references to the collective ingenuity and the sweat and toil of the masses involved in the building of the city. In the parlance of social anthropologists, this was another

Figure 30 Images of the Dragon King; (Left) from the Nine-Dragon Wall, Forbidden City; (Right) from an undated Chinese woodblock printing

Source: Jin, *Beijing de chuanshuo* (2003 ed.), pp. 9, 29.

example of people using "recycling" as a mechanism to cope with changes without sacrificing core values in a socialist state.[58]

Whatever the original sources, it is clear that since the beginning of the twentieth century this historical legend has been widely transmitted among many walks of life in the nation's capital in oral and written forms and has recently even been dramatized in murals in public buildings and featured in films. In all its versions the old Yuan Dadu legend remained intact: the guardian deity of the imperial capital was still the mythologized Nazha, but the principal agent in this drama, Liu Bingzhong, has been replaced by the mythical Ming imperial adviser Liu Ji (Liu Bowen). How did this come about? Liu Ji was never involved in the building of Peking nor had he previously lived there, so why did the modern legend make him the new hero in this fanciful setting, and what accounted for its sustained popularity in Peking folk culture and what purposes did it serve? Fiction may defy verification, but to make a story persuasive it has to have built-in logic. We shall examine Liu Ji's career, and trace the genesis and transformation of his legends that inspired the modern version of the Nazha or Nezha City legend.

Liu Bowen's Legends

Liu Ji is one of a few Chinese historical personages whose life has been so colored by later legends that he continues to have a grip on the Chinese conscience in modern times. A native of Qingtian 青田 county, Chuzhou 處州 prefecture, present-day Wencheng 文成 county, Wenzhou 溫州, Zhejiang, Liu Ji, courtesy-name Bowen, was born in 1311 into an impoverished scholar-gentry family. He achieved his *jinshi* degree in 1333 at the age of twenty-two, during the last reign of Yuan rule. An erudite and versatile scholar he was not only adept in the classics and literature, but also reputedly excelled in the pseudo sciences, such as astrology, geomancy, mathematics, divination, and the like. However, his great gifts did not land him a successful official career under the Yuan because of his strong character and trenchant criticism of the corrupt officialdom. After a string of junior county and prefectural administrative appointments, during which he incurred the enmity of several senior officials, in 1356 he was employed as a secretary by the chief of the Jiangzhe 江浙 Branch Central Secretariat, the Mongol general Shimo Yisun 石抹

宜孫 (?–1360), to assist him in the defense of Chuzhou against the raids of roving bandits. However, his successes did not win him recognition from the Yuan authorities, and grudgingly he forsook his official career and retired from office in 1357. He spent his time writing a provocative political discourse called *Yulizi* 郁離子, 2 *juan*, expounding his social and political views and unveiling his criticism of the malfeasant administration while awaiting an opportunity to serve as a leader of destiny. There was no shortage of fortune-seekers amid the collapse of the Mongol order, when leaders of humble social origins such as Chen Youliang 陳友諒 (1320 or 1321–1363), Zhang Shicheng 張士誠 (1321–1367), Fang Guozhen 方國珍 (1319 or 1320–1374), Zhu Yuanchang, and others rose up in the lower Yangzi region and central provinces and engaged in fierce military confrontations against one another for hegemony. With political foresight and bold calculation, Liu Ji threw in his lot with Zhu Yuanchang, the future Ming dynastic founder.[59]

After joining Zhu Yuanchang's camp at Yingtian, later Nanking, as adviser and strategist in 1360, Liu Ji counseled in two significant ways that led to the success of the future Ming emperor. In the political realm he persuaded Zhu to sever allegiance with Han Liner, the titular "emperor" of the Song state under which he had been serving, and become an independent contender. In the military sphere he advised Zhu to take the preemptive offensive against his nemesis Chen Youliang instead of Zhang Shicheng in view of Chen's pretension and strength. He was credited with the ingenious military schemes which decimated Chen's troops first in June 1360 at the sea-land battle inside Longwan 龍灣 (northwest of Nanking) and later in August 1363 at Poyang 鄱陽 Lake (Jiangxi), where Zhu Yuanchang eliminated his principal adversary. He reportedly also improvised a brilliant stratagem against Zhang Shicheng, leading to his capitulation at his capital Pingjiang 平江 (Suzhou) in late 1366. After Zhu was invested the Prince of Wu in 1364, he appointed Liu Ji director of the Astronomy Bureau, entrusting him with the design of the future capital of Nanking, and later named him vice censor-in-chief of the reorganized Censorate. Following Zhu Yuanchang's enthronement in 1368, Liu Ji remained as head of the Censorate and continued to advise on state and military affairs. During the next three years he was involved in drafting regulations for a new military organization, the *weisuo* 衛所 or "guard system", the compilation of a new code of law, a new calendar, and a treatise on rituals, and in other related scholarly matters. It appears that he offended the emperor with his unrestrained remonstrance and antagonized his colleagues with trenchant criticisms, particularly Li Shanchang 李善長 (1314–1390), the right prime minister, and Hu Weiyong 胡惟庸 (?–1380), assistant administrator of the Central Secretariat, who were jealous of his status and accomplishments. Ming Taizu once proposed to offer Liu the office of prime minister, but he declined for fear of aggravating the enmity of his rivals. In 1371, after being invested as the Earl of Chengyi 誠意 (Utmost Sincerity) in recognition of his service, Liu Ji pleaded ill-health and obtained permission to retire. He died at home three years later at the age of sixty-four. Rumor suggested that he was poisoned by Hu Weiyong, but there was no substantive proof. He was belatedly awarded the canonized name Wencheng (Cultured and Meritorious) by Emperor Shizong in 1514, and his descendants inherited his earldom up until the end of the dynasty. His literary collection, *Chengyibo Liu Wencheng gong wenji* 誠意伯劉文成公文集, in 24 *juan*, was compiled by his descendants in the early sixteenth century and is included in the *Siku quanshu* collection along with a few other items attributed to his authorship (Figure 31).[60]

The development of the Liu Ji legends unfolds as a long, winding, and multifaceted interplay between facts and fantasies in a continuum of official apotheosization and popular mythologization. The legendary cycle originated with the exaggeration of Liu Ji's contribution as Ming Taizu's chief adviser at both the élite and the popular levels in accordance with a distinct yet mutually acceptable impression of a scholar-hero in the Chinese tradition. In successive turns it was embroidered by the scholar-historians' dramatization of his role in the Ming founding in the stereotyped *topoi* of imperial advisers established in traditional historiography, and was simultaneously enhanced by the popular imagination of the man as a mythical hero endowed with occult powers indigenous to the conception in the folk traditions. In time this cumulative process commingled the mythologization of historical personages and contemporary events at different levels, and disseminated the legends throughout a broad spectrum of Chinese society with a wide range of impact and response.[61]

Liu Ji's legends germinated from the numerous anecdotes

Figure 31 Portrait of Liu Ji (Bowen)

Source: *Chengyibo Liu Wencheng gong wenji* (*SBCK* ed.), preface.

circulating in his locality about his prodigious abilities and spectacular achievements, which grew in dimension and in intensity in the years after his death. Basic to these were the stories about his prescient prediction of the rise of Zhu Yuanchang as the dynasty founder and the outcome of the latter's campaigns against his principal adversaries such as Chen Youliang and Zhang Shicheng, some of which he personally participated in, by observing the cosmological signs and through executing ingenious strategies. They were first recorded in Liu's biographical account, the "Chengyibo Liugong xingzhuang" 誠意伯劉公行狀, purportedly composed by his clansman Huang Bosheng 黃伯生 (?–1385) in 1383, but which are suspected to have been forged later in his name to dramatize Liu Ji's meritorious contribution in order to promote the status of his descendants.[62] These miraculous episodes were further embroidered with additional fantasies by the imaginative authors of pseudo-historical, semi-fictional miscellanies since the sixteenth-century under the pervasive influence of popular Buddhism and Daoism. They include Du Mu 都穆 (1459–1525), *Dugong tanzuan* 都公談纂; Zhu Yunming 祝允明 (1461–1527), *Yeji*; Lu Can 陸粲 (1494–1551), *Gengsi bian* 庚巳編; Liang Yi 梁億 (*jinshi* 1511), *Chuanxin lu* 傳信錄; Zhang Han 張翰 (1511–1593), *Songchuang mengyu* 松窗夢語; Dong Gu 董穀 (*juren* 1516), *Bili zacun* 碧里雜存; Wang Wenlu 王文祿 (1503–1586), *Longxing ciji* 龍興慈記; Song Lei 宋雷, *Xiwu liyu* 西吳里語; Yang Yi 楊儀, *Gaopo yizuan* 高坡異纂; Wang Tonggui 王同軌, *Ertan leizeng* 耳談類增, and others.

These miscellaneous works feature many fanciful stories and uncanny episodes regarding Liu Ji's extraordinary abilities and ingenious wisdom as manifested in political, military, and social events through the skillful application of his superior knowledge of astrology, geomancy, physiognomy, military tactics, and divination. As well as using local myths, many of the semi-historical, fictional trappings in the stories about Liu Ji were drawn partly from existing fantasies and partly conjured up by imaginative authors drawing on historical accounts and folkloric traditions.[63] The most bizarre story is that Liu foresaw the Jianwen emperor's tragic fate and so when Ming Taizu asked him about the political future, he presented a sealed basket to be stored away inside the imperial palace, asking that it not be unlocked for consultation until a catastrophe struck. When the Prince of Yan's army marched into Nanking, Jianwen in desperation unsealed the basket in which he found Buddhist garb, a monk's certificate, and a razor. He thus followed the instruction to impersonate a Buddhist monk and fled to safety. This episode provided the *topoi* of several instances of Liu Ji leaving a cryptic message in a sealed container presaging future political events to be revealed when disasters arrived.[64] In various ways these miraculous and uncanny stories apotheosized the man 's extraordinary abilities: his political perspicacity, tactical ingenuity, and versatility in the pseudo sciences, and in time transformed Liu Ji from a historical scholar-hero into a semi-mythical personality.

The dramatization of Liu Ji assumed a more definite form with the appearance of the *Yinglie zhuan* 英烈傳 (The Romance of the Ming Dynasty Heroes), an anonymous late Ming historical novel featuring the dynastic founding and comparable to the *Sanguozhi yanyi* 三國志演義 (The Romance of the Three Kingdoms) for the Three Kingdoms period. The authorship of the earliest version of this work, entitled *Huang Ming kaiyun yingwu zhuan* 皇明開運英武傳 in 8 *juan* remains unknown, but it was traditionally ascribed to Guo Xun 郭勛 (1475–1542) and was first printed in 1591. A later version, subtitled *Yunhe qizong* 雲合奇縱, 20 *juan*, was credited to the editorship of the late Ming novelist Xu Wei 徐渭 (1521–1593), with a preface dated 1616. It was in the latter that the work evolved from a popular historical narrative to become a full-fledged romance with dramatic and fictitious episodes and descriptions. Synthesizing the existing tales and anecdotes with the novelist's imagination, the anonymous author recast Liu Ji in the model of the Han and Sanguo heroes Zhang Liang and Zhuge Liang as an ingenious adviser-tactician endowed with Daoist occult powers and clairvoyant insights, inspiring many stories and strange tales.[65]

The stories about Liu Ji in the *Yinglie zhuan* begin with a fictitious claim that he was the grandson of Liu Bingzhong, thereby strengthening his popular appeal by establishing an intimate relationship with his legendary namesake. The source of Liu Ji's intelligence was also fictionalized by adapting the stories of Zhang Liang and contemporary anecdotes. He is said to have derived his knowledge of military tactics and statecraft from a "divine book" he found in a cave guarded by a monkey; it was the same book that was passed to Zhang Liang, Han Gaozu's close adviser, from the famous Daoist hermit the Yellow-stone Elder (Huangshi gong 黃石公). Liu Ji's capacity as adviser-tactician to Zhu Yuanchang, the future Ming founder, was also highly fictionalized by adapting the story of Zhuge Liang in *The Romance of the Three Kingdoms.* As adviser at the June 1360 battle of Longwan against Chen Youliang, Liu reportedly entrapped Chen's navy in the lake through an ingenious scheme and used magical spells to invoke a favorable wind and set the enemy fleet ablaze. There, ascending a Daoist altar in a black robe, waving his precious sword and chanting incantations, he is the look-alike of Zhuge Liang using the same feat to destroy the armada of his rival Zhou Yu 周瑜 (175–210) of Wu at Chibi 赤壁 (A.D. 208) in the *Three Kingdoms.* Another story relates the famous episode of Yelu Chucai 耶

律楚材 (1189–1243) who sought to dissuade the Mongol conqueror Chinggis Qan from further campaigning in the western region by citing warning of a strange single-horned animal *jueduan* (i.e. unicorn, most probably a rhinoceros). It portrays Liu Ji giving similar advice to the Ming general Li Wenzhong 李文忠 (1339–1384) by revealing his dream about the same animal when Li campaigned against remnants of the Mongol armies in late 1370 in Mount Hongluo 紅羅山 in Jinzhou 錦州, modern Liaoning, in order to exaggerate Liu's prescient knowledge. The last episode about Liu Ji relates that he became apprehensive of Ming Taizu's intentions when, accompanying Taizu on a visit to the temples of the worthy ministers of the past, he heard that the emperor had rebuked Zhang Liang for failure to serve Han Gaozu well, and thereby requested to retire from office. This was also adapted from a popular story about this famous Han imperial adviser (Figure 32).[66]

The fictionalization of Liu Ji in the *Yinglie zhuan* laid the groundwork of the popular conception of the man in the ensuing legends. It soon inspired Peking opera actors, storytellers, and popular singers in the capital to animate many of the dramatic stories with additional fantasies and theatrical twists. Themes such as *Zhan Taiping* 戰太平 (Battling at Taiping), *Dang Liang* 擋諒 (Warding off Chen Youliang), and *You Wumiao* 遊武廟 (A Visit to the Temple of War Gods), directly adapted from the *Yinglie zhuan,* were particularly popular. They played an equally significant role in transmitting and embroidering Liu Ji's legends in dramatic form among the popular audience from the late Ming onward.[67] In the meantime, Liu Ji was further dramatized in the *Xu Yinglie zhuan* 續英烈傳, a five-*juan* sequel to its namesake compiled by a certain Konggu daoren 空谷道人 in the early Qing dynasty. Commencing with Ming Taizu's appointment of his grandson Zhu Yunwen as successor, thereafter the Jianwen emperor, the novel terminates with the events in the middle reign of Shenzong, the Wanli emperor. Adapting the earlier stories it relates that at the time of the imperial designation, Liu Ji presented the Ming founder with an almanac called *Dongming li* 東明曆 (The Dongming Almanac) foretelling, among other future events, the misfortune of his grandson and proposing the means of remedy. Following his advice the emperor asked that three monk's certificates, three suits of monk's garb replete with hat and footgear, and a razor be sealed in a basket to be stored in a secret chamber

Figure 32 Liu Bowen dressed in a Daoist garment performing ritual before an altar in *Yinglie zhuan*

Source: Xu Wei, *Yunhe qizong* (1616 ed.), *tuxiang*, 10a.

inside the palace. It turned out that they provided the tools for the Jianwen emperor and his two loyal companions to escape in disguise from the mutinous army of the Prince of Yan on the fall of the capital as Liu Ji had predicted, accentuating the myth of his prescience.[68]

In another development, Liu Ji's legends proliferated with the appearance of large numbers of pseudo scientific writings attributed to his authorship or editorship, including such subjects as astrology, geomancy, military stratagem, physiognomy, and divination. A dozen and more known items have been catalogued separately in the *Mingshi yiwenzhi* 明史藝文志 and also the *Siku quanshu zhongmu* 四庫全書總目. Some of the more popular, which are still extant, include the *Qinglei tianwenfenye (zhisheng) zhishu* 清類天文分野(直省)之書, 24 *juan*, a treatise on the origin of the Ming prefectural divisions said to have been demarcated according to their correspondence with the location of the celestial stars; the *Baiyuan(jing) fengyu (zhanhou) tu* 白猿(經)風雨(占候)圖, 1 *juan*, a discourse on prognostication based on observation of the cosmological phenomena; the *Sanming qitan ditiansui* 三命奇談滴天髓, 1 *juan*, a treatise on physiognomy; the *Dili (kanyu) manxing*, 3 *juan*, and the *Zuoyuan zhizhi (tujie)* 佐元直指(圖解), 10 *juan*, two important treatises on geomancy; the *Guanxiang wanzhan* 觀象玩占, 10 *juan*, and the *Qimen tunjia* 奇門遁甲, various *juan*, two treatises on divination; the *(Liu Bowen xiansheng) Baizhanqilue* (劉伯溫先生)百戰奇略, 10 *juan*, a treatise on military stratagem; and the *Shaobing ge* 燒餅歌 (Baked Cake Ballad), a widely circulated book of prophecy in modern times. Such putative writings not only inflated Liu Ji's reputation for scholastic acumen in the pseudo sciences but also incorporated the legends of eminent historical personages, notably Zhang Liang and Zhuge Liang, into his life by crediting him with joint authorship or editorship. Examples are the *Huangshi gong sushu sanlue* 黃石公素書三略 and the *Zhuge Zhongwuhou bingfa xinyao* 諸葛忠武侯兵法新要, two well-known works on military stratagem. The dating and authorship of these writings can only be conjectured. Some of them date from the late Ming, others are perhaps of Qing origin, and some are even of recent production either of new fiction or extraction from older texts. It is also difficult to explain the motives of the putative authors. They may have doctored these works in Liu Ji's name to gain publicity, or to satisfy the craving for fantasy and melodrama at the lower levels of society with an eye on profit. In any case they have contributed significantly to the intensification and popularization of Liu Ji's mythology into the twentieth century.[69]

In a somewhat different contemporaneous setting, Liu Ji also became involved in a Mongolian legend of the building of Peking. Popular belief at this time among the Mongols was that the Yongle emperor was not the son of Ming Taizu but the posthumous child of the last Yuan emperor Toghōn Temür by his Qonggirad consort, known as Gongfei 碽妃 in Chinese unofficial literature. The emperor met and married her upon the fall of Dadu when she was already several months pregnant and she gave birth to a son sometime afterward. While there was much speculation on the subject in Chinese miscellanies since the sixteenth century, the rumor of the Mongol maternity of the Yongle emperor was mainly transmitted in several Mongolian historical narratives and folkloric tales popular among the Mongol residents in north China, and among those around Peking in particular. A more detailed version is given in a Mongolian manuscript circulated in the late Qing entitled "Book of the Story of How Emperor Yung-lo of the Great Ming Built the City of Peking—The Yuan Prince—the True Prince" in English translation. The Yuan Prince (i.e. Prince of the Mongols) refers to the future Yongle emperor, thought to be the actual son of Toghōn Temür, and the True Prince refers to the Hongwu emperor's other son, the future Jianwen emperor allegedly born to the same Mongol consort.

According to this story Ming Taizu, having seen in a dream that his son (the future Yongle emperor) was in fact the son of the Mongol qaghan, sent him off to Nankou 南口, the defile north of future Peking, with a thousand soldiers, instructing him to hold it from the Mongol attack. When the Prince received the order, and aware of how hard the task would be, he opened a sealed "envelope" (a pouch or bag) which his Mongol mother had given him for advice. There he found a piece of paper saying that when he was banished to Nankou, he should make Liu Bowen minister and follow his instructions. Thus he pleaded with the emperor to allow Liu to accompany him and the request was granted, along with one thousand old soldiers and one thousand exhausted horses. The story relates that after the prince had reached his destination, as he was riding out alone with his bow and arrows one day, he met a man of extraordinary bearing, with a swarthy face, dressed in a black robe and riding a black horse. The man took away his weapons and shot one arrow each into the four directions. Then he announced that there was an abundant treasure of gold, silver, and jewels in the spots hit by the arrows, and asked the prince to make Liu Bowen minister and found a great city there according to his proposed plan. With this order the strange man gave the prince his red spear and vanished.[70]

None of the episodes described here, as discussed in detail in Chapter 3, is historically authentic. In reality although the Yongle emperor was born of a Mongol consort from the Qonggirad tribe she was not the *qatun* of Toghōn Temür, and therefore he was not the posthumous son of the last Yuan emperor. Liu Ji died in 1375, long before Zhu Di was installed as the Prince of Yan, and so he could not have had any part in the building of Peking. However, this eerie Mongolian folktale skillfully extracts historical facts and mingles them with legendary elements. By pairing Yongle with Liu Ji, it was able to exploit the rich legend of the early Ming hero, particularly his role in designing the imperial city in Nanking, and create a story of his contribution to building the city in Peking. The part about the strange black rider shooting arrows into four directions to mark the site of the city evoked the Mongolian custom of "siting by bowshot", i.e. using the flight of arrows for allotting the site of a building or the size of fiefs, and complemented the story of city planning. Without question the most sensational element was the infusion of the Liu Bowen story, which not only animated the saga but also provided an indispensable linkage of the Peking legend with the most mythologized personage in recent history.

In yet another development, Liu Ji's legends were emphasized by the political activists or dissidents in the Ming-Qing transition and in the late Qing, who exploited Liu's historical and popular renown to fabricate political prophecies to advance their propaganda. In the late Ming, at a time of sociopolitical chaos, several literary miscellanies carried accounts about the discovery of Liu Ji's alleged "salvation epigraph" (*jiujiebei wen* 救劫碑文) engraved on steles and revealing his premonitions and predictions of the future. After the demise of the Ming, some anti-Manchu dissidents produced prophecies in Liu Bowen's name predicting the fate of the descendants of the Ming emperor Wanli (Shenzong) and the suicide of the last emperor Chongzhen (Sizong 思宗, r. 1628–1644) upon the fall of Peking to the invasion of the rebel leader Li Zicheng 李自成 (1605–1645), which terminated the dynasty. These prophetic messages strongly appealed to the populace who in times of upheaval sought relief and salvation from the supernatural deities. Liu Ji, as a mythologized imperial adviser of the Ming founding and gifted in divination and prognostication, became an instant Han ethnocentric patron and prophet-savior.[71]

Likewise, during the late Qianlong and later Jiaqing 嘉慶 (1796–1820) reign when many provinces of China were plunged into social and economic turmoil, Liu Ji was again utilized by the anti-Manchu sectarian organizations championing the restoration of Ming rule in order to attract a following. The Heaven and Earth Society (*Tiandihui* 天地會), a prominent "*fan Qing fu Ming*" 反清復明 triad society based in Jiangxi, Fujian, Guangdong, and Guangxi in the last two centuries, took the initiative. Both Zhuge Liang and Liu Bowen were deified by members of the society as their patron saints. As shown by surviving documents, along with Zhuge Liang, Liu Bowen was apotheosized as a sagacious strategist and efficacious prognosticator. Liu, in particular, was claimed to have bequeathed a secret plan in a "sealed packet" popularly known as *jinnang* 錦囊 (damask purse) for toppling the Qing regime and had left prognostications about the demise of Manchu rule.[72] At the same time a considerable amount of prophetic verses attributed to Liu Bowen about impending sociopolitical upheavals and the means of salvation emerged in different localities in north and central China. A prototype of the more mature ballad called *Liu Bowen xiansheng shishi ge* 劉伯溫先生時世歌 (Mister Liu Bowen's ballad on current events) surfaced in the mid-eighteenth century and was incorporated into a comprehensive sectarian "precious volume" (*baojuan* 寶卷) called *Sanjiao yingjie zongguan tongshu* 三教應劫總觀通書 (A General Interpretation of Response to Kalpic Change according to the Three Religions) allegedly compiled by Liu Bing 劉冰, a follower of the millenary Buddhist Yuandun 圓(元)頓 sect in the late Qianlong reign. This scripture, a revision of the original circulating among the White Lotus-Maitreya sects in Hebei and Shandong during the fifteenth century, was proscribed as the heretical text that inspired the great anti-Manchu Eight Trigrams Uprising of 1813 but is still extant. At the same time, sporadic prophetic messages ascribed to Liu Ji continued to circulate in many parts of troubled China. All these gave impetus to the birth of the *Shaobing ge* (Baked Cake Ballad), a fully-fledged prophecy book about the fortunes of Chinese society since the Ming dynasty doctored in his name probably as early as the mid-nineteenth century.[73]

In its present form, most editions of the *Shaobing ge* ascribed to Liu Bowen were published in the latter part of the Guangxu reign, but they are not clearly dated. One of the earliest dated editions, printed in Shanghai in 1897, carries the title page of *Liu xiansheng "Jingui jinnang"* 劉先生「金櫃錦囊」(Mister Liu's "Golden Casket and

Damask Purse"), with similar contents. Several other editions, including some with the varied title of *Dishi wenda ge* 帝師問答歌 (Ballad of Dialogue between the Emperor and the Teacher) and using the Yellow Emperor's putative chronology for dating, were published in Tokyo at the end of the Qing dynasty. Since the later Republican period, apart from existing as an individual publication, the work has been included in the *Zhongguo yuyan wu* (*qi* or *ba*) *zhong* 中國預言五(七、八)種 (Five, Seven, or Eight Samples of Chinese Prophecies), or *Zhongguo erqiannian (qian) zhi yuyan* 中國二千年(前)之預言 (Chinese Prophecies in Two Thousand Years), a compendium of Chinese prophecies attributed to several earlier prominent historical personages besides Liu Bowen. The compiler, a certain Li Zhong 李中 from Tiaoxi 苕溪 (?), claimed in his cryptic preface that this collection of prophecies was originally held in the custody of the Manchu inner court, but was disposed outside after the allied Sino-French troops gutted the Summer Palace of the Forbidden City in 1859; a copy was obtained by a foreign soldier, it was later passed to an English lady and, after another change of hands, the work was obtained by a certain Chinese literati and disseminated to the public. The first edition of *Zhongguo yuyan qizhong* 中國預言七種 was published in Shanghai in the 1930s and it was successively reprinted in numerous editions along with other related titles in many localities in China and in Hong Kong and Taiwan down to this day.[74]

Shaobing ge derives its title from a fictive meeting between Ming Taizu and Liu Ji. Taizu was taking a bite of a "baked cake" and, hearing of his confidant-adviser's arrival, covered it with a bowl and asked him to identify the hidden object. Unhesitatingly Liu gave the correct answer. Astonished by his prescience, Taizu asked Liu Bowen to divulge the fortunes and misfortunes of the dynasty and beyond. Liu gave predictions of events for six hundred years after his death. Many of those concerning the Ming were allegedly fulfilled. They included episodes like the usurpation of the Prince of Yan, the tragedy of the Jianwen emperor, Yingzong's captivity by the Mongols at the battle of Tumu, the last Ming emperors being the descendants of the Wanli emperor, the suicide of the Chongzhen emperor, the rebellion of Li Zicheng, and the termination of the dynasty by the Manchu invasion. The alleged fulfillment of these prophecies was indicated by brief explanatory notes inserted in the text and the same technique was extended to cover the Qing by entering the reign-name to those periods in which the prophecy was claimed to have been fulfilled. In most extant editions the last reign-name that appears in these notes is Guangxu, and the prophetic messages thereafter are cryptic and illusive, alluding to social and political chaos caused by the intrusion of the Hu 胡 people (i.e. northern barbarian, but also alluding to other hostile foreigners) and the advent of peace and happiness after their elimination. This would suggest that the book in its present form may have been compiled and printed at the end of Qing since all prophecy books must indicate their *post facto* fulfillment by reference to actual happenings in order to win the confidence of the readers (Figure 33).[75]

According to my investigations, *Shaobing ge* evolved from the legend of the early Ming Daoist Zhang Zhong 張中, alias the Iron-cap Master (Tieguan daoren 鐵冠道人), a learned Daoist and prescient prognosticator who served Ming Taizu as adviser and followed him in military campaigns against his rivals before the dynastic founding. He allegedly invoked occult power in devising tactics to overwhelm the enemy and accurately predicted the outcome of several decisive battles. The emperor personally wrote favorable accounts about him and asked the Hanlin academician Song Lian 宋濂 (1310–1381) to draft his official biography. In due course, stories about the Daoist's prescient abilities and his accurate predications of key political events of the dynasty began to circulate. It was reported, for instance, in Zheng Xiao's 鄭曉 (1499–1566) *Jinyan* 今言 (1566), and in Gu Qiyuan's 顧起言 (1565–1628) *Kezuo zhuiyu* 客座贅語 (1617), that he had left a prophetic tract called *Zhengbing ge* 蒸餅歌 (Steamed Cake Ballad) accurately predicting, *inter alia*, the dethronement of the Jianwen emperor and the tragic Tumu incident. This work was also cited in Zhang Zhong's biography in Zha Jizuo's 查繼佐 (1601–1676) private Ming history *Zuiwei* lu 罪惟錄 where the title was given as *Quebing ge* 缺餅歌 (Cracked Cake Ballad) but the contents were not revealed (Figure 34).[76]

A close scrutiny of these stories indicates that they provided the principal sources for the *Shaobing ge*. For instance, the episode about a meeting between Ming Taizu and the Daoist during which the emperor tested his clairvoyance by concealing the cake he was eating under a bowl, and the Daoist passing muster and divulging several predictions about the future events of the dynasty. It shows that the

Figure 33 Liu Bowen prognosticating before Ming Taizu in *Shaobing ge*

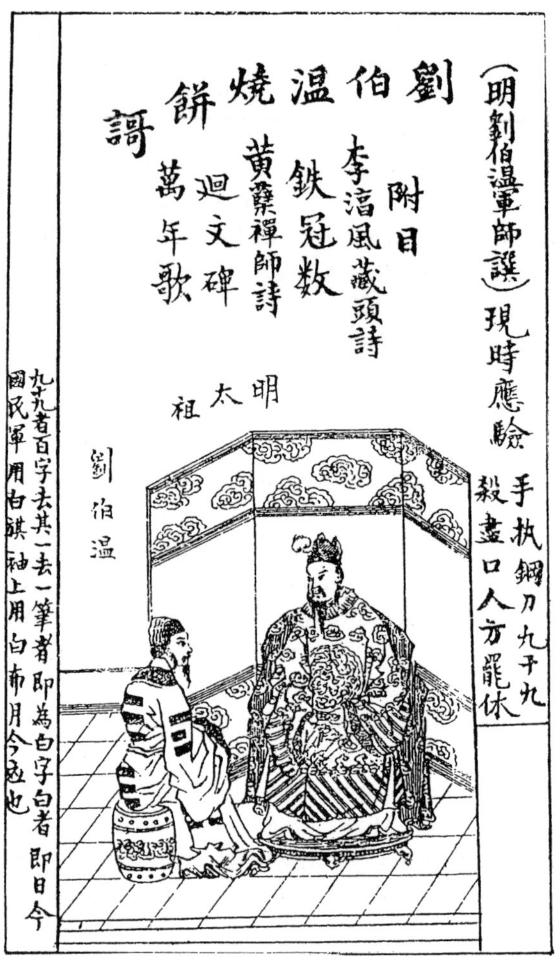

Source: Book cover, undated Showa ed. Tokyo.

initial compiler or compilers of the *Shaobing ge* craftily ascribed these stories about Zhang Zhong to Liu Bowen and changed the title from *Zhengbing* to *Shaobing*, with the addition of stories about the latter's prophecies, apparently because Liu had been deified as an anti-Manchu hero and commanded greater appeal to the populace than

Figure 34 Portrait of the Iron-cap Daoist Zhang Zhong

Source: Shangguan Zhou, *Wanxiaotang huazhuan* (1750), p. 175.

the early Ming Daoist who seemed to have lost his historical relevance. This development probably occurred before the Guangxu period. According to the miscellany *Jianqingshi suibi* 劍青室隨筆 by a certain Wang Liumen 王柳門 from Nanking in the late Qing, some copies of the *Shaobing ge* in vogue in his time were ascribed to Zhang Zhong and entitled *Zhengbing ge*, but other copies, either bearing the title *Zhengbing* or *Shaobing*, were assigned to the authorship of Liu Bowen.[77]

It is futile to attempt to identify the original compiler(s) or editor(s) of the *Shaobing ge*. A columnist writing in a January 1898 issue of the *Taiwan Ririxinbao* 臺灣日日新報, a Taiwanese newspaper published under Japanese rule, citing passages from Liu Ji's alleged prophecy—to which he gave the varied title of *Chibing ge* 吃餅歌 (Eating Cake Ballad)—suggested that it was probably forged by a former adviser of the leaders of the Taiping Heavenly Kingdom 太平天國 in order to drum up anti-Manchu propaganda, but this is speculative at best. However, the anonymous compiler or editor of *Shaobing ge* was very likely an individual who was affiliated with an anti-Manchu organization, whether it was a triad society or a sectarian sect, or was a sympathizer to its cause. This is obvious by the frequent use of ethnocentric and anti-foreign language as well as the invective against the Hu barbarians in the text, and there are also other paths of reference.[78] For example, in the famous anti-Manchu nationalist manifesto by Zou Rong 鄒容 (1885–1905), the *Gemingjun* (Revolutionary Army) dated 1903, he quoted a couplet from the *Shaobing ge* at the end of the text: "Brandish ninety-nine big swords, slaughter the 'Tartars' until they are all eliminated" (*Shouzhi dadao jiushijiu, zhajin Dazi fangbashou* 手執大刀九十九，殺盡韃子方罷手) as a prophecy of victory over the Qing rulers. Here the term "Tartars" (Dazi) is used as a pejorative, racist epithet for the Manchus, in contrast to the more general reference to Hu aliens used in other editions of the *Shaobing ge*, attesting to more intense political propaganda. Moreover, several 1911 editions of the *Shaobing ge* published in Tokyo adopted the Yellow Emperor's name as the chronology of dating, which was used by some of the revolutionaries at that time to promote their nationalist cause.[79]

Along with the prophecy, "killing the Tartars" became the theme of a series of folk stories about a plot devised by the ethnic Han Chinese to kill the hated Mongols on Mid-Autumn day and topple the Yuan dynasty, which emerged in the late Qing and early Republican period. They describe how the peasants, tipped off by a message found hidden in the stuffing of a moon cake on the night of the popular annual festival, rose up in rebellion, slaughtered the Tartars and ended the Mongol rule. Many of these stories attributed Liu Bowen to be the ingenious schemer and they have since become the most talked about folktales celebrating the Mid-Autumn festival even down to the present-day. There was no historical basis for these assertions—the Yuan dynasty was not toppled by a Han Chinese popular uprising on Mid-Autumn day and Liu Ji played no role in planning the rebellion. The stories were probably forged by the nationalistic anti-Manchu revolutionaries to further their cause of killing the Tartars, be they Mongols or others. In making Liu Bowen their champion hero in these historical uprisings to advance Han Chinese restoration, these folk stories further buttressed the legend of his clairvoyance and deepened his mythology.[80]

In any event, *Shaobing ge* remained a most popular prophecy book and was widely consulted and circulated in China and overseas Chinese communities at a time of sociopolitical crises when people in despair were yearning for guidelines or promises of salvation and deliverance. Several editions with annotations indicating the alleged fulfillment of Liu Bowen's prognostications appeared, further enhancing its popularity and broadening its circulation. Through the popularization of the *Shaobing ge* and its subsequent manipulation the public came to conceive of Liu Ji as a mystical prophet-savior who would re-emerge in troubled times to provide direction to soothe their fears and ease their anxiety. In due course, additional prophecies were doctored in Liu Ji's name in response to mass hysteria during periods of sociopolitical upheaval, proclaiming the fulfillment of his predictions of events as recent as the Cultural Revolution in mainland China, making him a kind of Chinese Nostradamus. This development marks the climax of the mythologization of Liu Ji from a historical adviser-tactician to the Ming founder into a larger-than-life mystical prophet-savior of the masses with a durable legacy in contemporary Chinese society.[81]

Nezha Cheng Legend Analyzed

The growth of Liu Ji's multifaceted legends provides an indispensable background for an investigation into the reborn Nazha City legend bearing his name in modern Peking's folk culture. To understand how this Ming hero was grafted onto the Yuan Dadu legend as one who designed Peking in partnership with the mythical Nezha, we need to re-examine the background that nourished and facilitated the transformation of this legend. Four factors merit consideration.

First, Peking was again elevated as the principal imperial capital in the Ming and restored to its former supreme status after an interruption of only thirty years. Moreover, since it was built on the site of Yuan Dadu, even though it did not preserve much of Dadu's architectural monuments and buildings, it retained many of the political, religious, and cultural institutions as well as the historical precedents, social customs, and folkloric traditions of the Mongol-Yuan dynasty. At the same time, as the principal capital, it developed and nourished its own Han Chinese institutions, customs, and traditions at the imperial, the literati, and the popular levels that blended with, or refurbished, the existing establishments and interacted with those of the subsidiary capital at Nanking. These traditions were inherited by the Manchu rulers of the Qing who reinstated Ming Peking as the imperial capital. They not only engaged in extensive renovation and expansion, especially in the Forbidden City and the western suburbs, but also developed and nurtured indigenous institutions and traditions that merged with and reinforced the Han Chinese establishments inherited from the Ming. Despite the sociopolitical disjuncture caused by the intrusion of the Manchu bannermen, there was much continuity in many of the developments in Peking down to the modern era.

Second, the building of Peking, like that of the earlier imperial cities founded in the region, though following the classical Wangcheng model in architectural design, was constrained by particular topographical and environmental problems. Besides the protracted droughts caused by the unpredictable continental climate, the paramount problem that beset Peking was inadequate water supply exacerbated by excessive demand and together with other man-made construction obstructions. Ming Peking faced not just the same problem of water supply as that faced by Dadu's palace- and imperial-cities, plus the silting of the Grand Canal that hampered the passage of the grain boats, but also more severe problems in water supply in general. This was caused by the construction of Yongle's mausoleum, the Changling, which disrupted the tributaries from Baifu Spring and impaired the Yuan irrigation system that supplied water to the city. Thus Peking had to depend solely on water originating from the Jade Spring Hill, which flowed through the West Lake into the Jishui Pool and emptied through different waterways into the imperial-city as well as the Grand Canal. The flow was inadequate, especially during periods of drought, and water shortage remained a constant problem throughout the Qing and the Republican period as the population expanded. The lack of water and the misery it caused had completely infiltrated the public consciousness and manifested itself in religious worship and folk culture.

Third, against the unique background of the building of Ming Peking, a variety of religious cults and mythologized personalities became the subject of worship in both the formal and the popular religious establishments. Apart from the Daoist paragon the Dark God Zhenwu or the mythologized Chinese war god Guan Yu 關羽 (160–219), whose temples and memorials numbered several hundreds in the capital, the equally prominent and ubiquitous deity was the Dragon King whose temples, Longwangmiao, rivaled the above deities in number as well as in grandeur. Moreover, there was a sacred Black Dragon's alleged abode called Heilongtan inside the Yongding Gate which was an equally popular site of worship for the pious and faithful.[82] It is striking that many temples in Peking that had a well outside often housed the spiritual tablet of the Dragon King in the altar of worship, and that many conspicuous wells had a mini temple or altar built nearby to offer sacrifice to the spiritual dragon. At a later date the Dragon King also emerged as the spiritual protector of a number of professional guilds in the city, particular the water carriers' guild and the firemen's guild. Thus the omnipresence of these temples and memorials devoted to the dragon genii reflected the particular concern of the residents—the water problem—and their anxiety for divine blessing.[83] In addition, praying for rain in Peking was also a very regular occurrence in the local communities because of persistent drought, and as attested by a late Ming gazetteer, the *Dijing jingwu lue* 帝京景物略 by Liu Tong 劉侗 (?–1637) and Yu Yizheng 于弈正 (?–c. 1635), it involved various elaborate rituals paying homage to the Dragon King before the temples, with both adults and children participating. Similar ceremonies were continued in the Qing and through the Republican period as one of the most popular and lasting religious festivities in Peking and its vicinity even down to present times.[84]

Fourth, as a result of intense mythologization from the Song through the Yuan, Nazha had already made a strong impact on Dadu with the germination of the legend of city planning associated with Liu Bingzhong. In the Ming his popularity in Peking was evidently enhanced by the Daoist metamorphosis of Nazha in the *Soushen guangji* into one of the highest-ranking Daoist immortals under the Jade Emperor endowed with extraordinary supernatural powers. The stories of his turbulent battle in the Eastern Sea with the dragon genii over control of the watery world were particularly sensational, the more so because people in Peking continually faced water shortage and the Dragon King became one of the most widely worshiped deities in the capital. It also explained why Nazha, as the latter's rival, was a popular idol of worship in the Eastern Peak Temple and other temples.[85] A Nezha Temple built near the Black Dragon Pool inside the Yongding Gate in the early Qianlong period—which later became part of what was known as Taoranting (Pavilion of Merriment) and survived into the 1950s before it was razed to make room for the Taoranting Public Park—also vividly attests to their antagonistic relationship.[86] In addition the continued popularization of the religious novels *Tales of the Investiture of Gods* and *Journey to the West* dramatizing Nazha's various exploits, as well as their adaptation in dramas and storytelling, further ingrained his miracles in the popular conception. They played an indispensable role in the transformations of the Nazha City legend.

There were enough grounds, therefore, for refurbishing the legend of Yuan Dadu in a new form from the perspective of popular tradition. Peking remained an imperial capital and needed a guardian protector, especially one who would subdue the dragon genii who allegedly controlled the water resources and caused trouble. None would be more capable than the miraculous Nezha who was still a popular deity. All the major ingredients in the Dadu legend would have remained attractive to the popular imagination in the Ming and post-Ming society with the exception of the old hero Liu Bingzhong who, as a champion of the Mongol cause, was no longer relevant in Chinese society after the Han ethnic restoration. What was needed to resuscitate the old legend was none other than a new hero, a mythologized personage who could be the equal of Liu Bingzhong and form a partnership with Nazha to protect the city from external threat and exorcize the dragon genii to assure water supply. The new hero, Liu Bowen, was found and the Nazha City legend was given a new lease of life. But how did Liu Bowen provide the perfect match and how were his own legends, as they developed, commingled so effectively with that of his predecessor and with the prevailing Nezha legend?

As already noted, by virtue of intense mythologization, Liu had enthralled a large segment of the Peking population as a nationalistic larger-than-life historical personage who performed miracles as an astrologer, geomancer, and above all as a prophet-savior. Some of

Liu Bowen's attributes, therefore, were easily infused into the popular culture of Peking, but how he superseded Liu Bingzhong as the hero receiving assistance from Nezha to design the imperial city was a product of the fortuitous convergence of various disparate circumstances. Some of the incidents recounted were inadvertent mingling of fiction and fantasies over periods of time, but others were spun from the creative reworking of the existing mythology by various agents of the popular tradition in the imperial capital. In this regard, a key point to be raised would be: Liu Bowen had already died when Peking was built and he visited Yuan Dadu only once when he went there to take the palace examination, so why did the legend associate him with the imperial capital and credit him with the city planning? Did he have any connection with old Peking in general, and the building of the capital there in particular?[87] In fact Liu Ji had no direct connection with Peking, and all the legends associating him with the imperial capital emanated from outside, were mingled together, and were grafted onto him in the course of transmission.

There are at least four different sources of the legend: first, the historical background of Liu Ji designing the city of Nanking as the Ming capital; second, the popular legend derived from Liu Ji's involvement in the building of the capital; third, the story of Liu Ji building a city in Peking transmitted by the Mongols residing around the capital; and finally, the attribution of Liu Ji as Liu Bingzhong's grandson through a faked genealogy. Molding these various sources together recast Liu Ji into the hero who designed the imperial city plan with Nezha's assistance.

The legends about Liu Bowen which connect him with the building of Peking were derived, first of all, from his designing of the capital city at Nanking which is well documented in historical records. It has been pointed out that when Zhu Yuanchang, while still the Prince of Wu, ordered the expansion of Yingtian as the future capital, Liu Ji was put in charge of the project. He designed a regular concentric walled city north of Mt. Zhong to the east of the old city and its construction was completed in 1367, a year before the founding of the dynasty. Two groups of palaces and halls were built in the compound. There were three great halls in the front (south), and two inner palaces in the rear (north); then in 1399, under the Jianwen emperor, a hall was added between these two inner palaces, making altogether six palaces and halls of the Forbidden City. When the Yongle emperor ordered the construction of the palace-city he specifically asked that the palaces and halls of Nanking be replicated in order to provide a symbolic link between his imperial residence and that of his father's and so enhance the legitimacy of his succession. This factual and symbolic link was to lay the ground for the Liu Bowen legends, derived from the building of Nanking, which would penetrate into and proliferate in Peking.[88]

Second, various strange legends arose from Liu Ji's involvement in the building of the capital and some made allusion to the usurpation of the Jianwen emperor's throne by the Prince of Yan, the future Yongle emperor. For instance, a story has it that after Liu proposed Yingtian as the future capital and chose the reclaimed Yanque Lake for the site of the central palace, he was dismayed when the emperor ordered that the foundation piles be moved back as they were too close to the edge of the lake, claiming that it would harm the geomancy and that the capital would be moved away before long.[89] Another story alleges that Liu used the occasion of the inspection tour with Zhu Yuanchang of the tower on the walled city upon its completion to divulge the dynastic fortune. It is said that when the future emperor, marveling at the invincibility of the lofty walls, wondered if anyone could intrude, Liu sighed: "No one possibly can, except the 'swallows'!" "Swallow" (*yan* 燕), being a pun on the Prince of Yan, alluded to the future Yongle emperor who launched a military campaign to usurp the throne from the imperial grandson.[90]

In addition, there was a story claiming that Liu Ji sited the future burial ground of Ming Taizu on the grave of the Liang dynasty eminent monk Baozhi 寶誌 (418–514), where the emperor happened to sit as they jointly toured Mt. Zhong in search of the future interment site. Liu reported that the monk's grave was a "dragon's cave", a site of auspicious geomancy. The tomb was then exhumed, revealing the monk's well-preserved body as a seated normal person. Sacrificial rites were therefore offered and the monk's remains were lavishly reburied five *li* away. The original site became Taizu's mausoleum, the Ming Xiaoling 孝陵 ("Filial Tumulus"), where he was interred after his death.[91] These stories not only accentuated Liu Ji's miraculous attributes as geomancer and prognosticator in the building of Nanking, but also connected him vicariously with Peking, the next imperial capital, since some of them made allusions to his prognostication of the victory of the Prince of Yan in the succession power struggle.

Third, the story of Liu Ji being ordered to build a city in Peking in the legend about the Prince of Yan's encounter with the strange swarthy-faced man transmitted by the Mongols residing around the capital provided an important catalyst in the evolution of the new version of the Nazha City legend. Neither reliable history nor fictional accounts associated Liu Bowen with the building of Peking, which was done in Yongle's reign when Liu had already been dead for more than thirty years. The significance of the Mongolian legend is that, by making Liu join the Prince of Yan as his adviser journeying to the site of the future capital, though historically untenable, it put them in the same time frame, and the fictive assertion linked Liu Bowen to the building of Peking. Although there was no mention of Nezha in this legend, a later simplified Chinese rendition transmitted by E. T. C. Werner in his *Myths and Legends of China* shows that it was apparently adapted from an oral version of this Mongolian source. It reports that Liu presented to the Prince of Yan a message concealed in a "sealed packet". It was a sketch of the Nezha City and the Prince followed the instructions and successfully built the city. The latter represents an interesting blending of Mongolian and Chinese folklore and supplies an indispensable nexus in the evolution of the Liu Bowen legend associating him with Nezha and the building of Peking in an entirely different time frame and setting.

Fourth, the attribution of Liu Ji as Liu Bingzhong's grandson in the seventeenth century historical romance *Yinglie zhuan* was an equally important catalyst in the crystallization of the legend of Liu Bowen building the Nezha City. It first appeared as local gossip, which sought to apotheosize the man in a broader historical setting. Its adaptation into the late Ming historical romance solidified his fictive blood relationship with the most mythologized namesake in recent history. Following the *Yinglie zhuan* and its sequel, Liu Ji's career was given yet another fictionalized treatment in a well-publicized Qing drama called *Jianhuang tu* 建皇圖 (Plan for Enthroning a Ruler) ascribed to Zhu Zuochao 朱佐朝. There it was also claimed that Liu was the grandson of Liu Bingzhong and was hailed for his versatile ingenuity and scholarly erudition. A late Qing novelette featuring Liu Ji's meritorious service under Zhu Yuanchang entitled *Zai jinpao* 再錦袍 (Re-donning the Damask Robe) by an anonymous author also made a similar claim for Liu Ji.[92] As a result, Liu Ji appropriated the legend of this illustrious Yuan statesman and mythologized hero and thus became his substitute as the new hero associating with Nezha in building the city in Peking. Using this relationship as the premise, the legend makers were able to revive the old tradition and infuse it into the growing legend of Liu Bowen to develop even more dramatic stories. Except for the presence of a faked genealogy it would be next to impossible to associate Liu Ji with Liu Bingzhong and to remold his legend to resuscitate the old mythology of Peking in Liu Bowen's name.

There is another puzzle in the reworked Nazha City legend. As first reported by Jin Shoushen, the contemporary version of the story features Liu Bowen and his fellow imperial adviser Yao Guangxiao competing to design the city of Peking. They each separately saw the apparition of Nezha and each was simultaneously inspired to draw a plan in the likeness of his transformed body with three heads, eight arms, and two feet. Since the two plans were exactly the same, neither won exclusive credit, and Yao was so irate that he ran away to become a monk, leaving Liu to build the city alone. However, Jin also reports a slightly modified version of the story which disparaged Yao Guangxiao. The story says that as Yao was making his sketch of the city by modeling it on Nezha, a breeze suddenly arose, blowing away the lapel of Nezha's jacket, so distorting his vision of the body, and therefore Yao's sketch of the northwestern corner of the outer city wall was not a proper corner but slanted off to the west. Thus his drawing was judged inferior to Liu Bowen's, making Liu the winner. (According to Beijing's city map, the northwestern corner of the outer wall from Desheng Gate to Xizhi Gate slanted off to the west at an oblique angle because it followed the contour of the Jishui Pool, which formed the boundary of the city wall. This topographical feature was twisted in fiction to disparage Yao Guangxiao.)[93] (Figures 26, 27) But why was Yao Guangxiao inserted into the story? Why did the story make him inferior to Liu Bowen for having committed a blunder in his drawing of the city plan? Was the episode a deliberate dramatic invention, or were there any historical precedents?

It seems that pairing one character against another for contrasting purposes was a familiar motif in Chinese historical novels in order to heighten the drama. This is also reflected in theatrical performance, such as Peking opera, where the main actor is always matched with a supporting actor who plays an antithetical and often debased role in order to bolster the leading character. Pairing Liu Bowen with Yao Guangxiao was one such example, but why choose Yao Guangxiao? There are historical reasons besides fictional and theatrical orchestration.

Historically, Yao was the former Monk Daoyuan, a versatile and learned man adept in the classics, philosophy, belle-lettres, astral-geography, and military science. He gained access to Zhu Di in his late forties as a monk-in-attendance at the Yan fief and won the confidence of the Prince who was plotting to unseat the Jianwen emperor. As trusted adviser, Daoyuan allegedly cajoled the Prince and devised the stratagem in the campaign against the emperor, playing a leading role in the eventual usurpation. After the Prince was enthroned as the Yongle emperor in 1402 he appointed Daoyan head of the central Buddhist registry, and two years later elevated him to the rank of junior preceptor to the heir apparent. He was then restored to his lay surname, granted the personal name Guangxiao, and from then on was known as Yao Guangxiao. The emperor also awarded him a residence and two female attendants, but he declined. He stayed in his old abode, the Qingshou monastery, wore his Buddhist habit, and donned his official robe only when he attended an audience (Figure 35).

In 1404 Yao was ordered to assist in the compilation and revision of the thesaurus, *Wenxian dacheng* 文獻大成 (Complete Collection of Literature). When completed in late 1407 it was renamed *Yongle dadian* 永樂大典 (Great Literary Repository of the Yongle Reign), and consisted of 22,937 *juan*. In November 1411 he was entrusted by the emperor with the supervision of the second revision of his father's reign records, the *Taizu shilu* 太祖實錄 (Veritable Records of Taizu), which was completed in June 1418, in 257 *juan*. Yao, however, died a month earlier, at the age of eighty-three. He was ennobled as the Duke of Rongguo 榮國 and given the posthumous name Gongjing 恭靖 (Reverent and Tranquil). The emperor granted him a state funeral according to Buddhist rites and personally wrote a tomb inscription in his memory. The stele was erected at Yao's grave in Fangshan county outside Peking in 1426. A month later, Yao's name tablet was placed in the Ancestral Temple along with the image of three other meritorious officials in the emperor's service. Late in 1530 Yao's tablet was moved to his former residence, then known as

Figure 35 Portrait/Statue of Monk Daoyuan (Yao Guangxiao)

Source: (Right) Portrait, *Palace Museum Weekly*, No. 102 (September 19 1931); (Left) Statue, Tang, *Jiudu wenwulue, Mingji lue*, p. 9.

Da Xinglongsi 大興隆寺, but after the monastery was destroyed by fire in 1535 it was removed to the Da Longshan Huguosi 大隆善護國寺, which survived until 1957. Yao Guangxiao was the author of three short Buddhist treatises, including the famed *Daoyu lu* 道餘錄, a treatise refuting the Neo-Confucian arguments against Buddhism by the Song masters Zhu Xi and the Cheng brothers. He also left a collection of poems, *Taoxuzi shiji* 逃虛子詩集, in 10+1 *juan*, and a collection of essays, *Taoxu leigao* 逃虛類稿, 5+1 *juan*, both of which are rare although Qing manuscript copies are available.[94]

Yao was often compared to Liu Ji because they were both eminent imperial advisers and erudite scholars although they served different emperors. It is also possible that he was given a role in the Liu Bowen/Nezha City legend because of his emulation of Liu Bingzhong, Qubilai's eminent adviser, who was the pivotal figure in the original legend. But public opinion was strongly hostile to Yao Guangxiao for siding with the usurper who dethroned the legitimate emperor, and also for his virulent attack on Neo-Confucianism in defense of Buddhism. This negative attitude was reflected in pejorative comments and unfavorable accounts about him in historical as well as fictional miscellanies. The deprecation of Yao Guangxiao in order to bolster Liu Ji's stature in the Peking folktale underscored some of these historical realities in factitious form (see Chapter 4).[95]

Nonetheless Yao Guangxiao also had never been involved in the building of Peking, so why was he presented in the story alongside Liu Ji? Fanciful imagination aside, the pairing of Liu and Yao had a precedent in a pseudo-historical episode about the building of the imperial city in Nanking reported in Lu Can's *Gengsi bian.* The work claims that when it was decided to build the palaces, Ming Taizu summoned three people: a Daoist, Liu Bowen, and the Iron-cap Daoist Zhang Zhong for consultation. It is said that without knowing what the others would do each submitted exactly the same plan, to the amazement of all, but the details are not revealed. Zhang Zhong, as noted earlier, was the celebrated Daoist prognosticator who allegedly authored the prophetic ballad *Zhengbing ge,* which was later expropriated to become the *Shaobing ge* attributed to Liu Bowen. As the story proliferated it migrated north and mingled with the Peking story, but the trio who allegedly drew up the city plan for Nanking was reduced to just Liu Bowen and Yao Guangxiao. Here Yao replaced the Iron-cap Daoist as Liu Ji's competitor because he was historically more relevant than Zhang Zhong who, having had his place as prognosticator assumed by Liu Ji, had apparently lost his historical luster as well as his relevance to Peking.[96] The background information shows that despite its fictionality, this rejuvenated legend incorporated old historical material representing a conscientious blending and synthesis of many different sources.

Finally, a puzzling question: when did this illustrious reborn legend take shape, who were the legend makers or, more specifically, who synthesized the historical information and religious traditions and further embroidered them with additional fiction and imaginative animation to revive the old legend? Lacking documentary evidence, the clue may lie in the timing of the maturation of Liu Bowen's mythology, particularly the Mongolian legend concerning his role in the building of a city in Peking, the legend about his being an efficacious prognosticator, and above all his being a Han ethnocentric anti-Manchu prophet-savior. The reason is that whereas the old legends associated with Liu Bingzhong and those of Nezha feuding with the dragon genii perpetuated by popular novels were very familiar to the residents of Beijing, they lay dormant in the public consciousness until the rise in popularity of the Liu Bowen legends. The latter, as already noted, were largely a product of the "anti-Manchu, Ming-restoration" propaganda after the mid-eighteenth century and were intensified in the late nineteenth century with the propagation of the *Shaobing ge* prophecy book and emerging prophecies attributed to Liu Bowen predicting the demise of the Manchus. Thus the rebirth of the legend in Liu Bowen's name was evidently related to the prestige of his cultist mythology and it enjoyed wide acclaim on the wings of Liu's legends down to the contemporary period, even though the Peking legend could command appeal by its unique popular Nezha tradition without Liu Bowen.

The creators or perpetuators of this resurgent legend have remained nameless and have left no trace of their authorship. However, they must have been residents of Peking deeply immersed in Nezha's historical and religious traditions in the imperial city/ national capital, and also obsessed with the Liu Bowen legends and their implication for Peking as well as Chinese folk culture in general. Is it possible that the people who created and propagated the new Nezha City legend were inspired by those who created and propagated the political prophecies in Liu Bowen's name? Or would the latter have recycled the old legend in Liu's name in order to perpetuate his mythology and accentuate his impact? Regardless, they were all part of the cult of Liu Bowen and the connection between these two groups of propagandists is very obvious. Nevertheless, despite their fanfare, these legends and fanciful stories were not isolated incidents in Peking's popular culture; they have to be understood within the broad picture of the political, socioeconomic, and cultural setting of Peking as it was transformed from a traditional imperial city into a modern national capital.

In fact, in the aftermath of the demise of the imperial order, when Peking was groping for a new intellectual and cultural identity as the capital of the Republic or just as a cosmopolitan city of north China (when the national capital was installed in Nanking), the revival of the famous old legend in a new form and new spirit is truly significant. These Peking folklorists, including Manchu descendants and native Chinese residents, were evidently literary people familiar with the nostalgia and the longing of local people—the old and the young, men and women, the literate and illiterate—for old memories of the city, new forms of culture, for traditional drama and modern entertainment, and they disseminated the stories through various means of oral communication, particularly in popular singing and storytelling, before they were written down and transmitted in the vernacular. It is striking that there were a number of Peking folk songs bearing Liu Bowen's name and featuring various miraculous stories perpetuating his legends, including the famed story of his designing the Eight-armed Nezha City. They were chanted and popularly performed in public places in the early Republican period, but many had been lost. Undoubtedly these animated folk songs provided the inspiration and some of the sources for the emergence of fully-fledged folktales about Liu Bowen building the Nezha City of Peking, and furthered their development.[97]

However, it should be noted that the prevalence of these popularized stories and legends in Peking since the Republican period was an integral part not only of the new intellectual ferment among the older and younger generation of educated people, but also of the rise of new forms of popular culture predicated on the collapse of the dynastic order and the ensuing urban transformation in the imperial capital. In former times, the public spaces created by religious temples and outdoor altars provided the main venues for social contacts and business transactions, and served as arenas for the circulation of material and cultural products as well as for public entertainment. These were vastly expanded in the Republican period, which saw not only a blooming commercial center in the Front Gate and the business sectors along the southern inner walls, but also a flourishing market and entertainment center in the Heavenly Bridge District bordering the famous imperial altars, which significantly transformed the old urban culture with the emergence of many varied forms of material cultural and creative popular entertainment. These new public spaces thus supplemented the private quarters of the Peking residents for the dissemination and multiplication of the stories and legends about the supernatural origins of their own city and their own environment. Such legends were far more powerful at the spiritual level and in popular entertainment than were the silent, imposing, and distant imperial monuments around them.[98]

The Liu Bowen building the Nezha City story remained popular after the founding of the People's Republic in 1949 through the promotion of folklore studies in the new capital city Beijing in the wake of the Marxist-Maoist socialist revolution. The movement activated various research teams to seek new sources of folktales and facilitated publication of various collections of Peking folklore. The appearance of the complete collection of Jin Shoushen, with "The Eight-armed Nezha City" as the lead story based on his miscellaneous drafts of the bygone days, is a major contribution. Though laced with the Communist parlance stating that these stories associated with Liu Bowen presented "the oral literature created by the working masses of Peking to illustrate their collective ingenuity and the contribution of their blood-and-sweat labor", Jin's folktales of old Peking were vividly written in the local vernacular and comprised the first complete text of the new version of the stories. All later versions draw on the same material even though there were minor modifications of detail. These folktales inundated the press after the Cultural Revolution, especially over the last two decades.[99]

It is apparent that the publication of these folktales has enhanced the popularity of the Liu Bowen building the Nezha City legend and has imputed new meaning to an old tradition in a socialist state through the recycling efforts of the folklorists. In a sense, it is new wine in an old bottle. Furthermore, through the artwork of interested translators, Jin Shoushen's *Beijing Legends* are now available in translations in both Japanese and English, enlivening and substantiating the older accounts of Werner and Arlington/ Lewisohn. In the 1980s, after China embarked on its open-door reform policy, Zhang Ding 張仃, an eminent painter affiliated with the Qinghua 清華 School of Fine Arts in Beijing, produced a mural depicting Nezha feuding with the dragon genii with Beijing city in the background called "Nezha naohai" 哪吒鬧海 (Nezha Stirring up the Sea), but with Liu Bowen conspicuously absent. It was mounted inside the "foreign visitors" lounge of the Capital International Airport c. 1985 and stayed there for several years. This monumental artistic display, together with the foreign language translations of the stories, has certainly greatly facilitated the dissemination of the Nezha City legend to the international audience, although its religiosity has at times been dismissed as superstition by the atheistic governmental authorities. Nonetheless, in one form or another, the legend is persistently mentioned in scholarly and popular writings about old Peking, and it has certainly reached a larger popular audience through various media of visual and oral communications. Its popularity in folk culture remains undiminished.[100]

PART II

"Siting by Bowshot": Locating the City of Ming Peking

Chapter 3

The Mongolian Story of How Emperor Yongle Built the City of Peking

The Historical Background

As a lesser companion to the Nezha City saga, but equally riveting and with its own distinctive features, the legend dubbed as "siting by bowshot, locating the city of Ming Peking", presents yet another popular tradition in the continued mythologization of the building of the imperial capital. The gist of the story is that the location of the capital city was chosen by the flight of an arrow based on the Mongolian nomadic tradition of siting by bowshot as used to allot lands, establish property ownership, and site monuments. In its initial form the story, entitled "How Emperor Yongle of the Great Ming Built the City of Peking", was an integral part of a legend about the Mongol maternity of the Ming emperor Yongle in vogue since the seventeenth century. A review of this intriguing legend is essential to an understanding of the genesis and evolution of the Mongolian story of how the Ming emperor built the city of Peking, and its aftermath.

As an integral part of the Mongolian tradition, a belief flourished in north China since the seventeenth century claiming that the Yongle emperor Zhu Di, the Prince of Yan, was actually the posthumous son of the last Yuan emperor Toghōn Temür by his Qonggirad *qatun* (consort or princess). She was said to have been already pregnant when she was captured by Zhu Yuanzhang, the Hongwu emperor or Ming Taizu, at the fall of Dadu in September 1368. She became the latter's consort and disguised her newborn as the Chinese emperor's own son by miraculously prolonging the pregnancy. This unexpected son grew up to be a strong prince, but was sent away to Peking when the Hongwu emperor became suspicious of his paternity. The prince eventually built a city at the end of the Great Wall and settled there. When his purported adoptive father died some years later, the prince led an army and returned to Nanking. He seized the emperor—his Chinese "brother" the Jianwen emperor Zhu Yunwen, but in actual history his nephew —who had been installed there, and ascended the throne of the Ming dynasty.

Several accounts in the same vein can be dated between the seventeenth and eighteenth centuries. They include the Mongolian chronicles bLo-bzaṅ bsTan-'jin's *Altan Tobchi*; *Altan Tobchi* (brevior); Saghang-sechen's *Erdeni-yin Tobchi*; Rasipungsugh's *Bolor Erike*; *Altan kürdüun mingghan kegesütü bichiq*; and Becingge's Chinese Mongolian clan record *Menggu shixi pu* 蒙古世系譜.[1] Most of them claim that the Mongol princess was two or three (lunar) months pregnant when she met the Hongwu emperor and that her pregnancy was prolonged by about ten more months. All of this, however, is sheer fabrication. According to the official sources Zhu Di, Hongwu's fourth son, was born in the twentieth year of the Zhizheng era of Toghōn Temür, that is in 1360. The prince was therefore eight years old when his father founded the new dynasty and the last Yuan emperor fled with the remnants of his court back to Mongolia. Although the assertion that his natural mother was Empress Ma 馬 (1332–1382) was evidently faked in the official records, and he was probably born to a Mongol consort, Zhu Di's mother could not possibly have been one of the last Yuan emperor's spouses captured by the Ming armies. No member of the Mongol-Yuan court was seized by Zhu Yuanzhang's forces until the fall of Dadu.[2]

In all likelihood the claim was conjured up as a psychological consolation for the loss of Mongol supremacy in China after a century of domination. The late Reverend Antoine Mostaert and other scholars have observed that the legend probably originated among the Mongol communities around the Peking region and later was disseminated back to Mongolia. From its inception as pure hearsay it was retold and transmitted through various agents—most likely shamans and storytellers—and inspired embellishments and imaginative embroidery before being written into the chronicles. It must have provided great sentimental satisfaction to the Mongols, who could thus indulge in the belief that despite the fall of the Yuan empire, the great qans in reality still ruled China for three more centuries. The Mongol ancestry of the Ming dynasty remained a popular subject in Mongolian and Inner Asian folktales down to the early twentieth century.[3]

However, our investigation must take into account the vicissitudes encountered by the Mongol tribesmen in north China after the conquest of Dadu by Zhu Yuanzhang's forces and the flight of Toghōn Temür to Mongolia. The last Yuan emperor took only a remnant of his court and army with him, leaving behind, according to *Edeni-yin Tobchi* and *Altan Tobchi*, thirty-four of his forty *tümen* (divisions) of troops in China, which would have amounted to several hundred thousand able bodies. Under Ming Taizu's conciliatory and pragmatic policies, the Mongols were allowed to live in their pastoral communities and large groups were organized into military units under their own commanders to serve the Chinese rulers. Many Mongols were employed at the Ming court as imperial guards, eunuchs, officers in the metropolitan police forces, and emissaries to foreign countries, and even as ranking officials in the civil bureaucracy.[4]

Shortly after Zhu Di was sent in April 1380 to Peking (then known as Beipingfu) to preside over the fief of Yan—he had already been invested as the Prince of Yan for ten years—he consciously promoted relations with the Mongol commanders and their rank-and-file soldiers, and won their allegiance. With the aid of the Mongol cavalry from the Uriyangqad guards the prince seized Daning on the Great Wall northeast of Peking during his "punitive" campaign against the Jianwen court at the end of 1399. This campaign, known as *jingnan* ("to clear away disasters"), succeeded in unseating his nephew the emperor in July 1402.[5] Thus after his enthronement he extended patronage to the Mongols settling in China. The cavalry constituted a solid core of the imperial troops, and additional Mongol officers staffed his court and commanded various military guards on the northern frontiers. By this time there must have been over a quarter of a million Mongols settling in China, with probably one-third of them scattered around the Peking area. This population was further bolstered by a steady influx of Mongol tribesmen who traveled across the desert to surrender to the Chinese authorities because of the favorable treatment they received. The trend continued until the middle of the fifteenth century. The presence of such a large Mongol population around Peking and the intimate role the Mongols played in Chinese court affairs are germane to an understanding of the evolution of the Mongolian legend on the founding of Peking.[6]

The claim of the Yongle emperor's Mongol ancestry is not, however, completely devoid of historical substance. His mother was not Toghōn Temür's *qatun*, but she was probably an imperial consort from a Mongol tribe. Although such official records as the imperial chronicle *Tianhuang yudie* 天潢玉牒 ("Jade Record" of the Imperial Generation) and the reign chronicle *Taizu shilu* (Veritable Records of Taizu) and *Taizong shilu* 太宗實錄 (Veritable Records of Taizong) state that Yongle was the fourth son of Taizu born to Empress Ma, this claim has been exposed by historians as a politically motivated fiction. Yongle needed to support his pretensions to legitimate succession after the demise of the Jianwen emperor, victim of the coup d'état, who allegedly died in a fire set in the imperial palace during the fall of Nanking. Invoking the first principle in the *August Ming Ancestral Injunctions* (*Huang Ming zuxun* 皇明祖訓)—that only the eldest surviving heir by the primary consort qualified to be the imperial successor—certainly solidified his claim to legitimate succession to the dynastic founder. However, rudimentary records do exist that attest to the contrary—Yongle was most likely born to a Mongol woman from the Qonggirad tribe even though he may have been raised by Empress Ma.[7]

A primary source on the purported Mongol maternity of the Yongle emperor was the record of the Court of Imperial Sacrifices at Nanking compiled by Shen Ruolin 沈若霖, entitled *Nanjing taichangsi zhi* 南京太常寺志 (1623), which contained a roster of the spirit tablets of the Ming imperial forbears. This work is now lost, but according to late Ming scholars such as He Qiaoyuan 何喬遠 (1558–1632), Tan Qian 談遷 (1594–1658), Li Qing 李清 (1602–1683), and Zhang Dai 張岱 (1597–1679), who had access to the record, Emperor Yongle's natural mother was a consort called Gongfei (consort Gong), whose surname Gong (variants: Weng and Wang) was evidently the Chinese transcription of the first syllable of the Mongolian word Qonggirad or Khungirat. An early Qing scholar, Liu Xianting 劉獻廷 (1648–1695), claimed in his *Guangyang zaji* 廣陽雜記 that this lady Gongfei was indeed Toghōn Temür's consort. Given the large numbers of Mongols serving the Yongle emperor, and the fact that some such as eunuchs had easy access to the inner court, palace secrets like this may have leaked out into the Mongol communities and fueled legends about the Chinese emperor's descent from Toghōn Temür.[8]

Anatomy of the Folkloric Legend

An oral version of the legend about the building of Peking under the Yongle emperor was recorded by Mostaert in his *Textes oraux ordos*, a corpus of Mongolian folklore that he collected in the Ordos in southern Inner Mongolia between 1905 and 1925. It is entitled "The Yuan Prince, the True Prince". The "Yuan Prince" (Yuan Taizi 元太子, Prince of the Mongols) refers to the future Yongle emperor, thought to be the actual son of Toghōn Temür born to his Mongol *qatun*, and the "True Prince" (Zhen Taizi 真太子) refers to the Hongwu emperor's other son born to a Chinese consort.[9] A parallel written version was transcribed twice in 1907 from even older manuscripts, which Mostaert had also acquired and added to his collection. Original authorship is not indicated, but the roots of this manuscript tradition probably go back to the eighteenth or nineteenth century. Henry Serruys examined one of the copies and published an English translation in 1972. It carries a longer Mongolian title, *Dayiming yuwa lowa gaghan begejing qota-(n)i bayighulughsan üliger-un debter—Yuwa (n) tayise—Jing tayise* (Book of the Story of How Emperor Yung-lo of the Great Ming Built the City of Peking—The Yuan Prince—The True Prince). The full text is included in Appendices (2).[10] In contrast to the oral version, the main focus of this written version is laid in the story of the building of Peking under the Yuan Prince. A later manuscript containing a slightly different version of the same story was discovered in the Ordos in the 1970s, and was recently studied by a Chinese scholar Yang Haiying 楊海英, who published a romanized transcription and a Japanese translation in 2003.[11]

In a mixture of legend and history, the story highlights several facts and pieces of fiction in a Sino-Mongolian setting. It begins with the anti-Mongol Chinese uprisings on the eve of the Mid-Autumn festival in the 1360s; the Ming emperor Zhu Hongwu's capture of Dadu and Toghōn Temür's hurried departure; the pregnant Mongol *qatun*'s marriage to the Ming emperor without revealing her pregnancy; and the birth of the posthumous son the "Yuan Prince" and another son fathered by the Ming emperor named the "True Prince". Concerned about the enmity between his two sons, the Ming emperor dispatched the Yuan Prince to the area of future Peking to establish a fief. Before this, on her sick bed, the Mongol *qatun* gave the prince two letters in separate sealed envelopes with instructions that he open one in a time of suffering and the other one in a time of success. In great distress, the prince unsealed the first letter and, following the instruction, pleaded with the emperor for the service of adviser Liu Bowen. His request was granted. After arriving at the designated locality the Prince of Yan met a burly swarthy-faced black rider who took away his bow and arrows, then shot an arrow in each of the four directions, admonishing the prince to appoint Liu Bowen in charge of building the capital city in the area where the arrows had fallen and where caches of gold, silver, and jewels would be found. With the building of the great city—to be known as Peking—the prince set up his own fief in the region. But soon he learned of the death of his father in Nanking and hurried there with a company of soldiers to pay homage. At this time the "True Prince" had already ascended the throne, but upon learning of the arrival of his elder brother and remembering their earlier enmity, the prince was frightened and hanged himself. The story ends with the Yuan Prince returning to Peking where he was enthroned in succession to his late father as Emperor Yongle of the Great Ming dynasty and inaugurated a lineage of thirteen generations of successive rulers.

The following excerpts from Serruys's translation highlight the legend, beginning with the Yuan Prince's birth through his adulthood and exile to the Nankou Pass, followed by the building of the city of Peking, and finally the Prince's enthronement as the Yongle emperor of the Great Ming. Each subsection is provided with a brief introduction and is followed by analysis. (Note: The Wade-Giles spellings have been replaced by the *pinyin* system to maintain consistency, and the translation has been stylistically modified whenever necessary.)[12] In light of the extant source materials from both the Mongolian and Chinese traditions, it is possible to trace the origin of some of the episodes given in the manuscript and to distinguish fact from fiction in order to evaluate the legend's historical background and cultural implications.

The story begins when the Ming Hongwu emperor took for himself a spouse (*qatun*) of the last Yuan emperor, Toghōn Temür, unaware that she was already pregnant. The Mongol princess earnestly prayed to the "Three Jewels" deities and prolonged the pregnancy, so that when she gave birth to a boy the paternal identity was not suspected. He was given the name Yuan Prince by a soothsayer, and before long another son was born, to be called the True Prince.

I

> Thereafter—at the time that the *qatun* was living with Toghōn Temür *qaghan* she was pregnant with a child—she said, "If I give birth soon, they will certainly kill [the child]." So she prayed fervently in silence to the Three Jewels, and as a result she gave birth to a son twelve months after her marriage to Zhu Hongwu 朱洪武 (i.e. the Hongwu emperor). When [the emperor] had the boy examined by a soothsayer, [the latter] declared, "This boy's fortune is extremely auspicious; he will succeed to the government of his father and protect the people." And so he gave him the name Yuan Prince. But when the ministers said [to the emperor], "If one considers the name Yuan Prince given by the soothsayer to this boy, it means 'Prince of the Mongols,' and because he is certainly a son of the Mongol *qaghan*, you are not allowed to raise him." The emperor became angry and said threateningly, "[The rule is that] a man is born when he has been nine months in his mother's womb; since this son of mine has only been born twelve months after I met with the *qatun*, how would he be a descendant of the Mongol [*qaghan*]?" None of them found anything to answer [to this]. When another son was born the soothsayer was ordered to examine him and he said: "This boy's fortune will be worse than his elder brother's." Thus he named him True Prince. This means Prince of the Chinese. As the two boys gradually grew up there was no harmony between them and they quarreled and fought continuously. At that time the mother *qatun* became sick and at the moment of death she called the elder son, the Yuan Prince, and handed him two letters [in separate] envelopes, saying: "This is my last will. In time of success read one envelope; in time of suffering read the other envelope."[13]

It is clear the claim that the Ming Yongle emperor was the posthumous son of Toghōn Temür was derived from the prevailing Mongolian legend nurtured and transmitted in the above-mentioned seventeenth- and eighteenth-century Mongolian chronicles and other oral traditions. Most of these older versions state that the *qatun* was two or three months pregnant when she met Ming Taizu, and her pregnancy was prolonged by ten months. Although neither oral nor written versions of the present legend indicates how long she had been pregnant, both state a twelve-month prolongation, thus giving a total of fourteen months. This minor alteration buttresses the drama of the pregnancy and strengthens the impression that Ming Taizu believed he had fathered the new-born child.[14] The statement that the Mongol princess prayed fervently to the "Three Jewels" and, as a result, gave birth to a son twelve months after her marriage to the Hongwu emperor, reflects a sacred Buddhist tradition. The "Three Jewels" (*ghurban erdeni*) refers to Triratna, or the "Three Precious Ones" (*sanbao* 三寶)—Buddha, Dharma (Law), and Sangha (the monastic order). In the Mongolian context, despite unavoidable Sinitic influence, the worship of the Three Jewels apparently drew inspiration from Tibetan Lamaism and would continue to do so in the extant Mongolian chronicles.[15] In the present legend the Mongol princess' prayer obviously refers to the Lamaist tradition because of the last part of the story, in which she is said to have exhorted the *qaghan*'s son in her will that he should, when becoming great-*qaghan*, "revere the Three Jewels in the Sacred Ornament and make them an object of sacrifice". The "Sacred Ornament" here approximates the Mongolian expression *oroi-yin chimeg*, which literally is equivalent to the Chinese term *dingdai* 頂戴 or *dingli* 頂禮. It refers to anything which one reveres and treasures above anything else. Serruys erred by stating that the term was the title of the highest lama at the Yuan court.[16]

There are parallels in Chinese folklore of the story that the Ming emperor had asked a soothsayer to examine the fortune of both the boys given birth by his *qatun*. The first child was found to be extremely auspicious and was thus given the name "Yuan Prince". The second child's fortune was less auspicious than his elder brother and he was given the name "True Prince". Similar anecdotes occur about the fortune-tellers' prognostication for the Prince of Yan, later the Yongle emperor, and the imperial grandson, the Jianwen emperor. According to the tomb inscription of the prominent Ming physiognomist Yuan Gong 袁珙 (1335–1410), Yuan was once asked to identify the Prince among a line-up of army officers; he immediately singled him out, hailing him as a future "Son of Heaven in times of peace" with "the physique of a *dragon* and the gesture of a *phoenix*", and predicting that by the age of forty, when his beard had grown to reach his belly, he would ascend the throne.[17] The story about the imperial grandson, the future Jianwen emperor, was less auspicious. It is said that when he was born, noticing that he had a flat skull, the Ming emperor already presaged his ill fortune. He therefore placed a set of tonsuring tools and a black robe in a sealed container, asking that it not be opened until catastrophe struck. Thus when the imperial grandson, then emperor, was confronted by the armies of the Prince of Yan who had seized the capital city and sought refuge, he unsealed the container for advice and, following the hints, disguised himself as a Buddhist monk and eluded the pursuit of the enemy to reach safety. It appears that these miraculous stories were conjured up *post facto* by the protagonists of the Prince of Yan and the apologists of the Jianwen emperor to dramatize their contrasting fortune in the outcome of the civil war.[18]

The supposed enmity between the Yuan Prince and the True Prince in this Mongolian legend was an imaginative creation making judicious use of contemporary Chinese political history. Although most of the extant Mongolian chronicles concurred on the Mongol paternity of the Yuan Prince, they asserted that the True Prince was born to the Ming emperor's Chinese empress. In the legend discussed here, however, the Yuan prince and the True Prince are presented as half-brothers by different fathers but by the same mother. The former was the posthumous son of Toghōn Temür conceived by his *qatun*, and the latter by the same Mongol consort after she became the Hongwu emperor's empress; their genetic differences account for their disparate characters. The written version of the present legend was a bit ambiguous on this matter, but the oral version clearly stated that the Mongol empress gave birth to another son, who came to be known as the True Prince.[19] However, in actual history it was very different. The future Yongle emperor Zhu Di, known here as the Yuan Prince, was not the eldest son of Taizu but his fourth son, who was invested as the Prince of Yan in 1370. It is true that he had not been on cordial terms with his brothers (Taizu had twenty-six sons and the eldest was Zhu Biao 朱標 [born 1355], the heir-apparent who died prematurely in 1392), and the prince against whom he was pitted in his struggle for the throne was not his sibling. The archrival was his nephew, Zhu Biao's eldest son Zhu Yunwen, who was appointed the imperial grandson by Ming Taizu shortly after Zhu Biao's death and who later succeeded his grandfather to become the Jianwen emperor.[20] Thus "True Prince" evidently alludes to the Jianwen emperor, who was the eldest surviving son of Zhu Biao by his primary consort. The discord and enmity between the two princes, which had already taken the form of frequent violent attacks and quarrels in their boyhood, set the stage for the open confrontation between Zhu Di and Zhu Yunwen that occurred upon Taizu's death. The *jingnan* campaign that the Prince of Yan initiated in August 1399 against his nephew was intended "to clear away disasters" and after three years of bitter civil war the prince succeeded in seizing the throne in July 1402. The legend thus made intelligent use of the most dramatic and violent political feud among members of the imperial family in the early part of the Ming dynasty. The historical premise continued to develop the legend of Yongle's Mongol ancestry and related it to the popular tradition about the building of Peking.[21]

Further along in the tale the Hongwu emperor has an ominous dream and learns that the Yuan Prince is in fact the son of the Mongol qaghan.

II

> Thereafter, Emperor Zhu Hongwu one night [as he was] asleep, [saw] in a dream one black striped snake and one yellow striped snake violently attack each other and come to rest on the emperor's two knees. The black striped snake on the right side attacked the yellow striped snake on the left side who fainted and was hardly [able to] rise and stagger back. Having had such a dream, he woke up and became suspicious, as he called in the soothsayer to have him examine [the omen]. [The soothsayer] immediately thought, "The emperor will evidently know." [Then] both the Yuan Prince and the True Prince, quarrelling and attacking each other, came before the emperor—the Yuan Prince, resting [on the emperor's] right knee, and the True Prince, resting on his left knee. The two pleaded the cause of their quarrel and walked out. The Emperor, very suspicious, called his many ministers together and when he told them the dream and the fact that the two sons had come to quarrel, the ministers declared, "If the elder and the younger brothers were

> certainly sons of one father, there would be no reason [for them] to be in discord; if one considers the name given by the soothsayer and the fact that he is not at peace now with the True Prince, one can be sure of the fact that the Yuan Prince is the son of the Mongol qaghan, and one must decide how to do away with him!" Thereupon the emperor said: "Ever since his childhood I have loved and cherished this boy as my own son; in addition to this [I want to consult with you] on the means to remove him without doing him any harm". As he was thus deliberating, the ministers said: "Tell him to occupy and hold the defile of Nankou, the pass through which comes our enemy, the Mongols. Give the Yuan Prince a thousand soldiers and send him [there].[22]

The episode of the ominous snakes is not unique. It appeared in earlier sources. In both versions of the *Altan Tobchi*, for example, the emperor had a dream in which two dragons fought, the eastern dragon beating the western one. The soothsayer who was asked to interpret the omen declared that the loser was his son by the Chinese empress and the winner was his son by the Mongol princess. This is most likely the source of the emperor's dream. However, according to Jagchid Sechin the concept of the dragon as the symbol of the *qaghan* (emperor) did not exist among the Mongols and such belief must have been the result of Sinitic influence.[23] In fact there are similar episodes in Chinese sources. In a sixteenth-century miscellany on the dethroned Jianwen emperor, the *Gechu yishi* 革除遺事 by Huang Zuo 黃佐 (1490–1566), Ming Taizu is said to have had a dream, seeing two dragons feuding with each other in the inner palace. The winner was the yellow dragon and the loser was the white dragon. When he awoke he saw his grandson playing with the Prince of Yan; the grandson was dressed in white, thus he realized that the latter must be the loser in a fight against his uncle. In yet another contemporaneous literary collection called *Suiyan* 隨言, compiled by the prefect of Suizhou 隨州, Huguang, the Ming emperor is said to have once had a similar dream in which he saw two dragons crawling in front of the court. One was aroused and snarled, while the other recoiled and lowered its head. When he awoke he found his eldest son Zhu Biao and his fourth son Zhu Di playing together. Such stories of the Ming emperor's dream prognosticating the triumph of the Prince of Yan over the Jianwen emperor must have spurred popular imagination in the making of the Mongolian legend.[24]

In contrast, the story that Ming Taizu, after learning the Yuan

Prince's identity, followed the advice of his ministers and sent him to Nankou was concocted from legends that are rooted in history. Zhu Di was in fact sent to Beipingfu by his father and was enfeoffed there as the Prince of Yan in 1370 (but for ten years did not reside there). However, this was to guard against possible Mongol intrusions, not exile for having offended the emperor. The notion of the prince's "exile" apparently came from Mongolian sources. In several Mongolian chronicles the future Yongle emperor is said to have founded Köke Qota, the "Blue City" "outside the Wall", after having been sent there by his father. The precedent for this was Toghōn Temür's building of Bars Qota, the "Tiger City", on the Kerülen River after fleeing from Dadu when the Yuan fell. Later Yongle returned with his Mongol armies to capture the empire from his "younger brother"—a reference to the *jingnan* campaign. In this portrayal the Yuan Prince's departure to the north has the character of an exile and it probably inspired the legend presented here, which makes it banishment to Nankou, the famous pass north of Peking.

One further point—Serruys suggested that the "Blue City" allegedly founded by the Yongle emperor may also be a projection into the past of the Blue City built by Altan-qan of the Temud, and named Guihua cheng 歸化城 (literally "Return-to-civilization City") in 1575. If true then this element in the Mongolian chronicles is of a rather late date.[25]

III

The decision was made, and immediately the emperor called in the Yuan Prince and told him, "Since it is likely that the armies of the Mongol enemy will come through the Nankou pass, you, my son, take a thousand soldiers and hold it." As [the emperor] said this, [the Yuan Prince] received the order with a bow and left; then he thought: "Now has come my time of suffering." Opening one of the envelopes given by his mother, he read, "When you are banished to guard the Nankou defile, make Liu Bowen minister, take him along, and follow his instructions." Thereafter the Yuan Prince, presenting himself in his father's presence, bowed and said weepingly, "I, your son, upon the order of my father, the emperor, will immediately proceed to the border but do me the favor [of allowing me] Liu Bowen." The emperor, because from the beginning he had

> favored him greatly, and thinking that he was his son, weakened and gave him Liu Bowen. When the ministers picked the troop, they gave him 1,000 crippled and old soldiers, with 1,000 worn cuirasses and weapons, and 1,000 emaciated and exhausted horses. [They] made him set out from the city of Nanking, but beforehand they had ordered the boats of the Yellow River to be gathered up.[26]

The source of this episode about the Yuan Prince's opening his late mother's "sealed envelope" and the subsequent request for the service of Liu Bowen is derived from the Chinese popular tradition that mythologized this imperial adviser. In the written version of our story, the Mongolian word for "envelope" is *qabtargh-a bichig*, literally meaning "container-letter". According to Serruys it comes from the Turkic word *gap*, or *xap*, the "pouch, bag" that Mongols hung on their belt for carrying articles or messages.[27] However, the episode of the hidden message in the "sealed envelopes", one to be opened in times of "suffering" and the other in times of "happiness", is clearly inspired by the Chinese popular lore about Liu Bowen's "sealed packet" (*jinnang*, literally "embroidered purse"). It was a familiar *topos* in Ming and Qing popular stories: an enlightened elder leaves a cryptic message in a *jinnang* to the uninitiated with instructions for handling an unexpected situation, but asking that these not be revealed prematurely.

In several late-Ming semi-historical miscellanies Liu Bowen, who had been mythologized as an efficacious prognosticator, is claimed to have left, at the injunction of Ming Taizu, a mysterious message in a sealed container to the future Jianwen Emperor that saved his life from the armies of the Prince of Yan upon the fall of the capital Nanking at the end of the *jingnan* campaign. The story has the similar contents as those cited earlier about the Ming emperor who, having seen the inauspicious skull of his imperial grandson upon his birth and fearing for his misfortune, placed a set of tonsuring tools and a black robe in a sealed container, asking that it not be opened until catastrophe struck. In so doing Ming Taizu appeared to have acted on his own instincts, but in the present context Liu Bowen was inserted into the story, becoming the one who gave such prescient advice to the emperor. After the Yan armies had overrun the capital the Jianwen emperor, heeding Liu's advice, unsealed the container and found the tools. Thus he disguised himself as a Buddhist monk and escaped through an underground tunnel to safety. There are also other stories about Liu Bowen leaving behind accurate prognostications of several catastrophic political events in "sealed packets" through the end of the Ming. Furthermore, as well as the prophecy book *Shaobing* ge ascribed to Liu Bowen, we find among the surviving documents of the late Qing secret anti-Manchu Heaven and Earth Society frequent references to Liu's bestowing a *jinnang* on the faithful with messages presaging the political upheavals of the dynasty and strategies for exterminating the Manchus. The "sealed envelopes" episode was therefore a skillful adaptation of contemporary Chinese popular tradition surrounding this legend-encrusted icon.[28]

Without question, the introduction of Liu Bowen into the story provides the most important catalyst so far. From the historical standpoint the presence of Liu Bowen as minister of the Yuan Prince was anachronistic, since Liu Ji had already passed away in the early years of Ming Taizu's reign. This new plot was evidently inspired by the historical precedent in which the future Yongle emperor was assigned the Buddhist monk Daoyuan by his father to be his adviser when he was the Prince of Yan. The monk, later known by his bestowed name as Yao Guangxiao, was a crafty adviser and sagacious tactician who had made an important contribution to the prince's imperial pretension.[29] In this altered setting, the legend makers put Liu Bowen in Yao Guangxiao's place and added fanciful details. There were good reasons for the addition of this ingenious twist to the story. Liu Bowen, the most celebrated legendary figure of the early Ming, still enjoyed unsurpassed popularity in later times. He was also renowned for his role in planning the new capital at Yingtian (Nanking), thus generating enthralling stories about the building of the city. Though legends also swirled around Yao Guangxiao, he was generally considered by historians to be inferior to Liu Bowen in ability and status. Moreover, in the popular imagination, his role in the Yongle emperor's usurpation cast him as a villain. In the above episode the legend makers adroitly put the suggestion to appoint Liu Bowen in the mouth of the Yuan Prince's Mongol mother. Consequently Liu Bowen's stature in the Mongolian perception grew and also, most importantly, it facilitated the incorporation of many bizarre stories about him into Mongolian contexts to substantiate this legend.

IV

> As they gradually progressed and supplies and silver came close to being exhausted, pigeons numerous beyond count, [which had followed them] at the time they left the city of Nanking, were covering the sun. [Every time] the Yuan Prince shot and killed one of them, it turned into a silver ingot. With those many pigeons flying and following, [the army] proceeded and when it came near the city of Jiu-jiu (unidentified), the pigeons failed to appear. The Yuan Prince and his following arrived at the road to Nankou and temporarily halted. One day, taking his bow, the Yuan Prince rode out alone. As he was going [around] searching in the neighborhood of the city of Jiu-jiu, where the pigeons had stopped following, all of a sudden he met a man with an extraordinary bearing, with a swarthy face, dressed in a black robe and riding a black horse. He said [to the Yuan Prince], "Son, give [me] your bow and arrows", and shot one arrow each into the four directions. He said, "There is an abundant treasure of gold, silver, and jewels in the spots hit by the arrows; also give this red spear of mine to Liu Bowen; should silver [come to be] wanting, [then] if he sticks this spear into the earth, underneath at a depth of an elbow, a variety of jewels will come out. Make Liu Bowen head minister and at this place found such a great city with four corners after the number of the four seasons; with nine gates in the exterior city [wall] after the number of planets; with eight gates in the interior double city [wall] after the number of the "diagrams;" with twelve large streets, after the number of the year (rather a reference to the months?); with 360 lanes (*qutung*), after the number of the days; with twenty-seven (or twenty-eight) great tribunals (*yeke yamu*), after the number of the (zodiacal) constellations. In a golden palace in the middle of the city set up a throne of jade [adorned] with nine interlaced dragons, and sitting down on it become Emperor yourself!" With this order [the old man] gave [the Yuan Prince] a red spear and departed and was seen no more.[30]

By all counts, the most sensational part of the legend about the building of Peking lies in the story of the Yuan Prince's encounter with the mysterious swarthy-faced black rider in the barren regions of Yan. Who could this spiritual man be? In an earlier study I suggested that he might refer to the famous Dark God Zhenwu who was closely associated with the future Yongle emperor and Ming Peking. The Dark God, originally known as Xuanwu, emerged as the guardian of the north in a Daoist tradition of Han times, but the name was changed to Zhenwu in the Song (1012) to avoid the tabooed name of the dynastic founder's legendary ancestor Zhao Xuanlang 趙玄朗. The deity was worshiped for the protection he provided against external aggression. He was elevated in 1304 to the status of High Lord of the Dark Heaven by the Yuan emperor Temür, and was also patronized by the Ming emperors. In his traditional image in Song literature and religious statues the Dark God is depicted with loose hair, wearing a black robe, holding a sword, and treading upon a tortoise and a snake. Yongle had claimed that the Dark God helped him in August 1399 to defeat the imperial armies outside his fief at the start of his *jingnan* campaign to seize the throne. As a result the Dark God was revered as the guardian-protector of the Forbidden City. A bronze statute of the deity was housed in the Fengtian and Qin'an Hall respectively in the palace-city. He was also honored in the Zhenwu Temple erected outside the Bei'an Gate of the imperial-city in 1415, and another temple was completed in 1418 on a grand scale in the Daoist sacred site at Mount Wudang 武當 (ancient name Taihe 太和) in northwest of modern Hubei (Figure 36).[31] He was also commonly worshiped in Shanxi and Inner Mongolia and a number

Figure 36 Bronze statues of the Dark God from Mt. Wudang's Zhenwu Temple

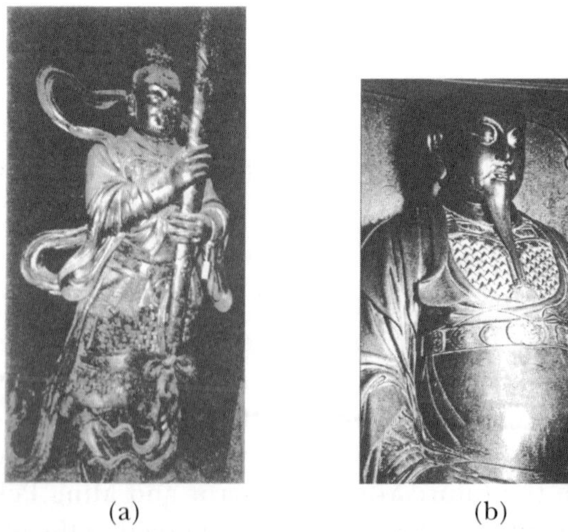

(a) (b)

Source: Wang Zilin, *Zijin cheng fengshui*, pp. 275(a), 276(b).

of temples were erected in his name in Wanquan 萬全, Xuanhua 宣化, and Datong 大同 during the Ming and Qing. In light of this historical background the identification of the black rider with the Dark God is quite credible.[32]

However, recently a Chinese scholar Zhong Han 鍾焓 has proposed that this strange spiritual man in the Mongolian legend might have evoked King Vaiśravana, the acclaimed father of Nazha in Tantric Buddhism, rather than the Dark God. The rationale is that in Mongolian religious belief, under the strong influence of Tibetan Buddhism, Vaiśravana was prominently revered not only as the Heavenly King, but also as Kubara, the god of wealth and ruler of the northern quarters in Brahmanic mythology. In Buddhist traditional hagiography King Vaiśravana appeared as a swarthy-faced, angry looking armor-clad deity, holding a forked halberd or spear in his hand. In Tibetan Buddhist images, he was moreover seen as riding a lion or a black or white horse. As Kubara he was often depicted in the same ferocious looking profile, donning armor and headgear and holding a red spear but was riding a black horse with white hoofs (Figure 37). In these considerations, King Vaiśravana could very well inspire the creation of the mysterious black rider in the Mongolian legend.[33]

This argument is quite sound if it is placed in an isolated context, but Vaiśravana's adventurous deeds bear little relevance to the historical exploits of the Prince of Yan, his seizure of the throne, and the building of Peking after his enthronement as the Yongle emperor. It seems therefore that the Dark God Zhenwu, who had been deified by the Yuan emperor Temür and who was closely related to the Prince of Yan in legends and became a superior deity of worship in Peking, in north China and Inner Mongolia, would supply a more fitting model for the folkloric creation in the Mongolian legend. But King Vaiśravana, given his strong presence in Mongolian and Tibetan Buddhist legends and the similarity of his profile with that of the black rider, should not be lightly dismissed. A fusion of the images of both the Dark God and King Vaiśravana might have provided the inspiration for the riveting Mongolian legend.

Leaving aside the question of the identify of the black rider, his instructions about the building of the imperial capital evidently derived from a specific Mongolian tradition with historical roots: the custom adopted by the great qan for allotting land to meritorious

Figure 37 Statuettes of Vaiśravana as Kubara, God of Wealth

Source: Getty, *The Gods of Northern Buddhism,* Plate XLVIII.

clansmen. There is a vivid account of this procedure in the *Yuanshi* biography of Chinqai (Zhenhai 鎮海). When Chinggis Qan decided to distribute the land around the Jin capital of Yanjing, after it fell into Mongol hands in May 1215, as a reward to his favorite lieutenant, he asked Chinqai to stand in the center of the rectangular city and shoot an arrow toward each of the four corners, and all the fields, ponds, and houses within the perimeter of the fallen arrows would be awarded to him.

It is also reported that when Qubilai Qaghan decided to build the Da Shengshou Wan'ansi 大聖壽萬安寺 (Great Wan'an Monastery for the Emperor's Birthday) in Dadu in 1271, he stood atop the White Pagoda which was the epicenter of the monastery and shot an arrow in each direction to determine the perimeter. It was completed in 1288 and has been measured as 160,000 square meters (or 0.16 sq. km.) based on the direction and flight of the arrow. According to Mongolian custom, arrows were used to signify ownership or occupation of property , and the flight of a bowshot was also a conceptualized unit of measurement for distance.[34] It should be noted that not just the strange black rider's building design but also his instructions to dig where the arrow had fallen in order to unearth treasures attests to yet another Mongolian custom—that of burying booty in large underground pits, a practice shared by other northern tribal peoples. These indigenous nomadic customs apparently inspired the development of the legend. It ran parallel to, but did not necessarily draw on, as Zhong Han suggests, the modern Chinese legend of the living god of wealth Shen Wansan who allegedly turned over his treasure horde to finance the building of Peking under duress (see later).[35]

A similar and important connection exists regarding the city plan. Not only does it reveal Mongolian astral-cosmological concepts, but also the way those concepts adapted Chinese cosmological tradition in relation to city planning. The Mongols, like the Chinese, were ardent believers in the supreme authority of the cosmos and the intimate relationship between the natural order and human affairs. Thus their design of the layout of the imperial capital, the residence of the Son of Heaven and symbolic domain of Heaven's authority, conformed to the arrangements of the celestial order as conceptualized by the Mongols. That is evidently why the black rider's plan called for the building of a great city "with four corners, after the number of the seasons; with nine gates in the exterior city [wall], after the number of planets; with eight gates in the interior double city [wall], after the number of the 'diagrams'; with twelve large streets, after the number of the months; with 360 lanes (*qutung*, that is, *hutong*), after the number of the days; with twenty-seven (or twenty-eight) great tribunals (*yeke yamu*), after the number of the (zodiacal) constellations." This is a rare Mongolian document of idealized city planning, and it reveals distinctive Sinitic influence.

The city plan goes beyond the ideal. By and large it reflects the actual layout of Yongle's eventual city of Peking as corroborated by Chinese sources. The stated number of gates (nine and eight) in both the exterior city wall and the interior city double-wall (that is, the Forbidden City) matches exactly those built in Yongle's time.[36] In our legend, however, such arrangements are couched in a mystical explanation drawn on Chinese as well as Tibetan sources. The nine gates in the exterior city wall, said to correspond to the number of planets, allude to the Tibetan planet system rather than the Chinese, which, since the Tang period, had a seven-planet system. The reference to the number of the "diagrams" (that is, trigrams, known as *gua* in Chinese) is evidence of Mongolian knowledge of the Chinese cosmological concepts elucidated in the *Book of Changes.*[37] The *Yijing* had a profound impact on city planning in imperial times. In the Mongol-Yuan era, for instance, when Liu Bingzhong designed and built the city of Kaiping (Shangdu) in 1256–1259, he placed two Buddhist monasteries respectively in the *qian* (northwestern) and *gen* (northeastern) cardinal points of the rectangular city according to the circular sequence of the "Diagram of the Posterior Heavens" in the *Book of Changes.* Again, in his design of Dadu as shown earlier, Liu assigned the Ancestral Temple to the *zhen* (eastern) cardinal point and the Celestial Master Palace to the *gen* cardinal point.[38]

The number of streets and lanes in the plan is apparently idealized, since there were far more than "twelve streets" and "360 *qutung*" as the Ming and Qing developed the city of Peking. While the designing of the twelve large streets, said to correspond to the number of the months requires no explanation, that of the 360 lanes, said to correspond to the number of days, attests to Tibetan influence. The Tibetans, besides following the Chinese tradition of calculating 365 days in a year, had also adopted a 360-day system, a practice that they imported from India in the eleventh century. The other proposal, that of designing twenty-seven (twenty-eight in the oral version of the legend) great tribunals (*yeke yamu*) after the number of zodiacal constellations, was an apparent attempt to match the twenty-eight lunar lodges (*xiu*) in ancient Chinese cosmology.[39] In a nutshell, the city plan in this legend not only reflects a conscious appeal to Mongolian ideas about the celestial order and human relationship, but also contributes to an understanding of the role of the multiple cosmological principles behind the actual building of Peking.

V

> Hearing this order, the Yuan Prince greatly rejoiced, and taking the spear he told the event to Liu Bowan. They all moved to the places where those arrows had been shot and found the four arrows. When they dug the ground underneath, they found and took countless great treasures of gold, silver, and jewels [that were] coming out [of there]. Recognizing among the thousand soldiers five men who were proficient in the principles of craftsmanship, he made them ministers. Through [the activities of] those jewelers, he assembled the many under his power; with Liu Bowen showing and instructing, [they started to] build [the city]. Before long they completed the construction of one great city having nine gates according to what the man on the black horse had said. Then [Liu] made the Yuan Prince "Little Emperor" and made him sit on the jade throne with nine interlaced dragons in the golden palace, and he called the city Peking. With the treasures of various jewels that had come out of the ground where the red spear had been fixed, Liu Bowen filled the emperor's treasury. Because exceedingly great favors and rewards were being given to many poor people, all the people of the four quarters loyally followed [the Little Emperor].[40]

In light of the Mongolian-inspired fiction about the origin of Peking it is not surprising that these details concerning its construction under Liu Bowen's supervision are largely imaginative. Nevertheless some of the fanciful descriptions conjured up by the legend-makers were either allusions to historical events or reflections of verifiable situations. In these cases, since historically Liu Bowen was not involved in the building of Peking, any valid historical references from which the legend could draw could be only those of the building of the imperial capital at Nanking, and later that of

Peking under the Yongle emperor. Such references illustrate the synthesis of legendary and historical materials, and the following analysis might shed important light on the interplay of fact and fiction.

First of all, no records indicate the discovery of, or search for, hidden underground treasures used in building the capital during Yongle's reign. However, this element of the story may allude to the historical fact that in the construction of Peking many wealthy families were either asked to make contributions of cash and provisions, or were forced to emigrate there to strengthen the new capital. Records show, for instance, that between 1402 and 1405, after the decision was made to build the capital city, orders were given to transfer to the Peking region ten thousand civilian households from Shanxi, an unknown number of wealthy families from ten commanderies including Zhili (i.e. Nanking) and Suzhou, and households from nine provincial administration commissions in Zhejiang and other provinces to the Peking region. Their contribution of wealth and culture must have been very substantial.[41]

In this context, popular stories about the building of Nanking under Ming Taizu that must have come northward with these households transferred from the southeast may have also provided inspiration for the development of the Peking legend. The most famous of these concerned Shen Fu, alias Shen Wansan, an extraordinarily affluent landlord and merchant from Suzhou who is enveloped in bizarre legend. He is said to have both accumulated a fortune in gold, silver, and jewels through magical and unscrupulous means and to have made various contributions to the emperor, including funds for one-third of the cost for building the city of Nanking. It is not surprising, as elaborated in Chapter 4, that several modern Beijing folktales, enlivened by the Suzhou elements, portray Shen Wansan as a wealthy man in a pauper's disguise who was harassed by government officials to reveal his hidden treasures for the construction of the imperial capital.

Second, although the legend makers deliberately tried to exaggerate the role of Liu Bowen and his work force, many of the claims in the story are not supported by evidence. There is no factual basis for the assertion that five men out of the 1,000 soldiers engaged in the construction were chosen by Liu Bowen for their proficiency in craftsmanship and made ministers. It seems possible that this alludes to those officials and soldiers who were rewarded for their merits with promotion in rank and gifts after the completion of the city.[42]

Finally, the claim that after the completion of Peking Liu Bowen made the Yuan Prince "Little Emperor" and put him on the jade throne decorated with interlaced dragons is pure fantasy. Serruys noted that the form of address accorded to Yongle—Little Emperor—was a logical title since according to the story his adoptive father, the Hongwu emperor, still reigned in Nanking at that time. Nevertheless it must be perceived as a slight to the Chinese imperial tradition since only the Son of Heaven could be addressed as emperor and the dragon throne was reserved exclusively for the august monarch. But the implication is clear once we see that in the original version of the story "Little Emperor" reads "*bagh-a gaghan*", which includes the title *gaghan*, a Mongol supreme ruler descended from the great Chinggis Qan.[43] In this context the legend made the Yuan Prince, and by implication the future Yongle emperor, a predestined Mongol *qaghan* whose claim went beyond China and the title of Emperor of the Ming dynasty. The building of Peking under Liu Bowen's supervision thus presaged the restoration of Mongol rule under Toghōn Temür's own blood, albeit in Chinese disguise!

VI

At that time, when the Hongwu emperor died in the city of Nanking, the Yuan Prince, in the company of his many ministers and the 1,000 soldiers, went to the city of Nanking to view and honor the remains of his father. But even before that, the younger brother, the True Prince, had mounted his father's throne. But now hearing that his elder brother, the Yuan Prince, was arriving with soldiers, [he did not] understand the situation; he remembered their former enmity and said, "For sure he has come to kill me and take away the government." Reduced to this extremity, he hung himself and died. When the Yuan Prince arrived at the city of Nanking, in great mourning he performed the ceremonies and offered sacrifices at the tomb of his father the emperor. Thereupon he intended to meet with his younger brother, the True Prince. He inquired [about him], and his ministers told him the circumstances of his death; he wept very bitterly, and said, "Now that my younger brother has died, there is

> no more use!" . . . Thereafter he selected and appointed a governor to the city of Nanking with orders to administer it, and thereafter he came back and entered by the south gate of the city of Peking. Selecting an auspicious day, he became Great Emperor, taking the name of Emperor Yongle of the Great Ming. He ruled over the thirteen great provinces of the Chinese and inaugurated the government of the country of the Great Ming. . . . Thereafter Emperor Yongle was ruling over the great government and in his absolute prosperity he opened one [that is, the other] letter left him by his mother and read it. Its contents were: "You, son, are really the offspring of Toghōn Temür qaghan of the Mongols: as a result of my very devout prayer to the Three Jewels, you were born after being in my womb for twelve months, [and so] you were able to stay alive and become a man; later when you become great-qaghan, remember your ancestry, act with due concern for the Mongols, and revering the Three Jewels in the Supreme Ornament make them an object of sacrifice."[44]

As a conclusion to the career of the Yuan Prince in exile in Nankou and the building of the city of Peking, the last episode of the legend relates the circumstances under which the Prince ascended the throne of the Great Ming dynasty. The narrative is set against the background of the *jingnan* campaign initiated by the Prince of Yan against his nephew the Jianwen emperor, which led to the former's triumphant capture of Nanking. Here the story begins with the death of the Hongwu emperor and the accession of the Jianwen emperor, and concludes with the enthronement of the prince after the suicide of the emperor. Since the aim of the story is to enhance Yongle's Mongolian affinities and his legacy to the Mongol communities, the bulk of the description is concocted in the best light possible. For this reason, historical events not favorable to the prince were discarded or significantly altered; the account is, in its own way, as skewed as the official records on the *jingnan* episode compiled by the Yongle emperor's court historians.[45]

According to accepted reconstructions of Taizu's death at Nanking by modern historians, the new emperor, Zhu Yunwen, faithfully executed the will of his grandfather by imploring the princes to observe mourning in their own fiefdoms and forbidding the officials to leave their garrison posts for the imperial capital. The Prince of Yan defied the injunction and arrived in Nanking from Beipingfu with a military contingent with the announced purpose of observing mourning. He was intercepted at the outskirts of the capital and was told he could enter with only a few of his attendants. The prince spurned the precondition and so departed, against his wishes. However, in the Mongolian manuscript version of the legend the prince is said to have both entered the capital with an army without incident and proceeded immediately to view and honor the remains of his late father. The Jianwen emperor is disguised in the person of the True Prince, who had ascended the throne immediately after his father's death. When he heard of the Yuan Prince's coming he was so apprehensive about their former enmity that he hanged himself. This narrative merely reworks the historical material to dramatize the fortunes of the Yuan Prince. It omits any references to the subsequent "punitive campaign" launched by the Prince of Yan against the Jianwen emperor and instead harks back to the earlier story of the discord between the two princes to explain why the emperor was so worried about the Yuan Prince as to take his own life.

It is pure fiction that the Jianwen emperor, apprehensive of the Prince of Yan's arrival in Nanking, "hanged himself". In fact according to official records, he apparently died in a fire set in the imperial palace at the fall of the capital in July 1402; unless, as Chinese popular legends have it, he escaped in the disguise of a monk and lived out his natural years. The emperor's alleged death by hanging could have been extrapolated for dramatization from the tragedy of the last Ming emperor Chongzhen (Sizong), who hanged himself at Coal Hill (renamed Scenic Hill) in the palace-city after the roaming bandits of Li Zicheng stormed into Peking in April 1644.[46] It is also not accurate, as the Mongolian legend asserts, that after the Prince of Yan had appointed a governor to administer Nanking, he returned to Peking and installed himself as the Great Emperor of the Ming dynasty. In reality, after the successful coup d'état, the Prince ascended the throne in Nanking in July 1402, buried the Jianwen emperor, proclaimed the era of Yongle starting the following year, changed the name of his fief from Beiping to Peking, making it the capital in January 1403, and instructed his eldest son Zhu Gaozhi (later Emperor Renzong) to proceed to the Northern Capital in February 1404, appointing him as heir-apparent in May. The Prince, now emperor, did not return to Peking until March 1409, almost seven years after the successful insurrection.[47]

Interestingly, while the legend makers avoided any allusion to the Prince of Yan's violent campaign to unseat the Jianwen emperor in order to give him an honorable name in history, the story concludes with a reference to the other "sealed envelope" from the prince's Mongol mother. Earlier, the prince had opened one envelope marked for the occasion of "suffering", through which he got the advice to employ Liu Bowen as minister. Having ascended the throne he unsealed the other envelope reserved for the occasion of "happiness". The message in it revealed that he was in fact the son of Toghōn Temür and admonished him "to remember [his] ancestry, act with due concern for the Mongols, and [by] revering the Three Jewels in the Supreme Ornament make them an object of sacrifice" when he becomes the great qaghan. The worship of the Three Jewels in the Sacred Ornament, which attests to Mongolian veneration of Tibetan Lamaism, here underscores a special relationship between two ethnically close peoples. The story thus has a dramatic happy ending, one which was obviously intended to strengthen the stature of the Mongols, if not also to exhort the rulers of China to be generous to their antagonists. Ironically, however, the historical Yongle emperor became known for his ruthless campaigns against the Mongol tribes on the northern frontiers during his reign.[48]

Seen in this light, this Mongolian legend about the building of the city of Peking under the Yongle emperor presents a vivid case of multifaceted adaptation of Han Chinese folkloristic traditions that had significant political and cultural implications. It is futile to attempt to establish any dates for the legend's formation, but it could not have taken shape earlier than the seventeenth-century legend of Yongle's Mongol father Toghōn Temür, which was accentuated by the growing Chinese suspicion since the previous dynasty about their ancestor's Mongol maternity. Most probably oral communications played a great role in transmitting the story through various popular agents at different stages, with both embellishments and substance added during the eighteenth and nineteenth centuries. The dates of the first written version of the legend also cannot be determined, but it is certain that a long period of evolution preceded the appearance of the manuscript texts in the late nineteenth century.

Leaving dates aside, the legend is a conspicuous ethnocentric expression of Mongol supremacy in political as well as cultural contributions. To be sure, the outstanding folk hero was a Chinese, the eminent imperial adviser Liu Bowen, not a Mongol. However, the story is clearly Mongol-centered because it was Toghōn Temür's spouse, the purported mother of the future Yongle emperor, who left in her will instructions to the prince to employ Liu Bowen as minister. Moreover, although the mysterious swarthy-faced black rider who gave a plan to the prince for building Peking under Liu Bowen's supervision was adapted from the legends of probably both the Dark God and King Vaiśravana, his type was also that of a spiritual elder with extraordinary wisdom and supernatural powers in the Mongolian folk tradition. In this way Chinese legendary material was judiciously exploited to buttress the superior role of the Mongol people in the building of a majestic city that was generally assumed to have been exclusively a Chinese achievement.

Impact on the Nezha Cheng Legend

The legend presented here not only vividly captured the imagination of the Mongol communities in north China, it also left a significant impact on the Chinese popular tradition about the building of Peking. We have already noted that in modern times the legend of Liu Bingzhong's invoking the Nazha deity in the building of Dadu has been recast into Liu Bowen's designing the Nezha City of Peking. The source is in the late Yuan, but it appears that many of the miraculous details attributed to Liu Bowen (namely his contest with Yao Guangxiao) were later accretions, occurring perhaps as late as the nineteenth century.[49] Although many details of the old and new Nazha/Nezha City legends have already been made available it is valuable to reexamine the linkage between the two popular traditions to further our understanding of how this riveting legend was transformed from one generation to the next in light of the present Mongolian legend.

We do not need to review the enduring popularity of Nezha in Peking. His stature as a guardian-protector of capital cities and exorcist of the dragon genii remained steadfast, but Liu Ji's emergence as the new hero in the legend is a product of changed circumstances. On the one hand, with the decline of Dadu after the fall of the Mongol regime, the legendary Liu Bingzhong as a Yuan dynasty hero became less attractive to the Chinese, who were now ruled by their own native dynasty. On the other hand, as the imperial city Peking was being built, many of the old legends about the region, especially stories of Nazha's exorcizing the dragon family to relieve the inhabitants from water shortages, were revitalized. In these situations a new hero in tune with the time was needed.

By all counts, the choice of Liu Bowen was most appropriate. First, Liu had been an outstanding imperial adviser and versatile scholar under Ming Taizu and began to be mythologized as a Chinese national hero with supernatural capabilities since the late Ming. Second, historically Liu Bowen was the principal planner of the imperial capital in Nanking and its Forbidden City was later replicated in Peking, thus making him conceptually easy to relate to the building of the new capital under the Yongle emperor. Third, in the course of mythologization he became confused as Liu Bingzhong's grandson, and this mistaken identity greatly facilitated the commingling of their legends. To sum up, Liu Bowen possessed unique qualifications for replacing Liu Bingzhong as the new hero in the transformation of the legend. However, what cemented that connection, it seems, is the Mongolian legend that we have examined. Though making no mention of Nezha, the Chinese version of the legend re-establishes the concrete relationship between Liu Bowen and the Yongle emperor, which is the nexus of the legend of the building of Peking.[50]

This connection, already suggested in Chapter 2, is clearly revealed in a crude version of the contemporary Chinese legend recorded by E. T. C. Werner under the title "Legend of the Building of Peking" in his *Myths and Legends of China* cited earlier.[51] It adapts many of the Mongolian folkloristic elements of the earlier tradition by supplying new twists and plots. Yet there are important differences. No mention is made of the Mongolian ethnicity of the Prince of Yan's mother. All we read is that "One of the consorts of Hung Wu [Hongwu], the Lady Weng, had a son named Chu-ti [Zhu Di]." Nor is there mention of her fear of a threat from Taizu's other son by his Chinese empress. Yongle's mother is given merely as "Lady Weng", as if she were a Chinese woman. (This name evidently derived from late-Ming accounts that her surname was Gong, Weng, or Wang.) In this Chinese version the cause of the empress' jealousy was merely the favors that Taizu showered upon Lady Weng's son, the future Yongle emperor. The empress then schemed to have him sent to Yan province. The Mongolian version, examined above, claims that the dying mother gave her son two "sealed envelopes", one to consult in times of "suffering". The present version here states: "Ere he departed, however, a Daoist priest, called Liu Bowen, who had a great affection for the Prince, put a sealed packet into his hand, and told him to open it when he found himself in difficulty, distress, or danger." Thus Liu Bowen takes a pivotal role in advising the future Yongle, and here is actually the one to hand over the instructions. The focus has fallen squarely within the Chinese popular tradition.[52]

Moreover, we get details of the city plan that are quite different from those of the Mongolian version. The Chinese legend says: "The name of the country in which the place was situated was Yan. It was a mere barren wilderness, with very few inhabitants; these lived in huts and scattered hamlets . . . Having found the packet (that the old Daoist priest had given him), he hastily broke it open to see what instructions it contained; taking out the first paper which came to hand, he read the following: 'When you reach Peip'ing Fu (Beipingfu) you must build a city there and name it No-cha Ch'eng (*Nezha cheng*), the City of No cha (Nezha) . . . On the back of this paper is a plan of the city.'" Money was raised from wealthy supporters and we are informed about foundations made "of layers of stone", walls "forty-eight *li* in circumference, fifty cubits in height, and fifty in breadth", a "stone-paved moat, in which the lotus and other flowers bloomed", and a geomantic layout that was "similar to that of Chin-ling (Jinling, i.e. Nanking)". Neither the principles of arrangement (geomantic and metaphysical), nor the relative positioning of architectural elements, is given. But the legend at least gives credit to Liu Bowen's plans, whatever they may have been.

All considered, the Mongolian legend clearly provided much inspiration, as well as new sources, for the development and transformation of the Liu Bowen/Nezha City legend. It inspired the blending of Liu Bingzhong's Dadu and Yongle's and Liu Bowen's Peking—a blend of Mongolian and Chinese elements that persists in today's legends. What is striking in the modern version of the legend of Liu Bowen's part in building the Nezha City, however, is that we find no trace of the Mongolian popular tradition, let alone its linkage with Liu Bingzhong's Dadu. This shows a thorough "Sinification" process through incorporation of the powerful legend of Liu Bowen, a great scholar-hero in the modern Chinese consciousness. It is only through the survival of the Mongolian texts of the legend in various forms that remnants have been preserved that bear witness to the interplay of Han Chinese and Mongolian traditions in the evolutionary process.

Seen in this context, this Mongolian legend about the Yongle emperor sheds significant light on both the Mongols' perception of their political stature vis-à-vis the Han Chinese and their fancied role in the building of a majestic capital city. The latter was conceived as an integral part of their heritage, and this is expressed forcefully by the propagation of the Yongle legend among Mongol communities in the Ordos and around Peking. While indulging in self-serving mythology about Mongolian blood in the veins of the Ming emperors, the indigenous legend drew heavily on Chinese ingredients and skillfully synthesized them to create a Mongol-centered folklore. It was indeed an impressive achievement, and as a result the legend enjoyed extensive popularity. Furthermore it helped develop a singular mythology concerning Liu Bowen's building of the Nezha City which is still retained among residents in Beijing today. The Mongolian importance in all of this must be placed in a broader Han-Mongol historical and cultural perspective for a judicious appraisal.

Another Mongolian Legend

Attention should be drawn to an oral version of yet another Mongolian legend about the founding of Peking. This legend, with some significant variations from the earlier versions, was provided by a modern Mongol informant and was recorded by the late Professor Owen Lattimore and published in the *Central Asiatic Journal* in 1979. The narrator's name was Arash, who, according to Lattimore, was not a local but a Jakhchin from the Altai. It was thought that had he been a local man he would almost certainly have told the story somewhat differently. The transcribed text (using the Wade-Giles romanization system for Chinese nomenclature; Lattimore's explanatory notes are presented in brackets) reads:[53]

> Togon Tömör (Toghōn Temür), last Emperor of the Mongol dynasty in China, had his capital at Ta T'ung, in northern Shansi. [Local pronunciation, Dai T'ung. I have more than once heard it called "the ancient capital", or confused with Peking, in Mongol folk tales.] He was

driven out by a Khitad deerem baatar, or Chinese bandit hero, who made himself the new emperor. Togon Tömör fled to Outer Mongolia, underground, through a cave. [This may be a reference to the Yün-kang 雲崗 temple caves, near Ta T'ung.] He left his Empress behind, and she was four months gone with child. The Khitad baatar summoned her before him and when he saw that she was well-grown and pleasing, decided to take her for his own empress. Then he saw that her belly was big and said to her, "Your stomach is properly big." She answered him and said, "When my Lord, the Emperor fled, I was sick with terror and anxiety, and my belly is swelled up with my sickness; it is not, for instance, a child."

Then the Khitad baatar said no more, but the Empress prostrated herself before Heaven and said: "Now I have in my belly the true child of the true Emperor of the Mongols; and if he is born when I am a slave in the hands of this Khitad baatar he will be killed. Therefore if the race of the Mongols has become bad, let him be killed; but if you, God [Burkhan] still favor the blood [literally yas, 'bone'] of Chinghis, let the term of the child in my belly be extended from ten [lunar] months to twelve months. Then perhaps the Khitad baatar will think it his own child and spare it."

So the Khitad baatar took her as his empress, and her stomach stayed about the same. Then it began to get bigger and the Khitad baatar thought, "Maybe she has been telling me lies. Maybe it is the child of the Mongol in her belly;" but he said nothing. After six months [i.e. when the child should have been at full term] it was not born. After ten months, still it was not born. Only after twelve months [i.e. a pregnancy of sixteen months] it was born. The Khitad baatar thought, "Is this really my child?"; but then he thought, "No, twelve months, that is the term of camels, not of human beings. It cannot be the child of the Mongol." So he acknowledged it as his own. Later he had another son, really his own, by the same empress, and the two boys grew up together.

Then one day the Khitad baatar had a dream. Two dragons, one yellow and one black, came to his feet and crawled up to his knees. The yellow one was at his right knee and the black one at his left knee. The dream troubled him, for he feared a bad omen. So he called a diviner to interpret the dream for him. When he had told the dream, the diviner asked him:

"Which dragon was at the right knee and which at your left?"

"The yellow dragon was at my right knee, and the black at my left."

The diviner said, "The dream has a meaning, but I do not dare to tell it."

"No, tell it; no harm will come to you."

"No, I am afraid to tell it; better not say anything about it."
"No, tell it you must."

So the diviner interpreted the dream: "The two dragons are your two sons; but one is not your true son. The yellow dragon is a Mongol son; the black one is your own son [i.e. khara Khitad, 'black Chinese']; but the false son is your heir; he is at your right knee and stands between your own son, who is at your left knee, and his inheritance."

Then the Khitad baatar was much troubled. The Mongol son who had been passed off on him was known by all to have been born twelve months after his mother had been taken by Khitad baatar. To kill him and favor the second son would lead to dynastic quarrels. To let him live would be to pass on the inheritance to the son of his Mongol predecessor and defraud his own rightful son. The only method was to dismiss both princes. So he called them to him and told them that they need not wait for his death to settle their inheritance. Both could go out and found their own kingdom. So the two sons went to Peking, which was then only a small unimportant place and build the city which is now Peking.

Lattimore notes in conclusion: "Here the story ends, a little lamely, but it ends in a way which points to a continuation, telling of the succession struggle after the death of the founder of the Ming Dynasty." But he too stopped here without venturing further analysis of the folkloric contents or historical sources.

In light of this narration, it is evident that the present legend retains the hard core of the stories as transmitted in the earlier legends in both oral and literary forms recounted by Mostaert and others. There were stories about the flight of Toghōn Temür from his capital, leaving his pregnant empress behind; the empress's betrothal to Zhu Yuanzhang, the new Ming emperor pejoratively dubbed as "Chinese bandit hero"; the empress's offering prayers to God to prolong the pregnancy and so to ease the emperor's suspicions; Zhu Yuanzhang's initial suspicion of the child's Mongol paternity but later acceptance as his own blood; the emperor's dream about the quarrels of two dragons—the yellow and the black dragon—and the diviner's interpretation of it as the enmity between his Mongol and Chinese sons; and the emperor's decision to send his Mongol son to guard the Nankou defile in the northwestern border where he built the city which is now Peking. The present legend carries many similar features but there are also apparent variations in presentation.

In the opening statement Toghōn Temür is again said to have a capital known as Da T'ung, as in earlier versions of the legend. This was a mistake for, as pointed out by Serruys, it was caused by a misreading of the transcription of the Yuan capital Dadu from "Dayidu" to "Dayitung", hence it was erroneously identified with Datong in modern Shanxi. The transmitter of the legend apparently lacked the historical knowledge of the Yuan capital to make the correction.[54] The error had already appeared in the written version of the legend and was repeated in the oral version, as well as in other Mongolian folktales. With regard to the story of the pregnancy, here it says that the empress was already four months pregnant when she met Zhu Yuanzhang upon the fall of Dadu, which is one or two months longer than reported in the *Altan Tobchi*. Then, through her successful prayer to God [Burkhan], she was able to give birth after what the Ming emperor believed to be twelve months of pregnancy, but in fact it was after sixteen months of pregnancy. Thereafter it also states clearly that the empress soon raised another son then known as the Chinese son whereas the previous was known as the Mongol son.

The setting of the Chinese emperor's dream of the two dragons and the diviner's interpretation closely followed the earlier legends, but the characters and symbols were different. Earlier versions mention two different colored snakes resting on the emperor's knee: on the right was a black striped snake, symbolizing the Yuan (Mongol) prince, and on the left was a yellow striped snake, symbolizing the True (Chinese) prince—they had been violently quarrelling and attacking each other. In actual history, the former alluded to the future Yongle emperor and the latter to the dethroned legitimate Jianwen emperor.[55] However, in the present legend the snakes were replaced by dragons, and the role of the colored symbols was reversed. In the Ming emperor's dream he saw two dragons coming to his feet and crawling up to his knees, on the right was a yellow dragon and on the left was a black dragon. No violent activities between the two were reported. The diviner subsequently revealed that the two dragons were actually his two sons. The yellow dragon on the right was the Mongol son and the black dragon, who sat on the left, was the Chinese son, without making further comment on this. Hearing this, the emperor was deeply troubled and decided that the best way was to dismiss both princes; thus he called in his two sons and told them not to wait for his death to settle their inheritance. Instead, both could go out and found their own kingdom. The story in the legend then proceeds with the two princes both going to Peking where they build a city bearing this name, but unfortunately the narrator did not give further details and, as Lattimore noted, he continued telling of the succession struggle between the two princes after the death of the founder of the Ming dynasty.[56]

The present legend hence reveals the unabated popularity of the Mongolian versions of the stories about the Mongol maternity of the Yongle emperor and the founding of the city of Peking related to his exile after quarrelling with his Chinese brother born to the same empress. The significant departure in this narration from the previous versions, however, is that both princes, the Mongol as well as the Chinese, were dismissed from the succession contest and that only the Mongol son was sent away to hold the Nankou defile on the northwestern border against enemy attacks and later built the capital city there with the aid of his Chinese adviser Liu Bowen. The Chinese prince was kept at the side of the Ming emperor and ascended the throne upon the death of his father. The divergence perhaps attests to the narrator's unfamiliarity with actual history as the story was told and retold through generations with unavoidable variations and simplifications. But the legend has kept alive an illustrious Mongolian popular tradition on the fringe of the Sinitic world about the building of Peking.

Chapter 4

The Stories of Liu Bowen, Yao Guangxiao, and Shen Wansan Building the City of Peking

The Folkloric Background

Against the backdrop of the enthralling legend of Liu Bowen building the Nezha City of Peking, and that of the Mongolian story of how the Yongle emperor built the capital, a cluster of equally dramatic and riveting folktales relating to the building of the city and its aftermath flourished. The following presents two stories concerning the role of Liu Bowen and his colleagues Yao Guangxiao and Shen Wansan in building the imperial city that have similarly captivated more recent residents of Beijing. The stories narrated in the Peking vernacular are contained in two major collections of Beijing folklore, the *Beijing fengwu chuanshuo* 北京風物傳說, edited by the Beijing Branch of the Chinese Association for Folk Literature Research (1983); and the *Beijing fengwu chuanshuo gushi xuan* 北京風物傳說故事選, edited by Wang Wenbao 王文寶 (1983).[1] The first story, "Liu Bowen built the City of Peking", begins with Liu Bowen's plot of siting the city by bowshot, alluding to the infusion of Mongolian social customs which have already been examined. Other sub-plots like Liu Bowen's feuds with the Dragon King and the martyrdom of the fictionalized hero Gao Liang against the vicious Dragon were either inspired by or drawn from similar folktales spun off from the Nezha City legend. The second story, "How was the City of Peking built?", though mentioning Liu Bowen, shifted the focus to his nemesis Yao Guangxiao, a former Buddhist monk who became a confidant of the Yongle emperor but who was thought in popular perception to be inferior to Liu Bowen. The story relates how he was given charge of the building of the capital by the Prince of Yan and how he sought out Shen Wansan to make him reveal his hoarded treasures in order to finance the city's construction.

It appears that these stories of unknown origin and date were disseminated through oral transmission and were recorded and buttressed by contemporary folklorists who might have recycled other dramatic episodes from early Ming popular stories about personalities and events involved in the building of the imperial capital. The first story was reportedly related by an elderly storyteller in Beijing in front of the Daoist shrine Pantao Palace 蟠桃宮 at a "temple fair" in the early nineteen sixties. This temple fair was usually held during the fifteenth day of the first month of the lunar year and was popularly attended by city residents.[2] The locals flocked there not only to buy and sell but also to meet their relations and friends, make social contacts, and revel in all sorts of folk entertainment. Storytelling was one of the most popular forms of oral entertainment, and the story of the building of old Peking associated with the legendary Liu Bowen and other luminary early Ming personalities would naturally draw a substantial crowd. The second story, of unknown folkloric origin, was probably crafted by storytellers fusing historical anecdotes about Yao Guangxiao and fictional episodes about the early Ming wealthy landlord and businessman Shen Wansan into vernacular narratives for popular consumption.

Yao Guangxiao, formerly the monk Daoyuan, was a celebrated personality in the Yongle reign. His Buddhist background and close relationship with the Ming emperor as confidant-adviser is well documented in historical literature,[3] and his fictional relationship with Liu Bowen in the Nezha legend of Peking has already been explored. Shen Wansan, on the other hand, was an extraordinarily wealthy but mysterious person of the late Yuan and early Ming and his many exploits remain deeply wrapped in fiction and legend. That he was assigned to a prominent role in building Peking in contemporary folklore requires an investigation of the historical background.

Shen Wansan was the sobriquet of Shen Fu, courtesy-name Zhongrong 仲容, an elder son of Shen You 祐 (佑), a rich landowner who moved the family from his native Wuxing 吳興 county in Huzhou 湖州, Zhejiang, to settle in the Zhouzhuang 周莊 canton of the Changzhou county of Suzhou, modern Jiangsu, in the early fourteenth century. His immediate descendants became the wealthiest Shen clansmen of the region, and probably the entire country. Shen Fu's popular name Wansan (Ten Thousand and Three) or Wansan Xiu 萬三秀, as well as that of his younger brother Gui 貴 (courtesy-name Zhonghua 仲華), Wansi 萬四 (Ten Thousand and Four), originated from the custom of the family and their kinship as well as the household ranking system of the Yuan and Ming.[4] In that period male offspring were named first in the order of seniority in the family, then in that of the kinship ranking system, which ranged from *shi* 十 (ten), *bai* 百 (hundred), *qian* 千 (thousand) to *wan* 萬 (ten thousand) according to generation, and also in the official household five-grade ranking system from *ge* 哥, *qi* 畸, *lang* 郎, *guan* 官, to *xiu* 秀—*ge* being the lowest grade and *xiu* the highest in terms of education and property. In Shen Fu's case, he was named *san* because he ranked third in seniority in his family, and was known as Wansan either because he belonged to the *wan* generation in the Shen kinship system, or possibly because he belonged to the wealthy *wanhu* 萬戶 (myriarch) household in the Yuan. He was also known as Shen (Wansan) Xiu because he belonged to the *xiu* grade in the Ming household ranking system based on his education and property.[5] There are no ascertainable birth or death dates for Shen Fu in the extant records, but the tomb inscriptions of his son Shen Mao 茂 and his nephew Shen Hanjie 漢傑 (Shen Gui's eldest son) date them in 1306–1376 and in 1320–1371 respectively. Therefore Shen Wansan may have been aged between seventy and eighty at the time of the founding of the Ming had he still been alive, and died shortly afterward. The assertion in the gazetteer *Wujiang zhi* 吳江志 that he already died during the time when Zhang Shicheng, who declared himself as the Prince of Cheng 誠王, ruling the state of Zhou under the reign-title Tianyou 天佑(祐) (1354–1357), lacks collateral evidence. He definitely spent most of his life in the Yuan after the reign of Qubilai Qaghan and may have lived only the first few years under the Ming dynasty.[6]

Shen Wansan evidently built his wealth on the inheritance from his father who was said to have possessed a large tract of high-yield arable land in his native and adjacent counties. It has been speculated that Shen, who allegedly managed the estates of some local wealthy landowners, also took over much of their fertile land, which they abandoned to avoid persecution amid the popular uprisings at the end of the Yuan. One such rumored benefactor was

Lu Deyuan 陸德原, a member of the wealthy landed gentry who allegedly dispersed his wealth to Shen and another close friend toward the end of his life, but there is no concrete proof. A skillful financial manager with an extraordinary endowment, Shen Wansan was able to multiply his wealth in leaps and bounds through not only expansion of profitable land, intensive tenant farming, developing and selling estates, engaging in grain transportation through the Grand Canal, and regional as well as overseas trade, but also through usury, charging high interest rates.[7] Since the mid-Ming, there had been various fabulous and sensational stories about his wealth in anecdotal miscellanies that proliferated into the Qing and inspired fantastic legends. Foremost, it was alleged that Shen built the most luxurious walled villa with a perimeter of seven hundred and twenty paces in his native place that rivaled that of a prince. A three-storied building in different heights rose above the walls, adorned with glamorous, exquisite architectural designs and surrounded by fabulous botanic and stone decorations. The residence was replete with collections of wares and objects in gold, silver, jewels, precious stones, and rare items of treasures. Other sumptuous residences and bridges allegedly built by Shen were also found in Suzhou and later in the Ming capital Nanking, and his landholdings and estates were omnipresent in the Suzhou and Nanking area. Despite some exaggeration, the Shen brothers were hailed as the richest men in the lower Yangzi region in the Yuan-Ming transition, and their name became synonymous with wealth and fortune in the popular imagination up to the recent century (Figure 38).[8]

With his extraordinary wealth, said to have rivaled that of a state, Shen Wansan was evidently wary of the jealousy of the ruler of becoming the target of requisition and suppression. As early as the dynastic founding, he and his brother were reportedly twice summoned by Ming Taizu and were coerced into contributing several thousand teals of silver and tens of thousands of bushels of grain to the state. It is probable that when Taizu instituted the "tax captain" (*liangchang* 糧長) system in 1371, Shen Wansan and his brother were among the rich landowners appointed to this position for the collection and deliverance of tax grain. One account reports that Taizu ordered Shen to make an annual submission of one thousand *ding* 錠 (ingot) of silver, one hundred catty (*jin* 斤) of gold, and much of the imperial army's armor, horses, and grain supplies

Figure 38 Shen Wansan as the fisherman receiving help from the Dragon King in a Qing woodblock print

Source: Jin, *Beijing de chuanshuo* (2003 ed.), p. 115.

were taken from his estate. Another story alleges that he was later indicted for a certain offense and was sent in exile to Liaoyang 遼陽 to perform garrison duties.[9] In addition, according to some late Ming accounts and the *Mingshi* biography of Empress Ma, Shen Wanshan reportedly offered to pay for one-third of the cost of building the capital city of Nanking, and also to give monetary awards to the imperial army. Ming Taizu rebuffed the latter offer and ordered his arrest, accusing him of meddling in the imperial prerogatives, but Shen escaped death through the empress's intervention and was instead exiled to Yunnan. Other accounts allege that he was executed and his estates and treasures were confiscated. However, while his contribution to building Nanking, even if true, was excessively enveloped in legends, the assertion about his exile to Yunnan and subsequent death was preposterous because the Ming government was not then in control of Yunnan. It may have been mistakenly identified with the indictment of Shen's son-in-law Gu Xuewen 顧學文 for collusion with the alleged rebellion of General Lan Yu 藍玉 in

1393; he was executed and the Shen household's estates and properties, including much of Shen's fabled treasures, were seized by the authorities. This dealt a severe blow to Shen Wansan's family fortune and it took the next two generations to rehabilitate it.[10]

There are several fanciful stories in Ming and Qing miscellanies about how Shen Wansan, portrayed as a poor fisherman, suddenly becomes rich. Foremost was the story that he acquired a strange bowl that accumulated treasures. It is said that when he was poor, he once had a dream in which hundreds of frogs appealed to him to spare their lives. At dawn, seeing a fisherman was about to kill the frogs for food, he bought them and released them in the pond. The next day, startled to see the frogs congregating around an earthen bowl croaking, he took the bowl away to use as his washing bowl, but when his wife dropped a silver object in it, it filled with countless pieces of silver. It happened again and again without fail and Shen Wansan became exceedingly rich. The bowl was known as the "treasure-accumulating bowl" (*jubaopan* 聚寶盆). Next was the story that Shen Wansan caught several pieces of the rare "crow-shaped rock" (*wuya-shi* 烏鴉石) in his net one day when he was out fishing; each fetched him several tens of thousands of coins, thus he obtained the capital to engage in maritime trade, which made him very prosperous. There was also the story that late one night, while gazing at the sky from his fishing boat, Shen saw the Big Dipper falling down, immediately he stretched his gown and caught the star's "handle". At dawn an elder leading seven men carrying loaded baskets arrived, asked him to look after them, and disappeared. When Shen lifted the covers he found numerous horse-shoe shaped gold nuggets and thus became extraordinarily rich. Yet another story of Shen Wansan finding treasures involved the famed Daoist patriarch Zhang Sanfeng 張三豐 who allegedly lived through the Yuan and Ming periods. It is said that Shen, in his humble days as a fisherman, unexpectedly ran into a hulking bearded Daoist who introduced himself as Zhang Sanfeng and who divulged to him the secrets of longevity and the arts of cultivation. Shen showed no interest and instead asked the famed Daoist for a way to get out of poverty. The Daoist consented and, through the craft of alchemy by smelting different drugs and materials, produced hot liquid solutions that changed metal and iron into gold and silver. Thus initiated, Shen Wansan set up a furnace and kept smelting day and night, and became the richest man in the country in due course. This is recorded in the forged collected works of Zhang Sanfeng compiled by an early Qing Daoist and is therefore of late and dubious origin.[11]

Without question the "treasure-accumulating bowl" episode was the most spectacular and it generated famed legends about Shen Wansan's building of the city of Nanking. In addition to the earlier assertions that Shen put up one-third of the cost of the construction, various accounts yield more specific though unverifiable information about his contributions. It has been said that several of the city's southeast walled gates, such as the south gate, called Jubao 聚寶, were built by Wansan, and so were the gates from Hongwumen 洪武門 to Shuiximen 水西門 (popular name for Sanshan 三山 Gate). It is also said that after building the south gate, Shen placed the "treasure-accumulating bowl" under the gate in order that it would sustain the "ruler's emanation" (*wangqi*) and so gave it the name Jubaomen. However, this is preposterous because the gate was named after the mountain to the north, which was so-called well before the Ming dynasty. The precious bowl was allegedly used for other purposes. It is said that after confiscating Shen Wansan's properties and condemning his display of wealth, Ming Taizu buried his "treasure-accumulating bowl" under one of the city gates in order to suppress its evil influence. On the other hand it is said that when Taizu gave order to build the city gates of Nanking, one of them was so close to the water that it could not stand erect, but when the emperor placed the "treasure-accumulating bowl" underneath the problem was solved. Another story relates that when the Shuixi Gate was plagued by the depredations of the *zhu(po)long* 豬(婆)龍 ("pig-dragon") sea creatures (crocodiles?), the emperor placed the bowl there and the disturbance ceased. All these legends imputed a prominent role to Shan Wansan in building Nanking and made it easy to connect him with the building of Peking.[12]

Such melodramatic popular gossip and anecdotes about Shen Wansan's wealth, adventures, and misfortune, fused with those about his siblings, descendants, and clansmen, made him a legendary larger-than-life figure in late modern Chinese history. As a prominent tycoon prospering in Suzhou, Shen and his family were certainly celebrities in Peking and some of their confiscated treasures and art objects allegedly found their way into the imperial depot and powerful officials' collections in the northern capital. A significant part of the Peking legend about Shen Wansan not only hailed him for making financial contributions to build the imperial city, but also apotheosized him as a "Living God of Wealth" (*huo caishen* 活財神) in local folk belief. Inside the famed Daoist White Cloud Shrine in the Western District of Peking there was a "Caishen" Hall, and Shen Wanshan was the deity of worship (Figure 39).[13] His alleged revelation of hidden treasures under physical torture was prominent in several folktales about his contributions to the building of Peking. The most interesting of these were those about the origin of the Shicha Sea and about how Liu Bowen and Yao Guangxiao built the capital city. But Shen Wansan had never been to Peking, so how was he involved in this gigantic undertaking? The main reason, it seems, was his close association with Ming Taizu and his alleged contribution of funds to build the city and gates of Nanking; as

Figure 39 Shen Wansan as the God of Wealth in a Qing clay figurine

Source: Jin, *Beijing de chuanshuo* (2003 ed.), p. 115.

Nanking was so closely connected with Peking, this inspired legend-makers to co-opt him in the story of his revealing the hidden treasures to build the imperial capital. The fact that Liu Bowen had been credited with designing the city of Nanking, and that he had been assigned to such a prominent role in building Peking would also make Shen Wansan's association with him and his nemesis Yao Guangxiao a natural outcome in fictional imagination.

As shown in the translation of the two stories about the building of Peking included in Appendices (4), (5), there are some overlaps in narration since they are all related to the building of the capital city. While Liu Bowen and Yao Guangxiao were the leading actors in each story, the role of Shen Wansan was featured in both pieces, although it was treated in greater detail in the second story. To avoid repetition, the following summaries of the first story, "Liu Bowen built the city of Peking", will leave out Shen Wanshan who will receive full attention in the second story, "How was the City of Peking built? " along with Yao Guangxiao, the principal actor. Attention will be given to the historical background and, whenever available, literary sources on the real or imagined characters, supernatural beings and dramatic events, as well as an examination of the process of fictionalization and development of the legends.

"Liu Bowen Built the City of Peking"

Liu Bowen, Xu Da, and Shen Wansan

The story holds that when the Prince of Yan contemplated building a northern capital he solicited grand minister Liu Bowen's advice. Liu resisted, suggesting to the Prince that he should ask the great general Xu Da to take charge. The Prince thus sent for the general. Upon Xu's arrival, Liu said to him, "Harness your divine strength to shoot an arrow toward the north; wherever the arrow falls, build the capital there." Xu consented and, standing outside the palace, he drew the bow with all his might and shot toward the north. Meantime Liu Bowen and his attendants sailed northward in a boat along the Grand Canal following the path of the arrow. The single arrow, as it turned out, streaked far away and landed in Nanyuan 南苑 (South Park), about twenty *li* (11.4 km) south of present-day Beijing. At that time eight households of minor wealth lived there. They were alarmed by the fallen arrow, and worried that if the capital were built there, all their houses and fields would be confiscated.

At this juncture one of these wealthy élite came up with a clever idea. He said, "Why don't we just shoot the arrow away?" Everyone applauded; and so he shot the arrow toward the north and it landed at the Houmen (Rear Gate) Bridge 後門橋 of present-day Beijing. We learn also that people there erected a stone epitaph with the inscription: "Bei-jing cheng" (Peking City) under the bridge, marking the spot of the fallen arrow. Just then, Liu Bowen, tracking the flight of the arrow by sea all the way up to Peking, had prognosticated where the arrow had fallen and took his men to the South Park, asking the households for the arrow. Realizing they could not cover up the incident, they confessed. They begged Liu Bowen not to build the capital there and promised to make amends by providing funds which they thought would not be too excessive.

In response Liu said, "Well, I don't necessarily need to build the capital here, but I shall build it on the spot of the fallen arrow that you shot and you should bear all the expenses!" The wealthy men yielded, and so Liu proceeded to the location of the fallen arrow; then he produced the city plan he had drafted earlier and ordered the laborers to start construction. But none foresaw that even before the completion of a single walled tower the rich élite of the South Park would be reduced to utter destitution. Thereafter Liu Bowen prognosticated again and sent for his attendants to find an eccentric wealthy man known as Shen Wansan to make him turn over his treasure of gold and silver. In the story Shen appeared as a beggar wearing rags and carrying a broken earthen bowl under his armpit, but having found him, Liu apprehended his real worth instantly and gave the order to beat him until he confessed and revealed his cache of treasure. The act was repeated two to three times, and Peking was built as a result. The same story appears again with further details in the other story that focused on Yao Guangxiao's role in building Peking.[14]

Summing up, these episodes present a fictionalized account of Liu Bowen and Xu Da, two eminent personalities of Ming Taizu's reign, against the background of the building of Peking under the Yongle emperor. Historically Liu Ji (Bowen) spent his most important political career under Taizu and died in 1375, when the future Yongle emperor was only a fifteen-year-old prince at his Yan fief. He had never been in Ming Beipingfu and therefore left no legacy there. Liu Bowen was associated with the Prince of Yan and credited with a primary role in building Peking because, as noted earlier, he was fictionalized as an adviser of the future emperor, then a young prince alleged to have been fathered by Toghōn Temür in the aforementioned Mongolian legend of the Mongol maternity of the Yongle emperor. It is said that when Ming Taizu suspected of his son's Mongol paternity and exiled him to the region later known as Peking, he also sent Liu Bowen to join his company and Liu was given charge of building a walled city on the advice of a mysterious swarthy-faced black rider whom they encountered in the wilderness.[15] As a result, in the Chinese folktales about the building of Peking, starting with the Nezha City story, Liu Bowen became the primary city planner and his role is repeated in the present story about the building of Peking.

As the story begins, when the Yongle emperor asked Liu Bowen for advice on building the capital, he recommended General Xu Da for the task. When the general arrived (i.e. in Nanking, where the emperor still resided), Liu suggested that he shoot an arrow toward the north with his "divine strength" and the place where the arrow landed would be the site of the future capital. The alleged place, Southern Park, was the historical southern part of the inner city of Peking (i.e. the Xuanwu District) where many wealthy landlords and businessmen resided.[16] The narrator, however, enhances the drama with an unexpected twist. It is said that when the landlords saw the fallen arrow, worrying that the city would be built on their lands, one of the more resourceful of them found an ingenious solution by shooting the arrow back, hoping that it would resolve their problem. The returned arrow landed at the Houmen Bridge near the lower Jishui Pool in the northwestern corner of the city, but the shrewd Liu Bowen was not deceived. He picked up the arrow and went back to threaten the landlords, forcing them to contribute funds for the construction if they did not want to see the capital city being built in their midst where the arrow originally landed. The landlords reluctantly consented.

None of these actually happened. Historically, although both were contemporaries and had served the Ming founder in various capacities, Liu Ji did not have an intimate working relationship with Xu Da and neither Liu nor Xu were involved in rebuilding the

Beiping prefecture. But in the eyes of modern Chinese they were paragons of civil and military officials under Ming Taizu and had made significant contributions. Some of the folk songs circulating in Peking/Pei-p'ing in the early Republican period, for instance, paired Liu Bowen with Xu Da as the two most meritorious civil and military officials of the early Ming dynasty. This close relationship is evident in fictional imagination.[17] Xu Da's fictitious arrow shot, on the other hand, reflects the traditional sociopolitical custom of siting by bowshot among the Mongols and the nomadic tribesmen as alluded to in the foregoing legend of the Mongol maternity of the Yongle emperor. That he shot an arrow to the north and let the landing of the arrow decide the site of the future capital was evidently an ingenious though fanciful adaptation of the Mongolian custom in a Sinitic context. He shot only in one direction, which deviates from the aforementioned Mongolian legend on the building of Peking, but was in accord with a common nomadic practice to establish property rights and use the distance of a bowshot as a conceptualized unit of measurement as noted earlier.[18] This nomadic custom moreover found expression in Shanxi folktales in the late Qing and early Republican periods. For instance an episode from Datong features the renowned late Tang early Song archer-warrior Yang Liulang 楊六郎 (Yang Ye 楊業, ?–986) who allegedly shot an arrow to demarcate the boundary of the Xiongnü 匈奴 settlement in Daqingshan 大青山 in his negotiation with the Khitan envoys. Another episode claims that the Ming founder Zhu Yuanzhang awarded his meritorious general Hu Dahai 胡大海 (?–1362) the land covered by the flight of a bowshot in Linxian 林縣, Henan, wherein he could exterminate the people who had bullied him in his humble days, resulting in a terrible bloodshed.[19]

Xu Da was a natural choice in this romanticized role in light of his military career, his connection with Peking, and especially his relationship with the Prince of Yan, the future Yongle emperor. A native of Zhu Yuanzhang's Hao prefecture, Xu joined his band as sub-commander in 1353 at the age of twenty-one, when Zhu was still under the command of Guo Zixing in the anti-Yuan uprisings. He distinguished himself in many of Zhu Yuanzhang's successful campaigns, becoming one of the most senior military commanders at the founding of the Ming dynasty in 1368. As emperor, Zhu awarded him the dukedom of the state of Wei 魏國 and named him right chief councilor and junior tutor to the heir-apparent. In the summer of that year Xu Da was one of two generals leading the expeditionary army against the Mongol court in the north and seized Dadu after the last Yuan emperor Toghōn Temür deserted the capital in September. Dadu, renamed Beipingfu, then came under Xu Da's military command. To defend the city against attack by the recalcitrant Mongol tribesmen, he rebuilt the northern face of the outer wall with two gates 5 *li* to the south behind the old canal, which originated in the northwestern mountains and ran around the rectangular capital city. The northwestern corner of the wall, however, was slanted along the canal until it reached the Jishui Pool near the Desheng Gate, and hence it altered the shape and reduced the length of the western walled city by two-fifths. In 1370, when Ming Taizu invested his fourth son Zhu Di as the Prince of Yan, Xu assumed the protection of his fiefdom and in 1376 his eldest daughter (later Empress Xu, 1362–1407), then sixteen-years of age, was married to the Prince, thus becoming a member of the imperial family. After taking up residence in his fief in 1380 the Prince came under Xu Da's direct influence and gained his military experience from patrolling the border under the general's direction for several years until Xu's death in 1385 (Figure 40).[20]

It is fitting, therefore, to draw Xu Da into the picture when the Yongle emperor gave orders to build the imperial city in Peking, although historically Xu had died more than twenty years earlier. The ingenious narrator not only made Xu Da the archer who shot the arrow at Liu Bowen's recommendation, but also had the returned arrow (after the original arrow was shot back by the shrewd landlord in the South Park) land at the Houmen Bridge, which was located at the eastern outlet of the lower Jishui Pool (part of the Shicha Sea) north of the Bei'an Gate (known as Di'anmen in the Qing) which was within Xu Da's military command. The bridge, originally named Wanning but popularly known as Haizi, was built in the Yuan dynasty across the Pool and the Tonghui Canal (which ran southward through the imperial-city before it joined the tributaries of the Grand Canal). It was also known as Houmen Bridge because it was situated north of the rear gate of the Yuan imperial-city. A medium-size arched bridge, it was built with white marble and legend has it that the bottom of the bridge was a stone tablet inscribed with two characters: "Bei-jing", and that when the water level reached that

Figure 40 Portrait of Xu Da

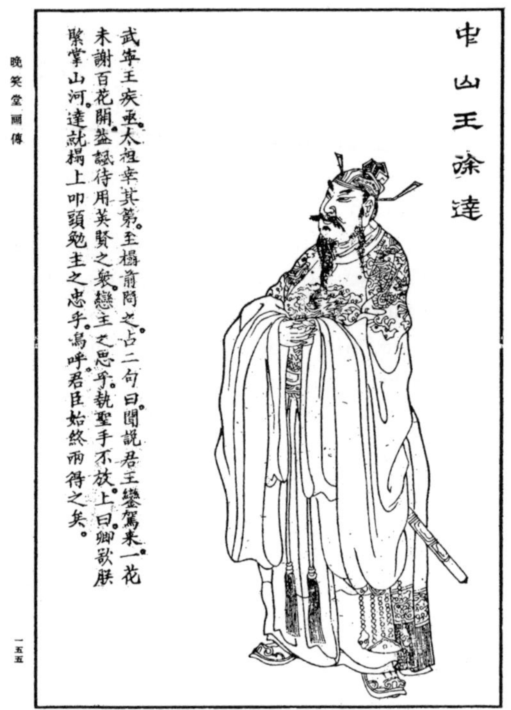

Source: Shangguan Zhou, *Wanxiaotang huazhuan*, p. 155.

point, Peking would be in danger of flooding. That is probably why in the story it is said that people there erected a stone epitaph with the inscription "Bei-jing cheng" (Peking City).

It is amusing that the Houmen Bridge, by virtue of the existence of a stone tablet allegedly inscribed with the words "Bei-jing" also inspired legend. In the diagram of the anatomy of Nezha's body said to be represented by various sites in the city of Peking reported by Arlington and Lewisohn, while the Shicha Sea represents Nezha's bladder, the Houmen Bridge is purported to be his "membrum virile". This is fanciful to the extreme.[21] Lin Yutang, who cited several examples of the "playfulness of belief" among the Pekingese about their environment in his *Imperial Peking*, has this to say on the Houmen Bridge: "Another example is the stone tablet under the bridge at Chungkulou (Zhonggulou 鐘鼓樓, i.e. the Bell and Drum Tower), near the Houmen Gate. It is associated with Liu Po(Bo)wen, adviser to the first Ming emperor and an astrologer, like Nostradamus, credited with supernatural powers of foretelling the future. . . . At Liu's suggestion, the tablet under the bridge was inscribed with the words 'Peking City' as a method of outwitting the gods. If the gods should be angry and determine to drown the city, they would see, when the flood reached the level of the tablet under the bridge, that 'Peking City' was already under water. They would then desist and be satisfied."[22] It is an ingenious vicarious expression of the local residents' concern over the water problems of their city.

These episodes represent a very careful dovetailing of fact and fiction with skillful adaptation of a popular Mongolian custom that vividly reveals the imagination of the story's author and transmitter. The aftermath of the bowshot incident, from how Liu Bowen browbeat the rich landowners into contributing funds for building the city to how he bullied the legendary wealthy Shen Wansan, was inspired by the popular legend about this eccentric rich man seen in the follow-up story of how Yao Guangxiao built the city of Peking. The present story, after relating how Liu Bowen found Shen Wansan and obtained his hoarded treasures for the construction, unveils Liu Bowen's head-on confrontation with the vicious Dragon King who thrived with his extended family in the underground waters of the capital city, which significantly enriches the legend.

Liu Bowen, the Dragon King, and Warrior Gao Liang

When Liu Bowen was sailing north tracking the flying arrow and was about to reach Peking, a wave suddenly rose up and a gigantic tortoise surfaced; the creature put its front flippers on the bow, almost capsizing the boat. He immediately recognized it as the transformed Dragon King and asked what he wanted. The Dragon King inquired if Liu was planning to build the capital city on his own domain, and if so what would he be compensated with. Liu said the Prince would repay him handsomely, but the Dragon retorted that he would want a position for each of his nine sons and grandsons. Liu realized that this was not possible but feigned that he would make arrangements when the time came. Thus satisfied, the Dragon King turned around and dove into the sea so Liu Bowen's boat continued northward. After the completion of the city of Peking, at Liu Bowen's invitation the Prince of Yan ascended the dragon throne and became the Yongle emperor.

Then one day a report came that an elderly man had been waiting at the palace entrance with several youngsters, demanding to see Liu Bowen. They were the Dragon King and his family. On seeing Liu the Dragon King exclaimed that they had arrived to claim the positions he had promised. In response Liu laughed heartily, saying that he had already made the arrangements. What he did was to assign the dragon sons and grandsons "positions" on ornamental pillars, on obelisks, on the eaves of houses, and on shadowed walls. After that he barked out his command: "Take your places!" The nine dragon sons and grandsons immediately streaked to their assigned positions and each one of them was stuck there. All the lively dragons thus became stone-engraved, brick-tarred, and oil-painted inanimate objects. The Dragon King was furious but seeing he was no match in a fight with Liu Bowen angrily departed, vowing revenge with a death curse on all the people in the city.

The vengeance came sooner than expected. On the next day, before Liu Bowen had risen, a messenger hurried in with a report, saying that the water in all the wells and rivers had dried up and people were rioting. Liu Bowen immediately realized it was the evil plot of his nemesis. Thus he summoned his soldiers and asked for a brave warrior to defeat the Dragon King and take back the water. Immediately, a burly man named Gao Liang came forward to accept the task. Knowing that the Dragon King would pack up all the water in two pouches and attach them to the cart he and his wife were pushing out of the city, Liu reminded Gao Liang that when he emerged from the Xizhi Gate he should hurry toward the west, catch the person pushing a small cart, use a spear to slit the water pouch placed on the left of the cart, then turn around and rush back. He said he would wait for him on the walled tower of the Gate but warned him not to turn around to take a look when he was running back after the job was done.[23]

In this segment of the story, the fancied episodes about Liu Bowen's encounter with the Dragon King, his shenanigans in tricking his nemesis and transforming his sons and grandsons into dead objects of architectural decoration, and the subsequent revenge of his arch rival by packing the water of Peking away were inspired by the earlier legend about the miraculous Tantric Buddhist child deity Nezha battling with the vicious sea creature in a fierce confrontation. As noted earlier, the saga was first featured in the late Yuan Daoist biography of Nazha in the *Huitu Shoushen guangji* and was transmitted in the Ming Buddhist-Daoist collection *Sanjiao yuanliu Soushen daquan.* It tells the story of Nezha who, while bathing in the Eastern Sea, accidentally trampled on the Crystal Hall, and enraged the Dragon King. The Dragon King challenged him to a duel but in seven days of fierce fights Nazha killed his nine dragon sons and finally confronted his nemesis and killed him, unleashing much chaos in the subterranean world. These episodes were subsequently adapted with subplots and trappings in the seventeenth-century popular novel *Tales of the Investiture of Gods,* and again in modified forms in the renowned *Journey to the West,* followed by further embroidery by storytellers and theater performers, thereby helping to increase and sustain the popularity of the Nazha/Nezha City legend.[24]

In adapting these materials, the characters and events have been transformed to fit into the content of the story to achieve the desired dramatic efforts. In the current story Liu Bowen has replaced Nezha as the main character who used all his wisdom and tricks to subdue the Dragon King to save the residents of Peking from thirst. It is a shrewd subplot spun out of the Nazha City legend through an ingenious adaptation of folkloric and historical materials. For example, the description of how Liu Bowen, responding to the Dragon King's request to appoint a "position" to each of his nine sons and grandsons at court, tricked them by asking them to stand in line and, when he barked a command, all of them streaked to their assigned positions on ornamental pillars, on obelisks, on the eaves of houses, and on shadowed walls and were stuck there as dead objects. In actual fact, however, there were ornaments of small dragons in various features on many of such monuments and buildings in the Forbidden City and the imperial-city in old Peking. These omnipresent figures, seen as "supernatural scarecrows", were meticulously crafted and vivaciously colored in harmony with the *yinyang* and Five Agents/Phases theories. But they did not serve as symbols of the dragon family as alleged in the popular legend; rather, they were symbols of the imperial ruler and imperial authority since the identification of the "dragon cult" with the emperor institution in the Han dynasty.[25]

In the follow-up subplot Liu Bowen did not play a direct role in confronting the Dragon King when he learned that his nemesis had packed all the water of Peking out of the city. Instead, a soldier from his guards by the name of Gao Liang responded, volunteering to undertake the hazardous assignment of recovering the water from the dragons. Thereupon Liu Bowen gave this brave warrior a set of instructions and a specific warning not to look back when he had accomplished his task. The episode, as discussed later, was inspired by a folktale with more elaborate details entitled "Gao Liang's Race for Water", which is a spin-off of the Liu Bowen building the Nezha City legend.[26] Gao Liang was evidently a fictionalized figure, but his name was taken from the famous Gaoliang 高粱 River which flowed into the Shicha Sea (the lower lake of the Yuan Jishui Pool) of the imperial-city from its source in the northwestern mountains. It provided not only an important inland waterway but was also a major source of water supply for the residents. An impressive stone bridge bearing the same name spanned the Gaoliang River about half of a *li* north of the Xizhi Gate, within the present-day Haidian District of Beijing outside the northwestern walls of the outer-city. Gao Liang, meaning "tall" and "bright", was homophonic with *gaoliang*, the name of a type of Chinese sorghum, but transforming the name of a river and a bridge into that of a fictionalized person playing such a dramatic role in the story of Liu Bowen feuding with the dragons to recover the water stolen from Peking was an ingenious adaptation of a historical legacy.

The Gaoliang River was a famed ancient waterway which was known as the Yu 玉 or Chang 長 (Jade or Long) River since the Qing dynasty. The River was already well known in the Jurchen-Jin as the inland waterway transporting supplies between the capital city Zhongdu and its summer palace located to the southwest (site of Yuan Dadu). According to the Yuan gazetteer *Xijin zhi*, the Gaoliang River originated in the mountains of Changping county; it flowed southeast to Gaoliangdian 高粱店 (which gives the river its name) and, having crossed Wanping 宛平 county, entered Dadu from the northwest through the north watergate of the Heyi Gate into the Jishui Pool. It provided a major source of water supply for the Yuan imperial capital. The Gaoliang Bridge, which derived its name from the river, was built in 1292 during the reign of Qubilai Qaghan to replace an old stone bridge. The bridge, an impressive camel back structure supported by three arches, spanned the banks of the southern end of the Gaoliang River before it flowed into the walled city through the Jishui Pool/Shicha Sea and the extended canals. It was at the confluence of tributaries through which ships and traders supplied the capital and its suburbs.[27]

In the same year as the bridge was built, the ingenious hydraulic engineer Guo Shoujing launched a massive plan to expand the waterway communications between Dadu and its suburbs. He channeled the water from the Jade Spring Hill into the Urn Hill Lake, which flowed into the Gaoliang River, and emptied it into the Jishui Pool. In addition, Guo dredged the old canal which descended from the Jishui Pool's outlet around the eastern walls of the imperial-city and exited through the Wenming Gate in the south to join the Grand Canal. The new Tonghui Canal thus completed a navigable waterway linking Dadu with Tongzhou on the Grand Canal, allowing the transport of provisions from the southeastern provinces. In the Ming the Gaoliang River and Tonghui Canal performed the same functions until the Jiajing era with the enclosure of the southern section of the walled outer-city and extension of the walls to the southern suburbs. The flow of water from the Gaoliang River was thus blocked at the Jishui Pool/Shicha Sea, and the linkage of the canal in the imperial-city with the Grand Canal was terminated. The situation remained relatively the same under the Qing. However, from the time of the Kangxi emperor, who developed the fabulous western parks, the Gaoliang River was given more attention as it provided a convenient passage to these new sites. The Gaoliang Bridge thus received special treatment. It was renovated in the Qianlong era and its banks were planted with willow trees and lined with exquisite embankments, creating an efficient facility and serene environ for travelers and visitors to and from the capital. It remains a well-known historical site and a favorite tourist attraction.[28]

Seen in this context, naming the brave warrior Gao Liang, which instantly reminded people of the famous river, underscores the ingenious design of the storyteller that made the utmost imaginative use of historical sources and topographical features. Not only were the Gaoliang River and Gaoliang Bridge well known to the local residents down to the present day as important in facilitating transportation, the fact that they played a significant role in inland waterway transport and in providing water resources to the imperial-city provided a strong historical context for the proliferation of the legend. It was an important addition that highlighted the drama and enriched the mythology of the feuds between Liu Bowen and the Dragon King in the legend of the building of Peking.

Gao Liang, Shen Wansan, and the Dragon King

When Gao Liang received Liu Bowen's order, he grabbed his long spear, left the Xizhi Gate, and rushed toward the west. He soon saw a small hand-cart stopped by the roadside and an elderly couple were resting under a tree nearby. He realized they were the transformed Dragon King and his wife. The dragon couple, angered by Liu Bowen taking the life of their sons and grandsons with his treacherous scheme, decided to move away and take all the water in the city with them in revenge. They had packed the water up in two different pouches, then fastened them to a cart and left the city. Immediately Gao Liang stealthily raced toward the cart and thrust his spear right into the water pouch, then turned around and dashed away. But in his rush he made a grave mistake. He only speared the water pouch on the right side. There were two water pouches on the cart, the left contained the sweet water and the right contained the brackish water. Later on Peking had many salty wells, which was attributed to Gao Liang slitting the wrong water pouch! As to the left water pouch still in the Dragon King's cart, later it filled Jade Spring Hill and ever since the water gushing from there was very sweet and tasty.

The Dragon King was enraged by Gao Liang's surprise strike. In revenge he waved his hands and torrents of water gushed out of the water pouches, surging in the direction of Gao Liang. Terrified by the thunderous roaring behind his back, Gao dared not turn around but kept running for his life. However, with the Xizhi Gate in sight, Gao relaxed and turned around for a quick look to see what had happened. As he turned his head a huge wave suddenly swept over him, drowning him instantly. Gao Liang drowned in the flood because he did not heed Liu Bowen's warning. Later a bridge, named Gaoliang Bridge, was built in his memory at the very spot where he died. Standing on the city tower and seeing that the flood had engulfed Gao Liang and was rolling toward the city gate, Liu Bowen was very worried that the water might destroy Peking. He immediately gave orders to close the gates as tightly as possible. The flood water was thus prevented from entering the city. Part of it flowed south along the waterway, and part of it flowed underground into the city. The wells and rivers of the city were all filled with water, and the residents were overjoyed and no longer feared dying of thirst.

But the Dragon King would not give up. He snuck into the city through the underground streams and found a well near a newly built bridge. He brought the water with him, and when it was unleashed it would gush upward drowning the entire city. When people heard the water rushing into the well they hurriedly reported to Liu Bowen. Liu immediately realized what had happened. He sent men to find Shen Wansan, took him to the well and asked him to press the water down. Shen pleaded in tears, claiming that he was a poor beggar and in no way could he take on the Dragon King. But Liu kept insisting and finally Shen Wansan yielded. He untied the cord around his neck from which his broken earthen begging bowl was suspended and thrust the bowl with its mouth facing down into the well. Instantly the water level from the well receded and the rushing of the water also gradually diminished—the Dragon King was trapped under the bowl. The Dragon King yelled at Liu Bowen, wondering if he could ever come out, and Liu responded that he could when the nearby bridge grew old. But Liu Bowen played another trick. He gave a name to the bridge built near the well, calling it Beixinqiao 北新橋 (which could be read as Buxinqiao 不新橋), meaning that this bridge can never grow old, and thus the Dragon King can never hope to come out again.[29]

The source of the episode about Gao Liang following Liu Bowen's instructions to chase the Dragon King and his wife to recover the stolen water was again the popular folktale "Gao Liang's Race for Water". It begins with the complaint among Peking's older residents that they lived in a bad place because it was a briny sea known as Bitter Sea Youzhou. People had to reside in the western and northern hills, leaving the Bitter Sea to the Dragon King and his extended family, and they lived a wretched life. After this brief remark, it tells how a boy named Nezha who appeared in a red jacket and short pants came to the Bitter Sea to rescue the people. He fought the Dragon King and his son nine times on each of the nine days, eighty-one fights in all; he captured the Dragon King and his wife, while their son, daughter-in-law and grand-children fled. After this the water slowly ebbed away and soil emerged. Nezha sealed up the different outlets to the sea, confining the Dragon King and his wife in a large lake, then built a big white pagoda overlooking it so that ever after they had to stay there to guard it. With the water ebbing away the name Bitter Sea was changed to Youzhou, and people returned. They built houses and settled down; villages sprang up and market-towns bloomed. Before long the dragon's son who had fled had become the King. He and his wife took refuge with their son and daughter in a lake at the foot of the western hills, but as they saw the people of Bitter Sea Youzhou increasing from day to day, they were exasperated. They wanted to go out and flood the place which was no longer called the Bitter Sea.

Thereafter the story relates that the new Dragon King and his wife reacted angrily when they heard that a city called Peking was to be built in Youzhou, and that Liu Bowen and Yao Guangxiao had drawn a plan to build an "Eight-armed Nezha City". He and his wife then hatched a plot to drain away all the water before the city was finished so that people would die of thirst. The next day, dressed like peasants going to the market in town, they set out with their son and daughter and a wheel-barrow loaded with vegetables and snuck into Peking.

They dumped all the vegetables and went around the town where the Dragon boy drank all the sweet water there and the Dragon girl all the bitter water. They then transformed themselves into two fish-scale water-panniers and laid down one on each side of the wheel-barrow. With the Dragon King pushing and his wife pulling it, they went boldly out of the Xizhi Gate. When Liu Bowen was informed of the report that all the wells in the city had dried up, he immediately realized it was the vicious revenge of the Dragon King and so he started organizing a rescue plan and a smart-looking young mason named Gao Liang volunteered his services.[30]

In the present version, Gao Liang appears as a soldier from Liu Bowen's guardsmen rather than a mason as in the original story. This puts his fight with the Dragon King in a more martial context. The details about Gao Liang tracking down the dragon couple and their hand-cart carrying the water pouches outside the Xizhi Gate, mistakenly thrusting his spear into the water pouch that carried the brackish water, and provoking the wrath of the Dragon King who unleashed a flood from the water pouch that drowned him and caused other havoc, are similar to the original version despite some minor variations. Moreover, the whole episode was set against the backdrop of the Jade Spring Hill, Jishui Pool, Xizhi Gate, and the Gaoliang Bridge, where many events concerning Peking's water supply, irrigation, and transportation had taken place, and the bizarre episodes in the story reflect some of the dire historical realities. The story's allegation that Peking had many salty wells because Gao Liang had slit the wrong water pouch, and that the Dragon King threw the water pouch with the sweet water into the Jade Spring Hill, which explains why the water there was still sweet and tasty, presents another example of ingenious fictionalization through imaginative recycling of folkloric legends. The fact that Peking's residents in the west districts of the old imperial-city tasted the "sweet" water was because they had access to the fresh and clear water cascading from Jade Spring Hill into the Jushui Pool and Gaoliang River, whereas the water which residents in other parts of Peking normally drank was water running through the canals and tapped from the wells, which was usually a kind of brackish, salty water. This had been the situation before the advent of the modern water supply system in the early twentieth century, but the stark reality of daily livelihood was sanitized in playful folkloric fantasies.[31] The claim that people paid tribute to Gao Liang's martyrdom by naming the bridge after him is utterly preposterous since the bridge was already known as Gaoliang—the name of a Chinese sorghum—when it was built in the Yuan, although in modern times it was also unofficially called Gaoliang (tall and bright) in deference to the old legend.

The final part of the story about Liu Bowen seeking Shen Wansan's assistance to exorcize the unrepentant Dragon King when he snuck into the city intending to flood it drew upon fanciful tales about Shen Wansan himself. It is said that when people reported hearing the water rushing in a well Liu Bowen immediately sent Shen to the well, asking him to press down the water. Shen at first resisted, pleading that he was only a poor beggar and could not match the Dragon King, but finally yielded under Liu's persistence. Then he released the cord that tied his broken earthen begging bowl around his neck, thrust the bowl mouth facing down into the well and it instantly pressed the water down, trapping the Dragon King under the bowl. This particular scene was apparently inspired by the legend, as noted earlier, about Shen Wansan's possession of a "treasure-accumulating bowl" which enabled him to produce valuable objects and subdue demons, and which was seized by Ming Taizu after confiscating Shen's estates and treasures on the charge of a serious crime he allegedly committed. It was reported that when some sea creatures known as *zhu(po)long* (crocodiles?) were spotted under the waterway of the Shuixi (formal name Sanshan) Gate of Nanking causing a disturbance, Ming Taizu used the power of old Shen's magic bowl to suppress them and this succeeded. It was not clear how this was accomplished, but it was obvious that the mythology of Shen Wanshan associated with Nanking came to be exploited by the Peking legend-makers in developing these stories.[32]

As to the concluding remark about Liu Bowen promising the Dragon King who was trapped under the well near the newly built bridge that he could come out again when the bridge grew old, but then changing the name of the bridge to "not growing old" and thus preventing the Dragon King from realizing his wish, was a clever subplot. The name of the bridge, Beixinqiao, originally means "North New Bridge" but when the storyteller read it as *buxin* this changed the meaning drastically, producing a dramatic effect. The bridge, probably built in Ming times, was located at the northeastern corner of the intersection of the five *li* long east-west street from Dongzhimen to the Drum Tower and the ten *li* long north-south street from Chongwenmen to the end of the northern city, in what is known as the Dongchengqu 東城區 in present-day Beijing. But the bridge no longer exists and it has become the name of an avenue. At the center was the Jingzhongmiao 精忠廟 (Temple of Sustained Loyalty) built in 1827 honoring the Song general Yue Fei 岳飛 (1103–1142), but the locals also conveniently called it Longwangmiao 龍王廟 (Dragon King Temple); inside the temple was a well, where legend says the Dragon King was trapped by Liu Bowen with the magic of Shen Wanshan. The temple, however, was razed in the last decade to make room for the construction of a commercial mall, now known as Beixinqiao shangchang 北新橋商場.[33]

It should be noted there is a longer version of the Beixinqiao story which was focused on Yao Guanxdiao's fight against the dragon and son in the building of Peking, infused with the legend of the deified General Yue Fei. It was said that like Liu Bowen scheming to subdue the Dragon King, Yao Guangxiao also learned that the old dragon and his son had snuck under the well near the Beixin Bridge plotting treachery. Yao rushed to the scene and challenged the dragons to a sword fight; he felt the strain of fighting two opponents and slowed after a few rounds, but suddenly he heard a loud grunt from the old dragon with blood dripping from his leg and the shouting of General Yue that he was coming to his rescue. Yao tried to find General Yue to no avail. He put the frightened senior dragon in chains and placed him and his son under the well, and built a temple over it to pay tribute to the General, hence it became known as Jingzhongmiao.[34] Inspired by the Liu Bowen and the dragon saga, it has become an integral part of the legend of Yao Guangxiao building the city of Peking.

"How was the City of Peking Built?"

Yao Guangxiao and the Prince of Yan

This story begins with a legend that the Prince of Yan was very jealous of Liu Bowen and was always trying to find an excuse to kill him. One day the prince put a difficult question to his adviser and asked for an answer. He said that he intended to lead a northern campaign and wanted to know where and when he should end the campaign. Liu Bowen told the prince that when he reached the place where people eat blood-tainted rice, use mud pots to cook their meals, and straw to cover their pots, the soldiers should lay down their arms. He said that he had a map, and a sealed letter, asking the prince to read them when the battle was over. It turned out that when the prince carried the campaign to the border fortresses of Youzhou (ancient name of Peking), the soldiers who ate only red *gaoliang* rice, with no iron pots to prepare meals, were undernourished and many fell sick and perished. The prince had to call off the campaign as Liu Bowen had forewarned and so had no pretext to harm him. At this juncture the Prince of Yan opened Liu Bowen's map; it was a plan for the building of the city of Peking. Then he unsealed the letter. In it Liu Bowen recommended an adviser named Yao Guangxiao for the construction of the city and suggested that if he had no money for the undertaking, he should seek out a resourceful man named Shen Wansan. The prince then gave order to look for both men, but there was no trace of them after several months' search.

Then one day as the prince went hunting on the west side of the capital he arrived at a place where the old trees on the hill jutted into the sky, clouds and mists swirled around, and rushing streams roared. He decided to take a rest in this valley, which turned out to be the site of the famous Tanzhou Monastery 潭州寺. Hearing of the Prince's arrival, all the monks, old and young, came out to the gate to greet "His Highness" with the most solemn ceremony. Among the crowd was a neatly dressed old monk holding up a "nine-link" goblet (*jiulingbei* 九連杯) in his hands. He knelt on the ground and proclaimed: "Your servant Yao Guangxiao bowing to meet Your Highness." It is said that the monk was originally called Yao Guanghui 姚廣慧. He was an Ordinary Grand Master (zhong dafu 中大夫) under Emperor Taizu but because he could not get along with his colleagues, he retired to the hills and changed his name to avoid trouble. When the prince heard the name Yao Guangxiao he immediately dismounted and clasped Yao's hand, and they went into the monastery together. Brushing aside his offer to sit on a "treasured seat" (*baozuo* 寶座), the prince invited Yao to occupy it, and made a bow to him, calling him "adviser" and pleading with him to leave the monastery to build the city of Peking. Yao Guangxiao immediately knelt down and kowtowed, declining the request. But when the prince tossed Liu Bowen's design on the ground and asked him to take a look, Yao was so frightened that he could not decline again but promised to accept the task. After all, Liu Bowen was his master and he could not refuse.[35]

It seems odd that the story starts with a statement that the Prince of Yan hated Liu Bowen so much that he always wanted to kill him, especially since historically they were totally unrelated and in the earlier Peking legend the Prince held him in high regard as his chief adviser. A likely explanation is that in telling a story that focused on Yao Guangxiao, the nemesis of Liu Bowen, the author opted to debase Liu by turning the Prince of Yan against him in order to bolster Yao's stature, even though in the follow-up subplots on the building of Peking he is still under Liu's thumb. The prince's northern campaign apparently alludes to his participation in a major expedition against remnants of the Mongol Northern Yuan court of Toghus Temür (r. 1378–1388) in the spring of 1390 outside the borders of Peking together with his brother Zhu Gang 朱棡 (1358–1398), the Prince of Jin, and other senior ranking generals. The operation turned out to be a success, with the capture of the ringleaders.[36] In the present story, however, the situation appears rather gloomy. The alleged exchange between the prince and Liu Bowen about the campaign and Liu's advice to suspend the battle when they reached a place of intolerable abject living conditions near the future city of Peking, and of how what he predicted eventually came true, were historically groundless. They are only imaginative fictional interpolations to lay the groundwork of the story of the building of the capital city. Nonetheless, starting the story with the Prince of Yan's campaign against the Mongols and relating it to the building of Peking attests to the prominence of the Mongolian elements in the evolving legend of the construction of the capital.

It is also fiction that Liu Bowen presented a map and a sealed letter to the prince, asking him to read them when the battle was over, and that when the prince did so after he halted the campaign on the border of Youzhou he found in the map a plan for building the city of Peking and the letter recommended an adviser named Yao Guangxiao to take charge of the building and to find Shen Wansan should he lack money for the construction. However, this was directly inspired by the aforementioned Mongolian story which relates that before the Prince of Yan departed from Nanking on exile to the north a Daoist priest named Liu Bowen put a "sealed packet" into his hand, instructing him to open it for consultation when he found himself in distress or danger. When the prince arrived in Nankou in what was later Peking, he was distressed at its barren wilderness, with few inhabitants and no city wall to protect the people. Thus he unsealed the packet and found Liu's instructions, which read: "When you reach Pei-p'ing Fu you must build a city there and name it Nocha Ch'eng, the City of No-cha. . . . On the back of this paper is a plan of the city; you must be careful to act according to the instructions accompanying it."[37] Thereafter the Prince followed the instructions and a spacious, magnificent capital city was built. This Mongolian story reveals few details of the city plan other than its name, but the extrapolation of the story significantly bolstered Liu Bowen's role in advising the prince to appoint Yao Guangxiao and find Shen Wansan for assistance in building Peking, and established a solid linkage between the present story and other stories that spun off from the Nezha City legend.

In the ensuing episode about the Prince of Yan's surprise visit to the Tanzhou Monastery on a hunting trip to the west side of the capital where he met Yao Guangxiao and pleaded with him to serve as adviser in charge of building Peking, much of the imaginative details about their encounter were conjured up against some specific historical background about the monk and his relationship with the future Yongle emperor. The Tanzhou Monastery was a fictionalized name of the famed historical Tanzhe Monastery 潭柘寺 situated at the foot of Mount Tanzhe some 90 *li* northwest of the old capital, in what has been dubbed one of the "Ten most exquisite sites of Tanzhe" (*Tanzhe shijing* 潭柘十景) in the southeastern section of the Mentougou District 門頭溝區 outside Beijing. Allegedly founded in the Jin dynasty (265–420), the monastery was named Jiafusi 嘉福寺 and was renamed Longquan 龍泉 under the Tang. It was regarded as the oldest monastery in Peking and popular wisdom says: "First there was Tanzhe, later there was Youzhou (i.e. Peking)." Tanzhe was the popular name known to local residents since the Ming dynasty, but it was never the formal name of the monastery. It was so called because there was a pool in the rear known as Qinglongtan 清龍潭, believed to be a dragon's residence, and there were *zhe* trees planted in the front. The monastery was named Da Wanshou 大萬壽 as a center of Chan Buddhism in 1141 under the Jurchen-Jin; it was known by the same name in the Yuan but the formal name was changed back first to Longquansi and later to Jiafusi in the Ming dynasty. During the Qing, the monastery enjoyed the patronage of Emperor Kangxi and his successors. In 1692, after the completion of an extensive renovation, the emperor gave the monastery the new name Xiuyun Chansi 岫雲禪寺, but the old name Tanzhe remained popular into the twentieth century. In 1957 it was listed among the first-class historical monuments under state protection with extensive restoration; it suffered colossal damages during the "Cultural Revolution" but has since been restored and expanded as a state visitors' park.[38]

Besides its prominence in the spread of Buddhism, the Tanzhe Monastery attracted much attention from scholars and historians because of its association with Yao Guangxiao who, although his regular abode was at the Qingshou Monastery in Peking during his service with the Yongle emperor, often sought temporary refuge at the Tanzhe Monastery because of its serene hermitic environment.

He had left a few memorial poems about the monastery and his meetings with eminent monks, some visiting from Japan. According to the gazetteer *Tanzheshan Ziuyunsi zhi* 潭柘山岫雲寺志 compiled in the late Qing, the Monastery nestled at the foot of the famed Tanzhe mount in a wooded and spacious valley with the landmark "dragon pool" and its murmuring downhill stream in the backyard. A phalanx of magnificent Buddhist halls and pavilions complemented by lofty arches and exquisite stone bridges spread out in a north-south, east-west orientation over seven hectares of scenic and serene landscape. With extensive renovations undertaken in the Qing dynasty, the Tanzhe Monastery has since become not only a center of Buddhist faith but also an attractive locale for tourists.[39] The description in the present story does not sufficiently reflect the grandeur and serenity of the Tanzhe Monastery and its prominence in the spread of Buddhism in the Ming and Qing, but it does provide an important historical backdrop for the development of the fictional episodes.

In the present account Yao Guangxiao was given the name Guanghui who was claimed to be a monk of grand order under Taizu who retired to the hills because he failed to get along with his colleagues. Yao humbly prostrated himself to receive the prince but the prince treated him most courteously when he realized the monk was the man he wanted. In real history, however, Yao was appointed by Taizu as a monk-in-attendance to the Prince of Yan at his fief in Beipingfu and fostered a close relationship with him, and the fact that he asked to be allowed to retire from official duties after the prince's enthronement as the Yongle emperor was of his own accord, not because he had incurred enmity from his colleagues.[40] He also died before work started on the building of Peking. It is a fictitious but ingenious plot, therefore, to present Yao Guangxiao as earnestly declining to become the prince's adviser to leave the monastery to build the city of Peking, but when the prince tossed Liu Bowen's design on the ground Yao was so frightened that he could not refuse to comply because Liu was his revered mentor. It supplements well the earlier folk story about Liu Bowen and Yao Guangxiao competing to design the plan for building the Nezha City in which Liu won because his drawing presented a proper square. The dramatization subtly reflects the inferior status of Yao Guangxiao to Liu Bowen in both later Ming literary and popular perception in general and in the competition to produce a design for the building of Peking in particular.

The Prince of Yan and Shen Wansan

However, though finding Yao Guangxiao who agreed to serve as his adviser, the Prince of Yan still lacked the money to build the city of Peking so he started to search for Shen Wansan as Liu Bowen had advised earlier. The prince first charged two junior officials with the task of finding Shen and gave them a three months' deadline, warning that if they failed their mission they would lose their heads. Time flew by quickly and only three days remained but there was no sign of the man. Then one day, one of the officers went out for a walk and wandered to the Donghua Gate. It was the only place in the imperial-city open to the public. There were many porters, carrying rations or precious goods for the imperial household, or serving as messengers. Many petty traders and hawkers also went there to run small businesses like selling bean curd, making fried dough sticks or selling hot cakes. One day a burly porter, stripped to his waist and with a load on his shoulders, walked away having eaten a hot cake. The hawkers yelled, accusing him of not paying. The man rebuffed them saying how he, Shen Wansan, could eat without paying. When the junior official heard the name he was overjoyed. He immediately paid the charge on his behalf and, having made sure he was Shen Wansan, told him that he had been looking for him for three months because the imperial master wanted his presence.

Seeing the half-naked dark burly porter, the Prince of Yan could not believe that the man before him was the living God of Wealth Shen Wansan. Still, he personally removed his handcuffs and asked him for money to build the city of Peking. Flabbergasted, Shen asked the prince not to poke fun, saying that he was only a porter, barely making enough to feed himself and not even having anything to wear. How could he have money hoarded at home? But the prince raised his eyebrows and threatened him on the pain of death to turn over his gold and silver. Shen again denied his wealth so the prince looked at Yao Guangxiao and gave the order to beat up Shen Wansan. Though beaten to a pulp and streaming with blood, Shen still said he had nothing. In frustration the prince ordered his men to put Shen in a cangue, placing a gong in his hand, parading him around under guard, and forcing him to chant aloud: "Don't act like me Shen Wansan, not doling out money to build the city of

Peking!" and then striking the gong three times. But after parading for three days there was still no result.

Then on the fourth day, the soldiers again dragged Shen Wansan out on parade. After going out of the Di'an Gate, Shen was so worn out by the torture that he was almost dead. Struggling for breath he soon collapsed on the ground, but the soldiers kept whipping him. Then a white-haired old man came forward and intervened. He pulled out his own smoke-pouch and invited Shen to take a puff. But Shen had no strength to smoke. He flung the pouch on the ground, saying to the old man: "I'm staying right here!" meaning that he would die there no matter what. But when the soldiers heard the word "here" they dashed to report to the officials that Shen Wansan had just spoken, hinting that the cache of gold and silver must be there. All the soldiers started digging on the spot where Shen had laid down and found 480,000 taels of silver. This time the prince was really exhilarated and ordered the soldiers to drag Shen Wansan along and follow his steps. After a few paces Shen collapsed again. The soldiers dug up ten vaults of silver at that spot, all together there were 1,800,000 taels. Afterward the ground was left with ten pits and when they were filled with water they became known as Shijiaohai 十窖海 (Ten Vaults Sea), which in later times came to be called Shichahai 十察海.

The Prince of Yan was still dissatisfied. The guards again chained and paraded Shen Wansan out to the Tian'an Gate, and when Shen reached the Gold Fish Pond on the west side of the Rainbow Bridge he again fainted. On that spot the soldiers started digging and found a golden vat filled with gold bars, totaling about 480,000 taels. When Shen awoke they whipped him again, and when he collapsed they resumed digging. In all they dug out nine vats of gold bars, each with the same amount, and the total number of taels of gold corresponded to the amount of silver found in the Di'an Gate. Together, they inspired the legend of "Nine Vats and Eighteen Vaults". The place came to be known as the Gold and Silver Pond (Jinyinchi 金銀池) and in later times, when goldfish were reared in the pond, it became known as the Gold Fish Pond (Jinyuchi 金魚池). The prince then planned to construct the city wall and summoned all the skilled builders, but no wall plaster could be found. Yao Guangxiao then reported that it was only available in Shanxi—far away from Peking. As horses and mules were not sufficient to haul the plaster, people were ordered to stand in a line, back to back, each passing to the next baskets of plaster from Shanxi. However, even after all the hilltops in Shanxi—three hundred and thirty-three in total—were leveled, the city walls still lacked three feet of plaster. Yao Guangxiao then laid out Liu Bowen's design of the city and found a line surrounding the four sides of the wall. He reported it to the prince and dredged the earth surrounding the four sides of the city walls and piled them upon the wall. Thus the city wall was completed, with the Hucheng Canal surrounding the four sides of the city.[41]

This part of the story, focusing on the Prince of Yan's search for Shen Wansan for money to build the city of Peking, culminates in a series of folkloric episodes about the construction of the capital that started with the prince's acquiring the services of Yao Guangxiao. Neither in history nor in fiction was the prince connected with Shen Wansan who came from a different generation, but the latter was known to Liu Bowen and Yao Guangxiao; hence the two were joined through the latter's recommendation. Historically the building of Peking was an imperial enterprise of the highest order; enormous financial, human, and material resources had been allocated and, unlike Taizu's building of Zhongdu at Fengyang that had to be aborted because of financial shortfall, this was not the case for Peking. However, the Yongle official records did show that early on affluent households from ten districts of Nanking and Suzhou and from nine of the provincial administration commissions of Zhejiang and other provinces, as well as ten thousand able-bodied households from Shanxi, had been ordered to migrate to live in Peking to strengthen its financial base and work force. Moreover, the requisition of construction materials, such as lumber from Sichuan, coal from Shanxi, stone from the nearby Xishan and Fangshan, bricks from Hebei, Shandong, Nanking, Jiangsu, and Anhui, and other commodities from the south of the Yangzi region, must have enforced great hardship to people on the supply and transportation route.[42] The intense effort to find Shen Wansan in order to secure money from him for the construction hence alluded to the general picture of the socioeconomic deprivation that the capital building brought to the population.

Indeed Shen Wansan, a scion of the wealthy landowning family in the Zhouzhuang canton of Suzhou who had built a tremendous fortune in the southern Nanking region during the late Yuan and early Ming, would be an ideal candidate for fictionalization in this context. But Shen Wansan's association with Liu Bowen and the Prince of Yan in the legend of the building of Peking, except for the reference to the source of his wealth, was based on his dealings with Ming Taizu and the building of Nanking. He is alleged to have made a substantial contribution toward building the southwest walled gates of Nanking and, as local rumor had it, he left his "treasure-accumulating bowl" buried under the southern gate, hence it was named the Jubaomen. In the meantime, with Liu Bowen being identified in legend with the building of Peking, and given the close relationship between Nanking and Peking, there is sufficient rationale and ample fictional material to involve Shen Wansan in the process. It is striking that in both versions of the story, the folkloric motif of a "god of wealth" disguised as a poor beggar was invoked.[43] Shen Wansan appeared as either a filthy beggar wearing rags and carrying a broken earthen bowl tied with a cord around his neck, or as a half-naked dark burly porter roaming in the Donghua Gate area looking for work and food. In both instances he feigned lack of any knowledge about hoarded treasure and only after being severely beaten did he confess and reveal the site of the hidden caches of gold, silver, and jewels. In light of the sufferings of Shen Wansan and his clansmen under the Ming emperor despite their financial contributions, these fictitious trappings would suggest that wealthy people in early Ming were wary of wanton persecution by the authorities and tried to conceal their identity or to hide their fortune underground in order to protect themselves. Indeed in the anecdotic miscellanies about Shen Wansan there are stories that the source of his wealth derived from the discovery of hidden treasures or that he had left some of his treasures hidden underground, providing sensational episodes for dramatization.[44]

It should be noted however, the details of the officials' search for Shen Wansan and of dragging him around in order to find the hidden treasure, were adapted from a much longer folktale about the Shicha Sea, connecting the digging for Shen's hidden treasures which resulted in a large number of pits on the ground with the origin of Peking's famed inland lakes in the northwestern part of the outer city. They underscored the fictional imagination of the author or tellers of the story, particularly their ability to dovetail Shen Wansan's route of movement with the unique topographical features of the city— the extraordinary scenic lakes and pools—to exaggerate the extent of his involvement with the capital building. The following episodes provide excellent testimony.[45]

To begin with, it is ingenious that the story set the successful search at the Donghua Gate, which was the only area of the imperial-city in Qing times open to common people. The fact that Shen Wansan disguised himself as a burly porter and was apprehended among the crowd in the imperial-city served well to concoct a figure from among the local rich needed by an imperial ruler committed to building his new capital. Shen Wansan was dragged along a route that covered a vast span of the city. But it was all within a region of lakes and pools, which facilitated the fictional dramatization. The first stop was outside the Di'anmen, the rear walled gate of the imperial-city southeast of the Shichahai. There a cluster of three large inland lakes in the northwestern corner of the outer city served as the anchorage of the grain boats traveling between the canals and as one of the main reservoirs of the city's water supply. It was said that being beaten, Shen twice collapsed and pointed to two different locations where treasure was hidden. After digging, not only were ten vaults of silver found—amounting to 480,000 taels in each find and 4,800,000 taels in total, the excavation also left ten large pits in the ground and, as the story was told, later when water filled these pits they became the Shicha Sea.[46]

The second spot where Shen Wansan was dragged was outside the Tian'anmen south of the imperial-city. As the soldiers kept whipping him, he collapsed twice near the Gold Fish Pond on the west side of the Rainbow Bridge. (The bridge was actually named *hong* 紅, meaning "red" but here the text reads *hong* 虹 as "rainbow".) At the first spot the soldiers dug out a golden vat filled with gold bars, also totaling 480,000 taels, and in the second spot they dug out nine vats of gold bars, each with similar amount of gold. In time these episodes inspired the legend of "Nine Vats and Eighteen Vaults" and these pits were said to be still visible in recent years. As a result the place came to be known as the Gold and Silver Pond and was also known as the Gold Fish Pond. These two instances were indeed bizarre but were well calculated to manipulate the popular imagination through the use of Peking's famed scenery. In the latter case, the Gold and Silver Pond was a fictionalized name for a cluster of small ponds actually known as Gold Fish Pond, which was dug in the Jurchen-Jin dynasty and was originally named Jincao 金草 chi or Golden Grass Pond where willow trees were planted along the banks. In the Ming and Qing it became known as Jinyuchi as it was primarily used to rear goldfish. It was a fanciful distortion of the name of a scenic spot to accentuate the drama of Shen Wansan's revelation of his hidden treasures.[47]

As to the final episode about the Prince of Yan planning to construct the city wall but finding no wall plaster and so acting on Yao Guangxiao's report to have it hauled from Shanxi, there was some half-truth in the story in view of the fact that plaster and coal had been imported from Shanxi during the construction of the capital, and a large labor force and transportation facilities had been mobilized. But the claim that even after all the hilltops in Shanxi were leveled the city wall still lacked three feet of plaster and Yao, by looking at Liu Bowen's design of the city, found a line surrounding the four sides of the wall and, therefore, he proposed to the prince to dredge the earth surrounding the four sides of the city wall and piled them upon the wall, is without historical merit. Thus the city wall was completed, with the Hucheng Canal (presumably filled with water after its sides were dug to provide earth for the city wall in the fictional imagination) surrounding the four sides of the city.[48] The episode was craftily exaggerated to give some credit to Yao Guangxiao for implementing Liu Bowen's design by ingeniously completing the city wall.

The Folkloric Legacy

In summary, it is clear that the Mongolian folktale relating the legend of the Mongol ancestry of the Yongle emperor provided the context for the story of the Prince of Yan's building of the city of Peking, while the episodes of siting by bowshot and putting Liu Bowen in charge of the construction became an inspiration to the Chinese folktales about the building of the imperial capital. The motifs not only refurbished the old Nazha City legend by coalescing the fictive relationship between the Prince of Yan and Liu Bowen and producing new episodes, but also inspired similar stories about the building of Peking spun off from the Liu Bowen legend and infused with other historical and semi-historical personalities and supernatural beings. It is apparent that whereas the Mongolian folkloric tradition impacted on the Chinese, the Chinese folklore also skillfully adapted the counter tradition and conjured up new episodes through an ingenious extrapolation of historical and folkloric materials.

Without question, the concocted relationship between the Prince of Yan and Liu Bowen established through the alleged Mongol mother of the prince in the Mongolian legend provided the catalyst for the story of the building of Peking in the Mongolian folktale as well as adaptation by the Chinese in their folkloric tradition. Her giving of two sealed "envelopes" to the prince, one of which contained instructions to ask his father the Taizu emperor to appoint Liu Bowen as his companion, and the other to be opened when the prince faced difficulties or danger, laid fertile ground for further fictional spinning. In the Mongolian context, it gives rise to the story of the prince's encounter with the mysterious swarthy-faced black rider while hunting in the wilderness in the company of Liu Bowen, the rider's shooting of arrows for siting, his revelation to the prince of the silver and jewels hidden in the spots hit by the arrows, and the advice to appoint Liu Bowen to build a great city there. The description of the city plan matches the basic architectural layout of the city of old Peking, and it emphasizes the correspondence with the planets and stars in the celestial constellation and the Eight Trigrams of the *Book of Changes*. It portrays an extrapolation of the cosmological principles in the layout of traditional Chinese imperial cities with explicit Mongolian trappings.

In the first Chinese folktale "Liu Bowen built the City of Peking", the impact of the Mongolian folkloric tradition, besides cementing the fictive relationship between the Prince of Yan and Liu Bowen, is most riveting in the episode of general Xu Da shooting an arrow to determine the site of the future capital and how that arrow was subsequently picked up by a local wealthy landlord to re-shoot it elsewhere. The motif is not a direct extrapolation from the above-mentioned Mongolian folktale but a borrowing from a related Mongolian custom about using the flight of the bowshot as a medium for allotting lands, determining property rights, and for siting when building monuments, a practice that was be documented as late as the seventeenth century. In the Chinese case, the adaptation of the nomadic custom of using the bowshot for siting was also reinforced by the Chinese popular lore of historical war heroes showing off their archery skill in comparable situations. The Chinese, however, did not use an arrow either for geomantic siting or for divination purposes as did the Mongols and other Altaic peoples.[49] The intrusion of this episode into the Chinese folktale about the building of Peking attests to the preponderance of nomadic traditions, though highly Sinicized, within the Chinese storytelling medium.

This ingenious adaptation of the Mongolian or other nomadic folkloric tradition at the start of the Chinese folktale was amicably matched with a string of miraculous episodes co-opted by the skillful storyteller about Liu Bowen's feud with the Dragon King, and the assistance offered by the fictionalized personages Shen Wansan and Gao Liang in building Peking and subduing the dragon to secure the water supply of the residents. These were inspired by the legend about Nezha battling with the Dragon King and his sons for control of the water in the Eastern Sea, which provided the impetus for the famed story of Liu Bowen building the Nezha City and its spin-off episodes. However, notwithstanding the fictitious and miraculous trappings, the various subplots in these stories vividly reflected the urban morphology of Peking—the prominence of lakes, pools, ponds in the palace-, imperial-, and outer-cities—and the disparate qualities of its water resources. In the latter case, the poor quality of much of Peking's underground water, which was caused by the silted conditions of the river beds, and the superior quality of the water cascading from the western hills like that at the Jade Spring Hill that flowed into the imperial- and palace-cities, played into the hands of legend-making. The phenomenon was explained in terms of Gao Liang's failure to recapture the water taken away by the Dragon King in two water bags, that he only broke the brackish water bag whereas the sweet water bag was carried off by the dragon to the Jade Spring Hill. This seamless interfacing of disparate episodes from both the Mongolian and Chinese traditions vividly attest to the ingenuity of the storytellers and the interplay of myth and reality in the popular perception of the building of Peking.

The other Chinese folktale "How was the City of Peking Built?", focusing on the relationship between the Prince of Yan, the monk-cum-adviser Yao Guangxiao and the mysterious Shen Wansan, was again a spin-off from the story of Liu Bowen building the Nezha City. This is quite clear from the ending of the story where it says that when Liu Bowen and Yao Guangxiao were competing with their plans for Peking, Yao's drawing looked exactly like that of Liu Bowen except for a minor flaw. Hence Yao could not claim exclusive credit and, greatly discouraged, goes off to be a monk. In the present story focusing on Yao Guangxiao, the Prince of Yan found Yao in the Tanzhe Monastery and succeeded in persuading him to build the city of Peking only by tossing Liu Bowen's design on the ground. It is said that on seeing the plan, Yao was so frightened that he found no way to resist but promised to accept the task as Liu Bowen was his master and he could not but comply. The rest of the story relates how the Prince of Yan, running out of money to build the city, asked Yao for a solution and Yao recommended finding Shen Wansan. Shen was a wealthy man who disguised himself in rags, and was believed to have hoarded vast amounts of gold and silver in secret places. The details of how the officials roamed around the city searching for Shen Wansan and having found the man, who appeared as a dark burly porter, beat him almost to death until he revealed his treasure were recycled from anecdotes and folktales about Shen's mysterious sources of wealth traceable to the literary miscellanies of the late Ming through the early Qing. The latter part of the story was also presented in summary fashion in the earlier story of Liu Bowen building the city of Peking, indicating the close connection between these two stories.

As in the earlier cases, the present story of how the city of Peking was built extracted elements from the daily lives of traders in the outer-city as well as the peculiar topographical features of the environs in the palace- and imperial-cities, which heightened the drama and made the story more believable. In the former case, the search for Shen Wanshan amid the markets and the crowded and busy Donghua Gate draws a sharp contrast with the serene monastic environs of Yao Guangxiao's abode in the Tanzhe Monastery and is a good illustration of the insertion of authentic details into a fictional story. In the latter, Shen Wansan's revelation of his hoard of gold, silver, and jewels and their subsequent excavation, which resulted in a number of vaults in Peking which were later filled by rain and through flooding gave birth to the belief that this was how many ponds and pools were formed in the city. In reality these ponds and pools were unique topographical features created by the geological and environmental evolution of nature over the millennia and were not man-made phenomenon. In the case of Shen Wansan's exploits, though it is entirely a Chinese phenomenon, it also smacks of traces of the afore-mentioned Mongolian folklore where the swarthy-faced black rider who shot arrows for siting also informed the Prince of Yan how to obtain hidden caches of gold, silver, and jewels to finance the building of the capital. The section of the story where a mysterious rider revealed that such treasure would be found where his arrows landed, and that Liu Bowen should dig up the ground at those spots, parallels the Chinese story of Shen Wansan's revelation of his hoard and the resultant environmental impact. This instance thus again provides evidence of the lingering Mongolian impact in the folk tradition about the building of Peking.

Moreover, it is worth noting that such nomadic tradition of siting by bowshot in its Sinitic adaptation also found expression in a folktale about the building of the Ming capital Nanking. This is seen in the story "Ying jia jian" 鷹夾箭 ("The Falcon Gripping the Arrow"), about the siting of the imperial-city at Nanking under Ming Taizu as transmitted in modern folklore. According to standard historical texts, the double-walled capital city of Nanking was built on the advice of Taizu's confidant Liu Ji, who had chosen the site south of Mt. Zhong in the autumn of 1366, two years before the founding of the new dynasty. In 1369 workers began construction of the new capital east of the Baixia Gate 白下門 of the old city; it included a walled imperial-city and palace-city with a perimeter of sixty-one *li* (34.7 km). The imperial-city was completed in the fall of 1373, but construction continued into the 1380s. The imperial-city and new palaces of Nanking were to provide the blueprint for the Forbidden City of Peking when the Yongle emperor ordered that the new city should be a replica of his father's old establishment. Folklore tells a different story of the building of Nanking.[50]

The episode in "Ying jia jian" about the siting of Nanking differs from the information in historical texts. We do not know its origin nor its course of transmission, but it was apparently popularly told and retold in Nanking and Fengyang, which was Zhu Yangzhang's native place in modern Anhui. Although the central theme is the origin of Nanking, the folktale begins with the building of a new Ming imperial-city Zhongdu at Fengyang. Its construction is said to have been ordered in 1369, and work continued during the next five years aimed at completing a grand metropolis for the national capital. But the project is said to have been abruptly suspended in

1375 when the emperor realized that both the people and his own treasury were exhausted. Contrary to the assertion in the folktale, Zhongdu was never completed but Fengyang remained a special administration of the imperial families throughout the Ming dynasty.[51]

The "Ying jia jian" episode begins with a fictitious claim of the completion of Zhongdu. It relates that after the completion of the walled city at Fengyang, Ming Taizu, with a coterie of civil and military officials, arrived at the site from Nanking for a jubilant inspection in preparation for transferring the main capital. As the emperor was basking in the exuberant applause of his ministers, his principal adviser Liu Bowan remained glum and silent. Dumfounded, the emperor demanded an explanation. Liu instantly fell on his knees, explaining that he was deeply distressed by the inauspicious geomancy.

Looking to the north, Liu explained that the city was exposed to the swamps of the Fangqiu Lake 方丘湖. If an enemy were to attack, the bushy willows would easily conceal a large army of invaders. Turning to the northwest, he pointed out the strategic Mount Ma'an 馬鞍山 (Horse Saddle). If an enemy were to launch an assault from its summit with cannon, the cannon balls would easily bombard the city. Therefore, he begged that the capital be built elsewhere. The emperor then inquired about the site, and Liu responded that it should be built at "the space of the fallen arrow" (*yijianzhidi* 一箭之地) .When the emperor pressed him for an explanation, Liu asked him to shoot an arrow southeastward, saying that the location of the fallen arrow should be the site of the new capital. Impressed by his knowledge of geomancy, the emperor did as told, drawing a bow with all his strength, and the arrow streaked toward the southeast like lightning, traveling forty-five *li* (25.6 km). As its flight weakened, a golden falcon suddenly swooped down from the air, gripped the arrow with its beak, and flew in the same direction the arrow had been traveling. Finally, after departing Fengyang and traversing the Yangzi River, the falcon arrived at Nanking and loosened its grip, whereupon the emperor's arrow fell into the city. Several days later, people came forward with a report of the sighting of the arrow, and so the emperor realized that it was the will of the spirits that the capital should be built in Nanking. It turned out that the golden falcon was the avatar of the Grand White, or Golden Star ([*Taibai*] *jinxing* 太白金星), the brightest star in the east to be on duty in the Celestial Palace that day. Having overheard the conversation between the emperor and Liu Bowan, the star-avatar presaged the arrow's falling into Nanking, and so he transformed himself into a falcon to ensure its occurrence for Taizu's sake. It is for this reason that the story came to be known by its title.[52]

Naturally, such a tale has no parallel evidence. According to historical records, when Liu Ji was entrusted with the design of the new palace and capital city at Nanking, he applied geomantic siting and located an auspicious site that laid south of Mt. Zhong and the Baixia Gate of the historical capital. The Zhongdu city at Fengyang was patterned after Nanking and in fact was built later, not earlier, than the latter. The Ming founder soon abandoned the thought of making his native place of Fengyang the main capital and suspended construction there. The interpolation of the story of Zhongdu, with an allusion to the Mongolian custom of siting by bowshot, is intriguing. It could have first started as part of the legend of the building of Peking, which was much influenced by the Mongolian folk tradition and, in the course of transmission, because of the close affinity between Peking and Nanking as dual capitals, the Peking legend came to be infused with that of the building of Nanking, although the two stories could also have developed independently. It is an ironic twist of popular imagination that Ming Taizu, the anti-Mongol Chinese dynastic founder, became enveloped in legends of Mongolian origin, though these legends have been blurred by intensive Sinification over the centuries.

Epilogue

Indeed, the evolution of the legends of the building of old Peking over the last several centuries—the Nazha/Nezha City legend of Yuan Dadu and Ming Peking, as well as the Mongolian legend of siting the capital by bowshot and spin-off episodes in Chinese folklore—reveal a rich popular tradition surrounding the urban development of this grandiose imperial city. Although these traditions originated with the building of Qubilai Qaghan's Great Capital in the heyday of Mongol rule, the legends drew upon an intermingling of heterogeneous influences for their growth and efflorescence. Juxtaposed with but distinct from the official and élite traditions of imperial city planning and urban culture, these unique popular traditions presented an admixture of Buddhism and Daoism, worship of spiritual deities, mythologized historical and fictionalized personages, Han Chinese as well as non-Han folk beliefs and sub-cultures. They were transmitted, recycled, and disseminated through a variety of literary media, oral and written popular literature as the imperial city grew and expanded over time, and they left an indelible imprint on Peking's intellectual and cultural heritage as it reemerged in the modern world.

Jeffrey Meyer dichotomizes the mythical structure of traditional Peking into two distinct but interrelated systems: the "warp" of astral/cosmic symbolisms of the high tradition and the "weft" of a complex system of popular beliefs and legends. They represented general patterns and classic design, and specific, unique events of a place, even though they shared some general plans. Although I do not subscribe to the "sacred city" thesis or what made a locality a "sacred place" in reference to old Peking, Meyer's binary classification, which underscores the symbiosis of high culture and popular culture in traditional Chinese civilization, is very useful to my own work. In reviewing the ideological component of imperial city planning and the architectural layout in both Yuan Dadu and Ming Peking, particularly the latter, which is sumptuously documented in historical accounts and visual in splendid extant monuments, it is evident that despite occasional deviations, they followed the general patterns of astral/cosmic symbolism and classical designs and left a durable legacy of cosmopolitan idealism. At the same time, old Peking is also distinguished for the profusion of miraculous stories and bizarre legends with specific motifs and traditions. Some are about local sites, monuments, towers, altars, temples, wells, lakes, walls, and other places, which Meyer dubs "local sacrality"; others are about the city as a whole, such as the legends and folktales about the building of Peking, which presented a different mythical structure. In some cases, while divine beings and *homo religious,* such as the legendary sage kings, mythologized heroes and the mythical dragon and strange animals, provided general models, many of the stories and legends were not derived from a cosmic pattern, but from unique mythical local events, leaving a particular mark, sacred or otherwise, for the city of Peking. These popular traditions are quite distinct from the official or élite traditions.

Meyer attaches much value to the myths and legends of old Peking. He said, "they give us a precious insight into how the masses of ordinary folk experienced Peking, how its monuments, temples, walls, and towers came to be important in their everyday lives. A few of the best of them reveal an understanding of human nature that transcends the particularities of time, race, and culture. . . . The legends give us the weft of the tapestry of the Chinese capital: the substance, color, and specificity that make Peking different from all other past capitals of China."[1] What then may have been the source of the mythical events that produced the stories and legends about the building of old Peking that made them so specific and appealing? We need to delve into the historical development of Peking, the events and personalities surrounding the building of the imperial city, its natural resources, as well as the impact of the transformation of the old capital in modern times.

First, a unique feature of old Peking was that an imperial city was built four times over several centuries under alien ruling dynasties, the Liao, Jin, Yuan, and Qing of the Khitans, Jurchens, Mongols, and the Manchus respectively. Only Ming Peking was founded as the capital city of the restored Chinese dynasty, but it was again replaced by an alien ruler, the Manchus, who renovated the Ming capital and expanded it. Although Han Chinese ideological component and architectural tradition were kept intact throughout Peking's history, and Chinese city planners—such as Liu Bingzhong, were employed in the planning of Dadu, the imperial city construction under alien rule could not but be affected by its political vicissitudes and by the non-Han religious beliefs and cultural traditions. The prominence of the Nazha story and its mythical role in the building of Yuan Dadu was an integral part of the mythologization of Liu Bingzhong as the confidant of Qubilai Qaghan. As such, the story was not just a history of Peking but also part of the intellectual and cultural development of the Mongol-Yuan dynasty.

Second, related to the above, Ming Peking also fell under strong Mongolian influences after Yuan rule as remnants of the Mongol tribes, starting with the Oirat-Mongols who had intruded into the outskirts of the capital and taken the Yingzong emperor captive in September 1449, constantly threatened the northern borders until the end of the dynasty. At the same time, a large Mongol population stayed in China after the expulsion of the Yuan court. They spread across the northern provinces and around Peking in their grassland settlements. A sizable contingent served at court as eunuchs and minor officials, and large numbers of them served in the Ming military units and even local administrations. Their storytellers and narrators were responsible for developing and nurturing stories and legends of the Mongol maternity of the Ming emperor Yongle, his being born as the posthumous son of Toghōn Temür, his exile to Peking, and his building the capital city there in the Mongolian context. Over time they penetrated into Chinese communities and inspired culturally integrated stories and legends about the building of Peking.

Third, apart from historical and human factors, old Peking was strongly susceptible to the impact of ecological and climatic factors in historical development because of its physical environs and urban morphology. Although the city was surrounded by rivers and inhabited by lakes and pools, Peking continually faced severe water problems. The water from the northeastern mountains was not sufficient to flood the waterways of the city to facilitate communication with the outside. The waterways also failed to provide adequate supply to the residents of the imperial- and palace-cities, and the situation became acute in times of drought or excess flooding. These natural and physical factors accounted for the profusion of stories and legends about Peking's sources of water, the river, the lake, or the well, and about the divinities, spirits, and mythical heroes who were believed to control water resources. In general, many stories and legends about Peking reflected the people's concern surrounding their environment and livelihood and were not necessarily inspired by imagination and fantasy.

Finally, in order to understand the evolution of the legends of old Peking it is vital to pinpoint, if possible, the historical sources and particular circumstances under which the stories and legends took root. In so far as those about the building of Peking's imperial cities are concerned, the most prominent of them, the Nazha/Nezha City legends, surfaced near the end of the dynasty when the more liberalizing environment gave the popular tradition a greater leverage to rejuvenate and flourish. The same timing also applied to the Mongolian legend about the Yongle emperor as the last Mongol qaghan's posthumous son building a capital city in Peking while he was in exile, which flourished around the metropolitan region in the late nineteenth and early twentieth centuries. The rest of the folktales that perpetuated the Nezha City or the Mongolian "siting by bowshot" legend flourished between the Republican and the Communist period in the midst of the residents' nostalgia of the heritage of old Peking while craving for a new cultural identity of their city in an epoch of tumultuous political and physical transformation.

Against this general background, we will revisit the legends about the building of old Peking, identify their common and individual characteristics, trace their sources of origin and transformation, and reexamine how they were created and maintained, and what made them unique and lasting.

As the earliest but perennial legends of the building of old Peking, the Nazha City legend of Yuan Dadu ascribed to Liu Bingzhong and its refurbished modern version, the Eight-armed Nezha City legend of Ming Peking ascribed to Liu Bowen present a remarkable narration of the city's urban development. Viewing the two as an interconnected entity, the legend is distinguished for the unique characteristics of its mythical structure—the intimate linkage of supernatural deities with mythologized historical and fictitious personalities, unambiguous connection with the historical and environmental realities of the imperial city, and aspiration of the residents to their daily concerns. The evolution of the two legends is also remarkable for the degree of adaptation of new sources and traditions, the incorporation of which rejuvenated the tradition. In both instances, the supernatural deity Nazha, later known as Nezha, remained the divine guardian-protector of the imperial city, but the mythologized hero who invoked his supernatural assistance in the planning of the city was changed from Liu Bingzhong to Liu Bowen when the legend was transposed from the Yuan to Ming and modern times, as historical realities and contemporary relevance warranted. There was an unmistakable dynamism of adaptation and refurbishment that had infused much new blood to sustain the longevity and popularity of the legend.

The Yuan legend was an integral part of the saga of the building of the Mongolian Great Capital under Qubilai Qaghan on the city plan of his erudite Buddhist-Daoist adviser Liu Bingzhong. Nazha, the supernatural Buddhist child deity who had undergone a mythical transformation in the Tang and Song through infusion of Daoist legends and Chinese popular lore, making him also one of the highest-ranked Daoist immortals, remained popular in Yuan society. In Buddhist hagiography he was hailed for his prodigious powers and magical spells to suppress evils and wicked spirits, and for his heroic deeds to protect the earthly king and his kingdom. However, in Daoist popular literature he was praised for his ferocious battles against the Dragon King and his sons in the Eastern Sea to deprive them control of the watery world. It is obvious that the reason he was infused into the legend of the building of Dadu when Liu Bingzhong designed eleven walled gates of the outer-city was to symbolize his transformed body—three heads, six arms, and two feet. Nazha would serve Dadu well as a divine guardian-protector and battle the dragons to provide water for the population, the shortage of which was a dire reality facing the imperial city. However, Liu Bingzhong was to claim equal credit for invoking the presence of Nazha by designing a city plan in his likeness, otherwise he would not have descended to earth to intervene. The development of the Nazha City legend was hence inseparable from the unfolding mythology of the legend-laden Chinese adviser to the Mongol qaghan. It is intriguing that the legend-makers not only rallied Liu Bingzhong and Nazha to address Dadu's water resources, but also used the eleven walled gates, which Liu designed to represent the child deity's body, to prognosticate the one hundred and ten years' duration of the Yuan regime, tying the legend to the champion of anti-Mongol rule and eventual Han restoration. The latter presents a different layer of the significance of the popular legend of old Peking in a sociopolitical perspective that spilled over to the later centuries.

In the case of the resurrection of the Yuan legend in the late Qing and early Republican period in the name of Liu Bowen building the Eight-armed Nezha City of Ming Peking, the development signaled not just a continued adulation of Nazha/Nezha's divine powers and reverence for his miraculous feats, but also an ingenious exploitation of the mythology of the Ming hero and champion of Han ethnocentrism. The fascination of the old Peking residents with Nezha as a supernatural deity is not difficult to understand in light of the preponderance of his riveting legend in the urban environment. The story of his fierce and victorious confrontation with the Dragon King and his sons in the Eastern Sea perpetuated by Daoist literature and popular novels must have heightened their yearning for his presence to subdue the sea demons thought to dominate the lakes and pools in Peking and drain away the precious water. The intrusion of the Liu Bowen mythology, however, not only enlivened the legend but also added a new dimension of drama. He became the *homo religious* to replace the old hero Liu Bingzhong invoking the presence of Nazha to be the guardian-protector of the imperial city because the former, a servant of the fallen Mongol-Yuan dynasty much hated by the ethnic Chinese, was no longer relevant to Ming Peking. By virtue of the manipulation of the powerful mythology of Liu Bowen, who in popular belief was hailed as an ingenious astrologer, geomancer, and prognosticator foretelling the demise of Manchu rule, and who was claimed to be related to Liu Bingzhong and to the Mongolian legend of the Yongle emperor building the city of Peking, the old Yuan legend was given a new lease of life. The wide impact of Liu Bowen's mythology in late Qing and Republican China was therefore inseparable from the triumphant return of the old legend of Dadu in new form.

By contrast, the Mongolian story of the building of Peking under the Yongle emperor, known as "siting by bowshot, locating the site of the city of Peking", did not fall within the mainstream of the legends about Peking but it was no less important. "Siting by bowshot" represented a uniquely Mongolian social and cultural tradition and it also had significant sociopolitical implications. In its original form, it was a nomadic custom to be applied not only to siting monuments, but also to award land grants to worthies and to determine property rights. The earliest known application of such a practice in Peking was ordered by Chinggis Qan when he decided to award the land around Yanjing to his favorite lieutenant Chinqai for his meritorious service. He asked Chinqai to stand in the center of the rectangular city and shoot an arrow toward each of the four corners, and all the fields, ponds, and houses within the perimeter of the fallen arrows would be awarded to him. The prevalence of such a custom among the Mongol communities in north China since Yuan rule apparently provided a powerful source of inspiration to the development of the legend.

However, in the present case, the story was part of the popular Mongolian legend of the Mongol maternity of the Yongle emperor in vogue in Mongolia and in north China since the seventeenth century. As presented in the Mongolian story of "How Emperor Yongle of the Great Ming Built the City of Peking", the future Chinese emperor, believed to be the posthumous son of Toghōn Temür, was "exiled" by Ming Taizu to the Peking region to defend the border and build a capital city. He was accompanied by the erudite imperial adviser Liu Bowen. The story relates that one day shortly after they had reached the destination, they encountered a mysterious swarthy-faced black rider—probably a fusion of the famous Dark God and King Vaiśravana in Mongolian disguise. He took away the prince's bow and arrows and shot in four directions, asking him to instruct Liu Bowen to build the city at the place where the arrows fell. The prince then put his sagacious adviser to the task, and a majestic city was thus built, becoming the capital Peking when the prince was enthroned as the Ming emperor. The design of the city, though adopting that of the Chinese imperial capital, reflected the Mongolian concept of cosmology and correspondence between the heavenly order and seasons and the architectural layout. As shown in the detailed textual analysis, the legend fused the Mongolian tradition about siting by bowshot in the building of monuments with the mythology of the Mongol maternity of the Yongle emperor, and incorporated the miraculous stories about Liu Bowen designing the capital of Nanking transmitted to Peking through various channels.

The significance of this Mongolian story of the building of Peking cannot be separated from the political implications of the legend about the Mongol ancestry of the Yongle emperor, which was conjured up in a brew of Mongolian hearsay and Chinese sources. It served as a psychological consolation to the Mongol communities, where it was believed that even though the empire was lost to the Chinese, it was still ruled over by descendants of Chinggis qan's bloodline through the Yongle emperor. In this context, the building of Peking was seen as the revival of the old Yuan capital, it was chosen by the Mongolian custom of siting by bowshot, and though they incorporated the Chinese adviser Liu Bowen into the execution of the building, it was a Mongol enterprise. It therefore had special meaning to the Mongol communities, but the story also provided an indispensable catalyst to the refurbishment of the old Chinese legend of Nazha City because of the injection of Liu Bowen. It solidified the relationship between Liu Bowen and the Yongle emperor and the building of Peking, which did not exist in actual history, and legitimated the replacement of Liu Bingzhong with Liu Bowen as the planner of the imperial city in the rejuvenated legend in the modern century.

As to the other popular stories that perpetuated the legend of the building of Peking that have enjoyed considerable publicity, they were inspired, on the one hand, by the Mongolian legend of the siting of Peking by bowshot, and on the other hand, by the refurbished version of the Nezha City legend ascribed to Liu Bowen. In various ways they were buttressed with spin-off materials about concocted historical events, mythologized personalities, and fictionalized episodes from popular traditions unique to Peking. Assuming the center of all activities, Liu Bowen found company in several historical and fictionalized figures of various persuasions. The former were the early Ming general Xu Da, the Yongle emperor's Buddhist adviser Monk Daoyuan (Yao Guangxiao), and the legendary wealthy landlord and businessman from Suzhou, Shen Wansan. The latter were the enigmatic hero Gao Liang, Liu Bowen's fictionalized chief assistant, and Liu's principal antagonists, the mythical Dragon King and his sons. Each of them was assigned a specific role in cementing the various parts of the miraculous story conjured up and embroidered by the folklorists and narrators to enrich the ensuing legends.

The first story, "Liu Bowen Built the City of Peking", consists of four major episodes. It begins with General Xu Da administering the bowshot, and Liu Bowen following the flight of the arrow to locate the site for building the city. Then, short of money, Liu coerced the wealthy Shen Wansan who was disguised as a beggar, to surrender his hoard of gold and silver to finance the building. It follows that the Dragon King, lord of the sea, resenting the building of the city on his turf, tried to smuggle all the water out of the city, but Liu Bowen put a stop to this vicious plot with the help of the fictitious hero Gao Liang and recovered the water. It concludes with Liu Bowen's final assault against the Dragon King—who hid under a well with the water collected from the streams—with Shen Wansan's help by thrusting his magic earthen begging bowl down the well, trapping the Dragon King at the bottom. In a nutshell, under the veil of imaginative fantasy, the story reflected certain historical realities about Peking and the residents' aspiration. For instance, the siting of the city by bowshot reflects a Mongolian popular belief about the origin of Peking, while Liu Bowen's coercion of the wealthy Shen Wansan for money alludes to the forced requisition of financial and human resources for the building of the capital. The fierce battles Liu Bowen waged against the vicious supernatural Dragon King to recover the stolen water, on the other hand, vividly attest to the people's worry over the shortage of water. It was a piece of bitter-sweet drama concerned about the place and the people.

The last story, "How Was the City of Peking Built?", is focused on the role of the monk Yao Guangxiao executing the building of the city with the wealth of the legendary Shen Wansan. In this story the familiar fictitious role of Liu Bowen and Yao Guangxiao was reversed; Yao emerged as the principal actor, recommended by Liu Bowen to the Yongle emperor to take charge of the building based on his city plan. This time the emperor was given a more direct role: he was credited with finding and persuading Yao Guangxiao to assume charge, and with seeking the wealthy Shen Wansan to surrender his hoarded treasure to finance the construction. As the event unfolded, Shen Wansan became the center of the drama. He was found by the guards, and, with the emperor watching, Yao Guangxiao gave the order to put him in chains and repeatedly whipped him until he revealed his hidden treasure, which would facilitate the completion of the project. The story hence fully exploited the legend of Shen

Wansan's wealth and skillfully conjured up imaginative episodes about his financial role in the building of Peking. As noted before, these episodes vividly alluded to the heavy burden shouldered not only by the wealthy but also by the commoners in the course of the construction of the capital, details rarely revealed in the historical sources. It is ingenious that the story also glossed Shen Wansan's exploits with Peking's unique urban morphology, that the excavation of his cache of treasure left many pits in the ground and when they were later filled with water through flooding, they became the famous Shicha Sea in the imperial city to enhance the drama of folk culture.

In summary, credit must go to those ingenious folklorists and storytellers who were veteran residents of old Peking or its vicinity and were well-versed in the history and popular culture of the place for recreating and propagating these fanciful stories and legends about the building of the imperial capital. In one form or another, they were recycling centuries-old myths and legends about the exploits of the supernatural deity Nazha, the Dragon King, the mythologized heroes Liu Bingzhong, Liu Bowen, and to some extent Yao Guangxiao and Shen Wansan in the building of the capital city over different periods of time. Each of these characters had a specific role in the adventure, and their laborious exploits and miraculous feats were embedded in the popular lore of the place. According to Madeleine Dong's definition, this recycling of myths and legends was not only an attempt to recapture the treasured symbols of an older culture, which appealed to the elderly city folk, but was also an effort to transform these old symbols into modern forms of urban culture without sacrificing their core values.[2] They were at the heart of a concerted process of refurbishment of bygone culture and values not only to establish a new identity for the residents of Peking, but also to meet their aspiration and material needs as they were undergoing a multitude of changes at the collapse of the dynastic order and under the pressure of modernization. The new cultural scene was much a product of, if not also facilitated by the spatial and socioeconomic transformation of, the old city and rapid urban development in the early twentieth century. This modern arena created new public spaces of expanded markets, leisure parks, and entertainment centers that supplemented the traditional "temple fairs" and other religious festivities such as pilgrimages to the city's sacred sites of worship as the venue for the display and communication of artistic and cultural representations across a broad section of society. It gave a new lease on life to the old stories and legends, and enriched the traditional urban culture in a meaningful way to different generations of residents.

This idea of recycling also applies to the Mongol storytellers who propagated the legend of the Yongle emperor as Toghōn Temür's posthumous son and the story of the emperor building the capital city in Peking on a plan provided by a mysterious black rider who administered the nomadic custom of siting by bowshot. It was an attempt to placate the Mongols who lived in Peking or its vicinity and who were surrounded by Chinese culture and Chinese communities by incorporating their history and myths into the building of Peking to give them a legitimate share of the place. In so doing these non-Han traditions were integrated into the Chinese traditions impacting the city's multiethnic communities. At the same time, through the shamans and storytellers who ventured into the Mongolian deserts, the same story and legend were transmitted in various forms beyond the Sinitic world. It is striking that this engrossing mythology was subsequently adapted by the Chinese folklorists and storytellers into equally uncanny stories about the building of Peking, thereby presenting an interesting case of intercultural transfusion. It not only preserves the non-Han heritage in the sedentary communities, but also enhances the ethnic diversity of urban culture in modern Peking.

All in all, these engrossing legends of the building of the imperial city unfolded the "weft" of the tapestry of old Peking in Meyer's typology, and, under embedded layers of imaginative fantasies and fictional trappings propagated by the recycling of the folklorists and storytellers, they subtly gave expression to human feelings, their nostalgia for the bygone, their love and concern of the place, their needs, and their aspirations for the future. A product of continuous commingling of strands of multifaceted popular culture unique to Peking, including the reciprocal adaptations of Han Chinese and Mongolian traditions, these stories and legends flourished as the bridge between the popular culture of the old order and the new world of the Chinese capital city. They present a vivid mirror of the past in the minds of the present; they will not only remain a durable cultural legacy of old Peking, but also constitute an integral part of the modern urban culture of new Beijing as it undergoes transformation to become one of the world's greatest capital cities.

PART III

Appendices

Appendices

1. The Eight-armed Nezha City (1)

Everyone calls Peking the Eight-armed Nezha City. They say only Eight-armed Nezha could have subdued the evil dragons in Bitter Sea Youzhou. How did Peking come to be built as an Eight-armed Nezha City? There's a folktale about this in the legend.

When the Emperor decided to build a northern capital, Peking, he assigned the task to the Minister of Works. Panic-stricken, the minister promptly petitioned the throne: "Peking was originally the Bitter Sea Youzhou, and the dragons there are too vicious for your humble servant to subdue. I beg Your Majesty send military advisers instead!" The Emperor thought that made sense. Peking could not be built unless there was a genius with knowledge of heaven and earth, who knew about both the spirits above and the devils below. So he summoned his military advisers, "Which of you can go and build the northern capital for me?" His advisers eyed each other for a while, not daring to respond, but finally someone had to answer, and Chief Adviser Liu Bowen volunteered, "I'll go!" Deputy Adviser Yao Guangxiao also volunteered, "I'll go too." The Emperor was truly excited, certain that these two brilliant advisers had the ability "to subdue dragons and tigers". He thus sent them off to build Peking.

Liu Bowen and Yao Guangxiao took the imperial rescript and arrived at Youzhou where Peking now stands. After putting up in a hostel, they went out every day to survey the terrain and figure out how to build the city in such a way that the dragons could not make trouble. However, Chief Adviser Liu and Deputy Adviser Yao had nothing but contempt for each other.

"Deputy Adviser Yao," proposed Liu, "let's live apart, you in the west city, I in the east. Each of us must think of a plan, then in ten days' time we'll meet at a place, and, sitting back to back, draw our plans for the city. Then we'll compare the two to see if they match."

Yao Guangxiao knew perfectly well that Liu Bowen hoped to shine and reap all the credit. "Very well," he said with a grim smile. "You're right, Chief Adviser, that's what we should do."

So the two advisers parted company. For the first two days, though the two of them were living apart and neither went out to survey the terrain, both heard a voice saying, "Just copy me and you'll do fine." The voice sounded like a child's, and the words were clearly repeated time and again. Who was talking? There was no one around. "Just copy me"—what did that mean? Neither Adviser Liu nor Deputy Adviser Yao had a clue.

On the third day they both went out to survey the terrain again. Wherever Adviser Liu went he saw a child in a red jacket and short pants walking ahead of him. When Liu hurried up, so did the child; when he slowed down, so did the child. At first he paid no special attention to this, but then he started wondering about it. He deliberately stood still. Well, how extraordinary! So did the child. Liu couldn't really figure out what the boy was up to. How about Deputy Adviser Yao? He too saw a child like that, and couldn't figure out what the boy would do.

Back in their different hostels, again both advisers heard a voice in their ears. "Just copy me and you'll do fine." Liu in the east city and Yao in the west city wondered: Can this child in the red jacket and short pants be Nezha? That doesn't seem like him—Nezha was supposed to have eight arms. They both came to the same decision: If I meet that boy tomorrow, I'll take a good look at him.

On the next day, the fourth day after they had reached their agreement, Liu Bowen went out after breakfast for a stroll with an assistant. Why did he take an assistant today? He hoped that the assistant could help him see if it was Nezha. Yao Guangxiao in the west city had the same idea. Both men had heard the same voice, seen the same child, and today they saw him again. Still wearing a red jacket and short pants, but not the same jacket as the previous day: this one was more like a cape with a lotus-leaf edge, and from the two shoulders dangled soft silken fringes which rustled in the wind like arms. At the sight of them Liu suspected that this must be the Eight-armed Nezha. He hurried forward to catch hold of the child and have a closer look; but the faster he chased him the faster the child ran away, reiterating, "Just copy me and you'll do fine!" Then he rushed off and vanished completely.

When Liu's assistant saw him chasing down the road, he did not know what had happened. He called after him, "Commander! Commander! Why are you running?"

Liu stopped to ask him, "Did you see a child in a red jacket and short pants?"

"Nay," said the assistant. "All this time I've been following you and haven't seen a soul."

Then Liu Bowen knew for sure that it was Nezha.

As for Yao Guangxiao, exactly the same thing had happened to him.

The two commanders returned to their hostels. Liu thought: "Copy me" must mean draw a plan of a city like the Eight-armed Nezha, so as to subdue the dragons in Bitter Sea Youzhou. Fine! Let's see how you handle this, Yao Guangxiao. If you can't produce such a plan, you're not fit to be an imperial adviser! Yao in the west city was thinking at the same time: Now we'll soon see you lose your title "Chief Adviser"!

On the ninth day Liu sent word to Yao: "At noon tomorrow, in the center of the city, we'll draw our plans by sitting back to back. Please be there punctual." And Yao concurred.

At noon on the tenth day, in a big empty square in the center of the town, two tables and two chairs were set out, the chairs back to back, and the two advisers arrived.

Liu asked, "Which way do you want to face, Deputy Adviser?"

Yao answered, "You live in the east city, Chief Adviser, so you should sit facing east. Your humble one will sit facing west."

When they had taken their seats, the assistants supplied them with paper, brushes, ink, and inkstones. They picked up the brushes and drew their plans stroke by stroke. Just before sunset both finished their plans of the city, and each picked up the other's to examine it. Then both of them burst out laughing, because their plans were identical, each being an Eight-armed Nezha City.

Yao Guangxiao asked the Chief Adviser to explain his Eight-armed Nezha City.

Liu said, "This walled gate in the center due south is Zhengyangmen, Nezha's head. A head should have two ears, and those gates to its east and west are Nezha's ears. The two wells inside Zhengyangmen are his eyes. On the east side of the Zhengyangmen, the Chongwenmen, Dongbianmen, and the Chaoyangmen,

Dongzhimen on the east side of the city's walled gates are four of Nezha's arms. On the west side of the Zhengyangmen, the Xuanwumen, Xibianmen, and the Fuchengmen, Xizhimen on the west side of the city's walled gates are Nezha's other four arms. The Andingmen and Deshengmen in the north are his feet."

Yao Guangxiao nodded, saying, "Yes, of course. But does Nezha have only eight arms, no heart, liver, spleen, lungs or kidneys?"

Liu Bowen's face turned red. "Of course he has!" he retorted. "How could a dead Nezha subdue evil dragons?" He pointed irately at his plan. "Look, brother. The rectangular Imperial-city is Nezha's viscera, and Tian'anmen at its entrance is the way into his viscera and leads in the other direction to Zhengyangmen, his brain. The long, level road between them is Nezha's gullet."

With a laugh Yao Guangxiao drawled, "Don't get mad, Chief Adviser. I can see your plan is most carefully worked out. The two roads running south and north on both sides of the viscera are Nezha's main ribs, and the *hutong* (alleyways) branching off are his lesser ribs—correct? You've really worked it out to the last detail!"

Although provoked, Liu Bowen had to stay calm. At any rate, the plan for an Eight-armed Nezha City had been drawn, and neither adviser could claim all the credit. Chief Adviser Liu did not mind about this, but Deputy Adviser Yao became so downcast that he went off to live as a monk, waiting to see how Liu would build Peking.

What Liu Bowen did not foresee was that the building of Peking would enrage the vicious dragons, which led to "Gao Liang's Race for Water" and many other stories.

* Translated from Jin Shoushen, *Beijing de chuanshuo* (Beijing: Beijing chubanshe, 1981), pp. 3–8; cf. Gladys Yang, *Beijing Legends* (Peking: Panda Books, 1982), pp. 10–17.

2. The Eight-armed Nezha City (2)

The people of Peking have said Peking is an Eight-armed Nezha City. The building of Peking took place in the early years of the Ming dynasty. At that time the emperor was called the Prince of Yan. In the fourth year of Yongle he gave an order to start building the Imperial City with its palaces and halls; and he dispatched his ministers to Sichuan, Huguang, Jiangxi, Zhejiang, Shanxi, and other places to collect timber [for its construction]. In the fourteenth year of Yongle, he assembled [officials to give] opinions on the building of the entire city of Peking. Legend has it that at that time, the Prince of Yan had two advisers at his disposal: the Chief Adviser was Liu Bowen, the Deputy Adviser was Yao Guangxiao. The Prince of Yan ordered them to design a plan for the city of Peking. After receiving the imperial order, they set out to survey the terrain.

Arriving at the center of the city, they drew a line from north to south. Then they stood [at the mid-point] back to back, one walked toward the east, and the other toward the west, each covered 5 *li*, marking the edge of the city. Next they drew a line along the places they had covered from east to west and intersecting the north-to-south line, forming the shape of the character *shi* (i.e. "ten", which looks like a cross). Then they stood back to back on the same intersection, one walked toward the south, and the other toward the north, each covered 7 *li*, marking the northern and southern edge of the city. After that they drew a frame around the miles of terrain they had covered [as city boundaries] and each returned home.

On the second day, the two men again went out. Chief Adviser Liu Bowen was thinking that since the terrain of the city had been measured out in paces, it was about time to draw the plan. If the plan could be drawn, he would claim the top honor. He thought that with his capability as Chief Adviser he was certainly far superior to the Deputy Adviser in every field. Therefore, in a job like drawing the city plan, it need not be a collaborative effort but rather each should draw his own plan. Yao Guangxiao was also thinking that if he worked with Liu Bowen, people would attribute the plan to the abilities of the Chief Adviser. Therefore, he could not draw the plan with Liu Bowen.

Thus when the two came together, Liu Bowen said to Yao Guangxiao: "Deputy Adviser, since we have already paced the terrain on foot, it is about time we draw the plan. Let's part company and each of us will come up with his own idea. Seven days later, we will meet here, then we'll sit back to back and draw our own plan on the spot. What do you think?"

Hearing this, Yao Guangxiao thought that would work perfectly. He responded: "No problem, Chief Adviser. You have a good point, let's do it this way." The two advisers thus split up.

Liu Bowen lived on the east side. After returning home, he could neither eat nor sleep, his mind was consumed with the thought of drawing a plan. But after mulling the problem for three days he still could not come up with an idea. Yao Guangxiao lived on the west side. After returning home he too failed to eat or sleep, obsessing with how to draw a plan for the city of Peking. The two of them each pondered for three days, but could come up with nothing.

Later, thoroughly exhausted, a muddled sleep came upon Liu Bowen. Deep in this sleep Liu Bowen seemed to hear someone talking. After carefully listening, the voice seemed to say: "Just copy me, just copy me." Having awakened, he saw nothing. Yao Guangxiao had the same experience. But when he woke up, there was nothing.

Three more days passed by in a blink; soon it was the last day—they had to go to the city center to draw their plans. Emerging from his house, Chief Adviser Liu Bowen was still heavy headed, but continued to deliberate on the way. Suddenly he saw a red-clad child walking ahead of him. When he speeded up, so did the child; when he slowed down, so did the child. He started wondering who this red-clad child was, and so he ran after him. Deputy Adviser Yao Guangxiao was also on his way to the meeting. He too saw a red-clad child. This child was also walking ahead of him. When he speeded up, so did the child; when he slowed down, so did the child. Thus he too ran after the child. As the two advisers were chasing the child, they bumped into each other; they had arrived at the rendezvous. Liu Bowen said: "Now we can each start drawing the plan." Yao Guangxiao nodded, and the two sat together back to back. Liu Bowen sat facing east, and Yao Guangxiao sat facing west. The two took out some paper, laying them before their eyes and started drawing. As they were concentrating on their thoughts, gazing at the paper, suddenly the image of the red-clad child emerged before their eyes: his head was well-combed with little curls, his legs are half naked, with bare feet, still wearing the red jacket and pants each had seen earlier. His red jacket was like a cape with a lotus-leaf edge, and from the two shoulders dangled soften silken fringes which, when rustled by the wind, looked like several arms. Thus it dawned on the two men: wasn't this the Eight-armed Nezha? Both were simultaneously exhilarated, but neither made a sound, and each continued drawing on his own.

Liu Bowen drew the head first, then the arms and legs until every part of the body was done. Yao Guangxiao did the same. He too started sketching from the head, stroke by stroke. But when he made his last stroke, a breeze suddenly arose, blowing away the lapel of Nezha's jacket, but Yao just quickly sketched it in again.

Having finished, the two exchanged their drawing. When they took a look, both burst into laughter. As it turned out, the two plans were exactly identical, each being the Eight-armed Nezha City. The only exception was that in Yao Guangxiao's drawing, the northwestern corner of the city wall did not form a ninety-degree angle but slanted from north to west.

Yao Guangxiao asked Liu Bowen to explain his Eight-armed Nezha City.

Liu said, "This gate in the center due south is Zhengyangmen, Nezha's head. The gates to its east and west are Nezha's ears. The two gates inside Zhengyangmen are his eyes. On the east side of the Zhengyangmen, the Chongwenmen, Dongbianmen, and the Chaoyangmen and Dongzhimen on the east side of the city wall are four of Nezha's arms. On the west side of the Zhengyangmen, the Xuanwumen, Xibianmen, and the Fuchengmen and Xizhimen on the west side of the city wall are Nezha's other four arms. The Andingmen and Deshengmen in the north are his feet."

Yao Guangxiao then enquired, "But where is Nezha's heart, liver, spleen, lungs, or kidneys?"

"Well, they are in the Imperial-city," Liu Bowen retorted. Yao Guangxiao still wanted to ask more questions. Sensing his attitude, Liu realized Yao wanted to criticize his own plan, and so he held up the drawing, pointing at where Yao Guangxiao had sketched a slanted line, saying: "This is where you have gone wrong, how could the city-wall be slanted?" Embarrassed, Yao Guangxiao replied: "Chief Adviser, you may not know that the shape of Nezha was in fact askew!" Arguing with each other to no avail, they took the drawings to see the Prince of Yan. Upon inspection, the Prince said: "Well, you two are really my advisers. Liu Bowen's drawing is a proper square; he should stay as Chief Adviser. Yao Guangxiao's drawing has a diagonal line. He may as well stay as Deputy Adviser."

Liu Bowen then asked: "When it comes to building the city, which plan should set the standard?" Pointing at the drawing, the Prince of Yan responded: "The east city will follow your plan, and the west city will follow Yao Guangxiao's."

In this way work began on the building of the city. After it was done, it revealed that Yao Guangxiao's slanted lines were exactly the slope from the Deshengmen west to the Xizhimen. Even to this day, the northwestern corner of Peking's city wall is still slightly slanted, and lacking a ninety-degree angle at that corner (see Figures 26, 27)!

* Translated from *Beijing de chuanshuo,* ed. Zhang Zichen and Li Yuenan (Shanghai: Shanghai Wenyi chubanshe, 1982), pp. 1–5.

3. Book of the Story of How Emperor Yung-lo of the Great Ming Built the City of Peking—The Yüan Prince—The True Prince (*Dayiming yuwa lowa gaghan begeǰing qota-i bayighulughsan üliger-ün debter —Yuwa(n) tayise—J̌ing tayise)*

After the Great Ancestor, the Fortunate Saintly Chinggis-qaghan of old, circulating [his influence] endowed with the prestige of great power, assembled many tribes and provinces under his domination, and established the government of the Great Yüan country, generation after generation succeeded each other, and thirteen great qaghans sat [on the throne]. At the end, in the period of Toghōn-temür qaghan, over [every] ten Chinese families one Mongol lama ruled who treated them as slaves. Those lamas abused the boys of the families under their jurisdiction and when a girl was about to marry, they took and abused her saying they were first taking the premices. Angered at being so grievously opposed by this shameful and licentious behavior, those Chinese on the fifth of the fifth month of the forty-second [*sic*] year of Toghōn-temür qaghan, conspired: "At the same hour we will kill the lamas ruling severally [over us] and destroy the government of the Mongols." As they had made such an agreement, but did not get ready on that very same day, they decided to make their move on the fifteenth of the intercalary eighth month of the same year: setting a day, on the fifteenth of the intercalary eighth month, as soon as the moon rose, they would kill all the supervising lamas and with their heads and livers they would worship the moon.

Thereafter, the Chinese, appointing a man with perfect power and skill, named Chu Hung-wu as their commander, readied a large army in the various provinces, and when they attacked Toghōn-temür qaghan, no matter how much opposition he offered, his forces were insufficient and the Chinese army encircled and laid siege to the City of Dayitung (*sic* for Dayidu, i.e. Peking). At that time, as Toghōn-temür qaghan discussed a means to get away with the minister Tulbutu-mergen, son of chancellor Dologhan, the minister said this: "A word my father spoke was this: 'When [all] means fail, there is a tunnel underneath the rock behind [the palace: the city?] leading towards the Mongol plains'." The qaghan took his jade seal, made the great empress come along, and with the minister Tulbutu-mergen, the three of them found that tunnel, and as [the qaghan] put the seal on the rock, it left [its] impression.

From there, reaching the plain of Kinar, they found three horses which they mounted and rode off unseen.

When Chu Hung-wu together with his soldiers entered the city and discovered that the gaghan was not there, and found the tunnel and the imprint of the seal, he knew that the qaghan had fled, and he left in pursuit [with] his army.

As the three of Toghōn-temür [etc.] traveled, when they arrived at the River Tuul (i.e. the Tuula River), and the river was widely flooded with no means to cross, they crossed peacefully over a golden bridge sent down from heaven. When the Chinese troops arrived, as the bridge was no more to be seen, they were unable to cross and returned.

Toghōn-temür qaghan built the City of the Tiger on the bank of the River Kerülen and remained there governing the Mongol tribes.

When Chu Hung-wu entered Toghōn-temür qaghan's interior palace, there was a little *qatun* of Toghōn-temür qaghan's who had been left behind; that *qatun* being young and beautiful and very intelligent went ahead to meet Emperor Chu Hung-wu: she bowed and knelt and showed her respect by performing the rites; and as she spoke beautiful words [expressing her] joy and happiness, Chu Hung-wu's heart was really captured! When he expressed his desire to marry this *qatun*, altogether his ministers warned him that one should not make friends with the friend of an enemy, he did not listen and made her his empress; then suspecting and fearing the Mongols, he appointed a minister in the City of Dayitung with orders to administer it, and [himself] moved away, and when he arrived at Nanking he made it his capital.

Thereafter—at the time that the *qatun* was living with Toghōn-temür qaghan she was pregnant with a child—she said: "If I give birth soon, they will certainly kill [the child];" so she prayed fervently in silence to the Three Jewels, and as a result she gave birth to a son twelve months after her marriage to Chu Hung-wu. When [the Emperor] had the boy examined by a soothsayer, [the latter] declared: "This boy's fortune is extremely auspicious, he will succeed to the government of his father and protect the people," and so he gave him the name Yüan Prince. But when the ministers said [to the Emperor]: "If one considers the name Yüan Prince given by the soothsayer to this boy, it means 'Prince of the Mongols,' and because he is certainly a son of the Mongol qaghan, you are not allowed to raise him," the Emperor became angry and threateningly said: "[This rule is that] a man is born when he has been nine months in his mother's womb; since this son of mine has only been born twelve months after I met with the *qatun*, how would he be a descendant of the Mongol [qaghan]?" To this, all found nothing to answer.

When another son was born and the soothsayer was made to examine him, he said: "This boy's fortune will be less good than that of his elder brother's," and he named him True Prince. This means Prince of the Chinese.

As the two boys gradually grew up there was no harmony between them and they quarreled and fought continuously. At that time the mother *qatun* became sick and at the moment of death she called the elder son, the Yüan Prince, and handed him two letters [in separate] envelopes saying: "This is my last will: in time of success read one envelope; in time of suffering read the other envelope."

Thereafter Emperor Chu Hung-wu one night [as he was] asleep, in a dream [he saw] one black striped snake and one yellow striped snake violently attack each other and come to rest on the Emperor's two knees. The black striped snake on the right side attacked the yellow striped snake on the left side that fainted and was hardly [able to] rise and stagger back. Having had such a dream, he woke up and becoming suspicious, as he called in the soothsayer to have him examine [the omen], [the soothsayer] immediately thought: "The Emperor will evidently know". [Then] both the Yüan Prince and the True Prince, quarrelling and attacking each other, came before the Emperor: the Yüan Prince resting [on the Emperor's] right knee, and the True Prince, resting on his left knee—the two pleaded the cause of their quarrel and walked out. The Emperor, very suspicious, called his many ministers together and when he told them the dream and the fact that the two sons had come to quarrel, the ministers declared: "If the elder and the younger brothers were certainly sons of one father, there would be no reason [for them] to be in discord; if one considers the name given by the soothsayer and the fact that he is not at peace now with the True Prince, one can be sure of the fact that the Yüan Prince is the son of the Mongol qaghan, and one must decide how to do away with him!" Thereupon the Emperor said: "Ever since his childhood I have loved and cherished this boy as my own son; in addition to this [I want to consult with you] on the means to remove him without doing him any harm." As he was thus deliberating, the ministers said: "Tell him to occupy and hold the defile of Nan-k'ou, the pass through which come our enemy, the Mongols, and giving the Yüan Prince a thousand soldiers send him [there]; if you order the boats taken out of the Yellow River, the Yüan Prince is likely to fall in the river and drown; should he turn around and come back, according to the law he would have to be put to death on the grounds that he has disobeyed an [imperial] order."

As they said this, the decision was made and immediately the Emperor called in the Yüan Prince and told him: "Since it is likely that the armies of the Mongol enemy will come through the Nan-k'ou pass, you, my son, take a thousand soldiers and hold it." As [the Emperor] said this, [the Yüan Prince] received the order with a bow and left; then he thought: "Now has come my time of suffering" and opening one of the envelopes given by his mother, he read: "When you are banished to guard the Nan-k'ou defile, make Liu Pai-wen minister, take him along, and follow his instructions."

Thereafter the Yüan Prince, presenting himself in his father's presence, bowed and, weeping, said: "I, your son, upon the order of my father, the Emperor, will immediately proceed to the border but do me the favor [of allowing me] Liu Pai-wen." The Emperor, because from the beginning he had favored him greatly, thinking that he was his son, weakened and gave him Liu Pai-wen.

When the ministers picked the troop to give him, they gave him a thousand crippled and old soldiers, with a thousand worn cuirasses and weapons, and a thousand emaciated and exhausted horses, made him set out from the city Nanking, but beforehand they had ordered the boats of the Yellow River to be gathered up.

As the Yüan Prince traveled with his soldiers and reached the Yellow River, bridges, ships, and vessels were absolutely gone;

stopping in the neighborhood, he sent a man to see if the river had frozen over or not; when the man came back and reported that the river was not frozen, he put him to death on the spot. Every morning [the Yüan Prince] sent a man to see, but as soon as they came back and said that the river was not frozen, they were all put to death.

Six days went by in this way; on the seventh day, one man on his way to look thought: "Our Yüan Prince is in the habit of killing [every] man who reports that the river is not frozen; how could it freeze now in the heat of the dog-days of the sixth [lunar] month? Since I am going to die anyway, instead of [me] being killed alone, all will die!" So thinking, he returned and reported that the river was solidly frozen; thereupon immediately all moved on and when they arrived at the bank of the river, [the Yüan Prince] called that same man and asked him: "Where is the frozen spot? Pass there!" The man answered: "Here," and as he entered [the water] surprisingly it was indeed frozen, and all passed at once successfully and without harm.

As they gradually progressed and supplies and silver came close to being exhausted, pigeons numerous beyond count [which had followed them] at the time they left the city of Nanking, were covering the sun. [Every time] the Yüan Prince shot and killed one of them, it turned into a silver ingot. With those many pigeons flying and following, [the army] proceeded and when it came near the city of Jiu-Jiu, the pigeons failed to appear. As the Yüan Prince and his following arrived at the road to Nan-k'ou, and temporarily halted, one day taking his bow, the Yüan Prince rode out alone; and as he was [going around] searching in the neighborhood of the city of Jiu-Jiu where the pigeons had stayed behind, all of a sudden he met a man with an extraordinary bearing, with a swarthy face, dressed in a black robe and riding a black horse; saying [to the Yüan Prince]: "Son, give [me] your bow and arrows," he shot one arrow each into the four directions, and said, "There is an abundant treasure of gold, silver, and jewels in the spots hit by the arrows; also give this red spear of mine to Liu Pai-wen: should the silver [come to be] wanting, if he sticks this spear into the earth, underneath at a depth of an elbow, a variety of jewels will come out; make Liu Pai-wen head minister and at this place found such a great city with four corners after the number of the four seasons; with nine gates in the exterior city [wall] after the number of planets; with eight gates in the interior double city [wall] after the number of the "diagrams;" with twelve large streets after the number of the year; with three hundred and sixty lanes after the number of the days; with twenty-seven great tribunals after the number of the [zodiacal] constellations. In a golden palace in the middle of the city set up a throne of fade [adorned] with nine interlaced dragons, and sitting down on it become Emperor yourself!" Giving this order he gave him a red spear and departed and was seen no more.

Hearing this order, the Yüan Prince greatly rejoiced, and taking the spear he told the event to Liu Pai-wen; they all moved to the places where those arrows had been shot, and finding the four arrows, when they dug the ground underneath, they found and took countless great treasures of gold, silver, and jewels coming out [of there].

Recognizing among the thousand soldiers five men who were proficient in the principles of craftsmanship, he made them ministers; through [the activities of] those jewelers, he assembled the many under his power; with Liu Pai-wen showing and instructing, [they started to] build [the city]: before long they completed the construction of one great city having nine gates according to what the man on the black horse had said; then [Liu] made the Yüan Prince "Little Emperor" and made him sit on the jade throne with nine interlaced dragons in the golden palace, and he called the city Peking.

With the treasures of various jewels that had come out of the ground where the red spear had been fixed, Liu Pai-wen filled the Emperor's treasury and as exceedingly great favors and rewards were being given to many poor people, all the people of the four quarters loyally followed [the Little Emperor].

At that time, when Emperor Chu Hung-wu died in the city of Nanking, the Yüan Prince, in the company of his many ministers and the thousand soldiers, went to the city of Nanking to view and honor the remains of his father. But even before that, the younger brother, the True Prince, had mounted his father's throne, but hearing that his elder brother, the Yüan Prince, was arriving with soldiers, without understanding the situation, he remembered their former enmity and said: "For sure he has come to kill me and take away the government," and, reduced to this extremity, he hung himself and died.

When the Yüan Prince arrived at the city of Nanking, in great mourning he performed the ceremonies and offered sacrifices at the tomb of his father the Emperor; thereupon when he intended to meet with his younger brother, the True Prince, he inquired [about him], and his ministers told him the circumstances of his death; he wept very bitterly, and said: "Now that my younger brother has died, there is no more use!" and he selected and appointed a governor to the city of Nanking with orders to administer it, and thereafter he came back and entered by the south gate of the city of Peking. Selecting an auspicious day, he became Great Emperor taking the name of Emperor Yung-lo of the Great Ming: he ruled over the thirteen great provinces of the Chinese and inaugurated the government of the country of the Great Ming.

Thereafter Emperor Yung-lo was ruling over the great government and in his absolute prosperity he opened [the other] one letter left him by his mother and read it. Its contents were: "You, son, are really the offspring of Toghōn-temür qaghan of the Mongols: as a result of my very devout prayer to the Three Jewels, you were born after being in my womb for twelve months, [and so] you were able to stay alive and become a man; later when you become great-qaghan, remember your ancestry, act with due concern for the Mongols, and revering the Three Jewels in the Supreme Ornament make them an object of sacrifice."

Learning this he became secretly greatly concerned with the Mongols. At that time, the Chinese people had the custom of raiding and bringing [prisoners back] from Mongolia, to cut off their heads and cut out their livers and hearts and offer them to the moon on the fifteenth of the eighth month. When Emperor Yung-lo said to stop this [practice] once and for all, because the hatred of the Chinese was exceedingly great, when he absolutely discontinued [the practice] of killing and sacrificing Mongols, he decided to make it a rule to cut [into pieces] a watermelon and a moon cake and to offer them.

Thereafter, Emperor Yung-lo sent a special official to invite His Highness the Saintly Tsong-kha-ba from the region Üi-tsang, but the Saint did not come; when in his stead he sent His Highness J̌amǰin chorǰi sakiy-a yeshi, the Emperor greatly revered him and made him the object of his offerings. His Highness J̌amǰin chorǰi let the multitude see wonderful miracles, and with the rasayana of the supreme doctrine he instructed first the Emperor and the Empress,

[then] a countless multitude of people; making them pass [into salvation] he led them unto the manifest and high way; and as he widely and greatly spread the Religion, descendants of the descendants of Emperor Yung-lo succeeded each other, became thirteen generations of great Emperors, and ruling over the Chinese people they protected the government.

May [all] be well and prosper.

May good merit spread,

And [all] hoped-for achievements will come true.

Copy finished on the nineteenth of the fourth [lunar] month of the thirty-third year of the era Badaraghultu törö (May 30 1907).

* Transcription and translation of the Mongolian text by Rev. Henry Serruys, C.I.C.M., originally published in *Analecta Mongolica*: The Mongolian Society Occasional Papers, No. 8 (Bloomington, Ind., 1972), pp. 30–59. Note: The Wade-Giles spelling system is used in this translation.

4. Liu Bowen Built the City of Peking

This is the story that spread as the Prince of Yan swept across north China in his military conquests. The Prince of Yan originally lived in the city of Nanking. When he began the planning for his new capital in the north, he summoned minister Liu Bowan, asking him where it should be built. "Let's invite General Xu Da to take charge," Liu Bowen said. The Prince of Yan then sent for Xu Da. Liu Bowen said to Xu Da: "Harness your divine strength to shoot an arrow toward the north, wherever the arrow falls, build the capital city there." Xu, having thus given his promise, went outside the imperial hall, mounted an arrow on his bow, and shot toward the north. Liu Bowen immediately took some attendants in a boat and sailed northward along the Grand Canal, following the path of the arrow's flight.

This arrow streaked far away landing at South Park (Nanyuan) about twenty odd *li* south of present-day Peking. Eight households of minor wealth lived in the vicinity. When they saw the arrow falling, they were greatly alarmed, worried that if the capital were built there, all their houses and fields would be confiscated. One of the wealthy households had an idea: "Why don't we just shoot the arrow away?" Everyone thought it was clever and so he shot the arrow toward the north. The arrow landed at a place called Rear Gate Bridge

(Houmenqiao). It was said that there was a stone tablet under the Rear Gate Bridge, engraved with the three characters "Bei-jing cheng" (Peking City). The exact spot where the arrow fell was under the bridge.

Liu Bowen and his men followed the arrow to South Park. By counting on his fingers to prognosticate, he figured that the arrow ought to have fallen there. He dispatched his men to find the eight wealthy households, pressing them for the arrow. Upon interrogation, they confessed, and repeatedly beseeched Liu Bowen, saying: "As long as you are not going to build the capital city here, we'll accept whatever deal you may propose." After some consideration, Liu Bowen said: "All right! I could decide not to build the capital city here, and could build it wherever the arrow has fallen, but the cost of the capital's construction will be borne by you!" The rich men did some calculating, and figuring they were all wealthy and that building a capital city would not be too expensive, they accepted the deal.

When Liu Bowen found the site of the fallen arrow; he took out the plans he had prepared and summoned artisans to start work. The walled tower of the Xizhi Gate was the first edifice to be built, and its construction was all funded by the eight wealthy households of South Park. No one foresaw that even before the completion of a single walled tower, the rich élite of the South Park would be reduced to utter destitution. What was to be done? Counting on his fingers again, Liu Bowen sent for his attendants and said: "Go find a man by the name of Shen Wansan [who knew about the hoarded treasure]!" Two days later, they found him. Shen Wansan was brought before Liu Bowen at Shichahai. At that time places like Shichahai (Shicha Sea), Beihai (North Sea), and Zhongnanhai (Central and South Sea) were flat fields with no water. Who was this Shen Wansan? He was a filthy beggar who wore rags and carried a broken earthen bowl under his armpit, which he secured with a cord around his neck. "We have no money to build the city of Peking, you've got to think of some way!" Liu Bowen told Shen Wansan as soon as he saw him. Wansan was greatly shocked when he heard the demand, and repeatedly grunted: "I'm a pauper begging for food, how could I have the money!" Liu Bowen gave him an angry stare, taunting him: "No money? No way! Beat him up." His attendants thus rained heavy blows on San Wansan with batons. At first San Wansan repeatedly wailed begging for mercy, but after being so badly beaten, he stretched out his legs and pointed to the ground: "There are silver ingots in the ground, go and dig them up." Liu Bowen sent men to dig, and found a huge vat. Removing the lid, they found shiny silver ingots inside. Liu Bowen thus spent them to build the city. But before long, these silver ingots were also used up. So he asked that Shen Wansan be brought before him again whereupon Shen was tied down and beaten. Being badly beaten, Wansan again pointed to the ground, saying: "There are silver ingots, you people just dig." After digging, silver ingots were found again. After repeating the same scenario two to three times, Peking was built, but the interior of the city was left with many huge pits as a result of the digging for silver. Later Liu Bowen ordered that water be drained into these pits, which created the present-day Shicha Sea, North Sea, and Central and South Sea.

When Liu Bowen was sailing north tracking the flying arrow, and had almost reached Peking, a wave rose up and a gigantic tortoise surfaced. When the creature put its front flippers on the bow, the boat was tipped sidewise. Rushing out of his cabin, Liu Bowen instantly recognized the tortoise as the transformed Dragon King and asked: "What do you want from me?" The Dragon King replied: "Are you planning to build the capital city here? This is my own turf; you are now seizing it, what kind of sweet deal are you giving me?" "Wait till the Prince of Yan has established his capital here, he'll heartily repay you." Liu snapped. "Ah, no. You've got to mean what you said. If you wish to build the capital city here, you must offer a position to each of my nine sons and grandsons!" demanded the Dragon King. Hearing thus, Liu Bowan thought, if the dragons were to take over the capital city, where would be the real Dragon King—the Prince of Yan—sit? He mused again, well, why not just promise him and wait for the outcome. Thus he gave the promise: "All right, I'll make the arrangement when the time comes." Greatly delighted, the Dragon King said: "I'll find you after the completion of the capital city." After that he turned round and dived into the river, and the ripples of wave subsided. Liu Bowen's boat continued northward.

After the completion of the city of Peking, Liu Bowen invited the Prince of Yan to take up residence there—the Prince ascended the dragon throne and became emperor of the millennial years. On this day, someone came to report that an elderly man had been waiting at the palace entrance with several youngsters, yelling that he wanted to see Liu Bowen. When Liu emerged from the palace, he realized that the Dragon King was standing there with his nine sons and grandsons. Seeing Liu, the Dragon King exclaimed: "Liu Bowen, you promised to offer positions to my sons and grandsons. Now I have brought them to meet you!" Liu laughed, saying, "I've already made all the arrangements!" Liu Bowen was really invincible; he assigned the dragon sons and dragon grandsons positions on ornamental pillars, on obelisks, on eaves of houses, and on shadowed walls. As soon as the positions were assigned, he barked out his command: "Take your places!" The nine dragon sons and grandsons immediately streaked to their assigned positions and each one of them was stuck there. All the lively dragons became stone-engraved, brick-tarred, and oil-painted inanimate objects. The Dragon King was mad as hell, vowing to get even. Liu Bowen stared at him angrily and exclaimed: "I have campaigned in the north and south and have fought many battles; with my abilities to prognosticate by counting on fingers and by summoning the wind and invoking the rain, would I fear you?" The Dragon King realized that he was no match in a fight, and so angrily retorted: "Liu Bowen, just wait and see. I won't rest until people in the whole city are dead." This said, he turned round and vanished.

On the morning of the second day, when Liu Bowen was about to rise, the messenger hurried in with a report: "Your Excellency, early this morning the water in all the wells and rivers dried up, people have no water to drink and are rioting!" Liu Bowen immediately counted on his fingers and realized that it was the evil plot of the Dragon King. He summoned his soldiers, and asked: "Who has the guts to nail the Dragon King and take back the water?" Immediately a burly man marched out of the column, holding a bow. "I'm ready to go," he said. Liu Bowen then reminded him: "When you emerge from the Xizhi Gate, dart toward the west, catch the one who pushes a small cart, use your spear to slit the water pouch placed on the left of the cart, then turn round and dash back. I'll wait for you on the walled tower of the Xizhi Gate and open the gate for you. Please remember never turn round for a look when you are running back." The burly man nodded and turned away.

Who was this burly man? His name was Gao Liang. Grabbing his long spear as he left the Xizhi Gate, he rushed toward the west. Racing about twenty or so *li* in one breadth, he saw in the distance a small hand-cart stopping by the roadside. Not far from the cart an elderly couple sat under a tree enjoying the cool shade—they were the transformed Dragon King and his wife. After Liu Bowen took the lives of the dragon sons and grandsons, the Dragon King angrily returned to the Dragon Palace, where, upon seeing his wife, he laid bare everything to her. The old lady, who doted on her sons and grandsons, wailed loudly, pleading with her husband to find a way to get even. The Dragon King said , "Let's move our home away from here and take the city's water with us, there won't be a single drop of water in Peking, and in a few days, people will die of thirst. We'll be avenged!" Hearing this, the old lady thought it was a good idea, and ceased crying. On the early morning of the next day, the Dragon King and his wife were very busy. They took the entire city's water and packed it up in two different pouches, then fastened the water pouches to a cart and pushed the cart out of the city. After toiling for two hours they felt a bit tired and hot. "Let's take a rest before continuing." While the Dragon King and his wife were taking a rest under the tree, Gao Liang also arrived. Gao Liang stealthily raced toward the cart, but he was also a bit scared because he was worried the Dragon King might see him. When he reached the water cart, without any hesitation he thrust the spear into the water pouch, then withdrew his spear, turned round and dashed away. But he made a bad mistake! He only speared the water pouch on the right side. There were two water pouches on the cart, the left contained the sweet water, and the right contained the brackish water. Later on the city of Peking had many salty wells, and it was said this was because Gao Liang had slit the wrong water pouch! What about the left water pouch? Later it filled the Yuquan Mount, and ever since the water gushing out from there was very sweet and tasty.

As the Dragon King was resting under the tree, he suddenly heard the sound of water, and when he raised his head, seeing that Gao Liang had slit the water pouch and was dashing back, he unleashed a barrage of abuse: "Little rascal, watch me drown you!" The Dragon King waved his hands, and torrents of water gushed out of the water pouches, surging in the direction of Gao Liang. When Gao heard the thunderous roaring behind his back he was terribly frightened, he dared not turn round, and kept running for his life. With the Xizhi Gate in sight, Gao Liang relaxed and thought it might not cause much harm if he just turned round for a quick look to see what had happened. As he turned his head, his steps slowed down, and suddenly a thirty-foot-high wave swept over him, drowning him instantly. Because Gao Liang did not take Liu Bowen's admonition to heart, he was drowned in the flood. Later a bridge named Gaoliang Bridge was built in his memory at the very spot where he drowned.

Standing on the city tower and seeing that the flood was about to engulf Gao Liang as it rolled toward the city gate, Liu Bowen was very worried that the water might destroy Peking. He immediately gave the order to close the gates as tightly as possible. The flood water thus could not enter the city; part of it flowed south along the waterway, and part of it flowed underground into the city. The wells and rivers of the city were all filled with water, and the citizens of Peking were overjoyed, now that no one would die of thirst.

But how could the Dragon King back down now that his scheme had been foiled by Liu Bowen? The Dragon King snuck into the city through the underground streams. There were many vents in Peking, but Liu Bowen had put a weight on top of most of them, like the White Pagoda on the Qionghua Island of the North Sea, the White Pagoda in the White Pagoda Monastery, and others. The Dragon King found a vent in the neighborhood of the North New Bridge; it was a well. He brought the water with him, which when unleashed, would gush upward drowning the entire city. When people heard the water rushing in the well, they hurried to report to Liu Bowen. Counting on his fingers, Liu Bowen got an idea. He sent men to find Shen Wansan, and took him to the well. "You must figure out a way to subdue the Dragon King, pressing the water down for me!" Liu Bowen said to Wansan. Shen Wansan was worried and cried: "I'm only a beggar, how could I take care of the Dragon King! Are you not asking me the impossible?" Liu Bowen gave him an angry look, saying: "If you can't take care of the Dragon King, I'll beat you up." "Don't, don't; let me find a way," Shen Wansan repeated. Then he lowered his head and paced around for a solution.

The rushing of water from the well got louder and louder and was rising up to the edge of the well. Standing beside Shen Wansan, Liu Bowen was pushing him very hard. Suddenly Shen Wansan cracked a smile, saying: "I have a plan. I have a broken earthen begging bowl, see if it works." He untied the cord around his neck from which the bowl hung, and, grasping the end of the cord, he thrust the bowl with its mouth facing down into the well. After this was done, surprisingly the water level from the well slowly receded, and the rushing of the water gradually diminished. The Dragon King, who was trapped under the bowl, yelled: "Liu Bowen, you've gone too far. Now you have weighted me to the bottom, when can I come out again?" Liu quipped, "Sure, I could let you come out. There is a bridge not far away from this well, when the bridge grows old, you can come out!" Well, the Dragon King pondered: "This bridge is new but there must be a time when it will be old, so I can still come out in the future and flood Peking." Thereafter he stayed quiet, waiting for his time. Shen Wansan's earthen bowl was fastened deep under the well, and the cord that tied the bowl became a long and heavy iron chain. Shen Wansan tied the chain's lead to the platform of the well, and for many years the chain stayed there. Some curious people tried pulling it up, but only after a few tugs the water started rushing. They were so frightened that they let go of the chain and the sound stopped. Since then no one dared touch it; who is not worried the Dragon King may come out again?

Liu Bowen then gave a name to the bridge built near the well, calling it Beixinqiao; it means that this bridge can never grow old, thus the Dragon King can never hope to come out again. (Note: The name literally means North New Bridge, but phonetically it rhymes with *buxin*, which means "never growing old", hence the pun.) What about that Shen Wansan? He was never seen again after that.

* Translated from *Beijing fengwu chuanshuo*, ed. The Beijing Branch of the Chinese Association for Research on Popular Literature (Beijing: Zhongguo minjian wenyi chubanshe, 1983), pp. 1–7.

5. How was the City of Peking Built?

Legend has it that the Prince of Yan was most jealous of Liu Bowen, always trying to find an excuse to kill him. One day, the Prince of Yan asked Liu Bowen: "This time I am to lead a northern campaign, at what location would you say I should most fittingly end the campaign?" "When you reach the place where people eat blood-tainted rice, use mud pots to cook their meals, and straw to cover their pots, then you should lay down your arms. I have here a map, and a sealed letter. When you have suspended your battle, you should take them out for a look." Liu Bowen said.

In ancient times Peking was called Youzhou. When the Prince of Yan carried his campaign to the border fortresses of Youzhou, the soldiers could no longer bear the suffering. They ate hard red *gaoliang* rice, and.could not relieve themselves; many fell sick and perished. At wit's end, the Prince of Yan called off military action. What was said earlier about the blood-tainted rice actually refers to the red *gaoliang* rice. There were no iron pots to prepare meals, so earthen pots were used, and because there were no pot covers, straw stalks were used instead. Liu Bowen's forewarning was all fulfilled. The Prince found no pretext to kill him, and could do nothing about it.

At this time, the Prince of Yan unveiled Liu Bowen's drawings for inspection, which were a plan for the construction of the city of Peking. The city was called Beiping, and when Liu Bowen advised the Prince of Yan to build a capital there, it was renamed Peking. Having examined the plan, he also unsealed the letter. In it Liu Bowen recommended an adviser for the construction of the city. This adviser was a man named Yao Guangxiao. In the letter he also informed the Prince of Yan: "Here is a man of resources; if you have no money, don't worry, just find Shen Wansan." But where to find Yao Guangxiao and Shen Wansan? The Prince had a petulant temper, prone to beating and killing people on the spur of the moment. Many of his servants who were sent to find Yao Guangxiao but failed were killed. Thus, several months' search came to nothing. The Prince of Yan grudgingly put the matter aside for a while.

Hunting was a great pleasure of the prince's and he rode out every day. One day, the Prince came to the west side of the capital and arrived at a place where the old trees on the hill jutted into the sky, clouds and mists swirled around the trees, and rushing streams roared. He decided to take a rest in this valley for a while, where it turned out the famous Tanzhou Monastery was also located. The old and young monks of the monastery, hearing of the Prince of Yan's arrival, immediately put on their Buddhist garb and went out to the gate of the hill to greet the Prince. The bells and drums sounded in unison, even the hundred grasses were transformed into fairies, all were greeting His Highness (*qiansuiye*). Among the crowd was a very neatly-dressed old monk; holding up a "nine-link" goblet (*jiulianbei*) in his hands, he knelt on the ground and proclaimed: "Your servant Yao Guangxiao bowing to meet Your Highness." This monk was originally called Yao Guanghui; he was an Ordinary Grand Master (zhong dafu) under Emperor Taizu, but because he could not get along with his colleagues, he retired to the hills. He was afraid that his real name would cause trouble, so he called himself Yao Guangxiao. When the Prince of Yan heard the name Yao Guangxiao, he immediately dismounted, grabbed Yao Guangxiao with his left hand, and the two went into the monastery.

Yao Guangxiao had initially arranged a "treasured seat" (*baozuo*) for the Prince of Yan, but this time the prince did not accept and instead let him occupy it. Turning to Yao Guangxiao, the Prince of Yan made a bow, saying: "You are now my adviser, I am asking you to go down the hill to build the city of Peking." Hearing this, Yao immediately knelt down and kowtowed, insisting that he would not oblige. The Prince of Yan then tossed Liu Bowen's design on the ground, and said: "Just take a look!" Yao Guangxiao was so frightened and perspiration soaked his body, finding no way to desist but promise to accept the task. The fact was that Liu Bowan was his master, how could he not comply?

The Prince had Yao Guangxiao but still lacked the money to build Peking city. It was now time to search for Shen Wansan. The Prince of Yan charged two junior officials with the task of looking for Shen Wansan and gave them a three-month deadline. If they could not find him, they'll lose their heads. The days went by one after another until very soon the three months came to an end. The junior officials cursed their soldiers' ineptness, beating them with whips, and even killed several of them, but Shen Wansan was not to be found. Only three days remained. The officials were frustrated and felt as though their situation was described by the Chinese pun: "Fifteen buckets pumping water, seven up and eight down." They worried they would be beheaded but did not know what to do. One day, one of the officials went out for a walk to alleviate his boredom, and he wandered to the Donghua Gate. This area belongs to the Imperial-city and normally people were not allowed to trade there. But the Donghua Gate is an exception. There were many porters, and they were there carrying rations or precious goods for the imperial household, or serving as messengers. Since the emperor did not offer them meals, petty traders and hawkers were allowed to come here to run small businesses like vending bean curds, making fried dough sticks, or selling hot cakes. There was quite a crowd around, for porters could get several fried dough sticks and hot cakes for a handful of copper coins.

On this day, inside the Imperial-city, a burly porter stripped to his waist with loads on his shoulders, was seen chewing a hot cake and wiping his mouth, then walking away. The hawkers yelled: "Hey, you, porter, you didn't pay for the hot cake you're eating! Who are you?" This burly man turned round, gave an angry stare, and said: "You're blind, how could I, Shen Wansan, eat without paying? I always pay before I eat." When the junior official heard the name Shen Wansan, he was overjoyed, crying: "Here he is, the man so hard to find!" Immediately the officer drew some copper coins from his pouch to pay for the bill, and inquired: "You are Shen Wansan, aren't you? You almost cost me my life. I've been looking for you for three months, but haven't been able to find you. Now please follow me, my imperial master wants you to come to the palace." Shen Wansan was flabbergasted; he said: "I'm only a porter, what could the imperial master want with me. I'm not going!" Finally, having failed with all his persuasions, the junior official ordered the soldiers to put Shen Wansan in chains and send him to the palace.

Hearing that this half-naked dark burly fellow was Shen Wansan, the Prince of Yan was astonished: "How could this pauper resemble a living God of Wealth!" Still, he personally removed the handcuffs from Shen Wansan, and asked him for money to build the city of Peking. Shen said: "Imperial prince, are you making fun of me? I'm just a porter, I have just enough on hand to feed myself, I don't even have anything to wear. How would I have money hoarded at home?" The Prince of Yan raised his eyebrows, and shouted: "If you don't hand over your gold and silver, don't expect to live!" Shen Wansan replied that he did not have it. "So, he has none, what is to be done?" said the Prince of Yan as he eyed Yao Guangxiao and gave the order to beat Shen Wansan. But though he was beaten to a pulp and was streaming with blood, Shen Wansan still said he had nothing. In frustration, the Prince of Yan wanted to slay Shen with his own sword, but was afraid that killing him would be pointless. Then he ordered his men to put Shen Wansan in a cangue, placing a gong in his hand, parading him around under guard, and forcing him to chant aloud: "Don't act like me Shen Wansan, not doling out money to build the city of Peking!" Then "bang, bang, bang", he struck the gong three times. But even so, after parading for three days, there was no result.

On this (the fourth) day, the soldiers again dragged Shen

Wansan out on parade. After going out of the Di'an Gate from the north side, Shen Wansan was so worn out by the torture that he was almost dead, struggling breathlessly, and it was not long before he collapsed on the ground, but the soldiers kept whipping him. His head laid to the northeast and his feet landed facing toward southwest; nothing could revive him. Then a white-haired old man came forward, shouting out: "This man can only be handled gently. Now you've used your force to no avail." He pulled out his own smoke-pouch, offering Shen Wansan the invitation to take a puff. But how could Shen Wansan have the strength to take a smoke? He did not inhale, and swung the pouch on the ground, saying to the old man: "I'm staying right here!"—He meant that "I'd die here no matter what!" The soldiers, hearing the word "here", dashed to report to the officials: "Shen Wansan just spoke, he said 'right here', his cache of gold and silver must be there." Minutes later, all the soldiers were busily engaged, with shovels to the ground, and dug up 480,000 teals of silver. This time the Prince of Yan was really overjoyed. He said: "It never occurred to me that whenever he is beaten money comes out!" Thus he ordered the soldiers: "Drag him along following me." After a few paces, Shen Wansan collapsed again. The soldiers fetched the hoes and dug the ground, again digging up ten vaults of silver, altogether there were 4,800,000 teals of silver. Since then, the ground was left with ten pits, and when these pits were filled with water, they became known as Shijiaohai (Ten Vaults Sea), and in later times, though it is unclear exactly when, it came to be called Shichahai.

Yet, with money at hand, the Prince of Yan was still dissatisfied. The guards again chained and paraded Shen Wansan out to the Tian'an Gate from the south side, and when Shen reached the Gold Fish Pond on the west side of the Rainbow Bridge, he again fainted. On the spot where he collapsed, soldiers started digging, and dug out a golden vat filled with gold bars, totaling about 480,000 teals. When Shen Wansan awoke, they whipped him again, and when he collapsed they resumed digging. In all they dug out nine vats of gold bars. This inspired the legend of "Nine Vats and Eighteen Vaults" [in bygone years these pits were still visible in the city]. Because gold and silver were found, this place came to be known as the Gold and Silver Pond, and in later times, gold fish were reared in the pond, and so it became known as the Gold Fish Pond.

With the money gathered, the Prince of Yan planned to construct the city wall, and all who knew about wall building were summoned. But wall plaster could not be found. Adviser Yao Guangxiao said: "Wall plaster is only available in Shanxi." How far is Shanxi away from Peking! Even eight hundred heads of big horses and mules were not sufficient to haul the plaster, what could be done? The Prince of Yan ordered the people to stand in a line, back to back, three to five paces in between, each passing to the next baskets of plaster from Shanxi to Peking. It is said that there were three hundred and thirty-three hilltops in Shanxi, all were leveled, but the city walls still lacked three feet of plaster. Yao Guangxiao laid out the city design of Peking drawn by Liu Bowen, and found a line surrounding the four sides of the city walls. He reported it to the Prince of Yan, and dredged the earth surrounding the four sides of the city walls and piled them upon the walls. Thus the city walls were completed, with Hucheng Canal surrounding the four sides of the city.

* Translated from Wang Wenbao, ed., *Beijing fengwu chuanshuo gushi xuan*, pp. 1–6.

Glossary

Translation of Terms

ba 壩 = dam/embankment
bao 堡 = fortress
bo 泊 = small lake
cang 倉 = depot
cha 岔 = defile
chi 池 = pond
ci 祠 = memorial
dao 島 = island
dian 殿 = hall
fang 坊 = ward
fu 府 = subprefecture
ge 閣 = pavilion
gong 宮 = palace
gou 溝 = ditch
guan 館 = academy
guan 關 = pass
guan 觀 = shrine
hai 海 = sea
hang 行 = guild
he 河 = river/canal
hu 湖 = lake
jie 街 = street
ku 庫 = storehouse
ling 陵 = mausoleum
long 龍 = dragon
lou 樓 = tower
lu 路 = district
men 門 = gate
miao 廟 = temple
qiao 橋 = bridge
qu 區 = district
qu 渠 = small canal
quan 泉 = spring
shan 山 = mount/mountain/hill
shi 市 = market
si 寺 = monastery/court
ta 塔 = pagoda
tan 壇 = altar
tan 潭 = pool
tang 堂 = hall
ting 亭 = pavilion
wang 王 = king/prince
xian 縣 = county
yuan 園 (苑) = park
yue 嶽 = marchmount
zha 閘 = watergate
zhou 州 = prefecture

Notes

Abbreviations to Major Works and Editions

BIHP	*Bulletin of the Institute of History and Philology, Academia Sinica* 中央研究院歷史語言研究所集刊
BJTS	*Beijing tongshi* 北京通史
CSJC	*Congshu jicheng* 叢書集成
DMB	*Dictionary of Ming Biography*
JCS	*Journal of Chinese Studies, The Chinese University of Hong Kong* 香港中文大學《中國文化研究所學報》
MS	*Mingshi* 明史
MTZOSL	*Ming Taizong shilu* 明太宗實錄
MTZUSL	*Ming Taizu shilu* 明太祖實錄
QDRXJWK	*Qinding Rixia jiuwen kao* 欽定日下舊聞考
SBBY	*Sibu beiyao* 四部備要
SBCK	*Sibu congkan* 四部叢刊
SKQS	*Siku quanshu* 四庫全書
SKCMCS	*Siku quanshu cunmu congshu* 四庫全書存目叢書
TSD	*Taishō shinshū daizōkyō* 大正新修大藏經
XXSKQS	*Xuxiu Siku quanshu* 續修四庫全書
YS	*Yuanshi* 元史

Introduction

1. For a succinct survey of the famous ancient Chinese imperial capital cities see, among others, Murata Jirō, *Chūgoku no teito* (Kyoto: Sōgeisha, 1981); Dong Jianhong et al., *Zhongguo chengshi jianshe shi* (Beijing: Zhongguo jianzhugongye chubanshe, 1982); He Yeju, *Zhongguo gudai chengshi guihua shi luncong* (Beijing: Zhongguo jianzhu gongye, 1986); Nancy S. Steinhardt, *Chinese Imperial City Planning* (Honolulu: University of Hawaii Press, 1990); Yang Kuan, *Zhongguo gudai ducheng zhidu shi yanjiu* (Shanghai: Shanghai guji chubanshe, 1993); and Victor Cunrui Xiong, *Sui-Tang Chang'an: A Study in Urban History of Medieval China* (Ann Arbor: Center for Chinese Studies, The University of Michigan, 2000).
2. For a general account of the building of these imperial cities in the Beijing region see, among others, Hou Renzhi and Jin Tao, *Beijing shihua* (Shanghai: Shanghai Renmin chubanshe, 1980); *Beijing shi*, compiled by Department of History, Peking University (Beijing: Beijing chubanshe,

1985); Yan Chongnian, *Beijing: The Treasures of an Ancient Capital* (Beijing: Morning Glory Press, 1987); Li Shulan, *Beijing shigao* (Beijing: Xueyuan chubanshe, 1994); Hou Renzhi, *Beijing cheng de qiyuan yu bianqian* (Beijing: Yanshan chubanshe, 1997); Cao Zixi et al., eds., *BJTS*, 10 volumes (Beijing: Zhongguo shudian, 1994); and Hou Renzhi et al., eds., *Beijing chengshi lishidili* (Beijing Yanshan, 2000). For a useful bibliographical guide to primary sources for research on Peking's history and geography, see Wang Canzhi, comp., *Beijing shidi fengwu shulu* (Beijing chubanshe, 1985). Sketch maps of these imperial cities are available in the historical atlas of Beijing produced by Hou Renzhi et al., eds., *Beijing lishiditu ji* (Beijing chubanshe, 1985), Vol. I, pp. 27–28, 31–32, 33–34, 35–36. The most comprehensive collection of essays and notes relating to archaeological work and architectural monuments in historical Peking remains Su Tianjun, ed., *Beijing kaogu jicheng* (Beijing chubanshe, 2000), 10 volumes. The latest scholarly survey of Peking's historical development for popular reading is *Manbu Beijing lishi changhe*, edited by Beijingshi yanjiuhui et al. (Zhongguo shudian, 2004).

3. See briefly Hou and Jin, *Beijing shihua*, chaps. 1–2; *Beijing shi*, chap. 2; Hou, *Beijing lishiditu ji*, Vol. I, pp. 4–5; Yan, *Beijing*, chap. 1; and Hou, *Beijing chengshi lishidili*, chaps. 1, 2.
4. See briefly Hou and Jin, *Beijing shihua*, chaps. 2–4; *Beijing shi*, chaps. 2–3; Hou, *Beijing lishi ditu ji*, Vol. 1, pp. 11–21; Yan, *Beijing*, chaps. 2–3; and Hou, *Beijing chengshi lishidili*, chaps. 1–3. On the date of Zhou's conquest of Shang, hence that of the founding of Ji, David S. Nivison first proposed 1045 B.C.; it has since been confirmed by Hou Renzhi and others despite some lingering dissent among Chinese archaeologists. See Nivison, "The Dates of Western Chou", *Harvard Journal of Asiatic Studies*, 43.2 (December 1983), pp. 499–524; and Hou, "Beijing jiancheng zhizhi", *Beijing shehuikexue*, 1990.3 (August), pp. 2–4. Wang Canzhi earlier proposed 1057 B.C. but this has since been rejected. See Wang, "Beijing jiandu shi yu gongyuanqian 1057 nian"(1980), rpt. in *Wang Canzhi shizhi lunwenji* (Beijing Yanshan, 1991), pp. 308–315. On Ji's and Yan's development in later periods, see Cao, *BJTS*, Vol. 1 (Prehistory, Qin-Han to Nanbei-chao); and Xiang Yansheng, *BJTS*, Vol. 2 (Sui-Tang to Wudai), passim.
5. See Tuotuo et al., *Liaoshi* (Beijing: Zhonghua shuju, 1974), 1: 45; 40: 494. See also Wang Ling, *BJTS*, Vol. 3 (Liao Nanjing), pp. 28–33, 59–74.
6. See *Liaoshi*, 40: 495. See also Liu Yingli, *Da Yuan hunyi fangyu shenglan, juan shang* 上 (1307; Chengdu: Sichuan daxue chubanshe, 2003), p. 21; Xiong Mengxiang, *Xijin zhi jiyi*, edited by Rare Book Reconstruction Committee (Beijing: Beijing guji chubanshe, 1983), p. 1: "zhengli shuoming" (editorial notes). For information on the *fenye* system, see the works of Needham, Ho, Schafer, and Sun and Kistemaker cited in notes 14, 16, but in particular for

reference to Liao, see Jeffrey F. Meyer, *The Dragons of Tiananmen: Beijing as a Sacred City* (Columbia: University of South Carolina Press, 1991), pp. 125–127. Note that these authors translate the Chinese astronomical terms variably. Needham and Schafer translate *xiu* as "lodging"; Ho as "mansion"; and Sun and Kistemaker as "lodge". Meyer renders *xiu* (which was erroneously romanized as *su*) and *ci* indiscriminately as dwelling/habitation. Schafer translates *ci* as "(Jupiter) station"; and Sun and Kistemaker, as "(Jupiter) mansion". I have stated my preference in the text.

7. See *Liaoshi*, 18: 217; 40: 494. See also Wang, *BJTS*, vol. 3 , pp. 62–64. On the population records of Liao Nanjing see Han Guanghui, *Beijing lishirenkou dili* (Beijing: Beijing daxue chubanshe, 1996), pp. 48–59; and Hou, *Beijing chengshi lishidili*, pp. 253–258.
8. See Tuotuo et al., *Jinshi* (Zhonghua, 1975), 5: 97, 100; 24: 572–573. For details see Yu Guangdu and Chang Runhua, *BJTS*, Vol. 4 (Jin Zhongdu), pp. 44–57; Yu Jie and Yu Guangdu, *Jin Zhongdu* (Beijing chubanshe, 1989), chaps. 2, 3, 4, 6. See also the earlier work, George Kates, "A New Date for the Origins of the Forbidden City", *Harvard Journal of Asiatic Studies*, 7.3 (February 1943), pp. 180–202. On the population records of Zhongdu see Han, *Beijing lishi renkoudili*, pp. 59–67; and Hou, *Beijing chengshi lishidili*, pp. 258–263.
9. See *Jinshi*, 24: 572–573, 27: 682–688. For details see Yu and Chang, *BJTS*, Vol. 4, pp. 343–352; Yu and Yu, *Jin Zhongdu*, pp. 100–107, 129–146. On the water supply system in Zhongdu and development of its waterway communications see Hou Renzhi, "Beijing dushi fazhan guocheng zhong de shuiyuan wenti", in Hou, *Lishidilixue de lilun yu shijian* (Shanghai Renmin chubanshe, 1979), pp. 281–288; and Hou, *Beijingcheng de qiyuan yu bianqian*, pp. 66–73.
10. On the building of Yuan Dadu and Ming-Qing Peking see Chapters 1, 2.
11. On these uneventful dates in Peking's recent history see *Beijing lishi jinian*, compiled by Compilation Committee, Beijingshi shehuikexue yanjiusuo (Beijing: Xinhua shudian, 1984), pp. 268, 303, 360; and Xi Wuyi and Deng Yibing, *BJTS*, Vol. 9 (Republican era), pp. 444, 456, 470.
12. See briefly Paul Wheatley, *The Pivot of the Four Quarters: A Preliminary Enquiry into the Origins and Character of the Ancient Chinese City* (Chicago: Aldine Publishing, 1971), pp. 144–146; see also comments by Edward H. Schafer, *Pacing the Void: T'ang Approaches to the Stars* (Berkeley: University of California Press, 1977), pp. 54–56.
13. See Lü Buwei, ed., *Lushi chunqiu* (*SBBY* ed.), *juan* 4, 9; Sima Qian, *Shiji* (Zhonghua, 1959), *juan* 27; Liu An, *Huainan honglie jie* (*SBCK* ed.), *juan* 3, 6; Dong Zhongshu, *Chunqiu fanlu* (*SBBY* ed.), *juan* 13. For a succinct discussion of the philosophy of cosmological resonance or "stimulus and response between heaven and man", see John B. Henderson, *The*

Development and Decline of Chinese Cosmology (New York: Columbia University Press, 1984), pp. 22–28; and Charles Le Blanc, *Huai Nan Tzu: Philosophical Synthesis in Early Han Thought* (Hong Kong: Hong Kong University Press, 1985), pp. 191–206. See also Aihe Wang, *Cosmology and Political Culture in Early China* (Cambridge: Cambridge University Press, 2000), pp. 185–190.

14. The principal pre-Qin astronomical records were the star catalogues produced by Shi Shen 石申 and Gan De 甘德 of the Warring States period. They were used by astrologers until the sixth century and fragments are found in Fang Xuanling et al., *Jinshu* (Zhonghua, 1974), *juan* 11. They are important sources preceding *Shiji, juan* 27. The former has been translated in Ho Peng Yoke, *The Astronomical Chapters of the Chin-shu* (Paris: Mouton, 1966), "Text", pp. 43–120. A summary of these traditional records with charts is found in Wang Qi, *Sancai tuhui* (Taibei: Chengwen chubanshe, 1970), *juan* 1. For a modern reconstruction of the ancient Chinese "lunar lodges" systems and the celestial constellations see Joseph Needham et al., eds., *Science and Civilization in China* (Cambridge: Cambridge University Press, 1959), Vol. 3, pp. 232–262. See also briefly Ho Peng Yoke, *Li Qi and Shu: An Introduction to Science and Civilization in China* (Hong Kong: Hong Kong University Press, 1985), pp. 131–149. A complete list of the twenty-eight *xiu* and their coordinate stars is included in *Zhongguo dabaikequanshu: Tianwenxue* (Beijing: Zhongguo dabaikequanshu chubanshe, 1980), pp. 572–576. On the reconstruction of the *xiu* and the Five Palaces during the Han dynasty see Sun Xiaochun and Jacob Kistemaker, *The Chinese Sky during the Han: Constellating Stars and Society* (Leiden: Brill, 1997), pp. 5–27, 115–124. For examples of the symbolic correlations between the Five Agents/Phases and things in the natural and divine world see Ho, *Li, Qi and Shu*, chap. 3, especially p. 22, Table 1. For recent studies of the Five Agents/Phases theories see Michael Loewe, "Water, earth and fire: The symbols of the Han dynasty", rpt. in Loewe, *Divination, Mythology and Monarchy in Han China* (Cambridge: Cambridge University Press, 1994), pp. 55–60; and Wang, *Cosmology and Political Culture in Early China*, passim.

15. For the source of the two different versions of the circular sequence of the Eight Trigrams see, among others, Zhang Huang, *Tushu bian* (*SKQS* ed.), 2: 13a, 51a; see also Ho, *Li, Qi and Shu*, chap. 7, pp. 50–51. For a detailed discussion of this topic see François Louis, "The Genesis of an Icon: The *Taiji* Diagram's Early History", *Harvard Journal of Asiatic Studies*, 63.1 (June 2003), pp. 145–196.

16. On the *fenye* system see Needham, *Science and Civilization*, Vol. 3, pp. 281, 545; Henderson, *Development and Decline of Chinese Cosmology*, pp. 68–70; and Sun and Kistemaker, *The Chinese Sky*, pp. 106, 132. Henderson translated *fenye* as "field allocation". Sun et al. asserted that the system was developed by the political astrologer Liu Xin 劉歆 (53 B.C.–A.D. 23); this is probably

incorrect unless one is to believe that the *Zhouli* was doctored by Liu and his compatriot classicists at the end of Former Han as alleged. Earlier Edward H. Schafer erroneously rendered the term as "disastrous geography", which inadvertently confused our understanding of its meaning, but his representation charts are very useful. On the "twelve terrestrial branches" and "twelve Jupiter stations" celestial/terrestrial division systems and their correspondence with the twenty-eight lunar lodges see Ho, *The Astronomical Chapters*, pp. 113–120; Schafer, *Pacing the Void*, pp. 75–78; and Meyer, *The Dragons of Tiananmen*, pp. 125–127.

17. For sources on the Taiwei, Ziwei, and Taiweiyuan and their coordinating stars see *Shiji, juan* 27; *Jinshu, juan* 11; *Sancai tuhui, juan* 1, passim. See also the star list in *Zhongguo dabaike quanshu*: *Tianwenxue*, pp. 571–572. For modern astronomical interpretations of these enclosures of star constellations and their ideological significance see Ho, *The Astronomical Chapters*, pp. 71–85; and Sun and Kistemaker, *The Chinese Sky*, pp. 82–86, 124–135.
18. See *Shiji*, 27: 1289–1290; and Sun and Kistemaker, *The Chinese Sky*, pp. 96–97, 103, 122–123, 133, 164.
19. Modern scholars have translated Ziweiyuan variably. Needham and Ho translated it as Purple Forbidden Enclosure; Schafer as Grand Palace of Purple Tenuity, or in short form, as Purple Palace; and Meyer as Purple Hidden Enclosure. According to Ho, Taiweiyuan is composed of stars in Virgo, Leo, and Coma Barenices; Ziwei is composed of stars in Draco, Ursa Major, and Camelopardus; and Tianshiyuan is composed of stars in Hercules, Serpens, Ophiuchus, and Aquila in western constellations. See op. cit., p. 71n[d], and "Star Maps" 1, 2, 3 (pp. 163–165).
20. In this case see Zhu Changwen, *Wujun tujing xuji* (*SKQS* ed.), *shang*, 3b. See also Li Mingwan and Feng Guifen, eds., *Suzhou fuzhi* (Taibei Chengwen, 1970), 4: 3b.
21. On this particular passage of the *Kaogong ji* see Zheng Xuan and Jia Kongyan annotated, *Zhouli zhusuo* (*SKQS* ed.), 41: 35b–36b. For a detailed study of this text and the Wangcheng model see He Yeju, *Kaogong ji yingguozhidu yanjiu* (Zhongguo jianzhugongye, 1985), chaps. 1–3. For a pioneering but outdated study of the Chinese cosmological and archaeological models of imperial cities in Western scholarship see Arthur F. Wright, "The Cosmology of the Chinese City", in *The City in Late Imperial China*, edited by G. William Skinner (Stanford: Stanford University Press, 1977), pp. 33–73; see also Wheatley, *The Pivot of the Four Quarters*, chap. 5; and Steinhart, *Chinese Imperial City Planning*, pp. 33–36, 43–46, 66–67, 98–101, 158–160.
22. See the literature cited in Chapter 1, notes 24–27; Chapter 2, notes 18–23.
23. There is substantial English literature, but of varying quality, on fengshui. For a partial list see Ernest J. Eitel, *Feng-Shui, Principles of the Natural Science*

of the Chinese (Hong Kong/London: Trübner, 1873); J. J. M. de Groot, *The Religious System of China* (Leiden: Brill, 1892), Vols. 2, 3, passim; Needham, *Science and Civilization of China,* Vol. 2 (1956), pp. 359–363; Stephan Feuchtwang, *An Anthropological Analysis of Chinese Geomancy* (Vientiane: Vithagana, 1974); Andrew L. March, "An Appreciation of Chinese Geomancy", *Journal of Asian Studies,* XXVII. 2 (1968), pp. 253–267; Steven J. Bennett, "Patterns of the Sky and Earth: A Chinese Science of Applied Cosmology", *Chinese Science,* 3 (1978): 1–26; Stephen Skinner, *The Living Earth Manual of Feng-Shui: Chinese Geomancy* (London: Routledge & Kegan Paul, 1982); Richard J. Smith, *Fortune-Tellers and Philosophers: Divination in Traditional Chinese Society* (Boulder: Westview Press, 1991), pp. 131–172; Ole Bruun, *Fengshui in China* (Honolulu: University of Hawaii Press, 2003), chap. 1, and appendix. A sample of Chinese works relating to architecture are cited in notes 25, 27 below.

24. On the development of the geomancers' compass see de Groot, *The Religious System of China,* Vol. 3, bk. 1, part III, chap. XII, pp. 935–1056; Needham, *Science and Civilization in China,* Vol. 4 : I (1962), section 26(i), passim; Smith, *Fortune-Tellers and Philosophers,* pp. 13–72; and Skinner, *The Living Earth Manual of Feng-shui,* chap. 5, passim. On the term *kanyu* in Han times see Michael Loewe, "The term *K'an-yü* and the choice of the moment", rpt. in Loewe, *Divination, Mythology and Monarchy in Han China,* pp. 112–120.
25. For a selection of the essential fengshui literature see Chen Menglei et al., eds., *Gujintushu jicheng* (1726; Shanghai: Zhonghua shuju, 1934), *bowu bian, yishu dian, kanyu bu* 勘輿部, *juan* 651–678; Yongrong et al., eds., *Siqu quanshu zongmu tiyao* (Taibei: Taiwan Shangwu yinshuguan, 1965), *juan* 111. See also Yi Ding, Yu Lu, and Hong Yong, *Zhongguo gudai fengshui yu jianzhu xuanzhi* (Baoding: Hebei kexue jishu chubanshe, 1996), Appendix. For more complete collections see *Siku shushulei congshu* (Shanghai guji, 1991); and *Siku shushulei daquan* (Haikou: Hainan chubanshe, 1993).
26. For more detailed information see March, "An Appreciation of Chinese Geomancy", passim; Skinner, *The Living Earth Manual of Feng-shui,* chaps. 1–6; Smith, *Fortune-Tellers and Philosophers,* pp. 13–72; and Bruun, *Fengshui in China,* chap. 1.
27. For a sample of recent studies on the influence of the fengshui system in the building of Chinese capital cities see Wang Qiheng, ed., *Fengshui lilun yanjiu* (Tianjin: Tianjin daxue chubanshe, 1992); Yi Ding, Yu Lu, and Hong Yong, *Zhongguo gudai fengshui yu jianzhu xuanzhi*; Evelyn Lip, *Fengshui: Environments of Power, A Study of Chinese Architecture* (London: Academy Editions, 1996); and Wang Zilin, *Zijin cheng fengshui* (Beijing: Zijincheng chubanshe, 2005).
28. For a succinct account see Chen Xuelin, "Yuan Daducheng jianzhao chuanshuo tanyuan", *Hanxue yanjiu,* 5.1 (June 1987), pp. 95–127.
29. For details see Chen Xuelin, *Liu Bowen yu Nezha cheng—Beijing jiancheng de*

chuanshuo (Taibei: Dongda tushugongsi, 1996), Parts 3, 4. For a review of this work by a leading Beijing folklorist see Wang Wenbao, "Cong minjian chuanshuo tanxun Beijing cheng de jianzhi—du Chen Xuelin 'Liu Bowen yu Nezha cheng—Beijing jiancheng de chuanshuo'", *Minjian wenxue luntan*, 1998.1 (January), pp. 76–79. See also the same author, *Zhongguo minsu yanjiushi* (Harbin: Heilongjiang Renmin chubanshe, 2003), pp. 289–290.

30. See Chapter 3.
31. See Chapter 4.
32. Such as David Strand, *Rickshaw Peking: City and Politics in the 1920s* (Berkeley: University of California Press, 1989); Joseph W. Esherick, *Remaking the Chinese City: Modernity and National Identity, 1900–1950* (Honolulu: University of Hawaii Press, 2000); Wu Hung, *Remaking Beijing: Tianmen Square and the Creation of a Political Space* (Chicago: The University of Chicago Press, 2005); and Lillian M. Li, Alison J. Pray-Novly, and Haili Kong, *Beijing: From Imperial Capital to Olympic City* (New York: Palgrave Macmillan, 2007), among others.
33. Meyer's *The Dragons of Tiananmen: Beijing as a Sacred City*, like other works of this genre, was inspired by the theoretical model Mircea Eliade developed in his pioneering studies *Patterns in Comparative Religion,* translated by Rosemary Sheed (Cleveland: World, 1959); *The Sacred and the Profane, the Nature of Religion*, translated by R. Trask (New York: Harcourt Brace, 1959); and others. For recent scholarship on sacred space, either studies of specific cases or compartative treatments, see Meyer, "Bibliography", pp. 195–204, passim. He has given a summary of his treatment of Peking as a "sacred city" in the Introduction as well as in chaps. 4 and 5 of the book. The quotation is from p. 6.
34. A collaborative research project titled "Pékin, Ville Sainte—Structures Liturgiques et Sociétié Civile" initiated by Professor Kristopher Schipper, has been in progress in the Section des Sciences Religieuses, l'École Pratique des Hautes Études, Paris since the mid-1990s. Specimens of research products have been published in the journal *Sanjiao wenxian* 三教文獻, edited by Dr. Vincent Goossaert et al., and five issues have been in print since 1997. An international research conference on this subject: "Beijing as a Holy City: Liturgical Structures and a Civil Society" was held under its auspices in Paris in October 1999.
35. Naquin, *Peking: Temples and City Life, 1400–1900* (Berkeley: University of California Press, 2000), especially chap. 1, Introducing Peking, and Epilogue, In search of Old Peking. Cf. Review by Mary B. Rankin in *Harvard Journal of Asiatic Studies*, 62.1 (June 2001), pp. 218–230. The story of Nazha is mentioned in Naquin, p. 14 and p. 113n12. On the Nezha Temple in Taoranting inside the Yongding Gate, see Chapter 2, note 86.
36. Madeleine Yue Dong, *Republican Beijing: The City and Its Histories* (Berkeley:

University of California Press, 2003). See in particular the Introduction, chap. 6, "Recycling: The Tianqiao District", and Conclusion. On Jin Shousen's literary contribution to old Peking, see, ibid., pp. 59–62.

Chapter 1

1. See *YS*, l: 63, 6: 114; 7: 140; 157: 3694. For a succinct account of Qubilai's rise to power, his association with Chinese literati and adoption of Han methods of governance, see among others Zhou Liangxiao, *Hubilie* (Changchun: Jilin jiaoyu chubanshe, 1986), chaps. 4–6; Morris Rossabi, *Khubilai Khan: His Life and Times* (Berkeley: University of California Press, 1988), chaps. 2–3; and *The Cambridge History of China*, Vol. 6: *Alien Regimes and Border States, 907–1368*, edited by Herbert Franke and Denis C. Twitchett (Cambridge: Cambridge University Press, 1994), chap. 5.
2. Haiyun, lay name Song Yinjian 宋印簡, a native of Ningyuan 寧遠 in Shanxi, was the first Buddhist monk summoned by Qubilai to offer counsel on state affairs. For his biography see Nianchang, *Fozu lidai tongzai*, in *TSD*, No. 2036, 21: 701–702. See also the biography by Jan Yunhua 冉雲華 included in *In the Service of the Khan: Eminent Personalities of the Early Mongol-Yuan Period*, edited by Igor de Rachewiltz, Hok-lam Chan et al. (Wiesbaden: Harrassowitz Verlag, 1993), pp. 224–242.
3. For Zicong/Liu Bingzhong's traditional biographies, see Liu Bingzhong, *Cangchun ji* (*SKQS* ed.), *juan* 6, appendix; Su Tianjue, *Guo (Yuan) chao mingren shilue* (Zhonghua, 1996), 7: 111–114; *YS*, 157: 3687–3694. There is a modern biography by H. L. Chan included in *In the Service of the Khan*, pp. 245–269. For modern studies see Sun Kekuan, "Yuandai shenmi renwu Liu Bingzhong jiqi *Cangchun ji*", rpt. in Sun, *Menggu Hanjun yu Hanwenhua yanjiu* (Taibei: Taiwan Zhonghua shuju, 1959), pp. 99–106; Hok-lam Chan, "Liu Ping-chung (1216–1274): A Buddhhist-Taoist Statesman at the Court of Khubilai Khan", *T'oung Pao*, 53.1–3 (1967), pp. 98–146; Yuan Ji, *Yuan Taibao Cangchunsanren Liu Bingzhong pingshu* (Taiwan Shangwu, 1974); and Yan Jihe, "Shilun Liu Bingzhong de lishizuoyong", *Beijing shiyuan* (Beijing Yanshan, 1988), Vol. 4, pp. 242–256. Other studies concerning Liu Bingzhong's building of Dadu are cited elsewhere.
4. On these major achievements of Liu Bingzhong, see the studies by Chan and Yuan cited in note 3. For his role in the design and building of Shangdu, see briefly Chen Gaohua and Shi Weimin, *Yuan Shangdu* (Jilin jiaoyu, 1988), pp. 23–25, 118–119; and Ye Xinmin, *Yuan Shangdu yanjiu* (Huhhot: Nei Menggu daxue chubanshe, 1998), pp. 2–3, 25–26. See also Chapter 3, note 38.
5. On Möngke's campaign and death in Hezhou, Sichuan, see Yao Congwu, "Song Yu Jie shefang shancheng dui Mengguren ruqin de daji", rpt. in Yao, *Dongbei shi lucong* (Taibei: Zhengzhong shuju, 1959), Vol. 2, pp. 364–369;

and idem. "Yuan Xianzong (Menggehan) de daju zheng Shu yu tazai Hezhou Diaoyutai de zhansi", rpt. in *Yao Congwu xiansheng quanji* (Zhengzhong, 1982), Vol. 5, pp. 253–286.

6. For these achievements of Liu Bingzhong and his activities in later years, see the studies by Chan and Yuan cited in note 3. On Liu's recommendation for the adoption of the Chinese state title Da Yuan and its significance see Xiao Qiqing, "Shuo 'Da Chao': Yuanchao jianhao qian Menggu de Hanwen guohao", *Hanxue yanjiu*, 3.1 (June 1985), pp. 23–40; David M. Farquhar, *The Government of China under Mongolian Rule* (Stuttgart: Franz Steiner, 1990), p. 427. On his private home in Nanping Hill and the shrines he built in both Shangdu and Dadu, see *Xijin zhi*, p. 94; and Ye, *Yuan Shangdu yanjiu*, pp. 2, 189. Liu's *Cangchun ji* in the *SKQS* has been reproduced by the Shanghai guji chubanshe, 1987, as Vol. 1191 of the collection. For a bibliographical note see *Siku quanshu zongmu tiyao*, 166: 5–6.
7. For such biographical accounts see Liu Bingzhong, *Cangchun ji*, appendix (6), 15a–21b. The authors include Zhang Wenqian 張文謙 (1217–1283), Yao Shu 姚樞 (1203–1280), Tudan Gonglü 徒單公履, and Xu Shilong. See also Chen Ji (1314–1370), "Liu Wenzheng gong xiaoxiang bingxu" 劉文正公肖像并序, *Yibaizhai gao* (*SKQS* ed.), 12: 14a–15b. For the biography of the Duke of Zhou, see *Shiji*, 33: 1515–1523; for Zhang Liang, see *Shiji* 55: 2033–2049 and Ban Gu, *Hanshu* (Zhonghua, 1962), 40: 2023–2038; for Fang Xuanling, see Ouyang Xiu, *Xin Tangshu* (Zhonghua, 1975), 96: 3853–3858; for Du Ruhui, see ibid. 96: 3858–3866.
8. Xu Shilong, "Ji Taibao Liugong wen", in *Cangchun ji*, appendix (6), 20a–21b; also included in Su Tianjue, *Guochao* (*Yuan*) *wenlei* (*SBCK* ed.), 48: 7b–9a. For a full translation of the funeral odes and biographical information of the exemplary historical personalities comparable to Liu Bingzhong in respective fields of accomplishment see Chan, "Liu Ping-chung", pp. 104–108, note 10.
9. Tao Zongyi, (*Nancun*) *Chuogeng lu* (Zhonghua, 1959), 2: 26.
10. Ye Ziqi, *Caomu zi* (Zhonghua, 1959), 4: 83, 84.
11. In *Chuogeng lu*, the poem is said to have been written by the Daoist deity the Dark God Zhenwu, but in Cheng Minzheng, *Song yimin lu* (*SKCMCS* ed.), 15: 7b-8a, it is mentioned that in Ming times people attributed it to Liu Bingzhong. The poem was elucidated in Lang Ying, *Qixiu leigao* (Zhonghua, 1959), 27: 408–409, in which the author showed that Liu Bingzhong had accurately predicted the death of the last Mongol-Yuan emperor and the rise of the Ming dynasty founder.
12. 'Phags-pa was made imperial adviser by Qubilai Qaghan in 1260 and was recognized as the head of the Tibetan Buddhist church with the title of *Dabao fawang* 大寶法王 (Great Precious Prince of the Earth). Later he devised a new writing system for the Mongols based on the Tibetan alphabet

known as the 'Phags-pa Alphabet. For his biography, see *YS*, 202: 4517–4518; and also L. Petech, "'Phags-pa", in de Rachewiltz, *In the Service of the Khan*, pp. 646–654.

13. Zhu Guozhen, *Yongzhuang xiaopin* (Zhonghua, 1955), 6: 131; see also Jiang Yikui, *Chang'an kehua* (Beijing guji, 1982), 3: 67. According to these accounts not only was the grave of Liu Bingzhong plundered, those of his grandfather Liu Ze 劉澤, father Liu Run, and younger brother Liu Bingshu 劉秉恕 (1231–1290) were also violated. The credit for being able to predict the robbery and have the names of the culprits presciently inscribed on an epitaph buried inside the grave was not only attributed to Liu Bingzhong but also to his younger brother Bingshu, who was said to have excelled equally in mathematics. Earlier Shen Defu gave a similar story in *Wanli yehuo bian* (Zhonghua, 1959), 29: 758, but it referred to Liu Bingshu instead of Liu Bingzhong. On Liu Bingshu, see *YS*, 157: 2694–2695; see also Ziluo and Xiaoning, "Chudu 'Liu Bingshu muzhi'", *Wenwu chunqiu*, 1994.3 (March), pp. 86–89.
14. Imperially commissioned, *Lidai chenjian* (1426 ed.), 27: 1a. This work is a compendium of incidents in the lives of ancient officials serving as examples to be followed.
15. For Yao Guangxiao's biographies see *MS*, 145: 4079–4082; Fu Weilin, *Mingshu* (*CSJC* ed.), 160: 3155–3159. See also Makita Tairyō, "Dōen den shōkō", *Tōyōshi kenkyū*, 18 (October 1959), pp. 57–79; and Eugene Feifel, "Yao Kuang-hsiao", in *DMB*, Vol. II, pp. 1561–1565. On Yao's contribution to Prince of Yan's usurpation and his work of scholarship, see the references cited in Chapter 2, note 94. On the story of his foretelling the Prince's imperial pretension see Zhu Yunming, *Yeji* (*CSJC* ed.), pp. 43–44. Yuan Gong was the physiognomist who pointed out to Daoyan that he could become a Liu Bingzhong; see *MS*, 145: 4079. For the anecdote about Daoyan dreaming of chatting with Liu Bingzhong in his residence see Zheng Xiao, *Huang Ming mingchen ji*, in *Wuxue bian*, 31 (*XXSKQS* ed.), 10: 1b; and Li Zhi, *Xu Cangshu* (Zhonghua, 1959), 9: 148. Yao Guangxiao had written poems expressing his admiration for Liu Bingzhong; they are included in his poetic works *Taoxuzi shiji* (Qing manuscript), *shang*, 1; *xia* 下, 8, 9. First built in 1186 under the Jin, the Qingshousi was renamed Da Xinglongsi at its renovation in 1448; it was burnt down in 1535 but was restored in 1764 under its original name. It was demolished in 1954. The site is located at the north side of West Chang'an Street 長安西街, near the Telegraph Building in present-day Beijing. See *Jinri Beijing*, edited by Beijingshi shehui kexueyuan (Beijing Yanshan, 1991), Vol. II, pp. 382–383.
16. In many places Daoyuan is compared to Liu Bingzhong, such as *MS*, 145: 4079; Li Zhi, *Xu Cangshu*, 9: 148; Yu Shenxing, *Gushan bizhu* (Zhonghua, 1984), 17: 199; and *Siku quanshu zongmu tiyao*, 32: 5. For Qian Qianyi's

remark see Qian, *Liechao shiji xiaozhuan* (Shanghai: Gudian wenxue chubanshe, 1959), *run ji* 閏集, pp. 669–670; also quoted in Zhao Jishi, *Jiyuan jisuoji* (*XXSKQS* ed.), "Qushuiji: ershi" 驅睡寄：二氏, 10: 3b. On Zhu Yizun's comments see *Jingzhiju shihua* (*XXSKQS* ed.), 6: 5b.

17. Lang Ying, *Qixiu leigao*, 25: 377–378.
18. A reproduction of a Late Ming Fujian edition of the *Yuchi jing*, 2 *juan*, *fulu* 1 *juan*, entitled *Juan dili canbu pinglin tujue quanbei Pingsha Yuchi jing*, with Liu Ji's commentary, an "elaboration" (*zhengshi*) by Lai Congqian, and an amendment by Xu Zhimo, is included in *XXSKQS*, Vol. 1054. For a bibliographical note see *Siku quanshu zongmu tiyao*, 111: 67–68. Its authenticity, however, has been challenged by Jiang Pingjie, a Qing geomancer, in his "*Pingsha Yuchi* bianwei", included in Jiang's *Dili bianzheng*, with subcommentary (*shu*) by Zhang Xinyan (1863 ed.), Vol. 2.
19. This account is entered under the *jiawu* 甲午 (thirteenth) day of the twelfth month of the tenth year of Chenghua (January 20 1475) in *Ming Xianzong shilu*, edited by Zhang Mao et al. (Taibei: Zhongyang yanjiuyuan lishiyuyan yanjiusuo, 1963), 136: 2551. It is also recorded in Zhu Guozhen, *Yongzhuang xiaobin*, 32: 766. For a note on the *Liu Taibao xielou tianji* see Sakai Tadao, *Chūgoku zensho no kenkyū* (Tokyo: Kōbundō, 1960), p. 442.
20. Zhao Bingwen then served in the Yuan court as an academician of the Chaowenyuan 昭文院 (Glorification of Literature Academy). For his biography see Su Tianjue, *Zixi wengao* (Zhonghua, 1997), 22: 365–368. See also *YS*, 150: 3555.
21. See Zhu Xi, *Zhuzi yulei*, edited by Li Jingde (Taibeixian: Hanjing wenhua-shiye youxiangongsi, 1980), 2: 14a–14b.
22. On Zhuge Liang's well-cited metaphor see (Jin) Zhang Bo 張勃, *Wu lu* 吳錄, quoted in Li Fang et al., eds., *Taiping yulan* (Zhonghua, 1960), 156: 3a. It is also included in *Zhu Geliang ji* (Zhonghua, 1960), p. 178. For Bātur's remark see *YS*, 119: 2942. On the biographies of Muqali and his descendants see also de Rachewiltz, *In the Service of the Khan*, pp. 3–26.
23. The "Dadufu", reconstructed from the *Yongle dadian*, is included in *QDRXJWK*, 5: 88–91; the quotation is on p. 89. Li Yousun obtained an appointment as instructor of Confucian studies of the Hangzhou circuit in 1302 as a result of his submission of the rhapsody. See Huang Zongxi and Quan Zuwang, *Song Yuan xue'an* (*XXSKQS* ed.), 76: 19a–19b.
24. For references to Liu Bingzhong's role in the design of Dadu in the *Xijin zhi*, see pp. 2, 33 , 213. Other references are available in Liu's biographies cited in note 6. For recent studies see Chen, *Yuan Dadu*; Chen, "Yuan Dadu cheng jianzhao chuanshuo tanyuan"; Yan Jihe, "Liu Bingzhong zhuchi xiujian Dadu cheng", *Xuexi yu yanjiu*, 1983.10 (October), pp. 42–43; Wang Gang, *BJTS*, Vol. 5 (Yuan Dadu), passim; Yu Xixian, "*Zhouyi* xiangshu yu Yuan

Dadu guihua buju", *Kong Meng xuebao*, 76 (September 1998), pp. 169–188; and Hou, *Beijing chengshi lishidili*, pp. 86–104.

25. On the construction of Dadu see briefly Chen, *Yuan Dadu*, pp. 37–42; Wang, *BJTS*, Vol. 5, pp. 38–41; and Hou, *Beijing chengshi lishdili*, pp. 86–104. For a study of the bureaucracy in charge of the building program see Cary Y. Liu, "The Yuan Dynasty Capital: Imperial Building Program and Bureaucracy", *T'oung Pao*, 78 (1992), pp. 264–301. The surviving earthern walls are remnants of the northwestern Dadu walls along the Jiande and Suqing Gate; they were left when the Ming authorities moved the Yuan walls five *li* southward along the Jishui Pool. They have been dubbed *tucheng* (earthern city) and are now incorporated in the Dadu Remains Public Park (Yuan Dadu chengyuanyizhi gongyuan 元大都城垣遺址公園). On its location, see *Jinri Beijing*, Vol. I, pp. 357–358; and Hou Renzhi, *Hou Renzhi jiang Beijing* (Beijing chubanshe, 2003), pp. 101–102. On the estimated perimeter of Dadu, see Li Xieping, *Mingdai Beijing ducheng yingjian congkao* (Zijincheng chubanshe, 2006), pp. 96–97.
26. For details see *YS*, 64: 1588–1589; 66: 1659–1660. On Guo Shoujing's contribution to Dadu's hydraulic work and irrigation see Su Tianjun, "Guo Shoujing yu Dadu shuili gongcheng", *Ziran kexueshi yanjiu*, 1983.1 (March): 66–72; Cai Fan, *Beijing guyunhe yu chengshi gongshui yanjiu* (Beijing chubanshe, 1987), pp. 21–22; Duan Tianshun, *Yanshui gujin tan* (Beijing Yanshan, 1991), pp. 145–151; and Hou, *Beijing cheng de qiyuan yu bianqian*, pp. 96–100. For Guo's biography see *YS*, 164: 3845–3852; see also the biography by Ho Peng Yoke included in de Rachewiltz, *In the Service Service of the Khan*, pp. 282–299.
27. Liu Yingli's *Da Yuan hunyi fangyu shenglan, juan shang*, pp. 21–88, provided the first sketch information on Dadu. Besides the *Xijin zhi*, the basic sources for a reconstruction of Dadu's city plan are two late Yuan and early Ming accounts: Tao Zongyi, (*Nancun*) *Chuogeng lu, juan* 21: "Gongque zhidu"; and Xiao Yan, *Gugong yilu* (*SKCMCS* ed.). For modern studies on Dadu based on literary sources and archaeological finds see Zhao Zhengzhi, "Yuan Dadu pingmian guihua fuyuan de yanjiu" (1966), rpt. in *Kejishi wenji*, 2nd ser.: *Jianzhushi zhuanji* (Shanghai: Shanghai kexuejishu chubanshe, 1979), pp. 14–27; and Wang Puzi, "Yuan Dadu pingmian guihua lueshu", *Gugong bowuyan yuankan*, 1970.2 (May), pp. 61–82. See also Hou Renzhi, "Yuan Dadu cheng yu Ming-Qing Beijing cheng", rpt. in idem, *Lishi dilixue de lilun yu shijian*, pp. 175–182; Chen, *Yuan Dadu*, passim; and Wang, *BJTS*, Vol. 5, passim. On the sketch maps of Dadu see Hou, *Beijing lishditu ji*, Vol. I, pp. 27–28. For Western studies on this subject see Nancy S. Steinhardt, "Imperial Architecture under Mongolian Patronage: Khubilai's City of Daidu", PhD dissertation, Harvard University, 1981; and Steinhardt, "The Plan of Khubilai Khan's Imperial City", *Artibus Asiae*, 44.2–3 (1983), pp. 137–158.

28. *Xijin zhi*, p. 8. Cf. *Da Yuan hunyi fangyu shenglan, juan shang*, p. 22.
29. *Xijin zhi*, pp. 32–33. All the office buildings and religious monuments mentioned in this text are found in the map of Dadu in Hou, *Beijing lishiditu ji*, Vol. I, pp. 27, 28 (Illustrations, no. 1). For information on the Purple Palace Enclosure and the stars in the Privy Council Enclosure see the references cited in Introduction, note 17. As one of the seven stars in the Big Dipper constellation, the *Wuque* star was originally known as *Kaiyang* in *Shiji*, 27: 1291 (*Suoyin* 索隱); the name *Wuque* was used in Tang Tantric Buddhist texts; see (*Foshuo*) *Beidou qixing yanming jing* (*TSD*, No. 1307), 425b, 426a. For information on the Eastern Palace in the celestial divisions, and on the *Gui*, which is the twenty-third lunar lodge, see briefly, Needham, *Science and Civilization*, Vol. 3, pp. 234–237; and also Sun and Kistemaker, *The Chinese Sky*, pp. 119–122. It is not certain, however, whether the term *Guihu* is an alternate name for the *Gui* lunar lodge inside the Eastern Palace. This term cannot be found in the extant astrological records.
30. *Xijin zhi*, pp. 8–9; *Da Yuan hunyi fangyu shenglan, juan shang*, pp. 26–27. See also *YS*, 6: 114; 7: 140; 9: 185. On the sites of the Secretariat, the Bureau of Military Affairs, and the Censorate, see Xu Pingfang, "Yuan Dadu Shumiyuan zhi kao", and "Yuan Dadu Yushitai zhi kao", rpt. in *Zhongguo lishikaoguxue luncong* (Taibei: Yunchen wenhuashiye gufen youxiangongsi, 1995), pp. 192–197, 198–204; see also the same author's "Yuan Dadu Zhongshusheng zhi kao", *JCS*, N.S. 6 (1996), pp. 385–391. On the Heavenly Master Shrine, later known as the Revered Truthful Myriad Longevity Shrine, see Miao Quansun et al., eds., *Shuntian fuzhi* (Beijing daxue chubanshe, 1983), pp. 74–75. Shortly afterward the Shrine was put under the charge of the Daoist patriarch's successor Zhang Liusun 張留孫 (1248–1321), who subsequently founded the Xuanjiao 玄教 (sect) of Yuan Daoism. See Sun Kekuan, *Yuandai Daojiao zhi fazhan* (Taizhong: Donghai daxue, 1969), pp. 157–163. A corresponding shrine was built in Shangdu, see Ye, *Yuan Shangdu yanjiu*, pp. 187–188.
31. This aspect of the correlation between Dadu's official buildings and religious monuments and the celestial constellations was also mentioned in Zhu Weisun's "Dadu fu". The lost text was reconstructed from the *Yongle dadian* and is preserved in *QDRXJWK*, 6: 88–91. For details see Yu, "*Zhouyi* xiangshu yu Yuan Dadu guihua buju", pp. 175–181.
32. *Xijin zhi*, p. 213.
33. See Jiang Xunyuan, "Lun Beijing Yuan Ming Qing sanchao gongdian de jicheng yu fazhan", rpt. in *Zijin cheng jianzhu yanju yu baohu*, edited by Yu Zhuoyun (Zijincheng chubanshe, 1995), p. 88. On these walled gates in Yuan Dadu see Tao Zongyi, (*Nancun*) *Chuogeng lu*, 21: 250–251. The line from the commentary of the *li* hexagram is quoted from Wang Bi and Kong Yingta annotated, *Zhou Yi zhushu* (*SKQS* ed.), 3: 13a–15a. Translation follows

The I Ching or Book of Changes, The Richard Wilhelm Translation rendered into English by Cary F. Baynes (Princeton: Princeton University Press, 1967), pp. 119, 536.

34. See Xu, "Yuan Dadu Zhongshusheng zhi kao", pp. 390–391.
35. *Xijin zhi*, p. 33.
36. See Wang Zhilin, *Zijin cheng fengshui* (Zijincheng chubanshe, 2005), pp. 179–180, citing the view of Guan Lu, *Guanshi dili zhimeng*, a second-century treatise on geomancy quoted from the Qing imperial encyclopedia compiled by Chen Menglai, *Gujintushu jicheng, Bowu bian, Yishu dian, juan* 655: *Kanyu bu, huikao* 彙考, 5: 11b–12a.
37. On this doomed late Yuan hydraulic project at Dadu see *YS*, 66: 1659–1660. For a detailed analysis see Cai, *Beijing guyunhe*, pp. 21–32.
38. On Emperor Huizong's *Genyue* see James M. Hargett, "Huizong's Magic Marchmount: The *Genyue* Pleasure Park of Kaifeng", *Monumenta Serica*, 38 (1988–1989), pp. 1–48. On the perimeter of Dadu's imperial- and palace-cities, see Li, *Mingdai Beijing ducheng yingjian congkao*, pp. 96–100.
39. *Xijin zhi*, p. 4, gives only twenty-nine *xiangtong* in Dadu, which seems too few. Its Sino-Mongolian equivalent was *qutung*, derived from *qudugh*, meaning "well", alluding to a place of residence. In the Ming the Chinese adaptation *hutong* 衚衕 appeared; the characters were later simplified into 胡同 and many of the historical alleyways known by this term still survive in present-day Beijing. For details see Zhang Qingchang, *Hutong ji qita* (rev. ed.) (Beijing: Beijing yuyan daxue chubanshe, 2004), pp. 1–6, 11–14, 30–36.
40. On the waterways of Dadu and its irrigation system see Hou, "Yuan Dadu cheng yu Ming-Qing Beijing cheng", pp. 175–182; see also Su, "Guo Shoujing yu Dadu shuili gongcheng", passim. On Dadu's wards and its markets see Wang, *BJTS*, Vol. 5, pp. 42–45, 199–206; and Shi Weimin, *Dushi zhong de youmumin—Yuandai chengshi shenghuo changjuan* (Changsha: Hunan chubanshe, 1996), pp. 48–58. On the development of *hutong* see also Weng Li, *Beijing de hutong* (Beijing Yanshan; rev. ed., 1992), pp. 43–57; and Zhang, *Hutong ji qita*, pp. 1–6, 77–78. For additional information on the problems of water supply in Dadu see Cai, *Beijing guyunhe*, chap. 3; and Tuan, *Yanshui gujintan*, pp. 145–151. On Dadu's sketch maps, see Hou, *Beijing lishi dituji*, Vol. I, pp. 27–28. On the estimated Dadu population in Yuan times see Han, *Beijing lishirenkuo dili*, pp. 81–84.
41. For a study of the impact of the *Yijing* on Dadu's city plan see Yu, "*Zhouyi* xiangshu yu Yuan Dadu guihe buju", passim; and briefly Hou, *Beijing chengshi lishidili*, pp. 101–103.
42. The names of these eleven walled-gates are recorded in *Da Yuan hunyi fangyu shenglan, juan sheng*, p. 26, *Xijin zhi*, p. 2. On Huang Wenzhong's remark in his "Dadu fu" see Zhou Nanrui, ed., *Tianxia tongwen ji* (*SKQS* ed.),

16: 3a. Shao Yong's remark is found in the "Guanwu waibian" 觀物外編 of his *Huangji jingshi shu* (*SKQS* ed.), 13: 19b.

43. On the original and extended meaning of the *kan* trigram see *Zhou Yi zhushu*, 3: 12a–13b. Cf. Baynes and Wilhelm, *The I Ching or Book of Changes*, pp. 114–118, 530–535.

44. On Marco Polo's impression of Dadu in his *Description of the World* see Zhang Ning, "*Makeboluo xingji* zhong de Yuan Dadu", in *Makeboluo jieshao yu yanjiu*, edited by Yu Shixiong (Beijing: Shangwu yinshuguan, 1983), pp. 85–106. For a recent study on Dadu's urban culture and city life see Shi, *Dushi zhong de youmumin*, passim. On the socioeconomic structure of Dadu and commercial activities see Hou, *Beijing chengshi lishidili*, chaps. 7(1), 8(4).

45. See Ye Ziqi, *Caomu zi*, 3 *shang*, 41; 3 *xia*, 63; 4 *xia*, 83. See also Jiang Yikui, *Chang'an kehua*, 1: 2.

46. See Zhang Yu, *Zhang Guangbi shiji* (*SBCK xubian* ed.), 3: 15b. This reference was first cited by Otagi Matsuo, "Gen no Daitō", *Rikishi kyōiku*, 14.12 (December 1966), pp. 61–62; and then elaborated by Chen, *Yuan Dadu*, pp. 50–51. Cf. Chen, "Yuan Dadu cheng jianzhao chuanshuo tanyuan", pp. 96–97.

47. See Changgu Zhenyi, *Nongtian yuhua*, in *Baoyantang miji* (1922 ed.), *guang ji*, edited by Chen Jiru, p. 3b.

48. See Kong Qi, *Zhizheng zhiji* (Shanghai guji, 1987), 1: 1–2.

49. On Han Shantong, Han Liner, and the Great Song state see briefly, *YS*, 42: 891, 66: 1645; *MS*, 122: 3681–3684; and John W. Dardess, "Han Lin-erh", in *DMB*, Vol. I, pp. 485–488.

50. For general references on King Vaiśravana see Mochizuki Shinkō, *Mochizuki Būkkyō daijiten* (Tokyo: Sekai seiten kankō kyōkai, 1954–1958), Vol. 5, pp. 4304–4307; and E. T. C. Werner, *A Dictionary of Chinese Mythology* (1932; New York: The Julian Press, 1961), pp. 452–454 (under "Sida tianwang" 四大天王). On his name in Sanskrit see William Soothill, *A Dictionary of Chinese Buddhism Terms* (Delhi: Motilal Banarsidass, 1937), pp. 173, 306. The *Foshuo Chang Ahan jing* is in *TSD*, No. 1; references to the "Four Heavenly Kings" are found in *juan* 20: *Shiji jing* 世紀經. There are several modern studies on Vaiśravana, and some on him together with his son Nezha. See, among others, Matsumoto Bunzaburō, "Tōbatsu bishamon kō", *Tōhō gakuhō* (Kyoto), 10.1 (1939), pp. 12–21; Liu Ts'un-yan, *Buddhist and Taoist Influences on Chinese Novels*, Vol. I: *The Authorship of the Feng Shen Yen I* (Wiesbaden: Otto Harrassowitz, 1962), chap. XI; and Miyazaki Ichisada, "Bishamonten shinko no tōzen ni tsuite", rpt. in *Miyazaki Ichisada zenshū* (Tokyo: Iwanami shoten, 1992), Vol. 19, pp. 51–81. Miyazaki's work examines the Central Asian origin of Vaiśravana's name and the development of the "Heavenly King" temples or halls (Tianwangmiao or Tianwangtang) in China bearing his name since the Song dynasty, and the popularity of his cult of worship in

medieval Japan. For references on King Vaiśravana in Mongolia, Tibet, and Central Asia, see Chapter 3, note 33.

51. See *TSD*, No. 1248, p. 225c. For a detailed study of Bukong's biography and his translations of Sanskrit sutras see Chou I-liang, "Tantrism in China", *Harvard Journal of Asiatic Studies*, 8.3–4 (March 1945), pp. 284–307. See also Liu, *Buddhist and Taoist Influences on Chinese Novels*, chap. XI.

52. For general references on Nazha/Nezha see *Mochizuki Būkkyō daijiten*, Vol. 4, pp. 3994–3995; and Werner, *A Dictionary of Chinese Mythology*, pp. 247–249 (under "Li No-cha" 李哪吒). On his name in Sanskrit see Soothill, *A Dictionary of Chinese Buddhism Terms*, pp. 247–248. Naluojiupo is mentioned in Tanmuchen, trans., *Fosuoxingzan jing*, in *TSD*, No. 192, 1: 3c; and Nazha first appears in Bukong, trans., *Beifang Pishamen tianwang suijunhufa yigui*, in *TSD*, No. 1247, pp. 224c–225a. For modern studies on Nezha, besides the work of Liu Ts'un-yan (Liu Cunren) cited above, see Ho Kin-chung, "Nezha: Figur de l'enfant rebelle", *Études Chinoises*, 7.2 (Autumn 1988), pp. 7–26; Wan Shuyuan, "Nezha naohai gushi kaolun", *Dongfang wenhua*, 1 (Nanjing: Dongnan daxue chubanshe, 1991), pp. 76–86; and Nikaido Yoshihirō, "Nata taishi kō", in *Dōkyō no rekishi to bunka*, edited by Yamada Toshiaki and Tanaka Fumio (Tokyo: Yuzankaku shuppan kabushiki kaisha, 1998), pp. 167–196. The latest and most detailed study is Xiao Dengfu, "Nezha shuoyuan", included in *Diyijie Nezha xueshu yantaohui lunwenji*, edited by Guoli Zhongshan daxue Qingdai xueshuyanjiu zhongxin (Gaoxiong, Taiwan, 2003), pp. 1–63. His comments on Nezha's name and on his siblings appear in pp. 18–19 and pp. 30–37. This symposium volume is the most comprehensive study of Nezha in history, fiction, folklore, and in popular worship, particularly in contemporary Taiwan. A sample of literary sources on Nezha is collected in *Zhongguo minjian zhushen*, edited by Lu Zongli and Luan Baoqun (Taibei: Taiwan Xuesheng shuju, 1991), Vol. II, pp. 1022–1031.

53. See *TSD*, No. 1247, pp. 224c–225a.

54. See *TSD*, No. 1247, p. 225a. On the evolution of Nazha/Nezha's portrait in Buddhist and Daoist literature see Chen Qingxiang, "Nezha tuxiang yuanliu kao", in *Diyijie Nezha xueshu yantaohui lunwenji*, pp. 91–116.

55. See *TSD*, No. 1249, p. 228c. This episode is also mentioned in the biography of Bukong composed by the monk Huilang 慧朗 entitled "Tang Jingzhao Daxingshansi Bukong zhuan" 唐京兆大興善寺不空傳 included in Zanning, *Song Gaozeng zhuan*, in *TSD*, No. 2061, 1: 714a. Both Matsumoto Bunzaburō and Chou I-liang concur that the story in the legend is entirely groundless. See Matsumoto, "Tōbatsu bishamon kō", passim; and Chou, "Tantrism in China", p. 305, n103.

56. See *TSD*, No. 1288, *shang*, 358b–358c.

57. See Xiao, "Nezha shuoyuan", pp. 18–19, n10.

58. See *TSD*, No. 2061, 1: 714a.

59. See *TSD*, No. 2126, *juan xia*, 254a–254b.
60. See Li Tao, *Xu Zizhitongjian changbian* (Zhonghua, 1979–?), 356: 8518; Qian Shuoyou, *Xianchun Lin'an zhi* (*SKQS* ed.), 73: 13a–14b; Mei Yingfa et al., eds., *Kaiqing Siming xuzhi* (*XXSKQS* ed.), 7a–7b; and Chen Menglei, *Gujintushu jicheng, Bowu bian, Shenyi dian, juan* 50: "Shenmiaobu 神廟部: huikao," 2: 13b. For other sources see Miyazaki, "Bishamoten shinko no tōzen ni tsuite", pp. 52–56.
61. The inscription on the epitaph of the Temple of Vaiśravana in Ninghua, Fujian, was composed by Huang Tao 黃滔 c. 920. It is preserved in the Ming gazetteer *Ninghuaxian zhi* 寧化縣志 and quoted in Chen Menglei, *Gujintushu jicheng, Bowu bian, Shenyi dian, juan* 54: "Shenmiaobu: zalu" 雜錄, 3a. For the other reference see *Da Tang San Zang qujing shihua* (Beijing: Wenxue gudian kanxingshe, 1954), 2b. On this new development of Vaiśravana's legend see Liu, *Buddhist and Taoist Influences on Chinese Novels*, pp. 219–220.
62. Daoyuan, *Jingde chuandeng lu*, in *TSD*, No. 2076, 25: 319c; 408a; Yuanwu Keqin, *Biyan lu* (also titled *Foguoyuanwu chanshi Biyuan lu*), in *TSD*, No. 2003, 9: 212a. On this new development of Nezha's legend see Nikaido, "Nata taishi kō," pp. 168–171; and Xiao, "Nezha shuo-yuan", pp. 37–39.
63. Puji, *Wudeng huiyuan* (Zhonghua, 1984), 2: 116.
64. See Hong Mai, *Yijian zhi* (Zhonghua, 1981), *Yijian sanzhi* 夷堅三志, *xin* 辛, pp. 1429–1439; *Daofu huiyuan*, 230: 1, in Baiyunguan Changchun zhenren, ed., *Zhengtong Daozang* (Taibei: Xinwenfeng chubangongsi, 1988), Vol. 51, p. 290. For other sources see Nikaido, "Nata taishi kō", pp. 171–175; and Xiao, "Nezha shuoyuan", pp. 39–40.
65. For details of Li Jing and Nazha's mythologization see Liu, *Buddhist Influences on Chinese Novels*, chap. II; and Liu Cunren, "Pishamen tianwang fuzi yu Zhongguo xiaoshuo zhi guanxi", rpt. in idem, *Hefengtang wenji* (Shanghai guji, 1991), Vol. II, pp. 1045–1052.
66. For a bibliographical note of these plays and chantables see Fu Xihua, ed., *Yuandai zaju quanmu* (Beijing: Zuojia chubanshe, 1957), pp. 78, 283; idem, *Mingdai zaju quanmu* (same publisher, 1958), pp. 253, 262; and Chen Naiqian, *Yuanren Xiaoling ji* (Zhonghua, 1962), p. 32. Qian Nanyang, *Song Yuan xiwen jiyi* (Shanghai gudian wenxue, 1956), p. 21. For background information see Wan, "Nezha naohai gushi kaolun", pp. 78–79; and Nikaido, "Nata taishi kō", pp. 173–175. On the portrayal of Nazha/Nezha in traditional drama see Huang Jingqin, "Nezha xiju xiangxiang tanshuo", in *Diyijie Nezha xueshu yantaohui lunwenji*, pp. 91–116.
67. This Ming edition of the *Huitu Sanjiao yuanliu Soushen daquan* was reproduced by the Lianjing chubanshiye gongsi in Taibei in 1980. On the Yuan origin of the Ming edition see the preface and postscript by Ye Dehui 葉德輝 (1864–1927), who was responsible for the printing of this work. For a modern scholar's appraisal see Ri Kenshō, *Maso shinkō no kenkyū* (Tokyo:

Taisan bunbutsusha, 1979), pp. 61–62; see also Li Weiguo, "Yuan Ming yiben *Soushen ji* sanzong yuanyuan yitonglun", in *Zhonghua wenshi luncong*, edited by Qian Bocheng (Shanghai guji, 1991), Vol. 48, pp. 243–257. A Yuan edition of the *Xinbian lianxiang Soushen guangji* has been reproduced in the *Huitu Sanjiao yuanliu Soushen daquan*, which includes the aforementioned Taibei Ming edition, by Shanghai guji chubanshe, 1990, but this Yuan edition does not include Nazha's biography. For an analysis of this story and its significance to the development of the Nezha saga see Wan, "Nezha naohai gushi kaolun", pp. 79–86; and Xiao Dengfu, "Nezha shuoyuan", pp. 40–44.

68. See *Huitu Sanjiao yuanliu Soushen daquan*, 7: 14a.
69. For a general reference on the Dragon/Dragon King in ancient Chinese mythology and their transformation in later times after combination with Indian mythology and Tantric Buddhism see Werner, *A Dictionary of Chinese Mythology*, pp. 185–197. See also, more recently, Liu Zixiong and Liu Jingrong, *Long yu Zhongguo wenhua* (Beijing: Renmin chubanshe, 1992), pp. 227–269; Michael Loewe, "The Cult of the Dragon and the Invocation for Rain", in Loewe, *Divination, Mythology and Monarchy in Han China*, pp. 142–159; and Annping Jing, *The Water God's Temple of the Guangsheng Monastery, Cosmic Function of Art, Ritual, and Theater* (Leiden: Brill, 2002), pp. 70–73, 164–168. For an analysis of the Buddhist worship of the *naga/nagas* as rain god see Lowell W. Bloss, "The Buddha and the Naga: A Study in Buddhist Folk Religion", *History of Religion*, 13 (1971), pp. 36–53; and Andrew Rawlinson, "Nagas and the Magic Cosmology of Buddhism", *Religion*, 16 (1986), pp. 135–153, among others.
70. A sample of these stories can be found, for example, in Jijiaye and Tan Yao, trans., *Zabaozang jing*, in *TSD*, No. 192, 7 (91): 483: "Luohan zhiye duo qu elong ruhai yuan" 羅漢祇夜多驅惡龍入海緣; and in Zhiqian, *Longwang xiongdi jing*; Zhu Haihu, *Foshuo Hailongwang jing*; and Yijing, *Fo wei Hailongwang shuofa yin jing*, in *TSD*, Nos. 597, 598, 599. See Wan, "Nezha naohai gushi kaolun", p. 86, n10.
71. The *Fengshen yanyi*, 100 *hui* (chapter), was first printed in the late Ming. A punctuated modern edition was published by the Zuojia chubanshe in Beijing in 1955. Liu Ts'un-yan identified Lu Xixing as its author in his study, *Buddhist and Taoist Influences on Chinese Novels*, cited in note 50 above. Liu has written Lu's biography: "Lu Hsi-hsing: A Confucian Scholar, Taoist Priest and Buddhist Devotee of the Sixteenth Century", rpt. in Liu Ts'un-yan, *Selected Papers from the Hall of the Harmonious Wind* (Leiden: Brill, 1976), pp. 175–202. Nazha's stories in the *Fengshen yanyi* are featured in chaps. 12–14. Wei Chuxian was the first to identify that the *Sanjiao yuanliu Soushen daquan* was the primary source for the stories of Nezha's confrontation with the Dragon King and his sons in the Eastern Sea. See *Fengshenbang gushi*

tanyuan (Hong Kong, privately published, 1960), Vol. II, p. 144. The *Xiyou ji*, 100 *hui*, was first printed in 1592. A punctuated modern edition was published by the Zuojia chubanshe in Beijing in 1954. Nazha's stories in *Xiyou ji* are featured in chaps. 4, 5, 51, 52, 61, 83; cf. Anthony C. Yu, *The Journey to the West* (Chicago: The University of Chicago Press, 1983), Vol. 4, Index, p. 463. On its author Wu Cheng'en's life see Liu Ts'un-yan, "Wu Ch'eng-en: His Life and Career", included in Liu's *Selected Papers*, pp. 259–355. For a comparative study of Nazha's stories in these two novels see Liu, "Pishamen tianwang fuzi yu Zhongguo xiaoshuo zhi guanxi", pp. 1081–1091. On the sources of the *Xiyou ji*, see Glen Dubridge, *The Hsi-yu-chi: A Study of Antecedents to the Sixteenth-century Chinese Novel* (Cambridge: Cambridge University Press, 1970); and Nakano Miyoko, *Xiyou ji de mimi*, translated by Wang Xiumin et al. (Zhonghua, 2002).

72. See Yin Junke, Yu Deyuan, and Wu Wentao, *Beijing lishi ziranzaihai yanjiu* (Beijing: Zhongguo huanjingkexue chubanshe, 1997), chap. 3, especially pp. 38–43 for statistical tabulation. On the Mongol-Yuan rulers' praying for rain to relieve drought see *YS*, 9: 189; 11: 226; 21: 463, 469; 23: 511; 24: 555, 558; 27: 602; 30: 668; 33: 732; 43: 913; 50: 1070–1071. See also note 76 below.

73. *Xijin zhi*, p. 214. For additional information on this popular ritual which prevails into modern times see Chen, "Jiu Beijing de qiyu yu silong: Guanshi jili yu minjian xisu", *JCS*, N.S. 12 (2003), pp. 217–219.

74. *Xijin zhi*, p. 2. On the construction of the Dam or Embankment Canal and its vicissitudes see *YS*, 64: 1590; 183: 4211; see also Cai, *Beijing guyunhe*, pp. 36–48. On the grain transport systems under the Yuan dynasty see *YS*, 93: 2363–2366. See also H. Franz Schurmann, *Economic Structure of the Yuan Dynasty* (Cambridge, MA: Harvard University Press, 1967), chap. I; and Yang Yumei, *Yuandai haicao liangyun changxing yingsu zhi tantao* (Taibei: Liren shuju, 1986), chap. 5.

75. The location of the Longwangtang is mentioned in *YS*, 64: 1592. The Jishui Pool in Ming times is mentioned in Jiang Yikui, *Chang'an kehua*, 1: 12–17. For descriptions of the cock-and-lion stone statues in the rear of the Huitong (Huiquan)ci inside the Jishui Pool see Zhang Cixi, *Yanjing fangguzhi*, quoted in Chen Zongfan, *Yandu congkao* (Beijing guji, 1991), pp. 413–416; and Ma Zixiang, *Lao Beijing lüxing zhinan* (Beijing Yanshan, 1997), pp. 140–141. (Note Zhang's work published in the *Jing Jin fengtu congshu* [Beijing, Shuangzhao lou, 1938] does not include this reference.) On the historical development of Jishui Pool see also Wang Weijie, Ren Jiasheng et al., *Beijing huanjing shihua* (Beijing: Dizhi chubanshe, 1989), pp. 70–73; and Hou Renzhi et al., eds., *Shichahai zhi* (Beijing chubanshe, 2003), pp. 19–23.

76. On the Black Dragon Pool sacrificial prayer see Ouyang Xuan, *Guizhai wenji* (*SBCK* ed.), 10: 9a–10b; cf. *QDRXJWK*, 94: 1580; 131: 2104–2105. The Yuan "dragon deity" seals mentioned here were discovered under the Zhengyang

Gate (i.e. Front Gate) in Qing times. See Wu Changyuan, *Chengyuan shilue* (Beijing guji, 1981), 16: 341; Dai Lu, *Tengyin zaji* (Beijing guji, 1981), 5: 47.

77. *Xijin zhi*, p. 214; and Zheng Sixiao, *Xinshi* (Shanghai: Zhina neixueyuan, 1933), *xia*, 74a. Zheng's dates are based on the research of Yao Congwu who had written three essays evaluating Zheng's life and works; see in particular, "Zheng Sixiao yu 'Tiehan Xinshi' guanxi de tuice", in *Yao Congwu xiansheng quanji* (Taibei Zhengzhong, 1982), Vol. 7, pp. 139–149. After the text of the *Xinshi* was discovered, Gu Yanwu (1613–1682) suggested that it may have been a doctored work by an anonymous Ming loyalist, and his opinion has swayed many later scholars since. Some modern scholars share Gu's opinion, but others have given a more positive view of the work. For a recent study confirming *Xinshi*'s historical value see Yang Ne, "*Xinshi* zhenwei bian", *Yuanshi luncong*, 5 (1993), pp. 235–242.
78. See Yang Weizhen, *Tieyai gu yuefu* (*SKQS* ed.), 5: 6b–7a. For Yang Weizhen's biography see *MS*, 285: 7308–7309; and also Edmund H. Worthy, Jr., "Yang Weizhen", in *DMB*, Vol. II, pp. 1547–1553.

Chapter 2

1. On the development of former Yuan Dadu during the early Hongwu period, see Hou and Jin, *Beijing shihua*, pp. 97–98; *Beijingshi*, pp. 207–208; Xie Mincong, *Beijing de chengyuan yu gongque zhi cai yanjiu* (Taiwan Xuesheng, 1980), pp. 25–26; and He Shude, *BJTS*, Vol. 6 (Ming), chap. 1, sec. 1. See also Wang Jianying, "Lun cong Yuan Dadu dao Ming Beijing de yanbian he fazhan", *Yanjing xuebao*, N.S. 1 (1995), pp. 61–64. On Xu Da's rebuilding of the northern outer walls of Dadu, see *MTZUSL*, 34: 611–612. For details, see Li, *Mingdai Beijing ducheng yingjian congkao*, pp. 10–19, 37–48.
2. See *MTZUSL*, 47: 435–436; 54: 1060; 127: 2024–2025; Sun Chengze, *Chunming mengyu lu* (1761; Hong Kong: Longmen shudian, 1965), 6: 8b–9a, 50a–50b. For details, see Wang Puzi, "Yan wangfu yu Zijin cheng", *Gugong bowuyuan yuankan*, 1 (February 1979), pp. 70–77; and Li, *Mingdai Beijing ducheng yingjian congkao*, pp. 182–185.
3. On Zhuge Liang's alleged comment see Chapter 1, note 22. For a succinct account of Nanjing's history of capital building see Gu Zuyu, *Dushi fangyu jiyao* (Zhonghua, 1955), 20: 898; and Zhu Jie, *Jinling guji tukao* (Shanghai: Shangwu yinshuguan, 1935), chap. 1. See also other modern studies on Nanjing cited in note 6 below.
4. See *MTZUSL*, 3: 29–30, 41–43, The *shilu* credits the remark to Tao Ao but not to Feng Guoyong. However, an anonymous biography of Tao, and the biography of Feng composed by Wang Shizhen (1526–1590) included in Jiao Hong, *Guochao xianzheng lu* (Taiwan Xuesheng, 1965), 6: 48a–49b and 6: 1a–7b give credit to both. See also Tao's biography in *MS*, 136: 3925–3927, and Feng's in 129: 3795–3796.

5. See Yao Tongshou, *Lejiao siyu* (Zhonghua, 2001), p. 60.
6. On the design and building of the new capital at Yingtianfu, later known as Nanking, see *MTZUSL*, 21: 295; 22: 317; 115: 1888; 220: 2227; 201: 3007; 243: 3534; *MS*, 1: 14, 2: 30, 32; 40: 910. See also briefly, Cheng Sigong and Wang Huayi, eds., (*Wanli*) *Yingtian fuzhi* (*SKCMCS* ed.), 3: 4a–4b; Lü Yanzhao and Yao Nai, eds., *Chongkan Jiangning fuzhi* (Taibei Chengwen, 1974), 5: 12b–13a; and Wang Huanbiao et al., eds., *Shoudu zhi* (Nanjing: Zhengzhong shuju, 1935), pp. 71–73. According to *MTZUSL*, 21: 295, Liu Ji was one of Zhu Yuanzhang's confidants entrusted with the siting of the capital city. A few later anecdotal miscellanies claimed that during the construction and after the completion of the imperial city, Liu made an ominous prophecy of the move of the capital to the north, i.e. Peking by alluding to the usurpation of the Prince of Yan. See Liang Yi, *Chuanxin lu*, in *Guochao molie jiyi*, edited by Zhu Dangmian (1553), 1: 15b; Zhang Han, *Songchuang mengyu* (Zhonghua, 1985), 5: 92; and also anonymous, *Jianzhu congbian* 剪燭叢編, quoted in Wang Xinyi, *Liu Bowen nianpu* (Shanghai Shangwu, 1936), p. 70 (cf. note 77 below). There are several important studies on Nanking. See, among others, Zhu Xie, *Jinling guji tukao* (Shanghai Shangwu, 1935); F. W. Mote, "The Transformation of Nanking, 1350–1400", in Skinner, *The City in Late Imperial China*, pp. 101–153; *Jiangxu chengshi lishi dili*, edited by Department of Geography, Nanjing Normal College (Nanjing: Jiangsu kexue jishu chubanshe, 1982), chap. I; and *Jinling shichao tiwangzhou—Nanjing juan*, edited by Gao Shusen and Zhao Jianguang (Beijing: Zhongguo Renmin daxue chubanshe, 1991). An expanded history of Nanking under the Ming comparable to that of Peking is still wanting. On the construction of Zhongdu at Fengyang see Wang Jianying, *Ming Zhongdu* (Zhonghua, 1992), and also Chapter 4, note 51.
7. A one-volume gazetteer of the walled city of Nanking compiled by the Ministry of Rites with a preface by Du Ze 杜澤 dated 1395 is extant. See *Hongwu jingcheng tu zhi* (Nanjing: Zhongshe, 1929). For details of the structure of the walled city see Ji Shijia, "Mingdu Nanjing chengyuan luelun", *Gugong bowuyuan yuankan*, 1984.2 (May), pp. 70–81; Zhang Quan, "Mingchu Nanjing cheng de guihua yu jianshe", in *Zhongguo gutu yanjiu*, edited by Zhongguo gutu xuehui (Hangzhou: Zhejiang Renmin chubanshe, 1986), pp. 171–202; and Xu Hong, "Mingchu Nanjing huangcheng gong cheng de guihua, pingmianbuju jiqi xiangzheng yiyi", *Guoli Taiwan daxue jianzhu yu chengxiang xuebao*, 7 (December 1993), pp. 79–96. The perimeter of the walled imperial-city is given as 59 *li* in *MTZUSL*, 82: 1481, but as 96 *li* in Li Xian, ed., *Da Ming yitongzhi* (1461), 6: 1a. The perimeter of the unwalled outer-city is given as 180 *li* in *Da Ming yitongzhi*, but is revised as 120 *li* by modern scholars. See Xu Hong, "Mingchu Nanjing de dushi guihua yu renkou bianqian", *Shihuo yuekan*, 10.3 (March 1980), p. 112, notes 109, 114.

8. For official accounts of the usurpation by the Prince of Yan of the Jianwen emperor, and his enthronement as the Yongle emperor, see *MTZOSL, juan* 1–9: "Fengtian jingnan shiji" 奉天靖難事蹟; and briefly *MS, juan* 4, 5. Wang Chongwu had published definitive studies on the *jingnan* episode and its historiographical issues. See *Ming jingnan shishi kanzheng gao* (Lizhuang, Sichuan: Guoli Zhongyang yanjiuyuan lishiyuyan yanjiusuo, 1945); and idem, *Fengtian jingnan ji zhu* (Shanghai Shangwu, 1948). For a general account see David B. Chan, *The Usurpation of the Prince of Yen, 1398–1402* (San Francisco: Chinese Materials Center, 1975, passim); and briefly Hok-lam Chan, "The Chien-wen, Yung-lo, Hung-hsi and Hsüan-te Reign, 1399–1435", in *The Cambridge History of China*, Vol. 7, *The Ming Dynasty*, Part I, edited by F. W. Mote and Denis Twitchett (Cambridge: Cambridge University Press, 1988), pp. 184–202, 214–218. On the issues of the legitimation of the Yongle emperor see Chapter 3, note 7.
9. On the rationale for transferring the imperial capital to Beipingfu see also Wu Han, "Mingdai jingnan zhiyi yu guodu beiqian", *Qinghua xuebao*, 10.3 (October 1935), pp. 917–939; Edward L. Farmer, *Early Ming Government, The Evolution of Dual Capitals* (Cambridge, MA: Harvard University Press, 1976), chaps. 4–5; Yan Chongnian, "Ming Yongledi qiantu Beijing shuiyi", rpt. in idem, *Yanbu ji* (Beijing Yanshan, 1989), pp. 342–364; and Wan Yi, "Lun Zhu Di yingjian Beijing gongdian, qiantu de zhuyao dongji ji hougu", rpt. in *Zijin cheng yingshanji*, edited by Gugong bowuyuan (Zijincheng chubanshe, 1992), pp. 52–61.
10. These essays have been collected in *QDRXJWK*, 6: 91–96. For other similar essays see ibid, 6: 96–101. These three essays are also found in the literary works of the respective authors: Yang Rong, *Wenmin ji* (*SKQS* ed.), 8: 1a–9b; Jin Shan (Youzi), *Jin Wenjing gong ji* (*SKQS* ed.), 6: 1a–6b; and Li Shimian, *Gulian wenji* (*SKQS* ed.), 1: 1a–7b. For Yang Rong's biographies, see *MS*, 148: 413841; Charles O. Hucker, "Yang Jung", in *DMB*, Vol. II, pp. 1519–1522; for Jin Youzi see *MS*, 147: 4126; for Li Shimian see *MS*, 163: 442123; Hucker, "Li Shi-mien", in *DMB*, Vol. I, pp. 865–868.
11. See *MTZOSL*, 92: 1202. According to Jiang Yikui, *Chang'an kehua*, 4: 82, the geomancer identifying the site was Wang Xian 王賢, a native of Ningyang 寧陽, Shandong. *QDRXJWK*, 137: 2196 also mentions an anonymous staff member of the Yan fief as a possible candidate, but the *shilu* provides the authoritative source. See also Hu Hansheng, *Ming shisan ling* (Beijing: Zhongguo qingnian chubanshe, 1998), pp. 25–26, especially note 1. According to Wang Zilin, *Zijin cheng fengshui*, chap. 11, which gives a thorough geomantic treatment of the mausoleums, Mount Tianshou's name was derived from the precepts of an auspicious site of burial in Guo Pu, *Zangshu* (*SKQS* ed.). For details of the thirteen Ming imperial mausoleums, see note 31 below.

12. *MTZOSL*, 231: 2235–2236. This rescript was dated the *wuchen* 戊辰 (fourth) day of the eleventh month of the eighteenth year of Yongle (December 8 1420). The emperor attended the new court to receive audience on the *jiazi* 甲子 (first) day of the first month of the following year (February 2 1421). See *MTZOSL*, 233: 2247.
13. See Wang, *Zijin cheng fengshui*, passim. The *Renzixuzhi zikao dili xinxue tongzong* was reprinted in 1583, reproduced in the *Gogong zhenben congkan*, Vol. 411, by the Hainan chubanshe in Haikou, Hainan, in 2000. Wang made substantial citations of this work but he seriously erred in identifying Xu Shanshu with his namesake, an early Ming Confucian scholar whose biography is contained in *MS*, 152: 4190, hence erroneously placing Xu and the book's authorship in the Yongle period. The Xus were natives of Dexing 德興, Jiangxi, and they claimed to have spent thirty years laboring on this work. See their prefaces to the reprinted edition.
14. See *Zijin cheng fengshui*, chaps. 1, 2, 3, 5. The reference to the explanation of the *qian* hexagram is from *Zhouyi* (*SBCK* ed.), *shang jing* 上經, *qian zhuan* 乾傳, 1: 2b. The original phrase, an explanation of the second *nine* line of the hexagram "jian long zai tian" 見龍在田 ("The dragon is appearing in the field") by Confucius, reads "long de er zheng zhong zhe ye" 龍德而正中者也 ("There he is, with the dragon's powers, and occupying exactly the central place"). See the translation by James Legge, *I Ching, Book of Changes*, edited with introduction by Ch'u Chai with Winberg Chai (New Hyde Park, NY: University Books, 1964), pp. 57, 410.
15. See *Zijin cheng fengshui*, chaps. 4, 6, 7, 10. On Yongle's deification of Zhenwu and its legends, see Chapter 3, note 31. According to my own study, the face of the Dark God in the bronze stature was cast in the likeliness of the Yongle emperor with his typical black walrus moustache to buttress the divinity of the august ruler. See Chen Xuelin, "'Zhenwu shen', 'Yongle xiang' chuanshuo suyuan", rpt. in Chen, *Mingdai renwu yu chuanshuo* (Hong Kong: The Chinese University Press, 1997), chap. 5. It became a source of inspiration for the Mongolian legend about the Dark God's role in designing the plan for the building of Peking.
16. For details see *MTZOSL*, 16: 294; 17: 301; 22: 415; 46. 714; 57: 835; 182: 1964–1965; 218: 2169; 232: 2244; *MS*, 7: 96, 99, 100; 40: 884. See also Hou and Jin, *Beijing shihua*, pp. 97–99; *Beijing shi*, pp. 207–210; Xie, *Beijing de chengyuan*, pp. 25–33; He, *BJTS*, Vol. 6, chap. 3. For additional information see Li, *Mingdai Beijing ducheng yingjian congkao*, pp. 10–63, 242–296; on Chen Gui's role in the capital construction see ibid., pp. 250–256. On Ruan An's architectural contribution see Chen Zhaodi, "Mingdai jiechudi jianzhu guimojia Ruan An", *Xuelin manlu*, 7 (March 1983), pp. 243–248; and Zhang Xiumin, *Zhongyue guanxishi lunwenji* (Taibei: Wenshizhe chubanshe, 1992), pp. 47–54, 115–129.

17. See *MTZOSL*, 229: 2227; 236: 2263; *Ming Renzong shilu*, edited by Zhang Fu et al. (Taibei, 1963), 8 x*ia*: 272; *Ming Yingzong shilu*, edited by Sun Jizong et al. (Taibei, 1963), 65: 1240; 85: 1696; *MS*, 7: 99; 8: 108; 10: 132. See also Xie, *Beijing de chengyuan*, p. 84; Farmer, *Early Ming Government*, p. 123. On Peking's *xingzai* designation and related issues see Xu Hong, "Ming Beijing xingbu zhi", *Hanxue yanjiu*, 2.2 (December 1973), pp. 569–598.
18. There are a number of gazetteers on the planning and layout of Ming Peking from which modern studies are drawn. See, for example, Sun Chengze, *Chunming mengyu lu*; idem, *Tianfu guangji* (Hong Kong: Longmen, 1968); *QDRXJWK*; and Zhang and Miao, *Shuntian fuzhi* (1885). For a bibliographical note see Wang, *Beijing shidi fengwu shulu*, passim. For a descriptive account of old Peking with detailed annotations, see Chen Zongfan, *Yandu congkao*. On the correspondence of Ming Peking's central north to south axis with Yuan Dadu, see Li, *Mingdai Beijing ducheng yingjian congkao*, pp. 297–332. On the sketch maps of Ming Beijing see Hou, *Beijing lishi ditu ji*, Vol. I, pp. 35–36. For more detailed city maps of Ming-Qing Peking with elaborate identifications based on literary and archaeological research see *Ming Qing Beijing cheng tu*, edited by Xu Pingfang (Beijing: Ditu chubanshe, 1986).
19. See Sun Chengze, *Chunming mengyulu*, 6: 10a–17a; *Tianfu guangji*, 5: 46–51; *QDRXJWK*, 33: 494–496; *Shuntian fuzhi*, 3: 18b–27a. For general studies on the Ming Forbidden City, see, Zhu Xie, *Beijing gongjue tushuo* (Shanghai Shangwu, 1938), chaps. 1–4; Hou, "Yuan Dadu cheng yu Ming Qing Beijing cheng", pp. 189–197; idem, "Zijin cheng zai guihua sheji shang de jicheng yu fazhan", rpt. in *Zijin cheng yingshanji*, pp. 7–15; Wang, "Lun cong Yuan Dadu dao Ming Beijing de yanbian he fazhan", pp. 61–64; and Li, *Mingdai Beijing ducheng yingjian congkao*, pp. 113–134, 242–296. See also briefly Hou and Jin, *Beijing shihua*, pp. 210–214; Xie, *Beijing de chenghuan*, chap. 4; He, *BJTS*, Vol. 6, chap. 3, sec. 1; and Hou, *Beijing chengshi lishi dili*, chap. 5, sec. 1. On the eunuch Ni Zhong's mission, see Wu Menglin and Liu Jingyi, "Ji yanjiu Mingdai Beijing yingjianshi de zhongyao zhishi", in *Beijing yu zhongwai gudu duibi yanjiu*, edited by Beijingshi shehuikexueyuan lishisuo (Beijing Yanshan, 1992), pp. 337–339.
20. On the origin of the correlation of the celestial Purple Palace Enclosure with the earthly imperial ruler's residence *jinzhong* or *jinnei* that coined the name *Zijin cheng* see *Jinshu*, 11: 290 (cf. Ho, *The Astronomical Chapters*, p. 71); and *Shiji*, 6: 271; *Hanshu*, 81: 3355; Fan Ye, *Hou Hanshu* (Zhonghua, 1965), 59: 1912; and Ouyang Xiu, *Xin Tangshu*, 120: 2020. For details of the Han reconstruction of the Chinese sky and the genesis of the celestial-terrestrial correspondence system see the references cited in the Introduction, notes 14–17. On the formal use of the name *Zijin cheng*, see Li, *Mingdai Beijing ducheng yingjian congkao*, pp. 104–112. The most authoritative study on the

architecture of the Forbidden City was written by Yu Zhuoyun, a senior engineer associated with the Palace Museum for several decades. See Yu, *Zijin cheng gongdian* (Hong Kong: Shangwu yinshuguan, 1982); and idem, *Zijin cheng gongdian—jianzhu he shenghuo de yishu* (same publisher, 2002). A comprehensive large-size pictorial book on the Forbidden City is Yan Chongnian's *Beijing*. Additional studies are available in *Zijin cheng jianzhu yanjiu yu baohu*, edited by Yu Zhuoyun; and *Zhongguo Zijin cheng xuehui lunwenji*, 1st ser., edited by Shan Shiyuan et al. (Zijincheng chubanshe, 1995, 1997).

21. See Yu, *Zijin cheng gongdian*, pp. 24–28; Xie, *Beijing de chengyuan*, pp. 231–232. On the influence of the *yinyang* and Five Agents/Phrases theories on the construction of the Forbidden City see Yu, *Zijin cheng gongdian—jianzhu he shenghuo de yishu*, pp. 29–33; Xie, op. cit., chap. 7; and Jiang Shunyuan, "Wuxing, sixiang, sanyuan, erji—Zijin cheng," rpt. in *Qingdai gongshi tanwei* (Zijincheng chubanshe, 1991), pp. 251–260. Additional studies are available in Yu, *Zijin cheng jianzhu yanjiu yu baohu*; Shan, *Zongguo Zijin cheng xuehui lunwenji*, lst ser.; and more thoroughly in Wang, *Zijin cheng fengshui*, passim. For a preliminary exposition of the subject in English see Meyer, *The Dragons of Tiananmen*, chaps. 2–4.
22. On these two clusters of markets and trade centers see briefly He, *BJTS*, Vol. 6, pp. 94–95; and Hou, *Beijing chengshi lishi dili*, pp. 229–230.
23. See briefly Yu, *Zijin cheng gongdian*, pp. 26–28; idem, *Zijin cheng gongdian—jianzhu he shenghuo de yishu*, pp. 29–33; Xie, *Beijing de chengyuan*, pp. 231–232; 237–238. For a study of Mount Wansui see Cheng Lianzhang, "Wansuishan de shezhi yu Zhijin cheng weizhi kao", rpt. in Yu, *Zijin cheng jianzhu yanjiu yu baohu*, pp. 240–248. On the Jinshui Canal see Hou Renzhi, "Beiping Jinshuihe kao", *Yanjing xuebao*, 30 (June 1946), pp. 107–133.
24. See briefly Yu, *Zijin cheng gongdian*, pp. 26–28; idem, *Zijin cheng gongdian—jianzhu he shenghuo de yishu*, pp. 29–33; Jiang, "Wuxing, sixiang, sanyuan, erji —Zijin cheng", pp. 254–255; and Meyer, *The Dragons of Tiananmen*, chap. 3. For additional references see Wang Qiheng, "Zijin cheng fengguang xingshi jianxi", rpt. in Yu, *Zijin cheng jianzhu yanjiu yu baohu*, pp. 94–104; and Lou Qingxi, "Zijin cheng jianzhu de secai xue", rpt. in Shan, *Zhongguo Zijin cheng xuehui lunwenji*, lst ser., pp. 279–283.
25. For color photographs and illustrations of the palaces, halls, altars, and temples of the Forbidden City as visual evidence of the impact of the Five Agents scheme on architectural design and ornamental decoration see Yu, *Zijin cheng gongdian*; idem, *Zijin cheng gongdian—jianzhu he shenghuo de yishu*; and Yan, *Beijing*, passim.
26. Passage quoted from Xie, *Beijing de chengyuan*, p. 232; translated in Roderick MacFarquahar, *The Forbidden City* (New York: Newsweek, 1972), p. 72.
27. For details see some of the references cited in note 19 above. See also briefly

Hou and Jin, *Beijing shihua*, pp 102–104; *Beijing shi*, pp. 214–216; He, *BJTS*, Vol. 6, chap. 3, sec. 2. On the varying accounts of the imperial-city in Ming and Qing official records, see Li, *Mingdai Beijing ducheng yingjian congkao*, pp. 64–134. For a brief historical account of the Tian'an Gate see Hou, *Lishi dilixue de lilun yu shijian*, pp. 227–252; for details see Lu Bingjie, *Tian'anmen* (Jinan: Shandong huabao chubanshe, 2004). On the sketch maps see Hou, *Beijing lishi ditu ji*, Vol. I, pp. 33–34.

28. On the construction of the walled gates of the inner-city in the Zhengtong reign and of the walled gates of the outer-city in the Jiajing period see *Ming Yingzong shilu*, 23: 471, 54: 1047; *Ming Shizong shilu*, edited by Zhang Rong et al. (Taibei, 1965), 396: 6960–6965; 397: 6982–6983; 403: 7060–7061; *MS*, 40: 884; Sun Chengze, *Chunming mengyu lu*, 3: 3a–4b; *Tianfu guangji*, 4: 39–40; *QDRXJWK*, 4: 66–67; *Shuntian fuzhi*, 1: 8a–10b. See also Hou and Jin, *Beijing shihua*, pp. 103–104; *Beijing shi*, pp. 208–210; Xie, *Beijing de chengyuan*, pp. 35–40; and Chen Zongfan, *Yandu congkao*, pp. 16–23. For the sketch maps see Hou, *Beijing lishi ditu ji*, Vol. I, pp. 31–32. For an authoritative study of the city walls and gates of old Peking see Osvald Sirén, *The Walls and Gates of Peking* . . . (London: John Lane Ltd., 1924); Chinese translation by Xu Yongquan, *Beijing de chengchang he chengmen* (Beijing Yanshan, 1985). There is a recent study of Peking's walls based on Siŕen's work with a collection of watercolor paintings by Zhang Xiande, *Ming Qing Beijing chengyuan he chengmen* (Shijiazhuang: Hebei jiaoyu chubanshe, 2003), especially pp. 1–170.
29. On the development of the *hutong* in the Ming see Chapter 1, note 39; Chapter 3, note 39.
30. For details see Sun Chengze, *Chunming mengyu lu*, 5: 1a–4b; *Tianfu guangji*, 2: 19–21; and Zhang Jue, *Jingshi wucheng fangxiang wutong ji* (Beijing chubanshe, 1982). On the commercial activities of Ming Beijing see Hou and Jin, *Beijing shihua*, pp. 118–123; *Beijing shi*, pp. 157–163; He, *BJTS*, Vol. 6, chap. 4, sec. 1; chap. 10, sec. 3; and also Luo Baoping, "Ming Qing shiqi Beijing shichang chutan", *Beijing shiyuan*, Vol. 4 (1988), pp. 242–256. On the vicissitudes of the Huitongguan see Zhao Lingyang, "Mingdai Huitongguan", *Dalu zazhi* , 41.5 (July 1970), pp. 17–30. For an account of the *miaohui* and related commercial activities see Guo Zisheng, *Beijing miaohui jiusu* (Beijing: Zhongguohuaqiao chubanshe, 1989); and Zhao Shiyu, *Kuanghuan yu richang: Ming Qing yilai de miaohui yu minjian shehui* (Beijing: Sanlian shudian, 2002). See also the best account on temple building and festivities in English in Susan Naquin, *Peking: Temples and City Life*, passim. On the development of the Guozijian in Ming Beijing see Lin Liyue, *Mingdai de Guozijian sheng* (Taibei: Taiwan Shifan daxue lishiyanjiusuo, 1979); and also He, *BJTS*, Vol. 6, chap. 14, sec. 1, 6.
31. For an account of the thirteen Ming imperial mausoleums in Peking see Gu

Yanwu, *Changping shanshui ji* (Beijing guji, 1982), *shang*, pp. 4–14; Sun Chengze, *Chunming mengyu lu*, 7: 3a–4b; *Tianfu guangji*, 40: 55257; and Tang Yongbin, *Jiudu wenwulue* (Beiping: Shizhengfu mishuchu, 1935), "Lingmulue" 陵墓略, pp. 1–7. On modern studies see Xie Mincong, *Zhongguo lidai diwang lingqin kaolue* (Taiwan Xuesheng, 1980), pp. 167–171; and Hu Hansheng, *Ming shisan ling daguan* (Beijing Zhongguo qingnian, 1993); idem, *Ming shishan ling* (same publisher, 1998). See also Ann Paludan, *The Imperial Ming Tomb* (Hong Kong: Oxford University Press, 1991), with colored illustrations.

32. On the waterways of Peking, the problem of water supply, and the hydraulic projects to improve the water resources see *MS*, 85: 2110–2113; and Sun Chengze, *Chunming mengyulu*, 69: 1a–4b; *Tianfu guangji*, 36: 474–476; *Shuntian fuzhi*, 46: 7b–9a. For modern studies see, among others, Hou, "Beijing tushi guocheng zhong de shuiyan wenti", rpt. in idem, *Lishi dilixue de lilun yu shijian*, pp. 296–303; Cai, *Beijing guyunhe*, chaps. 2, 3, 5; and Wang and Ren, *Beijing huanjing shihua*, pp. 62–65.
33. On the imperial decrees ordering the migration of people into Peking and related issues in the Yongle reign see *MTZOSL*, 12 *xia*: 217, 22: 415; 34: 604; 46: 714; see also *MS*, 5: 76, 6: 80, 81, 82; *Shuntian fuzhi*, 49: 3b.
34. According to the census data, the population in Peking peaked at the beginning of the Wanli reign with 179,200 households and 851,000 individuals, but declined to around 700,000 individuals in 1629. For details see Hou, *Beijing chengshi lishi dili*, pp. 270–280; and Han, *Beijing lishi renkou dili*, pp. 104–110, 258–269.
35. The basic source for the study of Qing Peking is the monumental *Rexia jiuwen* compiled by Zhu Yijun in 42 *juan* in 1686. It was revised and expanded by an imperial commission headed by Yu Minzhong in 1785–1787 and was known as *Qinding Rixia jiuwen kao* (*QDRXJWK*) in 169 *juan*. A modern edition was printed by Beijing chubanshe in 1981. A simplified work is the gazetteer, *Shuntian fuzhi*, 100 *juan* (1885). For a comprehensive account of Qing Peking see Wu Jianyong, *BJTS*, Vol. 7; Wei Kaizhao and Zhao Huirong, *BJTS*, Vol. 8; and Chen Zongfan, *Yandu congkao*, passim. See briefly Hou and Jin, *Beijing shihua*, chap. 10; *Beijing shi*, pp. 331–358; Xie, *Beijing de chengyuan*, chaps. 3–6. On the population of Qing Peking see also Hou, *Beijing chengshi lishi dili*, pp. 280–289; and Han, *Beijing lishi renko dili*, pp. 110–129, 269–281. For sketch maps see Hou, *Beijing lishi ditu ji*, Vol. I: 41–54.
36. There are several important monographs on the development of and changes in Peking from late Qing to the contemporary period. See in particular Zhao Shiyu, *Fuxiu yu shenqi*: *Qingdai chengshi shenghuo changjuan* (Hunan chubanshe, 1996); Hsueh Feng-hsuan, *Beijing*: *The Nature and Planning of a Chinese Capital City* (New York: Wiley, 1995); Shi Mingzheng,

Zouxiang jindaihua de Beijing cheng—chengshi jianshe yu shehui biange (Beijing daxue chubanshe, 1995); and, most recently, Madeleine Yue Dong, *Republican Beijing*. For excellent reminiscences of old Peking from a contemporary perspective see Deng Yunxiang, *Zengbu Yanjing fengtu ji* (Zhonghua, 1998), 2 vols. On the urban transformation of Peking since the late Qing, and the fate of the imperial city walls under the People's Republic, see Wang Bin and Xu Xiushan, *Beijing jiexiang tuzhi* (Beijing Zuojia, 2004), chaps. 7–9, and appendices; and Wang Jun, *Chengji* (Beijing Sanlian, 2003), passim.

37. For details see Yin, Yu, and Wu, *Beijing lishi ziran zaihai yanjiu*, chaps. 4, 5. See also Chen, "Jiu Beijing de qiyu yu silong", pp. 197–216. For citations of the Kangxi and Qianlong emperors' edicts on these occasions see pp. 208, 209.
38. See Chen, "Jiu Beijing de qiyu yu silong", pp. 197–205, 208–216, 217–221. See also note 84 below.
39. There are several important studies in Chinese, Japanese, and English on this humiliating mid-Ming debacle against the Mongols which had grave political and military consequences. For English see F. W. Mote, "The T'u-mu Incident of 1449", in *Chinese Ways in Warfare*, edited by Frank A. Kierman, Jr. and John K. Fairbank (Cambridge, MA: Harvard University Press, 1974), pp. 243–272, 361–369; and also Philip de Heer, *The Care-taker Emperor . . .* (Leiden: Brill, 1986), passim.
40. For Yang Ziqi's poem see Qian Qianyi, ed., *Liechao shiji* (1652 ed.), 7: 12a.
41. On Xin Xiuming's memoirs see *Lao taijian de huiyi* (Beijing Yanshan, 1992), p. 97.
42. See Alphonse Favier, *Peking: histoire et description* (Lille: Société de Saing-Augustin, 1900), p. 22. This mistake was repeated later in Juliet Bredon: *Peking: A Historical and Intimate Description of Its Chief Places of Interest* (Shanghai: Kelly and Walsh, Ltd., enlarged and revised ed., 1931 [first published in 1919]), p. 21.
43. For example, see the text of popular songs (no longer extant) titled *Xiu fadeng* 綉花燈 (Embroidered Flower Lamp), *Shieryue dajiang ming* 十二月古人名 (Names of Generals Arranged in Twelve Months), or *Shisanyue guren ming* 十三月古人名 (Names of Ancient Personages Arranged in Thirteen Months) recorded in Li Jiarui and Liu Fu, eds., *Zhongguo suqu zongmu gao* (Beiping: Guoli Beiping yanjiuyuan, 1932), Vol. I, p. 277; Vol. II, pp. 837, 838, 1260; see also Fu Xihua, ed., *Beijing chuantong quyi zonglu* (Zhonghua, 1962), pp. 877–878. The *Xiufadeng* piece originated from Jinan, Shandong; the rest were all from Peking, then known as Pei-p'ing. Cf. note 97 below.
44. See E. T. C. Werner, *Myths and Legends of China* (London: George G. Harrap, 1924), pp. 227–230. On the Mongolian source of this story see Antoine Mostaert, *Textes oraux ordos*, Monumenta Serica Monograph Series I

(Peiping: The French Bookstore, 1937), pp. 133–136; and the same author's French translation: *Folklore ordos*, Monumenta Serica Monograph Series II (1947), pp. 189–195. See also Chapter 3, note 10.

45. See Werner, *Myths and Legends of China*, pp. 232–234.
46. See Chen Hongnian, *Gudu fengwu* (Taibei Zhengzhong, 1960), pp. 140–142. The author fled Pei-p'ing for Taiwan in 1949 and subsequently wrote many short pieces on various topics about his reminiscences of the old capital. They were mostly published in newspapers and magazines and were later collected in the present volume after his death in 1965. For other similar reminiscences which mention the Nezha city legend see Bai Tiezheng, *Lao Beiping de gutianer* (Taibei: Huilong chubanshe, 1977), pp. 167–170; Yang Mingxian, *Chengmen yu hutong* (Taibei: Chunwenxue chubanshe, 1982), p. 1; and others.
47. I have not seen Yan Gongshang's *Beipinghua yuhui* myself. This information comes from Wang Tong, "'*Beiping yuhui*' ji qita", in *Shijie ribao* (World Journal) (U.S.A.), September 22 1983, "Renjian xianhua" column. According to the author, Yan's work was published in Pei-p'ing in the 1930s.
48. See Dong, *Republican Beijing*, pp. 11–12.
49. See L. C. Arlington and William Lewisohn, *In Search of Old Beijing* (Peking: Henri Vetch, 1935), p. 28. The authors did not cite their sources, and the work was probably based on folktales collected by local Chinese informants. It should be pointed out that earlier Western accounts about Peking already linked Liu to the building of the imperial city, but they neither mentioned the *Nezha cheng* legend nor elaborated on it as did the later works. See note 42 above.
50. Arlington and Lewisohn, *In Search of Old Beijing*, pp. 175–176.
51. Arlington and Lewisohn, *In Search of Old Beijing*, pp. 338–339.
52. These two were Lamaist monasteries. On their locations see Wu Changyuan, *Chenyuan shilue*, 12: 240, 242; *QDRXJWK*, 107: 1775–1776. See also *Jinri Beijing*, Vol. II, pp. 412, 420.
53. On the Houmen Bridge and related legend see Chapter 4, note 22.
54. See Jin Shoushen, *Beijing de chuanshuo* (Beijing: Tongsu wenyi chubanshe, 1957), pp. 3–8, Appendices (1). There are two later enlarged editions under the same title published by Beijing chubanshe, in 1981 and 2003 respectively. In both editions, the pagination for the Nezha City story remains the same. The 2003 edition includes additional old pictures and an account of the author's life and works by Yang Liangzhi, "Jin Shoushen he ta de zhushu," pp. 189–208. There are both Japanese and earlier English translations of this book as well as an adaptation in modern literary Chinese by a scholar in Taiwan based on the earlier editions. On the "Eight-armed *Nezha cheng*" story see Muramatsu Ichiya, *Pekin no densatsu* (Tokyo: Heibonsha, 1976), pp. 63–72; Gladys Yang, *Beijing Legends* (Beijing: Panda

Books, 1982), pp. 10–17; and Huang Xiandang, *Beiping de chuanshuo* (Taibei: Changchunshu shufang, 1979), pp. 77–85. For the second version of the story, see note 56. A short biographical profile of Jin Shousen also appears in the preface to his posthumous publication, *Beijing tong* (Beijing: Dazhong chubanshe, 1999).

55. In an earlier retelling of Jin's story entitled "Bazhishou de Nezha zhicheng" 八隻手的哪吒之城, the Taiwan scholar Huang Xiandeng added a rough sketch of the imaginary Nezha superimposed on the plan of Peking, showing the correspondence of different parts of his body with the specific walled gates of the imperial-city. See *Beiping de chuanshuo*, p. 40, but it is less interesting than the Nezha picture shown on the cover of the *Beijing Legends*. It was short-sighted of the Beijing Foreign Languages Press to replace in the 2005 edition of this book the old cover with a picture of the Palace Museum (entrance to the Forbidden City), hence diminishing its folkloric representation.

56. See Zhang Zichen and Li Yuenan, eds., *Beijing de chuanshuo* (Shanghai: Shanghai wenyi chubanshe, 1982), pp. 1–5.

57. See Jin, *Beijing de chuanshuo*, pp. 14–21; cf. Yang, *Beijing Legends*, pp. 24–31.

58. For comments on Jin Shoushen's works on Beijing culture see note 54 above; see also Dong, *Republican Beijing*, pp. 259–260.

59. For Liu Ji's traditional biographies see *MS*, 128: 3777–3782; and Lei Xi and Wang Fen, eds., *Qiantian xianzhi* (1876), 10: 3a–6b. They are based on Huang Bosheng: "Chengyibo Liugong xingzhuang" 誠意伯劉公行狀 (Venerable Liu's "Account of Conduct" [1383?]); and Zhang Shiqie 張時徹 (1500–1577): "Chengyibo Liugong shendao beiming" 誠意伯劉公神道碑銘 (Venerable Liu's "Spiritual-way Epitaph with Inscription" [1567]). Both are contained in the first *juan* of Liu Ji's literary collection, *Chengyibo Liu Wencheng gong wenji, 20 juan*, various editions. For modern works see *Liu Bowen nianpu* (1936); amended by Hao Zhaoju, *Zengding Liu Bowen nianpu* (Zhengzhou: Zhongzhou guji chubanshe, 1990); and Liu Deyu, *Ming Liu Bowengong shengping shiji shiyi* (Taibei, privately published, 1976). Other more recent biographical sketches include Hok-lam Chan, "Liu Chi", in *DMB*, Vol. I, pp. 932–938; Hao Zhaoju and Liu Wenfeng, *Liu Bowen quanzhuan* (Dalin: Dalin chubanshe, 1994); and Zhou Qun, *Liu Ji pingzhuan* (Nanjing: Nanjing daxue chuban she, 1995). The latest addition is Yang Ne, *Liu Ji shiji kaoshu* (Beijing: Beijing tushuguan chubanshe, 2004). It is a meticulous attempt to rectify Liu's biographical data against fictional interpolations and mythological trappings.

60. On Liu Ji's political career under Ming Taizu and his later years see the biographical references cited earlier. Hu Weiyong, later promoted prime minister, was executed by Ming Taizu on a trumped-up allegation of high treason in February 1380. One of the charges was that he had sent poison to the ailing Liu Ji and caused his death. For details of the allegation and refutation see Wu Han, "Hu Weiyong dang'an kao", *Qinghua xuebao,* 15

(June 1934), pp. 163–205; and Wang Zhiping, "Liu Ji zhisi kaoyi", *Jingshi jikan*, 2.3 (April 1942), pp. 59–60. The *SKQS* edition of Liu's *Chengyibo Liu Wencheng gong wenji* has been reproduced by the Shanghai guji chubanshe in 1987 as Vol. 1225 of the collection. For a bibliographical note see *Siku quanshu zongmu tiyao*, 169: 3.

61. Apart from the study on Liu Ji and the Nezha City legend cited in Introduction, note 29 and elsewhere, I have published a number of academic papers on his legends. See Hok-lam Chan, "Liu Chi in the *Ying-lieh chuan*: The Fictionalization of a Scholar-hero" (1967); "Liu Chi (1311–1375) and His Models: The Image-building of a Chinese Imperial Adviser" (1968); "A Mongolian Legend of the Building of Peking" (1990); and "The Demise of Yuan Rule in Mongolian and Chinese Legends" (1992). These four essays have been reproduced in my *China and the Mongols: History and Legend under the Yuan and Ming* (Aldershot, Hampshire: Ashgate Publishing Ltd., 1999), chaps. V, VII, VIII, X. In addition, see my studies on the *Shaobing ge* cited in note 74 below. A summary of my work on the Liu Ji legends is given in Chen Xuelin, "Guanyu Liu Bowen chuanshuo de yanjiu", *Beijing shehui kexue*, 1998.4 (November), pp. 44–48. In addition see "Liu Bowen yu 'Bayue shiwu sha Dazi' gushi kaosu", *Bulletin of the Institute of Modern History, Academia Sinica*, 46 (December 2005), pp. 1–51. For other studies on Liu Ji's legends see Jiang Xingyu, "Zhu Ming wangchao shenhua Liu Bowen de lishi guocheng", *Hangzhou daxue xuebao* (*zhexue shehui kexue ban*), 14.1 (March 1984), pp. 98–104, 119; Zhou Qun, "Liu Ji—cong lishi dao shenhua de shanbian", *Dalu zazhi*, 96.3–4 (March–April 1998): 16–19, 46–48; Wang Jianchuan, "Liu Bowen chuanshuo yu *Shaobing ge*, jiantan 'Tieguantu chen' de xingcheng", *Taiwan zongjiaoyanjiu tongxun*, 4 (October 2002), pp. 161–194; and Yang, *Liu Ji shiji kaoshu*, passim.

62. According to Yang Ne, judged by the contents, Wang Bosheng's "Chengyibo Liugong xingzhuang" (see note 59 above) may not have been written by Wang himself in 1384 as claimed and it was not publicized until 1404. It was replete with exaggerated statements and falsified episodes intended to inflate Liu Ji's contribution to the Ming founding in order to promote the family's status. See Yang, *Liu Ji shiji kaoshu*, pp. 169–170.

63. For a sample of these stories see Du Mu, *Dugong tanzuan* (*CSJC* ed.), *shang*, 4; Zhu Yunming, *Yeji*, pp. 1–3; Lu Can, *Gengsi bian* (Zhonghua, 1987), 7: 75, 86; 10: 116, 118; Liang Yi, *Chuanxin lu*, 1: 10b, 15a, 15b, 16b; Zhang Han, *Songchuang mengyu*, 5: 90, 92; Dong Gu, *Bili zacun* (*CSJC* ed.), *shang*, 16; Wang Wenlu, *Longxing ciji*, in *Jilu huibian*, edited by Shen Jiefu (Shanghai Shangwu, 1938), 13: 3b, 4b; Song Lei, *Xiwu liyu*, in *Shiyuan congshu*, ser. 6, edited by Zhang Junheng (1916 ed.), 3: 52b; Yang Yi, *Gaopo yizuan*, in *Shuoku*, edited by Wang Wenru (Taibei: Xinxing shuju, 1964), *xia*, 1a–1b; Wang Tonggui, *Ertan leizeng* (*XXSKQS* ed.), 19: 2a–2b, and others.

64. See Liang Yi, *Chuanxin lu*, 1: 15a; Wang Mi, *Dongchao ji*, in *Baicheng*, edited by Sun You'an (Taibei: Yiwen yinshuguan, 1967), Vol. 8, 5b; and He Qiaoyuan, *Mingshan cang* (Taibei Chengwen, 1970), "Chenlin ji 臣林記: Liu Ji", 8b.
65. For a bibliographical note on the earlier editions of the *Yinglie zhuan* see Sun Kaidi, *Zhongguo tongsu xiaoshuo shumu* (Beijing Zuojia, 1957), pp. 56–58; Zhao Jingshen and Du Haoming, eds. and annot., *Yinglie zhuan* (Shanghai: Siluan shuju, 1955) (based on the 159l, 1628 and 1616 editions), preface; Liu Ts'un-yan, *Chinese Popular Fiction in Two London Libraries* (Hong Kong: Lung Men Bookstore, 1967), pp. 281–282; and Zhao Jingshen, *Zhongguo Xiaoshuo congkao* (Jinan: Qilu shushe, 1983), pp. 176–209.
66. See *Yinglie zhuan*, pp. 89–91, 94–95, 155ff, 200ff, 21–11, 326ff, 414ff, 441ff. See also Chan, "Liu Chi in the *Ying-lieh chuan*", pp. 29–38.
67. On the stories adapted from the *Yinglie zhuan* and performed in Peking opera and storytelling see Wang Dacuo, *Xikao* (Shanghai Dadong, 1934), 14 *ce*: "You Wumiao"; "Dang Liang"; 24 *ce*: "You Wumiao"; "Liu Ji cichao" 劉基辭朝 (Liu Ji Resigning from the Court); Tao Junqi, *Jingju jumu chutan* (Zhonghua, 1962), p. 231; and Gong Debo, *Xiju yu lishi* (Taibei: Sanmin shuju, 1967), pp. 552–561. For details see Zhao, *Zhongguo xiaoshuo congkao*, pp. 169–175; see also Chen Ruheng, *Shuoshu shihua* (Shanghai: Zuojia chubanshe, 1958), p. 132.
68. The *Xu Yinglie zhuan*, 5 *juan* in 34 sections (*hui*), is available in several modern editions. For a bibliographical note see Sun, *Zhongguo tongsu xiaoshuo shumu*, p. 59. An early Qing edition, with the full title *Xiuxiang Yongle dingding quanzhi Xu Yinglie zhuan*, has been reproduced in *Guben xiaoshuo congkan*, 15th ser., vol. 1 (Zhonghua, 1991). The stories referred to here appear in *juan* one, pp. 36–40; *juan* five, pp. 351–355. For details see Wang, "Liu Bowen chuanshuo yu 'Shaobing ge'", pp. 188–193.
69. For bibliographical notes on these putative works see *MS*, 98: 2431, 2441, 2443, 2444; *Siku quanshu zongmu tiyao*, 109: 24, 110: 57, 60; 111: 67, 68, 69; 130: 52; and *Qingtian xianzhi*, 12: 17a–30b, 33b. See also Wang, *Liu Bowen nianpu*, pp. 106–109; and Hao, *Zengding Liu Bowen nianpu*, pp. 204–207.
70. For details see Chapter 3, II–IV.
71. For a sample of these sources see Ji Liuqi, *Mingji beilue* (Zhonghua, 1984), 1: 17–18, 20: 465–466, 23: 662–663; Zhao Jishi, *Jiyuan jisuoji* (*XXSKQS* ed.), 5 ("Mie Shu qiyi" 滅蜀奇異), 22b; 6 ("Fenlu ji shou kao" 焚廬寄・壽考), 8a–3b; Sun Zhilu, *Ershen yelu* (*SKCMCS* ed.), 7.2a; Wan Yan, ed., *Chongzhen changbian* (Taiwan Xuesheng, 1985), 59.13b; Tan Qian, *Guoque* (Beijing guji, 1958), 100: 6044; and Zou Yi, *Mingji yiwen* (*XXSKQS* ed.), 1.36a–36b.
72. See Xiao Yishan, *Jindai mimi shehui shiliao* (Guoli Beiping yanjiuyuan, 1935), 4: 11b; 5: 3b–4a; 6: 16b. See also *Tiandihui*, edited by the Research Institute of Qing History, People's University of China and No. 1 Historical Archives

of China (Zhongguo Renmin daxue, 1980), Vol. I, p. 7. There are several important studies on the Heaven and Earth Society in recent scholarship. See, among others, Zhuang Jifa, *Qingdai Tiandihui yuanliu kao* (Taibei: Gugong bowuyuan, 1981); Qin Baoqi, *Qingqianqi Tiandihui yanjiu* (Zhongguo Renmin daxue, 1988); He Zhiqing, *Tiandihui zhiyuan yanjiu* (Beijing: Shehui kexue wenxian chubanshe, 1996); Dian Murray/Qian Baoqi, *The Origins of the Tiandihui: Chinese Triads in Legend and History* (Palo Alto, CA: Stanford University Press; 1993); and Barend J. Ter Haar, *Ritual and Mythology of the Chinese Triads: Creating an Identity* (Leiden: Brill, 1998).

73. For a list of these alleged Liu Bowen prophetic verses, some of which were allegedly inscribed on steles, see Wang, "Liu Bowen chuanshuo yu 'Shaobing ge'", pp. 170–173; and idem, "*Tuibei tu, Wugong jing, Shaobing ge ji qita*", preface to *Ming Qing minjian zongjiao jingjuan wenxian xubian*, edited by Wang Jianchuan et al. (Taibei Xinwenfeng, 2006), pp. 11–13. Two manuscripts of the *Sanjiao yingjie zongguan tongshu* transcribed respectively in 1792 and 1876 were recently discovered by Li Shiyu in Shandong. See Li, "*Sanjiao yingjie zongguan tongshu* chutan", *Taiwan zongjiaoyanjiu tongxin*, 6 (October 2002), pp. 261–318. Liu Bowen's alleged prophecies are cited in op. cit., pp. 284–285; 298–318. For a study of the Eight Trigrams Uprising in the Jiaqing reign see Susan Naquin, *Millenarian Rebellion in China: The Eight Trigrams Uprising of 1813* (New Haven: Yale University Press, 1976), especially Part III.

74. On the purported preface by Li Zhong relating the alleged transmission of the Chinese prophecies including the *Shaobing ge* in the late Qing see, among others, *Zhongguo yuyan qizhong* (subtitled *Zhongguo erqian'nian* [*qian*] *zhi yuyan*) (n.d., copy in Sichuan Provincial Library, Chengdu); and Zhu Xiaoqin, ed., *Zhongguo yuyan bazhong* (Shanghai: Guangyi shuju, 1947), "post preface" (*ba* 跋), pp. 102–105. In other editions such as the undated *Zhongguo erqian'nian zhi yuyan*, this post preface was restored to the main preface. I have published several studies on the *Shaobing ge*, see Chen Xuelin, "Tu Liu Bowen *Shaobing ge*", in *Shou Luo Xianglin jiaoshou lunwenji* (Hong Kong, privately published, 1970), pp. 163–190, "Die Prophezeiung des Liu Ji (1311–1375): Ihre Entstehung und ihre Umwandlung im heutigen China", *Saeculum*, 25.4 (1974): 338–366; "Liu Bowen *Shaobing ge* xinkao", in *Luo Xianglin jiaoshou jinian lunwenji* (Taibei Xinwenfeng, 1993), pp. 1363–1403; and "Dongying kanxing de Zhongguo yuyanshu shuping", *Shisou—Qingzhu jianxiao sanshizhounian xueshulunwenji* (Department of History, The Chinese University of Hong Kong, 1993), pp. 169–201. See also Wang, "Liu Bowen chuanshuo yu 'Shaobing ge'", pp. 177–183; and idem, "*Tuibei tu, Wugong jing, Shaobing ge ji qita*", pp. 11–18.

75. See *Liu Bowen Shaobing ge* included in *Liu xiansheng "Jingui jinnang"*

(Shanghai: n.p., 1897); *Tuibei tu suoyin* (here the *Shaobing ge* is titled *Dishi wenda ge*) (Tokyo: n.p., 1917), and in Zhu, ed., *Zhongguo yuyan bazhong,* passim.

76. On Zhang Zhong's biographies see Song Lian, *Song xueshi wenji* (*SBCK* ed.), 9: 4a–5a; and *MS,* 299: 7640. On the stories of Zhang Zhong's prophecies and the genesis of the *Zhengbing ge* and relationship with the *Shaobing ge* see Zheng Xiao, *Jinyan* (Zhonghua, 1984), 6: 179–180; Gu Qiyan, *Kezuo zhuiyu* (Zhonghua, 1987), 2: 38; and Zha Jizuo, *Zuiwei lu* (*SBCK,* 3rd ser.), 26: 2a. For details see Hok-lam Chan, "The Prophecy of Chang Chung: The Transmission of the Legend of an Early Ming Taoist", *Oriens Extremus,* 20.1 (June 1973), pp. 65–102.

77. See Wang Liumen, *Jianqingshi suibi,* in *Nanjing wenxian,* 2nd ser. (Nanjing: Nanjingshi wenxian weiyuanhui, 1947), p. 14. See also Dunhuan, "*Xiaosanwuting suibi*: *Shaobing ge*", *Guocui xuebao,* 75 (1911), "*Congtan*", p. 1.

78. For the Taiwanese columnist's comments on the alleged authorship of Liu Ji's *Shaobing ge* see *Taiwan Ririxinbao,* No. 176, Meiji 31/12/3 (January 14 1899) (Chinese edition). He was responding to a notice alleging the fulfillment of some of Liu's prophecies published in Taiwan in no. 166 of the same newspaper, Meiji 31/1/20 (January 1 1899). Both texts are cited and discussed in Wang, "Liu Bowen chuanshuo yu 'Shaobing ge'", pp. 178–180.

79. Zou Rong's *Geming jun* has been translated by John Lust as *The Revolutionary Army: A Chinese Nationalist Tract of 1930* (Paris: Mouton & Co., 1968). The reference to the *Shaobing ge* is found on p. 127. It is striking that this reference was deleted from later editions of the *Geming jun.* See Chen, "Tu Liu Bowen *Shaobing ge*", pp. 189–190; "Liu Bowen *Shaobing ge xinkao*", pp. 1381–1388.

80. For details see Hok-lam Chan, "The Demise of Yuan Rule in Mongolian and Chinese Legends", rpt. in Chan, *China and the Mongols,* chap. V; see also Chen Xuelin, "Liu Bowen yu 'Bayueshiwu sha Dazi gushi kaosu'", passim.

81. See Chen, "Tu Liu Bowen *Shaobing ge*", pp. 189–190; "Liu Bowen *Shaobing ge xinkao*", pp. 1381–1388.

82. For an inventory of these temples which dated back to the Ming, most of which were refurbished in the Qing, see *Beijing simiao lishi ziliao,* compiled by Beijingshi Danganguan (Beijing: Zhongguo dang'an chubanshe, 1997), Index, p. 723 (Guandimiao 關帝廟), p. 730 (Zhenwumiao 真武廟), p. 719 (Longwangmiao), p. 719. This was compiled from the records of temples registered with the Nationalist government in 1928, 1936, and 1947. For a useful earlier index to temples in Beijing based on a social survey see Xu Daoling, ed., *Beiping miaoyu tongjian* (Guoli Beiping yanjiu yuan, 1936), 2 vols. On references to Guandimiao, Zhenwumiao, and

Longwangmiao see also Naquin, *Peking: Temples and City Life,* Glossary–Index, pp. 793, 799, 815.

83. For details see Li Qiao, *Zhongguo hangyeshen chongbai* (Beijing: Zhongguo huaqiao chuban gongsi, 1990), pp. 286–288. On the role of the water-carriers' guild in providing water to the residents of Peking in the late Qing and early Republican period see Qiu Zhonglin, "*Shuiwouzi*: Beijing de gongshuiyezhe yu minsheng yongshui", in *Zhongguo de chengshi shenghu,* edited by Li Xiaodi (Taibei Lianjing, 2005), pp 243–256.
84. On the rain-praying rituals and festivities in homage to the Dragon King in Peking since the Ming see Liu Tong and Yu Yizheng, *Dijing jingwu lue* (Beijing guji, 1980), p. 71; and also Chang Renchun, *Lao Beijing fengqing jiqu* (Beijing chubanshe, 1993), pp. 83–84. For details see Chen, "Jiu Beijing de qiyu yu silong", pp. 197–216.
85. Nezha was worshiped together with his father, the Pagoda-wielding Heavenly King, in the Eastern Peak Temple in Peking. On his statues see Anne S. Goodrich, *The Peking Temple of the Eastern Park: The Tung-yueh miao in Peking* (Nagoya: Monumenta Serica, 1964), pp. 221, 261.
86. The Nezha Temple inside the Yongding Gate near the Altar of Ancestral Agriculture in what was later known as Taoranting was built c. 1738 by the Sash and Girdle Manufacturing Guild (Tiaodaihang), which chose Nezha as its spiritual progenitor. See Li, *Zhongguo hangye shen yanjiu,* pp. 199–201. For details of the temple see Chen Xuelin, "Beijing waicheng Nezha miao tansu", *JCS,* N.S. 10 (2001), pp. 151–169.
87. Contemporary Chinese scholars on Peking history, including the leading authority Hou Renzhi, when asked to comment on the popular belief in Liu Bowen building the Nezha city, chose to dismiss this as hearsay instead of speculating on the origins of the legend in a scholarly manner. See Hou, "Beijing cheng he Liu Bowen de guanxi", *Beijing ribao* (*Peking Daily*) July 31 1962; see also Jiang Weitang, "Liu Bowen yu Beijing—Liu Bowen xingjian Beijing cheng, kanding shisanling zhisuo zhengwei", ibid, September 8 1999.
88. See Xu, "Mingchu Nanjing huangcheng gongcheng de guihua", pp. 91–92.
89. On this miraculous story see Liang Yi, *Chuanxin lu,* 1: 15b; Zhang Han, *Songchuang mengyu,* 5: 92; He Qiaoyuan, *Mingshan cang,* "Chenlin ji: Liu Ji", 8b; Cao Chen, *Shehua lu,* 6: 45; and anonymous, *Jianzhu congbian,* cited in Wang, *Liu Bowen nianpu,* p. 70.
90. See Liang Yi, *Chuanxin lu,* 1: 5b. When the story first appeared in the *Fengtian jingnan ji,* an official version of the Prince of Yan's *jingnan* campaign against the Jianwen emperor (p. 216), it was an anonymous Daoist who made such a prediction. As the story was transmitted, Liu Ji at first replaced the Daoist, but later the prediction was also ascribed to the Iron-cap Daoist Zhang Zhong. For the latter see Guo Zizhang, *Yuzhang shu* (1608), quoted in Chen Qingling and Tong Fan, eds., *Linchuan xianzhi* (1870), 53 *shang*: 7a.

91. On the legend of Liu Ji siting the mausoleum of Ming Taizu in Mt. Zhong over the Liang dynasty eminent monk Baozhi's grave by observing auspicious geomancy see Zhu Yunming, *Yeji*, p. 91; Zhang Han, *Songchuang mengyu*, 5: 92; and Dong Gu, *Bilu zacun*, 9a–9b. After transferring the monk's remains to a different site to make room for his own mausoleum, the emperor ordered a new monastery to be built in his honor, known as Linggusi 靈谷寺. He personally wrote an account entitled "Linggusi Ji", now included in his literary works, *Ming Taizu yuzhi wenji* (Taiwan Xuesheng, 1964), 14: 18b–20a. For a description of Taizu's mausoleum see *Ming Xiaoling*, edited by Nanjing Bowuyuan (Beijing: Wenwu chubanshe, 1981).
92. On Zhu Zuochao's *Jianhuang tu* see *Quhai zhongmu tiyao*, edited by Huang Wenchang and collated by Dong Kang (Kowloon: Hanxue tushu gongyingshe, 1967), p. 1350. The *Zai jinpao* is reprinted in several modern editions of Liu Bowen's prophecy book the *Shaobing ge*, for example *Liu Bowen Shaobing ge* (*quanben*) (Hong Kong: Da'nan chubanshe, 1976?), pp. 1–19.
93. On this story see Zhang and Li, *Beijing de chuanshuo*, pp. 1–5; cf. Chen, *Liu Bowen yu Nezha cheng*, pp. 120–121.
94. For Yao Guangxiao's biographies see Chapter 1, note 15. On his political contribution to Yongle's usurpation and subsequent career see Heinz Friese, "Der Mönch Yao Kuang-hsiao (1335–1418) und seine Zeit", *Oriens Extremus*, 7 (1960), pp. 158–184; idem, "Das *Tao-yu-lü* des Yao Kuang-hsiao", *Oriens Extremus*, 8 (1961), pp. 42–56; David B. Chan, "The Role of the Monk Tao-yen in the Usurpation of the Prince of Yen", *Sinologica*, 6.2 (1959): 83–100; Shang Chuan, "Mingqu zhuming zhengzhijia Yao Guangxiao", *Zhongguo shi yanjiu*, 1983.3 (August): 119–130; and Xu Zuosheng, "Ming shenmi mouseng Yao Guangxiao lun", *Dongnan wenhua*, 1990.4 (August), pp. 7–11. The Da Longshan Huguosi was the former Chongguobeisi 崇國北寺 built in 1284. It was generally known as Chongguosi 崇國寺 under the Yuan and early Ming. It was renamed Da Longshansi at its renovation in 1429, and then Da Longshan Huguosi at another renovation in 1472. For a detailed account see Tong Xun, *Fojiao yu Beijing simiao wenhua* (Beijing: Zhongyang Minzu daxue chubanshe, 1997), pp. 199–211 (pp. 206–211 on Yao Guangxiao).
95. On the unfavorable and damaging accounts of Yao Guangxiao in Ming-Qing miscellanies see, for example, Wang Shizhen, *Mingqing jiji*, in Shen Jiefu, ed., *Jilu huibian*, 99: 6a; Du Mu, *Dugong tanzuan*, *shang*, 15–16, Dong Gu, *Bili zacun*, *shang*, 21–23; Shen Defu, *Wanli yehuo bian*, 1: 12; Cao Canfang, *Xunguo zhengqi ji* (*SKCMCS* ed.), 3: 1a; Meicun yeshi (pseudo.), *Luqiao jiwen*, in *Taiwan wenxian congkan*, no. 127 (Taibei: Taiwan yinhang jingji yanjiushi, 1961), p. 54; and *Mingshu*, 160: 3158. See also Wang, *Ming jingnan shishi kaozheng gao*, pp. 39–41.

96. On this story see Lu Can, *Gengsi bian*, 10: 211–212; Yang Yi, *Gaobo yizuan, zhong*, 1b. See also Wang Qi, *Baishi huibian* (Taibei Xinxing, 1969), 52: 15b–16b; and Zhou Hui, *Xu Jinling suoshi, shang*, 10. According to these accounts, the other Daoist was named Huang Chuwang 黃楚望; his drawing of the palaces of Nanking is also said to be exactly the same as that produced by Liu Ji and Zhang Zhong, but again no details are revealed.
97. These popular songs variably took the title of *Qianli ju* 千里駒 (A Thousand *Li* Horse), *You Wumiao* (Touring the Temple of Warriors); *Xiuhua deng* (Embroidered Flower Lamp); *Shisan yue guren ming* (Names of Ancient Personages Arranged in Thirteen Months); *Chongzhen guanhua Tieguan tu* 崇禎觀畫鐵冠圖 (The Chongzhen Emperor Inspecting the Painting of the Charts submitted by the Iron-cap Daoist), *Liu Bowen*; *Shieryue dajiang ming* 十二月大將名 (Names of Great Generals Arranged in Twelve Months); *Liu Bowen Jingui jin'nang* (Liu Bowen's "Golden Casket and Damask Purse"); and others. See Li and Liu, *Zhongguo suqu zongmu gao*, Vol. I , pp. 86, 277; Vol. II, pp. 837, 838, 939, 1092, 1260; and Fu Xihua, ed., *Beijing chuantong quyi zonglu* (Zhonghua, 1962), pp. 876, 877, 878, 885. Unfortunately, none of these popular songs concerning Peking have survived. For a useful description see Deng Yunxiang, "Beijing suqu yu Beijing fengsu", in idem, *Shuiliu renzai conggao* (Zhonghua, 2001), pp. 65–95.
98. See briefly Hou, *Beijing lishidili*, chap. 5; Zhao, *Fuxiu yu shenqi*, chap. 12; and Naquin, *Peking: Temples and City Life*, chap. 16; Dong, *Republican Beijing*, chap. 6.
99. As well as being continued in the writings of Jin Shousen, Zhang Zichen, and Li Yuenan cited in the footnotes above, these stories are also collected in works such as *Beijing fengwu chuanshuo*, edited by Zhongguo minjian wenyi yanjiu hui, Beijing fenhui; Wang Wenbao, ed., *Beijing fengwu chuanshuo gushi xuan* (Fuzhou: Fuzhou Renmin chubanshe, 1983), and others. See also Chen, *Liu Bowen yu Nezha cheng*, Appendix: "Source Materials".
100. On the Japanese and English translations of Jin Shoushen's *Beijing Legends*, see note 54 above. The mural depicting Nezha and Beijing City originally mounted in the "foreign visitors" lounge of the Capital International Airport was reproduced photolithographically in *Beijing baikequanshu: caitu: dituji* (Beijing: Aolinpike chubanshe, 1991), p. 76; see also Chen, *Liu Bowen yu Nezha cheng*, p. 32. This mural was withdrawn from display in the early 1990s when the Airport was expanded. It was not returned afterward and has not been on public exhibition since. However, references to the *Nazha/Nezha cheng* legend continue to appear in recent popular works on Beijing. See Shi Lianfang, *Beijing jiexiang diming tan* (Taibei: Wangwenshe gufen youxiangongsi, 1995), pp. 96–97; Zhang Qingchang, *Beijing jiexiang mingqing shihua* (Beijing yuyan wenhua daxue, 1999), pp. 22–23, 154–

155; and others. In addition, Jin Shoushen's *Beijing de chuanshuo* was recently reissued in an expanded edition with related old photos and biographical information, attesting to the continued popularity of the legend.

Chapter 3

1. For details see *Altan Tobchi, A Brief History of the Mongols*, Scripta Mongolica (Cambridge, MA: Harvard University Press, 1952), Vol. II, pp. 125–126; C. R. Bawden, *The Mongol Chronicle Altan Tobchi* (Wiesbaden: Otto Harrassowitz, 1955), pp. 67–68, 154–155; cf. Kobayashi Takashirō, *Mōko Ōgonshi* (Tokyo: Seikatsu sha, 1941), pp. 89–90; Jagchid Sechin, *Menggu Huangjin shi yizhu* (Taibei Lianjing, 1979), pp. 186–188; Zhu Feng and Jia Jingyan, trans., *Hanyi Menggu Huangjin shigang* (Huhehot: Nei Menggu Renmin chubanshe, 1985), pp. 46–48; *Erdeni-yin Tobchi*: *Mongolian Chronicle*, Scripta Mongolica 2 (Cambridge, MA: Harvard University Press, 1956), Vol. II, p. 264; Vol. III, p. 260; cf. Daoruntibu, trans., (*Xinyi Jiaozhu*) *Menggu yuanliu* (Nei Menggu Renmin, 1980), 8: 464; *Bolor Erike*: *Mongolian Chronicle*, Scripta Mongolica 3 (Cambridge, MA: Harvard University Press, 1950), pp. 118–119; Walter Hessig, ed., *Altan kürdün mingglan gegesütü bichig*; *Eine Mongolische Chronik von Siregetü Guosi Dharma* [1739 ms] (Kopenhagen: Munksgaard, 1958), pp. 36–37; and *Menggu shixi pu*, a Chinese abridged edition of the *Menggu jiapu* prepared by Zhang Ertian (1939 ed.), 2: 7b–8a. In *Erdeni-yin Tobchi*, however, the Mongol princess was seven months pregnant when she met the Hongwu emperor and gave birth to a normal son three months later, thus raising doubts about the paternity of the child.
2. Zhu Di, the future Yongle emperor, was born on the *guiyou* 癸酉 (seventeenth) day of the fourth month of the *gengzi* 庚子 year, i.e. May 2 1360. See *MTZUSL*, 8: 94; *MTZOSL*, 1: 1; cf. F. W. Mote, "Chu Ti", in *DMB*, Vol. I, p. 355. The claim of Yongle's maternity by Empress Ma was methodically faked in the official records to support his claim of legitimate succession to his father's throne. For details see note 7 below.
3. Modern scholarship has commented on this; see the works of the Reverends Antoine Mostaert and Henry Serruys cited in note 10 below. In addition see Yamamoto Mamoru, "Eiraku Tei to Kenbun Tei: Eiraku Tei no Mōko denki", in Yamamoto, *Ryōtō no tama* (Mukden: Manshu jidai sha, 1944), pp. 107–117; and Zhou Qingshu, "Ming Chengzu shengmu Hongjilashi shuo suo fanying de tianmingguan", *Nei Mengu daxue xuebao* (*zhexue shehuikexue ban*), 1987.3 (July), pp. 1–18 (especially pp. 1–4). Zhou's study is insightful about the possible Chinese origin of the Mongolian legend. Owen Lattimore collected an oral version of the legend in Inner Mongolia in

1934, although it leaves out the story of how the city was built. See note 53 below.

4. According to a recent study by Hong Jinfu, the so-called forty *tümen* of the Mongol troops in Mongol-Yuan China as reported in the *Erdeni-yin Tobchi* and *Altan Tobchi,* and in earlier Yuan and Ming sources actually meant forty miliarch divisions (*wanhu*), which have been erroneously read and rendered as four hundred thousand (*sishiwan* 四十萬) households. See Hong Jinfu, "Sishiwan Menggu shuo lunzheng gao", in *Meng Yuande lishi yu wenhua: Meng Yuanshi xueshu yantaohui lunwenji,* edited by Xiao Qiqing (Taiwan Xuesheng, 2001), Vol. I, pp. 245–305. On the large number of Mongols left by Toghōn Temür in China see Henry Serruys, "The Mongols in China during the Hung-wu Period (1368–1398)", *Mélanges Chinois et Bouddhiques,* 11 (1959), pp. 47–50. Serruys's work, drawing extensively on the *Ming shilu,* is the best study of Mongols in China under Ming Taizu.
5. For details of the *jingnan* campaign launched by Zhu Di, the Prince of Yan, against his nephew the Jianwen emperor, and related historiographical issues, see Chapter 2, note 8. On the issues of the legitimacy of the Prince's accession as the Yongle emperor see also the references cited in note 7 below.
6. On Zhu Di's recruitment of Mongol cavalry into the imperial forces and extensive patronage of the Mongols settling in China after his ascension see Henry Serruys, "Mongols Ennobled during the Early Ming", *Harvard Journal of Asiatic Studies,* 22 (1959), pp. 209–260; and idem, "The Mongols in China, 1400–1450", *Monumenta Serica,* 26 (1968), pp. 233–305.
7. The maternity of the Yongle emperor and his legitimate claim were subjects of heated debate among Chinese historians in the1930s. Zhu Xizu accepted the Yongle official records' claim that he was born to Ming Taizu's spouse Empress Ma, for which see Xie Jin, ed., *Tianhuang yudie,* in *Jilu huibian,* 12: 9b, 11b; and *MTZUSL,* 1: 1. Fu Sinian, however, disputed the records and suggested that the emperor's natural mother was an imperial consort known as Gongfei, probably a Korean woman, based on private accounts. For the pros and cons of the argument see Zhu Xizu, "Ming Chengzu shengmu zhiyibian", [*Guoli*] *Zhongshan daxue wenshixu yanjiusuo yuekan,* 2.1 (1939), pp. 1–13; and Fu Sinian, "'Ba Ming Chengzu shengmu wenti huizheng' pingda Zhu Xizu xiansheng ", *BIHP,* 6 (1936), pp. 79–86. See also Li Jinhua, "Ming Chengzu shengmu wenti huizheng", *BIHP,* 6, pp. 45–77; and Wu Han, "Ming Chengzu shengmu kao", *Qinghua xuebao,* 10 (1935), pp. 631–646. Wu concurred with Fu but was uncertain about Gongfei's ethnicity. Later Shao Xunzheng concluded that she was a Mongol from the Qonggirad clan; see J. S. Shaw [Shao Xunzheng], "Historical Significance of the Curious Theory of the Mongol Blood in the Veins of the Ming Emperors", *Chinese Social and Political Sciences Review,* 20.4 (1937), pp. 492–

498. This is supported by Zhou, "Ming Chengzu shengmu", pp. 1–4, 12–14. For details of Emperor Yongle's attempt at legitimation see Hok-lam Chan, "Legitimating Usurpation: Historical Revisions under the Ming Yongle Emperor (r. 1402–1424)", in *The Legitimation of New Orders: Case Studies in World History*, edited by Phillip Yuen-sang Leung (Hong Kong: The Chinese University Press, 2007), pp. 75–158.

8. On private accounts concerning Gongfei (Weng/Wangfei) based on the *Nanjing taichangsi zhi*, see He Qiaoyuan, *Mingshan cang*, "Dianmou ji" 典謨記, 6: 1a; Tan Qian, *Zaolin zazu, yi ji* 乙集, 1a; idem, *Guoque* 12: 847; Zhang Dai, *Taoan mengyi* (Shanghai guji, 1982), 1: 1; Li Qing, *Sanyuan suibi* (*puyi fuzhi* 補遺附識) (Zhonghua, 1982), p. 249; Zhu Yizun, *Baoshuting ji* (*SBCK* ed.), 44: 16b–17a; and Liu Xianting, *Guangyang zazhi* (Zhonghua, 1957), p. 82. He Qiaoyuan and his three contemporaries stated that Yongle's mother was Gongfei, without specifying if she was a Mongol. Zhu Yizun thought she was a Korean; and only Liu Xianting (who wrote the name Weng 甕-fei) and *Erdeni-yin Tobchi* (*Menggu yuanliu*) claimed she was a Mongol consort of Toghōn Temür. See Li, "Ming Chengzu", pp. 55–60; and Zhou, "Meng Chengzu shengmu", pp. 12–13. The latter claims that Gong/Wengfei was a Qonggirad woman. None of the above explains the meaning of "Weng". However, the Mongolian genealogy *Menggu shixi pu* (see note 1) claims she was so called because she hid herself in a *weng* 甕 (earthen jar) from the Ming army but was captured and presented to Zhu Yuanzhang. This speculation was apparently influenced by the *Altan Tobchi* which states regarding the Qonggirad queen of Uqaghatu Qaghan (i.e. Toghōn Temür) that: ". . . the queen went into a barrel and was left behind. This barrel the Chinese call *qang* and the Mongols call *butung*." (trans. Bawden, *Altan Tobchi*, p. 154).

9. After the founding of the Qing dynasty, the Ordos was reorganized into the Yikezhao meng (alliance) in 1649. It was placed under the administration of Suiyuan 綏遠 province in 1928 and of the Inner Mongolia Autonomous Region since 1949. It is an Inner Mongolian highland embraced by the Yellow River on the west, north, and east, and the Chinese customarily called it the Hetao 河套 region. See briefly *Yikezhao meng zhi*, compiled by Editorial Committee of the Gazetteer of the Yikezhaomeng (Beijing: Xiandai chubanshe, 1995), Vol. I, "Introduction", pp. 1–4.

10. See Antoine Mostaert's Latin transcription, *Textes oraux ordos*, Monumenta Serica Monograph Series I (Peiping: The French Bookstore, 1937), pp. 133–136; the French translation of the verbatim text of the legend by the same author, *Folklore ordos*, Monumenta Serica Monograph Series II (Peiping: The Catholic University, 1947), pp. 189–195; its Japanese translation by Isono Fujiko, *Orudosu kōhi shū: Monkuru no minkan denshō* (Tokyo: Heibonsha, 1966), pp. 32–41; and Henry Serruys, "A Manuscript Version of the Legend

of the Mongol Ancestry of the Yung-lo Emperor", in *Analecta Mongolica, Dedicated to the Seventieth Birthday of Professor Owen Lattimore*, edited by John G. Hangin and U. Onon, Publications of the Mongol Society Occasional Papers no. 8 (Bloomington: Mongol Society, 1972), pp. 19–61. For a bibliographical note see Henry Serruys, "A Catalogue of Mongol Manuscripts from Ordos", *Journal of the American Oriental Society*, 95.2 (April–June 1975), p. 199 (ms. Nos. 6, 64). The contents of the oral (the definitive) and written (the more elaborate and refined) versions are much the same. For a Chinese translation and extensive study of this document see Chen Xuelin, "Menggu 'Da Ming Yongledi jianzao Beijing cheng' gushi tanyuan", *BIHP*, 75.3 (September 2004), pp. 515–572.

11. For details of this later version, see Yō Kaiei, "*Monkuru* ni okeru ōchō kōtaikan ni kansuru ichi shiryō—'En Taishi to Shin Taizi no monogatari' o chōshin ni—", *Jimbun ronshū: Shizoka Daigaku Jimbun gakubu, Shakai gakka gengo bunka gakka kenkyū hōkoku*, 54.2 (2003), pp. 23–65. Note: In this version the Yuan Prince is written as Yuan (distant) Taizi (遠) 太子, i.e. the prince from a distant land.
12. Serruys, "Manuscript Version", pp. 31–37 (text), pp. 42–48 (translation).
13. Serruys, "Manuscript Version", pp. 31–32 (text), pp. 42–43 (translation).
14. See Mostaert, *Textes oraux ordos*, pp. 133–136; idem, *Folklore Ordos*, pp. 189–195; and Serruys, "Manuscript Version", pp. 20–21.
15. For primary sources, see, for example, *Guoqu xianzai yinguo jing*, in *TSD*, No. 189, *juan* 3; and *Zengyi Ahan jing*, in *TSD*, No. 125, *juan* 48. Cf. Mochizuki, *Mochizuki Bukkyō dai jiten*, Vol. 2, p. 1648; and Soothill, *A Dictionary of Chinese Buddhist Terms*, p. 63. The "Three Precious Ones" (*sanbao*) is frequently mentioned in the Mongolian text *Çigula kereglegçi tegüs udqa-tu śastir* (*Penyi biyong jing* 本義必用經) and the seventeenth-century Mongolian chronicle *Erdeni tunumal neretü sudur orosiba*. The former is a Buddhist treatise composed by Manjusiri guosi Siregetü çorji and the latter, subtitled *Çakravarti Altan Qaghan-tu tuguji*, authorship unknown, is a biography of Altan Khan (1507–1583), the most powerful Mongol ruler during the Ming dynasty. See Walter Hessig's succinct "Ein Quellenbezug der Altan Khan Biographie", *Menggu shi yanjiu*, 1 (July 1985), pp. 185–192. However, in the Yuan (distant) Taizi story examined by Yang Haiying, the Mongol princess is said to have offered prayers not to the "Three Precious Ones" but to heaven and earth and the seven northern polar stars. See Yō Kaiei, op. cit., pp. 39–40.
16. I am indebted to Dr. Okada Hidehiro 岡田英弘 of the Tōyō Bunko for elucidating the meaning of *oroi-yin chimeg* and pointing out Serruys' translation error in a private communication.
17. The tomb inscription, composed by the Daoist Daoyuan under the lay name Yao Guangxiao, is included in Jiao Hong, ed., *Guochao xianzheng lu* (Taiwan

Xuesheng, 1965), 70: 49a. The story of Yuan Gong foretelling the Prince of Yan's fortune by reading his features was retold in later sources. See, for example, *MTZOSL*, 1: 1–2; Zhu Yunming, *Yeji*, p. 44; and Lu Can, *Gengsi bian*, 1: 2–3. Cf. Wang, *Fengtian jingnan ji zhu*, pp. 2–4. For Yuan's biographies see also *MS*, 299: 7642–7643; and Hok-lam Chan, "Yüan Kung", in *DMB*, Vol. II, pp. 1638–1641.

18. On the origin of this story see Huang Zuo, *Gechu yishi*, included in Yuan Jiong, ed., *Jinsheng yuzhenji*, 1: 8a; see also Lang Ying, *Qixiu leigao*, 12: 185.
19. See Mostaert, *Textes oraux ordos*, pp. 133–134; idem, *Folklore Ordos*, pp. 190–191.
20. For the biographies of Zhu Yunwen and Zhu Di see the annals of Gongmindi 恭閔帝 and Chengzu in *MS*, *juan* 4–7; and also the literature cited in *DMB*, Vol. I, pp. 346–348. Major studies on the Yongle Emperor include Zhu Hong, *Ming Chengzu yu Yongle zhengzhi* (Taiwan Shifan daxue lishiyanjiusuo, 1988); Shang Chuan, *Yongle huangdi* (Beijing Renmin, 1989); Chao Zhongchen, *Ming Chengzu zhuan* (Beijing Renmin, 1993); Mao Peiqi and Li Chuoran, *Ming Chengzu shilun* (Taibei: Wenjin chubanshe, 1994); and Shih-shan Henry Tsai, *Perpetual Happiness: The Ming Emperor Yongle* (Seattle: University of Washington Press, 2001). For a political narrative of these two reigns see Chan, "The Chien-wen, Yung-lo . . . Reign", in *The Cambridge History of China*, vol. 7, part 1: *The Ming Dynasty*, pp. 184–205, 205–275. Zhu Biao was posthumously elevated to the imperial rank of Xiaokang huangdi (temple name Xingzong) by his son the Jianwen emperor in 1399. Biographies are in *MS*, 115: 3547–3550; and F. W. Mote, "Chu Piao", in *DMB*, Vol. I, pp. 346—348.
21. See Yamamoto, *Ryoto no tama*; Zhou, "Ming Chengzu shengmu"; and Chan, "Legitimating Usurpation", passim.
22. Serruys, "Manuscript Version", pp. 32–33 (text), pp. 43–44 (translation).
23. See Bawden, *Mongol Chronicle*, pp. 154–155; Kobayashi, *Mōko Ōgonshi*, pp. 89–90; Jagchid, *Menggu Huangjin shi*, pp. 186–188; and Zhu and Jia, *Huangjin shikang*, pp. 46–97.
24. On these stories see Huang Zuo, *Gechu yishi*, 1: 8a; and Fan Qin, *Suiyan* (1532), included in *Guangcang xuejiong congshu*, compiled by Ji Fotuo (i.e. Ji Juemi) (1916 ed.), *jialei*, ser. I, *shang*, 1b. Other similar episodes of Ming Taizu's dream about the two princes feuding are found in Chen Huai, *Wenjian manlu*, included in *Siming congshu*, ser. 4, edited by Zhang Shouyong (1936), *shang*: 2a–2b; Lang Ying, *Qixiu leigao*, 12: 185; and *Dayue shanren* (pseudo.), *Jianwen huangdi shiji beiyi lu* (also entitled *Jianwen yiji*) (Taiwan Xuesheng, 1969), p. 8.
25. See *Altan Tobchi*, Vol. II: 125–126; Bawden, *Mongol Chronicle*, p. 155 (p. 61 of the Mongolian text); *Bolor Erike*, Vol. III: 118; cf. Serruys, "Manuscript Version", pp. 22–24. For a brief history of Guihua cheng, now the old city of

Huhehot in Inner Mongolia, see Henry Serruys, "A Note on Two Place Names in Mongolia", in *Documenta Barbarorum: Festschrift für Walther Heissig zum 70. Geburtstag*, edited by K. Sagaster and M. Weiers (Wiesbaden: Otto Harrassowitz, 1983), pp. 370–373. See also Tai Xueji, *Huhehaote jianshi* (Zhonghua, 1981), pp. 42–47.

26. Serruys, "Manuscript Version", pp. 33–34 (text), pp. 44–45 (translation).
27. On the translation of *qabtargh-a bichig* as "container-letter" in this text see Serruys, "Manuscript Version", p. 53, n33. On the history of the Mongol word see idem, "*Ho-po, ho-pao* 'pouch': Tukic *gap, xap*", *Oriens Extremus*, 15 (1968), pp. 135–148.
28. For the story of the sealed container meant to help the future Jianwen emperor see Liang Yi, *Chuanxin lu*, l: 15a; Wang Mi, *Dongchao ji*, in *Baicheng*, Vol. 8, 5b; and He Qiaoyuan, *Mingshan cang*, "Tianmo ji", 5: 28a. On the *jinnang* purportedly left by Liu Bowen that predicted the demise of Manchu rule in the documents of the Heaven and Earth Society and the prophecy book attributed to him see Xiao Yishan, *Jindai mimi shehui shiliao*, 4: 11b; 5: 3b; and *Shaobing ge*, in Zhu, ed., *Zhongguo yuyan bazhong*, pp. 92–93.
29. For detailed information on Yao Guangxiao see Chapter 1, note 15; Chapter 2, note 94.
30. Serruys, "Manuscript Version", pp. 34–35 (text); pp. 45–47 (translation). In the oral version the number of "lanes" (*qutung*) is 361 and that of the "great tribunals" (*yeke yamu*) is 27. See Mostaert, *Textes oraux ordos*, p. 135; idem, *Folklore Ordos*, p. 194. *Qutung*, translated here as "lanes", is *hutong* (alleyways) in Chinese (from Mongolian *qudugh*, "well", i.e. place of residence). On the development of the *hutong* see Chapter 1, note 39. See also note 39 below.
31. The Yongle emperor recounted the Dark God's assistance in the *jingnan* campaign in two personally composed epitaphs to the deity. The first, "Zhenwumiao bei," was erected in Peking in 1415. The other, "Taiyue Taiheshan daogong bei" 太嶽太和山道宮碑, was erected in Mount Taihe (i.e. Mount Wudong), Hubei, but the inscription was not composed until 1418. See Wang Ji et al., comps., *Taiyue Taiheshan jilue* (1744 ed.), 5: 15a. Cf. Chen Yuan, *Daojia jinshi lue*, edited by Chen Zhichao and Zeng Qingying (Beijing Wenwu, 1988), pp. 1250, 1251. Several Ming references have the emperor receiving assistance from the Dark God, but private sources also credit his principal adviser the Monk Daoyuan (Yao Guangxiao). The latter's biography in Li Zhi, *Xu Cangshu*, 9: 148, claims he was instrumental in summoning the Dark God, his spiritual teacher, to guide the prince's course at the start of the punitive campaign in August 1399. See Chen, "'Zhenwushen', 'Yonglexiang' chuanshuo suoyuan", passim. On the popular Ming religious literature on Zhenwu see Zhou Shaoliang, "'Xinkan Wudang zuben leibian quanxiang qisheng shilu' shuji", *Wenxian*, 2 (1985), pp. 161–174. The Zhenwu Temple in Mount Wudang has been fully

documented in *Wudangshan zhi*, edited by the Compilation Committee (Beijing: Xinhua chubanshe, 1995), passim. For a sample of Zhenwu's images see Stephen Little et al., eds, *Taoism and the Arts of China* (Chicago: The Arts Institute of Chicago/The University of California Press, 2000), pp. 291–297. See also note 32.

32. On the Dark God's images and the Zhenwu temples in Shanxi and Inner Mongolia, see Willem A. Grootaers, "Les temples villageois de la région au sud de Tat'ong (Chansi nord), leurs inscriptions et leur historie", *Folklore Studies* 4 (1945), pp. 195–198; Grootaers, Li Shih-yu, and Chang Chi-wen, "Temples and history of Wan-ch'üan (Chahar). The geographical method applied to folklore", *Monumenta Serica*, 13 (1948), pp. 209–316; Grootaers, "The hagiography of the Chinese god Chen-wu", *Folklore Studies*, 11 (1952), pp. 139–182; Grootaers, Li Shih-yu, and Wang Fu-shih, *The Sanctuaries in a North-China city—A complete survey of the cultic buildings in the city of Hsüan-hua (Cahar), Mélanges Chinois et Bouddhiques*, 26 (Bruxelles, 1995), pp. 83; 232, plate 62.

33. See Zhong Han, "Xishou, zhihuan yu zhenghe—Menggu liuchuan de Beijing jiancheng gushi xingchengguocheng kaocha", *Lishi yanjiu*, 2006.4 (August), pp. 338–342. On King Vaiśravana's images in Brahmanic mythology and Buddhist hagiography, see the sources cited in Chapter 1, note 50. References to Vaiśravana as Kubera in Mongolia, Tibet, and Central Asia can be found in Alice Getty, *The Gods of Northern Buddhism . . .* (London: The Clarendon Press, 1928), pp. 157–160, plate XLVIII; Arthur Waley, *A Catalogue of Paintings Recovered from Tunhuang by Sir Aurel Stein* (London: The British Museum, 1931), pp. 41, 79; René de Nebesky-Wojkowitz, *Oracles and demons of Tibet . . .* (Graz, Austria: Akademische Drucku. Verlagsanstalt, 1975), pp. 68–82; and Walther Heissig, *The Religions of Mongolia* (Berkeley: University of California Press, 1980), pp. 93–101.

34. On the sources of this custom and practices see *YS*, 120: 1964; and Nianchang, *Fozu lidai tongzai* (*TSD*, No. 2036), 22: 723b. For details see Hok-lam Chan, "Bowshot for Siting: A Mongolian Custom and its Sociopolitical and Cultural Implications", *Asia Major*, 3rd series, 4.2 (1991), pp. 45–65. On the Mongolian use of arrows to signify ownership or occupation see Henry Serruys, "A Note on Arrows and Oaths among the Mongols", *Journal of the American Oriental Society*, 78.4 (1958): 287. On other related implications see Hok-lam Chan "'The Distance of a Bowshot': Some Remarks on Measurement in the Altaic World", *Journal of Sung-Yuan Studies*, 25 (1995), pp. 29–46.

35. See Zhong Han, op. cit., pp. 42–45. On Shen Wansan's stories, see Chapter 4.

36. For the layout and architecture of Peking as built under the Yongle emperor in light of the Mongolian legend, see the references cited in Chapter 2,

notes 18, 19; but in particular, Yu, *Zijin cheng gongdian*; and Xu, *Ming Qing Beijing cheng tu.*

37. For discussions on traditional Chinese cosmology applied to imperial city planning, see Introduction, passim. On Tibetan cosmological concept and the planet system, see Guan Dongsheng, ed., *Zhongguo minzu wenhua daguan —Zang, Menba, Luoba juan* (Beijing Zhongguo dabaike quanshu, 1995), chap. 9, passim.
38. On Liu Bingzhong's role in the building of Shangdu and his design of the city, see *YS*, 4: 60; 58: 1350; 157: 3693. Cf. Chan, "Liu Bingzhong", p. 127, notes 58, 59. Among several important studies of Shangdu are Ishida Mikinosuke, "Gen no Jōtō nit suite" (revised), in *Nihon Daigaku sōritsu shichijunen kinen rombunshu*, Vol. I (October 1960), pp. 271–239; Jia Zhoujie, "Yuan Shangdu diaozha baokao", *Wenwu*, 5 (1977), pp. 65–74; Chen and Shi, *Yuan Shangdu* (1988); and Ye, *Yuan Shangdu yanjiu* (1998); and Ye and Qimudedaoerji, eds., *Yuan Shangdu yanjiu lunwenji* (2003).
39. On the evolution of the *hutong* in Ming and Qing Peking, see (Cao) Ersi, "Beijing hutong congta", in *Beijing shi yanjiu tongxun zengkan* (Beijingshi yanjiuhui, 1981), pp. 45–86; Weng, *Beijing de hutong*, chaps. 2–3; and Zhang, *Hutong qi qita*, pp. 77–83. See also note 30 above. On the Tibetans' adoption of the Indian 360-day system, see Guan Dongsheng, op. cit., pp. 165–168.
40. Serruys, "Manuscript Version", pp. 35–36 (text); p. 47 (translation).
41. On Yongle's orders to transfer the civilians and wealthy households from different provinces to take up residence in Peking, see Chapter 2, note 33. See also Farmer, *Early Ming Government*, pp. 148–152.
42. For details, see Chapter 2, note 16.
43. Serruys, "Manuscript Version", p. 36 (text); p. 47 (translation).
44. Serruys, "Manuscript Version", pp. 36–37 (text); pp. 47–48 (translation).
45. The official record of the *jingnan* campaign compiled on the order of the Yongle emperor after the successful coup d'état against the Jianwen emperor is known as *Fengtian jingnan ji*. It was heavily doctored in favor of the Prince of Yan to lend justification to the campaign and legitimate his accession. For details, see the references cited in Chapter 2, note 8.
46. On the Ming official records on the alleged death of the Jianwen emperor, see *Fengtian jingnan ji zhu*, 4: 208; *MTZOSL*, 9 *xia*: 130; *MS*, 4: 66. Popular legends alleging that the dethroned emperor escaped in the disguise of a monk and lived out his natural years were propagated by various private histories about the Jianwen reign compiled during the sixteenth and seventeenth centuries. They include Zheng Xiao, *Jianwen xunguo ji*; Jiang Qing, *Jiangshi mishi* (1595); Tu Shufang (*jinshi* 1577), *Jianwen chaoye huibian* (1598); and Zhu Lu (1553–1632), *Jianwen shufa ni* (1621). There is sizeable literature on the Jianwen legends, which cannot be documented here, but see Meng Sen, "Jianwen xunguoshi kao", rpt. in Meng, *Ming Qingshi lunzhu*

jikan (Taibei: Shijie shuju, 1961), pp. 1–12; Lun Meng, "Jianwen xunguo kaoyi", *Furen xuezhi*, 3.2 (1932), pp. 1–62; and also Chan, "The Chien-wen, Yung-lo . . . Reign", in *The Cambridge History of China*, Vol. 7, Part 1, *The Ming Dynasty*, p. 203, note 39. The more recent work is Xu Zuosheng, "Jianwendi wangming hefang", rpt. in Xu, *Fanzha kaoshu lu* (Beijing Xueyuan, 2000), pp. 162–259. On the suicide of Sizong, the Chongzhen emperor, see briefly *MS*, 24: 335; Zhang Dexin and Tan Tianxing, *Chongzhen huangdi dazhuan* (Shengyang: Liaoning jiaoyu chubanshe, 1993), p. 393.

47. See *MTZOSL*, 9 *xia*: 135, 138; 10 *shang*: 145; 16: 294; 27: 499; 30: 539; 88: 1170; 89: 1179; see also *MS*, 5: 75; 6: 79, 81, 86. For a critical account of the events beginning from the purported death of the Jianwen emperor to the enthronement of the Prince of Yan, see Wang, *Fengtian jingnan ji zhu*, pp. 106–116. See also David B. Chan, *The Usurpation*, chap. 8.

48. Emperor Yongle personally commanded five major campaigns against the Eastern Mongol tribesmen led by Arughtai (?–1434) in 1410, 1414, 1422, 1423, and 1424. He died of illness during the last campaign at Yumuchuan north of Dolon, Inner Mongolia, in August 1242. See briefly *MS*, 6: 86–88, 91; 7: 93–94, 98, 100–104; 327: 8467–8469. For details, see D. Pokotilov, *History of the Eastern Mongols during the Ming Dynasty from 1368 to 1634*, translated by R. Lowenthal, Studia Serica Monographs, Series A, I (Chengtu: Western Union University of China, 1947), Part I, pp. 23–35; see also Shang, *Yongle huangdi*, pp. 195–206; Chao, *Ming Chengzu zhuan*, pp. 352–393. On Yongle's death, see *MTZOSL*, 273: 2469; MS, 7: 104; cf. Mote, "Chu Ti", in *DMB*, Vol. I, p. 355.

49. There are variations in modern folklore concerning Liu Bowen's building of Peking. See Arlington and Lewisohn, *In Search of Old Peking*, pp. 175–176, 338–339; Jin, *Beijing de chuanshuo*, pp. 3–8; Zhang and Li, *Beijing de chuanshuo*, pp. 1–5; Wang, *Beijing fenwu chuanshuo gushi xuan*, pp. 1–6; and *Beijing fengwu chuanshuo*, pp. 1–7. For details, see Chapter 2, passim.

50. See *Yinglie zhuan*, p. 89. Liu Ji was also alleged to be Liu Bingzhong's grandson in the anonymous late Qing novelette *Zai jingpao*, included in several modern editions of Liu Bowen's prophecy book *Shaobing ge*; cf. Chapter 2, notes 66, 92.

51. Werner, *Myths and Legends of China*, pp. 227–230. See also Verne Dyson, *Forgotten Tales of Ancient China* (Shanghai: The Commercial Press, 1927), pp. 202–203. The source of the story is not identified, presumably it was either derived from an oral account told to the author, or based on a written version collected by the author in Peking during the early Republican era. However, if the latter were the case, I have not been able to retrieve it. The cited phrases are from three paragraphs of the story that appeared in these pages of Werner's text.

52. In this new version of the legend, the episode of Liu Bowen's handing two sealed envelopes to the Prince of Yan was clearly a skillful recycling of popular stories in the late Ming and early Qing that had Liu leaving instructions to the Jianwen emperor in a sealed container to help him escape the Prince of Yan in the disguise of a Buddhist monk. See the references cited in Chapter 2, notes 64, 68.
53. Owen Lattimore, "A Mongol Legend of the Founding of Peking", *Central Asiatic Journal*, 23.3–4 (1979), pp. 237–239.
54. Serruys, "Manuscript Version", p. 30 (text); p. 40 (translation).
55. Serruys, "Manuscript Version", p. 32 (text); p. 43 (translation).
56. This is not unexpected because the building of Peking was not the central focus in the Mongolian legend, which was primarily concerned with the Mongol maternity of the Prince of Yan, and the struggle between the siblings (actually in real history between uncle and nephew) for the throne after the death of the dynastic founder.

Chapter 4

1. See *Beijing fengwu chuanshuo*, pp. 1–7; and Wang, *Beijing fengwu chuanshuo gushi xuan*, pp. 1–6.
2. *Beijing fengwu chuanshuo*, p. 7. This published version is based on the oral narrative of an elderly storyteller who performed at the "temple fair" in Pantaogong in Beijing. The narrative was transcribed in April 1961. For a description of the Pantao Palace see Tada Teiichi, *Beijing deming zhi*, translated by Zhang Zichen (Beijing: Shumuwenxian chubanshe, 1986), p. 89; Su, *Beijing Kaogu jicheng*, Vol. 3, pp. 1283–1285; and *Jinri Beijing*, Vol. II, p. 421. The shrine is located in the Dongbian Gate of present-day Beijing and is devoted to the worship of the legendary goddess Xiwangmu 西王母 (Queen Mother of the West). See also Naquin, *Peking: Temples and City Life*, pp. 426–427, 441, 628.
3. See Chapter 1, note 15; Chapter 2, note 94.
4. For studies on Shen Wansan's life and his family see the primary works of Shen Defu, "Cong Shen Wansan de zhuanjiziliao lun xiupu yu xungen", *Disijie Yazhouzupu xueshu yantaohui huiyijilu* (Taibei: Guoxue wenxianguan, 1989), pp. 403–536; and Gu Cheng, "Shen Wansan jiqi jiazu shijikao", *Lishi yanjiu*, 1991.1 (February), pp. 66–85. See also Wu Ren'an, "Mingchu Jiangnan shoufu Shen Wansan jili kaobian", *Suzhoudaxue xuebao* (*zhexue shehuikexue*), 1984.3 (September), pp. 118–119; Pan Qun, "Shen Wansan xingming jiguan kao", *Dongyue luncong*, 1992.5 (September), pp. 100–106; and Wang Ting, "Shen Wansan de zhenshijiashi jiqi chuanqi", *Jinan shixue*, 2 (December 2003), pp. 247–258. Wu Enpei has written a fictional account of Shen's life: *Jushang Shen Wansan* (Taiyuan: Beiyue wenyi chubanshe, 1997), but it has little historical value.

5. See Liu Yizheng, "Shen Wansan", *Shixue zazhi,* 1.2 (1929), pp. 1–3; see also Shen, "Cong Shen Wansan de zhuanji ziliao", pp. 416–420; and Wu Shiyong, "Shen Wansan bingfei shiming", *Shixue yuekan,* 2004.5 (May), pp. 123–125.
6. On the biographical records of Shen Fu, his son, his brother, and nephew see Liu Sanwu, *Liu Xiansheng Tanzhai shiwenji* (*SKCMCS* ed.), *xia,* 2b–3a; Wang Xing, *Banxuan ji* (*SKQS* ed.), 9: 16b–17a, 18b–24a; see also Mo Dan, *Wujiang zhi* (Taibei Chengwen, 1983), 12: 10b–11a; Ni Shimeng, *Wujiang xianzhi* (Chengwen, 1975), 56: 9a–10a; and Tao Xun et al., *Zhouzhuang zhenzhi* (*XXSKQS* ed.), 4 (*Renwu*): 15a–16a; 6 (*Zaji*): 1a–3b. The assumption that Shen Wansan died during the rule of Zhang Shicheng in Suzhou was based on *Wujiang zhi,* op. cit.; and *Wujiang xianzhi,* op. cit. Gu Cheng supported this view but Wang Ting expressed doubt and suggested that Shen lived into the early Ming. See Gu, "Shen Wansan jiqi jiazu shiji kao", pp. 67–76; and Wang, "Shen Wansan de zhenshi jiashi jiqi chuanqi", pp. 255–256.
7. See, in addition to Shen's biographical records cited in note 6, Huangfu Lu, *Jinfeng wenlue* (Ming manuscript), 6: 7b–8a; Huang Wei, *Pengchuang leigao* (*SKCMCS* ed.), 1 ("Fuyi ji"): 14a; Dong Gu, *Bili zacun, shang,* 10–11; and Kong Er, *Yunjiaoguan jitan* (*CSJC* ed.), pp. 7–8. See also Shen, "Cong Shen Wansan de zhuanji ziliao", pp. 426–434; and Pan Qun, "Shen Wanshan caifu laiyuan kao", pp. 89–91. On the rumor about Shen receiving the abandoned lands of the wealthy Lu and other families see Lang Ying, *Qixiu leigao,* 40: 584–585; Wang Qi, *Baishi huibian,* 173: 17a–17b; Zhu Guozhen, *Yongchuang xiaopin,* 17: 392; Mo Dan, *Wujiang zhi,* 7: 1a; and Tao Xun, *Zhouzhuang zhenzhi,* 4: 15a–15b, 6: 1a. See Shen, op. cit., pp. 478–490; and Wang, "Shen Wansan de zhenshi jiashi ji chuanqi", pp. 249–250.
8. For a collection of stories about Shen Wansan's wealth and other exploits see Chai E, *Fantianlu conggao* (Shanghai Zhonghua, 1936), 34: 18a–23b; Huang Zhigang, "Shen Wansan chuanshuo kao", *Dongfang zazhi,* 32.1 (January 1935), pp. 91–97; Qu Mi (Qu Duizhi), "*Yangheshi suibi*: Shen Wansan", *Zhonghe yuekan,* 4.6 (June 1943), pp. 82–84; and Qu Duizhi, *Renwu fengsu zhidu congtan, jia ji* (Hong Kong Longmen, 1968), pp. 181–187. On Shen's luxurious villa in his native place and the items of exotic treasures in his possession, some of which were later confiscated, see Huangfu Lu, *Jinfeng wenlue,* 5: 11a–11b; Lang Ying, *Qixiu leigao,* 8: 126–127; Wang Shizhen, *Jinyi zhi,* in *Jilu huibian,* 195: 3b–4a; Kong Er, *Yunjiaoguan jitan,* pp. 7–9; Tan Qian, *Zaolin zazu, zhi ji,* 11a; Chu Renhuo, *Jianhu ji* (*XXSKQS* ed.), *xu ji,* 4: 12a–12b; Mo Dan, *Wujiang zhi,* 7: 4a–4b; and Tao Xun, *Zhouzhuang zhenzhi,* 2: 23a. See also Shen, "Cong Shen Wansan de zhuanji", pp. 459–452; and Pan Qun, "Shen Wansan caifu laiyuan kao", pp. 87–89.
9. See Liu Sanwu, *Liu Xiangsheng Tanzhai shiwenji, xia,* 2b; Huang Wei,

Pengchuang leigao, 2: 14a; Wang Qi, *Baishi huibian*, 38: 2b; Mo Dan, *Wujiang zhi*, 7: 4a–4b; Ni Shimeng, *Wujiang xianzhi*, 56: 9a; and Tao Xun, *Zhouzhuang zhenzhi*, 4: 15b, 6: 3a. On Shen's alleged exile to Liaoyang see Du Mu, *Dugong tanzuan, xia*: 44; Wang Qi, *Baishi huibian*, 38: 2b–3a; Huangfu Lu, *Jinfeng wenlue*, 6: 7b–8a; and Xie Zhaozhi, *Wu zazu* (Zhonghua, 1959), 5: 133.

10. On the sources of Shen Wansan's alleged contributions to Ming Taizu in building the city of Nanking see Lang Ying, *Qixiu leigao*, 8: 126–127; Kong Er, *Yunjiaoguan jitan*, p. 12. They were adapted by Mao Qiling in *Mao Hanlinji*: *Shengchao tongshi shiyi ji* (*SKCMCS* ed.), 1: 4b–5a, biography of Empress Ma, and were repeated in Fu Weilin, *Mingshu*, 20: 243; and *MS*, 113: 3506–3507. For a critical reappraisal see Shen, "Cong Shen Wansan de zhuanji ziliao", pp. 454–458; and Wu, "Shen Wansan bingfei shiming", pp. 123–124. On Shen Wansan's alleged execution and confiscation of his estates and treasures see also notes 9, 13. Gu Xuewen's indictment and seizure of the Shen household properties are mentioned in Zhu Yuanzhang, *Nichen lu* (Beijing daxue chubanshe, 1991), 5: 301–304; Mo Dan, *Wujiang zhi*, 12: 10b–11a; and Ni Shimeng, *Wujiang xianzhi*, 56: 9a–10b. For details see Chen Gaohua, "Shen Wansan yu Lan Yu dang'an", in *Mingshi luncong*, edited by Wang Chunyu (Beijing: Zhongguo shehui kexue chubanshe, 1999), pp. 67–73; and Wang, "Shen Wansan de zhenshi jiashi jiqi chuanqi", pp. 247–259.

11. On these eerie episodes, especially Shen Wansan's acquisition of the "treasure-accumulating bowl", see Kong Er, *Yunjiaoguan jitan*, pp. 7–9; Xie Zhaozhi, *Wu zazu*, 3: 70; He Qiaoyuan, *Mingshan cang*: "Huozhi ji" 貨殖記, 2b–3a; Chu Renhuo, *Jianhu ji, yu ji* 餘集, 2: 5a–5b; and *Zhang Sanfeng xiansheng quanji* (Hangzhou guji, 1990), *fulu*, 1, pp. 329–330. See also Suzuki, "Chin Mansan setsuwa no bunseki", pp. 87–89; and Pan, "Shen Wansan caifu laiyuan kao", pp. 87–88. On the legend of Zhang Sanfeng and his putative works see Wong Siu Hon, *Investigations into the Authenticity of the Chang San-Feng Ch'üan-Chi* (Canberra: Australian National University Press, 1982).

12. On stories about Shen Wansen's contributions to building Nanking and the legend of the "treasure-accumulating bowl" see Lang Ying, *Qixiu leigao*, 8: 126–127; Xie Zhaozhi, *Wu zazu*, 3: 70; He Qiaoyuan, *Mingshan cang*: "Huozhi ji", 1a–1b; Zhang Dai, *Mingshi jique* (Taiwan Xuesheng, 1969), pp. 11–12; Zhou Hui, *Xu Jinling suoshi* (in *Jinling suoshi*), *shang*, 18a; Zhao Jishi, *Jiyuan jisuoji*, 10 ("Zhushuiji: ershi" 驅睡記 · 二氏): 3a–3b; and *MS*, 113: 3506–3507. On this episode in Nanjing folklore see Dong Zhiyong, ed., *Nanjing de chuanshuo* (Shanghai wenyi, 1984), pp. 96–97; and Gao and Shao, *Jinling shichao dihuangzhou*, pp. 124–128. For additional stories about the role of the "treasure-accumulating bowl" in combating evil creatures harassing the watergate of Nanking see note 32 below.

13. For some of Shen Wansan's confiscated treasures that went into the imperial depot and other places see Wang Qi, *Baishi huibian*, 173: 26a; Wang Shizhen, *Jinyi zhi*, in *Jilu huibian*, 195: 3b–4a; Zhu Guozhen, *Yongchuang xiaopin*, 17: 392; Jiang Yikui, *Chang'an kehua*, 2: 30; Zhou Hui, *Jinling suoshi* (Taibei Chengwen, 1983), 4: 2a; Tan Qian, *Zaolin zasu, zhi ji*, 11a; Ni Shimeng, *Wujiang xianzhi*, 56: 9a; and Tao Xun, *Zhouzhuang zhenzhi*, 6: 1b–2a.On the worship of Shen Wansan as the "Living God of Wealth" inside the White Cloud (Baiyun) Shrine and among the Peking residents see Ma, *Lao Beijing lüxing zhinan*, pp. 200, 202–203. On the history of this famous historic shrine dating back to the Yuan dynasty see Liu and Yu, *Dijing jingwu lue*, 3: 137–139; *QDRXJWK*, 94: 1575–1580. For modern impressions see Li Xiangdong, "Luetan Baiyun guan de xingshuai", in *Yanjing chunqiu*, edited by Beijingshi yanjiuhui (Beijing chubanshe, 1982), pp. 145–148; and Deng, *Zengbu Yanjing fengtu ji*, pp. 9–12.
14. See Appendices (4). The first part of this story, retitled "Xu Da yijian ding jingcheng" 徐達一箭定京城 (Xu Da's setting the site of the capital city with a single bowshot), was recently included in a collection of legends about the Forbidden City. See Li Min, ed., *Zìjin cheng chuanshuo* (Beijing: Jiefangjun chubanshe, 2002), pp. 6–8.
15. See Chapter 3, III, IV.
16. On the development of the historical Nanyuan see Wang Puzi, "Nanyuan jianzhi kaolue", *Zhonghe yuekan*, 5.9 (September 1944), pp. 19–32.
17. For these folk songs see *Qianli ju*, *Yu Woumiao*, *Chongzhen guanhua Tieguan tu*, *Shieryue guren ming*, and others. They are recorded in Li and Liu, *Zhongguo suqu zongmu gao*, Vol. I, pp. 86, 277; Vol. II, pp. 939, 1260. On these folk songs see also Chapter 2, note 97.
18. See Chapter 3, note 34.
19. On these episodes see "Yang Liulang de jian" 楊六郎的箭, included in *Datong minjian gushi jicheng*, ed., Datongshi Shidawenyi jicheng bangongshi (Datong: Shanxi Renmin chubanshe, 1989), p. 133; and Pan Yuxiu and Zheng Yuzhuo, eds., *Genzai Hongdong* (Beijing Zhongguo dang'an, 1998), pp. 228–231. They are cited in Zhao Shiyu, "Zuxian jiyi, jiayuan xiangzheng yu gunzu lishi—Shanxi Hongdong Dahuaishu chuanshuo jushi", *Lishi yanjiu*, 6.1 (February), pp. 52, 59.
20. For the biographies of Xu Da and Empress Xu see *MS*, 125: 3723; 113: 3509; see also their biographies by Edward L. Farmer, and Chou Tao-chi and Ray Huang in *DMB*, Vol. I, pp. 556–569; 60–67. For an account of the early years of the Prince of Yan see *MS*, 2: 24; 5: 69; and Mote, "Chu Ti", in *DMB*, Vol. I, pp. 355–357. See also Shang, *Yongle huangdi*, pp. 14–22; and Chao, *Ming Chengzu zhuan*, pp. 25–30.
21. For a note on the Houmen Bridge, now located in the Di'anmen waidajie of the Xicheng district of Beijing, see *Jinri Beijing*, Vol. II, pp. 550–551. See also

Li, *Mingdai Beijing ducheng yingjian congkao*, pp. 308–309. The rear walled gate of the imperial-city was known as Bei'anmen in the Ming and Di'anmen in the Qing. On the representations of Shicha Sea and Houmen Bridge in the Nezha City legend see Arlington and Lewisohn, *In Search of Old Peking*, p. 339.

22. See Lin Yutang, *Imperial Peking, Seven Centuries of China* (New York: Crown Publishers, 1961), p. 165.
23. See Appendices (4).
24. For details of the stories of Nezha's fierce confrontation with the Dragon King and his sons in the Eastern Sea in the *Fengshen yanyi* and the *Xiyou ji* see Chapter 1, notes 67, 68.
25. For graphic presentations of some of the "supernatural scarecrows" in monuments and buildings in the Forbidden City see Yu, *Zijin cheng gongdian* (1982); and Yan, *Beijing*, passim. For a scholarly study on the dragon motifs in architectural decorations in imperial Peking see Lou Qingxi, "Long de shijie—Zijincheng zhong longwen zhuangshi de yingyong", rpt. in *Zijin cheng yingshanji*, pp. 254–273.
26. See Jin, *Beijing de chuanshuo*, pp. 9–16; Yang, *Beijing Legends*, pp. 24–31.
27. On the Gaoliang River and the Gaoliang Bridge see *Xijin zhi*, p. 96; Jiang Yikui, *Chang'an kehua* 3: 45–46; Liu and Yu, *Dijing jingwu lue* 5: 191–195; *QDRXJWK*, 98: 1625–1639. For modern studies see Chang Zheng, "Jingcheng hechu Gaolianghe", *Shiyuan*, Vol. 1 (Beijing: Wenhua yishu chubanshe, 1982), pp. 35–43; Cai, *Beijing guyunhe*, pp. 35–39; and Hou, *Hou Renzhi jiang Beijiing*, pp. 75–82.
28. For modern impressions of the Gaoliang Bridge see Ma, *Lao Beijing lüxing zhinan*, p. 209; *Jinri Beijing*, Vol. II, p. 297; and Deng, *Zengbu Yanjing fengtu ji*, pp. 93–95.
29. See Appendices (4).
30. See Jin, *Beijing de chuanshuo*, pp. 9–16; Yang, *Beijing Legends*, pp. 24–31.
31. On the water supply problem and quality of water in Peking during the past centuries which provide the basis for the popular legend under discussion see Chapter 2, note 32. See also Wang and Ren, *Beijing huanjing shihua*, pp. 94–100; Duan Tianshun, *Yanshui gujintan* (Beijing Yanshan, 1991), pp. 1–56. For comments on the effect on Peking residents see Qiu Zhonglin, "Shuiwouzi: Beijing de gongshui yezhe yu minsheng yongshui (1368–1937)", pp. 220 284.
32. For details on Shen Wansan's "treasure-accumulating bowl" see note 12 above. On the story of Ming Taizu employing the magical treasure bowl to fend off the dragon-like sea creatures see Song Changbai, *Liuting shihua*, quoted *in Yu Yue, Chaxiangshi congchao* (*XXSKQS* ed.), 20: 2a–2b; and Chai E, *Fantienlu conggao*, 34: 18b. The current *Liuting shihua*, 32 *juan*, in *XXSKQS*, Vol. 1700, does not contain this reference. According to Lang Ying, who

reports an incident of disturbance caused by a creature known as *zhu(po)long* along the river bank of Nanking that often caused inundation, and the way to catch it, it was identified as a *tuo* 鼉, probably a member of the crocodile family, commonly known as Yangzi crocodile. See Lang Ying, *Qixiu leigao,* 12: 188–89. See also Suzuki, "Chin Mansan", pp. 18–20.

33. For a note on the Beixinqiao and the Jingzhongmiao see *Beijing simiao lishi ziliao,* pp. 129, 475–476. Note there is another Jingzhongmiao, this one built in the Ming, located at Jingzhongmiao Street in Qianmen. The two should not be confused. On the latter see pp. 181, 589. For more detailed descriptions of the two temples in the 1930s see Ma, *Lao Beijing lüxing zhinan,* pp. 73–74.
34. On this story see Jin, *Beijing de chuanshuo,* pp. 17–30; cf. Yang, *Beijing Legends,* pp. 32–36; and for a shorter version see Zhang and Li, *Beijing de chuanshuo,* pp. 57–61. An earlier version of the "North New Bridge" story, without identifying Liu Bowen and Yao Guangxiao, appears in Arlington and Lewisohn, *In Search of Old Peking,* p. 176. It should be noted that an anecdote about a "dragon" being trapped under the well which could never come out because of the name change of the bridge was already reported in a gossip column in a certain issue of the Peking newspaper *Shuntian shibao* 順天時報 in the 1920s, attesting to the earlier origin of the story. This is quoted in Chen, *Yandu congkao,* pp. 299–300.
35. See Appendices (5).
36. On this campaign see briefly *MTZUSL,* 252: 3641–3642; 253: 3641–3642; and *MS,* 327: 8466–8467. See also Pokotilov, *History of the Eastern Mongols,* pp. 14–15; Shang, *Yongle huangdi,* pp. 23–25; and Chao, *Ming Chengzu zhuan,* pp. 31–33.
37. Werner, *Myths and Legends of China,* pp. 227–230.
38. For details of the historical geography of the Tanzhe Monastery see Shen Mude, *Tanzheshan Xiuyunsi zhi, in Zhongguo Fosizhi huikan,* edited by Du Jiexiang, 1st ser., Vol. 44 (Taibei: Mingwen shuju, 1980), 1: 1a–16a; and Zhao Runxing and Yang Baosheng, *Tanzhesi* (Beijing Yanshan, 1986), passim. See also briefly *QDRXJWK,* 105: 1743–1749. For modern studies see Tong, *Fojiao yu Beijing shimiao wenhua,* pp. 38–57. See also Ma, *Lao Beijing lüxing zhinan,* pp. 186–187; and Deng, *Zengbu Yanjing fengtu ji,* pp. 297–299.
39. See Shen Mude, *Tanzheshan Xiuyunsi zhi*; Zhao and Yang, *Tanzhesi,* passim.
40. See Yao Guangxiao's biographies cited in Chapter 1, note 15; Chapter 2, note 94.
41. See Appendices (5).
42. On the forced migration of these wealthy households from northwest and southwest China to reside in Peking see the references cited in Chapter 2, note 33. On the requisition and transportation of construction materials see briefly Yu, *Zijin cheng gongdian* (2002), pp. 7–14.

43. For a survey of this folkloric motif in reference to Shen Wansan, see Lü Wei, *Yinyu shijie de laifangzhe—Zhongguo minjian caishen xinyang* (Beijing Xueyuan, 2001), pp. 220–228.
44. Zhu Yuanzhang was known to have an ingrained hatred for the powerful rich landowners and had resorted to extreme measures to liquidate them. Several of the alleged "high treason" cases involved wealthy people; the case of Shen Wansan's banishment for implication in Lan Yu's sedition and rebellion was only one of them. See briefly Wu Han, *Zhu Yuanzhang zhuan*, rev. ed. (Beijing Renmin, 1994), pp. 172–186; and more fully Chen Gaohua, "Shen Wansan yu Lan Yu dang'an", passim. For stories about Shen deriving his wealth from hidden treasures or leaving his treasures hidden underground see Huang Wei, *Pengchuang leiji*, 3: 1a–1b; Wang Qi, *Baishi huibian*, 38: 2b–3a, 173: 17a–17b; and Xie Zhaozhi, *Wu zazu*, 5: 133.
45. On these folktales about Shichahai see Jin, *Beijing de chuanshuo*, pp. 111–116; cf. Yang, *Beijing Legends*, pp. 49–53; and Zhang and Li, *Beijing de chuanshuo*, pp. 57–61.
46. On the Shicha Sea see Liu and Yu, *Dijing jingwu lue*, 1: 39–40; and Jiang Yikui, *Chang'an kehua*, 1: 12–17. On its changing names and its historical role for Peking see Wang and Ren, *Beijing huanjing shihua*, pp. 70–73; and Hou, *Hou Renzhi jiang Beijing*, pp. 88–100. For further information on its historical development, water resources utilization, and transportation, as well as recent development, see Hou Renzhi et al., eds., *Shichahai zhi* (Beijing chubanshe, 2003), Parts I and II, relevant chapters.
47. On the origin of the Jinyuchi see Liu and Yu, *Dijing jingwu lue*, 3: 102–103; *QDRXJWK*, 39: 943–944. The pond was situated to the southeast of Chongwenmen, north of the Altar of Heaven. It was made up of a number of small ponds superb for rearing goldfish; it was filled by the water flowing from the Hucheng Canal in the south through the connecting ditch known as Longxugou 龍須溝 which ran around the Altar of Heaven and the famed Heavenly Bridge. For a detailed account see Zhang Cixi, *Renmin shoudu de Tianqiao* (Beijing: Xiugengtang shudian, 1951), pp. 55–58.
48. For a study of the Hucheng Canal surrounding the Forbidden City see Shi Zhimin and Chen Yinghua, "Zijin cheng huchenghe ji weifang yange kao", in Yu, *Zijin cheng jianzhu yanjiu yu baohu*, pp. 229–239.
49. On this topic see Serruys, "A Note on Arrows and Oaths among the Mongols", pp. 287–288; and Chan, "Siting by Bowshot", pp. 54–55, note 2.
50. On the building of the imperial city of Nanking see Chapter 2, note 6.
51. On the construction of Zhongdu in Fengyang see *MTZUSL*, 45: 880; 99: 1685; *MS*, 2: 23, 30, 40, 912. For details see Wang Jianying, *Ming Zhongdu*, Part 4; *Fengyang gujin*, edited by Wu Tingmei and Xia Yurun (Hefei: Huangshan shushe, 1986), chap. 3. Liu Ji was one of Taizu's senior officials who advised against designating Fengyang as the national capital. Late in

1368, before retiring, he pleaded with the emperor: "Even though Fengyang is your majesty's native place, it should not be made into a capital." See *MS*, 128: 3780, based on Huang Bosheng, "Chengyibo Liugong xingzhuang", in Liu Ji, *Chengyibo Liu Wencheng gong wenji*, p. 8a. On Fengyang as an aspect of Taizu's geopolitical strategy see Farmer, *Early Ming Government*, pp. 455–451; and also Steinhardt, *Imperial City Planning*, pp. 66–69.

52. Excerpted in *Fengyang gujin*, pp. 206–207. The source has not been identified.

Epilogue

1. See Meyer, *The Dragons of Tiananmen*, p. 122.
2. See Dong, *Republican Beijing*, pp. 11–12. Excellent illustrations of such cultural activities in old Peking and new Beijing can be found in Deng Yunxiang, *Zengbu Yanjing fengtu ji* (1982), two volumes, and in several other volumes of his miscellaneous writings. Deng, who died in 1998 in his late seventies, was a long-time resident of Peking and a prolific writer of life and culture in the old capital city. It is a surprise that Deng's very scholarly writings are not cited in Dong's book.

Bibliography

Chinese Language

(a) Traditional Works

Ban Gu 班固. *Hanshu* 漢書. Beijing: Zhonghua shuju, 1962.

Bukong 不空, trans. *Beifang Pishamen tianwang suijun hufa yigui* 北方毘沙門天王隨軍護法儀軌. In *TSD*, No. 1247.

———, trans. *Pishamen yigui* 毘沙門儀軌. In *TSD*, No. 1249.

Cao Canfang 曹參芳. *Xunguo zhengqi ji* 遜國正氣紀. In *SKCMCS: shibu* 史部, Vol. 59. Tainanxian. Taiwan: Zhuangyan wenhuashiye youxiangongsi, 1996.

Cao Chen 曹臣. *Shehua lu* 舌華錄. Changsha: Yuelu shushe, 1985.

Changgu Zhenyi 長谷真逸. *Nongtian yuhua* 農田餘話. In *Baoyantang miji* 寶顏堂祕笈, *guang ji* 廣集, edited by Chen Jiru 陳繼儒, 1922.

Chen Huai 陳槐. *Wenjian manlu* 聞見漫錄. In *Siming congshu* 四明叢書, ser. 4, edited by Zhang Shouyong 張壽鏞, 1936.

Chen Ji 陳基. *Yibaizhai gao* 夷白齋稿. *SKQS* ed. Shanghai: Shanghai guji chubanshe, 1987.

Chen Menglai 陳夢雷, comp. *Gujintushu jicheng* (*Bowu huibian, Yishu dian, Shenyi dian*) 古今圖書集成(博物彙編，藝術典，神異典). Shanghai: Zhonghua shuju, 1934.

Chen Qingling 陳慶齡 and Tong Fan 童範, eds. *Linchuan xianzhi* 臨川縣志, 1870.

Cheng Minzheng 程敏政. *Song yimin lu* 宋遺民錄. In *SKCMCS: shibu*, Vol. 88.

Cheng Sigong 程嗣功 and Wang Yihua 王一化, eds. (*Wanli*) *Yingtian fuzhi* 萬曆應天府志. In *SKCMCS: shibu*, Vol. 203.

Chu Renhuo 褚人獲. *Jianhu ji* 堅瓠集. In *XXSKQS*, Vols. 1260–1262. Shanghai: Shanghai guji chubanshe, 1995.

Da Tang San Zang qujing shihua 大唐三藏取經詩話. Beijing: Wenxue gudian kanxingshe, 1954.

Dai Lu 戴璐. *Tengyin zaji* 藤陰雜記. Beijing: Beijing guji chubanshe, 1981.

Daofa huiyuan 道法會元. In *Zhengtong Daozang* 正統道藏, edited by Baiyunguan Changchun zhenren 白雲觀長春真人, Vol. 51. Taibei: Xinwenfeng chubangongsi, 1988.

Daoyuan 道原. *Jingde chuandeng lu* 景德傳燈錄. In *TSD*, No. 2076.

Dayue shanren 大嶽山人 (pseudo.). *Jianwen huangdi shiji beiyi lu* 建文皇帝事跡備遺錄 (also titled *Jianwen yiji* 遺跡). Taibei: Taiwan Xuesheng shuju, 1969.

Dong Gu 董穀. *Bili zacun* 碧里雜存. In *CSJC*, Vol. 2911. Shanghai: Shanwu yinshuguan, 1937.

Dong Zhongshu 董仲舒. *Chunqiu fanlu* 春秋繁露. *SBBY* ed.

Du Mu 都穆. *Dugong tanzuan* 都公談纂. In *CSJC*, Vol. 2899. Shanghai: Shangwu yinshuguan, 1937.

Fan Qin 范欽. *Suiyan* 隨言. In *Guangcang xuejiong congshu* 廣倉學窘叢書, *jialei* 甲類, lst ser., compiled by Ji Fotuo 姬佛陀 (i.e. Ji Juemi 姬覺彌), 1916.

Fan Ye 范曄, *Hou Hanshu* 後漢書. Beijing: Zhonghua shuju, 1965.

Fang Xuanling 房玄齡 et al. *Jinshu* 晉書. Beijing: Zhonghua shuju, 1974.

Fatian 法天 (Faxian 法賢). *Foshuo zuishang mimi nanatian jing* 佛說最上秘密那拏天經. In *TSD*, No. 1288.

(*Foshuo*) *Beidou qixing yanming jing* (佛說) 北斗七星延命經. In *TSD*, No. 1307.

Fotuo Yeshe 佛陀耶舍 and Zhu Fonian 竺佛念, trans. *Foshuo Chang Ahan jing* 佛說長阿含經. In *TSD*, No. 1.

Fu Weilin 傅維鱗. *Mingshu* 明書. Shanghai: Shangwu yinshuguan, 1936.

Ge Yinliang 葛寅亮. *Jinling fancha zhi* 金陵梵刹志. In *XXSKQS*, Vols. 718–719.

Gu Qiyan 顧起元. *Kezuo zhuiyu* 客座贅語. Beijing: Zhonghua shuju, 1987.

Gu Yanwu 顧炎武. *Changping shanshui ji* 昌平山水記. Beijing: Beijing guji chubanshe, 1982.

Gu Zuyu 顧祖禹. *Dushi fangyu jiyao* 讀史方輿紀要. Beijing: Zhonghua shuju, 1955.

Guoqu xianzai yinguo jing 過去現在因果經. In *TSD*, No. 189.

He Qiaoyuan 何喬遠. *Mingshan cang* 名山藏. Taibei: Chengwen chubanshe, 1970.

Hong Mai 洪邁. *Yijian zhi* 夷堅志. Beijing: Zhonghua shuju, 1981.

Hongwu jing cheng tuzhi 洪武京城圖志 (Preface 1395). Compiled by early Ming Ministry of Rites. Rpt. of Hongzhi 弘治 (1488–1505) edition. Nanjing: Zhongshe, 1929.

Huang Wei 黃暐. *Pengchuang leiji* 蓬窗類紀. In *SKCMCS*: *zibu* 子部, Vol. 251.

Huang Zongxi 黃宗羲; Quan Zuwang 全祖望, amended. *Song Yuan xue'an* 宋元學案. In *XXSKQS*, Vols. 518–519.

Huang Zuo 黃佐. *Gechu yishi* 革除遺事. In *Jinsheng yuzhen ji* 金聲玉振集, edited by Yuan Jiong 袁褧. *SKCMCS*: *shibu*, Vol. 47.

Huangfu Lu 皇甫錄. *Jinfeng wenlue* 近峰聞略. 8 *juan*. Ming manuscript (Preface 1543). Taibei: National Library.

Huitu Sanjiao yuanliu Soushen daquan 繪圖三教源流搜神大全. Undated Ming manuscript. Taibei: Lianjing chubanshiye gongsi, 1980.

Ji Liuqi 計六奇. *Mingji beilue* 明季北略. Beijing: Zhonghua shuju, 1984.

Jiang Pingjie 蔣平階. "*Pingsha Yuchi* bianwei" 平砂玉尺辨偽. In *Dili bianzheng shu* 地理辨正疏; subcommentary by Zhang Xinyan 張心言, 1863.

Jiang Yikui 蔣一葵. *Chang'an kehua* 長安客話. Beijing: Beijing guji chubanshe, 1982.

Jiao Hong 焦竑, ed. *Guochao xianzheng lu* 國朝獻徵錄. Taibei: Taiwan Xuesheng shuju, 1965.

Jijiaye 吉迦夜 and Tan Yao 曇曜, trans. *Zabaozang jing* 雜寶藏經. In *TSD*, No. 192.

Jin Shan 金善 (Youzi 幼孜). *Jin Wenjing gong ji* 金文靖公集. *SKQS* ed.

Kong Er· 孔邇. *Yunjiaoguan jitan* 雲蕉館紀談. In *CSJC*, Vols. 2952–2954. Changsha: Shangwu yinshuguan, 1937.

Kong Qi 孔齊. *Zhizheng zhiji* 至正直記. Shanghai: Shanghai guji chubanshe, 1987.

Konggu daoren 空谷道人. *Xiuxiang Yongle dingding quanzhi Xu Yinglie zhuan* 繡像永樂定鼎全誌續英烈傳. In *Guben Xiaoshuo congkan* 古本小説叢刊, 15th, lst ser. Beijing: Zhonghua shuju, 1991.

Lang Ying 郎瑛. *Qixiu leigao* 七修類稿; *xugao* 續稿. Beijing: Zhonghua shuju, 1959.

Lei Xi 雷銑 and Wang Fen 王棻, eds. *Qingtian xianzhi* 青田縣志, 1876.

Li Mingwan 李銘皖 and Feng Guifen 馮桂芬, eds. *Suzhou fuzhi* 蘇州府志 (1862) Taibei: Chengwu chubanshe, 1970.

Li Qing 李清. *Sanyuan suibi* 三垣隨筆. Beijing: Zhonghua shuju, 1982.

Li Shimian 李時勉. *Gulian wenji* 古廉文集. *SKQS* ed.

Li Tao 李燾. *Xu Zizhitongjian changbian* 續資治通鑑長編. Beijing: Zhonghua shuju, 1979–.

Li Xian 李賢. *Da Ming yitong zhi* 大明一統志 (1461). Taiyuan: San Qin chubanshe, 1990.

Li Zhi 李贄. *Xu Cangshu* 續藏書. Beijing: Zhonghua shuju, 1959.

Liang Yi 梁億. *Chuanxin lu* 傳信錄. In *Guochao moulie jiyi* 國朝謨略輯遺, edited by Zhu Dangmian 朱當㴐. 1553.

Liu An 劉安. *Huainan honglie jie* 淮南鴻烈解. *SBCK* ed.

Liu Bingzhong 劉秉忠. *Cangchun ji* 藏春集. *SKQS* ed.

———. *Juan dili canbu pinglin tujue quanbei Pingsha Yuchi jing* 鐫地理參補評林圖訣全備平沙玉尺經, 2 *juan, fuli* 附例 1 *juan*. Liu Ji 劉基 *zhu* 注, Lai Congqian 賴從謙 *zengshi* 增釋, Xu Zhimo 徐之鏌 *canbu* 參補. In *XXSKQS*, Vol. 1054.

———. *Shihan* 石函 *Pingsha Yuchi jing*, 6 *juan*, *houji* 後集, 4 *juan*. In *SKCMCS: bubian* 補編, Vol. 77. Jinan: Qilu shushe, 2001.

———. *Xinke* 新刻 *Shihan Pingsha Yuchi jing*, 6 *juan*. Li Feng 李峰 *zhujie* 注解. Haikou: Hainan chubanshe, 2003.

Liu Ji. *Chengyibo Liu Wencheng gong wenji* 誠意伯劉文成公文集. *SBCK* ed.

———. *Liu xiansheng "Jingui jin'nang"* 劉先生《金櫃錦囊》. Shanghai: n.p., 1897.

Liu Sanwu 劉三吾. *Liu xiansheng Tanzhai shiwen ji* 劉先生坦齋詩文集. In *SKCMCS: jibu* 集部, Vol. 25.

Liu Tong 劉侗 and Yu Yizheng 于弈正. *Dijing jingwu lue* 帝京景物略. Beijing: Beijing guji chubanshe, 1980.

Liu Xianting 劉獻廷. *Guangyang zazhi* 廣陽雜記. Beijing: Zhonghua shuju, 1957.

Liu Yingli 劉應李. *Da Yuan hunyi fangyu shenglan* 大元混一方輿勝覽, 3 *juan*.

Revised by Zhan Youliang 詹友諒. Edited by Guo Xingpo 郭聲波. Chengdu: Sichuan daxue chubanshe, 2003.

Lu Can 陸粲. *Gengsi bian* 庚巳編. Beijing: Zhonghua shuju, 1987.

Lu Xixing 陸西星 (?). *Fengshen yanyi* 封神演義. Beijing: Zuojia chubanshe, 1955.

Lü Buwei 呂不韋, ed. *Lushi chunqiu* 呂氏春秋. *SBBY* ed.

Lü Yanzhao 呂燕昭 and Yao Nai 姚鼐, eds. *Chongkan Jiangning fuzhi* 重刊江寧府志 (1811). Taibei: Chengwen chubanshe, 1974.

Mao Qiling 毛奇齡. *Mao Hanlin ji* 毛翰林集: *Shengchao tongshi shiyi ji* 勝朝彤史拾遺集. In *SKCMCS*: *shibu*, Vol. 122.

Mei Yingfa 梅應發 and Liu Xi 劉錫, eds. *Kaiqing Siming xuzhi* 開慶四明續志. In *XXSKQS*, Vol. 705.

Meicun yeshi 梅村野史 (pseudo.). *Luqiao jiwen* 鹿樵紀聞. In *Taiwan wenxian congkan* 臺灣文獻叢刊, No. 127. Taibei: Taiwan yinhang jingji yanjiushi, 1961.

(*Ming*) *Renzong shilu* (明) 仁宗實錄. Edited by Zhang Fu 張輔 et al. Taibei: Zhongyang yanjiuyuan lishiyuyan yanjiusuo, 1963.

(*Ming*) *Shizong shilu* 世宗實錄. Edited by Zhang Rong 張溶 et al. Taibei, 1965.

(*Ming*) *Taizong shihlu* 太宗實錄. Edited by Zhang Fu 張輔 et al. Taibei, 1963.

(*Ming*) *Taizu shilu* 太祖實錄. Edited by Yao Guangxiao 姚廣孝 et al. Taibei, 1962.

(*Ming*) *Xianzong shilu* 憲宗實錄. Edited by Zhang Mao 張懋 et al. Taibei, 1964.

(*Ming*) *Yingzong shilu* 英宗實錄. Edited by Sun Jizong 孫繼宗 et al. Taibei, 1963.

Mo Dan 莫旦, ed. (*Hongzhi*) *Wujiang zhi* (弘治) 吳江志 (1488). Taibei: Chengwen chubanshe, 1983.

Ni Shimeng 倪師孟 and Chen Xunxiang 陳荀纕, eds. *Wujiang xianzhi* 吳江縣志 (1747). Taibei: Chengwen chubanshe, 1975.

Nianchang 念常. *Fozu lidai tongzai* 佛祖歷代通載. In *TSD*, No. 2036.

Nie Chongyi 聶崇義. *Sanli tu jizhu* 三禮圖集注. *SKQS* ed.

Ouyang Xiu 歐陽修. *Xin Tangshu* 新唐書. Beijing: Zhonghua shuju, 1975.

Ouyang Xuan 歐陽玄. *Guizhai wenji* 圭齋文集. *SBCK* ed.

Puji 普濟. *Wudeng huiyuan* 五燈會元. Beijing: Zhonghua shuju, 1984.

Qian Qianyi 錢謙益. *Liechao shiji* 列朝詩集. 1652.

———. *Liechao shiji xiaozhuan* 列朝詩集小傳. Shanghai: Gudian wenxue chubanshe, 1959.

Qian Shuoyou 潛説友. *Xianchun Lin'an zhi* 咸淳臨安志. *SKQS* ed.

Sanjiao yuanliu Soushen daquan 三教源流搜神大全. Taibei: Lianjing chubanshiye kongsi, 1980.

Shangguan Zhou 上官周. *Wanxiaotang huazhuan* 晚笑堂畫傳 (1750). Beijing: Renmin meishu chubanshe, 1959.

Shen Defu 沈德符. *Wanlin yehuo bian* 萬曆野獲編. Beijing: Zhonghua shuju, 1959.

Shen Mude 神穆德, continued by Monk Yi'an 義庵. *Tanzheshan Xiuyunsi zhi* 潭柘

山岫雲寺志 (1878). In *Zhongguo fosi shizhi huikan* 中國佛寺史志彙刊, 1st ser., Vol. 44. Taibei: Mingwen shuju, 1980.

Siku shushulei congshu 四庫術數類叢書. Shanghai: Shanghai guji chubanshe, 1991–.

Siku shushulei daquan 四庫術數類大全. Haikou: Haikou chubanshe, 1993–.

Sima Qian 司馬遷. *Shiji* 史記. Beijing: Zhonghua shuju, 1959.

Song Changbai 宋長白. *Liuting shihua* 柳亭詩話. In *XXSKQS*, Vol. 1700.

Song Lei 宋雷. *Xiwu liyu* 西吳里語. In *Shiyuan congshu* 適園叢書, 6th ser., edited by Zhang Junheng 張鈞衡, 1916.

Song Lian 宋濂. *Song xueshi wenji* 宋學士文集. *SBCK* ed.

——— et al. *Yuanshi* 元史. Beijing: Zhonghua shuju, 1976.

Su Tianjue 蘇天爵. *Guo (Yuan) chao mingren shilue* 國(元)朝名人事略. Beijing: Zhonghua shuju, 1996.

———. *Zixi wengao* 滋溪文稿. Beijing: Zhonghua shuju, 1997.

———, ed. *Guochao (Yuan) wenlei* 國朝(元)文類. *SBCK* ed.

Sun Chengze 孫承澤. *Chunming mengyu lu* 春明夢餘錄. Hong Kong: Longmen shudian, 1965.

———. *Tianfu guangji* 天府廣記. Hong Kong: Longmen shudian, 1968.

Sun Jianai 孫家鼐 et al., eds. (*Qinding*) *Shujing tushuo* (欽定)書經圖說. 1905 ed.

Sun Zhilu 孫之騄. *Ershen yelu* 二申野錄. In *SKCMCS*: *shibu*, Vol. 56.

Taiwan Ririxinbao 臺灣日日新報, No. 176, Meiji 明治 31/12/3 (January 14 1899); No. 166, Meiji 31/11/20 (January 1 1899) (both Chinese edition).

Tan Qian 談遷. *Guoque* 國榷. Beijing: Guji chubanshe, 1958.

———. *Zaolin zazu* 棗林雜俎. 12 *juan*. In *SKCMCS*: *zibu*, Vol. 113.

Tanmuchen 曇無讖, trans. Ma Ming posha 馬鳴菩薩. *Fosuoxingzan jing* 佛所行讚經. In *TSD*, No. 192.

Tao Xun 陶煦, ed. *Zhouzhuang zhenzhi* 周莊鎮志 (1882). In *XXSKQS*, Vol. 717.

Tao Zongyi 陶宗儀. (*Nancun*) *Chuogeng lu* (南村)輟耕錄. Beijing: Zhonghua shuju, 1959.

Tuotuo 脫脫 et al. *Jinshi* 金史. Beijing: Zhonghua shuju, 1974.

———. *Liaoshi* 遼史. Beijing: Zhonghua shuju, 1975.

Wan Yan 萬言, ed. *Chongzhen changbian* 崇禎長編. Taibei: Taiwan Xuesheng shuju, 1985.

Wang Bi 王弼 and Kong Yingta 孔穎達 annotated. *Zhou Yi zhushu* 周易注疏. *SKQS* ed.

Wang Ji 王紀 et al., comp. *Taiyue Taiheshan jilue* 太嶽太和山紀略, 1744 ed.

Wang Liumen 王柳門. *Jianqingshi suibi* 劍青室隨筆. In *Nanjing wenxian* 南京文獻, ser. 2. Nanjing: Nanjingshi wenxian weiyuanhui, 1947.

Wang Mi 王泌. *Dongchao ji* 東朝記. In *Baicheng* 稗乘, edited by Sun You'an 孫幼安, Vol. 8. Taibei: Yiwen yinshuguan, 1967.

Wang Qi 王圻, ed. *Baishi huibian* 稗史彙編. Taibei: Xinxing shuju, 1969.

———. *Sancai tuhui* 三才圖會. Taibei: Chengwen chubanshe, 1970.

Wang Shizhen 王世貞. *Mingqing jiji* 名卿績紀. In *Jilu huibian* 紀錄匯編, edited by Shen Jiefu 沈節甫, *juan* 99–100. Changsha: Shangwu yinshuguan, 1938.

——. *Jinyi zhi* 錦衣志. In *Jilu huibian, juan* 195.

Wang Tonggui 王同軌. *Leizeng Ertan* 類增耳談. In *XXSKQS*, Vol. 1268.

Wang Wenlu 王文祿. *Longxing ciji* 龍興慈記. In *Jilu huibian, juan* 13.

Wang Xing 王行. *Banxuan ji* 半軒集. *SKQS* ed.

Wu Changyuan 吳長元. *Chenyuan shilue* 宸垣識略. Beijing: Beijing guji chubanshe, 1981.

Wu Cheng'en 吳承恩. *Xiyou ji* 西遊記. Beijing: Zuojia chubanshe, 1954.

Xiao Xun 蕭洵. *Gugong yilu* 故宮遺錄. In *SKCMCS*: *shibu*, Vol. 166.

Xie Jin 解縉, ed. *Tianhuang yudie* 天潢玉牒. In *Jilu huibian, juan* 12.

Xie Zhaozhe 謝肇淛. *Wu zazu* 五雜俎. Beijing: Zhonghua shuju, 1959.

Xijin zhi jiyi 析津志輯佚. Edited by Rare Book Reconstruction Committee. Beijing: Beijing guji chubanshe, 1983.

Xu Shanji 徐善繼 and Xu Shanshu 徐善述. *Renzi xuzhi zixiao dilixue tongzong* 人子須知資孝地理學統宗 (1564; 1583 reprint). In *Gugong zhenben congkan* 故宮珍本叢刊, Vol. 411. Haikou: Hainan chubanshe, 2000.

Xu Wei 徐渭(?), ed. *Yunhe qizong* 雲合奇縱 (Preface 1616).

Yang Rong 楊榮. *Wenmin ji* 文敏集. *SKQS* ed.

Yang Weizhen 楊維楨. *Tieya guyuefu* 鐵崖古樂府. *SBCK* ed.

Yang Yi 楊儀. *Gaopo yizuan* 高坡異纂. In *Shuoku* 說庫, edited by Wang Wenru 王文濡. Taibei: Xinxing shuju, 1964.

Yao Guangxiao 姚廣孝. *Taoxu leigao* 逃虛類稿. Qing manuscript. Nanjing: Nanjing Municipal Library.

——. *Taoxuzi shiji* 逃虛子詩集. Qing manuscript. Tokyo: Tōyō Bunko.

Yao Tongshou 姚桐壽. *Yuejiao siyu* 樂郊私語. *SKQS* ed.

Ye Ziqi 葉子奇. *Caomu zi* 草木子. Beijing: Zhonghua shuju, 1959.

Yijing 義淨, trans. *Fo wei Hailongwang shuofa yin jing* 佛為海龍王說法印經. In *TSD*, No. 599.

Yongrong 永瑢 et al. *Siku quanshu zongmu tiyao* 四庫全書總目提要. Taibei: Taiwan Shangwu yinshuguan, 1965.

Yu Minzhong 于敏中 et al., eds. *Qinding Rixia jiuwen kao* 欽定日下舊聞考. Beijing: Zhonghua shuju, 1981.

Yu Shenxing 于慎行. *Gushan bizhu* 穀山筆麈. Beijing: Zhonghua shuju, 1984.

Yu Yue 俞樾. *Chaxiangshi congchao* 茶香室叢鈔. In *XXSKQS*, Vol. 1198.

Yuanwu Keqin 圓悟克勤. *Baiyuan lu* 碧嚴錄 (*Foguoyuanwu chanshi Biyan lu* 佛果圓悟禪師碧嚴錄). In *TSD*, No. 2003.

Zanning 贊寧. *Song Gaoseng zhuan* 宋高僧傳. In *TSD*, No. 2061.

——. (*Da Song*) *Sengshi lue* (大宋) 僧史略. In *TSD*, No. 2126.

Zengyi Ahan jing 增一阿含經. In *TSD*, No. 125.

Zha Jizuo 查繼佐. *Zuiwei lu* 罪惟錄. *SBCK*, 3rd ser. ed.

Zhang Bo 張勃. *Wu lu* 吳錄. In *Taiping yulan* 太平御覽, edited by Li Fang 李昉 et al., *juan* 156. Beijing: Zhonghua shuju, 1960.

Zhang Dai 張岱. *Mingshi jique* 明史紀闕. Taibei: Taiwan Xuesheng shuju, 1969.

———. *Taoan mengyi* 陶庵夢憶. Shanghai: Shanghai guji chubanshe, 1982.

Zhang Ertian 張爾田. *Menggu jiapu* 蒙古家譜, 1939.

Zhang Han 張翰. *Songchuang mengyu* 松窗夢語. Beijing: Zhonghua shuju, 1985.

Zhang Jue 張爵. *Jingshi wucheng fangxiang wutong ji* 京師五城坊巷衙衕集. Beijing: Beijing chubanshe, 1982.

Zhang Sanfeng 張三丰. *Zhang Sanfeng quanji* 張三丰全集. Hangzhou: Zhejiang guji chubanshe, 1990.

Zhang Tingyu 張廷玉 et al. *Mingshi* 明史. Beijing: Zhonghua shuju, 1974.

Zhang Yu 張昱. *Zhang Guangbi shiji* 張光弼詩集. *SBCK xubian* 續編 ed.

Zhang Zhidong 張之洞 and Miao Quansun 繆荃蓀 et al., eds. *Shuntian fuzhi* 順天府志, 1885.

Zhao Jishi 趙吉士. *Jiyuan jisuoji* 寄園寄所寄. In *XXSKQS*, Vols. 1196–1197.

Zheng Sixiao 鄭思肖. *Xinshi* 心史. Shanghai: Zhina neixueyuan, 1933.

Zheng Xiao 鄭曉. *Huang Ming mingchen ji* 皇明名臣記. In *Wuxue bian* 吾學編, *juan* 31; *XXSKQS*, Vol. 424.

———. *Jinyan* 今言. Shanghai: Zhonghua shuju, 1984.

Zheng Xuan 鄭玄 and Jia Kongyan 賈公彥, annotated. *Zhouli zhusuo* 周禮注疏. *SKQS* ed.

Zhiqian 支謙, trans. *Longwang xiongdi jing* 龍王兄弟經. In *TSD*, No. 597.

Zhou Hui 周暉. *Jinling suoshi* 金陵瑣事 (includes *Xu* 續 *Jinling suoshi*). Beijing: Wenwu guji Kanxingshe, 1955.

Zhou Nanrui 周南瑞, ed. *Tianxia tongwen ji* 天下同文集. *SKQS* ed.

Zhu Changwen 朱長文. *Wujun tujing xuji* 吳郡圖經續記. *SKQS* ed.

Zhu Guozhen 朱國禎. *Yongchuang xiaopin* 湧幢小品. Beijing: Zhonghua shuju, 1959.

Zhu Haihu 竺海護, trans. *Foshuo Hailongwang jing* 佛說海龍王經. In *TSD*, No. 598.

Zhu Xi 朱熹. *Zhuzi yulei* 朱子語類, edited by Li Jingde 黎靖德. Taibeixian: Hanjing wenhuashiye youxiangongsi, 1980.

Zhu Yizun 朱彝尊. *Baoshuting ji* 曝書亭集. *SKQS* ed.

———. *Jingzhiju shihua* 靜志居詩話. In *XXSKQS*, Vol. 1698.

Zhu Yuanzhang 朱元璋 (Ming Taizu). *Ming Taizu yuzhi wenji* 明太祖御製文集. Taibei: Taiwan Xuesheng shuju, 1964.

———. *Nichen lu* 逆臣錄. Beijing: Beijing daxue chubanshe, 1991.

Zhu Yunming 祝允明. *Yeji* 野記. In *CSJC*, Vol. 2801. Shanghai: Shangwu yinshuguan, 1936.

Zhuge Liang 諸葛亮. *Zhuge Liang ji* 諸葛亮集. Beijing: Zhonghua shuju, 1960.

Zou Yi 鄒漪. *Mingji yiwen* 明季遺聞. In *XXSKQS*, Vol. 442.

(b) Modern Works

Anonymous. *Zai jinpao* 再錦袍. Rpt. in *Liu Bowen Shaobing ge* (*quanben*) 劉伯溫燒餅歌 (全本), pp. 1–19. Hong Kong: Da'nan chubanshe, 1976?

Anonymous, ed. *Zhongguo yuyan qizhong* 中國預言七種. Chengdu, Sichuan, n.d., Copy kept at Sichuan Provincial Library, Chengdu.

———. *Zhongguo erqian'nian (qian) zhi yuyan* 中國二千年 (前) 之預言. Shanghai: Huaxia zheli chanweishe, 1937 (?); Hong Kong reprint, n.d.

Bai Tiezheng 白鐵錚. *Lao Beiping de gudianer* 老北平的古典兒. Taibei: Huilong chubanshe, 1977.

Beijing baikequanshu: caitu, dituji 北京百科全書：彩圖、地圖集. Beijing: Aolinpike chubanshe, 1991.

Beijing fengwu chuanshuo 北京風物傳說. Edited by Zhongguo minjian wenyi yanjiuhui, Beijing fenhui 中國民間文藝研究會北京分會. Beijing: Zhongguo minjian wenyi chubanshe, 1983.

Beijing lishi jinian 北京歷史紀年. Compiled by Compilation Committee, Beijingshi shehui kexue yanjiu suo. Beijing: Xinhua shudian, 1984.

Beijing shi 北京史. Compiled by Department of History, Peking University. Beijing: Beijing chubanshe, 1985.

Beijing simiao lishi ziliao 北京寺廟歷史資料. Compiled by Beijingshi Dang'anguan. Beijing: Zhongguo dang'an chubanshe, 1997.

Cai Fan 蔡蕃. *Beijing guyunhe yu chengshi gongshui yanjiu* 北京古運河與城市供水研究. Beijing: Beijing chubanshe, 1987.

(Cao) Ersi (曹) 爾泗. "Beijing hutong congtan" 北京胡同叢談. *Beijing shi yanjiu tongxun zengkan* 北京史研究通訊增刊, pp. 45–86. Beijing: Beijingshi yanjiuhui. 1981.

Cao Zixi 曹子西, ed., with various authors for 10 separate volumes. *Beijing tongshi* 北京通史. Beijing: Zhongguo shudian, 1994.

Chai E 柴萼. *Fantianlu conggao* 梵天廬叢稿. Shanghai: Zhonghua shuju, 1936.

Chang Zheng 常征. "Jingcheng hechu Gaoliangqiao" 京城何處高梁橋. *Shiyuan* 史苑, Vol. 1, pp. 35–43. Beijing: Wenhua yishu chubanshe, 1982.

Chao Zhongchen 晁中辰. *Ming Chengzu zhuan* 明成祖傳. Beijing: Renmin chubanshe, 1993.

Chen Gaohua 陳高華. *Yuan Dadu* 元大都. Beijing: Beijing chubanshe, 1982.

———. "Shen Wansan yu Lanyu dang'an" 沈萬三與藍玉黨案. In *Mingshi luncong* 明史論叢, edited by Wang Chunyu 王春瑜, pp. 67–73. Beijing: Zhongguo shehuikexue chubanshe, 1997.

——— and Shi Weimin 史衛民. *Yuan Shangdu* 元上都. Changchun: Jilin jiaoyu chubanshe, 1988.

Chen Hongping 陳鴻平. *Gudu fengwu* 故都風物. Taibei: Zhengzhong shuju, 1970.

Chen Naiqian 陳乃乾. *Yuanren Xiaolingji* 元人小令集. Beijing: Zhonghua shuju, 1962.

Chen Pingyuan 陳平原 and Wang Dewei 王德威, eds. *Beijing: Dushi xiangxiang yu wenhua jiyi* 北京：都市想像與文化記憶. Beijing: Beijing daxue chubanshe, 2005.

Chen Qingxiang 陳清香. "Nezha tuxiang yuanliu kao" 哪吒圖像源流考. In *Diyijie Nezha xueshu yantaohui lunwenji* 第一屆哪吒學術研討會論文集, pp. 91–116. Edited by Guoli Zhongshan daxue Qingdai xueshu yanjiuzhongxin 國立中山大學清代學術研究中心 and Xinying Taizigong guanli weiyuanhu 新營太子宮管理委員會. Tainan, Taiwan: Guoli Zhongshan daxue Qingdai xueshu yanjiuzhongxin, 2002.

Chen Ruheng 陳汝衡. *Shuoshu shihua* 說書史話. Shanghai: Zuojia chubanshe, 1958.

Chen Shaodi 陳紹棣. "Mingdai jiechude jianzhu guimojia Ruan An" 明代傑出的建築規模家阮安. *Xuelin manlu* 學林漫錄, 7 (March 1983), pp. 243–248.

Chen Xuelin 陳學霖. "Tu Liu Bowen *Shaobing ge*" 讀劉伯溫燒餅歌. In *Shou Luo Xianglin jiaoshou lunwenji* 壽羅香林教授論文集, pp. 163–190. Hong Kong, privately published, 1970.

———. "Yuan Daducheng jianzao chuanshuo tanyuan" 元大都城建造傳說探源. *Hanxue yanjiu* 漢學研究, 5.1 (June 1987), pp. 95–127.

———. "Dongying kanxing de Zhongguo yuyanshu shuping" 東瀛刊行的中國預言書述評. In *Shisou—Qingzhu jianxiao sanshizhounian xueshu lunwenji* 史藪—慶祝建校三十週年學術論文集, pp. 169–201. Hong Kong: Department of History, The Chinese University of Hong Kong. 1993.

———. "Liu Bowen *Shaobing ge* xinkao" 劉伯溫燒餅歌新考. In *Luo Xianglin jiaoshou jinian lunwenji* 羅香林教授紀念論文集, pp. 1363–1403. Taibei: Xinwenfeng chubangongsi. 1993.

———. *Liu Bowen yu Nezha cheng—Beijing jiancheng de chuanshuo* 劉伯溫與哪吒城—北京建城的傳說. Taibei: Dongda tushugongsi, 1996.

———. "Liu Bowen jian Beijingcheng chuanshuo tanze" 劉伯溫建北京城傳說探賾. Rpt. in Chen, *Mingdai renwu yu chuanshuo* 明代人物與傳說, pp. 65–86. Hong Kong: The Chinese University Press, 1997.

———. "Guanyu Liu Bowen chuanshuo de yanjiu" 關於劉伯溫傳說的研究. *Beijing shehui kexue* 北京社會科學, 1998.4 (November), pp. 44–48.

———. "Beijing waicheng Nezhamiao tansu" 北京外城哪吒廟探溯, *JCS*, N.S. 10 (2001), pp. 151–169.

———. "Jiu Beijing de qiyu yu silong: Guanshi jili yu minjian xisu" 舊北京的祈雨與祀龍：官式祭禮與民間習俗. *JCS*, N.S. 12 (2003), pp. 183–222.

———. "Menggu 'Da Ming Yongledi jianzao Beijing cheng' gushi tanyuan" 蒙古〈大明永樂帝建造北京城〉故事探源. *BIHP*, 75.3 (September 2004), pp. 515–572.

———. "Liu Bowen yu 'Bayueshiwu sha Dazi' gushi kaosu" 劉伯溫與「八月十五殺韃子」故事考溯. *Bulletin of the Institute of Modern History, Academia Sinica* (中央研究院近代史研究所集刊), 46 (December 2005), pp. 1–51.

——. "'Zhenwushen, Yonglexiang' chuanshuo suyuan"「真武神、永樂像」傳説溯源. Rpt. in *Mindai renwu yu chuanshuo,* pp. 87–127.

Chen Yuan 陳垣. *Daojia jinshilue* 道家金石略. Edited by Chen Zhichao 陳智超 and Zeng Qingying 曾慶映. Beijing: Wenwu chubanshe, 1988.

Chen Zongfan 陳宗藩. *Yandu congkao* 燕都叢考. Beijing: Beijing guji chubanshe, 1991.

Cheng Jianjun 程建軍 and Kong Shangpu 孔尚樸. *Fengshui yu jianzhu* 風水與建築. Nanchang: Jiangxi kexue jishu chubanshe, 1992.

Dai Xueji 戴學稷. *Huhehaote jianshi* 呼和浩特簡史. Beijing: Zhonghua shuju, 1981.

Daoruntibu 道潤梯步, trans. (*Xinyi jiaozhu*) *Menggu yuanliu* (新譯校註) 蒙古源流. Huhehot: Nei Menggu Renmin chubanshe, 1980.

Datong minjian gushi jicheng 大同民間故事集成. Edited by Datongshi Shidawenyi jicheng bangongshi. Taiyuan: Shanxi Renmin chubanshe, 1989.

Deng Yunxiang 鄧雲鄉. *Shuiliu yunzai zagao* 水流雲在雜稿. Taiyuan: Beiyue wenyi chubanshe, 1992.

——. *Zengbu Yanjing fengtu ji* 增補燕京風土記. Beijing: Zhonghua shuju, 1998.

Dong Jianhong 董鑒泓 et al. *Zhongguo chengshi jiansheshi* 中國城市建設史. Beijing: Zhongguo jianzhu gongye chubanshe, 1982.

Dong Zhiyong 董志湧. *Nanjing de chuanshuo* 南京的傳説. Shanghai: Shanghai wenyi chubanshe, 1984.

Dunhuan 鈍宧 (pseudo.). "Xiaosanwuting suibi: Shaobing ge" 小三吾亭隨筆：燒餅歌. *Guocui xuebao* 國粹學報, 75 (1911): *Congtan* 叢談, p. 1.

Fu Si'nian 傅斯年. "Ba 'Ming Chengzu shengmu wenti huizheng' pingda Zhu Xizu xiansheng" 跋「明成祖生母問題彙證」平答朱希祖先生. *BIHP*, 6 (1936), pp. 79–86.

Fu Xihua 傅惜華. *Mingdai zaju quanmu* 明代雜劇全目. Beijing: Zuojia chubanshe, 1958.

——, ed. *Yuandai zaju quanmu* 元代雜劇全目. Beijing: Zuojia chubanshe, 1957.

Gao Shusen 高樹森 and Shao Jianguang 邵建光, eds. *Jinling shichao diwangzhou—Nanjing juan* 金陵十朝帝王州——南京卷. Beijing: Zhongguo Renmin daxue chubanshe, 1991.

Gong Debo 龔德柏. *Xiju yu lishi* 戲劇與歷史. Taibei: Sanmin shuju, 1967.

Gong Xianzong 龔顯宗. "Fengshen xiaoshuo Nezha xingxiang de yanhua" 封神小説哪吒形像的演化. In *Diyijie Nezha xueshu yantaohui lunwenji,* pp. 437–450.

Gu Cheng 顧誠. "Shen Wansan jiqi jiazu shiji kao" 沈萬三及其家族事跡考. *Lishi yanjiu* 歷史研究, 1991.1 (February), pp. 66–85.

Guan Dongsheng 關東升, ed. *Zhongguo minzu wenhua daguan: Zang zu, Mengba zu, Luoba zu* 中國民族文化大觀：藏族，門巴族，珞巴族. Beijing: Zhongguo dabaikequanshu chubanshe, 1995.

Gugong zhoukan 故宮週刊. Nos. 102 (September 19 1931). Beiping: Palace Museum.

Guo Zisheng 郭子昇. *Beijing miaohui jiusu* 北京廟會舊俗. Beijing: Zhongguohuaqiao chubanshe, 1989.

———. *Shijing fengqing—Jingcheng miaohui yu changdian* 市井風情——京城廟會與廠甸. Shenyang: Liaohai chubanshe, 1997.

Han Guanghui 韓光輝. *Beijing lishirenkuo dili* 北京歷史人口地理. Beijing: Beijing daxue chubanshe, 1996.

Hao Zhaoju 郝兆矩. *Zengding Liu Bowen nianpu* 增訂劉伯溫年譜. Zhengzhou: Zhongzhou guji chubanshe, 1990 (see also under Wang Xinyi).

——— and Liu Wenfeng 劉文峰. *Liu Bowen quanzhuan* 劉伯溫全傳. Dalin: Dalin chubanshe, 1994.

He Shude 賀樹德. *Beijing tongshi*, Vol. 6 (Ming Beijing).

He Yeju 賀鄴鉅. *Kaogong ji yingguozhidu yanjiu* 考工記營國制度研究. Beijing: Zhongguo jianzhu gongye chubanshe, 1985.

———. *Zhongguo gudai chengshi guihuashi luncong* 中國古代城市規劃史論叢. Beijing: Zhongguo jianzhu gongye chubanshe, 1986.

Hong Jinfu 洪金富. "Sishiwan Menggu shuo lunzhenggao" 四十萬蒙古說論證稿. In *Meng Yuande lishi yu wenhua: Meng Yuanshi xueshu yantaohui lunwenji* 蒙元的歷史與文化：蒙元史學術研討會論文集, edited by Xiao Qiqing, Vol. I, pp. 245–305. Taibei: Taiwan Xuesheng shuju, 2001.

Hou Renzhi 侯仁之. "Beiping Jinshuihe kao" 北平金水河考. *Yanjing xuebao* 燕京學報, 30 (June 1946), pp. 107–133.

———. "Beijing cheng he Liu Bowen de guanxi" 北京城和劉伯溫的關係. *Beijing ribao* 北京日報 (Peking Daily), July 31 1962.

———. "Beijing tushi fazhan guocheng zhong de shuiyan wenti" 北京都市發展過程中的水源問題. Rpt. in Hou, *Lishi dilixue de lilun yu shijian* 歷史地理學的理論與實踐, pp. 274–279. Shanghai: Renmin chubanshe. 1979.

———. "Lun Beijing jiancheng zhishi" 論北京建城之始. *Beijing shehuikexue* 北京社會科學, 1990.3 (August), pp. 2–4.

———. "Yuan Dadu cheng yu Ming Qing Beijing cheng" 元大都城與明清北京城. Rpt. in Hou, *Lishi dilixue de lilun yu shijian*, pp. 159–204.

———. "Zijin cheng zai guihua sheji shang de jicheng yu fazhan" 紫禁城在規劃設計上的繼承與發展. In *Zijin cheng yingshanji* 紫禁城營繕記, edited by Gugong bowuyuan 故宮博物院, pp. 7–15. Beijing: Zijincheng chubanshe, 1992.

———. *Beijing cheng de qiyuan yu bianqian* 北京城的起源與變遷. Beijing: Beijing Yanshan chubanshe, 1997.

———. *Hou Renzhi jiang Beijing* 侯仁之講北京. Edited by Yin Junke 尹鈞科. Beijing: Beijing chubanshe. 2003.

——— et al., eds. *Beijing lishi dituji* 北京歷史地圖集, Vol. 1. Beijing: Beijing chubanshe, 1985.

——— et al., eds. *Shichahai zhi* 什刹海志. Beijing: Beijing chubanshe. 2002.

Hu Hansheng 胡漢生. *Ming shisan ling daguan* 明十三陵大觀. Beijing: Zhongguo qingnian chubanshe, 1992.

———. *Ming shishan ling* 明十三陵. Beijing: Zhongguo qingnian chubanshe, 1998.

Huang Jingqin 黃敬欽. "Nezha xiju xingyang tansuo" 哪吒戲劇形樣探索. In *Diyijie Nezha xueshu yantaohui lunwenji*, pp. 331–372.

Huang Wenchang 黃文暘, ed., and collated by Dong Kang 董康. *Quhai zongmu tiyao* 曲海總目提要. Hong Kong: Hanxue tushu gongyingshe, 1967.

Huang Xiandeng 黃先登. *Beiping de chuanshuo* 北平的傳說. Taibei: Changchunshu shufang, 1979.

Huang Zhigang 黃芝崗. "Shen Wansan chuanshuo kao" 沈萬三傳說考. *Dongfang zazhi* 東方雜誌, 32.1 (January 1935), pp. 91–97.

Jagchid Sechin 札斯奇欽. *Menggu Huangjin shi yizhu* 蒙古黃金史譯註. Taibei: Lianjing shiye chubangongsi, 1979.

Ji Shijia 季士家. "Mingdu Nanjing chengyuan luelun" 明都南京城垣略論. *Gugong bowuyuan yuankan* 故宮博物院院刊, 1984.2 (May), pp. 70–81.

Jia Zhoujie 賈洲傑. "Yuan Shangdu diaozha baokao" 元上都調查報告. *Wenwu* 文物, 1977.5 (May), pp. 65–74.

Jiang Shunyuan 姜舜源. "Lun Beijing Yuan Ming Qing sanchao gongdian de jicheng yu fazhan" 論北京元明清三朝宮殿的繼承與發展. Rpt. in *Zijin cheng jianzhu yanjiu yu baohu*, edited by Yu Zhuoyun, pp. 80–93.

———. "Wuxing, sixiang, sanyuan, liangji—Zijin cheng" 五行, 四象, 三垣, 兩極—紫禁城. In *Qingdai gongshi tanwei* 清代宮史探微, edited by Qingdai gongshi yanjiuhui, pp. 251–260. Beijing: Zijincheng chubanshe, 1991.

Jiang Weitang 姜緯堂. "Liu Bowen yu Beijing—Liu Bowen xingjian Beijing cheng, kanding shisanling zhishuo zhengwei" 劉伯溫與北京—劉伯溫興建北京城、勘定十三陵之說證偽. *Beijing ribao*, September 8 1999.

Jiang Xingyu 蔣星煜. "Zhu Ming wangchao shenhua Liu Bowen de lishi guocheng" 朱明王朝神化劉伯溫的歷史過程. *Hangzhou daxue xuebao* 杭州大學學報 (*zhexue shehuikexue ban* 哲學社會科學版), 14.1 (March 1984), pp. 98–104, 119.

Jiangsu chengshi dili 江蘇城市地理. Edited by Department of Geography, Nanjing Normal College. Nanjing: Jiangsu kexue jishu chubanshe, 1982.

Jin Shoushen 金受申. *Beijing de chuanshuo* 北京的傳說. Beijing: Tongsuwenyi chubanshe, 1957. Rpt. in an enlarged edition published by Beijing chubanshe, 1981. Another new edition by the same press, 2003. The latter includes Yang Liangzhi 楊良志. "Jin Shousen he tade zhushu" 金受申和他的著述, pp. 189–208.

———. *Beijing tong* 北京通. Beijing: Dazhong chubanshe, 1999.

Jinri Beijing 今日北京. Edited by Beijingshi shehuikexueyuan. Beijing: Beijing Yanshan chubanshe, 1991.

Li Jiarui 李家瑞 and Liu Fu 劉復, eds. *Zhongguo suqu zongmu gao* 中國俗曲總目稿. Beiping: Guoli Beiping yanjiuyuan, 1932.

Li Jinhua 李晉華. "Ming Chengzu shengmu wenti huizheng" 明成祖生母問題彙證. *BIHP*, 6 (1936), pp. 45–77.

Li Min 李旻. *Zijin cheng chuanshuo* 紫禁城傳說. Beijing: Jiefangjun chubanshe, 2002.

Li Qiao 李喬. *Zhongguo hangyeshen chongbai* 中國行業神崇拜. Beijing: Zhongguo huaqiao chubangongsi, 1990.

Li Shiyu 李世瑜. "*Sanjiao yingjie zongguan tongshu* chutan" 《三教應劫總觀通書》初探. *Taiwan zongjiaoyanjiu tongxin* 臺灣宗教研究通訊, 6 (October 2003), pp. 261–318.

Li Shulan 李淑蘭. *Beijing shigao* 北京史稿. Beijing: Xueyuan chubanshe, 1994.

Li Weiguo 李偉國. "Yuan Ming yiben *Soushen ji* sanzhong yuanyuan yitonglun" 元明異本搜神記三種淵源異同論. In *Zhonghua wenshi luncong* 中華文史論叢, edited by Qian Bocheng 錢伯城, Vol. 48, pp. 243–257. Shanghai: Shanghai guji chubanshe, 1991.

Li Xiangdong 李向東. "Luetan Baiyunguan de xingshuai " 略談白雲觀的興衰. In *Yanjing chunqiu* 燕京春秋, edited by Beijingshi yanjiuhui, pp. 145–148. Beijing: Beijing chubanshe, 1982.

Li Xieping 李燮平. *Mingdai Beijing ducheng yingjian congkao* 明代北京都城營建叢考. Beijing: Zijincheng chubanshe, 2006.

(Liang) Zhengjiang (梁) 正江 and Ding Shan 丁山. *Taoranting* 陶然亭. Beijing: Beijing lüyou chubanshe, 1983.

Lin Liyue 林麗月. *Mingdai de Guozijian sheng* 明代的國子監生. Taibei: Taiwan Shifan daxue lishiyanjiusuo, 1979.

Liu Cunren 柳存仁. "Pishamen tianwang fuzi yu Zhongguoxiaoshuo zhi guansi" 毘沙門天王父子與中國小說之關係. In Liu, *Hefengtang wenji* 和風堂文集, Vol. II, pp. 1045–1052, 1081–1091. Shanghai: Shanghai guji chubanshe, 1991.

Liu Deyu 劉德隅. *Ming Liu Bowengong shengping shiji shiyi* 明劉伯溫公生平事蹟拾遺. Taibei, privately published, 1976.

Liu Yizheng 柳詒徵. "Shen Wansan" 沈萬三. *Shixue zazhi* 史學雜誌 (Nanjing), 1.2 (1929), pp. 1–3.

Liu Zhixiong 劉志雄 and Liu Jingrong 劉靜榮. *Long yu Zhongguo wenhua* 龍與中國文化. Beijing: Renmin chubanshe, 1992.

Liu Bowen Shaobing ge (*quanben*) 劉伯溫燒餅歌 (全本). Hong Kong: Da'nan chubanshe, 1976?

Lou Qingxi 樓慶西. "Long de shijie—Zijin cheng zhong longwen zhuangshi de yingyong" 龍的世界——紫禁城中龍紋裝飾的應用. Rpt. in *Zijin cheng yingshanji*, edited by Gugong bowuyuan, pp. 254–273.

———. "Zijin cheng jianzhu de secaixue" 紫禁城建築的色彩學. Rpt. in *Zhongguo Zijin cheng xuehui lunwenji*, 1st ser., edited by Shan Shiyuan et al., pp. 279–283.

Lu Bingjie 路秉傑. *Tian'anmen* 天安門. Jinan: Shandong huabao chubanshe, 2004.

Lü Wei 呂微. *Yinyu shijie de laifang zhe—Zhongguo minjian caishen xinyang* 隱喻世界的來訪者——中國民間財神信仰.Beijing: Xueyuan chubanshe, 2001.

Lü Zongli 呂宗力 and Luan Baoqun 欒保群, eds. *Zhongguo minjian zhushen* 中國民間諸神. Taibei: Taiwan Xuesheng shuju, 1991.

Lun Meng 倫明. "Jianwen xunguo kaoyi" 建文遜國考疑. *Furen xuezhi* 輔仁學誌, 3.2 (1932), pp. 1–62.

Luo Baoping 羅保平. "Ming Qing shiqi Beijing shichang chutan" 明清時期北京市場初探. *Beijing shiyuan* 北京史苑, Vol. 4, pp. 242–256. Beijing: Beijing chubanshe, 1988.

Ma Zhixiang 馬芷庠. *Lao Beijing lüxing zhinan* 老北京旅行指南 (1935). Beijing: Beijing Yanshan chubanshe, 1997.

Manbu Beijing lishi changhe 慢步北京歷史長河. Beijingshi yanjiuhui et al., eds. Beijing: Zhongguo shudian, 2004.

Mao Peiqi 毛佩琦 and Li Chuoran 李焯然. *Ming Chengzu shilun* 明成祖史論. Taibei: Wenjin chubanshe. 1994.

Meng Sen 孟森. "Jianwen xunguoshi kao" 建文遜國事考. Rpt. in Meng, *Ming Qingshi lunzhu jikan* 明清史論著集刊, pp. 1–12. Taibei: Shijie shuju, 1961.

Ming Xiaoling 明孝陵. Edited by Nanjing Bowuyuan. Beijing: Wenwu chubanshe, 1981.

Nakano Miyoko. See Wang Xiuwen.

Pan Qun 潘群. "Shen Wansan xingming jiguan kao" 沈萬三姓名籍貫考. *Dongyue luncong* 東岳論叢, 1992.5 (September), pp. 100–106.

———. "Shen Wansan caifu laiyuan kao" 沈萬三財富來源考. *Qilu xuekan* 齊魯學刊, 1993.4 (December), pp. 86–91.

Pan Yuxiu 潘玉修 and Zheng Yuzhuo 鄭玉琢, eds. *Genzai hongdong* 根在洪洞. Beijing: Zhongguo dang'an chubanshe. 1998.

Qian Nanyang 錢南揚. *Song Yuan xiwen jiyi* 宋元戲文輯佚. Shanghai: Shanghai gudian wenxue chubanshe, 1956.

Qin Baoqi 秦寶琦. *Qingqianqi Tiandihui yanjiu* 清前期天地會研究. Beijing: Zhongguo Renmin daxue chubanshe, 1988.

Qiu Zhonglin 邱仲麟. "Fengchen, jierang yu qiwei: Ming-Qing Beijing de shenghuo huanjing yu shiren de didu yinxiang" 風塵、街壤與氣味：明清北京的生活環境與士人的帝都印象. *Tsinghua Journal of Chinese Studies* (清華學報), N.S. 34.1 (June 2004), pp. 181–225.

———. "*Shuiwouzi*: Beijing de gongshuiyezhe yu minsheng yongshui" 水窩子：北京的供水業者與民生用水 (1368–1937). In *Zhongguo de chengshi shenghuo* 中國的城市生活, edited by Li Xiaodi 李孝悌, pp. 229–284. Taibei: Lianjing chubanshiye gongshi, 2005.

Qu Duizhi 瞿兑之. *Renwu fengsu zhidu congtan, jia ji* 人物風俗制度叢談，甲集. Hong Kong: Longmen shudian. 1968 rpt.

Qu Mi 渠彌 (Qu Duizhi). "*Yanghe shi suibi*: Shen Wansan" 養和室隨筆：沈萬三. *Zhonghe yuekan* 中和月刊, 4.6 (June 1943), pp. 82–84.

Shan Shiyuan 單士元 and Yu Zhuoyun 于倬雲, eds. *Zhongguo Zijin cheng xuehui lunwenji* 中國紫禁城學會論文集, lst ser., Jinian Gugong bowuyuan jianyuan qishizhounian ji *Zijin cheng jiancheng wubaiqishiwuzhounian* 紀念故宮博物館院建院七十周年暨紫禁城建成五百七十五周年. Beijing: Zijincheng chubanshe, 1997.

Shang Chuan 商傳. "Mingchu zhuming zhengzhijia Yao Guangxiao" 明初著名政治家姚廣孝. *Zhongguo shi yanjiu* 中國史研究, 1983.3 (August), pp. 119–130.

———. *Yongle huangdi* 永樂皇帝. Beijing: Renmin chubanshe, 1989.

Shen Defu 沈德輔. "Cong Shen Wansan de zhuanji ziliao lun xiupu yu xungen" 從沈萬三的傳記資料論修譜與尋根. *Disijie Yazhou zupu xueshu yantaohui huiyijilu* 第四屆亞洲族譜學術研討會會議記錄, pp. 403–536. Taibei: Guoxue wenxianguan, 1989.

Shi Lianfang 施連方. *Beijing jiexiang diming tan* 北京街巷地名談. Taibei: Wangwenshe gufen youxiangongsi, 1995.

Shi Mingzheng 史明正. *Zouxiang jindaihua de Beijing cheng—chengshi jianshe yu shehui biange* 走向近代化的北京城——城市建設與社會變革. Beijing: Beijing daxue chubanshe, 1995.

Shi Weimin 史衛民. *Dushi zhong de youmumin—Yuandai chengshi shenghuo changjuan* 都市中的游牧民——元代城市生活長卷. Changsha: Hunan chubanshe, 1996.

Shi Zhimin 石志敏 and Chen Yinghua 陳英華. "Zijin cheng huchenghe ji weifang yange kao" 紫禁城護城河及圍房沿革考. In *Zijin cheng jianzhu yanjiu yu baohu*, edited by Yu Zhuoyun, pp. 229–239.

Sirén, Osvald. See Xu Yongquan.

Su Tianjun 蘇天鈞. "Guo Shoujing yu Dadu shuili gongcheng" 郭守敬與大都水利工程. *Ziran koxueshi yanjiu* 自然科學史研究, 1983.1 (March), pp. 66–72.

———, ed. *Beijing kaogu jicheng* 北京考古集成. Beijing: Beijing chubanshe, 2000.

Sun Kaidi 孫楷第. *Zhongguo tongsuxiaoshuo shumu* 中國通俗小說書目. Beijing: Zuojia chubanshe, 1957.

Sun Kekuan 孫克寬. *Yuandai Daojiao zhi fazhan* 元代道教之發展. Taizhong, Taiwan: Donghai daxue, 1969.

———. "Yuandai shenmirenwu Liu Bingzhong jiqi *Cangchun ji*" 元代神祕人物劉秉忠及其藏春集. Rpt. In Sun, *Menggu Hanjun yu Hanwenhua yanjiu* 蒙古漢軍與漢文化研究, pp. 99–106. Taibei: Taiwan Zhonghua shuju, 1959.

Tada Teichi. See Zhang Zichen.

Tang Yongbin 湯用彬, ed. *Jiudu wenwulue* 舊都文物略. Beiping: Shizhengfu mishuchu, 1935.

Tao Junqi 陶君起. *Jingju jumu chutan* 京劇劇目初探. Beijing: Zhonghua shuju, 1962.

Tiandihui 天地會, Vol. 1. Edited by Research Institute of Qing History, People's University of China and Number One Historical Archives of China. Beijing: Zhongguo Renmin daxue chubanshe, 1980.

Tong Xun 佟洵, ed. *Fojiao yu Beijing simiao wenhua* 佛教與北京寺廟文化.Beijing: Zhongyang minzu daxue chubanshe, 1997.

Tuan Tianshun 段天順. *Yanshui gujintan* 燕水古今談. Beijing: Yanshan chubanshe, 1991.

Tuibei tu suoyin 推背圖索隱. Tokyo: n.p., 1917.

Wan Shuyuan 萬書元. "Nezha naohai gushi kaolun" 哪吒鬧海故事考論. *Dongfang wenhua* 東方文化, 1 (1991), pp. 76–86.

Wan Yi 萬依. "Lun Zhu Di yingjian Beijing gongdian, qiandu de zhuyao dongji ji houguo" 論朱棣營建北京宮殿，遷都的主要動機及後果. In *Zijin cheng yingshanji*, pp. 52–61.

Wang Bin 王彬 and Xu Xiushan 徐秀珊. *Beijing jiexiang tuzhi* 北京街巷圖志. Beijing: Zuojia chubanshe, 2004.

Wang Canzhi 王燦熾. "Beijing jiandu shi yu gongyuanqian 1057 nian" 北京建都始於公元前1057年. Rpt. in Wang, *Wang Canzhi shizhi lunwenji* 王燦熾史誌論文集, pp. 308–315. Beijing: Yanshan chubanshe, 1991.

——, comp. *Beijing shidi fengwu shulu* 北京史地風物書錄. Beijing: Beijing chubanshe, 1985.

Wang Chongwu 王崇武. *Ming jingnan shishi kaozheng gao* 明靖難史事考證稿. Lizhuang, Sichuan: Guoli Zhongyang yanjiuyuan lishiyuyan yanjiusuo, 1945.

——. *Fengtian jingnan ji zhu* 奉天靖難記注. Shanghai: Shangwu yinshuguan, 1948.

Wang Dacuo 王大錯. *Xikao* 戲考. Shanghai: Dadong shuju, 1934.

Wang Gang 王崗. *Beijing tongshi*, Vol. 5 (Yuan Dadu).

Wang Huanbiao 王煥鑣 et al., eds. *Shoudu zhi* 首都志. Nanjing: Zhengzhong shuju, 1935.

Wang Jianchuan 王見川. "Liu Bowen chuanshuo yu *Shaobing ge*: jiantan 'Tieguantu chen' de xingcheng" 劉伯溫傳說與《燒餅歌》：兼談「鐵冠圖讖」的形成. *Taiwan zongjiaoyanjiu tongxun*, 4 (October 2002), pp. 161–194.

——. "*Tuibei tu, Wugong jing, Shaobing ge* ji qita" 《推背圖》，《五公符》，《燒餅歌》及其他, preface to *Ming Qing minjian zongjiao jingjuan wenxian xubian* 明清民間宗教經卷文獻續編, edited by Wang Jianchuan, Che Xilun 車錫倫, Song Jun 宋軍, Li Shijie 李世瑜, and Fan Chunwu 范純武, pp. 1–24. Taibei: Xinwenfeng chubangongsi, 2006.

Wang Jianying 王劍英. *Ming Zhongdu* 明中都. Beijing: Zhonghua shuju, 1992.

——. "Lun cong Yuan Dadu dao Ming Beijing de yanbian he fazhan" 論從元大都到明北京的演變和發展. *Yanjing xuebao* 燕京學報, N.S. 1 (1995), pp. 61–64.

Wang Jun 王軍. *Cheng ji* 城記. Beijing: Sanlian shudian, 2003.

Wang Ling 王玲. *Beijing tongshi*, Vol. 3 (Liao Nanjing).

Wang Puzi 王樸子. "Nanyuan jianzhi kaolue" 南苑建置考略. *Zhonghe yuekan*, 5.9 (September 1944), pp. 19–32.

———. "Yuan Dadu pingmian guihua lueshu" 元大都平面規劃略述. *Gugong bowuyuan yuankan* 故宮博物院院刊, 1970.2 (May), pp. 61–82.

———. "Yan wangfu yu Zijin cheng" 燕王府與紫禁城. *Gugong bowuyuan yuankan*, 1979.1 (February), pp. 61–82.

Wang Qiheng 王其亨. "Zijin cheng fengguang xingshi jianxi" 紫禁城風光形勢簡析. Rpt. in *Zijin cheng jianzhu yanjiu yu baohu*, edited by Yu Zhuoyun, pp. 94–104.

———, ed. *Fengshui lilun yanjiu* 風水理論研究. Tianjin: Tianjin daxue chubanshe, 1992.

Wang Ting 王頲. "Shen Wansan de zhenshi jiashi ji chuanqi" 沈萬三的真實家世及傳奇. *Jinan shixue* 暨南史學, 2 (December 2003), pp. 247–259.

Wang Tong 汪侗. "'*Beipinghua yuhui*' ji qita" 《北平話語匯》及其他. In "Renjian xianhua" 人間閒話 column. *Shijie ribao* 世界日報 (U.S.A.), September 22 1983.

Wang Weijie 王偉傑, Ren Jiasheng 任家生, Han Wensheng 韓文生, Ma Zhenyu 馬振玉, and Li Tiejun 李鐵軍. *Beijing huanjing shihua* 北京環境史話. Beijing: Dizhi chubanshe, 1989.

Wang Wenbao 王文寶, ed. *Beijing fengwu chuanshuo gushixuan* 北京風物傳說故事選. Fuzhou: Fuzhou Renmin chubanshe, 1983.

———. "Cong minjian chuanshuo tanxun Beijing cheng de jianzhi—du Chen Xuelin 'Liu Bowen yu *Nezha cheng*—Beijing jiancheng de chuanshuo' " 從民間傳說探尋北京城的建置——讀陳學霖《劉伯溫與哪吒城——北京建城的傳說》. *Minjian wenxue luntan* 民間文學論壇, 1998.1 (January), pp. 76–79.

———. *Zhongguo minsu yanjiushi* 中國民俗研究史. Harbin: Heilongjiang renmin chubanshe, 2003.

Wang Xinyi 王馨一. *Liu Bowen nianpu* 劉伯溫年譜. Shanghai: Shangwu yinshuguan, 1936. Amended by Hao Chaoju 郝兆矩. *Zengding* 增訂 *Liu Bowen nianpu*. Zhengzhou: Zhongzhou guji chubanshe, 1990.

Wang Xiuwen 王秀文 et al., trans. Nakano Miyoko 中野美代子, *"Xiyou ji" de mimi* 《西遊記》的祕密. Beijing: Zhonghua shuju, 2002.

Wang Zhiping 王之屏. "Liu Ji zhisi kaoyi" 劉基之死考異. *Jingshi jikan* 經世季刊, 2.3 (April 1942), pp. 59–60.

Wang Zilin 王子林. *Zijin cheng fengshui* 紫禁城風水. Beijing: Zijincheng chubanshe, 2005.

Wei Juxian 衛聚賢. *Fengshenbang gushi tanyuan* 封神榜故事探源. Hong Kong, privately published by author, 1960.

Wei Kaizhao 魏開肇 and Zhao Huirong 趙蕙蓉. *Beijing tongshi*, Vol. 8 (Qing Beijing).

Weng Li 翁立. *Beijing de hutong* 北京的胡同. Revised ed. Beijing: Yanshan chubanshe, 1992.

Wu Enpei 吳恩培. *Jushang Shen Wansan* 巨商沈萬三. Taiyuan: Beiyue wenyi chubanshe, 1997.

Wu Han 吳晗. "Hu Weiyong dang'an kao" 胡惟庸黨案考. *Yanjing xuebao*, 15 (June 1934), pp. 163–205.

——. "Ming Chengzu shengmu kao" 明成祖生母考. *Qinghua xuebao* 清華學報, 10.3 (1935), pp. 631–646.

——. "Mingdai jingnan zhiyi yu guodu beiqian" 明代靖難之役與國都北遷. *Qinghua xuebao*, 10.3 (October 1935), pp. 917–939.

——. *Zhu Yuanzhang zhuan* 朱元璋傳. Rev. ed. Beijing: Renmin chubanshe, 1994.

Wu Jianyong 吳建雍. *Beijing tongshi*, Vol. 7 (Qing Beijing).

Wu Menglin 吳夢麟 and Liu Jingyi 劉精義. "Ji yanjiu Mingdai Beijingyingjianshi de zhongyao zhishi—'Neiguanjian Ni taijian shoucangji'" 記研究明代北京營建史的重要誌石——《內官監倪太監壽藏記》. In *Beijing yu Zhongwai gudu duibi yanjiu* 北京與中外古都對比研究, edited by Beijing shehuikexueyuan lishisuo, pp. 332–344. Beijing: Yanjing chubanshe, 1992.

Wu Ren'an 吳仁安. "Mingchu jiangnan shoufu Shen Wansan jili kaobian" 明初江南首富沈萬三籍里考辨. *Suzhoudaxue xuebao* 蘇州大學學報 (*zhexue shehuikexue ban*), 1984: 3 (September), pp. 118–119.

Wu Shiyong 吳士勇. "Shen Wansan bingfei shiming" 沈萬三並非實名. *Shixue yuekan* 史學月刊, 2004.5 (May), pp. 123–125.

Wu Tingmei 吳庭美 and Xia Yurun 夏玉潤, eds. *Fengyang gujin* 鳳陽古今. Hefei: Huangshan shushe, 1986.

Wudangshan zhi 武當山志. Compiled by *Wudangshan zhi* bianzuan weiyuanhui. Beijing: Xinhua chubanshe, 1994.

Xi Wuyi 習五一 and Deng Yibing 鄧亦兵. *Beijing tongshi*, Vol. 9 (Republican era).

Xiang Yansheng 向燕生. *Beijing tongshi*, Vol. 2 (Sui-Tang to Wudai).

Xiao Dengfu 蕭登福. "Nezha suyuan" 哪吒溯源. In *Diyijie Nezha xueshu yantaohui lunwenji*, pp. 1–66.

Xiao Qiqing 蕭啟慶. "Shuo 'Da Chao': Yuanchao jianhao qian Menggu de Hanwen guohao" 說"大朝":元朝建號前蒙古的漢文國號. *Hanxue yanjiu*, 3.1 (June 1985), pp. 23–40.

Xiao Yishan 蕭一山. *Jindai mimishehui shiliao* 近代秘密社會史料. Beiping: Guoli Beiping yanjiuyuan, 1935.

Xie Mincong 謝敏聰. *Beijing de chengyuan yu gongque zhi cai yanjiu* 北京的城垣與宮闕之再研究. Taibei: Taiwan Xuesheng shuju, 1980.

——, *Zhongguo lidai diwang lingqin kaolue* 中國歷代帝王陵寢考略. Taibei: Taiwan Xuesheng shuju, 1980.

Xin Xiuming 信修明. *Lao taijian de huiyi* 老太監的回憶. Beiping: Yanshan chubanshe, 1992.

Xu Daoling 許道齡, ed. *Beiping miaoyu tongjian* 北平廟宇通檢. Beiping: Guoli Beiping yanjiuyuan, 1936.

Xu Hong 徐泓. "Mingchu Nanjing huangcheng gongcheng de guihua, pingmianbuju jiqi xiangzhengyiyi" 明初南京皇城宮城的規劃，平面布局及其象徵意義. *Guoli Taiwan daxue jianzhu yu chengxiang xuebao* 國立臺灣大學建築與城鄉學報, 7 (December 1993), pp. 79–96.

———. "Ming Beijing xingbu zhi" 明北京行部志. *Hanxue yanjiu*, 2.2 (December 1973), pp. 569–598.

Xu Pingfang 徐蘋芳, ed. *Ming Qing Beijing cheng tu* 明清北京城圖. Beijing: Ditu chubanshe, 1986.

———. "Yuan Dadu Shumiyuanzhi kao" 元大都樞密院址考. Rpt. in Xu, *Zhongguo lishi kaoguxue luncong* 中國歷史考古學論叢, pp. 192–197. Taibei: Yunchen wenhuashiye gufen youxiangongsi, 1995.

———. "Yuan Dadu Yushitaizhi kao" 元大都御史臺址考. Rpt. in Xu, *Zhongguo lishi kaoguxue luncong*, pp. 198–204.

———. "Yuan Dadu Zhongshushengzhi kao" 元大都中書省址考. *JCS*, N.S. No. 6 (1996), pp. 385–391.

Xu Yongquan 許永全, trans. Aosiwu'erde Xirenlong 奥斯伍爾德・喜仁能 (Osvald Sirén), *Beijing de chengchang he chengmen* 北京的城牆和城門. Beijing: Yanshan chubanshe, 1985.

Xu Zuosheng 徐作生. "Jianwendi wangming hefang" 建文帝亡命何方. Rpt. in Xu, *Fancha kaoshu lu* 泛槎考述錄, pp. 162–259. Beijing: Xueyuan chubanshe, 2000.

———. "Ming shenmi mouseng Yao Guangxiao lun" 明神秘謀僧姚廣孝論. *Dongnan wenhua* 東南文化, 1990.4 (August), pp. 7–11.

Yan Chongnian 閻崇年. "Ming Yongledi qiantu Beijing shuyi" 明永樂帝遷都北京述議. Rpt. in Yan, *Yanbuji* 燕步集, pp. 342–364. Beijing: Yanshan chubanshe, 1989.

Yan Gongshang 嚴工上. *Beipinghua yuhui* 北平話語匯. Appendix: "Beiping de chuanshuo" 北平的傳說. Peiping: n.p., 1932?

Yan Jihe 顏吉鶴. "Liu Bingzhong zhuchi xiu Daducheng" 劉秉忠主持修大都城. *Xuexi yu yanjiu* 學習與研究, 1983.10 (October), pp. 42–43.

———. "Shilun Liu Bingzhong de lishizuoyong" 試論劉秉忠的歷史作用. *Beijing shiyuan* 北京史苑, Vol. 3, pp. 242–256. Beijing: Yanshan chubanshe, 1985.

Yang Kuan 楊寬. *Zhongguo gudaiducheng zhidushi yanjiu* 中國古代都城制度史研究. Shanghai: Shanghai guji chubanshe, 1993.

Yang Mingxian 楊明顯. *Chengmen yu hutong* 城門與胡同. Taipei: Chunwenxue chubanshe, 1982.

Yang Ne 楊訥. *Liu Ji shiji kaoshu* 劉基事蹟考述. Beijing: Beijing tushu guan chubanshe, 2004.

———. "*Xinshi* zhenwei bian" 「心史」真偽辨. *Yuanshi luncong* 元史論叢, 5 (1993), pp. 235–242.

Yang Yumei 楊育鎂. *Yuandai haicao liangyun changxing yinsu zhi tantao* 元代海漕糧運暢行因素之探討. Taibei: Liren shuju, 1986.

Yao Congwu 姚從吾. "Song Yu Jie shefang shancheng dui Menggu ruqin de daji" 宋余玠設防山城對蒙古入侵的打擊. Rpt. in *Dongbeishi lucong* 東北史論叢, Vol. 2, pp. 364–375. Taibei: Zhengzhon shuju, 1959.

———. "Yuan Xianzong (Menggehan) de daju zheng Shu yu ta zai Hezhou Diaoyucheng de zhansi". 元憲宗(蒙哥汗)的大舉征蜀與他在合州釣魚城的戰死. In *Yao Congwu xiansheng quanji* 姚從吾先生全集, Vol. 6, pp. 253–285. Taibei: Zhengzhong shuju, 1982.

———. "Zheng Sixiao yu 'Tiehan Xinshi' guanxi de tuice" 鄭思肖與「鐵函心史」關係的推測. In *Yao Congwu xiansheng quanji*, Vol. 7, pp. 139–149.

Ye Xinmin 葉新民. *Yuan Shangdu yanjiu* 元上都研究. Huhhot: Nei Menggu daxue chubanshe, 1998.

——— and Qimudedaoerji 齊木德道爾吉, eds. *Yuan Shangdu yanjiu lunwen ji* 元上都研究論文集. Beijing: Zhongyang Renmin daxue chubanshe, 2003.

Yi Ding 一丁, Yu Lu 雨露, and Hong Yong 洪湧. *Zhongguo gudai fengshui yu jianzhu xuanzhi* 中國古代風水與建築選址. Baoding: Hebei kexue jishu chubanshe, 1995.

Yikezhao meng zhi 伊克昭盟志. Edited by Editorial Committee of the Gazetteer of the Yikezhao meng. Beijing: Xiandai chubanshe, 1995.

Yin Junke, Yu Deyuan 于德源, and Wu Wentao 吳文濤. *Beijing lishi ziran zaihai yanjiu* 北京歷史自然災害研究. Beijing: Zhongguo huanjing kexue chubanshe, 1997.

Yu Guangdu 于光度 and Chang Runhua 常潤華. *Beijing tongshi*, Vol. 4 (Jin Zhongdu).

Yu Jie 于傑 and Yu Guangdu 于光度. *Jin Zhongdu* 金中都. Beijing: Beijing chubanshe, 1989.

Yu Xixian 于希賢. "Zhouyi xiangshu yu Yuan Dadu guihua buju" 周易象數與元大都規劃布局. *Kong Meng xuebao* 孔孟學報, 76 (September 1998), pp. 169–188.

Yu Zhuoyun. *Zijin cheng gongdian* 紫禁城宮殿. Hong Kong: Shangwu yinshuguan, 1982. This book has been abridged as *Zijin cheng gongdian—jianzhu he shenghuo de yishu* 紫禁城宮殿——建築和生活的藝術. Hong Kong: Shangwu yinshuguan, 2002.

———, ed. *Zijin cheng jianzhu yanjiu yu baohu* (*Gugong bowuyuan jianyuan qishizhounian huigu*) 紫禁城建築研究與保護(故宮博物院建院70周年回顧). Beijing: Zijincheng chubanshe, 1995.

Yuan Ji 袁冀. *Yuan Taibao Cangchunsanren Liu Bingzhong pingshu* 元太保藏春散人劉秉忠評述. Taibei: Taiwan Shangwu yinshuguan, 1974.

Zhang Cixi 張次溪. *Yanjing fangu lu* 燕京訪古錄. In Zhang, ed., *Jingjin fengtu congshu* 京津風土叢書. Beijing: Shuangzhao lou. 1938.

———. *Renmin shoudu de Tianqiao*人民首都的天橋. Beijing: Xiugengtang shudian, 1951.

Zhang Dexin 張德信 and Tan Tianxing 譚天星. *Chongzhen huangdi dazhuan* 崇禎皇帝大傳. Shenyang: Liaoning jiaoyu chubanshe, 1993.

Zhang Ning 張寧. "*Makeboluo xingji* zhong de Yuan Dadu"《馬可波羅行記》中的元大都. Rpt. in *Makeboluo jieshao yu yanjiu* 馬可波羅介紹與研究, edited by Yu Shixiong 余士雄, pp. 85–106. Beijing: Shangwu yinshuguan, 1983.

Zhang Qingchang 張清常. *Beijing jiexiang mingqing shihua* 北京街巷名稱史話. Beijing: Beijing Yuyan wenhua daxue chubanshe, 1999.

———. *Hutong ji qita* 胡同及其他. Rev. ed. Beijing: Beijing Yuyan daxue chubanshe, 2004.

Zhang Quan 張泉. "Mingchu Nanjing cheng de guihua yu jianshe" 明初南京城的規劃與建設. In *Zhongguo gudu yanjiu* 中國古都研究, edited by Zhongguo gudu xuehui, pp. 71–202. Hangzhou: Zhejiang Renmin chubanshe, 1986.

Zhang Xiande 張先得. *Ming Qing Beijing chengyuan he chengmen* 明清北京城垣和城門. Shijiazhuang: Hebei jiaoyu chubanshe, 2003.

Zhang Xiumin 張秀民. *Zhong Yue guanxishi lunwenji* 中越關係史論文集. Taibei: Wenshizhe chubanshe, 1992.

Zhang Zichen 張紫辰, trans. Tada Teiichi 多田貞一, *Beijing deming zhi* 北京地名志. Beijing: Shumu wenxian chubanshe, 1986.

——— and Li Yuenan 李岳南, eds. *Beijing de chuanshuo.* Shanghai: Shanghai wenyi chubanshe 1982.

Zhao Jingshen 趙景深. *Zhongguo xiaoshuo congkao* 中國小說叢考. Jinan: Qilu shushe, 1983.

——— and Du Haoming 杜浩銘, eds. and annot. *Yinglie zhuan* 英烈傳. Based on the 159l, 1628, and 1616 editions. Shanghai: Siluan shuju, 1955.

Zhao Lingyang 趙令揚. "Mingdai Huitongguan" 明代會同館. *Dalu zazhi* 大陸雜誌, 41.5 (July 1970), pp. 17–30.

Zhao Runxing 趙潤星 and Yang Baosheng 楊寶生. *Taizhesi* 潭柘寺. Beijing: Beijing Yanshan chubanshe, 1986.

Zhao Shiyu 趙世瑜. *Fuxiu yu shenqi: Qingdai chengshi shenghuo changjuan* 腐朽與神奇：清代城市生活長卷. Changsha: Hunnan chubanshe, 1996.

———. *Kuanghuan yu richang: Ming Qing yilai de miaohui yu minjianshehui* 狂歡與日常：明清以來的廟會與民間社會. Beijing: Sanlian shudian, 2002.

———. "Zuxian jiyi, jiayuan xiangzheng yu zuqun lishi—Shanxi Hongdong Dahuaishu chuanshuo jiexi" 祖先記憶、家園象徵與族群歷史——山西洪洞大槐樹傳説解析. *Lishi yanjiu*, 2006.1 (February), pp. 49–64.

Zhao Zhengzhi 趙正之. "Yuan Dadu pingmian guihuo fuyuan de yanjiu" 元大都平面規劃復原的研究. *Kejishi wenji* 科技史文集, 2nd ser.: *Jianzhushi zhuanji* 建築史專輯, pp. 14–27. Shanghai: Shanghai kexuejishu chubanshe, 1979.

Zheng Lianzhang 鄭連章. "Wanshoushan de shezhi yu Zijin cheng weizhi kao" 萬壽山的設置與紫禁城位置考. Rpt. in *Zijin cheng yingshanji*, pp. 62–75.

Zhong Han 鍾焓. "Xishou, zhihuan yu zhenghe—Menggu liuchuan de Beijing jiancheng gushi xingchengguocheng kaocha" 吸收，置換與整合——蒙古流傳的北京建城故事形成過程考察. *Lishi yanjiu*, 2006.4 (August), pp. 36–52.

Zhongguo dabaikequanshu: Tianwenxue 中國大百科全書：天文學. Beijing: Zhongguo dabaikequanshu chubanshe, 1980.

Zhongguo jianzhu jianshi 中國建築簡史. Edited by *Zhongguo jianzhushi* bianji weiyuan hui. Beijing: Beijing gongye chubanshe, 1962.

Zhou Liangxiao 周良霄. *Hubilie* 忽必烈. Changchun: Jilin jiaoyu chubanshe, 1986.

Zhou Qingshu 周清樹. "Ming Chengzu shengmu Hongjilashi shuo suo fanying de tianmingguan" 明成祖生母弘吉剌氏說所反映的天命觀. *Nei Menggu daxue xuebao* 內蒙古大學學報 (*zhexue shehuikexue ban*), 1987.3 (July), pp. 1–18.

Zhou Qun 周群. *Liu Ji pingzhuan* 劉基評傳. Nanjing: Nanjing daxue chubanshe, 1995.

———. "Liu Ji—cong lishi dao shenhua de shanbian" 劉基——從歷史到神話的嬗變. *Dalu zazhi*, 96.3–4 (March–April 1998), pp. 16–19, 46–48.

Zhou Shaoliang 周紹良. "'Xinkan Wudang zuben leibian quanxiang Qisheng shilu' shuji"「新刊武當足本類編全相啟聖實錄」書記. *Wenxian* 文獻, 2 (1985), pp. 161–174.

Zhu Feng 朱風 and Jia Jingyan 賈敬顏, trans. *Hanyi Menggu Huangjin shigang* 漢譯蒙古黃金史綱. Huhehot: Nei Menggu Renmin chubanshe, 1985.

Zhu Hong 朱鴻. *Ming Chengzu yu Yongle zhengzhi* 明成祖與永樂政治. Taibei: National Taiwan Normal University, 1988.

Zhu Xiaoqin 朱肖琴, ed. *Zhongguo yuyan bazhong* 中國預言八種. Shanghai: Guangyi shuju. 1947.

Zhu Xie 朱偰. *Beijing gongjue tushuo* 北京宮闕圖說. Shanghai: Shangwu yinshuguan, 1938.

———. *Jinling guji tukao* 金陵古蹟圖考. Shanghai: Shangwu yinshuguan, 1935.

Zhu Xizu 朱希祖, "Ming Chengzu shengmu zhiyi bian" 明成祖生母質疑辯. (*Guoli*) *Zhongshan daxue wenshixue yanjiusuo yuekan* (國立) 中山大學文史學研究所月刊, 2.1 (1939), pp. 1–13.

Zhuang Jifa 莊吉發. *Qingdai Tiandi hui yuanliukao* 清代天地會源流考. Taibei: Gukong bowuyuan, 1981.

Ziluo 子羅 and Xiaoning 曉寧. "Chudu 'Liu Bingshu muzhi'" 初讀《劉秉恕墓誌》, *Wenwu chunqiu* 文物春秋, 1994.1 (March), pp. 86–89.

Japanese Language

Ishida Mikinosuke 石田幹之助. "Gen no Jōtōni tsuite" 元の上都に就いて (revised). *Nihon Daigaku sōritsu shichijūnen kinen rombunshū* 日本大學創立七十年紀念論文集, Vol. I (October 1960), pp. 271–319.

Kobayashi Takashirō 小林高四郎. *Mōko Ōgonshi* 蒙古黃金史. Tokyo: Seikatsu sha, 1941.

Makita Tairyō 牧田諦亮. "Dōen den shōkō" 道淵傳小稿. *Tōyōshi kenkyū* 東洋史研究, 18 (October 1959), pp. 57–79.

Matsumoto Bunzaburō 松本文三郎. "Tōbatsu bishamon kō" 兜跋毘沙門考. *Tōhō gakuhō*, 東方學報 (Kyoto), 10.1 (1939), pp. 12–21.

Miyazaki Ichisada 宮崎市定. "Bishamonten shinko no tōzen nitsuite" 毘沙門天信仰の東漸について. In *Miyazaki Ichisada zenshū* 宮崎市定先生全集, Vol. 19, pp. 51–81. Tokyo: Iwanami shoten, 1991.

Mochizuki Shinkō 望月信亨, ed. *Mochizuki Būkkyō daijiten* 望月佛教大辭典. Tokyo: Sekai seiten kankō kyōkai, 1954–1958.

Mostaert, Antoine. *Orudosu kōhi shū: Monkuru no minkan denshō* オルドス口碑集：モンゴルの民間伝承, translated by Isono Fujiko 礎野富士子. Tokyo: Heibonsha, 1966.

Muramatsu Ichiya 村松一彌, trans. *Pekin no densatsu* 北京の傳說. Tokyo: Heibonsha, 1976.

Murata Jirō 村田治郎. *Chūgoku no teito* 中國の帝都. Kyoto: Sōgeisha, 1981.

Nikaido Yoshihirō 二階堂善弘. "Nata taishi kō" 哪吒太子考. In *Dōkyō no rekishi to bunka* 道教の歴史と文化, edited by Yamada Toshiaki 山田利明 and Tanaka Fumio 田中文雄, pp. 167–196. Tokyo: Yūzankaku. 1998.

Otagi Matsuo 愛宕松男. "Gen no Daitō" 元の大都. *Rikishi kyōiku* 歴史教育, 14.12 (December 1966), pp. 59–65.

Ri Kenshō 李獻璋. *Maso shinkō no kenkyū* 媽祖信仰の研究. Tokyo: Taizan bunbutsusha, 1979.

Saeki Yūichi 佐伯有一, Tanaka Issei 田仲一成, et al., eds. *Niida Noboru hakushi shu Pekin kōshō "Girudo" (Guild) shiryōshū* 仁井田陞博士輯《北京工商ギルド資料集》. *Tōyōgaku bunken senta sokan* 東洋學文獻センター叢刊, No. 33, Vol. 5. Tokyo: Tōkyo Daigaku Tōyōbunka kenkyūjo, 1980.

Sakai Tadao 酒井忠夫. *Chūgoku zensho no kenkyū* 中國善書の研究. Tokyo: Kōbundō, 1960.

Suzuki Tadashi 鈴木正. "Chin Mansan setsuwa no bunseki" 沈萬三説話の分析. *Shikan* 史觀, 72 (September 1965), pp. 2–36.

Takakusu Juniirō 高楠順次郎 and Watanabe Kaigyoku 渡邊海旭, eds. *Taishō shinshū daizōkyō* 大正新修大藏經. Tokyo: Taishō issaikyō kankōkai, 1924–1932.

Yamamoto Mamoru 山本守. "Eiraku Tei to Kenbun Tei: Eiraku Tei no Mōko denki" 永樂帝と建文帝の蒙古伝記. Rpt. in Yamamoto, *Ryōtō no tama* 遼東の珠, pp. 107–117. Mukden: Manshu jidai sha, 1944.

Yō Kaiei 楊海英. "*Monkuru* ni okeru ōchō kōtaikan ni kansuru ichi shiryō—'En Taishi to Shin Taizi no monogatari' o chūshin ni" モンゴルにおける王朝交替に關する一資料──「遠太子と真太子の物語」を中心に. *Jimbun ronshū: Shizoka Daigaku Jimbun gakubu, Shakai gakka gengo bunka gakka kenkyū hōkoku* 人文論集：靜岡大學人文學部、社會學科言語文化學科研究報告, 54.2 (2003), pp. 23–65.

Western Languages

Altan Tobchi, A Brief History of the Mongols. Scripta Mongolica. Cambridge, MA: Harvard University Press, 1952.

Arlington, L. C. and Lewisohn, William. *In Search of Old Peking.* Peking: Henri Vetch, 1935.

Bawden, Charles R. *The Mongol Chronicle Altan Tobchi.* Wiesbaden: Otto Harrassowitz, 1955.

Bennett, Stevan J. "Patterns of the Sky and Earth: A Chinese Science of Applied Cosmology". *Chinese Science,* 3 (1978), pp. 1–26.

Bloss, Lowell W. "The Buddha and the Naga: A Study in Buddhist Folk Religion". *History of Religion,* 13 (1971), pp. 36–53.

Bolor Erike: Mongolian Chronicle. Scripta Mongolica 3. Cambridge, MA: Harvard University Press, 1950.

Bredon, Juliet. *Peking: A Historical and Intimate Description of Its Chief Places of Interest.* Shanghai: Kelly and Walsh, Ltd., enlarged and revised edition, 1931 (first published in 1919).

Bruun, Ole. *Fengshui in China: Geomantic Divination between State Orthodoxy and Popular Religion.* Honolulu: University of Hawaii Press, 2003.

Chan, David B. "The Role of the Monk Tao-yen in the Usurpation of the Prince of Yen". *Sinologica,* 6.2 (1959), pp. 83–100.

———. *The Usurpation of the Prince of Yen (1398–1402).* San Francisco: Chinese Materials Research Center, 1975.

Chan, Hok-lam. "Liu Chi in the *Ying-lieh chuan*: The Fictionalization of a Scholar-hero". *Journal of the Oriental Society of Australia,* 5.1–2 (December 1967): 26–42.

———. "Liu Ping-chung (1216–1274): A Buddhhist-Taoist Statesman at the Court of Khubilai Khan". *T'oung Pao,* 53.1–3 (1967), pp. 98–146.

———. "Liu Chi (1311–1375) and His Models: The Image-building of a Chinese Imperial Adviser". *Oriens Extremus,* 15.1 (June 1968), pp. 34–35.

———. "The Prophecy of Chang Chung: The Transmission of the Legend of an Early Ming Taoist". *Oriens Extremus,* 20.1 (June 1973), pp. 65–102.

———. "Die Prophezeiung des Liu Ji (1311–1375): Ihre Entstehung und ihre Umwandlung im heutigen China". *Saeculum,* 25.4 (1974), pp. 338–366.

———. "A Mongolian Legend of the Building of Peking". *Asia Major,* 3rd ser. 3.2 (1990), pp. 65–93.

———. "Siting by Bowshot: A Mongolian Custom and its Sociopolitical Implications". *Asia Major,* 3rd ser., 4.2 (September 1991), pp. 53–78.

———. "The Demise of Yuan Rule in Mongolian and Chinese Legends". In *Altaic Religious Beliefs and Practices. Proceedings of the 33rd Meeting of the Permanent International Altaistic Conference,* edited by Géza Bethlenfalvy and Alice

Sárközi, et al., pp. 65–82. Budapest: The Research Group for Altaic Studies, Hungarian Academy of Sciences, 1992.

———. "'The Distance of a Bowshot': Some Remarks on Measurement in the Altaic World". *Journal of Sung-Yuan Studies*, 25 (1995), pp. 29–46.

———. *China and the Mongols: History and Legend under the Yuan and Ming* (Variorum). Aldershot, Hampshire: Ashgate Publishing Ltd., 1999.

———. "Legitimating Usurpation: Historical Revisions under the Ming Yongle Emperor (r. 1402–1424)". In *The Legitimation of New Orders: Case Studies in World History*, edited by Phillip Yuen-sang Leung, pp. 75–158. Hong Kong: The Chinese University Press, 2007.

Chou I-liang 周一良. "Tantrism in China". *Harvard Journal of Asiatic Studies*, 8.3–4 (March 1945), pp. 284–307.

De Groot, J. J. M. *The Religious System of China*, Vols. 2, 3. Leiden: Brill, 1892.

de Heer, Philip. *The Care-taker Emperor*. Leiden: Brill, 1986.

de Rachewiltz, Hok-lam Chan, Ch'i-ch'ing Hsiao et al., eds. *In the Service of the Khan: Eminent Personalities of the Early Mongol-Yuan Period*. Wiesbaden: Harrassowitz Verlag, 1993.

Dong, Madeleine Yue. *Republican Beijing: The City and Its Histories*. Berkeley: University of California Press, 2003.

Dudbridge, Glen. *The Hsi-yu-chi: A Study of Antecedents to the Sixteenth-century Chinese Novel*. Cambridge: Cambridge University Press, 1970.

Dyson, Verne. *Forgotten Tales of Ancient China*. Shanghai: The Commercial Press, 1927.

Eitel, Ernest J. *Feng-shui, or, The Rudiments of Natural Science in China* (1873). Singapore: Graham Brash, 1984.

Eliade, Mircea. *Patterns in Comparative Religion*, translated by Rosemary Sheed. Cleveland: World, 1959.

———. *The Sacred and the Profane, the Nature of Religion*, translated by Willard R. Trask. New York: Harcourt Brace, 1959.

Erdeni-yin Tobchi: Mongolian Chronicle. Scripta Mongolica 2. Cambridge, MA: Harvard University Press, 1956.

Esherick, Joseph W., ed. *Remaking the Chinese City: Modernity and National Identity, 1900–1950*. Honolulu: University of Hawaii Press, 2000.

Farmer, Edward L. *Early Ming Government, The Evolution of Dual Capitals*. Cambridge, MA: Harvard University Press, 1976.

Farquhar, David M. *The Government of China under Mongolian Rule: A Reference Guide*. Münchener Ostasiatische Studien Band 53. Stuttgart: Franz Steiner, 1990.

Favier, Alphonse. *Peking: histoire et description*. Lille: Societe de Saing-Augustin, 1900.

Feuchtwang, Stephan. *An Anthropological Analysis of Chinese Geomancy*. Vientiane: Vitagna, 1974. New edition, Bangkok: White Lotus Co. Ltd., 2002.

Franke, Herbert and Denis Twitchett, eds. *The Cambridge History of China*, Vol. 6: *Alien Regimes and Border States, 907–1368*. Cambridge: Cambridge University Press, 1994.

Friese, Heinz. "Der Mönch Yao Kuang-hsiao (1335–1418) und seine Zeit". *Oriens Extremus*, 7 (1960), pp. 158–184.

——. "Das *Tao-yu-lü* des Yao Kuang-hsiao". *Oriens Extremus*, 8 (1961), pp. 42–56.

Getty, Alice. *The Gods of Northern Buddhism; their history, iconography and progressive evolution through the Northern Buddhist countries*. Rev. ed. London: The Clarendon Press, 1928.

Goodrich, Anne S. *The Peking Temple of the Eastern Park: The Tung-yueh miao in Peking*. Nagoya: Monumenta Serica, 1964.

Goodrich, L. Carrington and Chaoying Fang, eds. *Dictionary of Ming Biography, 1368–1644*. 2 vols. New York: Columbia University Press, 1976.

Grootaers, W. A. "Les temples villageois de la région au sud de Tat'ong (Chansi nord), leurs inscriptions et leur historie". *Folklore Studies*, 4(1945), pp. 161–212.

——. "The hagiography of the Chinese god Chen-wu (The transmission of rural traditions in Chahar)". *Folklore Studies*, 11 (1952), pp. 139–182.

——, Li Shih-yu, and Chang Chi-wen 張冀文. "Temples and history of Wanch'üan (Chahar): The geographical method applied to folklore". *Monumenta Serica*, 13 (1948), pp. 209–316.

——, Li Shih-yu, and Wang Fu-shih 王輔世. *The Sanctuaries in a North-China city—A complete survey of the cultic buildings in the city of Hsüan-Hua Chahar. Mélanges Chinois et Bouddhiques*, 26 (1995), Bruxelles.

Haar, Barend J. Ter. *Ritual and Mythology of the Chinese Triads: Creating an Identity*. Leiden: Brill, 1998.

Hargett, James M. "Huizong's Magic Marchmount: The *Genyue* Pleasure Park of Kaifeng". *Monumenta Serica*, 38 (1988–1989), pp. 1–48.

Henderson, John B. *Development and Decline of Chinese Cosmology*. New York: Columbia University Press, 1984.

Hessig, Walter, ed. *Altan kürdün mingglan gegesülü bichig: Eine Mongolische Chronik von Siregetü Guosi Dharma* [1739 ms]. Kopenhagen: Munksgaard, 1958.

——. *The Religions of Mongolia*, translated by Geoffrey Samuel. Berkeley: University of California Press, 1980.

——. "Ein Quellenbezug der Altan Khan Biographie". *Menggushi yanjiu* 蒙古史研究, 1 (July 1985), pp. 185–192.

Ho Kin-chung. "Nezha: Figur de l'enfant rebelled". *Études Chinoises*, 7.2 (Autumn, 1988), pp. 7–26.

Ho Peng Yoke. *The Astronomical Chapters of Chin-shu*. Paris: Mouton & Co., 1966.

———. *Li, Qi and Shu: An Introduction to Science and Civilization in China.* Hong Kong: Hong Kong University Press, 1985.

Jing, Anning. *The Water God's Temple of the Guangsheng Monastery, Cosmic Function of Art, Ritual, and Theater.* Leiden: Brill, 2002.

Kates, George N. "A New Date for the Origins of the Forbidden City". *Harvard Journal of Asiatic Studies,* 7.3 (February 1943), pp. 180–202.

Lattimore, Owen. "A Mongol Legend of the Founding of Peking". *Central Asiatic Journal,* XXIII (1979), pp. 37–39.

Le Blanc, Charles. *Huai Nan Tzu: Philosophical Synthesis in Early Han Thought.* Hong Kong: Hong Kong University Press, 1985.

Legge, James, trans. *I Ching: Book of Change.* Edited by Ch'u Chai and Winberg Chai with introduction. New Hyde Park, NY: University Books, 1964.

Li, Lillian, Alison J. Dray-Novey, and Haili Kong. *Beijing: From Imperial Capital to Olympic City.* New York: Palgrave Macmillan, 2007.

Lin Yutang (林語堂). *Imperial Peking, Seven Centuries of China.* New York: Crown Publishers, 1961.

Lip, Evelyn. *Feng Shui: Environment of Power: A Study of Chinese Architecture.* London: Academy Editions, 1995.

Little, Stephen et al., eds. *Daoism and the Arts of China.* Chicago: The Art Institute of Chicago in Association with The University of California Press, 2000.

Liu, Cary Y. "The Yuan Dynasty Capital: Imperial Building Program and Bureaucracy". *T'oung Pao,* 78 (1992), pp. 264–301.

Liu Ts'un-yan. *Buddhist Influences on Chinese Novels,* Vol. I: *The Authorship of the Feng Shen Yen I.* Wiesbaden: Otto Harrassowitz, 1962.

———. *Chinese Popular Fiction in Two London Libraries* (倫敦所見中國小說書錄). Hong Kong: Lung Men Bookstore, 1967.

———. "Lu Hsi-hsing: A Confucian Scholar, Taoist Priest and Buddhist Devotee of the Sixteenth Century". Rpt. in Liu, *Selected Papers from the Hall of the Harmonious Wind,* pp. 175–202. Leiden: Brill, 1976.

———. "Wu Ch'eng-en: His Life and Career". Rpt. in Liu, *Selected Papers from the Hall of the Harmonious Wind,* pp. 259–355.

Loewe, Michael. *Divination, Mythology and Monarchy in Han China.* Cambridge: Cambridge University Press, 1994.

Louis, François. "The Genesis of an Icon: The *Taiji* Diagram's Early History". *Harvard Journal of Asiatic Studies,* 63.1 (June 2003), pp. 145–196.

Lust, John. *The Revolutionary Army: A Chinese Nationalist Tract of 1903.* Paris: Mouton & Co., 1968.

March, Andrew L. "An Appreciation of Chinese Geomancy". *Journal of Asian Studies,* 27.2 (1968), pp. 53–67.

MacFarquahar, Roderick. *The Forbidden City.* New York: Newsweek, 1972.

Meyer, Jeffrey, F. *The Dragons of Tiananmen: Beijing as a Sacred City.* Columbia: University of South Carolina Press, 1991.

Mostaert, Antoine. *Textes oraux ordos.* Monumenta Serica Monograph Series I. Peiping: The French Bookstore, 1937.

———. *Folklore ordox.* Monumenta Serica Monograph Series II. Peiping: The Catholic University, 1947.

———, trans. and annot. *Manual of Mongol Astrology and Divination.* Scripta Mongolica IV. Cambridge, MA: Harvard University Press, 1968.

Mote, F. W. "The T'u-mu Incident of 1449." In *Chinese Ways in Warfare,* edited by Frank A. Kierman, Jr. and John K. Fairbank, pp. 243–272, 361–369. Cambridge, MA: Harvard University Press, 1974.

———. "The Transformation of Nanking, 1350–1400". In *The City in Late Imperial China,* edited by G. William Skinner, pp. 101–153. Stanford: Stanford University Press, 1977.

——— and Denis Twitchett, eds. *The Cambridge History of China,* Vol. 7, part I: *The Ming Dynasty (1368–1644).* Cambridge: Cambridge University Press, 1988.

Naquin, Susan. *Millenarian Rebellion in China: The Eight Trigrams Uprising of 1813.* New Haven: Yale University Press, 1976.

———. *Peking: Temples and City Life, 1400–1900.* Berkeley: University of California Press, 2000.

Nebesky-Wojkowitz, René de. *Oracles and demons of Tibet: the cult and iconography of the Tibetan protective deities.* Graz, Austria Akademische Drucku. Verlagsanstalt, 1975.

Needham, Joseph et al., eds. *Science and Civilization in China,* Vols. 2, 3, 4. Cambridge: Cambridge University Press, 1956, 1959, 1962.

Nivison, David S. "The Dates of Western Chou". *Harvard Journal of Asiatic Studies,* 43.2 (December 1983), pp. 481–580.

Paludan, Ann. *The Ming Tombs.* Hong Kong: Oxford University Press, 1991.

Pokotilov, D. *History of the Eastern Mongols during the Ming Dynasty from 1368 to 1634,* translated by R. Loewenthal. Studia Serica Monographs, Series A. Chengtu: Western Union University of China, 1947.

Rawlinson, Andrew. "Nagas and the Magic Cosmology of Buddhism". *Religion,* 16 (1986), pp. 135–153.

Rossabi, Morris. *Khubilai Khan: His Life and Times.* Berkeley: University of California Press, 1988.

Schafer, Edward H. *Pacing the Void: T'ang Approaches to the Stars.* Berkeley: University of California Press, 1977.

Schurmann, Herbert Franz. *Economic Structure of the Yuan Dynasty.* Cambridge, MA: Harvard University Press, 1967.

Serruys, Henry. "A Note on Arrows and Oaths among the Mongols". *Journal of the American Oriental Society,* 78.4 (1958), pp. 279–284.

———. "The Mongols in China during the Hung-wu Period (1368–1398)". *Mélanges Chinois et Bouddhiques,* 11 (1959), pp. 47–50. Bruxelles.

———. "Mongols Ennobled during the Early Ming". *Harvard Journal of Asiatic Studies,* 22 (1959), pp. 209–260.

———. "The Mongols in China, 1400–1450". *Monumenta Serica,* 16 (1968), pp. 233–305.

———. "*Ho-po, ho-pao* 'pouch': Tukic *gap, xap*". *Oriens Extremus,* 15 (1968), pp. 135–148.

———. "A Manuscript Version of the Legend of the Mongol Ancestry of the Yung-lo Emperor". In *Analecta Mongolica: Dedicated to the Seventieth Birthday of Professor Owen Lattimore,* edited by John G. Hangin and U. Onon, pp. 19–61. Publications of the Mongol Society Occasional Papers 8. Bloomington: Mongol Society, 1972.

———. "A Catalogue of Mongol Manuscripts from Ordos". *Journal of the American Oriental Society,* 95.2 (April–June 1975), pp. 191–208.

———. "A Note on Two Place Names in Mongolia". In *Documenta Barbarorum: Festschrift für Walther Heissig zum 70 Geburtstag,* edited by K. Sagaster and M. Weiers, pp. 370–381. Wiesbaden: Otto Harrassowitz, 1983.

Shaw, J. S. (Shao Xunzheng 邵循正). "Historical Significance of the Curios Theory of the Mongol Blood in the Veins of the Ming Emperors". *Chinese Social and Political Sciences Review,* 20.4 (1937), pp. 492–498.

Sirén, Osvald. *The Walls and Gates of Peking: Researches and Impressions.* Illustrated with 109 photographs by the author and 50 architectural drawings made by Chinese artists. London: John Lane Ltd., 1924.

Sit, Victor F. S. (Xue Fengxuan 薛鳳旋). *Beijing: The Nature and Planning of a Chinese Capital City.* New York: Wiley, 1995.

Skinner, Stephen. *The Living Earth Manual of Feng-Shui: Chinese Geomancy.* London: Routledge & Kegan Paul, 1982; Arkana, the Penguin Group, 1989.

Smith, Richard J. *Fortune-Tellers and Philosophers: Divination in Traditional Chinese Society.* Boulder: Westview Press, 1991.

Soothill, William. *A Dictionary of Chinese Buddhism Terms.* Delhi: Motilal Banarsidass, 1937.

Steinhardt, Nancy S. "Imperial Architecture under Mongolian Patronage: Khubilai's City of Daidu". PhD dissertation, Harvard University, 1981.

———. *Chinese Imperial City Planning.* Honolulu: University of Hawaii Press, 1990.

———. "The Plan of Khubilai Khan's Imperial City". *Artibus Asiae,* 44.2–3 (1983), pp. 137–158.

Strand, David. *Rickshaw Peking: City and Politics in the 1920s.* Berkeley: University of California Press, 1989.

Sun Xiaochun and Jacob Kistemaker. *The Chinese Sky during the Han: Constellating Stars and Society.* Leiden: Brill, 1997.

The I Ching or Book of Changes. The Richard Wilhelm Translation rendered into English by Cary F. Baynes. Bollingen Series XIX. Princeton, NJ: Princeton University Press, 1967.

Tsai, Shih-shan Henry. *Perpetual Happiness: The Ming Emperor Yongle.* Seattle: University of Washington Press, 2001.

Tu Li-ch'en. *Annual Customs and Festivals in Peking,* translated and annotated by Derk Bodde. 2nd edition. Hong Kong: Hong Kong University Press, 1965.

Waley, Arthur. *A Catalogue of Paintings recovered from Tunhuang by Sir Aurel Stein.* London: The British Museum. 1931.

Wang, Aihe. *Cosmology and Political Culture in Ancient China.* Cambridge: Cambridge University Press, 2000.

Werner, E. T. C. *Myths and Legends of China.* London: George G. Harrap, 1924.

——. *A Dictionary of Chinese Mythology* (1932). Introduction by Professor Hyman Kublin. New York: The Julian Press, 1961.

Wheatley, Paul. *The Pivot of the Four Quarters: A Preliminary Enquiry into the Origins and Character of Ancient Chinese City.* Chicago: Aldine Publishing Company, 1971.

Wong Siu Hon. *Investigations into the Authenticity of the Chang San-Feng Ch'uan-Chi: The Complete Works of Chang San-Feng.* Canberra: Australian National University Press, 1982.

Wright, Arthur F. "The Cosmology of the Chinese City". In *The City in Late Imperial China,* edited by G. William Skinner, pp. 33–73. Stanford: Stanford University Press, 1977.

Wu Hung. *Remaking Beijing: Tiananmen Square and the Creation of a Political Space.* Chicago: The University of Chicago Press, 2005.

Xiong, Victor Cunrui. *Sui-Tang Chang'an: A Study in Urban History of Medieval China.* Center for Chinese Studies, The University of Michigan. Ann Arbor, Michigan, 2000.

Yan Chongnian. *Beijing: The Treasures of an Ancient Capital.* Peking: Morning Glory Press, 1985.

Yang, Gladys. *Peking Legends.* Beijing: Panda Books, 1982. Reprint. Beijing: Foreign Language Press, 2005.

Yu, Anthony C. *The Journey to the West,* vol. 4. Chicago: The University of Chicago Press, 1983.

Index

Chinese characters are given for items which are not glossed in the main text and Notes. Numbers in **bold** refer to pages with figures or maps.

Acheng, (Jin) Shangjing, 5
Altan kürdüun mingghan kegesütü bichiq, 174
Altan Tobchi, 175, 183, 205
Altan Tobchi (brevior), 174
Altan-qan of Temud, 184
Altar of Earth, see Ditan
Altar of Heaven, see Tiantan
Altar of the Moon, see Yuetan
Altar of the Sun, see Ritan
Altars of Mountains and Rivers, see Shanchuantan
Altars of Soil and Grain, see Shejitan
Amoghavajra (Monk Bukong), 67, 69, 71–73
An-ting Men, see Andingmen
Ancestral Altar of Agriculture, see Xian'nongtan
Ancestral Temple, see Taimiao
Andingmen (Gate of Fixed Peace), **101**, 111, 113, 114, 116, 127–129, **131**, 133, 266, 269
Anti-Manchu
- deified hero/prophet-savior (Liu Bowen), 152, 165
- dissidents, 148
- Eight Trigrams uprising, 149
- Heaven and Earth Society, 149, 186
- Ming restoration propaganda, 154, 166
- revolutionary movement, 118, 154, see also "*Fan Qing fu Ming*", Tiandihui

Anti-Mongol uprisings, on the eve of the Mid-Autumn festival, 154, 177, 270, 276, see also "Killing the Tartars" propaganda
Anxi, 71, 73, 80
Anzhen Gate, **49**, **54**, 61
Arash, narrator of Mongolian story of the building of Peking, 202
Ariq Böke, 39
Arlington, L. C. and William Lewisohn, 127, 168, 220
Astral-geography, concept in imperial capital construction, 4, 15, see also *Fatian xiangdi, Fenye,* Imperial cities
- Liu Bingzhong's knowledge of, 35, 44, 47, 52, 55

Astrobiology, see Berthelot, René, Sky-earth correspondence concept
Aśvaghosa (Monk Maming), 69
Azure Dragon, see Canglong

Ba [Dam or Embankment] Canal, 7, 50, **51**, **54**, 81
Badaraghultu törö, 277
bagh-a gaghan, 195, see also "Little Emperor"

Bagua, 10, 22, 192, see also Eight Trigrams
Baifu Spring, 50, 60, 115, 156
Baihu [White Tiger], 10, **11**, 22, 105
Bailian Pool, 7, see also Jishui Pool
Baita Monastery, 129, **131**
Baixia Gate, 245, 247
Baiyuan (jing) fengyu (zhanhou) tu, 146
Baiyunguan [White Cloud Shrine], 2, 114, 214
Baotian Ward, 55
Baozhi, grave in Mount Zhong, 160, 326n91
Baozuo ("treasured seat"), 232, 285
Bars Qota ["Tiger City"], 184, 271
Bātur (Bağatur), 37, 39, 45–46
"Bazhishou de Nezha zhizheng", 320n55
Bei Yuan 北元 [Northern Yuan], 87
Bei'anmen, 105, 130, 219
Beichen [Northern Asterism], 46
Beidou (Big Dipper), 53, 212
Beifang Pishamen tianwang suijun hufa yigui [Ceremonies in the Worship of the Heavenly King Vaiśravana of the North, the Protector of the Army], 69, see also Vaiśravana, Heavenly King
Beifang Pishamen tianwang suijun hufa zhenyan [The True Words of the Heavenly King Vaiśravana of the North, the Protector of the Army], 67, 70, see also Vaiśravana, Heavenly King
Beihai [North Sea], 110, 278, 279, 282
Beihai Park, 51
Beiji [North Pole], 10, 13, 14, 46
Beijing, xv, 1, 2, 5, 8, 35, 93, 118, 133, 147, 166, 168, 202, 207, 208, 215, 216, 224, 230, 234, 260, see also Peking
  as a "Holy City"/"Sacred City", xviii, 27, 28, 297n34
  city map, 162
  in Republican period, 30, 126
  modern folktales, 168, 194, 207
  storytellers in, 208
"Bei-jing cheng" [Peking City], 216, 219–221, 278
Beijing de chuanshuo (Jin Shoushen), 132–134, 319n54, see also under Peking, "The Eight-armed Nezha City"
Beijing de chuanshuo (Zhang Zichen/Li Yuenan), 134–136
Beijing fengwu chuanshuo, 207
Beijing fengwu chuanshuo gushi xuan, 207
Beijing Legends (Gladys Yang), 133, 134, 168, 266, see also *Beijing de chuanshuo* (Jin Shoushen), Peking legends
Beiping gongshi tu [Drawings of the palaces and chambers of Beiping], 88
Beiping(fu), 8, 43, 87, 91, 93, 175, 184, 196, 197, 217, 219, 235, 284, see also Dadu, Pei-p'ing Fu, Yan prefecture
Beipinghua yuhui, 126
Beisheng [Northern (Central) Secretariat], **54**, 55, 56
Beixinqiao, 227, 230, 231, 282, 283
Beixinqiao shangchang, 230
Bell Tower, see Zhonglou
Berthelot, René, 9
Bianliang (Kaifeng), 1, 23, 52, 60
Big Dipper, see Beidou
Bili zacun, 142
Bitter Sea Youzhou, 132, 227, 228,

263, 265, see also Dragons, Youzou
Biyan lu, 74
Black Dragon Pool
 in Taoranting, 30, 157, 158
 in Fangshan, 83, 120, see also Heilongtan
bLo-bzaṅ bsTan-'jin, *Altan Tobchi*, 174
Book of Changes [*Yijing*], 9, 10, 19, 20, 22, 35, 40, 41, 47, 56, 57, 61, 62, 96, 106, 192, 242
"Book of the Story of How Emperor Yung-lo of the Great Ming Built the City of Peking—The Yuan Prince—The True Prince" (*Dayiming yuwa lowa gaghan begej̆ ing qota-(n)i bayighulughsan üliger-ün debter—Yuwa (n) tayise—J̌ing tayise*), 147, 177
 text, 270–277, see also Mongolian legend of the Mongol maternity of the Yongle Emperor
Brahmanism, 67
Buddha, 67, 68 (Śākyamuni), 69, 72, 180
Buddhacarita-kāvya (*Fosuoxingzan jing*), 69
Buddhayaśas, 67
Buddhism, 36, 234, 235, 249, see also Chan Buddhism, Tantric Buddhism, Tibetan Buddhism (Lamaism)
 borrowed from Brahmanism, 67
 popular, influence of, 75, 112
 refutation of Neo-Confucian arguments against—by Zhu Xi, 164, 165
 under the Liao, 4
 White Lotus-Maitreya sects, 66, 149
 Yuandun sect, 149
Buddhist monasteries
 in Dadu, 61, 73
 in Jin Zhongdu, 5
 in Liao Nanjing, 4
 in Peking, 114
Buddhist *Tripitaka*, 69
Bukong (Monk), see Amoghavajra
Bureau of Military Affairs, 53, 55, 56, see also Shumiyuan
Burkhan (Mongolian God), 203, 205
Buxinqiao, 227, 230

"Caishen" Hall, 214
Cambulac (city of the Khans), 62, see also Dadu
Cangchun (Liu Bingzhong), 36
Cangchun ji, 40
Canglong [Azure Dragon], 10, **11**, 22, 105
Canling Zhongshu (councilor of the Secretariat), 39
Caomu zi, 41, 63
Celestial imperial court, correspondence with terrestrial counterparts, 15–17
Celestial Markets Enclosure, see Tianshiyuan
Celestial Master Palace, see Tianshigong
Celestial-terrestrial correspondence/ division systems, 4, 9, 12, 14, 22, 56, 57, 61, 96, 100, 103
 modification by Dadu, 55
Censorate, see Yushitai
Central and South Sea, see Zhongnanhai
Central Asia, 63
Central Capital, see Zhongdu
Central Palace, see Zhonggong, Zigong

Central Pavilion, see Zhongxinge
Central Secretariat, see Beisheng, Nansheng, Zhongshusheng
Chan Buddhism, 43, 234
  gongan (cases), 73
  Linji sect, 36
Chang [Long] River, see Yu [Jade] River
Chang'an, 1, 17, 23
Changgu Zhenyi, 64
Changling ["Longevity Tumulus"], 94, 98, 156, see also Yongle Emperor, Zhu Di
Changping, Hebei, **3**, 50, 94, 99, 114, 224
Changzhou, 42, 208
Chaobai River, 2, **3**
Chaoqianshi [Court's Front Markets], 106, 113
Chao-yang Men, see Chaoyangmen
Chaoyangmen
  (Nanjing), **92**
  (Peking), **101**, 111, 113, **116**, 129, **131**, 133, 265, 269
Chen (state), 88
Chen Gui, Earl of Taining, 98, 99
Chen Youliang, 139, 141, 143
Cheng, King of Zhou, 17
Cheng, Prince of (Zhang Shicheng), 209
Cheng Hao, 22
Cheng Yi, 22
Chengguangdian 承光殿 [Hall of Receiving Brightness], **112**
Chenghua reign (Ming), 118–119
Chenghuangmiao, 114
Chengqing Ward, 55
Chengtian [Received from Heaven] Gate, 110, **112**, **116**, see also Tian'anmen
Cheng-yang Men, see Zhengyangmen
Chengyi, Earl of (Liu Ji), 140
Chengyibo Liu Wencheng gong wenji, 140
"Chengyibo Liugong xingzhuang", 141, 320n59
Chengyunku 承運庫, **112**
Chengzong, Mongol ruler Temür, 96
Chengzu, see Zhu Di, Prince of Yan, Yongle Emperor
Chesi [Wagon Shop], 15
Chexiang Canal, 7
Chiang Kai-shek (Jiang Jieshi), xv, 8
Chibi, 143
Chibing ge [Eating Cake Ballad], 154
Ch'ien Men [Front Gate], see Qianmen
Ch'ien-ch'ing Kung, see Qianqing Palace
Ch'ien-ch'ing Men, see Qianqingmen
Chinese Nostradamus, see Liu Ji
Chinese Republic, founding of, xv, 8, 123
Chinggis Qan, 7, 39, 144, 191, 195, 203, 255, 256, 270
Chin-ling, see Jinling
Chinqai (Zhenhai), 191, 255
Ch'i-p'an Chieh, see Qipan Street
Chongguobeisi, 326n94
Chongguosi, 326n94
Chongren Gate 崇仁門, **49**, **54**, 61, **101**
Chongwenmen, **101**, 111, 113, **116**, **131**, 133, 230, 265, 269
Chongzhen emperor, see Ming emperor Sizong
Chongzhen reign, 119
Chongzhi Gate 崇智門, **49**
Chu Hongwu, see Zhu Hongwu
Chu Hung-wu, see Hongwu Emperor, Zhu Hongwu

Chuanxin lu, 142
Chung-ho Tien, 130
Chung-hua Men, see Zhonghua Gate
Chungkulou, see Zhonggulou
Ch'ung-wen Men, see Chongwenmen
Chunqiu fanlu [Luxuriant Dew of the Spring and Autumn Annals], 10
Chuogeng lu, 41
Chu-ti, see Zhu Di
Chuzhou, Zhejiang, 138
Cidu Monastery, 129, **131**
Coal Hill, see Jingshan, Meishan
"Coiling dragon" [*longpan*] and "crouching tiger" [*huju*], 46
Confucianism, 36
Confucius, 89
  political ideology, 110
Court of Imperial Entertainments, see Guanglusi
Crystal Hall [Shuijingdian], domicile of Dragon King in the Eastern Sea, 77, 223
Crystal Palace [Baotagong], domicile of Heavenly King Vaiśravana, 73, 79

Da Chao (Great Dynasty), 39
Da Guangmingdian 大光明殿 [Hall of Great Brightness], **112**
Da Longshan Huguosi, 164, 326n94, see also Yao Guangxiao
Da Ming (Great Brightness), 56, see also Great Ming
Da Ming Gate, 56, **104**, 110, **112**, 113, 128, **131**
Da Mingdian, 52
Da Nei [Great Interior] (Yuan), 51, 55, 56, 88, **104** (site)
Da Qing Gate, 110, 128, **131**
Da Shengshou Wan'ansi [Great Wan'an Monastery for the Emperor's Birthday], 191, see also White Pagoda Monastery
Da Song (State), 66, 88, 139, see also Han Liner
Da Song Sengshi lue, 73
Da Tang San Zang qujing shihua [Poetic Talk on Great Tang's "Three Tripitaka" Master Journeying to obtain the Scriptures], 74
Da Tianshou Wanningsi 大天壽萬寧寺, **54**
Da T'ung, see Datong
Da Wanshousi, 234, see also Tanzhe Monastery
Da Xinglongsi, 164, 300n15, see also Qingshousi
Da Yuan [Great great], 39, 270, see also Great Yuan, Yeke Mongghol ulus
Dabao fawang, 299n12, see also 'Phags-pa
Dadu (Yuan), xv–xvi, xviii, 1, 8, 23, 24, 25, 42, 80, 84, 91, 95, 97, 121, 122, 138, 157–159, 191, 199, 201, 224, 225, 249, 252, 254, see also Great Capital
  as imperial capital, 18, 35, 39, 48, 62, 63, 82
  as imperial city, 18, 47, 63, 64, 80, 156, 251, 253, 254
  blueprint for Ming Peking, 90, 93, 100, **101**, 113, 155
  building of capital city and city plan, 22, 35, 37, 42, 44–63, 192, 251, see also Liu Bingzhong, Qubilai gaghan
  city plan superimposed on "Diagram of the Posterior Heavens", **54**, 192

city plan superimposed on Jin Zhongdu, **49**
explanation of the eleven gates of outer-city walls in popular legend, 61, 62, 64, 65, 79, 253, see also Liu Bingzhong
fall to armies of Zhu Yuanzhang with Togōn Temür's flight, 85, 87, 147, 173, 175, 177, 184, 219
fang (ward) and markets in outer-city, 19, 60, 61
imperial-city (*huangcheng*), 18, 48, 50–52, 55–57, 59–61, 88, 102, 156, 219
lakes, rivers, canals, **51**
Nazha City legend, see main entry
outer-city (*waicheng*), 18, 48, 50, 55, 60, 62, 66, 79
palace-city (*gongcheng*), 18, 48, 51, 52, 55–57, 59–61, 88, 100, 102, 156
population in the capital city, 61–63, 81, 84
rain, flood and drought in the Mongol-Yuan reign, 61, 81, 83, 118
transcription of the name, 205, 271
"Dadu fu"
(Li Yousun), 46–47
(Huang Wenzhong), 62
Dadu Remains Public Park [Yuan Dadu chengyuan yizhi gongyuan], 48, 302n25
Dai T'ung, see Datong
Daidu (Mongolian for Dadu), 62
Dali kingdom, 37
Daluoxian (the highest-ranked immortal), 76
Dam or Embankment Canal, see Ba Canal
Dang Liang [Warding off Chen Youliang], 144
Daning Palace, 6, see also Wanning Palace
Dao'an (Monk), 40
Daofa huiyuan, 74
Daoism, 36, 43, 74, 77, 142, 249
in Han dynasty, 14
influence of, on Buddhist works, 73–75, 142
Daoist, hierarchy, 76
immortals, 74, 77
pantheon, 74
popular literature, 74, 253
shrines in Dadu, 61
shrines in Jin Zhongdu, 5
shrines in Peking, 114
Daoists, Quanzhen sect, 36
Daoyu lu, 164
Daoyuan (Monk), see Yao Guangxiao
Daqingshan, 218
Dark God, bronze stature image cast in the image of Emperor Yongle, 96, **97**, **188**, 313n15
assistance to Prince of Yan in the *jingnan* campaign, 333n31
images in temples, 334n32, see also Dark God Zhenwu
Dark God (Zhenwu), war god and guardian of the north, 75, 157, 187, 189, 199, 255
as Xuantian Shangdi [High Lord of the Dark Heaven], 96
poem allegedly written by, 299n11
Dark Warrior, see Xuanwu
Datong, Shanxi, 189, 218
Daxing [Great Posterity], **3**, 5
Dayan zhishu ("number of the total"), 19, 61

Dayidu (Dadu), 205, 271
Dayitung (*sic* for Dadu), 205, 271
Deshengmen, **101**, 111, 115, **116**, 128, 129, **131**, 133, 136, 162, 219, 266, 269, 270
Dharmaraksa (Monk Tanwuchen), 69
Dhritarāshtra [Chiguo tianwang] (East), 67
Di [root] (lunar lodge), 12
"Diagram of the Posterior Heavens", see *Houtian tu*
"Diagrams", 187, 192, 274, see also *Baqua*, Eight Trigrams
Dian (hall), 90, 102
Di'anmen, **104**, 105, **131**, 219, 237, 240, 287, see also Bei'anmen
Digunai, see Jin emperor Liang (Hailing wang)
Dijing jingwu lue, 157
Dili (kanyu) manxing, 22, 146
Ding (ingot), 210
Dingdai/Dingli ("Sacred Ornament"), 180
"Dingding dangdang panergui" [The Jingling Ghost in the Tub], 75
Directorate of Ceremonial, see Silijian
Directorate of Clothing Service, see Shangyijian
Directorate of Eunuchs, see Neigongjian
Dishi wenda ge (Ballad of Dialogue between the Emperor and the Teacher), 150, see also *Shaobing ge*
Ditan [Altar of Earth], 107, 111, **116**, 126
Dizhi [terrestrial branches], 4, see also "Twelve Terrestrial Branches"
Dong, Madeleine, *Republican Beijing*, 27, 30; on "recycling", 31, 126, 138, 258
Dong Gu, 142
Dong Huang Si [East Yellow Monastery], 129
Dong liugong [Six Eastern Palaces], **108**
Dong Zhongshu, 10
Dong'an Gate, 129, **131**
Dongbianmen, 113, 116, 133, 265, 269
Dongchengqu, 230
Donghuamen, 105, 129, **131**, 236, 239, 240, 244, 285
Dongjing, 1, 5, 17, 23, 73, see also Bianliang.
Dongming li [The Dongming Almanac], 144
Dongxi Shangjiang (East and West Upper Generals), 15
Dongxi Shangxiang [East and West Upper Ministers], 15
Dongyuemiao [Eastern Park Temple], 114, **131**, 325n85
Dongzhimen, **101**, 111, **116**, 129, **131**, 133, 230, 266, 269
Dou [dipper] (lunar lodge), 12
Dragon
  as a cosmological image of Fengshui, 22, 23 45–47, 95, 96
  as symbol of Chinese ruler but not among the Mongol gaghan, 183
Dragon(s)
  as mythical creature, 76, 96, 105, 107, 181, 183, 203–205, 250, 275
  as rain-maker, worshiped in Dadu, 81, 120, 121
  as spiritual deity in Tantric Buddhist sutra, 72, 73, 77–79

as spiritual sea creature, xvii, 30
in Bitter Sea Youzhou, 263, 265, 266, 279
in building of Peking legend, 125, 126, 132, 133, 136, 157, 158, 166, 168, 207, 221, 223, 224, 226, 228, 231, 234, 243, 253, see also Liu Bowen, Shen Wanshan, Yao Guangxiao
in Shangdu legend, 65, 66
"Dragon cult", identification with the emperor institution, 223
"Dragon deity" (*longshen*), 83
Dragon family (spiritual sea creatures), xvii, 30, 77, 84, 200, 222, 223, 230, 280, 281
Dragon genii, 79, 84, 157, 158, 166, 168, 199
Dragon King, xvi, xvii, 25, 26, 27, 67, 78, 129, 258, see also Dragon(s)
as spiritual protector of professional guilds in Peking, 157
battling with Buddhist child-deity Nazha/Nezha in the Eastern Sea in Daoist stories, 77, 79, 80, 122, 158, 243 ,253, 254, see also Nazha/Nezha
battling with Nazha/Nezha for control of lake water in Peking in popular stories, 122, 136, 227, 228
battling with Shen Wanshan and Yao Guangxiao over control of Peking's water, 229, 230, see also Shen Wanshan, Yao Guangxiao
feuding with Liu Bowen and battling with Gao Liang to seek control of Peking's water, 221–223, 226–231, 257, 279–283, see also Liu Bowen, Gao Liang
images of, **137**
revered in Dadu as deity for calming the waters, 81–83
worshiped as rain-praying deity in Peking, 120, 121, 159, see also Dragon(s), Longwangmiao, Longwangtang
Dragon King Hall, see Longwangtang
"Dragon Raising its Head", see *long taitao*
Dragon throne, 195, 222, 279
Dragon's "cave" (*longyue*), 23, 95, 96, 102, 106, 160, 166
Dragon's vein, 58, 96, 100, 106
Drought
in Ming, Qing Peking, 115, 118–120, 156, 157, 251
in Yuan Dadu, xx, 61, 81, 83
Drum Tower, see Gulou
Du Mu, 142
Du Ruhui, 40
Du Yu, 41
Duan Gate, 129, **131**
Duanli Gate 端禮門, **49**
Duanzong, Song emperor Zhao Shi, 122
Dugong tanzuan, 142
Dui (hexagram), 11
Dushi jiangjun [Single Tree General], 56

Eastern Jin, 88
Eastern Palace, 12, 13, 53
Edeni-yin Tobci, 175
Eight Trigrams, 10, 11, 21, 96, 106
xiantian and *houtian* arrangements, **12**, see also *Baiqua, Houtian tu, Xiantian tu*
"Eight-armed Nezha City", see

Beijing de chuanshuo, Liu Bowen, Nezha, Peking
"Erlangshen zuishe suomojing" (The Second Elder Deity in Drunkenness Shot at the Locking Devil's Mirror), 75
Ershiba xiu (twenty-eight lunar lodges/mansions), 10, see also *Xiu* (lunar lodges)
Ertan leizeng, 142
Ezhou (Wuchang, Hubei), 37

"*Fan Qing fu Ming*" triad society, 149, see also Tiandihui
Fang [ward], 2, 18, 19, 60, 61, 113, 116
Fang Guozhen, 139
Fang Xuanling, 40
Fangqiu Lake, 246
Fangshan, 2, **3**, 83, 120, 163, 238
Fatian (Monk), also known as Faxian, 72
Fatian xiangdi ["following the model of the sky and creating its counterpart on the earth"], 15, 55
Favier, Alphonse, 123
Feng Guoyong, 89
Fengchi Ward, 52, 53, 57
Fenghuolun (No Cha's "Wind and Fire" wheels), 129
Fengshen yanyi [Tales of the Investiture of Gods], 79, 121, 158, 223, 308n71
Fengshui (geomantic principle), 11
  definition and schemes, 19–24, 45, 47, 57–59, 96, 97, 106, see also under Forbidden City, Ming Peking
  English language literature on, 295n23
  School of Forms and Orientations, 21
Fengshui jia (*kanyu jia*), 20, see also geomancers
Fengtai 豐臺, **3**
Fengtian (Commanded by Heaven)-dian, 90
Fengyang, Anhui, see Zhongdu (Ming)
Fengyi Gate 豐宜門, **49**
Fenye (astral-geographical "field division" system), 4, 11–15
  translations of, 294n16
Five Agents: Wood, Fire, Earth, Metal, Water, 10, 23
Five Agents/Phases theories/schemes, 5, 9
  applied to geomancy, 11, 20, 22, 23, 96, 103
  symbolic correlations in architectural planning in Forbidden City, 106, 107, 109, 111, 223, see also *Yinyang/wuxing* theories/schemes
Five Palaces, see Central Palace (Purple Palace), Eastern Palace, Southern Palace, Western Palace, Northern Palace
Forbidden City (Ming Nanking), 91, 102, 117, 159, 200
Forbidden City (Ming Peking), 8, 18, 24, 57, 58, 91, 105, 100–110, 115, 117, 159, 188, 192, 223, 245
  city plan, plan within the Imperial-city, **104**, **108**
  fengshui features of architectural buildings in *yin/yang* and Five Agents symbolic correlative interactions, 94–97, 106–107, 109–110
  patterned after the celestial Purple Palace Enclosure, 96, 103, 105
Forbidden City (Qing Peking), 103,

106, 120, 123, 130, 150, 156, see also Ming Peking: palace-city, *Zijin cheng*
Former Han, 11, 15, 17
Foshuo Chang Ahan jing (Dirghāgama), 67
Foshuo zuishang mimi nanatian jing, 72
Fou-ch'eng Men, see Fuchengmen
Four advisors, see *Sifu*
Four animal images, **11**, see also Azure Dragon, Dark Warrior, Vermillion Bird, White Tiger
Four "Heavenly Kings", 64, 67, 73
Fuchengmen, **101**, 111, 113, **116**, 129, **131**, 133, 266, 269
Fuxi, 10
Fuzhou, Mount 覆舟山, **92**

Gaitian ("Covering Sky") cosmological theory, 46
"Ganying tongxie dutaizi Nazha" [The Responsive, Awe-inspiring Chief Prince Nazha], 74
Gao Liang, 126, 136, 207, 221, 222, 224–229, 243, 256, 257, 280–282, see also Dragon King, Liu Bowen
Gao Liang ganshui [Gao Liang's Race for Water], 136, 224, 227, 266, 280–282
Gaoliang (Chinese sorghum, tall and bright), 224, 229
Gaoliang Bridge, 224–226, 229, 282
Gaoliang rice, 231, 284
Gaoliang River, 7, 47, **49**, 50, **51**, **54**, 60, 87, **101**, 224, 225, 229
Gaopo yizuan, 142
Gate of Imperial Supremacy, see Huangjimen
Gechu yishi, 183
Gemingjun (Revolutionary Army), 154, see also Zou Rong
Gen (trigram/hexagram/cardinal direction), 11, 53, 56, 192
Gengsi bian, 142, 165
Genyue [Northeast Marchmount], 59
Geomancers, 19, 20, 44, 95, 100, 106, 138, 142, 145, 246
  School of Forms (*xingshi*), 21, 89
  School of Orientations (*fangwei*), 21, see also Wang Ji, Yang Yunsong
Geomancy, 19, 23, 24, see also Fengshui
  Liu Bingzhong's knowledge of, 36, 47, 63
  Liu Ji (Bowen)'s knowledge of, 138, 140, 142, 145, 146, 160
  Ming Peking, 94, 95, 109, 110, 123, 127, 128
  Yuan Dadu (Yan), 45, 46, 58, 59
Geomantic, applications, 11
  siting, 13, 20, 23, 24, 47, 52, 53, 57, 243, 247
God of Wealth (Shen Wansan), 191, 236, 239, 286, see also *Huo caishen*
Gold and Silver Pond, see Jinyinchi
Gold Fish Pond, see Jinyuchi
Golden Water Canal, see Jinshui River
Gong ["palace"], 10, 90, 102
Gong'an (cases), see under Chan Buddhism
Gongcheng ("palace-city"), 18, see also under Dadu (Yuan) and Peking (Ming)
Gongfei, 124, 146, 176, 329n7, 330n8, see also Lady Weng, and also under Zhu Di
Gongjing (Reverent and Tranquil) (Yao Guangxiao), 163

Gongyuan (Examination Hall), 114
Grand Canal, 7, 50, 59, 82, 87, 99, 113, 115, 156, 210, 215, 219, 225, 277
Grand Secretariat, 94
Great Brightness, 56, see also Da Ming
Great Capital, 8, 24, 35, 37, 46, 85, 249, 253, see also Dadu
Great Emperor of Heaven, see Tianhuang dadi, Yuhuang
Great Wall, 2, 174, 175
Great Yuan, 270, see Da Yuan
Gu Qiyuan, 151
Gu Xuewen, 211
Gu Yanwu, 310n77
Guan Luo, 20, 58
Guan Yu, 157
Guang'an Gate, 113
Guanglusi 光祿寺 [Court of Imperial Entertainments], **112**
Guangning Gate 廣寧門, **116**
Guangqu Gate, 113, **116**
Guangtai Gate 光泰門, **49**
Guangxi Gate, **49**, **51**, **54**, 61, 81
Guangxu reign, 119, 151,153
Guangyang zaji, 176
Guanshi dili zhimeng [Guan's Geomantic Indicator], 20
Guanxiang wanzhan, 146
Guanzi, 20
Guihu [Ghost Household] (lunar lodge), 53
Guihua cheng ["Return-to-civilization City"], 184
Guijintushu jicheng, 22
"Gulf of Beijing", 1
Gulf of Bohai, 1
Gulou [Drum Tower]
  (Yuan), 50, 61
  (Ming), **101**, 110, 113, 221, 230
Guo Pu, 20
Guo Shoujing, 48, 50, 81, 225
Guo Xun, 143
Guojijian (National College), 114

Hai, branch of *dizhi*, 13
Haidian 海淀 District, **3**, 118, 224
Hailing, Prince of (Hailong wang), see Jin emperor Liang (Digunai)
Haiyan, 89
Haiyun (Monk), visited Qubilai Qan with Zicong (Liu Bingzhong), 36, 297n2
Haizi, 82, 219
Hall of Audience, 17
Hall of Blessed Peace, see Qin'andian
Hall of Establishing Supremacy, see Jianjidian
Hall of Great Brightness, see Da Guangmingdian
Hall of Middle Supremacy, see Zongjidian
Hall of Peaceful Unity, see Jiaotaidian
Hall of Receiving Brightness, see Chengguangdian
Hall of Supreme Harmony, see Taihedian
Han (state), correlated with lunar lodges, 12
Han Chinese, xviii, 31, 62, 84,
  and non-Han Chinese culture, 28
  and Mongolian traditions, 202
  dynastic restoration, 121, 123, 155
  institutions, customs and traditions, 156
  folkloristic traditions, 198, 249
  popular uprising, 154
Han dynasty, 1, 2, 4, 9–15, 17, 19, 20, 22, 23, 84, 187, 223

Han Gaozu, 40, 143, 144
Han Liner, 66, 88, 139
Han Shantong, 66
Hangzhou, 89
Hanlin Academy, 55, 94
Hao prefecture, Anhui, 218
Haohua Gate 顥華門, **49**
Hata Men, 128, **131**, see also Chongwenmen
He Qiaoyuan, 176
Heaven and Earth Society, see Tiandihui
Heavenly Bridge, see Tianqiao
Heavenly Kings, see Maharajas-devas
Heavenly Purity Gate, **108**, see Qianqingmen
"Heilian Nazha" [Dark-face Nazha], 75
Heilongtan, 30, 157, see also Black Dragon Pool
Helu, King of state of Wu, 15
"Heterodox books" (*yaoshu*), 44
Heyi Gate, **49**, **54**, 62, 82, **101**, 224
Hezhou, Sichuan, 39
High Lord of the Dark Heaven, see Dark God Zhenwu
Homo religious, 250, 254
Hong Mai, 74
Honghaier ("Crimson Kid"), 79, see also Nazha
Hongluo, Mount, 144
Hongqiao [Rainbow Bridge], 237, 240, 287
Hongwu Gate, **92**, 213
Hongwu Emperor, 173, 174, 177, 179, 180, 182, 195, 196, 200, see also Ming Taizu, Zhu Hongwu (Chu Hung-wu), Zhu Yuanzhang
Hongwu reign, 8
Hou Men [Rear Gate]), 130, see also Bei'anmen, Di'anmen
Hou sangong [Rear Three Palaces], 102, 103
Houmenqiao [Rear Gate Bridge], **131**, 216, 217, 219, 220, 277, 278
Houshi (Rear Markets), 105
Houtian tu ("Diagram of the Posterior Heavens"), 10, **12**, **54**, 56, 61, 62, see also *Baigua,* Eight Trigrams
"How Emperor Yongle of the Great Ming Built the City of Peking", 25, 173, see also "Book of the Story of How Emperor Yung-lo of the Great Ming Built the City of Peking—The Yuan Prince—The True Prince"
"How was the City of Peking Built?", 26, 207, 215, 231–241, 243, 257, 283–288
Hsi-an Men, 129, 130
Hsi-chih Men, see Xizhimen
Hsi-hua Men, see Xihuamen
Hsuan-wu Men, see Xuanwumen
Hu Dahai, 218
Hu Weiyong, 140
Hua, Mount, 45
Huabiao ["ornamented pillars"], 105, 280
Huai River, 37, 89
Huailai, Hebei, 121
Huainan honglie [Great Works of King of Huainan], 10
Huainan Mountains, 23
Huairou, Hebei, **3**
Huakai [Stately Umbrella]-dian, 90–91
Huang Bosheng, 141
Huang Chuwang (Daoist), designing palaces of Nanking, 327n96
Huang Ming kaiyun yingwu zhuan, 143
Huang Ming zuxun [August Ming Ancestral Injunctions], 176

Huang Wenzhong, 62
Huang Zuo, 183
Huangcheng ("imperial-city"), see under Dadu (Yuan) and Peking (Ming)
Huangdao [Imperial Way]
(Dadu), 52
(Ming Peking), 102, 110, 129, **131**
Huangdi [August Emperor], 15, see also Yellow Emperor
Huangdi zhaijing, 20
"Huangdu dayitong fu", 94
Huangji Jingshi shu [Supreme Principles Governing the World], 62
Huangjidian [Hall of Imperial Supremacy], 96, 107, **108**, see also Taihedian
Huangjimen [Gate of Imperial Supremacy], 106, **108**
Huangshi gong [Yellow-stone Elder], 143
Huangshi gong sushu sanlue, 146
Huanzhe [Eunuch], 15
Hucheng [Protective] Canal, 5, 7, 60, 91, 102, 106, **108**, 111, 123, 238, 241, 288
Huguosi, 114
Huicheng Gate 會城門, **49**
Huilin (Monk), 40
Huitong Canal, 60, **104**, see also Yu Canal
Huitong (Huiquan)ci (Memorial), 82
Huitongguan [Hostelry for foreigners], 114
Huitu Sanjiao yuanliu Soushen daquan
[A Compendium of the Sources and Eminent Deities of the Three Teachings], 76, 78, 223, 307n67
Huizong, Northern Song emperor, 60
Huo caishen ("Living God of Wealth"), 191, 214, 236, 286, see also Shen Wanshan
Huojianqiang (No Cha's "Precious Spear), 129
Huotanzhou (Nazha's "fiery blanket spell"), 74
Hutong (alleyways), 60, 113, 192, 266, 304n39, 333n30, 335n39, see also Mongolian *qutung*
Huzhou, Zhejiang, 208

Imperial capital, xv, 1, 5–7, 15, 19, 24, 28, 29, see also (Yuan) Dadu, (Ming) Nanking, Peking
Imperial cities
cosmological concepts of, 8–15
planning of, 15–24, see also (Yuan) Dadu, (Ming) Peking
Imperial Garden, see Yuhuayuan
Imperial Way, see *Huangdao*
In Search of Old Peking, 127–130, see also Arlington, L. C. and William Lewisohn
Inner Mongolia, 24, 87, 121, 177, 188, 189
Institutions of Zhou, see *Zhouli*
Interior Golden Water Canal, see Nei Jinshui Canal
Islamic mosques in Peking, 114

Jade Emperor, 76, 77, 157, see also Yuhuang dadi
Jade Spring Hill, see Yuquan Hill
Jagchid Sechin, 183
J̌amǰin chorǰi sakiy-a yeshi, His Highness, 276
Ji [winnower] (lunar lodge), 4
Ji, first city founded in Beijing region, 2, **3**, 185

"Ji Taibao Liugong wen", 40
Jiafusi, 234, see also Tanzhe Monastery
Jiajing reign, 42, 111, 119, 148, 225, see also Ming emperor Shizong
Jiande Gate, **49**, **54**, 61
Jiang-Huai region, 46
Jiang Jieshi, see Chiang Kai-shek
"Jiangren yingguo", 17, see also Wangcheng model
Jianhuang tu [Plan for Enthroning a Ruler], 161
Jianjidian [Hall of Establishing Supremacy], **108**
Jiankang (Jianye), 88, see also Jinling, Nanking, Yingtian prefecture
Jianlou (arrow tower), 111
Jianqingshi suibi, 153
Jianwen Emperor (Zhu Yunwen), 8, 25, 43, 91, 114, 159, 163, 205
  dethronement, alleged death, and disappearance, 150, 174, 176, 180–183, 196–198, 335n46, see also Prince of Yan, Yongle Emperor
  legend in *Xu Yinglie zhuan*, 144–145
  Liu Ji's prediction of his fate by providing tools to escape in a monk's disguise, 142, 146, 185, see also Liu Ji
Jiao [horn] (lunar lodge), 12
Jiaotaidian [Hall of Peaceful Unity], 91, 95, 102, **108**
Jiaqing reign (Qing), 148
Jidu, *fengshui* features, 45, see also Yan prefecture
Jiedushi (military commissioners), 73
Jilong, Mount 雞籠山, **92**
Jin, Prince of (Zhu Gang), 232
Jin (catty), 210
Jin (Jurchen) rulers, 5, see also Jurchen-Jin dynasty/rule
Jin Shan (Youzi), 94
Jin Shoushen, 31, 132–134, 136–137, 162, 168
Jincaochi (Golden Grass Pond), 241
Jinchuan Gate 金川門, **92**
Jingde chuandeng lu, 74
Jingfeng Gate 景風門, **49**
Jingnan ("to clear away disasters"), 91, 96, 175, 182, 184, 185, 188, 196
Jingshan [Scenic Hill], **101**, **104**, 106, 197, see also Meishan, Wanshou/Wansuishan
Jingtai emperor, Ming Daizong Zhu Chiyu, 114
Jingzhongmiao [Temple of Sustained Loyalty], 230, 231, 342n33
Jinkou Canal, 7, 48, **49**, **51**, 58
Jinkou New Canal, **51**
Jinlianchuan, 24, 37, see also Kaiping, Shangdu (Yuan)
Jinling ["gold tumulus"], 46, 87–89, 201, see also Nanking, Yingtian prefecture
Jinnang (damask purse), 149, 185, 186, see also "sealed packet"
Jinshen [Cautious to Self]-dian, 91
Jinshi, 6
Jinshu, Monograph on Astronomy, 103
Jinshui [Golden Water] Canal, **49**, 50, **51**, **54**, 59, 60, 96, **101**, 115
Jinyan, 151
Jinyinchi [Gold and Silver Pond], 237, 240, 287
Jinyuchi [Gold Fish Pond], 237, 240, 241, 287, 343n47
Jinzhong/Jinnei ["forbidden interior"], 103

Jinzhou, 144
Jiqing district, 88
Jishichi/Jishishi ["cock-lion" pond/ rock], 82
Jishui [Gathered Waters] Pool, 7, **49**, 50, **51**, **54**, 60, 61, 82, 87, **101**, 111, 156, 162, 217, 219, 224, 225, 229
Jiu Shumiyuan jiaoshi, 61
Jiujiebei wen ["salvation epigraph"], 148
Jiu-jiu, 187
Jiulingbei (nine-link goblet), 232, 284
Journey to the West, see *Xiyou ji*
Jubao Gate, **92**, 213, 239
Jubaopan [treasure-accumulating bowl], 212, 213, 239
Jueduan (unicorn), 144
Jurchen-Jin dynasty/rule, 35, 41, 45, 50, 224, 231, 241, 250
Juyong Pass, 63

Kaifeng, see Bianliang
Kaiping, 24, 35, 37, 87, 192, see also Shangdu
Kaiyang star, 53
Kan (hexagram), 11, 62
Kang [neck] (lunar lodge), 12
Kangxi Emperor, Qing dynasty, 120, 225, 234
Kangxi reign, 117, 119, 120
Kanyu, 19, see also *Fengshui*
Kanyu jia, 20, see also *Fengshui jia*
Kaogong ji [Record of Construction], 17
Kerülen River, 104, 271
Kezuo zhuiyu, 151
Khanbalik (Turkic for Dadu), 62
Khitad deerem baatar (Chinese bandit hero alluded to Zhu Hongwu in a Mongolian legend)
dreaming of two dragons, yellow and black, crawling up to his knees, 204, see also "Mongolian legend of the founding of Peking"
marrying the pregnant Mongol empress, 203
Khitan(s), 4–5, 250, see also Liao dynasty
"Killing the Tartars" propaganda, 154, 155
Kinship ranking system in Yuan and Ming: *shi* (ten), *bai* (hundred), *qian* (thousand), *wan* (ten thousand), 209
Köke Qota ("Blue City"), 184
Kong Qi, 65
Konggu daoren, 144
Koryŏ, 4
Kubara, god of wealth in Brahmanic mythology, 67, 189
statuettes of Vaiśravana, **190**, see also Vaiśravana, Heavenly King
Kucha, 85
Kuhai Youzhou, see Bitter Sea Youzhou
Kui [stride] (lunar lodge), 12
Kun (trigram/hexagram/cardinal point), 11
Kunlun Mountain, 23, 46, 89, 95
Kunming Lake, 50, 115, 117, see also Wengshanbo
Kunninggong [Palace of Earthly Tranquility], 91, 102, **108**

Lamaist temples in Peking, 114
Lan Yu, 211
Later Han, 10, 15
Later Jin (state), 4
Later Qin kingdom, 67
Lattimore, Owen, 202, 204, 206
Left and Right Law Administrator

Celestial Gates stars, see Zuoyou Zhifa Tianmen
Lejiao siyu (Gossip from the Le Suburbs), 89
Li (hexagram), 11, 46, 57, 303n33
Li Huai, 42
Li Jing
in legend as father of Nezha, 64, 76, 79
as Pagoda-bearing Heavenly King (*Tuota tianwang* Li Jing), 75, 77
Li Mi, 41
Li Qing, 176
Li Shanchang, 140
Li Shimian, "Beijing fu", 94
Li Weisun, "Dadu fu", 46–47
Li Wenzhong, 144
Li Yuenan, 134
Li Zhong, 150
Li Zicheng, 148, 150, 197
Liang (state), 88
Liang (Digunai), Jin emperor Prince Hailing, 5, 6
Liang Yi, 142
Liangchang (tax captain), 210
Lianhua Pond, 5, 47, **49**, **51**, see also West Lake, Xihu
Liao dynasty, 4–5, 45, 250
Liao Junqing, 94
Liaoshi dilizhi, 4
Liaoyang, 211
Lidai chenjian [Mirror of Exemplary Officials in Successive Dynasties], 42
Liechi [Row of Shops], 15
Lin Yutang, *Imperial Peking*, 220
Linggusi, 326n91
"Linggusi Ji" (Zhu Yuanzhang), 326n91
"Little Emperor", 193, 195, 275, see also "Yüan Prince"
Liu [willow] (lunar lodge), 12
Liu An, 10
Liu Bing, 149
Liu Bingshu, 300n13
Liu Bingzhong (Liu Kan, Zhonghui, Zicong, Cangchun, Duke of Zhaoguo, Wenzhen, Liu Taibao), xvi, xviii, 7, 22, 24, 25, 35, 138, 199
as Monk Zicong, visiting Qubilai with Chan master Haiyun, and serving the gaghan, 36–40, see also Qubilai qaghan
building of Shangdu (Upper Capital) at Kaiping, 37, 65, 66, 83, 192
campaigning with Qubilai in Dali and Ezhou, 37
comparison with historical personalities, 40–41
decline in prestige in the Ming period, 121, 158, 159, 199
designing a new capital city at Zhongdu (later Dadu), 39, 65
designing eleven walled gates of Dadu allegedly to symbolize Nazha's three heads, six arms, and two feet in popular legend, 62, 65, 122, 253
knowledge of astrology and geomancy, 43, 44, 47, 57, 58
lay name reinstated, 39
legends and mytholization, 41–44, 258
Nazha City legend, 24, 25, 26, 63, 66, 79, 83, 84, 121, 126, 157–159, 161, 164, 166, 199, 201, 252–254, see also Nazha/Nezha City Legend
plan of building Dadu, 44–63, 65, 66, 100, 200, 201, 251, see also Dadu

portrait, **38**
proposing organization of Han Chinese-style administration, recommending dynastic title to Qubilai qaghan, 39, 42
relationship with Liu Ji (Bowen), 22, 44, 143, 159, 161, 162, 199, 200, 201, 256, see also Liu Ji
relationship with Yao Guangxiao, 43, 44, see also Yao Guangxiao
Liu Bowen, xvi–xviii, 25–27, 30, 44, see also Li Ji, Liu Pai-wen
alleged authorship of political prophecies and prophecy book *Shaobing ge*, 148–155, 186
as anti-Manchu hero, Han ethnocentric prophet-savior, 149, 152, 165, 166
as champion of restoration of Han Chinese rule, 149, 155, 166, 254
association with the Eight-armed Nezha in building the city of Peking in popular legend, 121, 124–126, 132–136, 138, 158, 159–162, 167, 168, 199, 200–202, 208, 252–254, 264–266, 268–270, see also Nezha, Nezha cheng legend
battling with the Dragon King over control of water resources in popular stories, 125, 126, 136, 207, 221–226, 243, 279–288, 230, see also main entry
chief adviser in building the city of Peking in popular stories, 100, 123, 124, 126, 132–135, 167, 207, 208, 214–218, 221, 222, 226, 236, 241, 253, 258, 263–266, 267, 268, 277–283, 284–288, see also under Peking (Ming)
competing with Yao Guangxiao in building the Eight-armed Nezha City of Peking, 132–136, 162, 163, 186, 199, 207, 215, 228, 231–233, 235, 243, 244, 263–266, 267–270, see also Yao Guangxiao
designing and building the capital city of Nanking, 89, 159, 160, 186, 193, 200, see also Nanking
development of legends, see Liu Ji
in Mongolian legend/story as adviser of the Yuan Prince to build the city of Peking, 124, 125, 146, 147, 159, 161, 165, 178, 181–187, 193–195, 198, 199, 201, 206, 255, 273–275, see also main entry
popular songs ascribed to him, 167, 327n97
portrait in *Shaobing ge*, **152**; in *Yinglie zhuan*, **145**
predicting the fate of the Jianwen emperor and providing tools for his escape, 142, 144–145, 185, 186, see also Liu Bowen
relation with Zhang Zhong, the Iron-cap Daoist, 152, 165, see also main entry
recommending Xu Da to site the capital of Peking by bowshot, 219, 277
summoning Shen Wansan to help build the capital city

of Peking, 221, 229, 257, 278, 279, see also Shen Wansan
"Liu Bowen Building the Eight-armed Nezha City", xvi, 25, 124, 167, 199, 202, 207, 208, 224, 243, 254
popularity of the story in People's Republic, 167, 168, see also Peking, "the Eight-armed Nezha City"
"Liu Bowen Built the City of Peking", xviii, 26, 207, (summary) 215–221, 242–244, 257, (text) 277–283
(*Liu Bowen xiansheng*) *Baizhanqilue,* 146
Liu Bowen xiansheng shishi ge [Liu Bowen's ballad on current events], 149
"Liu Bowen xiansheng zhizao Beijing cheng" [Mister Liu Bowen Building the City of Peking], 124
Liu Bowen zhizao babi Nezha cheng [Liu Bowen building the Eight-armed Nezha City], 25, see also "The Eight-armed Nezha City"
Liu Ji (Liu Bowen, Earl of Chengyi, Wencheng), vi–xviii, 8, 22, 25, 44
acclaimed grandson of Liu Bingzhong in faked genealogy, 143, 159, 161, 162, 200, see also Liu Bingzhong
as Ming Taizu's adviser and strategist, 138–140, 150, 155, 164
biographical sketch, 138–142, 148, 186, 216, 320n59
building the city of Peking and the Nezha cheng legend, 159–162, 164–165, 199, see also Liu Bowen, Nezha cheng legend
Chinese Nostradamus, 155, 221
designing and building the capital city Nanking, 89, 159, 160, 245, 247, 311n6, 326n91, see also Nanking
development of legends, 138–155, 148, 155, 159, 162
dramatization in *Yinglie zhuan* and *Xu Yinglie zhuan,* 143–145
in Mongolian legend/story of the building of Peking, 146–148, 159, 161, 199, see main entry
plan of No Cha's (Nezha's) body represented by sites in Peking, 128–130, see also Nezha, Nezha cheng legend
political prophecies, "salvation epigraph", and *shaobing ge,* 148–155, see also Liu Bowen, *Shaobing ge*
portrait, **141**
prediction of the fate of the Jianwen emperor and providing tools for his escape, 142, 144–145, 160, see also Liu Bowen
relationship with Xu Da, 216, 217, see also Xu Da
superior knowledge of astrology, geomancy, military stratagem, and divination, 89, 142 ,145, 146
writings and putative writings, 22 (see also Liu Bingzhong), 140, 146
Liu Kan, see Liu Bingzhong
Liu Pai-wen, 273–275, see also Liu Bowen
Liu Run, 36, 299n13

Liu Song period, 20, 41
Liu Taibao, see Liu Bingzhong
Liu Taibao xielou tianji [Liu Taibao divulging the hidden plans of Providence], 44
Liu Tong and Yu Yizheng, 157
Liu xiansheng "Jingui jinnang" [Mister Liu's "Golden Casket and Damask Purse"], 149, see also *Shaobing ge*
Liu Xianting, 176
Liu Ze, 299n13
Liuxing [moving stars], 23
"Living God of Wealth", see *Huo caishen*
Lize Gate 麗澤門, **49**
Lizheng Gate, **49**, **54**, 56, 57, 59, 62, 65, **101**
Long taitao [Dragon raising its head], 81, 83
Long/Longwang (dragon or dragon king), 67, 77, see also Naga(s)
Longfeng [Dragon and Phoenix], 66
Longfu Palace 隆福宮, **54**
Longfusi, 114
Longpan [coiling dragon], 46
Longquansi, 234, see also Tanzhe Monastery
Longshan (Dragon Hill), 115
Longshen, 83, see also "dragon deity"
Longwan, 139, 143
Longwangmiao [Dragon King Temple], 157, 230
Longwangtang [Dragon King Hall], **54**, 81, 82
Longxing ciji, 142
Longxue, see "dragon's cave"
Lou [lasso] (lunar lodge), 12
Lu (state), correlated with lunar lodges, 12
Lü Buwei, 9
Lu Can, 142, 165
Lu Deyuan, 210
Lu Xixing, 79
Luan Prefecture, 85, see also Kaiping, Shangdu (Yuan)
Lugou Bridge, **51**
Lugou River, 7, 48, **51**, see also Yongding River
"Lunar lodges" equatorial divisions system, 4, 9, 14, see also *Xiu*
Luopan [dial-plate], 20
Luoyang, 1, 17, 23
Luoyi, 17
Lüshi chunqiu [The Spring and Autumn Annals of Master Lü], 9

Ma, (Ming) Empress, 174, 176, see also Ming Taizu
Mingshi biography of, 211
mother of Liu Bingzhong, 36
Ma'an (Horse Saddle), Mount, 246
Madage, see Jin emperor Zhangzong
Maharajas-devas, four heavenly kings, 67, see also Dhritarāshtra, Virūdhaka, Virupaksha, and Vaiśravana
Manchu rule, 103, 123, 149, 254
Manchu rulers, 8, 122, 156, see also Qing rulers
Manchus, 31, 154, 166, 186, 250
Maoshan Daoist, 74
Marco Polo's *Description of the World*, 62
May Fourth Movement, 123
Meishan [Coal Hill], **101**, 106, 110, 197, see also Jingshan, Wanshou/ Wanshuishan
Menggu shixi pu (Becingge's Chinese Mongolian clan record), 174
"Menglie Nazha sanbianhua" [The

Three Transformations of the Ferocious Nazha], 75, 76
Mentougou (District), **3**, 234
Meyer, Jeffrey F., *The Dragons of Tiananmen*, 27–28, 249–250, 259
Miaofengshan 妙峰山, **3**
Miaohui, see "Temple fairs"
Middle Kingdom, see Zhongguo
Military Windings star, see Kaiyang, Wuquexing star
Ming (hexagram), 46
Ming dynasty/era/period, xv, xvi, 1, 8, 18, 21, 22, 29, 41, 42, 44, 65, 66, 76 ,89, 94, 98, 103, 110, 114, 118, 121, 122, 132, 149, 174, 175, 182, 195–197, 204, 206, 209, 213, 218, 230, 234, 241, 244, 246
Ming Peking, see Peking (Ming)
Ming Taizu, 8, 25, 43, 44, 46, 84, 87, 93, 124, 140, 142, 144, 175, 185, 186, 200, 216, 218
  asking Liu Ji to predict future dynastic events in popular stories, 150, 151, 184, see also Liu Bowen, Li Ji
  consulting with Liu Ji, Zhang Zhong, and a Daoist to build palaces in Nanking, 165, 194
  death in Nanking, 91, 178, 182, 196
  enfeoffing Zhu Di as Prince of Yan and building his residence in Beipingfu, 87, 88, 184, 219, see also Zhu Di
  folklore about the building of Nanking, 239, 245–247
  forcing Shen Wansan to contribute silver and grain to the state, and seizing his estates and treasures, 210–211, 213–214, 230, 239, see also Shen Wansan
  having a dream of fight between two dragons alluding to the Prince of Yan and his grandson Zhu Yunwen in popular stories, 147, 183, 205
  marrying a Mongol consort named Gongfei in Mongolian legend, 124, 173, 180, see also Toghōn Temür
  mausoleum (Xiaoling) in Nanking, 114, 160
  meeting with Liu Ji (Bowen) to receive prognostication on future events, **152**
  portrait, **90**
  sending Prince of Yan off to Nankou to establish a fief in Mongolian legend, 26, 147, 184, 217, 255, see also Prince of Yan
Ming Tombs, 114
Ming Xiaoling ("Filial Tumulus"), see Ming Taizu
Mingshi yiwenzhi, 146
Mingtang (Hall of Light), 105
Mochizuki Būkkyō daijiten, 69, 72
Mochou Lake 莫愁湖, **92**
Möngke qan, 39
Mongol invasion of Jin, 7, 36, 47
Mongol *qatun* (Toghōn-temür *qaghan*'s Qonggirad *qatun*), 148, 173, 176
  alleged marriage to Zhu Hung-wu and story of her pregnancy, 177–181, 271, 272, see also Toghōn Temür
Mongol (Yuan) rule, 36, 37, 63, 65, 81, 84, 138, 154, 195, 249, 251, 254, 255
Mongol storytellers, 259

Mongol-Yuan dynasty, 7, 81, 155, 156, 251, 254, see also Yuan Dynasty
Mongolia, 63, 174, 175, 255, 276
Mongolian and Inner Asian folktales, 175
Mongolian astral-cosmological concepts, 191, 255
Mongolian chronicles, 174, 180, 181, 184
Mongolian custom on arrow/bowshot, xix, 191, 242, 243, 254
    siting by bowshot, 26, 148, 173, 207, 241, 242, 245, 247, 249, 255–257, see also Mongolian legend, siting the capital city by bowshot by the swarthy-faced black rider
Mongolian folktales, 205
Mongolian legend, siting the capital city by bowshot by the swarthy-faced black rider, 26, 147, 148, 178, 187, 189, 199, 217, 242, 245, 249, 252, 254, 259, 274, 275
"Mongolian legend of the founding of Peking" (Owen Lattimore), 202–206
Mongolian legend/story of the Mongol maternity of the Yongle Emperor, and the building of Peking, xvii, 26, 125, 146, 147, 161, 173, 176–178, 202, 207, 217, 241, 242, 249, 251, 252, 255, 256, see also "Book of the Story of How Emperor Yung-lo of the Great Ming Built the City of Peking"
Mongolian *ordos*, 52
Mongols, 7, 31, 36, 41–43, 48, 62, 146, 147, 150, 154, 155, 159, 161, 174–176, 183, 191, 196, 198, 202, 203, 218, 233, 243, 250, 251, 259, 270–273, 276
Mostaert, Antoine, the Reverend, 174, 177, 204
Muqali, 37, 39, 46

Naga(s), 67, 73, 77, 78, see also *long, longwang*
"Naji [Nazha] taizi zhuan", 76, see also Nazha
Nana deva, 72, 73, 78
Nanhai (South Sea), 106, 110
Nanjing
    as Liao Southern Capital (Yanjing), xvii, 4, 5
    superimposed on Yuan Dadu and Ming Peking, **6**
    Jin Southern Capital, former Song capital Bianliang, 7
Nanjing taichangsi zhi [Record of the Court of Imperial Sacrifices at Nanking], 176
Nanking (Southern Capital), xv, 8, 26, 46, 87, 93, 98, 99, 114, 139, 142, 153, 166, 176, 210, 217, 311n6, see also Jiankang (Jianye), Jinling, Yingtian(fu)
    as imperial capital, 88–90, 193, 200
    as imperial city, 148, 165
    building the capital city under Zhu Yuanzhang, 88–90, 117, 148, 159, 160, 165, 211, 213, 215, 239, 246, 247, see also Ming Taizu
    city plan, **92**
    city plan designed by Liu Ji (Liu Bowen), 22, 25, 139, 148, 159, 200, 215, 247, see also Liu Ji, Liu Bowen
    impact of capital city on building Peking and its Forbidden City, 91, 100, 102, 103, 117, 159, 160, 193, 201,

274, 275, 276, 277, see also Forbidden City
imperial-city, 89, 91, 245
in Mongolian legend of the building of Peking, 124, 174, 185–187, 193, 195–197, 201, 233, 271, 273–276, see main entry
legend of building the capital city transmitted to Peking, 159, 160, 161, 213, 215, 230, 239, 245, see also Peking (Ming)
migration of wealthy households from metropolitan region to Peking, 117, 194, 238
palace-city, 8, 18, 89, 91, 96, 100, 103, 107, 160, 197, 245
Nan-k'ou, see Nankou
Nankou, **3**, 147, 178, 183, 184, 187, 204, 206, 233, 273, 274
Nanping Hill, 40
Nansheng [Southern Secretariat], 55
Nanyuan (South Park), 215, 216, 219, 277, 278
Naquin, Susan, *Peking: Temples and City Life*, 27, 28, 29, 30
Nata, 69, 72, see also Nazha
Nazha (Tantric Buddhist child-deity, third son of Heavenly King Vaiśravana), xvi, 35, 66, 69, 78, 80, 83, 84, 121, 138, 158, 289, 199, 251, 253, 254, 258, see also Vaiśravana
as third son of the Pagoda-bearing Heavenly King Li Jing, 64, 75, 79, see also Li Jing
birthday celebration, 83
body representing the layout of Ming Peking in popular legend, see Nezha, No-cha
body symbolizing Dadu's eleven walled gates in popular legend, 25, 61–62, 65, 132
body transformed in three heads, six/eight arms, and two feet, 24, 65, 74, 77
Chinese renderings of names in Sanskrit, 69
image in Chan Buddhist and Daoist works, 73–75; in Daoist biography as *daluoxin* under the Jade Emperor, 76, 77, 157
image in Yuan plays, 75, 76
legend of battling with Dragon King in the Eastern Sea in Daoist stories, 73, 76, 77, 79, 122, 223
legend of coming to Peking to capture dragons to relieve water shortage, 30, 200, see also Nazha cheng, Nezha cheng legend
portrait, **71**, **78**
profile, 66, 68, 69, 70–72
Nazha cheng (Nazha City), legend of Yuan Dadu, xvi, xviii, 24, 25, 35, 63–66, 121, 126, 137, 138, 155, 161, 162, 199, 241, 249, 252, 253, 256
mentioned in Yang Weizhen's *yuefu*, 84, 85, see also Nezha cheng (Nezha City) legend
"Nazha fa" [Nazha's Law], 75
"Nazha ling" [A Short Syllabic Lyric about Nazha], 75
"Nazhataizi yanjingji" [A Tale of Prince Nazha's Eyes], 75
Needham, Joseph, definition of fengshui, 19
Nei Jinshui [Interior Golden Water] Canal, **104**, 106, 107, **108**

Neigongjian 內宮監 [Directorate of Eunuchs], **112**
Neizhiranju 內織染局 [Palace of Weaving and Dyeing Service], **112**
Neo-Confucianism, 45, 164
Nezha
  as Eight-armed Buddhist child deity, **frontispiece**, xvi, xvii, xix, 25, 35, 69, 74, 79, 121, 124, 125, 127, 135, 136, 159, 200, 223, 243, 254
  body representing the layout of Ming Peking in popular legend, 126, 127, 130, 132, 162, 220, 264–266, 268–270, see also under No Cha
  image superimposed on city plan of Peking, **131**
  legend of battling with the Dragon King and dragons to retrieve stolen water in Peking, 136, 166, 168, 223, 227, 228
  portrait in *Beijing Legends*, **134**
  portrait in *Xiyou ji* (dubbed "Crimson Kid"), **80**
  statues in Peking's Eastern Park Temple, 325n85
Nezha cheng (Nezha City) legend, xvi–xx, 25, 26, 31, 123, 125, 126, 132, 133, 135, 137, 138, 161, 164, 166–168, 173, 199, 201, 202, 207, 208, 217, 223, 224, 233, 235, 243, 249, 252, 254–256, see also Nazha cheng legend, *Beijing de chuanshuo*, "The Eight-armed Nezha City" story
  analyzed, 155–169
  modified version, 134–136, 161, 162
"Nezha naohai" (Nezha Stirring up the Sea), **frontispiece**, xvii, 168
Nezha Temple, 30, 158, 325n86
Ni Zhong, 102, 314n19
"Nianxia qu" (Ballads from the Capital), 64
Nine Moving Stars, see *liuxing*
"Nine Vats and Eighteen Vaults", legend of, 237, 240, 287
Niu [cow/ox] (lunar lodge), 12
No Cha, body represented by the City of Peking, 127–130, see also under Nezha
Nocha ch'eng [City of No-cha], 124, 201, 233
Non-Han
  dynastic regimes, xv
  folk and religious beliefs, 249, 251
  popular culture and traditions, 28, 259
Nongtian yuhua (Conversations from plowing the field), 64
North New Bridge, 230, 282, 283, see also Beixinqiao
North Pole, see Beiji
North Sea, see Beihai
Northern Asterism, see Beichen, Beiji
"Northern Capital", xv, 8, 91, 98, 197, see also Peking
Northern (Central) Secretariat, see Beisheng
Northern Liang Kingdom, 69
Northern New Bridge, see Beixinqiao
Northern Palace, 12, 105
"Northern Peace" Prefecture, see Beiping(fu)
Northern Yuan, see Bei Yuan
Nourishing Heart Palace, see Yangxindian
Nuzhen, see Jurchen

Official household five-grade ranking system in Yuan and Ming, *ge, qi, lang, guan, xiu,* 209
Oirat-Mongols, 251
invasion of, 121, 251
Okada Hidehiro, 331n16
Ordos, 177, 202
Outer Mongolia, 203

Pagoda-bearing Heavenly King Li Jing, 75, 77, see also Li Jing, Nezha, Vaiśravana, Heavenly King
"Palace-city" [gongcheng], 18, see also under (Yuan) Dadu, (Ming) Peking
Palace of Earthly Tranquility, see Kunninggong
Palace of Heavenly Brightness, see Qianqinggong
Palace of Weaving and Dyeing Service, see Neizhiranju
Palace Museum, Peking/Beijing, 8, 58, 90, 93, 95, 103
Pantao Palace, 208
Pao-ho Tien, 130
Pei-p'ing (Northern Peace), xv, 8, 218, see also Beijing, Peking
Pei-p'ing Fu, 201, 233, see also Beiping(fu), Yan prefecture
"Pekin, Ville Sainte", xviii, 28, ("Beijing as a Holy City") 297n34
Peking, xv–xix, 1, 3, 8, 27, 28, 29, 30, 31, 124, 137, 202, 204, 218, 220, 231, 249, 251, 252
ancient site, **3**, English language literature on, 27–30
as a "sacred city", 27, 28, 249, see also Beijing
as imperial capital, 8, 18, 25, 30, 94, 97, 100, 103, 106, 114, 115, 117, 133, 138, 155, 156, 158–160, 167, 173, 189, 191, 194, 196, 208, 215, 220, 241, 255, 258, see also Peking (Ming) (Qing)
as Northern Capital, xv, 8, 91, 98, 197, 202, 214, 215, 263
compared with Nanking, 159, 160
folktales, folklore, popular culture in Republican period, 138, 155, 165–168, 258, 259
Mongol communities and population, 174–176, 202
names for, xv
residents of, 125, 126, 167, 254, 257, 258
salty wells, inland lakes, 226, 239, 282
segment of, under the Celestial Markets Enclosure, 14
storytellers and popular singers, 144
temples and city life, 29, 30
urban morphology, 243, 244, 258
Peking (Ming), xv–xviii, 1, 8, 18, 23–25, 57, 59, 83, 91, 93–95, 97–99, 103, 106, 111, 113–117, 121, 125, 128, 133, 136, 137, 156, 163, 165, 169, 184, 189, 192, 197, 200, 201, 204, 213, 214
as leading intellectual and cultural center, and consumer capital, 115, 117
as imperial city, 25, 26, 94, 95, 97, 100, 111, 114, 115, 127–129, 132, 134, 159, 166, 207, 214, 219, 223, 249, 250, 252, 253, 256, 258, 259
building of Peking, the stories of Liu Bowen, the Nezha City and Mongolian legends, 25–27, 44, 66, 100, 121–127, 128–133, 138, 146–148, 156, 157, 159–162, 165, 167, 173–175, 182, 187, 189, 191, 193, 195, 196, 198, 199, 206, 208, 216, 217, 221, 222, 226, 234, 236–238, 241, 243, 244, 249, 250, 256–258,

see also Liu Bowen, Nezha cheng legend, the Mongolian legend/story of the building of Peking
drought and floods, rain-praying sacrificial offerings to Dragon King, 118–121
fang (ward), lanes and *hutong*, 19, 60, 61, 113, **116**, 117
fengshui features in *yin/yang* and Five Agents symbolic correlative interactions in architectural planning, see Forbidden City
"imperial-city", 18, 100, 102, **104**–106, 110 (perimeter), **112**, 113, 115, 117, 120, 121, 123, 130, 156, 188, 219, 224, 225, 229, 236, 240, 243, 244, 266, 269, 285, 286
in Mongolian legend/story of the building of the capital city, see main entry
markets, "temple fairs" (*miaohui*), cultural, educational centers, religious buildings, 113–114
model from Nanking, 102, 160
north-south axis of the palace-imperial cities, 96, 102, 103, 107
outer-city (capital-city), 5, 18, 24, known as "great city" (*dacheng*) and "inner-city" (*neicheng*), 110, 111, 113–117, change in shape and southern extension of the walled city, 112, 113 (perimeter), 123, 225, 243, 244
palace-city, 8, 18, 91, 96, 100, 101, 102 (perimeter), 103, 107, 160, 197, 243, 244, see also Ming Forbidden City
plan of Imperial City, 25, 100, **101**, 102, 103, **104**, **108**, **116**, **119**, 128, **131**, 159
popular culture, 159, 166
population, 117, 118, 120, 156, 158, 175, 176, 194, 251
public work projects to increase water resources and improve transportation, 115
wailoucheng, *waicheng* and *neicheng*, 113
walled city, change in shape and southern extension, 112, 113 (perimeter), 123
water shortage and problems, 156, 158, 226, 229, 251, 252, 282
Peking (Qing), 8, 117–121, 133, 156, 192
bannermen, 118, 156
construction of "three mounts" and "five gardens", 117, 118
drought and floods, rain-praying sacrificial offerings to Dragon King, 118–121
Han and Manchu popular culture, 118
residence of Manchu rulers and family, 117, see also Peking (Ming)
Peking (Republican period), 8, 30, 31, 110, 115, 123–127, 137, 156–158, 166, 167, 218, 254
Peking, "the Eight-armed Nezha City", 132–136, 167, 168, 254, (text) (1) 263–266, (2) 266–270, see also Liu Bowen, Nezha cheng/city legend
Peking City, 221, see also Bei-jing cheng

Peking legend(s), xvi–xviii, 31, 132, 148, 166, 194, 214, 230, 232, 247, see also Mongolian legend/story of the Mongol maternity of the Yongle Emperor, and the building of Peking, Nezha cheng legend
Peking man (*Sinanthropus pekinensis*), 2, 127
Peking opera, 144, 162
Peking vernacular, 132, 207
Penglai Ward, 55
'Phags-pa, 42
  Alphabet, 299n12
Pingjiang, 139, see also Suzhou
P'ing-tse Men, 129, see also Fuchengmen, Pingze Gate
Pingze Gate, **49**, **54**, 61, 62, **101**, **131**, see also P'ing-tse Men
Pishamen tianwang, see also Vaiśravana, Heavenly King
Pishamen tianwang suijun hufa zhenyan [The True Words of the Heavenly King Vaiśravana, the Protector of the Army], 67
Pishamen yigui [Ceremonies in the Worship of Vaiśravana], 71
Poyang Lake (Jiangxi), 139
Pre-Qin schools of thought, Confucian, Daoist, and cosmologist, 9, 22
Privy Council Enclosure, see Taiweiyuan
Puji (Monk), 74
"Purple Bright Constellation with Polaris in the Center", 13, 91, 103, see also Ziweiyuan
Purple Palace Enclosure, see Ziweiyuan
Purple or Polar "Forbidden City", see *Zijin cheng*
Qabtargh-a bichig (container-letter), 185
Qaraqorum, 36
Qi (primal ether), 19, 22, 23, 47, see also *yuanqi*
Qi (state), 88
Qian (hexagram), 11, 96, 106, 192
Qian Qianyi, 43
Qianbulang (thousand-pace corridor), **104**, 110–111
Qianlong jingcheng quantu, **119**
Qianlong emperor, Qing dynasty, 120
Qianlong reign, 30, 117–119, 148
Qianmen [Front Gate], **104**, 106, 126, 128, **131**, 167
Qianqinggong [Palace of Heavenly Purity], 91, 107, **108**, 130
Qianqingmen [Heavenly Purity Gate], **108**, 130
Qianqun zuanzhuo (No Cha's "Heaven and Earth" diamond bracelet), 129
Qiansicang [A Thousand Granary], 82
Qidans, see Khitans
Qihua Gate, **49**, **54**, 61 62, **101**
Qimen tunjia, 146
Qin dynasty, 2, 13
Qin'andian [Hall of Blessed Peace], 96, **97**, **108**
Qing dynasty/era/period, xvi, 1, 5, 8, 18, 21, 29, 50, 83, 96, 103, 105–107, 110, 111, 113–115, 117–119, 121–123, 127, 129, 133, 144, 148, 150, 151, 153, 154, 156, 157, 186, 189, 192, 210, 218, 224, 225, 234, 235, 240, 241, 244, 250
Qing Peking, see under Peking (Qing)
Qinglei tianwenfenye (zhisheng) zhishu, 146

Qinglongtan, 234
Qingnang aozhi, 20
Qingshousi ["Double pagoda" Monastery], 43, 163, 234, 300n15, see also Da Xinglongsi
Qingshu [Lucid Summer] Palace, 110
Qingtian, Zhejiang, 138
Qinhuai River 秦淮河, **92**
Qionghua Island, 47, **49**, **54**, 59, **101**, **104**, 110, 282
Qipan [Chessboard] Street, 106, 113, 127, 128, **131**
Qonggirad (Khungirat) *qatun*, 173, see also under Toghōn Temür
Qonggirad (Khungirat) tribe, 26, 148, 176
Qubilai Qaghan, 40, 42, 50, 122, 209, 224, 241, 251
  accession in Kaiping in succession to Möngke Qan, 35, 39, 48, 65
  campaigning against Yunnan and invading Southern Song, 37, 46
  drought in Dadu during his reign, 81
  inviting Chan monk Haiyun and his disciple Zicong to Qaraqorum for consultation on governmental matters, 36, 37 (see Liu Bingzhong)
  ordering Zicong to design and build a subsidiary capital at Kaiping, 37, see also Shangdu and construct a new walled capital in Zhongdu (Yanjing), 8, 35, 53, 56, 63, 249, 253, see also Dadu
  portrait, **38**
  shooting an arrow to determine the perimeter of Dashengshou Wan'an Monastery in Dadu, 191
Quebing ge (Cracked Cake Ballad), 151
Qutun, see Mongol *qutun*
Qutung (alleyways), 60, 187, 192, 304n39, see also *hutong*, *xiangtong*

Rain-praying, in Ming, Qing Peking, see under Dragon King
Rainbow Bridge, see Hongqiao
Rasipungsugh, *Bolor Erike*, 174
Rear Gate Bridge, see Houmenqiao
Rear Three Palaces, see *Hou sandian*
Red Turban rebels, see anti-Yuan insurgents
Renzi xuzhi zikao dili xinxue tongzong (Essential Knowledge of the Principles of Geomancy and Philosophy of the Mind to Posterity), 95
Renzong, see Ming emperor Zhu Goxu
Republican period, 30, 110, 115, 125–127, 150, 154, 156, 157, 167, 218, 254
Revered True Myriad Longevity Palace [Chongzhen Wanshougong], 55
Rijingmen, 56
Ritan [Altar of the Sun], 111, **116**
Rongguo, Duke of (Yao Guangxiao), 163
Ruan An, 99, 111
Ruizhou, Liaoning, 35

"Sacred city", 27, 28, 249, 297n33
"Sacred Ornament" (*oroi-yin chimeg*) in Lamaist tradition, 180, see also *dingdai/dingli*

Saghang-sechen, *Erdeni-yin Tobchi*, 174, 175
Samarkand, 72
San dadian [Three Great Halls], 102, 105, 108, see also Fengtian, Huakai, Jinshen hall
San yuan [three sidereal regions], 13, see also Ziweiyuan, Taiweiyuan, Tianshiyuan
Sanguo, see Three Kingdoms
Sanguozhi yanyi [The Romance of the Three Kingdoms], 143, 144
Sanhai ("Three Seas"), 110, 130, **131**, see also Beihai, Zonghai, Nanhai
Sanjiao yingjie zongguan tongshu [A General Interpretation of Response to Kalpic Change according to the Three Religions], 149
Sanjiao yuanliu Soushen daquan, 76, 223
Sanming qitan ditiansui, 146
Sanshan (Shuixi) Gate, **92**, 230
Santai [Three Terraces], 105
"Sealed envelopes", story of, 147, 184–186, 198, 201, 242, 272, 273, see also "sealed packets"
"Sealed packets", story of, 124–125, 149, 161, 185, 186, 233, see also "sealed envelopes"
Serruys, Henry, 177, 178, 180, 184, 185, 195, 205
Shanchuantan [Altars of Mountains and Rivers], **101**, 111, 113, 120
Shang (state), 2
Shangdi (High Lord), 9, 14
Shangdu (Upper Capital) (Yuan), 24, 35, 37, 40, 44, 63, 65, 66, 83, 85, 87, 192, see also Kaiping
"Shangdu bishu" [Escaping Summer in Shangdu], 65, 66
Shanggu, 46
Shangshusheng [Presidential Council], 55
Shangyijian 尚衣監 [Directorate of Clothing Service], **112**
Shao, Duke of, Zhou Kingdom, 41
Shao Yong, 41, 56, 62
Shaobing ge [Baked Cake Ballad], 146, 165, 166, 186
  prophecy and authorship analyzed, 149–155
  modern scholarship, 321n61, 324n78, see also Liu Bowen, Zhang Zhong, *Zhengbing ge*
She-chi T'an, see Shejitan
Shejitan [Altars of Soil and Grain], 17, **54**, 61, **101**, **104**, 107, 109, 110, 120, 130, **131**
Shen [Spiritual] Hill, 50, 115, see also Longshan
Shen Fu, see Shen Wansan
Shen Gui (Wansi), 209
Shen Hanjie, 209
Shen Ruolin, 176
Shen Wanshan (Shen Fu; *zi* Zhongrong, alias Wanshanxiu), xvii, 26, 27
  alleged financial contribution to building the city of Nanking, 194, 211, 213, 239, 339n12, biographical profile and sources, 208–210, 337n4, 338n6
  helping Liu Bowen and Yao Guangxiao subdue the Dragon King to solve the water problem in Peking in popular stories, 229–30, 282–283
  portrait as a fisherman, **211**
  portrait as the God of Wealth,

214, see also *Huo caishen* ("Living God of Wealth")
stories about the sources of his wealth, 209–215, 338n8, see also "treasure-accumulating bowl"
summoned by Liu Bowen and Yao Guangxiao to help build the capital of Peking in popular stories, 207, 231, 233, 236, 278, 284, 285
unearthing hoarded gold and silver to build the city of Peking, 191, 216, 237–241, 243–245, 257, 258, 278, 279, 286, 287
Shen Wansi, 209
Shen You, 208
Shence Gate 神策門, **92**
Shengzong, see Yehlu Longxu, Liao emperor
Shenwu [Divine Warrior] Gate, 105, 123
Shenzong, Ming emperor Wanli, 114, 144
descendants of, 150
Shi [diviner's board], 19
Shich'a Hai, see Shichahai
Shichahai [Sea], **101**, 115, 130, 214, 219, 220, 225, 237, 239, 240, 258, 278, 279, 287
Shicheng Gate 石城門, **92**
Shier ci [twelve dwellings/ habitations of the lunar lodges], 4, 12
Shier gong [Twelve Palaces], 22
Shiji [Records of the Historian], 10, 12
Shijiaohai [Ten Vaults Sea], 237, 287
Shijing [Book of Songs], 9
Shijing Hill, **3**, 7, 58
Shimo Yisun, 138
Shiren Gate 施仁門, **49**
Shitou, Mount 石頭山 (Boulder), 88
Shizong
Jin emperor Wulu, 6, 47
Ming emperor Jiajing, 42, 100, 111, 140
Shoushi li (Yuan calendar) 39
Shu (State), 40
Shuang Huang [Double Yellow] Monastery, 129, see also Dong Huang Si, Xi Huang Si
Shuixi Gate, 213, 230, see also Sanshan Gate
Shujing [Book of Documents], 9
Shumiyuan [Bureau of Military Affairs], 53–55
Shun-chih Men, see Shunzhi Gate
Shuncheng Gate, **49**, **54**, 61, 62, **101**
Shundi, see Yuan emperor Toghōn Temür
Shuntian (Obedient to Heaven) prefecture, 98, 120
Shuntian shibao, 342n34
Shunzhi Gate, 128, **131**, see also Xuanwumen
Shunzhi reign (Qing), 117
Sifu [Four Advisers], 15
Silijian 司禮監 [Directorate of Ceremonial], **112**
Sima Qian, 9, 10, 13
"Single Tree General" [*dushi jiangjun*], 56
Sinitic
influence, 180, 183, 192
rites, 39
world, 206, 259
Sishenci (Shrine of Four Deities), 105
"Siting by bowshot, locating the city of Ming Peking", xvii, 25, 173,

254, see also Mongolian legend of the Mongol maternity of the Yongle emperor and the building of Peking
Six Eastern Palaces, see *Dong liugong*
Sixty-four Hexagrams, 23, see also *Bagua*, *Book of Changes*, Eight Trigrams
Sizong, Ming emperor Chongzhen, 148, 150, 197
Sky-earth correspondence concept, 9, 109, see also Celestial-terrestrial correspondence system
Son of Heaven (Tianzi), 9, 18, 28, 46, 48, 91, 95, 102, 103, 109, 181, 191, 195
Song (state), 88
Song, Mount, 45
Song dynasty, 1, 17, 21, 23, 39, 41, 45, 52, 60, 72–75, 79, 83, 157, 188, 218, 253
Song Gaozeng zhuan, 73
Song Lei, 142
Song Li, 98
Song Lian, 151
Songchuang mengyu, 142
Soushen guangji, 157, 223
South Park, see Nanyuan
Southern Capital, see (Liao) Nanjing, (Ming) Nanking
Southern Palace, 12, 13, 105 (Spring Palace), 15
Southern Secretariat, see Nansheng
Southern Song, 6, 37, 45, 46, 73
Spring Palace, 56
Sui dynasty, 2
Suiyan, 183
Suizhou, Huguang, 183
Sumeru, Mount, 73
Summer Palace of the Forbidden City, 150
Sun Quan, 46
"Supernatural scarecrows", 223, 341n25
Suqing Gate 肅清門, **49**, **54**, 62, 302n25
Suzhou, 15, 42, 83, 117, 139, 194, 208, 210, 213, 238, 256

Ta T'ung, see Datong
T'ai-ho Men, 129
T'ai-ho Tien, 130, see also Taihedian
Taibai jinxing (Grand White/ Golden Star), 246
Taibao (Grand Protector), 39, 53
Taifu (Grand Tutor), 40
Taihang Mountains, 1, 23
Taihe, Mount, 188, 332n31, see also Mount Wudang
Taihedian [Hall of Supreme Harmony], 96, 107, see also Huangjidian
Taimiao [Ancestral Temple], 17, 53, **54**, 55, 56, 61, **101**, **104**, 107, 109, 110, 163, 192
Taiping Gate 太平門, **92**
Taiping Heavenly Kingdom, 154
Taiwan Ririxinbao, 153
Taiweiyuan [Privy Council Enclosure], 13, 15, **16**, 17, 53, 56, 105
Taiye Pond, 47, 52, **54**, 59, 60, **101**, **104**, 110, **112**
Taiyi (Grand Monad), 9, 13, 14
Taiyi and Liuding Daoist deities, 40
Taiyi Guangfu Wanshougong [Grand One, Vast Prosperity, Myriad Longevity Palace], 40
Taizong, see Yehlu Deguang, Liao emperor; Zhu Di, Ming emperor Yongle
Taizong shilu (Veritable Records of

Taizong), 176, see also Zhu Di, Prince of Yan, Yongle Emperor
Taizu, see Ming Taizu
Taizu shilu (Veritable Records of Taizu), 163, 176, see also Ming Taizu
Tales of the Investiture of Gods, see *Fengshen yanyi*
Tan Qian, 176
Tang dynasty/period, 1, 2, 4, 17, 20, 21, 23, 41, 64, 67, 70, 71, 73, 75, 77, 88, 103, 192, 218, 234, 253
Tang Taizong, 40
Tang Xiu, 41
Tang Xuanzong, 73
Tanguts, 62
Tantric Buddhism, xviii, 25, 62, 64, 67, 75, 77, 80, 189
  sutra, 69, 70, 72, 73
Tanze shijng ("Ten most exquisite sites of Tanzhe"), 234
Tanzhe Monastery, 234, 235, 244
Tanzhe, Mount, 234, 235
Tanzheshan Ziuyunsi zhi, 235
Tanzhou Monastery, 232, 234, 284, see also Tanzhe Monastery
Tao An, 89
Tao Zongyi, 41
Taoranting [Pavilion of Merriment], 30, 158
Taoxu leigao, 164
Taoxuzi shiji, 164
Tartar City (Qing Peking), 127
Tashkand (Taskent), 72
Te-sheng Men, see Deshengmen
"Temple fairs" (*miaohui*), in Beijing, 114, 208, 258
Temür, Mongol ruler, see Chengzong
Ten Celestial Stems, 20
The Romance of the Ming Dynasty Heroes, see *Yinglie zhuan*
The Romance of the Three Kingdoms, see *Sanguozhi yanyi*
Three Great Halls, see *San dadian*
Three Jewels (*ghurban erdeni*) in the Sacred Ornament, 179, 180, 196, 198, 272, 276, see also "Three Precious Ones" (Triratna)
Three Kingdoms period, 20, 46, 143
"Three Precious Ones" (*sanbao*), i.e., Buddha, Dharma (Law), and Sangha (monastic order), 180
Three Seas: North Sea, Middle Sea, South Sea, see *Sanhai*
Tian'anmen, 56, 105, 111, 127, 129, **131**, 133, 237, 240, 266, 287, see also Chengtianmen
Tianbao era (Tang), 71
Tiandihui [Heaven and Earth Society], 149, 186, 322n72
"Tianguan shu", in *Shiji,* 9, 13
Tianhuang dadi [High God/Great Emperor of Heaven], 14, 15, 76, see also Jade Emperor, Yuhuang
Tianhuang yudie ("Jade Record" of the Imperial Generation), 176
Tianning Monastery, 36
Tianqiao [Heavenly Bridge], 30; (District), 167
Tianren ganying (stimulus and responses between heaven and man), 10
Tianshigong [Celestial Master Palace], 53, **54**, 55, 56
Tianshiyuan [Celestial Markets Enclosure], 4, 13, **14**, 15, **16**, 17, 61, 105
Tianshoushan [Mount of Heavenly Longevity], **3**, 94, 95, 96, 98, 100, 114
Tiantan [Altar of Heaven], 30, 99, **101**, 107, 111, 113, 120, 125

Tianwangmiao [Heavenly King's Temple] in Fujian, 73
Tianwangtang [Heavenly King's Hall] in Kaifeng, 73, see also Vaiśravana, Heavenly King
Tianyou reign, 209, see also Zhang Shicheng
Tianzhu (Heavenly Pillar) stars, 105
Tiaodaihang [Sash and Girdle Manufacturing Guild], 30, 325n86
Tibetan
  Buddhism, 56, 189
  Lamaism, 118, 180, 198
  planet system, 192–193
T'ien-an Men, see Tian'anmen
Tieya gu yuefu, 84–85
Tiger (cosmological image), 45
Toghōn Temür (Toghōn-temür qaghan), 25, 66, 81, 146, 174, 179, 181, 195, 196, 198
  flight from Dadu back to Mongolia, 85, 175, 177, 184, 202, 204, 219, 232, 270, 271
  in Mongolian story from the Ordos about his alleged posthumous son building the city of Peking, 270–273 , see also "Yuan Prince"
  in Mongolian story narrated by Arash, 203–205
  offering sacrificial prayers to Dragon in a year of drought, 83
  Qonggirad *qatun,* allegedly captured by Zhu Yuanzhang and married the Ming dynastic founder in Mongolian legend, 146–148, 173, 177, 199, see also Gongfei, Zhu Hongwu
  story of Qonggirad *qatun*'s pregnancy and birth of posthumous son alleged to be the Ming Yongle Emperor, 174, 176, 179, 203, 204, 251, 271, 272, 276
Toghus Temür, Mongol ruler, 232
Togon Tömör, see Toghōn Temür
Tonghui [Thorough and Beneficial] Canal, **3**, **49**, **51**, **54**, 59, 61, 82, 115, 219, 225
Tongxian 通縣, **3**
Tongxuan Gate 通玄門, **49**
Tongzhou, 7, 50, 225
Tongzi (Hucheng)-he 筒子 (護城) 河 [Protective Canal], **108**
Toutiao *hutong*, 114
"Treasure-accumulating bowl", see *Jubaopan*
"True Prince" (Chinese Prince), 147, 177–183, 195, 197, 205, 272, 273, 275, 276, see also Jianwen Emperor, Zhu Yunwen
Tsong-kha-ba, His Highness the Saintly from Üi-tsang, 276
Tuan Men, see Duan Gate
Tulbutu-mergen, son of chancellor Dologhan, 271
Tümen (divisions), 175
Tumu fortress, 121, 150
Tung-an Men, see Dong'an Gate
Tung-chih Men, 129, see also Dongzhimen
Tung-hua Men, see Donghuamen
Tung-yueh Miao, see Dongyue Temple
Tuotuo, 59
Tusi [Butcher Shop], 15
Tuul (Tuula) River, 271
Twelve Animals, 23
Twelve Branches of the calendar, 23
"Twelve dwellings/habitations"

(Jupiter station), 4, 12, 13, see also *Shier ci*
Twelve Palaces, see *Shier gong*
Twelve Terrestrial Branches, 4, 12, 13, 20, see also *Dizi*
Twenty-four Mountains, 23
Twenty-eight Lunar Lodges, 20

Upper Capital, see Shangdu
Uriyangqad guards, 175
Urn Hill, see Wengshan
Urn Hill Lake, see Wengshanbo

Vaiśravana, Heavenly King of the North, appearing in Nazha City legend, 64
as Pishamen tianwang, Duowen tianwang, 67–75, 189, 199, 255
father of Nazha, 80, 189, see also Nazha
feting the Buddhist priests in the Crystal Palace, 74, 79
images in Brahmanic mythology and Buddhist hagiography, 334n33
legend grafted on Tang general Li Jing to create the Pagoda-bearing Heavenly King, 75, 77, see also Li Jing
portrait in Tang Buddhist text, **68**
statuettes as Kubara, God of Wealth, **190**
worship of his image in Tang times, as chief of the Yakṣa, 73
Vermillion Bird, see Zhuque
Virūdhaka [Zengzhang tianwang] (South), 67
Virūpaksha [Guangmu tianwang] (West), 67
king of the Nagas, 73, 78

Waicheng ("outer-city"), see under (Yuan) Dadu and (Ming) Peking
Wailuocheng, 113
Wanhu (myriarch), 209
Wang Ji, 21
Wang Liumen, 153
Wang Shizhen, 310n4
Wang Tonggui, 142
Wang Wei, 20
Wang Wenbao, 207
Wang Wenlu, 142
Wang Xian, 312n11
Wang Zilin, 58, 95–97
Wangcheng (Zhou model), 17, **18** (*tu* 圖), 47, 51, 55, 56, 61, 90, 156
Wangqi ("ruler's emanation), 53, 213
Wanli reign, 114, 117–119, 144, see also Ming emperor Shenzong
Wanning Palace, 6, 51
Wanquan, 189
Wanshou/Wansuishan [Hill of Longevity/Myriad Years], 59, 96, **101**, **104**, 106, 110, **112**, see also Jingshan, Meishan
Wanyan clan, 5, see also Jurchens, Jin dynasty
Wei [tail] (lunar lodge), 4
Wei [winnower] (lunar lodge), 12
Wei (state), 46; Duke of (Xu Da), 218
Wei Gao, 41
Weisuo ("guard system"), 139
Wen, King, of Zhou kingdom, 10, 56, 62
Wencheng, Zhejiang, 138
Weng, Lady, 124, 200, see also Gongfei, Zhu Di
Wengcheng (protective wall), 111
Wengshan [Urn Hill], 7, 117

Wengshanbo [Urn Hill Lake], 7, 50, **51**, 58, 60, 115, 225, see also Kunming Lake
Wenmiao 文廟 [Confucius Temple], **101**
Wenming Gate, **49**, 50, **54**, 61, 62, 82, **101**, 225
Wenxian dacheng [Complete Collection of Literature], 163
Wenyu River, **3**, 7, **82**
Wenzhen [Cultured and Faithful] (Liu Bingzhong), 40
Wenzhou, Zhejiang, 138
Werner, E. T. C., *Myths and Legends of China*, "Legend of the Building of Peking", 124, 125, 127, 161, 200, 201
West Lake, see Lianhua Pool, Xihu
West Park, see Xiyuan
West River, 45
Western District, 2, 214
Western Hills, see Xishan
Western Palace, 12, 105, (Xigong) 99
Western zodiac (Capricorn, Aquarius, Pisces, Aries, etc.), 4
Wheatley, Paul, 9
White Cloud Shrine, see Baiyunguan
White Pagoda, 129, 191, 282
White Pagoda Monastery, 282, see also Da Shengshou Wan'ansi
White Tiger, see Baihu
Wu, King, of Zhou Kingdom, 2
Wu, Prince of (Zhu Yuanzhang), see also Ming Taizu, Zhu Yuanzhang
Wu (state), correlated with lunar lodges, 12
Wu Cheng'en, 79
Wu Men, see Wumen
Wu Zixu, 15
Wu'an, Mount, Henan, 36
Wudang, Mount, 188, see also Mount Taihe
Wudeng huiyuan, 74
Wudubu, see Jin emperor Xuanzong
Wufenglou (Five Phoenix Tower), 105
Wuhua Hill, 58
Wujiang zhi, 209
Wulu, see Jin emperor Shizong
Wumen [Meridian or Noon Gate], 90, 102, 105, **108**, 110, **112**, 129, 130
Wuquexing [Military Windings star], 53, see also Kaiyang star
Wuxing, see Five Agents/Phases theories/schemes
Wuxing (Zhejiang), 208
Wuyashi ("crow-shaped stone"), 212
Wuyun Ward, 55

Xi Huang Si [West Yellow Monastery], 129
Xi liugong [Six West Palaces], **108**
Xiangtong (alleyways), 60, see also *Hutong*, *Qutung*
Xiangtu changshui ["divining the land and testing the water"], 15
Xiangzhai [to inspect (the site) for a dwelling], 45
Xian'nongtan [Ancestral Altar of Agriculture], 30, 111, 126
Xiantian tu ["Diagram of the Prior Heavens"], 10, **12**, see also *Baigua*, Eight Trigrams
Xiao Dengfu, 69, 72
Xiao Mingwang, see Han Liner
Xibianmen, 113, **116**, 133, 266, 269
Xiejieshi, 61
Xihu [West Lake], 5, **49**, 156
Xihuamen, 105, 129, **131**

"Xijiang yue" [The Moon over the West River], 42
Xijin zhi, 44, 50, 52, 56, 81, 82, 224
Xijinfu, 4–5, see also (Liao) Nanjing, Yanjing
Xima Ditch, 5
Ximu dwelling (Sagittarius), 4
Ximu weijin [split wood to make a ferry], 5
Xin Xiuming, 122, 123
Xing [star] (lunar lodge), 12
Xingsheng Palace 興盛宮, **54**
Xingtai, Hebei, 35
Xingzai ("residence pro tempore"), 98, 99
Xingzhou, 35, 36
Xingzong, see Yelu Zongzhen, Liao emperor
Xinming (magic spell), 72
Xinshi [History written from the Heart], 83, see also Zheng Suonan, Zheng Sixiao
Xiong Mengxiang, 44, 52, 55, 57–59
Xishan [Western Hills], 48, 58, 59, 238
Xiu ([twenty-eight] lunar lodges), 4, 9, 10, 12, 14, 20, 23, 193, 292n6, see also Di, Dou, Ji, Jiao, Kang, Kui, Niu, Liu, Lou, Xing, Wei, and Zhang individual "lunar lodges"
Xiuyun Chansi, 234, see also Tanzhe Monastery
Xiwangmu (Queen Mother of the West), 337n2
Xiwu liyu, 142
Xiyou ji (Journey to the West), 79, **80**, 121, 158, 223; 308n71
Xiyuan [West Park], **104**, 110, **112**, 115
Xizhimen, **101**, 111, 113, **116**, 129, **131**, 133, 136, 162, 222, 224, 226, 228, 229, 266, 269, 270, 278, 280, 281
Xu, Empress, 94, 98, 219, see also Xu Da, Yongle Emperor
Xu Da
  Ming general, archer of bowshot, 26
  career under Yongle Emperor, 216–219
  extending the northern face of the outer walls of Dadu, 87, 111
  portrait, **220**
  story of shooting an arrow to locate a site to build the city of Peking, 215, 242, 257, 277
"Xu Da yijian ding jingcheng", 340n14
Xu Shanji, 95
Xu Shanshu, 95
Xu Shilong, 40
Xu Wei, 143
Xu Yinglie zhuan [Sequel to The Romance of the Ming Dynasty Heroes], 144
Xuanhao [murky hollow] (Jupiter station), 13
Xuanhua, 189
Xuantian Shangdi [High Lord of the Dark Heaven], 96
Xuanwu (Gate) District, 5, 217
Xuanwu [Dark Warrior], 10, **11**, 23, 105, 187, see also Dark God Zhenwu
Xuanwu Lake 玄武湖, **92**
Xuanwumen, **101**, 105, **108**, 111, 113, **116**, 128, **131**, 133, 266, 269, see also Shenwu Gate
Xuanyao Gate 宣曜門, **49**
Xuanzong
  Jin emperor, 7
  Ming emperor, 42, 99

Tang emperor, 71, 73
Xun (hexagram), 11, 106
Xuzhao (Monk), Chan master of Caodong school, 36

Yakṣa, 67, 68, 70, 73
Yan
as capital city, 45, 46, 65, 95, see also Yanjing
as Zhu Di's fief, 26, 124, 163, 175, 216
Yan (star), 4
Yan (state), 2, 4, 14
Yan, Prince of, see also Yongle Emperor, Yuan Prince, Zhu Di,
alleged posthumous son of Toghōn Temür's Qonggirad *qatun* in Mongolian legend, 25–26, 173, 180, 183, 200, see also Zhu Di
enfeoffed to Yan prefecture by Ming Taizu, 8, 87, 124, 148, 175, 181, 184, 219
enlisted Monk-in-attendance Daoyuan (Yao Guangxiao) as adviser, 43, 186, 235, see also Yao Guangxiao
enmity with the Jianwen Emperor and usurpation, 142, 145, 150, 160, 181, 185, 196–198
enthroned as the Yongle Emperor, 88, 189, 197, 222
exiled to Nankou with Liu Bowen as adviser to build a capital city in Mongolian legend, 147, 161, 178, 189, 201, 241, 242, see also Mongolian legend/story of the Mongol maternity of the Yongle Emperor, and the building of Peking
inviting Liu Bowen to build the city of Peking in popular legends, 207, 215, 218, 231–233, 239, 247, 277, 279, 284
inviting Yao Guangxiao to build the city of Peking, 235, 238, 243, 244, 284–288, see also Yao Guangxiao
seeking Shen Wansan to provide hidden wealth to build the capital city, 236–240, 243, 284, 288, see also Shen Wansan
"Swallow", a pun for the Prince, 160
Yan Gongshang, 126
Yan Mountains, 1, 23, 46
Yan prefecture (province), 4, 5, 14, 43, 45, 46, 47, 84, 124, 187, 200, 201, 216
Yang and *yin* ether, 22, 102
Yang Haiying, 177
Yang Liulang (Yang Ye), 218
Yang Rong, 94
Yang Weizhen, 84–85
Yang Yi, 142
Yang Yunsong, 20
founder of School of Forms of geomancy, 21
Yang Ziqi, 122
Yang-hsin Tien, see Yangxindian
Yangchun Gate 陽春門, **49**
Yangjiaoshi, 61
Yangxindian [Nourishing Heart Palace], **108**, 130
Yanjing, Liao Southern Capital (Nanjing), 4, 5
as Jin capital Zhongdu, 6, 191
as Yuan capital, future Dadu, 7, 24, 52, 255, see also Dadu, Zhongdu
Yangzi River, 87, 88, 117, 246

region, 139, 210, 238
Yanmoshan [Mount of Devils of Blazing Flames], 76
Yanque Lake, 89, **92**, 160
Yao, Lord/Emperor, 2, 17
Yao Guanghui, 232, 235, see also Yao Guangxiao.
Yao Guangxiao (Monk Daoyuan), xvii, 25–27, 208, 258
admirer and comparison with Liu Bingzhong, 42–44, 164
as monk-in-attendance and adviser of Prince of Yan, 163, 186, 207, 256
biographical sources, 300n15, 326n94
career under the Yongle emperor, 163–165
completing with Liu Bowen in building Peking's "Eight-armed Nezha City", 132–136, 162–165, 199, 214–216, 221, 228, 233, 263–266, 267–270, see also Liu Bowen
fighting against the Dragon King in legend of the building of Peking, 229–231, see also Dragon King
literary and scholarly writings, 163–164
portraits, **164**
seeking out Shen Wansen to contribute wealth for building Peking in folk stories, 231, 236, 238, 257, see also Shen Wansen
story of Prince of Yan inviting him to build the city of Peking, 231–235, 241, 243–244, 257, 284–285, 288, see also Prince of Yan
unfavorable public opinion for siding with Yongle's usurpation, 164–165, 186, 207
Yao Tongshou, 89
Yaoshu ("heterodox books"), 44
Ye Ziqi, 41, 63
Yeji, 142
"Yeke Mongghol ulus", 39, see also Da Yuan
Yeke yamu (great tribunals), 187, 192, 193, 275
Yellow Emperor, 15, 56, 150, 154
Yellow River, 1, 45, 185, 273
Yellow Sea, 23
Yelu Chucai, 143
Yelu Deguang, Liao emperor Taizong, 4
Yelu Longxu, Liao emperor Shengzong, 4
Yelu Zongzhen, Liao emperor Xingzong, 5
Yiheyuan parks, 118
Yijian zhi, 74
Yijianzhidi ("the space of the fallen arrow"), 246
Yijing, 9, 20, 21, 192, see also *Book of Changes*
Yin, branch of *dizhi*, 4
Yin and *yang*, interaction of cosmic forces in Forbidden City, 107, 109
"Ying jia jian" ("The Falcon Gripping the Arrow"), 245–247
Yingchang, 87
Yinglie zhuan [The Romance of the Ming Dynasty Heroes], 143–145, 161
Yingtian(fu) ("Responsive to Heaven" Prefecture), 87, 88, 89, 98, 139, 159, 160, 186, see also Nanking
Yingzong, Ming emperor Zhu Qizhen, 99, 111
captured by the Oirat-Mongols

at the battle of Tumu, 121, 150, 251
Yingzhou Island, 110
Yinyang and *wuxing* (Five Agents/ Phases) theories, 9, 10, 96, 103, 106, 223
"Yong Shizu", 122
Yongding River, 2, **3**, **7**, see also Lugou River
Yongdingmen [Eternal Security Gate], 30, 100, 113, **116**, 157, 158
Yongle dadian [Great Literary Repository of the Yongle Reign], 163
Yongle Emperor (Taizong, Chengzu), 8, 25, 88, 96, 136, 180, 181, 188, 195, 196, 205, 222, 276, 277, see also Zhu Di, Prince of Yan, Mongolian legend/story of the Mongol maternity of the Yongle Emperor, and the building of Peking
alleged posthumous son of Toghōn Temür by his Qonggirad *qatun* Gongfei in Mongolian legend, 124, 125, 146, 147, 160, 176, 179, 199, 200, 202, 205, 206, 217, 218, 252, 255, 256, 259, 329n7, see also Toghōn Temür
assigning Liu Bowen and Yao Guangxiao to building Peking, 217, 235, 256, 257, 263, see also Liu Bowen, Yao Guangxiao
building of the Ming capital in modern Beijing, xv, 25, 26, 27, 91, 94, 96, 98, 102, 114, 121, 132, 173, 189, 194, 196, 200, 216, 217, 219, 245
founding Köke Qota, outside the Great Wall in Mongolian legend, 184
how he built the city of Peking in Mongolian legend, 148, 173, 177, 178, 198, 206, 207, 241, 252, 254
mausoleum of, 156, see also Changling
portrait, **93**
relationship with Monk Daoyuan (Yao Guangxiao), 43, 163, 186, 207, 234
successors of, 99, 115, 277
Yongle, reign, 167, 197, 266
Yongzheng, reign, 94, 115, 208, 266
You Wumiao [A Visit to the Temple of War Gods], 144
You'an Gate, 113, **116**
Youdu, see Youzhou
Youzhou, 14, 228, 231, 233, 234, 263, 284, see also Bitter Sea Youzhou
as Liao Southern Capital (Nanjing), 4
as Sui-Tang city, 2
Yu (Jade or Imperial) Canal, **101**, **104**, 115, see also Huitong Canal
Yu (Jade or Long) River, 224, see also Chang River
Yu li (drought sacrifice), 120
Yuan Dadu, see Dadu (Yuan)
Yuan dynasty, xvi, 1, 22, 57, 76, 82, 88, 154, 156, 199, 209, 212, 219, 234, 250, 251, see also Mongol-Yuan dynasty
Yuan Gong, 180
Yuan plays on Nazha, 75
"Yüan Prince" (Prince of the Mongols), 147, 177–183, 186, 197
enmity with the True Prince, 181–183, 205, 272, 276
exiled to Nankou with Liu

Bowen as adviser and to build the capital city (Peking), 147, 184, 187, 193, 196, 273–275
succeeded as the "Little Emperor", 195, 275–276, see also Liu Bowen, Prince of Yan, Yongle Emperor
Yuan rule, see Mongol rule
"Yuan Taizi", see "Yuan Prince"
Yuan (distant) Taizi, 331n11
Yuanqi [Primal ether], 19
Yuanshi, 44, 191
Yuanshuai (marshals) in Daoist pantheon, 74
Yuanwu Keqin (Monk), 74
Yuchi jing (Jade Ruler Canon), 22, 44, see also Liu Bingzhong
Yue (state), correlated with lunar lodges, 12
Yue Fei (General Yue), 230, 231
Yuejingmen, 56
Yuequan [Jade Spring] Hill, 7, 50, **51**, 58, 60, 115, 156, 225, 226, 229, 243, 281
Yuetan [Altar of the Moon], 111, **116**
Yuhuang, 76, see also Jade Emperor, Tianhuang dadi
Yuhuayuan [Imperial Garden], 105, **108**
Yulizi, 139
Yün-kang temple caves, 203
Yunhe qizong, 143
Yunzhong, 45
Yushitai [Censorate], 53, **54**, 55, 56, 139
Yuyuan Pool, 7, **51**

Zai jinpao [Re-donning the Damask Robe], 161
Zang shu, 20
Zanning (Monk), 73
Zha [Watergate] Canal, 7
Zha Jizuo, 151
Zhan Taiping [Battling at Taiping], 144
Zhang [extended net] (lunar lodge), 12
Zhang Dai, 176
Zhang Ding, xvii, 168
Zhang Han, 142
Zhang Liang, 40, 143, 144, 146
Zhang Sanfeng (Daoist), 212, 213
Zhang Shicheng, 139, 141, 209
Zhang Yu, 64
Zhang Yun, 88
Zhang Zhong, Iron-cap Daoist (Tieguan daoren), alleged author of the prophecy book *Zhengbing ge* and *Shaobing ge*, 165, see also main entries
biographies, 151, 152
designing the palaces in Nanking with Liu Ji (Liu Bowen), 165, 327n96
portrait, **153**
predicting the rise of Prince of Yan, 325n90
Zhang Zichen, 134
Zhang Zongyan, 55
Zhanguo [Warring States] period, 4, 12, 20
Zhangyi Gate 彰義門, **49**
Zhangzong, Jurchen Jin emperor Madage, 7
Zhao, Duke of, Zhou kingdom, 2, 41
Zhao (state), Duke of (Liu Bingzhong), 40
Zhao Bingwen, 45
Zhao Feng, 41
Zhao Shi, see Southern Song emperor Duanzong
Zhao Xuanlang, 188

Zhao Yao, 88
Zhen (hexagram/cardinal point), 11, 53, 56, 192
Zhen Taizi, see "True Prince"
Zheng Sixiao, 83
Zheng Suonan (Sixiao), *Xinshi,* 83
birth and death dates of, and authenticity of *Xinshi,* 310n77
Zheng Xiao, 151
Zhengbing ge [Steamed Cake Ballad], 151–153, 165
Zhengde reign (Ming), 119
Zhengyangmen (Facing Brightness Gate)
(Nankjing), **92**
(Peking), 100, **101**, **104**, 106, 111, 113, 114, 116, **131**, 133, 265, 266, 269, see also Qianmen
Zhenshan [mount for suppression], see Jingshan, Meishan
Zhenwu, see Dark God, Xuanwu
Zhili (i.e. Nanking), 117, 194
Zhizheng era (Yuan), 174
Zhizheng zhiji [Faithful Record of the Zhizheng Era], 65
Zhong, Mount, 88, 89, **92**, 159, 160, 245, 247
Zhong dafu [Ordinary Grand Master], 232, 284
Zhong Han, 189, 191
Zhongdu [Central Capital] (Jin), xv, 5–7, 18, 47, **49**, **51**, 52, 60, 61, 224
Zhongdu (Ming), 44, 89, 91, 92, 100, 238, 245–247
Zhongdu (Yuan), 7, 8, 39, 42, 48, see also Dadu
Zhonggong [Central Palace], 10, 13, 103
Zhongguo [Middle Kingdom], 5, 63
Zhongguo erqiannian (qian) zhi yuyan, 150
Zhongguo yuyan wu (qi or *ba) zhong* [Five, Seven, or Eight Samples of Chinese Prophecies], 150
Zhonggulou [Bell and Drum Tower], 221, see also Zhonglou, Gulou
Zhonghai [Middle Sea], 110
Zhonghua Gate, 110, 128, 129, **131**, see also Da Ming Gate, Da Qing Gate
Zhongjidian [Hall of Middle Supremacy], **108**
Zhonglou [Bell Tower]
(Yuan Dadu), 53
(Ming Peking), 99, 100, **101**, 110, 113
Zhongnanhai 中南海 [Central and South Sea], 278, 279
Zhongshusheng [Central Secretariat], 52, 53, **54**, 55, 57, 140, see also Beisheng, Nansheng
Zhongxin zhi tai (Central Platform), 50
Zhongxinge [Central Pavilion], 50, **54**, 60
Zongren [Nobility's Servant], 15
Zongzheng [Nobility's Head Servant], 15
Zhou (state), 209, see also Zhang Shicheng
Zhou, Duke of, Zhou Kingdom, 17, 40, 89
Zhou kingdom, 2, 4, 41
correlated with lunar lodges, 12
Zhou Yu, 113
Zhoubi suanjing [Arithmetic of the Gnomon and the Circular Paths], 46
Zhouli [Institutions of Zhou], 9, 12, 17, 47
Zhouzhuang (canton), 208, 238

Zhouzi [loggerhead turtle] (Jupiter station), 13
Zhu Biao, 181–183
Zhu Di (Prince of Yan, Taizong, Chengzu, Yongle Emperor), see also Prince of Yan, Yongle Emperor
alleged posthumous son of Toghōn Temür's Qonggirad *qatun* in Mongolian legend, 124, 173, 174, 200, see also Mongolian legend/story of the Mongol maternity of the Yongle Emperor, and the building of Peking
enfeoffed by Ming Taizu as the Prince of Yan, 8, 87, 148, 175, 181, 184, 219
enmity with the Jianwen emperor and usurpation, 25, 43, 91, 163, 182–184
Zhu Fonian, 67
Zhu Gang, 232
Zhu Gaozhi, Ming emperor Renzong, 98, 197
Zhu Hongwu (Chu Hung-wu), 177, 179, 182, 270, 275, see also Hongwu Emperor, Ming Taizu, Zhu Yuanzhang
capturing Toghōn Temur's pregnant *qatun* at fall of Dadu and marrying her in Mongolian legend, 271, 272
story of dream of the fight between the black-striped snake (Yuan Prince) and the yellow-striped snake (True Prince), 182–183, 272–273, see also Mongolian legend/story of the Mongol maternity of the Yongle Emperor, and the building of Peking
Zhu Qiyu, see Ming emperor Jingtai
Zhu Qizhen, Ming emperor Yingzong, 99
Zhu Xi, 22, 45, 95, 164
Zhu Yizun, 43
Zhu Yuanzhang (Prince of Wu), 8, 66, 88, 139, 143, 175, 218, see also Hongwu Emperor, Ming Taizu, Zhu Hung-wu
capturing Toghon Temur's pregnant *qatun* at fall of Dadu and marrying her in Mongolian legend, 173, 174, 179, 204
commanding Liu Ji to build a capital city in Jinling (Nanking), 89, 151, 160
dubbed as "Chinese bandit hero" in a Mongolian legend of the building of Peking, 204, see also Hongwu Emperor, Ming Taizu, Zhu Hung-wu
Zhu Yunming, 142
Zhu Yunwen, see Ming emperor Jianwen
Zhu Zhanji, Ming emperor Xuanzong, 99
Zhu Zuochao, 161
Zhuge Liang, 40, 46, 88, 143, 146, 149
Zhuge Zhongwuhou bingfa xinyao, 146
Zhu(po) long (crocodile?), 213, 230, 341n32
Zhuque [Vermillion Bird], 10, **11**, 22, 105
Zi, branch of *dizhi*, 13
Zicong (Monk) (Liu Bingzhong), 7, 35, 36, 37, 39
Zigong [Purple Palace], 10
Zijin cheng [Purple or Polar "Forbidden City"], 8, 100, see

also Ming/Qing Forbidden City
Zijin cheng fengshui [Geomancy of the Forbidden City], 95–97
Ziweiyuan [Purple Palace Enclosure], 13–15, **16**, 52, 53, 55–57, 91, 96, 100, 103, 105, 295n19
Zongren [Nobility's Servant], 15
Zongzheng [Nobility's Head Servant], 15
Zou Rong, 154
Zuiwei lu, 151
Zuo'an Gate, 113, **116**
Zuoyou Zhifa Tianmen [Left and Right Law Administrator Celestial Gates stars], 53, 56, 105
Zuoyuan zhizhi (*tujie*), 146